DATE DUE

GAYLORD			PRINTED IN U.S.A.

Theoretical Foundations of Computer Science

Theoretical Foundations of Computer Science

Dino Mandrioli
Carlo Ghezzi

John Wiley & Sons

New York   **Chichester**   **Brisbane**   **Toronto**   **Singapore**

Library of Congress Cataloging in Publication Data:

Mandrioli, Dino.
   Theoretical foundations of computer science.

   Bibliography: p. 459
   1. Mathematics—1961- .   2. Electronic data
processing—Mathematics.   I. Ghezzi, Carlo.
II. Title.

QA39.2.M336 1987   004′.01   87-2118
ISBN 0-471-83834-9

Printed in the United States of America

10 9 8 7 6 5 4 3 2 1

Dino Mandrioli dedicates this book to
his father, Crisanto

Carlo Ghezzi dedicates this book
to the memory of his father, Giovanni, and
to his mother, Federica

Preface

The main topics of theoretical computer science are taught in most computer science and engineering curricula, but are not presented as a *foundation* for computer studies. Most courses—and their reference textbooks—are highly biased in their choice of topics. Very often they overemphasize traditional areas —such as formal languages and automata—and pay little or no attention to newer important topics—such as formal semantics or computational complexity.

The organization of this book results from our strongly held belief that theoretical computer science should be viewed as the cornerstone of computer science and engineering curricula. Computer specialists, in their everyday life, must be able to translate actual problems into abstractions based on the use of formal models, to manipulate such formal descriptions, and to reason about their properties in a rigorous way. This very special attitude differentiates the computer specialist from most other technical professionals.

For these reasons, we suggest that an exposure to theoretical computer science topics should be given in the early stage of computer science education, particularly at the undergraduate level. Theoretical topics *should not* be viewed as options that can be added late in the curricula. Rather, they must be viewed as the basis that will inspire and permeate all of the curriculum and, in particular, all other more practical courses.

This book is also based on another of our beliefs: computer science and engineering students should be equipped with a strong mathematical background. For computer studies, as for other traditional applied science and engineering studies, such a background must include the basics of calculus. In addition, the computer specialist's mathematical background should include several chapters of *discrete mathematics*, such as algebra, combinatorics and graph theory, mathematical logic, and possibly elements of the theory of recursive functions. Hopefully, schools will move to the point where these topics will be taught routinely in mathematics courses. Since this is not presently the case in most science and engineering schools, we decided to enlarge the set of theoretical computer science topics covered to include mathematical prerequisites as well.

In conclusion, the main purpose of this book is to present theoretical computer science as a unitary basis for all computer science studies. The ideal—though not exclusive—use of the text is to cover two semesters, as we discuss in the note for the instructor. The necessary prerequisites can be provided by introductory courses on programming, computer architecture, and mathematics. Advanced courses on programming, algorithm design, programming languages, and the like, can either follow or be taught in parallel. The text is also suitable for use in more traditional courses on theoretical computer science, which are usually taught at a more advanced level.

In more detail, there are two types of required prerequisites.

a. *Computer science prerequisites.*
   Basic concepts of programming and computer architectures and knowledge of a high-level programming language, such as Pascal.
b. *Mathematical prerequisites.*
   Elementary knowledge of calculus and very basic notions of algebra, combinatorics, and mathematical logic.

We have included *Chapter 0* to cover mathematical prerequisites. The level of coverage is shallow—in the form of a glossary—for the most standard topics such as basic concepts of algebra and combinatorics. It is self-explanatory for less common topics such as mathematical logic, axiomatization of arithmetic, and the theory of recursive functions.

The rest of the book concentrates on fundamental topics of theoretical computer science and is organized as follows.

Chapter 1 deals with the basic formalisms of theoretical computer science: automata and grammars. It also covers less standard topics, such as equations in language spaces and Petri nets. The style of the chapter is not a model-by-model or theorem-by-theorem description of theoretical concepts. Rather, its purpose is to enhance the reader's attitude to defining formal models and reasoning about them.

Chapter 2 deals with the concept of *computational power* of a formalism, specifically the issue of decidable and undecidable problems in the light of the fundamental Church's thesis.

Chapter 3 introduces *computational complexity* as a refinement of decidability. Complexity is a measure of cost of problem solutions, which depends on the computational device used for implementation of an algorithm. The differences and relationships between different models in complexity analysis are thoroughly investigated.

Chapter 4 deals with tools for formally defining *semantics* of programming languages. We introduce and contrast two main approaches: operational and denotational semantics.

Chapter 5 is an application of the concepts developed in Chapter 4, formally *proving program properties*; in particular, program correctness.

Chapter 6 deals with nondeterminism and concurrency. It is an introduction to the problems, difficulties, and impact on formal models, arising in the description of nondeterministic and (or) concurrent computations.

As this brief outline shows, the material presented in this text provides a wide-spectrum coverage of theoretical computer science. Our main goal has been to combine breadth with depth, in order to provide a *sound and complete theoretical basis* for computer science studies. This is especially evident in chapters 4 through 6, where we decided to include the basic concepts and introductory examples for each topic, but not all of the details needed for a practical application in a specific field. For instance, we provide the foundations of denotational semantics but not all of the enrichments needed to deal with a real programming language. Similarly, we outline the issues of nondeterminism and concurrency but leave a detailed discussion to the specialized studies.

We also decided to include a number of selected, more advanced topics that may shed light on some critical points or some promising research areas. Such topics, which are marked by an asterisk (*), throughout the text, can obviously be left to a more advanced readership or to a deeper rereading of the book because they often require a greater amount of mathematical background. Such material is not on any critical path of the book.

The book contains many exercises, at various levels of difficulty (some of them are marked by an asterisk). Besides routine exercises of mathematical type, which cover classical formal language and computability topics, others require the student to prove theorems or to criticize (or give) new formal definitions. Others require the student to translate a formal definition or a theorem into a computer program; still others require a mixture of theoretical and experimental work. Exercises play a very important role in the overall organization of the book.

The contents and organization of this book have been used experimentally in numerous courses both in universities (Politecnico di Milano and Università di Udine) and in intensive industrial courses. We have used both the entire text and monothematic subsets. In either case our message on the use and role of theoretical computer science in current programming practice went through clearly.

This book took shape in our minds over a period of about ten years. The first author gave it a written version and then the two of us reshaped it several times before reaching the current version. During this time, we have discussed the concepts we present in the book with several people including Giorgio Ausiello, Egon Börger, Stefano Crespi-Reghizzi, Mariangiola Dezani, Michael Harrison, Mehdi Jazayeri, Richard Kemmerer, and Giancarlo Mauri. Their influence and ideas appear throughout the book.

We owe special thanks to Claudio Citrini and to the reviewers, who gave us an immense number of suggestions, ranging from questions of overall organization to details of individual definitions or proofs.

We acknowledge the support we received from our editors and advisors at John Wiley & Sons. Richard Bonacci encouraged us to pursue the idea of a theoretical computer science textbook and gave us the initial support. Gene Davenport monitored the process that turned the initial rough draft into the book. Ann Meader and Susan Giniger were extremely helpful in the final editing stage.

Finally, we wish to thank the typists of Copisteria Teodosio for their collaboration in the never-ending typing and retyping of the book.

After all the support and suggestions we received from these people, if there are remaining obscurities or troublespots in the book, this is entirely our own responsibility.

CNR—the Italian Research Council—supported our work through its center CSISEI in Milano.

A Note for the Instructor

The suitability of our text for use both at the undergraduate and graduate level stems from the possibility of easily subsetting the book in several ways. Here are some examples.

1. One-semester undergraduate course. The purpose is to provide an overall view of theoretical topics. This is a chapter-by-chapter outline:
   - Chapter 0: Omit Section 0.2.4.2.
   - Chapter 1: Omit Sections 1.6, 1.7.3, 1.8 and the appendix. Several proofs may also be omitted.
   - Chapter 2: Omit Sections 2.7, 2.8, 2.9. In Section 2.10, Theorem 2.20 may also be omitted.
   - Chapter 3: Omit Sections 3.2.2, 3.3, 3.5, 3.6, 3.7, 3.8, 3.9, 3.10.
   - Chapter 4: Cover Sections 4.1 through 4.4 and give only hints on 4.5.
   - Chapter 5: Omit Sections 5.2.2, 5.3.1, 5.4, 5.5, 5.6, 5.7, 5.8.
   - Chapter 6: Omit the entire chapter.
   In addition, all marked parts should be omitted.

2. Two-semester undergraduate course. (Senior)
   All of the topics should be taught, except for the contents of marked sections.
3. Two-semester graduate course.
   All of the topics should be taught, except for the parts of Chapters 0, 1, 2, and 3 that may be known already, and including the contents of marked sections.

Another possibility is to select the contents of the book for use in a one-semester course with a strong bias towards specific topics of theoretical computer science.

For example, one might emphasize automata and formal languages by choosing Chapters 0 through 2 (marked sections included), parts of Chapter 3, and very little of Chapters 4 and 5. Of course, we recommend a more balanced distribution of topics, which follows the spirit of our choices.

We believe that exercises play an essential role for a thorough understanding of concepts of theoretical computer science. As we said, the text lists a large number of exercises explicitly, with outlines of solutions for critical exercises. Other exercises are left implicit in the text (e.g., in theorem proofs).

Dino Mandrioli
Carlo Ghezzi

Contents

CHAPTER 1   MODELS FOR COMPUTER SCIENCE: AUTOMATA AND GRAMMARS   43

CHAPTER 2   SOLVABLE AND UNSOLVABLE PROBLEMS   147

CHAPTER 3   THE COMPLEXITY OF COMPUTING   193

Notation and Symbols

Notation	Explanation
$\in$, $\notin$	Membership relation ("belongs to") and its negation ("does not belong to").
$\subseteq$, $\supseteq$, $\nsubseteq$, $\nsupseteq$	Containment relations and their negations.
$\subset$, $\supset$	Strict containment relations. $\supset$ also denotes logical implication.
$=$	Equality.
$\equiv$	1. Strong equality; 2. Logical equivalence.
$\forall$	For every.
$\exists$	There exists one element.
$\cup$, $\cap$	Union, intersection.
$\varnothing$	Empty set.
$-$	Besides the usual "minus" operator, it also denotes set difference.
$\overline{X}$	1. Complement of set X; 2. Vector of variables.

$\langle , \rangle$	Angular brackets enclose ordered (occasionally unordered) n-tuples of elements.
$A \times B$	Cartesian product of sets A and B.
$\{ , \}$	1. Curly brackets are used in the description of a set; various forms are $\{x_i\}$, $\{x\vert P(x)\}$, and $\{x_1, \ldots, x_n\}$ $\ldots$; 2. Sometimes they enclose possibly infinite sequences of elements.
$[\ \ ]$	1. Equivalence class; 2. Indexing of arrays in a programming language notation; 3. Set of monotonic functions: $[X \to Y]$ is the set of monotonic functions from X to Y.
$f \colon X \to Y$	f is a function from set X to Y.
D_f	Definition domain of function f.
I_f	Image of function f.
x^{-1}, f^{-1}	Inverse of element x, inverse of function f.
$\circ$	1. Generic (infix) operator; 2. Composition of two functions.
$\{f \vert f \colon X \to Y\}$	The set of functions from X to Y.
$\mathscr{P}(X), \mathscr{P}_F(X)$	Power set of set X, finite subsets of X.
$\approx$	Equinumerous relation.
$\aleph_0, 2^{\aleph_0}$	Denumerable cardinality, cardinality of continuum.
$\leq, <, \geq, >$	Order relations.
$\succ$	Well-order relation.
$\sqcup, \sqcap$	Lattice operations.
$\cancel{b}$	Blank symbol.
$\bot$	Conventional undefined element of any set.
Σ, Π	Sum, product over a set of elements.
R^+	Transitive closure of relation R.
R^*	Reflexive and transitive closure of relation R.
X^*	Free monoid generated by set X.
X^+	Semigroup generated by set X.
$X^{\hat{}}$	Set X augmented by the undefined element.

$\cup, ., *$	Operators building regular expressions. They are different symbols than $\cup, ., *$, respectively.
$S \bmod R$	S modulo, or S quotient relation R. It is also used as an operator in programming languages.
$\mathbb{N}, \mathbb{Z}, \mathbb{R}$	Natural numbers, integer numbers, rational numbers.
$\equiv_K$	Equivalence modulo K.
$\wedge, \vee, \neg, \supset, \equiv$	And, or, not, implication (but also strict containment), logical equivalence (but also strong equality).
T, F *true, false*	Logical values "true" and "false."
$\square, \$, *, \#$	1. Are used as special symbols in alphabets; 2. $\square$ also precedes a guarded command.
FA, PDA, TM, FT, PDT, PN	Finite-state automaton, pushdown automaton, Turing machine, finite-state transducer, pushdown transducer, Petri net.
NFA, NPDA, NTM, NFT, NPDT	Nondeterministic finite-state automaton, nondeterministic pushdown automaton, nondeterministic Turing machine, nondeterministic finite-state transducer, nondeterministic pushdown transducer.
ϵ	Empty string.
$\Rightarrow, \overset{k}{\Rightarrow}$	Derivation relation, derivation in k steps.
$\alpha \to \beta$	Production of a grammar (where α and β denote strings).
$A \to \alpha_2 \vert \alpha_2 \vert \ldots \alpha_\ell$	Short notation for $A \to \alpha_1, A \to \alpha_2, \ldots A \to \alpha_\ell$
$\mathscr{L}$	1. Family of languages; 2. List of statements.
$\mathscr{A}$	1. Formal theory for arithmetic; 2. Family of automata.
$\mathscr{E}$	Enumeration.
f_x	Function computed by the x-th Turing machine.
$\leq_r$	Reducibility relation between sets of numbers.
∞	Infinity.
x^R	Mirror image of the string x.

if-then-else(fi)	1. Keywords for a Pascal-like statement; 2. Notation for conditional functions.
$\underline{0}, \underline{1}$	Bottom and universal elements of lattices and Boolean algebras.
wf	Well-formed formula.
!	Factorial.
$\begin{pmatrix} x_1 & \cdots & x_n \\ y_1 & \cdots & y_n \end{pmatrix}$	Permutation.
$\binom{n}{r}$	Binomial coefficient.
$\vdash$	1. Logical deduction; 2. Transition relation.
$\overset{*d}{\vdash}$	Transition sequence of a pushdown automata not allowing further ϵ-moves.
MP Gen	Modus ponens $\Big\}$ rules of inference. Generalization
$\mathcal{T}, \mathcal{PC}, \mathcal{FT}, \mathcal{FPC}$	Formal theory, propositional calculus, first-order theory, first-order predicate calculus.
$|X|, |x|, |s|, |n|$	Cardinality of the set X, length of the string x, length (*ie.*, number of elements) of the sequence s, absolute value of the relative number n.
$\lfloor x \rfloor$	Maximum integer not exceeding the real number x.
$\lceil y \rceil$	Minimum integer greater than or equal to the real number y.
$\lim\limits_{n \to \infty} f(n)$	Limit of function f as n goes to infinity.
$\max\{x|C\}$	Maximum value among the elements of the set x satisfying condition C.
min	Minimum.
I/O	Input–Output.
$\Theta(f)$	Order of the function f.
$\log n$	Logarithm of n. Unless otherwise explicitly stated, $\log n$ denotes the base-2 logarithm.
DTIME(f), NTIME(f), DSPACE(f), NSPACE(f).	Classes of languages recognizable by Turing machines in time and space bounded by function f.

$\mathscr{P}, \mathscr{NP}$	Class of languages recognizable by a deterministic (nondeterministic) Turing machine in polynomial time.
SMALG, SMALM, SMALG$^+$, SMALM$^+$, SMALG$^-$.	Small Algol-like languages, Small Algol-like machines.
ID_M, ID_P	Set of the identifiers declared in a SMALG$^{(+)}$ main program, Set of identifiers declared in a SMALG$^+$ procedure.
$F \Leftarrow P[F]$	Definition of a recursive program P.
$\tau[F]$	Operator τ applied to function variable F.
Ω	Everywhere undefined function; $\Omega(x) = \perp$ for all x in any set.
FP, LFP	Fixed point, least fixed point.
$Sem, \mathscr{S}em$	Semantic functions.
$\{Pre\}P\{Post\}$	Asserted program (fragment); Pre is the precondition, $Post$ the postcondition, and P the program (fragment).
$\dfrac{A_1 \ldots A_n}{B}$	Rule of inference in correctness proofs: $A_1, \ldots A_n$; are the antecedents, B the consequent.
P_x^t	The result of substituting all free occurrences of variable x by term t in the formula P.
UB, LUB, LB, GLB	Upperbound, least upperbound, lowerbound, least lowerbound.
$\vDash_{\mathscr{I}} A(s)$	Assertion A is satisfied by the sequence s under the interpretation $\mathscr{I}$.
$a[lb..ub]$	The slice of array a consisting of the elements whose index is enclosed between lb and ub.
$\uparrow$	1. Marker of the position of a Turing machine head; 2. Marker of variable function symbols in computation rules.

CHAPTER ZERO

Mathematical Background

0.1 Mathematical Glossary

This section is intended to be a brief survey of basic mathematical definitions and terminology. Most of the notions contained therein should be already familiar from previous mathematical exposure so that little explanation and examples are supplied.

0.1.1 Sets, Relations, Functions

A *set* is a collection of *objects*. Any object x in a set X is called an *element* or *member* of X; x being an element of X will be denoted by $x \in X$, while the opposite will be $x \notin X$.

$X \subseteq Y$ will denote that X *is included into* or *is a subset of* Y; that is, all elements of X are also elements of Y. $Y \supseteq X$ is an equivalent notation to $X \subseteq Y$. $X = Y$ will denote that X is identical to Y, that is, all elements of X are also elements of Y and conversely; namely $X \subseteq Y$ and $Y \subseteq X$. $\neq$, $\nsubseteq$, and $\nsupseteq$ will respectively deny $=$, $\subseteq$, $\supseteq$. $X \subset Y$ will denote proper inclusion, that is, $X \subseteq Y$ but also $X \neq Y$. $X \supset Y$ is defined accordingly.

$X \cup Y$ (read "X union Y") denotes the set consisting of those elements belonging either to X or to Y. $X \cap Y$ (read "X intersection Y") denotes the set of elements belonging to both X and Y. Obviously $(X \cup Y) \cup Z = X \cup (Y \cup Z)$, that is, union is *associative*; and $X \cup Y = Y \cup X$, that is, union is *commutative*. The same holds for $\cap$. Furthermore, $X \cap (Y \cup Z) = (X \cap Y) \cup (X \cap Z)$, $X \cup (Y \cap Z) = (X \cup Y) \cap (X \cup Z)$, that is, union and intersection are mutually distributive.

$\emptyset$ denotes the *empty set*, that is, the conventional set with no elements. $X \cap \emptyset = \emptyset$ and $X \cup \emptyset = X$ for each X. $X - Y$ (*set difference*) is the set of all elements of X that do not belong to Y. X and Y are said to be *disjoint* if and only if $X \cap Y = \emptyset$.

$\mathscr{P}(X)$ denotes the *power set* of X, that is, the set of all subsets of X.

Let $b_1, b_2, \ldots, b_k$ be k objects: $\langle b_1, b_2, \ldots, b_k \rangle$ denotes the *ordered k-tuple* consisting of *exactly* $b_1, b_2, \ldots, b_k$ *in the above order*, that is, $\langle b_1, b_2, \ldots, b_k \rangle = \langle c_1, c_2, \ldots, c_k \rangle$ if and only if $b_1 = c_1$, $b_2 = c_2, \ldots, b_k = c_k$. A 2-tuple is also said a *couple*, or *pair*.

The *Cartesian product* $X_1 \times X_2 \times \cdots X_k$ denotes the set of all k-tuples $\langle x_1, x_2, \ldots, x_k \rangle$ with $x_1 \in X_1$, $x_2 \in X_2, \ldots, x_k \in X_k$. X^n denotes the Cartesian product of X with itself $n - 1$ times. Equivalently X^n is inductively defined by $X^1 = X$, $X^{n+1} = X^n \times X$.

An *n-ary relation* R on the sets $X_1, \ldots, X_n$ is a subset of $X_1 \times \cdots \times X_n$. The notation $R(x_1, \ldots, x_n)$ is sometimes used in place of $\langle x_1, \ldots, x_n \rangle \in R$. In this case we say that R *holds* for the *n*-tuple $\langle x_1, \ldots, x_n \rangle$. A 1-ary relation is also called a *property*. Let P be a property defined on a given set X: the notation $\{x \,|\, P(x)\}$ denotes the set consisting of all elements $x \in X$ such that property P holds for x.

$\forall x$ is an abbreviation for "for each x" and $\exists x (\not\exists x)$ is an abbreviation for "there (does not) exist x such that." For instance, let $\mathbb{N}$ denote the set of natural numbers. $\{x \,|\, \not\exists \langle y, z \rangle (y \neq 0,\ y \neq 1,\ z \neq 0,\ z \neq 1 \text{ and } x = y \cdot z)\}$ denotes the set of prime numbers.

A 2-ary relation is called a *binary relation*. If R is a binary relation, the infix notation xRy may be used in place of $R(x, y)$.

Given a binary relation R on sets X and Y, X is called the *domain* of R and Y is called its *range*. The *inverse relation* R^{-1} of R is the set of all ordered pairs $\langle y, z \rangle$ such that $\langle z, y \rangle \in R$. Let $R \subseteq X \times X$, that is, let X be both the domain and range of a binary relation R. In such a case we say that R is a relation on X. R is *reflexive* if xRx for all x. R is *symmetric* if xRy implies yRx, and R is *transitive* if xRy and yRz imply xRz. R is *irreflexive* if xRx does not hold for any x, and R is *antisymmetric* if xRy implies not yRx.

The *reflexive and transitive closure* R^* of R is defined by xR^*y if and only if $\exists x_0, x_1, \ldots, x_n$, $n \geq 0$ such that $x_0 = x$, $x_n = y$ and for any i, $i = 1, \ldots, n$, $x_{i-1} R x_i$. Thus for any R, xR^*x for each x. The *transitive closure* R^+ and the kth *power* R^k of R are defined as R^* with the differences that, $n \geq 1$ and $n = k$, respectively.

A binary relation that is reflexive, symmetric, and transitive is called an *equivalence relation*. Given an equivalence relation R on a set X, and given any y, with $y \in X$, define $[y]_R$ as the set of all z in X such that yRz. $[y]_R$ is called the *R-equivalence class* of y. It is easy to verify that $[y]_R = [z]_R$ if and only if yRz; and that, if $[y]_R \neq [z]_R$, then $[y]_R \cap [z]_R = \varnothing$, that is, different R-equivalence classes have no elements in common. Hence, the set X is completely partitioned into its R-equivalence classes. The *index* of R, denoted as *index(R)*, is the number of its equivalence classes, whether finite or infinite. The symbol R will be dropped from the notation $[x]_R$ when it is apparent from the context.

Reflexive and *irreflexive partial orders* over a set X are, respectively, reflexive and irreflexive, antisymmetric, and transitive relations on X. "Partial order" is used for either reflexive or irreflexive partial order. For any partial order R, two elements x, y, with x, $y \in X$, such that neither xRy nor yRx are said to be *noncomparable*. A (reflexive) total order is a (reflexive) partial order R such that, for any x and y either $x = y$, or xRy, or yRx.

Let R be a partial order on X and let B be a subset of X. An element $x \in X$ is called an *upperbound* of B if and only if for any $y \in B$, yRx holds. An upperbound x of B is called a *least upperbound* of B if and only if for any upperbound z of B, xRz holds. Similarly x is called a *lowerbound* of B if and only if for any $y \in B$, xRy holds and is called a *greatest lowerbound* if and only if for any lower bound z of B, zRx holds. An element y of B is called an *R-least element* of B if and only if yRz for every element z of B different from y. A *well-order* (or well-ordering relation) is a total order R on X such that every nonempty subset of X has an R-least element. For instance, the relation $<$ on the set of nonnegative integers is a well order; the relation $<$ on the set of nonnegative rational numbers is a total order but not a well order because the set of numbers of the type $1/n$ has no least element. A pair $\langle X, R \rangle$ such that R is a well order on X is called a *well-founded set*.

A *function* f with *domain* X and *range* Y (from X to Y), denoted as $f: X \to Y$, is a relation on $X \times Y$ such that for any $x \in X$ there is at most one $y \in Y$ such that xfy. Such an element y is denoted $f(x)$. In general, functions considered in this text are *partial*, that is, it may happen that for some x there is no y such that $y = f(x)$. In this case we say that $f(x)$ is *undefined*, and we write $f(x) = \perp$, where the special symbol $\perp$ means "undefined." The *definition domain* D_f of a function f is the set of all x such that $f(x)$ is defined (i.e., $f(x) = y$ for some $y \in Y$). The *image* I_f of f is the subset of Y consisting of all y such that $f(x) = y$ for some $x \in X$. For any function f, if $D_f = X$ then f is said to be *total*; if $I_f = Y$, then f is said to be *onto Y*. f is said to be *one to one* if and only if for any x, $x' \in X$, $x \neq x'$ implies $f(x) \neq f(x')$. A total, one-to-one function from X onto Y is called a *bijection* or *one-to-one correspondence* between X and Y. If f is one to one, its inverse relation f^{-1} is also a one-to-one function from Y to X. If f is a bijection, so is f^{-1}. Let $f: X \to Y$ and let $W \subseteq Y$.

The *inverse image* of W under f, denoted as $f^{-1}(W)$, is the set of all $x \in X$, such that $f(x) \in W$. Note that f does not need to be one to one. If f is a function with domain $X_1 \times X_2 \cdots \times X_n$ we write $f(x_1, \ldots, x_n)$ instead of $f(\langle x_1, \ldots, x_n \rangle)$.

For any set X, its *identity function* Id_X is defined as $\mathrm{Id}_X(x) = x$ for any $x \in X$.

Let $f: X \rightarrow Y$, $g: Y \rightarrow Z$ be two functions. Their *composition* $g \circ f: X \rightarrow Z$ is defined by $g \circ f(x) = g(f(x))$. For any two functions f, g, we write $f = g$ to say that they are identical (they are the same function); that is, $D_f = D_g$ and $f(x) = g(x)$ for any $x \in D_f$. Note that $f(x) = \bot$ implies $g(x) = \bot$, and conversely. If f is a bijection between X and Y, then $f^{-1} \circ f = \mathrm{Id}_X$ and $f \circ f^{-1} = \mathrm{Id}_Y$. If f is a bijection between X and Y and g is a bijection between Y and Z, then $g \circ f$ is a bijection between X and Z.

By an *n-place operation* (or operation with n arguments, or *n-ary operation*) on a set X, we mean a function from X^n to X. By convention a 0-place operation is a constant element of X.

Sets X and Y are said to be *equinumerous* (written $X \approx Y$) if and only if there is a bijection between X and Y. Clearly, $X \approx X$; $X \approx Y$ implies that $Y \approx X$; and $X \approx Y$ and $Y \approx Z$ imply that $X \approx Z$. If $X \approx Y$, one also says that X and Y have the *same cardinality*; and if X is equinumerous with a subset of Y, but Y is not equinumerous with any subset of X, one says that the cardinality of X is *smaller than* the cardinality of Y.

A set X is said to be *finite* if and only if it is empty or it is equinumerous with the set of all positive integers that are less than or equal to some positive integer n. In such a case X is said to have cardinality n. A set that is not finite is said to be *infinite*.

A set X is said to be *denumerable* if and only if it is equinumerous with the set $\mathbb{N}$ of natural numbers, that is, the set of nonnegative integers. A denumerable set is said to have cardinality $\aleph_0$. Any set equinumerous with the set of all subsets of a denumerable set is said to have cardinality $2^{\aleph_0}$ (or to have the cardinality of the continuum). The power set $\mathscr{P}(\mathbb{N})$ of the set $\mathbb{N}$ of natural numbers, and the set of all functions from $\mathbb{N}$ into itself have cardinality $2^{\aleph_0}$. A set is said to be *countable* if and only if it is either finite or denumerable. Clearly, any subset of a denumerable set is countable. $|X|$ will denote the cardinality of a set X. Let A and B be two finite sets. Then the cardinality of the set of all total functions with domain A and range B is $|B|^{|A|}$.

A *denumerable sequence* is a total function s whose domain is the set of positive, (or of the nonnegative) integers; one usually writes s_n instead of $s(n)$ and the argument n is called the *index* of s_n. A *finite sequence* is a function whose domain is $\{1, 2, \ldots, n\}$, for some positive integer n. Finite and infinite sequences are respectively denoted as $\{s_1, s_2, \ldots, s_n\}$ and $\{s_1, s_2, \ldots\}$. A *subsequence* ss of a denumerable sequence $s = \{s_1, s_2, \ldots\}$ is a sequence $\{ss_1, ss_2, \ldots\}$ such that for each j, with $j \geq 1$, $ss_j = s_i$ for some $i \geq 1$ and $ss_j = s_i$, $ss_{j'} = s_{i'}$, with $j > j'$ implies that $i > i'$. A subsequence of $s = \{s_1, s_2, \ldots\}$ is usually denoted by $\{s_{i_1}, s_{i_2}, \ldots\}$.

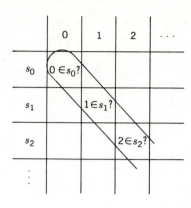

FIGURE 0.1 Diagonalization example.

It is important to notice that $2^{\aleph_0}$ is a greater cardinality than $\aleph_0$. In fact $2^{\aleph_0}$ is clearly not smaller than $\aleph_0$ (there is a trivial bijection between $\mathbb{N}$ and a subset of $\mathscr{P}(\mathbb{N})$). Suppose now by contradiction that they have the same cardinality. This implies that there exists a bijection $s\colon \mathbb{N} \to \mathscr{P}(\mathbb{N}) = \{s_0, s_1, \ldots\}$. Consider now the set $D \subseteq \mathbb{N}$ consisting of exactly those numbers n which do not belong to the set $s_n \in \mathscr{P}(\mathbb{N})$. Formally $D = \{n \mid n \notin s_n\}$. Figure 0.1 helps in understanding the definition of D; in fact, $0 \in D$ if and only if $0 \notin s_0$, $1 \in D$ if and only if $1 \notin s_1, \ldots$ D is a subset of $\mathbb{N}$, thus $D \in \mathscr{P}(\mathbb{N})$. Therefore there must exist an index i such that $D = s_i$ (the sequence s enumerates *all* subsets of $\mathbb{N}$). Consider whether or not $i \in s_i$. In the positive case, since $D = s_i$, i must not belong to s_i by definition of D: a contradiction. Similarly, in the negative case, $i \notin s_i$ implies by definition that i is in D, that is, in s_i: again, a contradiction. Thus $\mathbb{N}$ and $\mathscr{P}(\mathbb{N})$ are not equinumerous.

The above reasoning is called *diagonalization* (see Figure 0.1) and is due to Cantor. We will later realize that it is a fundamental proof technique in computation theory.

0.1.2 Basic Algebraic Structures

A *semigroup* is a pair $\langle S, \circ \rangle$, where S is a set and $\circ$ is an *associative operation* on S, that is, a function $\circ\colon S \times S \to S$ such that A1: $\forall x \forall y \forall z (\circ(\circ(x, y), z) = \circ(x, \circ(y, z)))$.

In general, $\circ$ is used with *infix notation*, that is, $x \circ y$ stands for $\circ(x, y)$.

A *monoid* is a semigroup such that there exists an element $u \in S$ which is a *right* and *left unit* with respect to $\circ$; that is, A2: $\forall x (x \circ u = u \circ x = x)$. A monoid has a unique unit u. In fact, suppose there are two such units u_1, u_2: we have $u_1 \circ u_2 = u_2 \circ u_1 = u_2$ because u_1 is unit and $u_2 \circ u_1 = u_1 \circ u_2 = u_1$ because u_2 is unit. Thus $u_2 = u_1$.

A *group* is a monoid where, for each $x \in S$, there exists an *inverse element* denoted by x^{-1} such that A3: $\forall x (x \circ x^{-1} = x^{-1} \circ x = u)$. For each x, x^{-1} is unique. In fact, suppose there exist x, x_1^{-1}, x_2^{-1} such that $x \circ x_1^{-1} = x_1^{-1} \circ x = u$,

$x \circ x_2^{-1} = x_2^{-1} \circ x = u$: thus $x_1^{-1} = x_1^{-1} \circ u = x_1 \circ (x \circ x_2^{-1}) = (x_1^{-1} \circ x) \circ x_2^{-1} = u \circ x_2^{-1} = x_2^{-1}$. Notice that $u^{-1} = u$: in fact, $u^{-1} = u^{-1} \circ u = u$.

Let $\langle S, \circ \rangle$ be a semigroup. For any $X \subseteq S$, X^+ denotes the subset of S *generated by* X, that is, the set of all elements $s \in S$ such that $s = x_1 \circ x_2 \circ x_3 \circ \cdots \circ x_n$ for some $n \geq 1$, $x_i \in X$. Notice that parentheses are not necessary in the foregoing notation, thanks to the associativity of $\circ$. Thus $x_1 \circ x_2 \circ x_3$ can be equivalently read as $(x_1 \circ x_2) \circ x_3$ or $x_1 \circ (x_2 \circ x_3)$. X^+ is a *subsemigroup of* S, that is, it is a semigroup with respect to $\circ$. In fact if $x_1, x_2 \in X^+$, then obviously $x_1 \circ x_2 \in X^+$.

If $\langle S, \circ, u \rangle$ is a monoid, then $X^* = X^+ \cup \{u\}$ is a submonoid of S and is called the *submonoid generated by* X. If $X^+ = S$, X is called a set of *generators of the semigroup* S. Similarly, X is called a set of *generators of the monoid* S if $X^* = S$.

For a given set X and operation symbol $\circ$, the set X^+ of all elements $s = x_1 \circ x_2 \cdots \circ x_n$ with $n \geq 1$ is called the *free semigroup* generated by X and $\circ$. In fact, if $s_1 = x_1 \circ \cdots \circ x_k$, $s_2 = y_1 \circ \cdots \circ y_r$, $s_1 \circ s_2 = x_1 \circ \cdots \circ x_k \circ y_1 \cdots \circ y_r$. If conventionally we add a *unit element* u to X^+ such that $x \circ u = u \circ x = x$ for every $x \in X$, we obtain the *free monoid* $X^* = X^+ \cup \{u\}$ generated by X and $\circ$.

Let $\langle S, \circ \rangle$ be a semigroup. A *congruence* on S is an equivalence relation C preserving the operation $\circ$, that is, such that xCy implies that $x \circ zCy \circ z$ and $z \circ xCz \circ y$, for each z. If C is a congruence on a semigroup S, the set of C-equivalence classes of S, called S *modulo* C or S *quotient* C and denoted $S \bmod C$ or S/C is made a semigroup by defining $[y] \circ [z] = [y \circ z]$ for any $y, z \in S$. The foregoing definition is well defined because $[y_1] = [y_2]$ if and only if $y_1 C y_2$. In such a case $[y_1] \circ [z] = [y_2] \circ [z] = [y_1 \circ z] = [y_2 \circ z]$ since $y_1 \circ zCy_2 \circ z$. Thus the definition does not depend on the choice of the element y (and z) within the class $[y]$ (and $[z]$). Furthermore, $([x] \circ [y]) \circ [z] = [x \circ y] \circ [z] = [x \circ y \circ z] = [x \circ (y \circ z)] = [x] \circ [y \circ z] = [x] \circ ([y] \circ [z])$. Thus S/C is a semigroup with respect to the operation $\circ$ defined on C-equivalence classes.

If S is a monoid, then S/C is a monoid as well, its unit being $[u]$. In fact, for each x, $[x] \circ [u] = [x \circ u] = [x] = [u \circ x] = [u] \circ [x]$. If S is a group, then S/C is a group as well. In fact, for each x, $[x]^{-1} = [x^{-1}]$ since $[u] = [x \circ x^{-1}] = [x] \circ [x^{-1}]$ and $[u] = [x^{-1} \circ x] = [x^{-1}] \circ [x]$. In such cases, S/C is called the *quotient monoid* and *quotient group*, respectively.

For example, let $\mathbb{N}$ and $\mathbb{Z}$ be the sets of natural numbers and the set of integers, respectively. $\langle \mathbb{N}, + \rangle$ is a semigroup and $\langle \mathbb{N}, +, 0 \rangle$ is a monoid. However, $\mathbb{N}$ is not a group with respect to the operation $+$. Instead, $\mathbb{Z}$ is a group, with respect to the operation $+$, unit 0, and inverse $-$ (for every x, x^{-1} is denoted $-x$). The elements 0 and 1 form a set of generators for $\mathbb{N}$.

Define the relation $\equiv_k$ on $\mathbb{N}$ by $x \equiv_k y$ if and only if the remainder of integer division of x by k equals the remainder of integer division of y by k, that is, there exist d_1, d_2, and r such that $x = d_1 \cdot k + r$, $y = d_2 \cdot k + r$ and $0 \leq r < k$. In such a case $[x] = [y] = [r]$. $\equiv_k$ is a congruence with respect to

$+$, that is, $x \equiv_k y$ implies $x + z \equiv_k y + z$. In fact, let $z = d_3 \cdot k + s, 0 \leq s < k$. Thus $x + z = d_1 \cdot k + r + d_3 \cdot k + s = (d_1 + d_3) \cdot k + s + r$, $y + z = d_2 \cdot k + r + d_3 \cdot k + s = (d_2 + d_3) \cdot k + r + s$. Let be $s + r = d \cdot k + c, 0 \leq c < k$. Thus $x + z = (d_1 + d_3 + d) \cdot k + c$, $y + z = (d_2 + d_3 + d) \cdot k + c$, that is, $[x + z] = [y + z] = [c]$.

$\mathbb{N}/\equiv_k$ is called the *class of remainders* modulo k. It is also a group by defining $-[x] = [-x]$. In fact, for any x, $[x] + (-[x]) = [x] + [-x] = [x - x] = [0]$.

Let X and Y be two semigroups or monoids or groups. A function $h: X \to Y$ is a (semigroup, monoid, or group, respectively) *homomorphism* if and only if, for any $x_1, x_2 \in X$, $h(x_1 \circ x_2) = h(x_1) \circ h(x_2)$. If X and Y are monoids and u, u' denote their respective units, then $h(u) = u'$ for any homomorphism from X to Y. In fact, for any x, $h(x) = h(x \circ u) = h(x) \circ h(u)$, $h(x) = h(u \circ x) = h(u) \circ h(x)$. Thus $h(u)$ is a right and left unit for Y. Furthermore, if X and Y are groups, then for any x, $h(x^{-1}) = h(x)^{-1}$. In fact $u' = h(u) = h(x \circ x^{-1}) = h(x) \circ h(x^{-1}) = h(x^{-1} \circ x) = h(x^{-1}) \circ h(x)$, that is, $h(x^{-1})$ is the inverse of $h(x)$.

If $h: X \to Y$ is a bijection and a homomorphism, then it is called an *isomorphism* between X and Y. If there exists an isomorphism between two semigroups, monoids, or groups, respectively, they are said to be *isomorphic*.

A *poset* (*partially ordered set*) is a pair $(S, \leq)$ where S is a set and $\leq$ a reflexive partial order on S. A *lattice* is a poset such that for any x, y, with $x, y \in S$, there exist a greatest lower bound (GLB) and a least upperbound (LUB) of x and y in S, respectively, denoted by $x \sqcap y$ and $x \sqcup y$. Furthermore there exists a *universal lower bound* $\underline{0}$ such that $\underline{0} \leq x$ for any $x \in S$.

A *Boolean algebra* is a lattice with a universal element $\underline{1}$ and complement operation $\neg: S \to S$ such that for every x, $x \sqcup (\neg x) = \underline{1}$, $x \sqcap (\neg x) = \underline{0}$. Equivalently a Boolean algebra can be defined as the 6-tuple $\langle S, \sqcup, \sqcap, \underline{0}, \underline{1}, \neg \rangle$, by considering the relation $\leq$ as an *abbreviation for $x \sqcap y = x$* (in fact, $x \sqcap y = x$ if and only if $x \leq y$).

0.1.3 Permutations and Combinations

A *permutation* p over n elements is a bijection from the set $\{1, 2, \ldots, n\}$ onto itself. A usual way to denote a permutation p is the following

$$p = \begin{pmatrix} 1, & 2, \ldots, n \\ i_1, & i_2, \ldots, i_n \end{pmatrix}$$

which means: $p(1) = i_1, \ldots, p(n) = i_n$. The set P_n of all permutations over n elements is clearly a group with respect to functional composition. A *cyclic permutation* over n elements is a permutation p such that there exists $k, 0 < k < n - 1$, such that $p(i) \equiv_n i + k$, for $1 \leq i \leq n$.

The notion of a permutation over n elements is immediately extended to *any* set of n elements $a_1 \ldots a_n$ by stating a natural bijection between $\{a_1, \ldots, a_n\}$ and $\{1, \ldots, n\}$.

The number of different permutations over n elements is $n!$ (read n *factorial*), where $n! = $ **if** $n = 0$ **then** 1 **else** $\prod_{i=1}^{n} i$.

Let S be a set. An r-*multiset* (or *bag*) of S is an unordered collection of r elements of S, with *possible repetitions*. Thus if S is $\{a, b, c, d, e\}$ a 5-multiset of S is $\{a, a, b, a, e\}$. An r-*combination* of S is an r-multiset of S where each element of S occurs once at most. A 3-combination of the above S is $\{a, c, d\}$. The number $C(n, r)$ of r-combinations of a set of n elements is thus the number of different ways of choosing r elements from a given set of n elements. It is $C(n,r) = \binom{n}{r}$ where $\binom{n}{r}$ denotes the binomial coefficient of the element t^r in the polynomial expansion of $(1 + t)^n = a_0 + a_1 t \ldots + a_r t^r \ldots a_n t^n$; that is, $\binom{n}{r} = a_r$. Also, $\binom{n}{r} = \dfrac{n!}{(n - r)! r!}$.

0.1.4 Graphs and Trees

A *graph* G is a pair $\langle V, E \rangle$, where V is a (usually finite) set of *vertices* (or *nodes*) and E is a set of *edges* (or *arcs*), each edge being a pair of vertices. If the edges are *ordered pairs*, then G is said to be *directed* (also called a *digraph*). If the edges are unordered pairs (namely, $\langle v_1, v_2 \rangle$ is considered to be the same object as $\langle v_2, v_1 \rangle$) then G is said to be *undirected*. Here we will refer to directed graphs, unless the contrary is explicitly stated. In any directed edge $\langle v_i, v_j \rangle$, v_i is called the *source* of the edge and v_j is called the *target* of the edge. An *S-labeled graph* —whether directed or not—is a graph whose edges are associated to a *label*, belonging to a given set S; that is, an edge is a pair $\langle \langle v_i, v_j \rangle, l \rangle$ when $\langle v_i, v_j \rangle$ is a pair of vertices and $l \in S$.

Graphs owe their name to the natural graphical representation that is used to represent them. So the graph $G = \langle \{A, B, C, D, E\}, \{\langle A, B \rangle, \langle B, A \rangle, \langle A, C \rangle, \langle C, E \rangle, \langle E, D \rangle, \langle D, A \rangle, \langle D, B \rangle\} \rangle$ is represented by Figure 0.2. If G were an undirected graph, it would be represented as in Figure 0.3, where the arrows of Figure 0.2 have been substituted by undirected edges and the two edges $\langle A, B \rangle$ and $\langle B, A \rangle$ have been collapsed into a single edge. Occasionally, several arcs may connect two given nodes. In this case, we speak of *multigraphs*. Multigraphs may be formally defined by means of multisets of the set of arcs.

A *path*—of *length n*— in a graph is a sequence of edges of the type $\{\langle v_0, v_1 \rangle, \langle v_1, v_2 \rangle, \ldots, \langle v_{n-1}, v_n \rangle\}$. Two vertices v and v' are said to be *connected*, or, equivalently, v' is said to be *reachable* from v, if and only if there exists a path such that $v = v_0, v_n = v'$. By convention, v is always connected to itself by a 0-length path. A *cycle* (or *cyclic path*) is a path such that $v_n = v_0$. Two

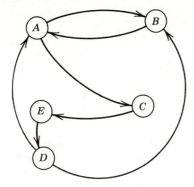

FIGURE 0.2 A directed graph.

nodes of a graph are said to be *adjacent* if and only if they are connected by a path of length 1, that is, they are the source and the target of some edge. A *directed acyclic graph* (DAG) is a digraph that does not contain cycles.

A *tree* is a DAG such that

1. There is exactly one mode n_0, called the *root*, which has no entering arcs, that is, such that there is no arc of the type $\langle n, n_0 \rangle$.
2. Any node $n \neq n_0$ is the target of exactly one edge.
3. Every node is reachable from n_0.

By virtue of the above definition, it is easily shown that there is at most one path connecting two any given nodes n and n'. Furthermore (if the tree is finite), there are *terminal nodes* with no exiting edges, that is, for any such node n there is no edge of the type $\langle n, n' \rangle$. Such terminal nodes are also called the *leaves* of the tree. If the edge $\langle n, n' \rangle$ belongs to a tree, n is called the *father* of n' and, conversely, n' is called a *son* of n. If a node n' is reachable from node n, n is called an *ancestor* of n' and n' a *descendant* of n. A node n together with all its descendants and connecting edges in a tree T is called a *subtree* of T, and n is

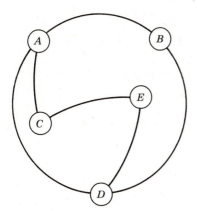

FIGURE 0.3 An undirected graph.

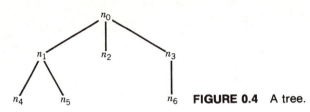

FIGURE 0.4 A tree.

the root of the subtree. Figure 0.4 provides an example of a tree. For simplicity, edges are implicitly assumed as downwards directed. A *binary tree* is a tree such that each node either is a leaf or has exactly two sons.

0.1.5 Alphabets, Strings, and Languages

An *alphabet* (or *vocabulary*) V is a finite set of elementary objects called *symbols* (or *characters*). Examples of alphabets are the alphabet of letters $\{a, b, c, \ldots, z\}$, the alphabet of decimal digits $\{0, 1, \ldots, 9\}$, the alphabet of binary digits $\{0, 1\}$, or the alphabet of the Pascal language. A *string* over an alphabet V is a finite sequence on V. A string $s = \{s_1, s_2, \ldots, s_n\}$ is usually denoted by the simpler notation $s_1 s_2 \ldots s_n$. Examples of strings over the alphabet $\{a, b, \ldots, z\}$ are *abzc, baa, ceabaazzc, love*. By convection, ϵ denotes the *empty string* (i.e., the string consisting of no symbols). Let x be a string. The notation $|x|$ denotes the *length* of x (i.e., the cardinality of its domain). For example, $|aba| = 3$, $|a| = 1$, $|\epsilon| = 0$, etc. If $x = s_1 s_2 \ldots s_n$ is a string, we say that the symbols s_i, $i = 1, \ldots, n$ *occur* in x at *position i*. So if $x = abaac$, a occurs in x at positions 1, 3, and 4, and the third occurrence of a in x is at position 4.

The *concatenation* $x \cdot y$, of two strings x and y consists of all characters of x followed by the characters of y. So, if $x = geo$, $y = rge$, $x \cdot y$ is *george*. Formally, concatenation is an operation on the set of strings defined in the following way: let $x = a_1 a_2 \ldots a_n$, $y = b_1 b_2 \ldots b_m$, with $n, m \geq 1$, then $x \cdot y = c_1 c_2 \ldots c_{n+m}$, with $c_i = a_i$ for $1 \leq i \leq n$, $c_i = b_{i-n}$ for $n + 1 \leq i \leq n + m$. By convention, for any x, $x \cdot \epsilon = \epsilon \cdot x = x$, that is, ϵ is a right and left unit with respect to $\cdot$. When no doubt may arise, one can write xy in place of $x \cdot y$. Notice that the concatenation operation is associative. Thus for any alphabet V the set of all strings over V is exactly the free monoid V^*.

A string x is called a *prefix* of y if there exists a string z such that $y = xz$. If $z \neq \epsilon$, then x is a *proper prefix* of y. Similarly, x is a (proper) *suffix* of y if there exists z such that $y = zx$ (with $z \neq \epsilon$).

Let x be any string. x^i denotes the concatenation of x with itself $i - 1$ times, that is, $x^0 = \epsilon$ (by convention), $x^{i+1} = x^i \cdot x$.

A *language* L over an alphabet V is a subset of V^*, that is, a set of strings on V. For instance, if $V = \{a, b, c\}$, the following are languages on V.

$L_1 = \emptyset$ (the empty language; i.e., the empty subset of V)

$L_2 = \{\epsilon\}$ (the language containing just the empty string; notice that $L_1 \neq L_2$)

$L_3 = \{a, b, c\} = V$ (the language whose elements are just the strings of length 1)

$L_4 = \{aa, ba, ab\}$

$L_5 = \{a, aaa, aaaaa, bc\}$

$L_6 = \{ab, aab, aaab, aaaab, \dots\}$ (the infinite language whose strings consist of any number of a's followed by a single b; L_6 can also be defined in the more compact way $L_6 = \{a^n b \mid n \geq 1\}$)

$L_7 = \{(ab)^n c^m \mid n \geq 1, m \geq 2\}$

$L_8 = \{a^n b^n \mid n \geq 1\} = \{ab, aabb, aaabbb, \dots\}$

Since languages are sets of strings the usual operations $\cup, \cap, -$ are implicitly defined, in particular the *complement* $\bar{L}$ of L denotes $V^* - L$. For instance, $L_7 \cap L_8 = \emptyset$, $L_1 \cup L_2 \cup L_8 = \{a^n b^n \mid n \geq 0\}$. Besides the Boolean operations $\cup, \cap, -$, the following operations are defined on languages.

The *concatenation* $L \cdot M$ (LM when no confusion may arise) of two languages L and M is defined as $L \cdot M = \{x \cdot y \mid x \in L, y \in M\}$, that is, any string of $L \cdot M$ is obtained by concatenating one string of L with one string of M. For instance $L_3 \cdot L_4 = \{aaa, aba, aab, baa, bba, bab, caa, cba, cab\}$. For any language L, L^i is defined similarly to the case of strings, that is, $L^0 = \{\epsilon\}$ (notice that $\emptyset^0 = \{\epsilon\}$), $L^{i+1} = L \cdot L^i$.

The *closure* or (*Kleene-star operation*), *, is defined on any language L by

$$L^* = \bigcup_{i=0}^{\infty} L^i = L^0 \cup L \cup L \cdot L \cup \dots$$

L^+ stands for $L^* - \{\epsilon\} = L \cup L \cdot L \cup \dots$

For instance $\emptyset^* = \{\epsilon\}$, $L_3^* = V^*$, the *universal* language,

$$L_8^+ = \{a^{n_1} b^{n_1} a^{n_2} b^{n_2} \dots a^{n_k} b^{n_k} \mid k \geq 1, n_i \geq 1 \text{ for } 1 \leq i \leq k\}.$$

Exercises

0.1 Enumerate the first 10 strings $x_1, \dots, x_{10}$ of L_7 by increasing length, that is, in such a way that $1 \leq i < j \leq 10$ implies $|x_i| \leq |x_j|$.

0.2 Is $L_6^* = V^*$?

0.3 For each language L, is $(L^*)^* = L^*$?

0.4 Prove that $L_7 = L_9^+ \cdot L_{10} \cdot L_{10}^+$, where $L_9 = \{ab\}^+$, $L_{10} = \{c\}$. In short, by avoiding useless brackets, $L_7 = (ab)^+ \cdot c \cdot c^+$.

0.5 Prove that, for any alphabet V, the set of languages over V, that is, $\mathscr{P}(V^*)$, is a boolean algebra by letting $\leq = \subseteq$, $\sqcup = \cup$, $\sqcap = \cap$, $\neg = \bar{}$.

0.6 Prove that concatenation is distributive with respect to union and intersection, that is, for every L_1, L_2, L_3, $(L_1 \cup L_2) \cdot L_3 = L_1 \cdot L_3 \cup L_2 \cdot L_3$ and $(L_1 \cap L_2) \cdot L_3 = L_1 \cdot L_3 \cap L_2 \cdot L_3$.

0.2   Basic Elements of Mathematical Logic

0.2.1   Introduction to Formal Theories

A formal theory is a way to make assertions in the form of mathematical formulas, to make deductions as a process of deriving formulas from other formulas, and to derive truths as formulas derived from truths. For instance the simplest reasoning "If John is hungry, then John will eventually eat something. John is hungry. Thus John will eventually eat something" could be represented by the self-explanatory sequence of formulas: "*John-hungry* ⊃ *John event-eat*; *John-hungry*; *John event-eat*," where the symbol ' ⊃ ' denotes logical implication.

The use of a formal notation to express our reasoning can have several advantages over informal descriptions given in natural language. For instance, the sentence "function f is not defined for every x" is ambiguous: it may mean either that f is never defined, or that there exists some value of x for which f is not defined. Instead, formal descriptions can be made unambiguous, consistent (noncontradictory), and complete. They are often more clear and more concise. These claims will be verified throughout the text.

Now we give a definition of the following basic concepts: formal theory, proof (or deduction), and theorem. In the next section we provide a first simple and important example of a formal theory, namely propositional calculus. In Section 0.2.3 we address first-order predicate calculi and theories. Finally, in Section 0.2.4 we briefly summarize a first-order theory that formalizes the familiar concepts of arithmetic and describes its very essential properties.

Our goal here is not to give a complete coverage of mathematical logic—a very large and relevant branch of mathematics—but only to give an introductory overview that will equip the reader with the minimum background that is needed to understand the rest of the book.

Definition 0.1

A formal theory $\mathcal{T}$ is a 4-tuple $\langle \mathcal{S}, \mathcal{WF}, \mathcal{A}, \mathcal{R} \rangle$ where

- $\mathcal{S}$ *is a countable set of* symbols. *A finite sequence of symbols is called an* expression *of $\mathcal{T}$.*
- $\mathcal{WF}$ *is a subset of the expressions of $\mathcal{T}$, called the set of* well-formed-formulas (*wfs*).
- $\mathcal{A}$ *is a subset of $\mathcal{WF}$, called the set of* axioms *of $\mathcal{T}$.*
- $\mathcal{R}$ *is a finite set $\{R_1, \ldots, R_n\}$ of relations among wfs,* called rules of inference. *For each R_i, if $R_i(W_1, \ldots, W_k, W)$ holds for some $W_1, \ldots, W_k, W$, then W is called a* direct consequence *of the set $\{W_1, \ldots, W_k\}$ by virtue of R_i.*

A wf W is a *consequence* in $\mathcal{T}$ of a set Γ of wfs if and only if there is a sequence $\{W_1, \ldots, W_n\}$ of wfs such that $W = W_n$ and, for each i, either W_i is an axiom, or W_i is in Γ, or W_i is a direct consequence by some rule of inference R_j of some subset of $\{W_1, \ldots, W_{i-1}\}$. Such a sequence is called a *proof* (or *deduction*) of W from Γ. The members of Γ are called the *hypotheses* (or *premises*) of the proof. The notation $\Gamma \vdash_{\mathscr{T}} W$ is used to denote the fact that W is a consequence of Γ in $\mathscr{T}$. The subscript $\mathscr{T}$ is avoided when no confusion may arise. If Γ is a finite set $\{W_1, \ldots, W_n\}$, we write $W_1, \ldots, W_n \vdash W$ instead of $\{W_1, \ldots, W_n\} \vdash W$. If Γ is the empty set $\varnothing$, it is customary to simply write $\vdash W$. In such a case, W is called a *theorem* of $\mathscr{T}$. $\qquad\qquad\square$

Intuitively, wfs are meaningful sequences of symbols. Axioms are formulas describing facts that are assumed as a priori true. Rules of inferences are elementary mechanisms supporting deductions. Theorems are formulas describing truths that can be derived from other statements, either a priori true or previously proved.

In all theories considered in this text one can easily give algorithms for

1. Stating whether or not a given expression is a wf.
2. Stating whether or not a given wf is an axiom.
3. Stating whether or not for a given $(k + 1)$-ary rule of inference R, a given set of wfs $\{W_1, \ldots, W_k\}$ and a given wf W, $R(W_1, \ldots, W_k, W)$ holds.

However, this does by no means imply *a priori* that one can find an algorithm to test whether or not a wf W is a theorem of $\mathscr{T}$. This fact is thoroughly investigated in the following chapters.

0.2.2 Propositional Calculus ($\mathscr{PC}$)

Propositional calculus ($\mathscr{PC}$) is the calculus of the truth of logical sentences. An example of such a calculus is the reasoning given previously in Section 0.2.1. A further example is the following: "It may not be the case that Mary is both alive and dead. Mary is not dead. Thus Mary is alive".

$\mathscr{PC}$ can be described as a formal theory in a very simple way. We define as follows the set of symbols of the theory and its wfs. Then we will digress to some background concepts before defining axioms and rules of inference.

1. *Symbols*
   The symbols of $\mathscr{PC}$ are:
   1.1 The *logical connectives* '¬' (logical operator *not*), '⊃' (logical *implies*), '∧' (logical *and*), '∨' (logical *or*), '≡' (logical *equivalence*).
   1.2 The *parentheses* '(' and ')'.
   1.3 A denumerable set $\{A_1, A_2, \ldots\}$ of *statement* (or *proposition*) *letters*.
2. *Well-formed formulas* (wfs)
   Among the infinitely many expressions, wfs of $\mathscr{PC}$ are defined as follows.
   2.1 All statement letters are wfs.
   2.2 If V and W are wfs of $\mathscr{PC}$, so are $(\neg V)$ and $(V \supset W)$, $(V \wedge W)$, $(V \vee W)$, $(V \equiv W)$.

2.3 No expression other than those derivable according to rules 2.1 and 2.2 is a wf.

Examples of wfs of $\mathscr{PC}$ are $(A_1 \supset A_2)$ and $((\neg A_1) \supset (A_2 \wedge A_1))$.

Before giving axioms and inference rules of $\mathscr{PC}$, a few remarks are in order. $\mathscr{PC}$ is intended to compute the truth of some logical statements. Thus we *interpret* $\mathscr{PC}$ wfs as statements that may be either true or false. More precisely each statement letter is interpreted as a *logical variable*, that is, a variable ranging its values in the domain $\{T, F\}$. Each wf containing letters $A_1, \ldots, A_n$ is associated to a *truth function* with domain $\{T, F\}^n$ and range $\{T, F\}$. Elementary truth functions are associated to logical connectives as specified by Table 0.1.

TABLE 0.1 Elementary Truth Functions

A		$\neg A$
T		F
F		T

A	B	$A \wedge B$
T	T	T
F	T	F
T	F	F
F	F	F

A	B	$A \vee B$
T	T	T
F	T	T
T	F	T
F	F	F

A	B	$A \supset B$
T	T	T
F	T	T
T	F	F
F	F	T

A	B	$A \equiv B$
T	T	T
T	F	F
F	T	F
F	F	T

TABLE 0.2   An Example

A	B	$(\neg(A \wedge (\neg B)))$
T	T	T
T	F	F
F	T	T
F	F	T

Then, the truth function W_F associated to any wf W is computed by composing the truth functions associated to the logical connectives of W according to its structure. For instance, the truth function of $(\neg(A \wedge (\neg B)))$ is specified by Table 0.2.

Definition 0.2

A wf is called a *tautology* if and only if its associated truth function always yields the value T. A wf is called a *contradiction* if and only if it always yields the value F. A wf is *satisfiable* if and only if it yields the value T in at least one case that is, for at least one element of its domain. Two wfs W, and V are said to be *logically equivalent* if and only if $(W \equiv V)$ is a tautology.   □

For instance, $(A \wedge (\neg A))$ is a contradiction and $(A \vee (\neg A))$ is a tautology. $(A \wedge B)$ is logically equivalent to $(\neg((\neg B) \vee (\neg A)))$.

Abbreviations and normal forms

As in the case of usual arithmetic expressions, we introduce the following conventions to avoid extra parentheses in wfs of $\mathscr{PC}$.

- The outermost parentheses pair can be omitted.
- When a wf contains only one type of binary connective (namely $\supset$, $\equiv$, $\vee$, $\wedge$), parentheses are omitted by association to the left: so $A \supset B \supset C \supset D$ stands for $(((A \supset B) \supset C) \supset D)$.
- The connectives are ordered by increasing precedence as follows: $\equiv$, $\supset$, $\vee$, $\wedge$, $\neg$. Thus $A \vee \neg B \supset C \equiv A$ stands for $(((A \vee (\neg B)) \supset C) \equiv A)$.

Notice now that for any wfs W and V the following logical equivalences hold.

e1. $W \wedge V$ is logically equivalent to $\neg(W \supset \neg V)$.
e2. $W \vee V$ is logically equivalent to $(\neg W) \supset V$.
e3. $W \equiv V$ is logically equivalent to $(W \supset V) \wedge (V \supset W)$.
e4. $W \wedge V$ is logically equivalent to $\neg((\neg W) \vee (\neg V))$.
e5. $W \vee V$ is logically equivalent to $\neg((\neg W) \wedge (\neg V))$.

These allow us to transform any wf of $\mathscr{PC}$ into a logically equivalent *normal form*, that is, a form that has the same logical meaning as the original formula but has a particular syntactic form. Three classical normal forms for wfs of $\mathscr{PC}$ are the following.

F1. ($\wedge$, $\vee$, $\equiv$)-*free form*: only the connectives $\neg$, $\supset$ are used.

F2. *Conjunctive normal form* (*CNF*): the wf is the conjunction, that is, the logical $\wedge$, of several *conjuncts*. Each conjunct is the *disjunction*, that is, the logical $\vee$, of several *literals*. Each literal is either a statement letter or its negation.

F3. *Disjunctive normal form* (*DNF*): the wf is the disjunction of several *disjuncts*, each being the conjunction of several literals.

For instance, the three normal forms of $(A \wedge B) \supset (C \wedge D)$ are

F1: $(\neg(A \supset \neg B)) \supset (\neg(C \supset \neg D))$
F2: $(\neg A \vee \neg B \vee C) \wedge (\neg A \vee \neg B \vee D)$
F3: $(\neg A) \vee (\neg B) \vee (C \wedge D)$

Exercises

0.7 Transform the following wfs into normal forms of type F1, F2, and F3.

  1. $A \equiv (B \vee (A \supset C))$
  2. $(B \supset A) \wedge (\neg B \supset (C \vee A))$

0.8 Give algorithms to transform any wf into normal forms F1, F2, and F3.

We can now complete the definition of $\mathscr{PC}$ as a formal theory. Axioms and inference rules are given with the purpose of obtaining truths as theorems of $\mathscr{PC}$. Let us restrict our attention to wfs in the ($\wedge$, $\vee$, $\equiv$)-free form. This has only the purpose of keeping the number of axioms to a minimum and does not cause any loss of generality. In fact, one can view any wf containing the connectives $\wedge$, $\vee$, $\equiv$ as an *abbreviation* for its corresponding normal form. These are the axioms and the only inference rule for $\mathscr{PC}$.

3. *Axioms*
   If V, W, and U are any wfs of $\mathscr{PC}$, then the following are axioms of $\mathscr{PC}$.

   A1. $V \supset (W \supset V)$
   A2. $(V \supset (W \supset U)) \supset ((V \supset W) \supset (V \supset U))$
   A3. $(\neg W \supset \neg V) \supset ((\neg W \supset V) \supset W)$.

4. *Rule of inference*
   The only rule of inference of $\mathscr{PC}$ is *modus ponens* (*MP*): W is a direct consequence of V and $V \supset W$.

Notice that $\mathscr{PC}$ has a denumerable set of axioms. In fact, A1, A2 and A3 are *axiom schemes* with V, W, U being *any* wf of $\mathscr{PC}$.

Example 0.1

Let us derive the deduction $A \supset B, B \supset C \vdash A \supset C$, which states the transitivity of logical implication.

1. The wf $(B \supset C) \supset ((A \supset (B \supset C))$ is an instance of axiom schema A1, where V is $B \supset C$, W is A. Thus it is an axiom.
2. Since $B \supset C$ is a hypothesis, we can apply MP, obtaining $A \supset (B \supset C)$.
3. $(A \supset (B \supset C)) \supset ((A \supset B) \supset (A \supset C))$ is an instance of A2 by letting $V = A, W = B, U = C$.
4. Since we have previously obtained $A \supset (B \supset C)$, which is the antecedent of the foregoing formula, we can apply again MP, obtaining $(A \supset B) \supset (A \supset C)$.
5. Since $A \supset B$ is an hypothesis, we apply again MP, finally obtaining $A \supset C$.

Notice that the foregoing deduction holds as well even if we substitute any wfs to statement letters A, B, C. Thus we obtained a *deduction schema* $V \supset W$, $W \supset U \vdash V \supset U$ for any wf V, W, U.

Exercise

0.9 Prove the following *theorem schemas* for any wfs, V and W.

1. $\neg\neg V \supset V$
2. $V \supset \neg\neg V$
3. $(V \supset W) \supset (\neg W \supset \neg V)$

The following statement, which is given without proof, helps derive proofs in $\mathscr{PC}$.

Statement 0.1 (Deduction Theorem)
If Γ is a set of wfs, V and W are wfs and $\Gamma, V \vdash W$, then $\Gamma \vdash V \supset W$. In particular, if $V \vdash W$, then $\vdash V \supset W$. □

Intuitively, the Deduction Theorem states that a hypothesis in a deduction logically implies the deduced formula. As an example, let us derive the deduction of Example 0.1 by using Statement 0.1. All what we need is the deduction $A \supset B, B \supset C, A \vdash C$. This is obtained in a trivial way. In fact, B follows from $A \supset B$ and A by MP; and C follows from $B \supset C$ and B by MP. Then we apply Statement 0.1 by letting $\Gamma = \{A \supset B, B \supset C\}$ and $V, W = A, C$ respectively.

Notice that the Deduction Theorem states a property of $\mathscr{PC}$, but *it is not a theorem of $\mathscr{PC}$*. In fact, it cannot even be stated as a wf of $\mathscr{PC}$. Sometimes properties of a formal theory, which are not proved *inside the theory* (i.e., as theorems of the theory itself), are called *metatheorems*. Instead, we use in this text the more general and informal term "statement."

Observe now that any axiom of $\mathscr{PC}$ is a tautology. This can be verified easily as an exercise. Furthermore, MP derives tautologies from tautologies, that is, if for any wfs V and W, $(V \supset W)$ and V are tautologies, so is W. Thus we have obtained the following important results.

Statement 0.2
All theorems of $\mathscr{PC}$ are tautologies. □

Statement 0.2 guarantees the *soundness* of $\mathscr{PC}$, that is, the fact that theorems of $\mathscr{PC}$ represent only true statements, a tautology being a formula that is true no matter which values have its arguments.

As a corollary of Statement 0.2, we derive the *consistency* of $\mathscr{PC}$. This means that for no wf V, both V and $\neg V$ are provable in the formal theory. In fact, if V were a tautology, $\neg V$ could not be a tautology and conversely.

The converse of Statement 0.2 holds too (we do not give its proof here).

Statement 0.3
All tautologies in $(\wedge, \vee, \equiv)$-free normal form are theorems of $\mathscr{PC}$. □

The above (meta)theorem states the *completeness* of $\mathscr{PC}$. This means that true statements are provable as theorems.

Soundness and completeness are quite relevant properties of $\mathscr{PC}$ since they guarantee that the given formal theory properly captures all "truths" about propositional calculus. We will realize later that such a pleasant fact cannot be obtained always.

Another positive consequence of Statements 0.2 and 0.3 is the possibility of testing a wf of $\mathscr{PC}$ to check whether or not it is a theorem by means of an algorithm. In fact, being a theorem is the same as being a tautology and testing a wf for being a tautology can be done by enumerating all possible (finite) truth assignments to statement letters occurring in the wf and by evaluating the corresponding truth function for each assignment.

0.2.3   First-Order Theories and Predicate Calculi

$\mathscr{PC}$ is the calculus of propositions as it allows to derive true statements from true statements. However, sentences like "John is hungry" are treated as atomic formulas that can be either true or false. No rules are given to investigate the truth of single statements like "Each natural number is odd." Consequently, simple deductions such as "All men are mortal. Socrates is a man. Thus Socrates is mortal" or "7 is greater than 5. 5 is greater than 3. Thus 7 is greater than 3" are not representable within $\mathscr{PC}$. In this section we outline the so-called *first-order theories and predicate calculi*[1] as an enrichment—in some sense—of $\mathscr{PC}$ that allow formalizing most logical and mathematical reasonings in a fairly natural way. As we did for $\mathscr{PC}$ we first define wfs of first-order theories, then we will consider their interpretation and validity, and finally we give axioms, rules of inference, and the main properties.

---

[1] For an explanation of the term "first order" see the bibliographic remarks at the end of this chapter.

Many first-order theories exist. For each first-order theory ($\mathscr{FT}$), the *set of symbols* contains

- a countable set $\{x_1, x_2, \ldots\}$ of *variable symbols*.
- a countable set $\{f_1^{n_1}, f_2^{n_2}, \ldots\}$ of *function symbols*, where the superscript n_i of the ith symbol denotes its *arity* (i.e., the number of its arguments). By convention, if $n_i = 0$, f_i is called a *constant symbol* and is denoted by a_i.
- a countable set $\{A_1^{n_1}, A_2^{n_2}, \ldots\}$ of *predicate letters*, where the superscript n_i denotes the arity of A_i and is greater than 0.
- the symbols $(,), \neg, \supset$ as in $\mathscr{PC}$, plus the *universal quantifier* $\forall$ (read "for any").

In order to define wfs of a $\mathscr{FT}$, let us first inductively define *terms*:

i. Variable symbols are terms.
ii. If $f_i^{n_i}$ is a function symbol and $t_1, t_2, \ldots, t_{n_i}$ are n_i terms (including the case where $n_i = 0$ (i.e., f_i is constant symbol), then $f_i^{n_i}(t_1, \ldots, t_{n_i})$ is a term.[2]

For example, let $\{x, y, z\}$ be a set of variable symbols, $\{a, b\}$ a set of constant symbols, and $\{f, g\}$, a set of function symbols, f with arity 1 and g with arity 2. Sample terms are $a, x, b, f(a), f(y), g(f(a), y), f(g(f(x), f(g(b, f(z)))))$.

Next, we define *atomic formulas* of a $\mathscr{FT}$ as expressions of the type $A_i^{n_i}(t_1, \ldots, t_{n_i})$, where $A_i^{n_i}$ is a predicate letter and $t_1, \ldots, t_{n_i}$ are terms.

Finally, we inductively define wfs of a $\mathscr{FT}$ as follows.

j. Every atomic formula is a wf.
jj. If V and W are wfs and x is a variable symbol, then $(\neg V)$, $(V \supset W)$ and $(\forall x V)$ are wfs.

Examples of wfs are $A(a, x), B(f(b)), (\forall y((\forall x A(y, x)) \supset B(g(x, a))))$ where symbols a, x, b, f, y, g are as above, A is a binary predicate letter and B a unary predicate letter.

In formulas of the type $(\forall x V)$, V being a wf, V is called the *scope* of the quantifier $\forall x$. In the foregoing examples, $A(y, x)$ is the scope of $\forall x$.

As for $\mathscr{PC}$, formulas of the type $V \wedge W, V \vee W, V \equiv W$ are defined as abbreviations for $\neg(V \supset \neg W)$, etc. Similarly, formulas involving the *existential quantifier* $\exists$ (read "there exists") are defined as abbreviations of formulas involving only the universal quantifier. Precisely, $(\exists x V)$ stands for $\neg(\forall x(\neg V))$.

The conventions on the omission of parentheses that were made in the previous section are restated here, with the additional convention that *quantifiers rank in increasing strength between* $\equiv$, $\supset$ *and* $\vee, \wedge, \neg$. Furthermore, we omit parentheses around quantified formulas when they are preceded by other quantifiers. Thus $\forall y B(y) \supset A(y, a)$ stands for $((\forall y B(y)) \supset A(y, a)), \forall z B(z) \vee A(x, z)$ stands for $(\forall z(B(z) \vee A(x, z))), \forall x \forall y \exists z C(x, y, z)$ stands for $(\forall x(\forall y(\exists z(C(x, y, z)))))$.

---

[2] From now on, in inductive definitions of the above type we will not state explicitly that only the objects built in such a way satisfy the definition.

Now that we have formulas, we must interpret them, that is, assign them a meaning. Remember that in $\mathscr{PC}$ interpreting a wf means to assign it a truth value. Accordingly, in $\mathscr{FT}$s, interpreting a wf will require giving values (or sets of values) to constant and variable symbols, assigning "real" functions to function symbols, and relations to predicate symbols in such a way that ultimately one can state whether a formula is true or false. To state all this precisely we need more definitions and explanation than was necessary for $\mathscr{PC}$.

Definition 0.3

Let $\mathscr{FT}$ be a first-order theory where X is the set of variable symbols, F is the set of function symbols, and PR is the set of predicate letters. An *interpretation* $\mathscr{I}$ of $\mathscr{FT}$ is a triple $\mathscr{I} = \langle D, \mathscr{F}, \mathscr{R} \rangle$, where

- D is a nonempty set, called the *domain* of the interpretation.
- $\mathscr{F}$ is a function that maps any element $f_i^{n_i}$ of F into a function $f_i: D^{n_i} \to D$ (if $n_i = 0$, then f_i is an element of D).
- $\mathscr{R}$ is a function which maps any element $A_i^{n_i}$ of PR into a n_i-ary relation of D. □

Furthermore, the symbols $\neg$, $\supset$ (and $\wedge$, $\vee$, $\equiv$) are interpreted as in $\mathscr{PC}$. We rely for awhile on reader's intuition to give universal and existential quantifiers their meaning.

As an example, consider a $\mathscr{FT}$ containing the binary predicate letter A, the unary function letter f, and the constant symbol a. As a first interpretation of the theory, assume that $\mathbb{N}$ (the set of naturals) is the domain of the interpretation, A is the relation "less than or equal to", (i.e., $\leq$), f is the "successor" function (i.e., $f(x) = x + 1$), and a is the value 0, respectively. Clearly the wf $A(x, z)$, interpreted as $x \leq z$, is true for some values of x and z and false for others. The wf $A(x, f(x))$ is true for any x, and thus also the wf $\forall x A(x, f(x))$ is true. Similarly, $A(x, y) \wedge A(y, z) \supset A(x, z)$ is true for any x, y, z, thus $\forall x \forall y \forall z A(x, y) \wedge A(y, z) \supset A(x, z)$ is also true. If now we change $\mathbb{N}$ into $\mathbb{Z}$ (the set of integers) leaving the rest of the interpretation unaffected, we see that some facts change. For instance $\forall x A(0, x)$ is false as $A(0, x)$ holds for same value of x but not for all of them.

These examples show the difference between quantified and nonquantified variables when we are stating the truth of a formula. For instance, a wf containing only quantified variables is either true or false, whereas a wf with some nonquantified variable is interpreted in general as a relation over D. Now we make these remarks more precise through the following definitions.

Definition 0.4

An *occurrence* of a variable x is said to be *bound* in a wf if and only if either it is the variable of a quantifier "$\forall x$" in the wf, or it is within the scope of a quantifier "$\forall x$" in the wf. Otherwise, the occurrence is said to be *free* in the wf.

A *variable* x of a wf W is said to be *free* in W if and only if it has some free occurrence in W. It is said to be *bound* in W if and only if it has some bound occurrence in W.

A wf is *closed* if and only if it has no free variables. The *closure* of a wf W is obtained from W by prefixing with universal quantifiers those variables (in any fixed order-say alphabetic or by decreasing subscript) that are free in W. □

For instance, consider the wfs

$W1$: $(\forall x A(x)) \supset B(x, y)$
$W2$: $\forall x(B(x, y) \supset \forall x A(x))$
$W3$: $(\forall y A(y)) \supset (\forall x \forall y B(x, y))$

The first and second occurrence of x in $W1$ are bound, while the third occurrence of x and the only occurrence of y are free. Thus x is *both free and bound* in $W1$, while y is free. All occurrences of x are bound in $W2$, while y is free. $W3$ is a closed wf. The closure of $W1$ is $\forall x \forall y (\forall x A(x)) \supset B(x, y)$. The closure of $W3$ is $W3$ itself.

Definition 0.5

Let $\mathcal{I}$ be an interpretation of a theory $\mathcal{FT}$, with interpretation domain D. Let $s = \{v_1, v_2, \dots\}$ be a denumerable sequence of elements of D and let t be a term of $\mathcal{FT}$ involving variable symbols $x_1, \dots, x_n$. We define the *evaluation* $eval(t, s)$ of t for s, in the following, inductive, way.

   i. If t is a constant symbol a, then $eval(t, s)$ is the interpretation of a, that is, $\mathcal{F}(a)$.
  ii. If t is the variable symbol x_i, then $eval(t, s)$ is v_i.
 iii. If t is $f_i^{n_i}(t_1, \dots, t_{n_i})$ then $eval(t, s)$ is $\tilde{f}_i(eval(t_1, s), \dots eval(t_{n_i}, s))$, where $\tilde{f}_i$ is the interpretation of $f_i^{n_i}$, that is, $\mathcal{F}(f_i^{n_i})$. □

Intuitively, $eval(t, s)$ is the result of substituting in t all occurrences of x_i by v_i, and then evaluating the functions that correspond in the interpretation $\mathcal{I}$ to the function symbols of t. For instance, if t is $f(g(g(x_2, a), x_1))$ and a, g, f are interpreted as '1', '+', and 'square', respectively, then for the sequence $s = \{0, 5, 3, 2, 1, \dots\}$, $eval(t, s)$ is $((5 + 1) + 0)^2 = 36$.

Now, we come to the key notion of *statisfiability* of a wf. Intuitively, a sequence s is said to satisfy a wf W if and only if the result of substituting all free occurrences of all x_i in W by the corresponding value v_i of s gives a true proposition under the given interpretation. The natural formalization of this definition is, as usual, of the inductive type.

Definition 0.6

Let $\mathcal{FT}$ be a theory, with an interpretation $\mathcal{I}$, and let s be a sequence of values in D.

   i. If V is an atomic wf $A_i^n(t_1, \dots, t_n)$ and R_i is the relation $\mathcal{R}(A_i^n)$ then the sequence s *satisfies* V under $\mathcal{I}$ if and only if $\langle eval(t_1, s), \dots, eval(t_n, s) \rangle \in R_i$.
  ii. s *satisfies* $\neg V$ if and only if s does not satisfy V.
 iii. s *satisfies* $V \supset W$ if and only if either s does not satisfy V or s satisfies W.

iv. *s satisfies* $\forall x_i V$ if and only if every sequence s' that differs from s in at most the ith component satisfies V.   □

Definition 0.7

Let $\mathscr{FT}$ and $\mathscr{I}$ be a theory and its interpretation, respectively. A wf V of $\mathscr{FT}$ *is said to be true for* $\mathscr{I}$ if and only if every sequence s of values in D satisfies V. In this case we write $\models_{\mathscr{I}} V$. V is said to be *false* for $\mathscr{I}$ if and only if no sequence s satisfies it.   □

To fully appreciate the foregoing definitions the reader is invited to reflect on the following statements S1 through S8 which naturally derive from them.

S1. V is false for a given interpretation if and only if $\neg V$ is true for that interpretation, and conversely.

S2. No wf can be both true and false for a given interpretation.

S3. If V and $V \supset W$ are true for a given interpretation, so is W.

S4. A sequence s satisfies $V \wedge W$ if and only if it satisfies both V and W. A sequence s satisfies $V \vee W$ if and only if it satisfies either V or W. A sequence s satisfies $V \equiv W$ if and only if it satisfies both V and W or neither.

S5. A sequence s satisfies $\exists x_i V$ if and only if there exists a sequence s' satisfying V that differs from s in at most the ith element.

S6. V is true (for a given interpretation) if and only if for any variable symbol x_i, whether occurring in V or not, $\forall x_i V$ is true (for that interpretation). Hence V is true if and only if its closure is true.

S7. If the free variables (if any) of a wf V occur in the list $x_{i_1}, \ldots, x_{i_k}$, and if the sequences s and s' have the same components in the i_1th, $\ldots$, i_kth places, then s satisfies V if and only if s' satisfies V.

S8. If V is closed, then, for any given interpretation, either V is true or $\neg V$ is true (i.e., V is false). If V is not closed, V may be neither true nor false for some interpretations.

In general, let V contain $x_{i_1}, \ldots, x_{i_k}$ as free variables. For a given interpretation $\mathscr{I}$, V defines a k-ary relation over D, consisting of those k-tuples $\langle v_{i_1}, \ldots, v_{i_k} \rangle$ of elements of D such that any sequence s having $v_{i_1}, \ldots, v_{i_k}$ as i_1th, $\ldots$, i_kth elements satisfy V. For example, let D be the set $\mathbb{N}$ of natural numbers, let f, A, B be interpreted as the multiplication, the equality, and the "less than" relation, respectively. Then the wf

$$\exists y A(x, f(y, z)) \wedge \exists y A(w, f(y, z)) \wedge$$
$$\neg \exists v (B(z, v) \wedge \exists y A(x, f(y, v)) \wedge \exists y A(w, f(y, v)))$$

is associated to the relation consisting of those values of x, w, z such that z is the greatest common divisor of x and w.

We have seen that, in general, the truth and satisfiability of a wf depends on its interpretation. However, in some case it may happen that a formula is true no matter how it is interpreted. For instance $\forall x(A(x, y) \vee \neg A(x, y))$ is true whichever interpretation is chosen. We can formalize this through the following definition.

Definition 0.8
A wf V is said to be *logically valid* if and only if it is true for every interpretation. A wf is said to be *contradictory* if $\neg V$ is logically valid. A wf V is said to be *satisfiable* if and only if there is an interpretation $\mathscr{I}$ for which V is satisfied by at least one sequence of values of D.

   A set Γ of wfs is said to *logically imply* V, or V is called a *logical consequence of* Γ, if and only if, in every interpretation, any sequence satisfying all wfs of Γ, also satisfies V. Two wfs V and W are said to be *logically equivalent* if and only if they logically imply each other.   □

The following statements are straightforward consequences of the above definition.

   S9. V is logically valid if and only if $\neg V$ is not satisfiable. Conversely V is satisfiable if and only if $\neg V$ is not logically valid.
   S10. If V is closed, then V is satisfiable if and only if it is true for some interpretation.
   S11. V logically implies W if and only if $V \supset W$ is logically valid.
   S12. V and W are logically equivalent if and only if $V \equiv W$ is logically valid.
   S13. If V is a logical consequence of a set Γ of wfs and all wfs in Γ are true in a given interpretation or logically valid, so is W.

Exercise

0.10   An *instance* of a wf of $\mathscr{PC}$ is a wf of $\mathscr{PC}$ where all occurrences of proposition letters are replaced by a wf of an $\mathscr{FT}$, all occurrences of the same letter being replaced by the *same* wf. Prove that any instance of a tautology is logically valid.

We can now proceed to axiomatize first-order theories, that is, to provide suitable axioms and inference rules such that some (or possibly all) "truths" of the theory can be derived as theorems. However, we should recall that some truths depend on the particular interpretation of the theory, while other—namely logically valid formulas—do not. For instance, let P denote any property in any theory. Then, if we know that property P holds for all elements of a set, we can deduce that P holds for any particular element of the set. Formally this can be described as deducing the wf $P(a)$ from $\forall x P(x)$, no matter what the interpretation of P and a is. Instead, the deduction of $A(x, z)$ from $A(x, y)$ and $A(y, z)$ is valid in arithmetic if A is interpreted as the relation "less than," but it is not valid if A is interpreted as "not equal to." Also, if we change the domain of interpretation from numbers to humans, the same deduction is valid if A is interpreted as "brother of" (assuming that a man is brother of himself), but it is not if A is "father of." Therefore, it is reasonable to divide axioms and inference rules into *logical axioms and rules of inference*, which are valid independent of the particular interpretation, and *proper axioms and rules*, which are specific of particular theories and depend on the way we interpret them. We describe and briefly comment as follows on the logical axioms and inference rules for $\mathscr{FT}$s. Then we will present a few simple examples of axiomatizations of particular theories. The next section is devoted to the axiomatization of classical arithmetic as a first-order theory.

Logical axioms and rules of inference of $\mathscr{FT}$s

Let U, V, and W denote any wfs of any $\mathscr{FT}$.

The following three *axiom schemas* are the same as for $\mathscr{PC}$ and are needed to support the same deductions on any propositions.

A1. $V \supset (W \supset V)$
A2. $(V \supset (W \supset U)) \supset ((V \supset W) \supset (V \supset U))$
A3. $(\neg W \supset \neg V) \supset ((\neg W \supset V) \supset W)$

Before giving the remaining logical axiom schemas we need some technical definitions.

Definition 0.9

Let V be any wf containing—among others—the free variables $x_1, \ldots x_n$ and let $t_1, \ldots t_n$ be terms. Then $V_{x_1, \ldots, x_n}^{t_1, \ldots, t_n}$ denotes the result of substituting all *free occurrences* of $x_1, \ldots, x_n$ in V by $t_1, \ldots, t_n$ respectively. □

For instance, let V be $(\forall x A(x, y)) \supset (\forall y B(x, y, z))$, let t_1 and t_2 be $f(v, x)$ and x, respectively. Then $V_{y, z}^{t_1, t_2}$ is $(\forall x A(x, f(v, x))) \supset (\forall y(B(x, y, x)))$.

Definition 0.10

Let V be a wf, t a term, and x and y two variables. Then t is *said to be free for x in V* if and only if no free occurrences of x in V are in the scope of any quantifier $\forall y, \exists y$, y being a variable occurring in t. □

For instance, the terms a and $f(a)$, a being a constant symbol, are free for any variable in any wf; the term $f(y)$ is free for x in $A(x)$, but not in $\forall y A(x)$; $g(x, y)$ is free for x in $(\exists z B(x, z)) \wedge A(x)$, but it is not free for x in $\exists y B(x, y) \supset A(x)$. A term t is free for any variable in V if none of the variables of t is bound in V. The term x is free for x in any wf.

Exercises

0.11 For the following pairs ⟨term, wf⟩ state whether the term is free for x in the wf or not.

1. $\langle x, \forall x \forall y A(x, y)\rangle$
2. $\langle f(x, y), \forall y A(x, y) \supset \forall x B(x)\rangle$
3. $\langle f(x, y), \forall x (A(x, y) \supset B(y))\rangle$
4. $\langle g(z, y), \forall x \forall z \forall y (C(x, y) \supset A(z, y))\rangle$

We can now give the remaining logical axiom schemas and inference rules of $\mathscr{FT}$s.

A4. $(\forall x V) \supset V_x^t$ if the term t is free for x in V.
A5. $(\forall x (V \supset W)) \supset (V \supset \forall x W)$ if V contains no free occurrences of x.

The logical rules of inference are

I1. *Modus ponens* (*MP*): as in $\mathscr{PC}$, W follows from V and $V \supset W$.
I2. *Generalization* (*Gen*): $\forall x V$ follows from V, x being any variable whether or not occurring in V.

The foregoing axioms and rules allow us to obtain the deduction "All men are mortal. Socrates is a man. Thus Socrates is mortal" within the framework of $\mathscr{FT}$s. In fact, the above reasoning can be translated into the following formal deduction: $\forall x (M(x) \supset D(x))$, $M(s) \vdash D(s)$, where predicate letters M and D are respectively interpreted as "being a man" and "being mortal," s is a constant letter interpreted as the individual "Socrates." The foregoing deduction can be obtained in the following way: $\forall x (M(x) \supset D(x)) \supset (M(s) \supset D(s))$ is an instance of axiom schema A4 since the term s is free for x in $M(x) \supset D(x)$; $M(s) \supset D(s)$ follows, by virtue of MP, from the above instance of A4 and from the hypothesis $\forall x (M(x) \supset (D(x))$; $D(s)$ follows by MP from $M(s) \supset D(s)$ and the hypothesis $M(s)$.

Before proceeding further some explanation is needed for the restrictions in A4 and A5. Intuitively, A4 states that if a property holds for any value of a variable, then it holds as well after substituting some term t for the variable symbol. For example, we can deduce $A(a, b)$ from $\forall x \forall y A(x, y)$. However, some caution must be used in the substitution. For instance, if we replace $\forall x \exists y A(x, y)$, with $\exists y A(y, y)$, by substituting the term y for x, we obtain something that is not logically valid. In fact, interpret A as the relation "not equal to" in the set of natural numbers. Thus $\forall x \exists y A(x, y)$ is true, while $\exists y A(y, y)$ is false. Thus $(\forall x \exists y A(x, y)) \supset (\exists y A(y, y))$ is not logically valid.

The reader who does not want to bother with the technicalities of Definition 0.10 when using axiom schema A4 may use the following little trick. Every time an instance of A4 is needed, use a variable not occurring in t as a quantified variable. This guarantees a priori that t is free for that variable in V. On the other hand, it causes no loss of generality since a wf W obtained from another wf V by replacing all bound variables of V with other *new* variables not previously occurring in V is clearly logically equivalent to V. For instance we can always replace $\forall x \exists y A(x, y)$ with $\forall z \exists v A(z, v)$.

In the case of A5, the imposed restriction is needed to prevent a wf of the type $\forall x(A(x) \supset A(x)) \supset (A(x) \supset \forall x A(x))$ from being an axiom.

Exercises

0.12 Show that $\forall x \exists y A(x, y) \vdash \forall z \exists v A(z, v)$.

0.13 Formalize the following reasonings as deductions in $\mathscr{FT}$s and prove them by means of A1 through A4 and I1, I2.

1. No man has three legs. Bobby has three legs. Thus Bobby is not a man.
2. No man can be both happy and hungry. John is a man and is hungry. Thus John is not happy.

Definition 0.11

A $\mathscr{FT}$ having only axiom schemas A1 through A5 and rules of inference I1, I2 is called a *first-order predicate calculus* ($\mathscr{FPC}$). $\qquad\square$

Intuitively, a $\mathscr{FPC}$ is a theory with no truth depending on particular interpretations. Thus it is not surprising that the following fundamental statement holds for any $\mathscr{FPC}$.

Statement 0.4

Any $\mathscr{FPC}$ is

- *Sound*, that is, every theorem is a logically valid wf.
- *Consistent*, that is, for no wf V, both $\vdash V$ and $\vdash \neg V$.
- *Complete*, that is, every logically valid wf is a theorem. $\qquad\square$

Without going into the technical proof of the statement, we invite the reader to verify—on an intuitive basis—the logical validity of axiom schemas A1 through A5 (recall Exercise 0.10). Clearly, rules I1 and I2 preserve logical validity, that is, if $\Gamma \vdash V$ and every wf of Γ is logically valid, so is V. Consistency is an obvious corollary of soundness, as, by contradiction, $\vdash V$ and $\vdash \neg V$, would imply both V and $\neg V$ being logically valid, that is, true under any interpretation. Instead, completeness is much harder to prove even on an intuitive basis and we simply state the property.

Exercise

0.14* Formalize the following reasoning in a $\mathscr{FPC}$. "Any barber of a town shaves exactly those men who do not shave themselves. Thus there is no barber in the town." State whether or not the fact that there is no barber in the town is a logical consequence of the first sentence.

We have seen that in $\mathscr{PC}$ the Deduction Theorem (Statement 0.1) allows us to obtain $\Gamma \vdash V \supset W$ from a deduction $\Gamma, V \vdash W$. Such a statement has been useful in making proofs easier. Thus it is natural to investigate whether or not it holds for $\mathscr{FT}$s as well. It turns out that the Deduction Theorem—as formulated by Statement 0.1—does not hold for $\mathscr{FT}$s. In fact, let V be $A(x)$, A being interpreted as the unary relation "is even" on natural numbers. Thus, on the one side we may build the deduction $A(x) \vdash \forall x A(x)$ through the rule I2 (*Gen*), but on the other side it is clear that $A(x) \supset \forall x A(x)$ is not true. In fact, any sequence of even numbers satisfies $A(x)$, but no sequence of numbers satisfies $\forall x A(x)$. Thus $A(x) \supset \forall x A(x)$ cannot be logically valid and therefore, by Statement 0.4, it cannot be a theorem of any $\mathscr{FPC}$.

This remarks sheds more light on rule I2. Actually, it supports the deduction of true formulas from true formulas (in fact, from the previous property S6, V is true if and only if so is $\forall x V$), but it does not have the meaning of a logical implication.

However, the Deduction Theorem can be restated in an appropriate formulation even within the framework of $\mathscr{FT}$s. We give it below (Statement 0.5) in two simplified but still useful versions without proof.

Statement 0.5
1. If a deduction $\Gamma, V \vdash W$ involves no application of the logical inference rule I2 (*Gen*), of which the quantified variable is free in V, then $\Gamma \vdash V \supset W$.
2. If $\Gamma, V \vdash W$ and V is closed, then $\Gamma \vdash V \supset W$.   □

Let us now give an example of the proper axioms of simple $\mathscr{FT}$s. For convenience we assume that $\mathscr{FT}$s have no proper rules of inference. Any time that the truth of W should be deduced from the truth of the set $\{V_1, \ldots, V_n\}$, the axiom $V_1 \wedge \cdots \wedge V_n \supset W$ can be stated allowing the deduction $\{V_1, \ldots, V_n\} \vdash W$ by means of *MP*.

Example 0.2

Let us formalize *partial orders* as a $\mathscr{FT}$. There is only one predicate letter A, with arity two. There are no function letters. In order to make the notation closer to its intended meaning we write $x < y$ in place of $A(x, y)$ and $x \not< y$ in place of $\neg A(x, y)$. However, the reader should carefully distinguish between the symbol "$<$" intended as a predicate letter and its (possible) interpretation as the relation "strictly less than."

    Proper axioms of partial orders are

P01: $\forall x(x \not< x)$. P01 is called the *irreflexivity* of $<$.
P02: $\forall x \forall y \forall z(x < y \wedge y < z \supset x < z)$. P02 is called the *transitivity* of $<$.[3]

---

[3] Notice that P01 and P02 are not axiom schemas but true axioms.

An example of a simple theorem in such a theory is

$$\forall x \forall y \forall z \forall v ((x < y \wedge y < z \wedge z < v) \supset (x < v)).$$

Its formal deduction is the following

1. $\forall x \forall y \forall z (x < y \wedge z \supset x < z)$ is P02.
2. $x < y \wedge y < z \supset x < z$ is obtained from 1 and from the following instance of A4:

    $$(\forall x \forall y \forall z(x < y \wedge y < z \supset x < z)) \supset (x < y \wedge y < z \supset x < z)$$

    by applying *MP* repeatedly, for x, y, and z.
3. $(x_1 < x_2 \wedge x_2 < x_3 \supset x_1 < x_3)$ is obtained from P02 and A4.
4. $\forall x_1 \forall x_2 \forall x_3(x_1 < x_2 \wedge x_2 < x_3 \supset x_1 < x_3)$ is obtained from 3 by repeated application of *Gen*.
5. $y < z \wedge z < v \supset y < v$ is obtained from 4 and A4.
6. $x < y, y < z, z < v \vdash x < v$ is derived in the following way:

    6.1 $y < z \supset (z < v \supset (y < z \wedge z < v))$

    This is an instance of the tautology $V \supset (W \supset (V \wedge W))$. (Verify as an exercise that the above formula of $\mathscr{PC}$ is actually a tautology.)

    6.2 $y < z \wedge z < v$ is obtained from 6.1 and from the hypotheses $y < z$ and $z < v$ by repeated application of *MP*.

    6.3 $y < v$ is obtained from 6.2 and 5 by *MP*.

    6.4 $x < v$ is obtained from $x < y$ and 6.3 by P02.
7. $x < y \supset (y < z \supset (z < v \supset x < v))$ is obtained from deduction 6 by repeated application of Statement 0.5 (Notice that *Gen* is not used in 6).
8. $x < y \wedge y < z \wedge z < v \supset x < v$ is an instance of the tautology $V \supset (W \supset (U \supset Y)) \equiv (V \wedge W \wedge U) \supset Y$.

    (Verify this as an exercise.)
9. Finally the thesis is obtained by repeated application of *Gen* to 8.

The reader is probably unhappy with such a long and tedious proof for such a simple statement. However, he or she should realize that so many trivial steps can be skipped in practice by an expert "theorem prover." Similarly, proofs in mathematics contain many statements of the type "it is clear that ... ." In such cases it is on the prover's responsibility to make sure that an apparently true fact can actually be proved in full detail.

Exercise

0.15 Prove that in partial-order theory

$$\forall x \forall y (x < y \supset \neg(y < x))$$

Hint: Use the tautology $V \supset (W \wedge \neg W) \equiv \neg V$.

Definition 0.12

A *model* of a $\mathscr{FT}$ is an interpretation of the theory such that all of its axioms are true. □

These are some simple and relevant consequences of Definition 0.12.

Statement 0.6
1. In a model of a $\mathscr{FT}$ all of the theorems of the theory are true. This follows from the fact that rules of inference *MP* and *Gen* preserve the truth of formulas in any interpretation.
2. If a theory has a model, then it is consistent. In fact, since theorems of the theory are true in an interpretation that is a model, no wf V can be such $\vdash V$ and $\vdash \neg V$, since V should be both true and false in the model. □

Any partially ordered set is a model of the theory whose proper axioms are P01 and P02. For instance, natural numbers, with the relation "strictly less than" are a model of that theory. However, this is not true if the relation is "less than or equal to." Another model of that theory is provided by the set of human beings with the relation "being an ancestor of," once it is stated that no human can be an ancestor of him or herself.

Example 0.3

The following is an axiomatization of monoids. There is one function letter with arity 2, one constant symbol, and one predicate letter with arity 2. As before, we denote them respectively by the symbols "$\circ$", "u", "$=$," using infix notation, to make formulas immediately understandable.

Proper axioms for monoids are the following

M1. $\forall x(x = x)$ — Reflexivity ⎫
M2. $\forall x \forall y(x = y \supset y = x)$ — Symmetry ⎬ Axioms of
M3. $\forall x \forall y \forall z(x = y \wedge y = z \supset x = z)$ — Transitivity ⎭ equality
M4. $\forall x \forall y \forall z(x \circ (y \circ z)) = ((x \circ y) \circ z)$ — Associativity of $\circ$
M5. $\forall x(u \circ x = x \wedge x \circ u = x)$ — Identity
M6. $\forall x \forall y \forall z((y = z) \supset$ — Substitutivity of
  $(x \circ y = x \circ z \wedge y \circ x = z \circ x))$ — equality

Clearly any monoid is a model of the foregoing theory.

Exercises

0.16 Prove that the identity is unique within the theory of monoids, that is,
  $\forall y(\forall x(x \circ y = x \wedge y \circ x = x) \supset y = u)$.
0.17 Give a $\mathscr{FT}$ for total, reflexive orders.

0.18   Give a $\mathscr{FT}$ for groups. Notice that axioms for groups must include axioms for monoids. However, M5 can be replaced by the "weaker" M5': $\forall x(u \circ x = x)$. Why?

0.2.4   A $\mathscr{FT}$ for Arithmetic and Its Functions

In this section we briefly sketch a major application of formal theories, namely the axiomatization of arithmetic, a very basic theory of almost any mathematical reasoning.

The section is divided into three subsections. Subsection 0.2.4.1 describes and briefly comments upon the classical Peano's axiom system for arithmetic: a $\mathscr{FT}$ named $\mathscr{A}$. Subsection 0.2.4.2 presents a major class of functions on natural numbers, that is, recursive functions. Subsection 0.2.4.3 gives the flavor of fundamental results on the axiomatization of arithmetics without going into formal and lengthy proofs.

0.2.4.1   Peano's Axioms

G. Peano was the first mathematician to suggest a set of "elementary truths" regarding natural numbers and their operations from which most of other truths could be deduced. An informal description of such truths is the following.

PE1. There is a natural number denoted by 0.

PE2. Let x denote any natural number. Then there is *another* natural number denoted as x', and called the *successor* of x.

PE3. Let x be any natural number. Then its successor x' is different from 0.

PE4. If the successors of two numbers x and y are equal, then x is equal to y.

PE5. (*Principle of Mathematical Induction*). Let Q be a property of natural numbers. If property Q holds for 0 (*basis of the induction*) and if the fact that property Q holds for any number x implies that the same property holds for x' (*induction step*), then Q holds for all natural numbers.

Notice that, informally, from PE1 through PE4 we can deduce that there are infinitely many natural numbers. In fact, from PE1 and PE2 we obtain the numbers $0, 0', (0')', \ldots$. Let 0^x and 0^y denote $((0')' \ldots)'$ with x and y strokes, respectively. If x is different from y, then 0^x must be different from 0^y, that is, they must denote two different numbers. Suppose, by contradiction, $0^x = 0^y$ and, say, $x > y$. Thus, by PE4 $0^{x-1} = 0^{y-1}, \ldots, 0^{x-y} = 0^{y-y}$ that is, 0 with just 0 strokes, that is, 0 itself, equals 0 with $x - y$ strokes, that is, $(0^{x-y-1})'$. But this contradicts PE3.

The principle of mathematical induction is a very powerful tool to prove properties of natural numbers. For instance, consider the well-known property P: $\sum_{i=0}^{n} i = n \cdot (n + 1)/2$. P holds in a trivial way when n is 0, which is the basis of the induction. Now, consider the induction step. Assume that P holds for any given n (inductive hypothesis): we are left to prove that P

holds for $(n + 1)$ as well. Now, $\sum\limits_{i=0}^{n+1} i = \sum\limits_{i=0}^{n} i + (n + 1)$. By the inductive hypothesis, the first part of the latter term equals $n(n + 1)/2$. Thus $\sum\limits_{i=0}^{n+1} i = n(n + 1)/2 + (n + 1) = (n \cdot (n + 1) + 2(n + 1))/2 = ((n + 1) \cdot (n + 2))/2 = (n + 1) \cdot ((n + 1) + 1)/2$ which proves the inductive step. Thus we can deduce that P holds for every n.

Mathematical induction will be used throughout this text as a major proof tool. It will be applied not only to the set of natural numbers but to any denumerable set. In fact, let a property hold for the first element of a denumerable set and let it hold for the $(i + 1)$th element under the condition it holds for the ith element. Then we can deduce that it holds for every element.

Let us restate now axioms PE1 through PE5 as a $\mathscr{FT}$ which will be called $\mathscr{A}$. The following axioms include also the axiomatization of basic arithmetic operations, namely addition and multiplication. $\mathscr{A}$ has only one binary predicate letter, one constant, one unary, and two binary function letters. As usual we denote them, respectively, as $=$, 0, $'$, $+$, $\cdot$, to make the notation closer to its intended meaning. Furthermore we will use the infix notation for binary symbols and we will write x' for $'(x)$; $x \neq y$ is an abbreviation for $\neg (x = y)$.
The proper axioms of $\mathscr{A}$ are:

PA1. $(x = y \wedge x = z) \supset y = z$
PA2. $x = y \supset x' = y'$
PA3. $0 \neq x'$
PA4. $x' = y' \supset x = y$
PA5. $x + 0 = x$
PA6. $x + y' = (x + y)'$
PA7. $x \cdot 0 = 0$
PA8. $x \cdot (y') = x \cdot y + x$
PA9. For any wf V the following wf is an axiom.

$$\left(V_x^0 \wedge \forall x(V \supset V_x^{x'})\right) \supset \forall x V$$

Axioms PA1 through PA9 allow us to derive most well-known properties of arithmetic in a rather trivial, yet sometimes tedious, way. Some examples of this are given in the sequel.

Example 0.4

The following wfs TH1 and TH2 are theorems of $\mathscr{A}$.

TH1: $x = x$. This is proved by the following deduction.
    1.1 $x + 0 = x$ (by PA5).
    1.2 $(x + 0 = x) \wedge (x + 0 = x) \supset (x = x)$. This is obtained from PA1 by replacing x, y, z, respectively, with $x + 0$, x, x. In more detail, let V be PA1. Deduce $\forall x \forall y \forall z V$ by repeated application of *Gen*. Let $V1$ be $\forall y \forall z V$ and consider the instance of A4, $\forall x V1 \supset V1_x^{x+0}$. Let $V2$ be $\forall z V_x^{x+0}$ and consider the instance of A4, $\forall y V2 \supset V2_y^x$. Finally, let $V3$

be $(V_x^{x+0})_y^x$ and consider the axiom $\forall z V3 \supset V3_z^x$. By repeated applications of MP, 1.2 is eventually obtained. Notice that the conditions for the validity of A4 are always satisfied as $x + 0$ is free for x in $V1$, and so on. In the following we will substitute any term t to variable x—provided t is free for x—in any wf without repeating this tedious sequence of deductions.

    1.3 $x = x$ (from 1.2 and 1.1, by virtue of MP).

TH2: $x = y \supset y = x$. This is proved by the following sequence of deductions.

    2.1 $((x = y) \wedge (x = x)) \supset y = x$ (from PA1, by substituting z with x).

    2.2 $(x = x) \supset ((x = y) \supset (y = x))$. This is obtained from 2.1 by applying the tautology $((A \wedge B) \supset C) \equiv B \supset (A \supset C)$.

    2.3 $x = x$ (from TH1).

    2.4 $x = y \supset y = x$ (from 2.2 and 2.3, by virtue of MP).

Exercise

0.19 Prove the following theorems.

    1. $x = y \wedge y = z \supset x = z$. (This theorem, along with TH1 and TH2 of Example 0.4, shows that the axioms for equality M1 through M3 stated in Example 0.3 are deducible in our system.)

    2. $x = y \wedge z = y \supset x = z$.

Example 0.5

$0 + x = x$ is a theorem, deduced as follows by using mathematical induction.

Basis of the Induction
$0 + 0 = 0$ is obtained from PA5 by substituting x with 0.

Induction Step
The following deduction derives the thesis $0 + x' = x'$ from the induction hypothesis $0 + x = x$.

1. $0 + x = x$

2. $0 + x' = (0 + x)'$ (from PA6 by replacing x with 0 and y with x)

3. $0 + x = x \supset (0 + x)' = x'$ (from PA2[4])

4. $(0 + x)' = x'$ (from 1, 3 and by MP)

5. $(0 + x' = (0 + x)') \wedge ((0 + x)' = x')$ (from 1 in Exercise 0.19)
   $\supset 0 + x' = x'$

6. $0 + x' = x'$ (from 5, 2, 4 through the application of an obvious tautology)

---

[4] From now on, we omit to specify obvious substitutions.

Finally we apply the Deduction Theorem to $0 + x = x \vdash 0 + x' = x'$ (verify that we are authorized to do this) and we obtain $0 + x = x \supset 0 + x' = x'$, which completes the induction step. Thus A9 allows us to deduce $\forall x(0 + x = x)$.

Exercise

0.20 Prove the following theorems.

1. $x = y \supset x + z = y + z$
2. $x + y = y + x$
3. $x \cdot y = y \cdot x$

The axiomatization PA9 of the principle of mathematical induction deserves a few comments. First, notice that it is an axiom schema, holding for any wf V, while PA1 through PA8 are true axioms. Second, observe that PE5 refers to a *property* Q, while PA9 refers to a wf V. The two terms are not totally equivalent, as a property is a unary relation on a set. Thus, for a given set S, the set of its properties is $\mathcal{P}(S)$. In the case of $\mathbb{N}$, $\mathcal{P}(\mathbb{N})$ has the cardinality $2^{\aleph_0}$. Instead, the set of possible wfs in any $\mathcal{FT}$ is denumerable. Thus PE5 and PA9 are not exactly the same. However, for our purposes, PA9 is a satisfactory axiomatization of the induction principle.

It is clear that arithmetic (i.e., natural numbers along with their usual operations) is a model of $\mathscr{A}$. Furthermore, all usual notations of arithmetic can easily be expressed in terms of previous symbols. For instance the relation $x < y$ (x is strictly less than y) is the interpretation of the wf $\exists z(z \neq 0 \land x + z = y)$.

Exercises

0.21 Give wfs expressing (i.e., whose interpretations in usual arithmetic are) the following relations.

1. $x \leq y$
2. $x > y$
3. $x \not< y$

0.22 Prove the following theorems.

1. $x \not< x$
2. $0 < x'$
3. $x < y \equiv x' \leq y$.

0.23 Give an axiom system for the algebra of integer numbers with usual operations of addition, subtraction, multiplication, and integer division.

0.24 Prove that for any wf V the following *Complete Induction Principle* is a theorem of $\mathscr{A}$ (based on PA9): $(\forall x(\forall y(y < x) \supset V_z^y) \supset V_z^x) \supset \forall x V_z^x$, where y and x are free for z in V.

0.2.4.2 Recursive Functions

Many relevant functions can be defined on natural numbers besides the successor, addition, and multiplication operations defined in Section 0.2.4.1. Among the $2^{\aleph_0}$ functions whose domain is $\mathbb{N}$ or $\mathbb{N}^k$ for some finite k, the class of *recursive functions* plays a major role. Recursive functions are defined by using a small set of *base* or *initial functions* and a small set of mechanisms to build new functions from existing ones. It will turn out that the set of functions that can be obtained in this way contains most interesting functions.

Definition 0.13

The following functions are called *base* or *initial functions*.

1. The *zero function*, $Z\colon \mathbb{N} \to \mathbb{N}$ defined as $Z(x) = 0$ for every x.
2. The *successor function*, $'\colon \mathbb{N} \to \mathbb{N}$ defined as $'(x) = x + 1$ for every x. For consistency with Section 0.2.4.1 we use the postfix notation x' instead of $'(x)$.
3. The *projection functions* $U_i^k\colon \mathbb{N}^k \to \mathbb{N}$, where $1 \le i \le k$, defined as $U_i^k(x_1, \dots, x_k) = x_i$ for any k-tuple $\langle x_1, \dots, x_k \rangle$. □

Definition 0.14

The following are operations to define new functions on the basis of other functions.

1. *Substitution* (or *composition*).
   Let $g\colon \mathbb{N}^k \to \mathbb{N}$, $h_i\colon \mathbb{N}^n \to \mathbb{N}$, with $1 \le i \le k$, be any functions. Then $f\colon \mathbb{N}^n \to \mathbb{N}$ defined as $f(x_1, \dots, x_n) = g(h_1(x_1, \dots, x_n), \dots, h_k(x_1, \dots, x_n))$ is said to be obtained by *substitution* (or *composition*) from $g, h_1, \dots, h_k$.
2. *Primitive Recursion.*
   Let $g\colon \mathbb{N}^n \to \mathbb{N}$, $h\colon \mathbb{N}^{n+2} \to \mathbb{N}$, with $n \ge 0$, be any two functions. Then $f\colon \mathbb{N}^{n+1} \to \mathbb{N}$ defined by the two equations

$$\begin{cases} f(x_1, \dots, x_n, 0) = g(x_1, \dots, x_n), \\ f(x_1, \dots, x_n, y') = h(x_1, \dots, x_n, y, f(x_1, \dots, x_n, y)) \end{cases}$$

   is said to be obtained by *primitive recursion* from g and h. (If $n = 0$ then g is a constant in $\mathbb{N}$).
3. *Minimalization* (*through the μ-operator*).
   Let $g\colon \mathbb{N}^{n+1} \to \mathbb{N}$, with $n \ge 0$, be any function. We denote by $\mu_y(g(x_1, \dots x_n, y) = 0)$ the least number y, if any, such that

$$g(x_1, \dots, x_n, y) = 0.$$

   In general, for any $n + 1$-ary relation R, we denote as $\mu_y(R(x_1, \dots, x_n, y))$ the least y, if any, such that R holds for $\langle x_1, \dots, x_n, y \rangle$. The function $f\colon \mathbb{N}^n \to \mathbb{N}$ defined as $f(x_1, \dots, x_n) = \mu_y(g(x_1, \dots, x_n, y) = 0)$ is said to be obtained from g by *minimalization* or by the *μ-operator*. □

Notice that if $f(x_1, \ldots, x_n) = \mu_y(g(x_1, \ldots, x_n, y) = 0)$, then $f(x_1, \ldots, x_n)$ is undefined, that is, $f(x_1, \ldots, x_n) = \bot$, whenever no y exists such that $g(x_1, \ldots, x_n, y) = 0$.

Definition 0.15

The class of *primitive recursive functions* is defined as follows.

1. All base functions are primitive recursive.
2. All functions obtained by composition or by primitive recursion from primitive recursive functions are primitive recursive.

The class of *partial recursive functions* is defined similarly by allowing also the use of the minimalization. $\qquad\square$

The generic term *recursive functions* will be used whenever a sharp distinction between primitive recursive and partial recursive functions will not be necessary.

The following examples should illustrate the power of the foregoing operations to define functions.

Example 0.6

The following are primitive recursive functions.

1. $f_1(x, y) = x + y$ is definable by means of primitive recursion as follows.

$$f_1(x, 0) = x$$
$$f_1(x, y') = f_1(x, y)'$$

In the above definition $f_1(x, 0)$, that is, $x + 0$, is defined by means of primitive recursion by using U_1^2 as function g; $f_1(x, y')$ is defined by using as function h the composition $U_2^2(y, f_1(x, y)')$.

3. $f_2(x, y) = x \cdot y$ is definable by means of primitive recursion as follows.

$$x \cdot 0 = 0 \qquad (g \text{ is the zero function})$$
$$x \cdot y' = x \cdot y + x \qquad (h \text{ is the function } h(x, y, z) = x + z)$$

3. $f_3(x) = \textbf{if } x > 0 \textbf{ then } x - 1 \textbf{ else } 0$ is definable as follows.

$$f_3(0) = 0$$
$$f_3(x') = x$$

4. $f_4(x, y) = \textbf{if } x \geq y \textbf{ then } x - y \textbf{ else } 0$ is definable as follows.

$$f_4(x, 0) = x$$
$$f_4(x, y') = f_3(f_4(x, y))$$

5. $f_5(x) = \sum_{i=1}^{x} i$ is definable as follows.

$$f_5(0) = 0$$
$$f_5(x') = x' + f_5(x).$$

The following are partial recursive functions.

6. $f_6(x) =$ **if** $x = 0$ **then** 0 **else** $\perp$ is definable by means of minimalization as follows.

$$f_6(x) = \mu_y(y + x = 0)$$

7. $f_7 =$ **if** $x > 0$ **then** $x - 1$ **else** $\perp$ is defined by

$$f_7(0) = f_6(0')$$
$$f_7(x') = x$$

Notice that f_7, unlike f_3, is a *partial function* over the domain $\mathbb{N}$ as it is not defined for $x = 0$.

8. $f_8 =$ **if** $x \geq y$ **then** $x - y$ **else** $\perp$ is defined by

$$f_8(x, 0) = x$$
$$f_8(x, y') = f_7(f_8(x, y))$$

9. $f_9(x) =$ exact square root of x, that is, the value y, *if any*, such that $x = y^2$ is definable as follows.

$$f_7(x) = \mu_y(x - y^2 = 0)$$

(Obviously the "square" function is primitive recursive.)

It is immediate to realize that all primitive recursive functions are total while some partial recursive functions are not.

Exercises

0.25 Show that the following functions are primitive recursive.

1. $f_{10}(x) =$ integer square root of x, that is, the value y, such that $y^2 \leq x < (y + 1)^2$.
2. $f_{11}(x, y) = |x - y| =$ **if** $x \geq y$ **then** $x - y$ **else** $y - x$.

0.26 Show that if f and g are n-ary partial recursive functions, so is the function h, given by $h(x_1, \ldots, x_n) =$ **if** $f(x_1, \ldots, x_n) \geq g(x_1, \ldots, x_n)$ **then** 1 **else** 0.

We have seen that induction is a powerful tool to prove properties on natural numbers. Similarly, primitive recursion is a powerful tool to build functions on natural numbers. These two conceptual tools are strongly related to one another, as shown by the following example.

Example 0.7

Let us prove by induction the associative property of addition, that is, for any $x, y, z, (x + y) + z = x + (y + z)$. We will not go into all the tedious details of the formal deduction since the reader should now be able to carry them out, if necessary. The induction is based on the variable z.

Basis of the Induction

We must prove that $(x + y) + 0 = x + (y + 0)$.
This in turn, can be proved by induction on y as follows

- $(x + 0) + 0 = x + (0 + 0)$ since $x + 0 = x$ and $0 + 0 = 0$.
- Let $(x + y) + 0 = x + (y + 0)$. Then $(x + y') + 0 = ((x + y)' + 0) = (0 + (x + y)') = (0 + (x + y))' = ((x + y) + 0)' = (x + (y + 0))' = (x + (y + 0)') = (x + (0 + y)') = (x + (0 + y')) = x + (y' + 0)$.

Induction Step

Assume, as the inductive hypothesis, that $(x + y) + z = x + (y + z)$. Then $(x + y) + z' = ((x + y) + z)' = (x + (y + z))' = (x + (y + z)') = x + (y + z')$. The proof is thus complete.

Exercise

0.27 Prove that for all x, y, and z, $x^{y+z} = x^y \cdot x^z$.

0.2.4.3* Some Fundamental Properties of the Axiomatization of Arithmetic

In this section we give an idea of some major results concerning the axiomatization of arithmetic. However, the reader interested in reaching a deeper and more complete understanding of these topics is urged to refer to a more specialized literature.

In Section 0.2.4.1 we intuitively claimed that the standard interpretation of arithmetic symbols over the set of natural numbers is a model for its axioms, that is, it is such that all of its axioms, including the logical axioms given in Section 0.2.3, and therefore all of its theorems, are true for that interpretation. If a theory has a model, then it is consistent since it may not happen that both $\vdash V$ and $\vdash \neg V$ for any wf V. In fact, V should be both true and false in the model. This fact is rigorously stated by the following statement.

Statement 0.7

$\mathscr{A}$ has a model and therefore $\mathscr{A}$ is consistent. □

However, we must warn the reader that Statement 0.7 cannot be proved as a theorem of the same theory, that is, there is no wf stating the consistency of $\mathscr{A}$, which can be deduced from its axioms. This fact is an instance of the following fundamental statement.

Statement 0.8 (Gödel Incompleteness Theorem)

$\mathscr{A}$ is *incomplete*, that is, there is a closed wf V such that neither $\vdash V$ nor $\vdash \neg V$.

□

Statement 0.8 has a very strong impact. In fact, notice that in any interpretation a closed wf must be either true or false. Thus Statement 0.8 means that there is some true formula of arithmetic that cannot be proved as a theorem of $\mathscr{A}$. This explains the word *incomplete*.

We will not give a proof of Statement 0.8, but we will try to give an idea of its underlying philosophy since it is a formalization of old philosophical paradoxes. Intuitively, the proof of Statement 0.8 consists of building a wf V asserting its own unprovability, that is, V is a formal statement of the fact that there is no proof of V in the theory. Now, since $\mathscr{A}$ has a model, in the model V must be either true or false. If V is true, then what is true is that there is no proof of V in $\mathscr{A}$. If V is false, then there is a proof of V, that is, $\vdash V$ and therefore V must be true in the model, a contradiction. Thus V is true in any model of $\mathscr{A}$, but this also implies that it is not provable in the same theory.

The construction of the above wf V uses a major technical tool, which is worth mentioning by itself. In fact, a method is given to describe numbers as terms of $\mathscr{A}$ and functions on natural numbers by means of wfs of $\mathscr{A}$. Also, natural numbers are associated to wfs, theorems, and proofs of $\mathscr{A}$ so that we can talk about the number of a wf, the number of a proof, etc. Such numbers can be computed as values of functions that—in turn—are represented by means of some wf. Let us briefly outline some key points of the above path.

Definition 0.16

For any natural number x, the *numeral* $\bar{x}$ is the term $0\,\overbrace{'\ldots'}^{x\ \text{times}}$, that is, the function letter "successor" applied x times to the constant 0.   □

Definition 0.17

A function $f: \mathbb{N}^n \to \mathbb{N}$ is said to be *representable* in $\mathscr{A}$ if and only if there is a wf V with free variables $x_1, \ldots, x_{n+1}$ such that for any natural numbers $k_1, \ldots, k_{n+1}$

1. If $f(k_1, \ldots, k_n) = k_{n+1}$, then $\vdash V_{x_1, \ldots, x_{n+1}}^{\bar{k}_1, \ldots, \bar{k}_{n+1}}$

2. $\vdash \forall x \forall y (V_{x_1, \ldots, x_{n+1}}^{\bar{k}_1, \ldots, \bar{k}_n, x} \wedge V_{x_1, \ldots, x_{n+1}}^{\bar{k}_1, \ldots, \bar{k}_n, y} \supset x = y)$ □

Notice that if f is total and representable, then for any $k_1, \ldots, k_n \vdash \exists x_{n+1} V_{x_1, \ldots, x_n}^{\bar{k}_1, \ldots, \bar{k}_n}$. In fact, for any $k_1, \ldots k_n$, there exists a k_{n+1} such that $\vdash V_{x_1, \ldots, x_{n+1}}^{\bar{k}_1, \ldots, \bar{k}_{n+1}}$. Thus one can deduce $\exists x_{n+1} V_{x_1, \ldots, x_{n+1}}^{\bar{k}_1, \ldots, \bar{k}_{n+1}}$. (In general, for any wf V and term t free for x in V, if $\vdash V_x^t$, then $\vdash \exists x V$). For instance, the zero function Z is represented by the wf $x_1 = x_1 \wedge x_2 = 0$, the addition function is represented by the wf $x_3 = x_1 + x_2$, etc.

Exercise

0.28 Show that all base functions are representable in $\mathscr{A}$.

Going through some technical details one can prove the following statement.

Statement 0.9
All partial recursive functions are representable in $\mathscr{A}$. $\qquad\qquad\square$

Thus we have been able to represent any partial recursive function through a wf of $\mathscr{A}$. The converse of Statement 0.9 is achieved by binding natural numbers bijectively to the elements of $\mathscr{A}$ and of any $\mathscr{FT}$ in the following way.

Definition 0.18
Let $\mathscr{T}$ be any $\mathscr{FT}$. Let $X = \{x_i\}$ denote the set of its variables, $A = \{a_i\}$ the set of constants, $F = \{f_i^{n_i}\}$ the set of function symbols whose arity is other than 0, $PL = \{A_i^{n_i}\}$ the set of predicate letters, S the set of symbols, that is, $X \cup A \cup F \cup PL \cup \{(,),,,\forall,\neg,\supset\}$; E the set of expressions, and SE the set of all sequences of expressions.

1. We define a bijective function $g: S \cup E \cup SE \to \mathbb{N}$ in the following way.
    1.1 $g(() = 3$, $g()) = 5$, $g(,) = 7$, $g(\forall) = 9$, $g(\neg) = 11$, $g(\supset) = 13$.
    1.2 For any x_i in X, $g(x_i) = 5 + 8 \cdot i$.
    1.3 For any a_i in A, $g(a_i) = 7 + 8 \cdot i$.
    1.4 For any $f_i^{n_i}$ in F, $g(f_i^{n_i}) = 9 + 8(2^{n_i} \cdot 3^i)$.
    1.5 For any $A_i^{n_i}$ in PL, $g(A_i^{n_i}) = 11 + 8(2^{n_i} \cdot 3^i)$.
2. Let $e = s_1 s_2 \cdots s_n$ be any expression in E.
    Then $g(e) = 2^{g(s_1)} \cdot 3^{g(s_2)} \cdots p_n^{g(s_n)}$, where p_i denotes the ith prime number, assuming $p_1 = 2$.
3. Let $se = \{e_1, e_2, \ldots, e_n\}$ be any sequence of expressions in SE. Then $g(se) = 2^{g(e_1)} \cdot 3^{g(e_2)} \cdots p_n^{g(e_n)}$. $\qquad\qquad\square$

It is an easy exercise to verify that g is total and one to one. In fact, different symbols are bound to different, odd numbers. Different expressions are bound to different even numbers whose unique factorization into the product of prime numbers has an odd exponent of 2. Different sequences of expressions have different numbers where the exponent of 2 in its factorization is even. Notice that the number of an expression consisting of a single symbol is different from the number associated to the symbol itself. The number $g(u)$, u being in $S \cup E \cup SE$ is called the *Gödel number* of u, in honor of the mathematician Kurt Gödel who invented this method. The method of stating a one-to-one function between elements of a mathematical theory and numbers is called *arithmetization* and has been quite fruitful in proving properties of several formalisms. We will see a major application in Chapter 2.

Among the Gödel numbers of a theory, and of $\mathscr{A}$ in particular, we are interested in the numbers of wfs, of proofs, and of theorems. A rather long but conceptually simple proof shows that the unary relations on $\mathbb{N}$ stating that a number x is the Gödel number of a wf, of an axiom, of a proof of $\mathscr{A}$ are primitive recursive[5].

For instance, the fact that x is the Gödel number of an expression consisting of a variable is expressed by the relation $\exists z(1 \leq z \wedge x = 2^{5+8z})$. As a further example let $E1$, $E2$, and $E3$ be the expressions whose Gödel numbers are z, x, y, respectively. Let $E1$ be the consequence of $E2$ and $E3$ by MP, that is, let $E3$ be $(E2 \supset E1)$. Let $x_1, \ldots, x_{i_x}$ be the *unique* integers such that $x = 2^{x_1} \cdots p_{i_x}^{x_{i_x}}$ and let $y_1, \ldots, y_{i_y}$, $z_1, \ldots, z_{i_z}$ be similarly defined. Then $y_1 = 3$, $y_2 = x_1, \ldots, y_{i_x+1} = x_{i_x}$, $y_{i_x+2} = 13$, $y_{i_x+3} = z_1, \ldots, y_{i_y-1} = z_{i_z}$, $y_{i_y} = 5$ and the relation $y = 2^3 \cdot 3^{x_1} \cdots p_{i_y}^5$ is such that its characteristic function is a primitive recursive function of x, y, z.

Exercise

0.29 Show that the relations expressing the facts that x is the Gödel number of a term of $\mathscr{A}$ and of an atomic wf of $\mathscr{A}$ are primitive recursive.

Further investigation starting from these facts leads to the proof of the following statement, which is the counterpart of Statement 0.9.

Statement 0.10
A function f on natural numbers, which is representable in $\mathscr{A}$, is partial recursive.   □

An obvious corollary of Statements 0.9 and 0.10 is that a function is partial recursive and total if and only if there is a wf V with free variables $x_1, \ldots, x_{n+1}$ such that for any numbers $k_1, \ldots, k_{n+1}$

1. if $f(k_1, \ldots, k_n) = k_{n+1}$ then $\vdash V_{x, \ldots, x_{n+1}}^{\bar{k}_1, \ldots, \bar{k}_{n+1}}$
2. $\vdash \exists x_{n+1} V_{x_1, \ldots, x_n}^{\bar{k}_1, \ldots, \bar{k}_n} \wedge \forall x \forall y (V_{x_1, \ldots, x_{n+1}}^{\bar{k}_1, \ldots, \bar{k}_n, x} \wedge V_{x_1, \ldots, x_{n+1}}^{\bar{k}_1, \ldots, \bar{k}_n, y} \supset x = y)$.

By means of Statements 0.9 and 0.10 one can build a wf of $\mathscr{A}$ stating its own unprovability along the following lines. First, consider the relation $R(u, v)$ stating that u is the Gödel number of a wf V having the free variable x and v is the number of a proof of V_x^u. Such a relation is primitive recursive and therefore can be represented by a wf WR, with free variables x and y representing u and v, respectively. Then, we can build the wf $W1$: $\forall y(\neg WR)$. $W1$ states that there is no proof of V_x^u, u being the Gödel number of V. Now, let $W2$ be the wf $\forall y(\neg WR_x^{\bar{m}})$, where m is the Gödel number of $W1$. Thus $W2$ states that there is no proof of the wf obtained from the wf whose Gödel number is m (i.e., $W1$) by

---

[5]A relation R is *primitive recursive* if and only if its characteristic function f_R given by $f_R(x_1, \ldots, x_n) = $ **if** $\langle x_1, \ldots, x_n \rangle \in R$ **then** 1 **else** 0 is primitive recursive. Partial recursiveness of R is defined in a similar way.

replacing the free variable x with $\overline{m}$. Such a wf is *W2* itself. Thus *W2* asserts its own unprovability.

The fact that $\mathscr{A}$'s consistency cannot be proved as a theorem of $\mathscr{A}$ itself can be shown in quite a similar way.

The deep philosophical essence of the reasoning that leads to Statement 0.8 can be applied to a variety of formalisms to show their limits. We will see more examples of this in Chapters 2 and 5. At this point the reader, even if convinced of the validity of Statement 0.8, could still suspect that it is due to an error in the construction of $\mathscr{A}$. In other words, the axioms PA1 through PA9 could be too weak, such that some true facts of arithmetic are not captured. Thus one could still hope to capture all truths by adding new axioms. However, it has been shown that arithmetic is *essentially incomplete*, that is, there is no way to *extend* $\mathscr{A}$ by adding new axioms in such a way that it remains consistent and, for any closed wf, V, either $\vdash V$ or $\vdash \neg V$. Since "arithmetic truths" are needed very often, for example, in programming practice, the negative impact of this fact is quite strong.

Chapter Summary

This chapter has provided some background material. First, in Section 0.1, we have briefly resumed the basic mathematical terminology. The notions of set, relation, function, group, lattice, string, and language have been recalled. Then, Section 0.2 has been devoted to supplying the necessary basis in mathematical logic to the reader who might be unacquainted with this theory. However, we did not intend to provide a comprehensive treatment of the field.

The notion of formal theory has been introduced as a tool to describe logical reasoning by means of mathematical formulas. A first and simple example of a formal theory is the calculus of propositions $\mathscr{PC}$, which introduces the use of logical connectives between sentences. Then, we have described first-order theories and predicate calculi, which allow the use of variables, functions, predicates, and quantifiers. Interpretations of first-order theories assign truth values to their sentences and axiom systems are supplied in order to derive the truths of a theory as theorems.

Arithmetic is a major example of a first-order theory. We have described an axiomatization of arithmetic which follows the lines suggested by Peano. We have introduced the major class of recursive functions on natural numbers and we have used them to show the intrinsic incompleteness, that is, the impossibility of deriving as theorems all truths of the theory.

Bibliographic Remarks

The mathematical concepts recalled in Section 0.1, with the possible exception of Section 0.1.5, are treated in depth in any introductory text on algebra. Let us mention for all the classical MacLane and Birkhoff (1970). The basic terminology of language theory is provided by any text on formal language, such as Hopcroft and Ullman (1969, 1979) and Harrison (1978).

Mathematical logic is a major field of mathematics that is rooted in the old philosophical works by Plato, Aristotle, Descartes, etc. However the strongest push towards its present mathematical formulation has been given at the end of 1800 and in the first half this century. Peano (1891) has given fundamental contributions especially in the axiomatic treatment of arithmetic. Gödel (1930, 1931, 1934) gave major contributions on complete and incomplete systems and showed incompleteness of arithmetic. Church (1936) and Rosser (1936) extended Gödel's results considerably.

Some classical texts we suggest for a thorough treatment of the field are Kleene (1952, 1967), Church (1956), and Mendelson (1964).

Chapters on mathematical logic have often been inserted within texts on theoretical computer science. For instance, see Manna (1974), Lewis and Papadimitriou (1981), and Manna and Waldinger (1985).

Finally, we mention that, recently, more sophisticated topics of mathematical logic than those introduced here have found relevant application in computer science (Pnueli (1979)). An important example is given by *higher-order theories*. In contrast to first-order theories, higher-order theories allow predicate letters to have other predicate letters or function symbols as arguments. Furthermore, quantification can be applied not only to variable symbols, but also to function symbols and to predicate letters. Hasenjaeger and Scholz (1961) provides background material on this topic.

CHAPTER ONE

Models for Computer Science: Automata and Grammars

1.1   The Use of Models in Engineering and Science

In most fields of engineering, design is based on the use of *models*. This is because it is often impossible, or impractical, to test whether a problem solution is adequate by directly applying it to the real world. For instance, building a bridge without any previous design decisions based on some modeling of the problem would be a crazy decision in most practical cases.

In some cases, the engineer may use *physical models*: observations and measures on a real bridge, yet strongly reduced in size, can help predict the behavior of the actual bridge to be built. Physical models, however, cannot solve all engineering problems for many reasons:

a. It may be difficult or highly expensive to build a physical model of the phenomenon under study.

b. A physical model may be helpful *after* all major design decisions have been taken, as an experimental tool for quality assurance. Building several different physical models to explore entirely different designs would be unacceptably expensive in most practical cases. Consequently, physical models are more supportive of design evaluation rather than design synthesis.

c. It may be difficult to translate the results of experiments performed on the model into results holding for the real case.

d. It may be difficult to achieve acceptable control over the accuracy of measures performed on the physical model.

Design can also be supported by the use of *formal models*. A formal model deals with *mathematical objects* that represent *abstractions* of the real entities to be modeled. Formal models allow the user to apply the rigor of mathematical reasoning in the derivation of properties of the entities being modeled. For example, a set of mathematical equations can describe the structure of the bridge and the forces applied to it. After solving such equations the designer can foresee internal efforts of the bridge to be designed.

Formal models basically require

1. To formalize the problem, that is, translate the real problem into a denotation within some mathematical formalism.

2. To solve the formalized problem by means of the tools provided by the chosen formalism.

3. To interpret the results obtained for the model in order to derive, or evaluate, design decisions.

Several errors can obviously occur during this process too, both during the informal steps 1 and 3 and during the computations of step 2. Thus, design of a complex engineering project often requires a careful use of several models of different types.

Models play an essential role also in every branch of science. The fundamental emphasis of modeling in science is more oriented towards interpretation of reality, whereas in engineering it is more oriented towards design. A model in science embodies our understanding of a certain phenomenon. As such, it abstracts away from many fine details and reflects only certain macroscopic properties of their aggregate behavior. It is exactly through abstraction that our models allow us to master the enormous complexity of real phenomena.

A model is adequate if the results we obtain by experimenting, or reasoning, on the model reflect observable properties of the phenomenon under study, within acceptable approximation limits. In other words, the abstraction embodied by the model captures exactly all properties of the phenomenon which are relevant in our studies. All best-known physical laws (such as the laws of motion, the laws of electricity, and the laws of thermodynamics) are models of physical phenomena that embody certain abstractions.

The next section explores these concepts further with the aid of simple examples. In Section 1.1.2 we discuss the use and role of models in computer science and we contrast them with the use of role of models in more classical fields of engineering and science.

1.1.1 Introductory Examples

Example 1.1

Consider the following problem: In a yard there are both chickens and rabbits. The total number is 20. Furthermore, the total number of legs is 60. How many chickens and how many rabbits are in the yard?

A student who knows about equations will probably reason along the following lines: "let x and y be the number of chickens and rabbits, respectively. The known facts about the animals in the yard can be represented by the following equations.

$$x + y = 20$$
$$2x + 4y = 60$$

The solution of the equations yields $x = 10$ and $y = 10$. Thus in the yard there are 10 chickens and 10 rabbits."

Solving this problem would be much more difficult for a student who is not familiar with equations. The reason of this difficulty is essentially in the inability to abstract away from the actual problem, that is, translating it into a suitable formal notation—the equations—that also provide some mechanical tools for its solution, for example, variable substitution.

Example 1.2

Suppose a ripe apple falls from the top of an h-meter-high apple tree. We want to evaluate the time t required by the apple to reach the earth.

Elementary physics suggests a simple abstraction of the phenomenon under study. The apple may be represented as a material particle; the only force applied to the material particle is its weight. According to Newton's gravity law, the apple has an acceleration $g = 9.81$ m/sec^2. Since the starting velocity of the apple is zero, the relation between h and t is represented by the following equation.

$$h = \tfrac{1}{2} \cdot g \cdot t^2 \tag{E1}$$

Equation (E1) shows that t depends only on h. From practical observations however, we all know that this is not true, in general, for any object. For example, the time t_a required by an apple is different from the time t_s required by a sheet of paper to reach the earth from the same height h.

In order to understand the reasons why we have fallen into this contradiction, we must go back to analyze carefully our formal model and the abstractions embodied therein. We have represented the falling object as a material particle subject only to gravitation. This means that the friction of the air has been ignored in the formal model. Practical observations show that this is a reasonable assumption in the case of the falling apple, but gives unacceptable results in the case of the falling sheet of paper.

As we already observed in the previous section, formal models give an abstract and simplified view of reality; the results we obtain by reasoning on models are an approximation of the results that can be observed in reality. If the deviation is too high, the model must be repeatedly refined, until a satisfactory approximation (i.e., a suitable abstraction) is reached.

Example 1.3

We are designing a parachute. Let h_m be the minimum height for parachuting and let h be the aircraft height. We want to know the maximum safety delay t_m after which the parachute must open in order to guarantee a safe descent.

Equation E1 can be used again as a model of the physical phenomenon under study in the initial phase of motion, until the parachute unfolds. Thus t_m must satisfy equation

$$h - h_m = \tfrac{1}{2}g \cdot t_m^2 \qquad\qquad\qquad (E2)$$

According to what we saw in Example 1.2, the value of t_m provided by equation E2 is certainly smaller than the real maximum admissible delay. However, since our purpose here is designing a safe parachute the model is perfectly adequate.

1.1.2   What About Models for the Computer Scientist?

Abstraction and modeling play a fundamental role in every branch of science and engineering. They play an even more essential role in computer science.

In many applications, computer programs are designed to replace manual procedures. This means that software designers must "reproduce," or "imitate," the "essential" behavior of the manual procedure into a computer program. Thus, computer programs are models of these manual procedures.

Software production, however, is not just programming, and computer programs are not the only kind of model issued during software production. Sound software engineering principles insist, among others, on the need for accurate requirements analysis and design. The result of requirements analysis is a requirements specification document stating exactly *what* the system is expected to do. In other words, this is a model that emphasizes the external behavior of our system. Similarly, design yields a software design document that specifies the decomposition into modules. This is another kind of model, which takes the overall software structure into account and abstracts away from details of the internals of each module.

In conclusion, software production proceeds through a series of models. Traditionally, these models are stated informally using natural language; very often they are incomplete, inconsistent, and ambiguous. Programs are the only exception. They must be formal, that is, they must conform to the syntax and semantics of the chosen programming language.

The evolution of software engineering, however, is towards the use of formal languages in all phases of software production. Formality is expected to improve not only program reliability and maintainability, but also the degree of automatic support that can be given to assist software production. Several examples of such formal languages have already appeared in the literature, but much research and experimentation is still needed before they will become truly practical tools. It is important to notice, however, that the foundations of all such languages are rooted into the theoretical concepts that will be explored in this text. The concepts we study here will provide the basis on which one can found the definition of rigorous, formal languages to be used for modeling in the various phases of software production.

Abstraction and modeling also play an essential role in understanding and designing computer systems. This is quite similar to what we see in other fields of science and engineering. For example, in order to understand, or even design, a new car it is not at all useful to model it as a set of molecules. The user of the care would like to model it as a collection of higher-level building blocks (*abstractions*), such as brake, steering wheel, clutch pedal, etc. The designer would use a different model, for example, one showing the mechanisms that connect the steering wheel with the wheels; this model will be in terms of yet another set of abstractions.

Similarly, in order to use a word processor on a personal computer, the user can view the computer system as sophisticated typewriter, equipped with a keyboard, a screen, and a printer, and providing a specific set of commands to format and manipulate texts. The designer of the word processor, on the other hand, requires a much more detailed view of the system, but still there is no need for viewing it at the level of the underlying hardware circuitery. Let us look at this point into some more detail.

Consider the CPU of a modern computer. It is a collection of an enormous number of semiconductor devices: some of them are of the type shown in Figure 1.1. The circuit of Figure 1.1 is a *formal model* of an actual device: It consists of ideal diodes, transistors, and resistors. These ideal components can be represented by suitable equations binding voltages and currents at their ends. According to the type of analysis the designer wants to perform on the model, these equations may exhibit different levels of precision. For example, a diode is sometimes represented by the diagram of Figure 1.2a and sometimes by the one of Figure 1.2b. The solution of the complete set of equations for the circuit of Figure 1.1 allows one to obtain the output voltage V_O as a function of the input voltages V_i, $i = 1, 2, 3$ (within the approximation of the used model).

It is well known, however, that the analysis of an actual computer by means of an electrical model would be impossible in practice because of the enormous

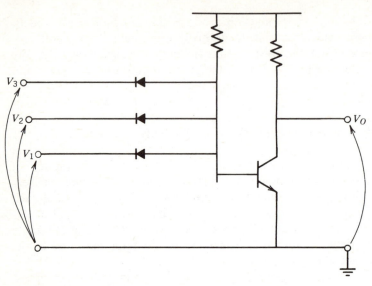

FIGURE 1.1   A circuit-level view of a CPU element.

amount of circuits involved. A further abstraction step leads to recognizing that only two voltage levels are actually of interest during the analysis of the above circuit. Let us call these voltage levels *high* and *low*, respectively (the actual values of *high* and *low* depend on the technology used for implementation). When all input voltages are *high* the output is *low*; if at least one input voltage is *low* then the output is *high*. Thus abstracting from actual voltage we can assume that V_i and V_O have either a conventional "0" value or a "1" value. The behavior of the circuit can then be modeled by a new and completely different model: the so-called **NAND** port, shown in Figure 1.3, which represents the boolean function **NAND**—**NOT AND**—(see Section 0.2.2).

Note that the change of model also implies a change of the formal tools to be used for studying properties of the model. Studying the behavior of a CPU in terms of circuits like the one shown in Figure 1.1 involves the use of differential

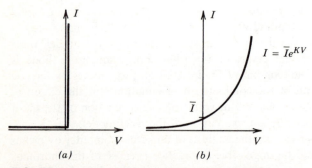

FIGURE 1.2   Two different models of a diode.

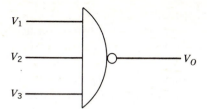

FIGURE 1.3   A NAND port.

equations on the domain of real numbers, whereas studying the behavior of a CPU viewed as a collection of building blocks like the one shown in Figure 1.3 involves the use of boolean algebra. In the latter case, we are able to represent a CPU as a collection of equations in terms of **AND**, **OR**, and **NOT** operators on Boolean variables. However, the number of involved variables and equations would still be unmanageable: More abstraction is definitely needed.

Several other abstraction steps and consequent changes of models will finally lead to the classical description of the CPU of a computer. The CPU is viewed as a collection of registers, each register being a finite sequence of flip-flops, each flip-flop being a device with two stable states called "0" and "1," respectively. Several operations, *load*, *store*, *add*, *shift*, etc. are defined on registers and on memory words. The fundamental aspect of this description is that, when reasoning on the CPU, the designer can rely only on the definition of operations like *load*, *store*, etc., with no care on, say, the law of motion of electrons in diodes during the execution of an operation.

This view of the CPU at the assembly language level may be appropriate if our purpose is programming in assembly language, or writing a compiler that translates input programs written in some higher-level language into assembly language. It is definitely not appropriate if our purpose is writing applications in some higher-level language, such as Pascal or Ada. In such a case, one might view the CPU as a processor that can manipulate typed data (integers, characters, reals, etc.) and whose repertoire of instructions includes the evaluation of complex expressions, assignments, conditionals, loops, subprogram calls with parameter passing, etc. In other words, our processor is viewed as an abstract processor that is able to interpret the instructions of the higher-level language directly.

So far, we have seen that the emphasis of modeling and abstraction in computer science is twofold. First, computer scientists need models to represent a computer system at different levels of abstraction, for understanding it, or designing it, or even using it. This is very similar to what happens in every other field of science and engineering. Second, the intrinsic essence of the computer scientist's job is building models: from purely abstract models, as in the case of formal specification languages, to concretely executable models, as in the case of programs.

The models used in traditional branches of engineering are based on a rather standard set of formal tools, particularly differential and integral calculus. Much more flexibility is needed by the computer scientist in the use of formal tools as design aids. The foregoing example of the CPU has already shown how the formalism to be used is likely to change when performing an abstraction step. We will show later that the design and analysis of software programs suggests the use of entirely different models.

The remaining sections of this chapter introduce two fundamental classes of computer science models: automata and grammars. Formal models are presented along with examples which motivate their use for practical modeling purposes. Also, fundamental properties of the various formalisms are discussed.

1.2   Finite-State Automata

The finite-state automaton (FA) is probably the simplest and most widely used computer science model. Intuitively, a FA is a system that can enter a finite set of different *states*. As a consequence of some *input*, which may range over a finite set of possible values, the FA operates a *transition* from one state to another.

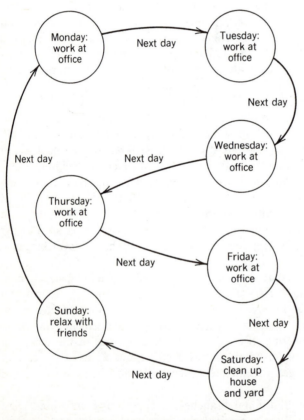

FIGURE 1.4 A FA modeling activities during a week.

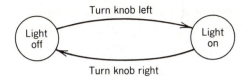

FIGURE 1.5 A FA modeling a light switch.

A graph provides an immediate representation of a FA: Nodes denote states and edges denote transitions. For instance, the graph of Figure 1.4 represents an automaton that models the activities of a person during a week. The graph of Figure 1.5 represents an automaton that models the behavior of a light switch.

Let us define a FA formally.

Definition 1.1

A *finite-state automation* (FA) is a triple $\langle Q, I, \delta \rangle$, where

1. Q is a finite set of *states*.
2. I is a finite set of *input symbols*.
3. δ is the—possibly partial—*next-state function* $\delta: Q \times I \to Q$ $\qquad\qquad$ □

It is immediate to state a correspondence with the foregoing graph representation: Nodes represent states and an arc labeled i is directed from q to $q' \in Q$ if and only if $\delta(q, i) = q'$. In the following the term, FA and its graphical representation will be interchanged freely without any explicit mention.

Let us now extend function δ to the domain $Q \times I^*$ in a natural way; that is, i.e., let $\delta^*: Q \times I^* \to Q$ be such that

$$\delta^*(q, \epsilon) = q \qquad \delta^*(q, xi) = \delta(\delta^*(q, x), i), x \in I^*, i \in I$$

δ^* defines the evolution of the automaton, starting from state q, as a consequence of any sequence of input values $x \in I^*$. For instance, in the case of the automaton of Figure 1.5 δ^* ("light-off," "turn-knob-left" "turn-knob-right") is "light-off."

Finite-state automata are extensively used in switching theory. For example, the so-called S–R flip-flop can be modeled by the FA shown in Figure 1.6. The flip-flop has two stable states, say 0 and 1, and two inputs S and R. At any clock instant, one of the inputs is applied. If S is applied, the state is set to 1; if

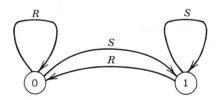

FIGURE 1.6 A S–R flip-flop.

R is applied, the state is reset to 0. Notice that the behavior of the flip-flop is described by the automaton no matter how the physical device is realized. Therefore, the automaton is an abstract model of the $S-R$ flip-flop.

Exercises

1.1   The channel selection switch of a television set can be turned both clockwise and counterclockwise to select among three possible channels. In the first case, channels A, B, and C are selected in the order. Model this using a FA.

1.2   Describe the following game by means of a FA-state. Two players, say A and B, alternatively throw a dice. At each turn, the winner of the previous turn—say A—plays first; then B plays. Let x and y, $1 \le x$, $y \le 6$ be the scores of A and B, respectively. A wins if $x > y$, otherwise B wins. Do not care about starting and ending the game.

1.3*   Describe an eight-bit shift register by means of a FA. (*Note.* This exercise requires elementary knowledge of hardware.)

1.2.1 Finite-State Automata as Language Acceptors

For modeling purposes, it is often quite useful to extend the FA definition with the notions of *initial* and *final* states. In particular, this is true when a FA is used to model the recognition of some sequences of items. For example, suppose you wish to describe the syntax of legal identifiers in the Pascal programming language: "A Pascal identifier is denoted by a sequence of digits and letters. The first character, however, must be a letter." A simple model would consist of a FA: Each character of the input stream would cause a transition of the FA and a legal input stream would cause an evolution of the FA from an initial state to

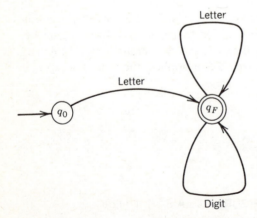

FIGURE 1.7 An acceptor of Pascal identifiers. The directed edges labeled "Letter" stand for a *n*-tuple of edges labeled $A, B, \ldots, Z$, respectively. Similarly, the edge labeled "Digit" stands for a *n*-tuple of edges labeled $0, 1, \ldots, 9$, respectively.

some final state. Intuitively, this is described by the graph of Figure 1.7, where q_0 is the initial state and q_F is the final state. In order to make the initial and final states clearly visible in the graph representation, the initial state q_0 are indicated by an arrow and the final states are indicated by a double circle.

The graph representation in Figure 1.7 models the structure of legal Pascal identifiers in terms of a hypothetical recognition process. The automaton reaches its final state q_F starting from its initial state q_0 if and only if the input stream is a legal Pascal identifier. In such a case, we say that our FA *recognizes*, or *accepts*, the input stream. The input stream is not recognized, or rejected, if the automaton does not reach its final state starting from its initial state. Here are some examples of streams accepted and rejected by the FA shown in Figure 1.7

Accepted	*Rejected*
ALPHA	512
ALPHA29	9AB3C
AB3C	17

Let us formally define a FA with initial and final states.

Definition 1.2

A *finite-state acceptor* (*recognizer*) is a quintuple $\langle Q, I, \delta, q_0, F \rangle$, where Q, I, and δ are as in Definition 1.1, $q_0 \in Q$ is called the *initial state* and $F \subseteq Q$ is called the set of *final states* (or *accepting states*). □

Definition 1.3

A *string* $x \in I^*$ is *accepted* (or *recognized*) by a finite automaton with initial and final states $\langle Q, I, \delta, q_0, F \rangle$ if and only if $\delta^*(q_0, x) \in F$. The *language accepted* (or *recognized*) by a finite automaton with initial and final states is the set of strings accepted by the automaton. If A is a finite-state acceptor, $L(A)$ denotes the language accepted by A. □

In what follows, the term finite-state automaton and the acronym FA will be used also in the case of a finite-state acceptor, whenever the existence of initial and final states will be clear from context. No ambiguity will ever arise because we refer to finite-state acceptors almost exclusively. Further examples of finite-state acceptors are given as follows.

Example 1.4

A sequence of bits represents an odd integer number if the least significant digit is a 1. This can be modeled by the FA shown in Figure 1.8, under the assumption that the automaton inputs digits from the most to the least significant.

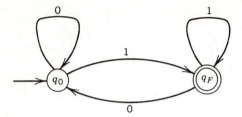

FIGURE 1.8   A finite-state acceptor of odd integers.

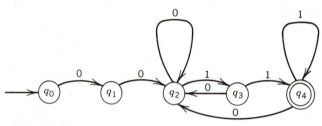

FIGURE 1.9   A finite-state acceptor.

Example 1.5

The FA shown in Figure 1.9 accepts sequences of 0 and 1 that start with at least two 0's and end with at least two 1's. Formally, the automaton accepts the following language:

$$L = \{0^n x 1^m | n \geq 2, m \geq 2, x \in \{0,1\}^*\}$$

Exercises

1.4   Build a FA accepting the language L over the alphabet $\{0,1\}$ defined in such a way that $x \in L$ if and only if x contains a sequence of at least three consecutive 0's.

1.5   Build a FA recognizing the following language.

$$L_1 = \{a^{2n}b^{3m}c | n \geq 1, m \geq 0\}$$

A string of L_1 consists of an even number of a's, greater than zero, followed by a number of b's that are multiples of 3, and followed by a single c.

1.6   Build a FA recognizing the following language L_2. $L_2 = L_1^*$, where L_1 is as in the previous exercise (see Section 0.1.5 for the definition of L_1^*).

1.7 Build a FA accepting the following language L.

$$L = \{0,1\}^* \cdot 00 \cdot \{0,1\}^* \cdot 11 \cdot \{0,1\}^*.$$

A string of L contains at least two consecutive 0's, followed, not necessarily immediately, by two consecutive 1's.

1.2.2 Finite-State Automata as Language Translators

Very often we need to model processes that produce an output as a consequence of some input. Computer programs are the most familiar case. For example, consider the following informal program specification:

> **An input text contains only lowercase letters and the special character $. The program should output the input text formatted as follows: The first letter after a $ is converted to uppercase. Two consecutive occurrences of $ are converted into a carriage return (*CR*). No more than two consecutive occurrences of $ can appear in the input text, except for a sequence of three $ that indicates the end of the input stream. The character $ is not reported in the output text; its occurrence in the input text is only due to formatting purposes.**

This lengthy and informal specification can be formalized by a FA with output that describes how an output is produced while the input text is recognized. Intuitively, the FA with output shown in Figure 1.10 is an abstract model of our program. Here, arcs are labeled by a pair $\langle a, y \rangle$ (shown as a/y) where a is an input character and y is a—possibly empty—output string.

Many informal, lengthy, and—very often—ambiguous, incomplete, and inconsistent program specifications can be converted into a more concise, precise, and formal notation using finite-state automata with output. A typical case is

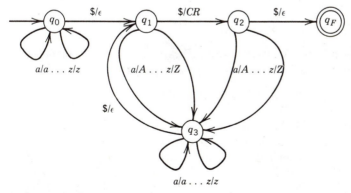

FIGURE 1.10 A FA with output.

represented by the problems of translation of an input into an output language. To emphasize this concept, finite-state automata with output are often called *finite-state transducers*.

Finite-state transducers (FT) can be defined formally starting from Definition 1.2.

Definition 1.4

A *finite-state transducer* (FT)—finite-state automaton with initial and final states, and output—is a 7-tuple $\langle Q, I, \delta, q_0, F, O, \eta \rangle$ where Q, I, δ, q_0, F are as in Definition 1.2, O is a finite set of *output symbols* and η is the (possibly partial) *output function*

$$\eta: Q \times I \to 0^*$$

Both functions δ and η are defined over the same definition domain. The FA *subjacent* to a FT is obtained by omitting O and η. □

In the graph representation of a FT, the value of η is added as a new label on arcs. Let $\delta(q, i) = q'$ and $\eta(q, i) = y \in O^*$; then i/y labels an arc connecting q and q'. The natural extension of $\eta, \eta^*: Q \times I^* \to O^*$, can be defined as follows:

$$\eta^*(q, \epsilon) = \epsilon$$
$$\eta^*(q, xi) = \eta^*(q, x) \cdot \eta(\delta^*(q, x), i)$$

Definition 1.5

Let T be a FT. The *translation* $\tau_T: I^* \to O^*$ associated to T is defined as

$$\tau_T(x) = \eta^*(q_0, x) \quad \text{if and only if } \delta^*(q_0, x) \in F$$ □

Thus T defines a translation only on the language recognized by its subjacent automaton.

Example 1.6

We wish to model a robot with two hands. The robot receives a sequence of dishes and cups, and operates as follows on receiving an item.

1. If both hands are free, the robot gets the item in its left hand, be it a dish or a cup.
2. If the robot's left hand holds an item, the new item it receives must be of a different type; in such a case the item is picked up by the right hand.
3. The robot puts the cup over the dish and outputs them.
4. When the input stream terminates, both hands of the robot must be free.

Figure 1.11 gives an informal pictorial description of the robot, while Figure 1.12

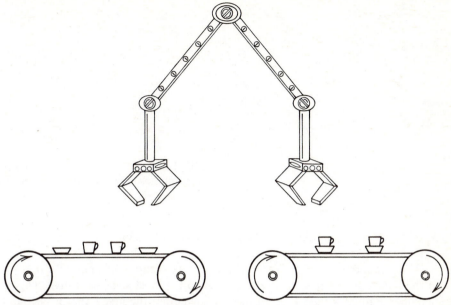

FIGURE 1.11   A robot assembling dishes and cups.

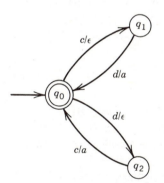

FIGURE 1.12   A FT modeling the robot of Figure 1.11.

gives a FT modeling the robot; here, c stands for cup, d stands for dish, and a stands for assembled item.

The automaton can be seen also as a *string transducer*: It accepts strings belonging to the set $\{cd, dc\}^*$ and *translates* them into strings belonging to $\{a\}^*$. More precisely, a sequence of n 2-character strings (cd or dc) are translated into a sequence of n a's.

Example 1.7

A commonly used internal binary representation for integers is called *two's-complement*. In this representation, positive integers are represented by their magni-

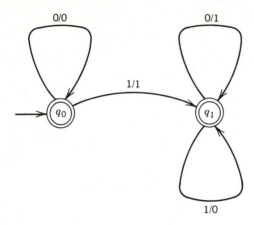

FIGURE 1.13 A FT performing negation of a number in two's–complement representation.

tude. The negation of a positive number is given by complementing every bit and then adding a 1 in the unit's position.

This is another equivalent way of performing negation of number n: Let us scan the binary representation from the least to the most significant digit. Digits are copied identically in output up to (and including) the first 1 that is encountered. From this point on, every digit is copied in complemented form.

Figure 1.13 illustrates a FT which models negation of a number in two's-complement representation.

Exercises

1.8   Design a FT that
   a. Recognizes the language $L = \{(ab)^n ccc(ba)^m | n \geq 1,\ m \geq 0\}$.
   b. Translates any string of the language into the string $d^{2n} e f^{\lfloor m/2 \rfloor}$, where n, m are the same numbers as in point a and, as usual, $\lfloor m/2 \rfloor$ denotes the integer truncation of $m/2$.

1.9   Design a FT that writes a \$ every time it recognizes, within the input stream $x \in \{a, b, 0, 1\}^*$, three consecutives b's with at least one 0 in the preceding five characters. For example, *abbabbb0a1bbb* should produce \$, *a0bbbb1ab01ab1abbb01bbb* should produce \$\$\$, etc.....

1.10   Build a program simulating the behavior of any FA A used as language recognizer. The program receives as input a description of the automaton to be simulated and the string x to be recognized. It produces as output a message stating whether $x \in L(A)$.

Hint: A can be described by a data structure consisting of

- A list of A's states, the first element of which being the initial state.
- A list of final states.
- A list of input symbols.
- A rectangular array of size $|Q| \times |I|$ representing the transition function δ.

Thus, simulating A's behavior means scanning the input string x and determining at each step the new value of A's current state, which is initialized at q_0. At the end of the string, it is necessary to test whether the current state is in F.

1.2.3 Properties of Finite-State Automata

Formal models are rigorous descriptions of certain phenomena. Deriving a formal model requires deep insight into the given phenomenon: The resulting formal model, in fact, embodies our understanding of the phenomenon in unambiguous, precise, and concise terms. As for any formalism, models can be manipulated. One can derive properties from formalisms, and through such properties one can get deeper and deeper insights into the phenomena being modeled. This section presents some basic properties of finite-state automata.

The properties described by Theorems 1.1 through 1.3 give insights into the kinds of languages which are recognized by finite-state acceptors (are they finite? infinite? what is their structure?).

Theorem 1.1
Let $A = \langle Q, I, \delta, q_0, F \rangle$ be a FA and let n be the cardinality of Q. The language recognized by A is nonempty if and only if A accepts a string x with $|x| < n$.

Proof
The "if" part of the theorem is trivial. To prove the "only if" part, let $x \in L(A)$ be a string such that $|x| \le |y|$, for every $y \in L(A)$. If $|x| < n$, then the result is proven. Thus assume that $x \ge n$. Since A performs a move on reading each element of x, A must pass through the same state more than once during recognition of x. Thus, we can find a state q in Q and write x as $x_1 x_2 x_3$, $x_2 \ne \epsilon$, in such a way that:

- $\delta^*(q_0, x_1) = q$
- $\delta^*(q, x_2) = q$
- $\delta^*(q, x_3) \in F$

This implies that $x_1 x_3 \in L(A)$. However, this contradicts the assumption that $|x| \le |y|$, for every $y \in L(A)$. In fact, if $y = x_1 x_3$, then $|x_1 x_3| < |x|$. ∎

Theorem 1.2
Let $A = \langle Q, I, \delta, q_0, F \rangle$ be a FA and let n be the cardinality of Q. The language recognized by A is infinite if and only if A accepts a string x with $n \le |x| < 2 \cdot n$.

Proof
If part
The proof of Theorem 1.1 shows that for $x \in L(A)$, $|x| \ge n$ implies the existence of a state q and strings x_1, x_2, x_3 with $x_2 \ne \epsilon$ such that $x = x_1 x_2 x_3$ and $\delta^*(q_0, x_1) = q$, $\delta^*(q, x_2) = q$, $\delta^*(q, x_3) \in F$. Thus $\delta^*(q_0, x_1 x_2^m x_3) \in F$ for any $m \ge 0$ and an infinite number of strings of the type $x_1 x_2^m x_3$ are in $L(A)$.

Only if part

If $L(A)$ is infinite, there exists $x \in L(A)$ such that $|x| \geq n$. Decompose x as $x_1 x_2 x_3$ as in the above "if part". If both $|x_1 x_3| < n$ and $|x_2| \leq n$, the thesis is proved. Otherwise, suppose first that $|x_1 x_3| \geq n$. If $|x_1 x_3| < 2n$ the thesis is proved because $x_1 x_3 \in L(A)$. Otherwise, the same decomposition is applied to $x_1 x_3$ and so on until a string y is found such that $y = y_1 y_2 y_3$, with $\delta^*(q_0, y_1) = q_1$, $\delta^*(q_1, y_2) = q_1$, $\delta^*(q_1, y_3) \in F$ and $|y_1 y_3| < n$. If $|y_2| \leq n$, the thesis is proved. Otherwise y_2 can again be decomposed as $z_1 z_2 z_3$ such that $z_2 \neq \epsilon$ and $\delta^*(q_1, z_1 z_3) = q_1$. The procedure continues until an y_2' such that $\delta^*(q_1, y_2') = q_1$ and $|y_2'| \leq n$ is actually found. ∎

The previous theorems are based on the fact that a FA can present loops in its graphlike representation. If it does not, the accepted language is finite; if it does, the accepted language is infinite. The possible presence of loops justifies also the following theorem, which describes an interesting property of languages recognized by FAs and somewhat generalizes Theorems 1.1 and 1.2.

Theorem 1.3 (Pumping Lemma)

Let A be a FA. There exists a constant k such that if $x \in L(A)$ and $|x| \geq k$, then x can be written as ywz, where $1 \leq |w| \leq k$ and $yw^i z \in L$, for every $i \geq 0$. ∎

The proof is left to the reader as an exercise. *Hint*: k is the number of states in A.

Now we turn to another class of problems concerning FAs. First of all, let us observe that there exist more than one FA that can recognize a given language. For example, Figure 1.14 shows a FA that recognizes exactly the same language that was recognized by the FA shown in Figure 1.7

Thus, two questions naturally arise. How can we decide whether two FAs recognize exactly the same language? Second, can we define some "canonical-form automaton," for example, a minimum-state automaton, and determine a procedure that transforms any FA into such canonical form? In the sequel, we give theorems that answer these two questions, starting from the latter.

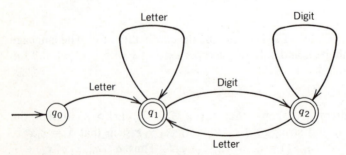

FIGURE 1.14   A FA accepting Pascal identifiers.

Theorem 1.4

Let $\mathscr{A}$ be the set of finite-state acceptors that recognize a given language $L \subseteq I^*$. Let $\bar{A} = \langle \bar{Q}, I, \bar{\delta}, \bar{q}_0, \bar{F} \rangle$ be a *minimum-state automaton* of $\mathscr{A}$, that is, such that $|\bar{Q}| \leq |Q|$ for each $A = \langle Q, I, \delta, q_0, F \rangle$. Then $\bar{A}$ is unique up to an isomorphism, i.e., a renaming of states.

Proof

In order to prove this theorem we need to investigate some interesting algebraic properties of languages and of FAs. A natural equivalence relation E_L can be associated to any language $L \subseteq I^*$. $x E_L y$ holds for any x and $y \in I^*$ if and only if either both or neither of x and y belong to L. It is immediate to verify that E_L is actually an equivalence relation on I^*. Now modify E_L into a new relation R_L defined as $x R_L y$ if and only if, for any z in I^*, either both or neither of xz and yz are in L. It is immediate to realize that R_L is an equivalence relation as well, and that $R_L \subseteq E_L$, that is, R_L implies E_L. Furthermore, R_L is a *right congruence* with respect to concatenation, that is, $x R_L y$ implies $xz R_L yz$ for any $z \in I^*$.

Consider now a FA A and define the relation R_A on I^* as $x R_A y$ if and only if $\delta^*(q_0, x) = \delta^*(q_0, y)$, that is, x and y lead A into the same state, when starting from q_0. It is immediate to realize that R_A is an equivalence relation and a right congruence as well as R_L. Furthermore, $x R_A y$ clearly implies $x R_{L(A)} y$ since A reaches the same state for x as for y, which either is in F or not. Thus we obtain the following statement.

Statement 1.5

For any FA A the relation R_A is a *refinement* of relation $R_{L(A)}$, that is, $R_A \subseteq R_{L(A)}$. Furthermore since R_A's index, that is, its number of equivalence classes, is equal to $|Q|$, for any language L accepted by some FA, R_L is of finite index. In general, $index(R_{L(A)}) \leq index(R_A)$. □

The converse result holds as well.

Statement 1.6

Consider any language L such that R_L is of finite index. A FA $A_R = \langle Q_R, I, \delta_R, q_{0R}, F_R \rangle$ can be built such that $L = L(A_R)$ and $|Q_R| = index(R_L)$.

In order to prove the statement we define
- $Q_R = \{[x] | x \in I^*\}$
- $\delta_R([x], i) = [xi]$ for any $[x] \in Q_R$, $i \in I$
- $q_{0R} = [\epsilon]$
- $F_R = \{[x] | x \in L\}$

It is easy to verify that
- The above definition is consistent as if $[x] = [y]$ for some x and $y \in I^*$, $\delta_R([x], i) = \delta_R([y], i)$ for any i, since R_L is a right congruence and either both $[x], [y]$ are in F_R or neither.
- $L(A_R) = L$, since $\delta_R^*([\epsilon], x) = [x]$, which is in F_R if and only if $x \in L$. □

The collection of Statements 1.5 and 1.6 is also known as the *Myhill–Nerode theorem*.

At this point we can complete the proof of Theorem 1.4 by observing that A_R is the minimum state automaton $\bar{A}$, up to a suitable renaming. In fact, let $\bar{q}$ be a state of $\bar{A}$. There must exist an x such that $\bar{\delta}*(q_0, x) = \bar{q}$ since otherwise $\bar{q}$ could be removed from $\bar{Q}$ without altering $L(\bar{A})$, thus contradicting the minimality of $\bar{A}$. Thus rename $\bar{q}$ as $[x]$ for such an x and verify the consistency of the definition through the fact that if $\bar{\delta}*(\bar{q}_0, x) = \bar{\delta}*(\bar{q}_0, y)$ then $xR_{\bar{A}}y$ and therefore $xR_L y$ because of Statement 1.5. Thus $[x] = [y]$.

The minimality of $\bar{A} = A_R$ follows then from the fact that $|Q_R| = index(R_L) \le index(R_A) = |Q|$ for any FA A recognizing L.   ∎

The FA A_R is called the canonical acceptor recognizing L since it is unique up to a renaming of its states. Note, however, that the proof of Theorem 1.4 states the existence of a minimal automaton without providing an explicit procedure to build it. In order to get a *constructive proof* of Theorem 1.4 we can proceed as follows. Let A be any FA.

i. First, eliminate all *useless states* from Q. A useless state q is such that either there is no x such that $\delta*(q_0, x) = q$ or there is no y such that $\delta*(q, y) \in F$. It is an easy exercise to derive an algorithm that performs the elimination.

ii. Then define an equivalence relation D on Q as qDq' if and only if for any x either both or neither of $\delta*(q, x), \delta*(q', x)$ are in F. D can also be easily tested by means of an algorithm since, as usual, if for some q and q', an x exists for which $\delta*(q, x) \in F$, $\delta*(q', x) \notin F$, then also an x' exists with the same property and with $|x'| < |Q|$.

iii. At this point, define the automaton $A' = \langle Q', I, \delta', q'_0, F' \rangle$ with $Q' = \{[q]\}$, that is, the set of equivalence classes of Q with respect to D, $\delta'([q], a) = [\delta(q, a)]$, and $F' = \{[q] | q \in F\}$.

As a simple exercise, one can verify that

- A' is well defined as the definition of δ' does not depend on the choice of the particular q in $[q]$.
- $L(A') = L(A)$.
- $Q' \le index(R_{L(A)})$. In fact, by contradiction suppose that $Q' > index(R_{L(A)})$. Then, since by Statement 1.5 R_A is a refinement of $R_{L(A)}$, there should exist $[q] \ne [q']$ and $x \ne y$, such that $xR_{L(A)}y$ and $\delta'*([q_0], x) = [q]$, $\delta'*([q_0], y) = [q']$. However, supposing $[q] \ne [q']$ (i.e., qDq' does not hold) there should exist a w such that $\delta*(q_0, xw) = \delta*(q, w) \in F$ and $\delta*(q_0, yw) \notin F$, or vice-versa. But this contradicts $xR_{L(A)}y$ because R_L is a right congruence.

Example 1.8

Consider the FA of Figure 1.14. It is immediate to realize that $q_1 D q_2$ since $\delta*(q_1, x) \in F$ as well as $\delta*(q_2, x)$ for any $x \in \{A, \ldots, Z, 0, 1, \ldots, 9\}*$. However, $q_0 D q_1$ does not hold because $\delta*(q_0, \epsilon) \notin F$ while $\delta*(q_1, \epsilon) \in F$. Thus, by

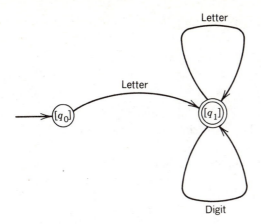

FIGURE 1.15 The result of minimizing the FA of Figure 1.14.

applying the above construction, we obtain the FA of Figure 1.15, which coincides with the FAs of Figure 1.7 up to a renaming of states.

Exercises

1.11 Minimize the FA subjacent to the FT of Figure 1.10.
1.12 Minimize the FA of Figure 1.16.

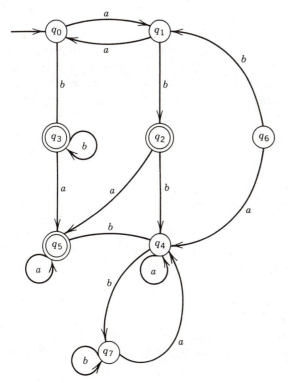

FIGURE 1.16 A FA to be minimized.

1.13   Devise a procedure to minimize FTs and build a program implementing it.
1.14   Minimize the FT of Figure 1.10.

Corollary 1.7
Given two FAs A_1 and A_2, $L(A_1) = L(A_2)$ if and only if their associated minimal automata $\bar{A}_1, \bar{A}_2$ are identical up to a renaming of states.   □

Theorem 1.4 and Corollary 1.7 are examples that show how the application of mathematical properties of a model can provide results of practical interest.

The following theorem shows that the class of languages accepted by FAs is *closed* under set operations; that is, the combination of languages in the class yields a language in the same class. Additional closure properties will be proved later.

Theorem 1.8
The class of languages accepted by finite-state automata is closed under

a. Intersection.
b. Complement with respect to I^*.
c. Union.

Outline of the proof

a. Intersection.
   Let $A_1 = \langle Q_1, I_1, \delta_1, q_{01}, F_1 \rangle$ and $A_2 = \langle Q_2, I_2, \delta_2, q_{02}, F_2 \rangle$ be two FAs. Assume that $I_1 = I_2 = I$ and Q_1, Q_2 are disjoint. This does not cause any loss of generality since we can always let $I = I_1 \cup I_2$, and suitably rename the states of A_1 obtaining two automata equivalent to A_1 and A_2, respectively, and satisfying the assumption. The FA $A = \langle Q, I, \delta, q_0, F \rangle$ accepting $L(A_1) \cap L(A_2)$ is constructed as follows.

   - $Q = Q_1 \times Q_2$
   - $q_0 = \langle q_{01}, q_{02} \rangle$
   - $F = \{\langle q', q'' \rangle | q' \in F_1, q'' \in F_2\}$
   - $\delta(\langle q_1, q_2 \rangle, a) = \langle q_1', q_2' \rangle$
     if and only if $\delta_1(q_1, a) = q_1', \delta_2(q_2, a) = q_2'$

b. Complement.
   Let $A = \langle Q, I, \delta, q_0, F \rangle$ be a FA. First, construct a FA A' by adding a new state $\bar{q}$ to A such that the next-state function of A' leads to $\bar{q}$ whenever it is undefined in A. Furthermore, it remains in $\bar{q}$ for every input symbol. The FA accepting $\overline{L(A)} = I^* - L(A)$ is identical to A', except that final and non-final states are interchanged.

c. Union.
   Let A_1, A_2 be two FAs. Then $L = L(A_1) \cup L(A_2) = \overline{\overline{L(A_1)} \cap \overline{L(A_2)}}$.
   Thus, according to (a) and (b), L is accepted by a FA.   ■

Exercise

1.15 Complete the proof of Theorem 1.8 by showing that the FAs defined in (a) and (b) actually accept $L(A_1) \cap L(A_2)$ and $L(A)$, respectively. In addition, give a construction to build a FA accepting the union of the languages accepted by two FAs.

1.3 Extending Finite-State Automata: The Pushdown Automaton

Let us go back to the robot of Example 1.6 that assembles dishes and cups: if the robot is already holding a dish and receives one more dish, it is unable to accept it and fails. Thus, let us augment the robot with a stack (initially empty). If the robot is already holding a dish (cup) and receives one more dish (cup) it can put the new item on the top of the stack, waiting for receiving a cup (dish). We assume that any number of dishes (cups) can be put on top of each other without causing any trouble. When both hands are free and a dish (cup) is received, if the stack contains cups (dishes), the robots gets one of them from the top of the stack and assembles the two items as before. When the robot halts, both hands must be free and the stack must be empty, to make sure that an equal number of dishes and cups have been received. Note: at any time the stack does not contain both dishes and cups (see Figure 1.17).

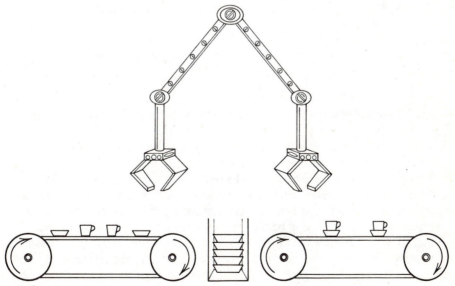

FIGURE 1.17 A robot assembling dishes and cups by using a stack.

If we assume that the stack can contain an unbounded number of items, no finite automaton can model this new robot. Thanks to their limited number of states, finite automata can distinguish only among a finite number of different configurations. On the other hand, it is intuitively clear that a configuration of the robot with, say, 157 dishes in the stack is different from a configuration with 158 dishes in the stack because in the former case the robot would halt after receiving exactly 157 cups (if its hands are initially free) whereas in the latter case it would not.

Let us introduce a new class of automata, more "powerful" then the FAs, which enables us to model our modified robot. Such automaton is called *pushdown automaton* (PDA) because it is like a FA, but is augmented with an auxiliary memory that is structured as a pushdown store (or stack). Items can be inserted and extracted from the stack according to a last-in-first-out (LIFO) policy.

Definition 1.6

A *pushdown automaton* (PDA) is a six-tuple $\langle Q, I, \Gamma, \delta, q_0, Z_0 \rangle$ where

1. Q is a finite set of *states*.
2. I is a finite set of *input* symbols.
3. Γ is a finite set of symbols, such that $\Gamma \cap I = \varnothing$, called *auxiliary symbols* (or *stack symbols*).
4. δ is the—possibly partial—*transition mapping*

$$\delta: Q \times (I \cup \{\epsilon\}) \times \Gamma \to Q \times \Gamma^*$$

   such that if $\delta(q, \epsilon, A)$ is defined, then $\delta(q, i, A)$ is undefined, for the same q and A, and for any i.
5. $q_0 \in Q$ is the *initial state*.
6. $Z_0 \in \Gamma$ is the *initial stack symbol*. It is the symbol that initially appears on the stack.   □

Before formally defining the behavior of a PDA, let us explain it in an intuitive way. Let us first go back to the behavior of a FA. The sequential scanning of the input string performed by a FA can be implemented by an ideal device provided with a *scanning head*. Initially, the scanning head is positioned at the beginning of the input string that is supposed to be written on a *tape*; q_0 is the initial state of the device. At each step, corresponding to a new time instant in a time space represented by natural numbers, the head scans a new character and the device commutes to state $\delta(q, i)$, q being the previous state and i being the scanned symbol. If $\delta(q, i)$ is undefined the machine stops. When the input string has been completely scanned, if the automaton is in a final state, the string is accepted, otherwise it is rejected. Figure 1.18 gives a rough view of the idealized device.

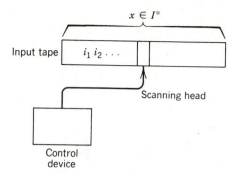

FIGURE 1.18 Finite-state automaton.

Exercise

1.16 Extend the foregoing model to depict finite-state transducers.

A PDA is just a FA augmented by an auxiliary memory device structured as a stack (see Figure 1.19). During the evolution of the PDA, the scanning head reads the input tape from left to right as for finite-state automata; the control device is in one of the states of Q, and the stack contains elements of Γ. The move (or transition) of the automaton is a function of the scanned symbol i, the present state q and the symbol on top of the stack. The move consists of

- Moving the scanning head rightwards.
- Commuting to a new state q'.
- Substituting the symbol on top of the stack with a (possibly empty) string of symbols of Γ.

Characters are pushed onto and popped from the stack according to a LIFO

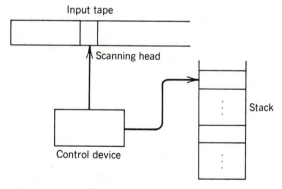

FIGURE 1.19 Pushdown automaton.

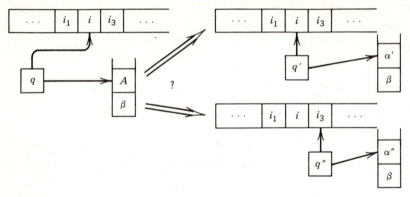

FIGURE 1.20 A nondetermined move of a PDA.

policy. The automaton may also perform a move without scanning any symbol: Formally, this means that $\delta(q, \epsilon, A)$ may be defined. The constraint that if $\delta(q, \epsilon, A)$ is defined then $\delta(q, i, A)$ must be undefined for each i, has been stated in order to make moves univocally determined. If this constraint were not stated, the automaton could choose among several possible moves in a nondeterministic fashion, as Figure 1.20 illustrates. We return to the issue of nondeterminism in Section 1.7. Here, and in what follows, formal models are all deterministic.

1.3.1 Pushdown Automata as Language Acceptors

The behavior of a PDA as an acceptor is described formally by the following definitions:

Definition 1.7
A *configuration* of a PDA is a triple $c = \langle q, x, \gamma \rangle$ with $q \in Q$, $x \in I^*$, $\gamma \in \Gamma^*$. q is the current state, x is the unread portion of input string, and γ is the contents of the stack.   □

Definition 1.8
For a given PDA, A, the binary *transition relation* $\vdash_A$ in the space of possible A's configurations is defined by $c = \langle q, x, \gamma \rangle \vdash_A c' = \langle q', x', \gamma' \rangle$ if and only if either

a. $x = ay$, $x' = y$, $\gamma = A\beta$, $\gamma' = \alpha\beta$ and $\delta(q, a, A) = \langle q', \alpha \rangle$
   or
b. $x = x'$, $\gamma = A\beta$, $\gamma' = \alpha\beta$ and $\delta(q, \epsilon, A) = \langle q', \alpha \rangle$ □

Note that the symbol A in $\vdash_A$ denotes the automaton and should not be confused with a nonterminal. It is omitted when obvious.

As we noticed before, point 4 of Definition 1.6 guarantees that for any c there exists at most one c' such that $c \vdash c'$. Also, notice that no move is possible if the stack is empty.

Acceptance of a string by a PDA can be defined by introducing the notion of a set of final states, as we did before for finite automata.

Definition 1.9

A *pushdown acceptor* (*recognizer*) is a 7-tuple

$$A = \langle Q, I, \Gamma, \delta, q_0, Z_0, F \rangle$$

where Q, I, Γ, δ, q_0, and Z_0 are as in Definition 1.6, and $F \subseteq Q$ is the set of accepting states. The string $x \in I^*$ is accepted by the automaton if and only if $\langle q_0, x, Z_0 \rangle \overset{*}{\underset{A}{\vdash}} \langle q, \epsilon, \gamma \rangle$ for some $q \in F$, $\gamma \in \Gamma^*$.

The *language accepted* (*recognized*) by a PDA is the set of strings accepted by the PDA. If A is a PDA, $L(A)$ denotes the language accepted by A. □

For simplicity, the term "pushdown automaton" and the acronym PDA will be used to refer to a pushdown acceptor whenever this will be clear from the context.

Example 1.9

A Pascal-like programming language structures programs in a nested fashion. The nesting structure is given by the following keywords and symbols:

if ... **fi**	(conditionals)
do ... **od**	(loops)
begin ... **end**	(sequences)
(...)	(expressions)

The special symbol $ denotes the end of the program.

We want to specify formally the intuitive idea of a correct nesting and balancing of keywords and symbols.

A PDA will serve our purposes. When an **if**, **do**, **begin**, or '(' will be encountered on the input stream, a I, D, B, or P, respectively, will be pushed onto the stack. When a **fi**, **od**, **end**, or ')' will be encountered, a I, D, B, or P, respectively, will be expected to be on top of the stack for correct matching. If this is the case, the topmost stack symbol will be popped off and processing will proceed.

Formally, we can specify our PDA as follows.

$Q = \{q_0, q_1\}$, where q_0 is the initial state.

$I = \{\mathbf{if}, \mathbf{fi}, \mathbf{do}, \mathbf{od}, \mathbf{begin}, \mathbf{end}, (\,,\,), \$\}$.

$\Gamma = \{I, D, B, P, Z_0\}$, where Z_0 is the empty stack symbol.

$F = \{q_1\}$.

Function $\delta(q, i, A)$ is undefined for $q = q_1$ and any values $i \in I$ and $A \in \Gamma$; the values of $\delta(q_0, i, A)$ are described by Table 1.1 for the various values of i and A.

TABLE 1.1   The Transition Function of a PDA

A \ i	if	fi	do	od	begin	end	(	)	$
I	q_0, II	q_0, ϵ	q_0, DI		q_0, BI		q_0, PI		
D	q_0, ID		q_0, DD	q_0, ϵ	q_0, BD		q_0, PD		
B	q_0, IB		q_0, DB		q_0, BB	q_0, ϵ	q_0, PB		
P	q_0, IP		q_0, DP		q_0, BP		q_0, PP	q_0, ϵ	
Z_0	q_0, IZ_0		q_0, DZ_0		q_0, BZ_0		q_0, PZ_0		q_1, ϵ

A PDA can be described by a graph. Nodes represent states of the automaton, edges represent transitions. If $\delta(q, a, A) = \langle q', \alpha \rangle$, then there is an edge directed from q to q' and labeled $a, A/\alpha$.

Example 1.10

The following PDA recognizes the language $L = \{ a^n b^n | n \geq 1 \}$, the set of strings consisting of any positive number of a followed by the *same* number of b.

$$A = \langle \{ q_0, q_1, q_2 \}, \{ a, b \}, \{ Z, Z_0 \}, \delta, q_0, Z_0, \{ q_2 \} \rangle$$

where δ is described by the graph in Figure 1.21.

In order to convince ourselves that A does recognize L, we can submit a few test cases and observe the sequence of moves of the automaton. For example, let us process the input string *aaabbb*:

$$\langle q_0, aaabbb, Z_0 \rangle \vdash \langle q_0, aabbb, ZZ_0 \rangle \vdash$$
$$\langle q_0, abbb, ZZZ_0 \rangle \vdash \langle q_0, bbb, ZZZZ_0 \rangle \vdash \langle q_1, bb, ZZZ_0 \rangle \vdash$$
$$\langle q_1, b, ZZ_0 \rangle \vdash \langle q_1, \epsilon, Z_0 \rangle \vdash \langle q_2, \epsilon, \epsilon \rangle$$

Instead, the string *aaabb* is rejected as A would halt in the configuration

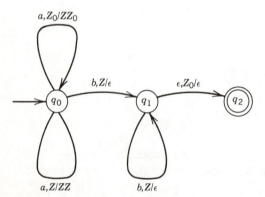

FIGURE 1.21 A graph describing a PDA.

$\langle q_1, \epsilon, ZZ_0 \rangle$, which is not an acceptance configuration because $q_1 \notin F$. The reader is invited to verify the behavior of A on other test cases.

If testing does not entirely convince us that A indeed solves the problem as stated, we might pursue formal verification. For example, we might try to prove the following facts f1 through f5 (see Exercise 1.17).

f1. $\forall n, \langle q_0, a^n, Z_0 \rangle \overset{*}{\vdash} \langle q_0, \epsilon, Z^n Z_0 \rangle$

f2. $\langle q_0, b, Z^n Z_0 \rangle \vdash \langle q_1, \epsilon, Z^{n-1} Z_0 \rangle$

f3. $\langle q_1, b^i, Z^i Z_0 \rangle \overset{*}{\vdash} \langle q_1, \epsilon, Z_0 \rangle$

and

$\neg \langle q_1, b^i, Z^j Z_0 \rangle \overset{*}{\vdash} \langle q_1, \epsilon, Z_0 \rangle$ if $i \neq j$

f4. $\langle q_1, \epsilon, Z_0 \rangle \vdash \langle q_2, \epsilon, \epsilon \rangle$

f5. The conjunction of f1, f2, f3, and f4 clearly implies that

$$\langle q_0, x, Z_0 \rangle \overset{*}{\vdash} \langle q_2, \epsilon, \epsilon \rangle \text{ if and only if } x = a^n b^n, n \geq 1.$$

Exercises

1.17 Prove facts f1 through f5. *Hint*: Use induction.

1.18 Define a PDA that recognizes $L = \{ a^n b^{2n} | n \geq 0 \}$.

1.19 Describe a PDA that recognizes a language L of brackets. The alphabet I of L is

$$I = \{ (,), [,], \langle, \rangle, . \}$$

Brackets must be properly nested, and nesting can be at any depth. Symbol "." represents the end of the string.

1.20 Show that the PDA of Figure 1.22 recognizes the language

$$L = \{ wcw^R | w \in \{ a, b \}^* \},$$

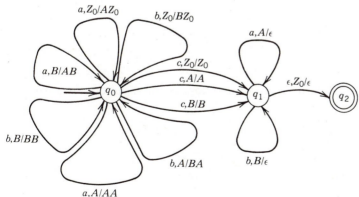

FIGURE 1.22 A PDA accepting $\{ wcw^R \}$.

where w^R denotes the *reverse* or mirror image of w, that is, w read from right to left.

1.21 Build PDAs recognizing the languages

$$L_1 = \{ a^n b^m a^m b^n | n, m \geq 1 \}$$

$$L_2 = L_1^*$$

$$L_3 = \{ a^{n_1} b^{n_1} a^{n_2} b^{n_2} \cdots a^{n_k} b^{n_k} | k \geq 1, n_i \geq 1 \text{ for } 1 \leq i \leq k \}$$

1.22* Write a nonrecursive Pascal program that recognizes the language introduced in Example 1.9. Show how you can write a recursive solution. In particular, show that in this case you do not need to handle a stack explicitly, but you can simply do the job using the stack of procedure activation records that is automatically handled by the language processor.

1.3.2 Pushdown Automata as Language Translators

As we did for FAs, it is possible to extend PDAs in order to let them generate output. Pushdown automata with output (which will be called *pushdown transducers*) are abstract models of translators, intrinsically more powerful than finite-state transducers.[1]

Definition 1.10

A *pushdown transducer* (PDT) is a 9-tuple

$$T = \langle Q, I, \Gamma, \delta, q_0, Z_0, F, O, \eta \rangle$$

where Q, I, Γ, δ, q_0, and F are as in Definition 1.9, O is a finite set of *output values*, η is the *output mapping* $\eta: Q \times (I \cup \{\epsilon\}) \times \Gamma \to O^*$ defined whenever δ is defined. The pushdown automaton A obtained from a pushdown transducer T by eliminating O and η is called the *automaton underlying or subjacent T*. □

Definition 1.11

A *configuration* of a PDT T is a quadruple $c = \langle q, x, \gamma, z \rangle$ where $q \in Q$, $x \in I^*$, $\gamma \in \Gamma^*$, $z \in O^*$. The *transition relation* $c \vdash_T c'$ with $c = \langle q, x, \gamma, z \rangle$, $c' = \langle q', x', \gamma', z' \rangle$ is defined as we did for $\vdash_A$ in Definition 1.8, with the following additions:

$$z' = z\bar{z}$$

$$\bar{z} = \eta(q, a, A) \text{ in case (a)}$$

$$\bar{z} = \eta(q, \epsilon, A) \text{ in case (b)}$$ □

---

[1] We formally compare the power of FAs and PDAs in Section 1.3.3.

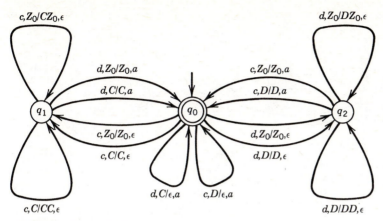

FIGURE 1.23 A PDT modeling the robot with a stack.

Definition 1.12

A *translation* $\tau\colon I^* \to O^*$ is associated to T in the following way.

$\tau(x) = z$ if and only if $\langle q_0, x, Z_0, \epsilon \rangle \overset{*}{\underset{T}{\vdash}} \langle q, \epsilon, \gamma, z \rangle$, $q \in F$, and,

for no $q', \gamma', z', \langle q, \epsilon, \gamma, z \rangle \vdash \langle q', \epsilon, \gamma', z' \rangle$.[2] □

A graph description for a PDT can be easily obtained as an extension of the notation used for PDA. In the PDT case, arcs are labeled by a four-tuple $\langle a, A, \alpha, z \rangle$ (written $a, A/\alpha, z$) where a, A and α are as in the case of a PDA, z is the output string.

Example 1.11

Let us go back to our modified robot assembling dishes and cups. The unbounded stack, which could not be modeled by the finite memory of a FA, can be modeled by the pushdown store of a PDA. The PDT modeling the robot can be described as follows.

1. $Q = \{q_0, q_1, q_2\}$, where states have the following intuitive meaning.
   q_0: both hands are free
   q_1: left hand holds a cup, right hand is free
   q_2: left hand holds a dish, right hand is free
2. $I = \{d, c\}$, where d stands for dish and c stands for cup.
3. $\Gamma = \{Z_0, D, C\}$. The pushdown store models the robot's stack. Z_0 is the initial stack symbol. $D(C)$ represents the dish (cup) when it is put apart onto the stack for later assembly.
4. $O = \{a\}$ where a stands for assembled item.
5, 6. δ and η are defined in Figure 1.23.

---

[2] This restriction is assumed to make the definition of τ univocal.

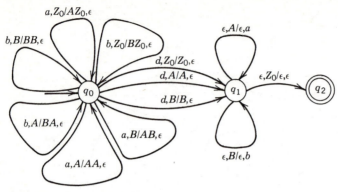

FIGURE 1.24   A PDT reversing a string.

The reader is invited to examine the graph of Figure 1.23 carefully and to simulate the behavior of the automaton in several test cases.

Example 1.12

Suppose you wish to translate a string x of the type wd, $w \in \{a, b\}^*$ into w^R the reverse of w. Thus, for example, $x = aabbabad$ would be translated into $ababbaa$. The following PDT T does the job.

$$T = \langle \{q_0, q_1, q_2\}, \{a, b, d\}, \{A, B, Z_0\}, \delta, q_0, \{q_2\}, \{a, b\}, \eta \rangle$$

where δ and η are described in Figure 1.24.

Intuitively, T scans the input string in state q_0 and stores an A (B) into the stack if an a (b) is encountered. On reading d, T switches to state q_1, where the output is produced without any further reading. If an A (B) is on top of the stack, an a (b) is output. Where Z_0 appears on top of the stack, T enters its final state q_2.

Exercises

1.23 Prove formally that the PDT of Example 1.12 actually performs the claimed translation.

Hint: Use induction to prove

1. $\langle q_0, w, Z_0, \epsilon \rangle \overset{*}{\underset{T}{\vdash}} \langle q_0, \epsilon, W^R Z_0, \rangle$, where W denotes the result of replacing lowercase letters in w by uppercase equal letters, and W^R denotes the reverse of W.
2. $\langle q_0, d, XZ_0, \epsilon \rangle \underset{T}{\vdash} \langle q_1, \epsilon, XZ_0, \epsilon \rangle$ for any $X \in \{A, B\}^*$.
3. $\langle q_1, \epsilon, XZ_0, \epsilon \rangle \overset{*}{\underset{T}{\vdash}} \langle q_1, \epsilon, Z_0, x \rangle$, where x denotes the result of replacing uppercase letters in X by corresponding lowercase equal letters.
4. $\langle q_1, \epsilon, Z_0, x \rangle \underset{T}{\vdash} \langle q_2, \epsilon, \epsilon, x \rangle$ for any $x \in \{a, b\}^*$.

1.24 Build a PDT realizing the translation

$\tau(a^n b^m c^m) = d^{3m} e^n$, for $m, n \geq 1$.

(It does not matter what the output is if the input string is not of the foregoing type.)

1.3.3 Properties of Pushdown Automata and Their Relation to Finite-State Automata

In Section 1.3 we have given informal arguments to support the claim that pushdown automata are more powerful than finite-state automata. By "more powerful" we mean that the class of problems we can solve by means of pushdown automata is larger than the class of problems we can solve by means of finite automata. Let us consider two formalisms *F1* and *F2*, which define language acceptors. *F1* is more powerful than *F2* if the set of languages accepted by members of *F1* includes the set of languages accepted by members of *F2*.

In what follows, we will prove formally that pushdown automata are more powerful language acceptors than finite-state automata. The proof is a direct consequence of the following two theorems.

Theorem 1.9
The language $L = \{a^n b^n | n \geq 1\}$ can be accepted by a PDA but cannot be accepted by an FA.

Proof
We know from Example 1.10 that L is accepted by a PDA. We must show now that L cannot be accepted by any FA. In fact, suppose there exists a FA A such that $L(A) = L$. Since Q is finite there exist $q \in Q$, and two natural numbers n_1 and n_2 with $n_1 \neq n_2$, such that

$\delta*(q_0, a^{n_1}) = \delta*(q_0, a^{n_2}) = q.$

On the other hand $a^{n_2} b^{n_2} \in L$ implies $\delta*(q, b^{n_2}) \in F$. Therefore, $\delta*(q_0, a^{n_1} b^{n_2}) = \delta*(q, b^{n_2}) \in F$; but this implies that $a^{n_1} b^{n_2} \in L$: a contradiction.   ∎

Exercise

1.25 Give an alternative proof of Theorem 1.9 by applying the Pumping Lemma (Theorem 1.3).

Hint: Show (by contradiction) that the hypothesis that L be recognized by some FA would lead to the fact that either strings of the type $a^n (a^r b^s)^k b^{n+r-s}$ or strings of the type $a^{n+k} b^n$ or strings of the type $a^n b^{n+k}$ are in L.

Theorem 1.10
Any language accepted by a FA can also be accepted by a PDA.

Proof
For a given FA $A = \langle Q, I, \delta, q_0, F \rangle$ it is immediate to build a PDA $\bar{A} = \langle \bar{Q}, \bar{I}, \bar{\Gamma}, \bar{\delta}, \bar{q}_0, \bar{Z}_0, \bar{F} \rangle$ such that $L(\bar{A}) = L(A)$. Just define $\bar{Q} = Q$, $\bar{I} = I$, $\bar{\Gamma} = \{Z_0\}$, $\bar{F} = F$, $\bar{\delta}(q, i, Z_0) = \langle \delta(q, i), Z_0 \rangle$ for all q, i. ∎

Exercise

1.26 Prove that PDTs are more powerful language translators than FTs.

Let us point out another difference between FAs and PDAs. FAs must scan an input symbol at any move. This implies that they always scan the whole input string unless a state is entered for which δ is not defined for the current input symbol. However, notice that δ can be easily made a total function by adding a suitable error state q_E to Q and defining $\delta'(q, i) = q_E$ whenever δ is undefined and $\delta'(q_E, i) = q_E$ for any i. Thus we can assume that a FAs always scan the whole input.

The same does not hold in general for PDAs, even if we add a suitable error state as for FAs. In fact, it may happen that a PDA in some configuration enters an infinite sequence of ϵ-moves, (i.e., of non-input-consuming moves). For instance, if a PDA were in a configuration $c = \langle q, x, AZ_0 \rangle$ and $\delta(q, \epsilon, A) = \langle q, AA \rangle$, it would enter the never-ending sequence of configurations $\langle q, x, AZ_0 \rangle \vdash \langle q, x, AAZ_0 \rangle \vdash \langle q, x, AAAZ_0 \rangle \dots$. Fortunately, this unpleasant behavior of a PDA can be removed, if needed, by the construction described below.

Definition 1.13
Let A be a PDA.

$\langle q, x, \alpha \rangle \overset{*d}{\underset{A}{\vdash}} \langle q', y, \beta \rangle$ denotes that

$\langle q, x, \alpha \rangle \overset{*}{\underset{A}{\vdash}} \langle q', y, \beta \rangle$ and, for $\beta = Z\beta'$, $\delta(q', \epsilon, Z)$ is undefined.   □

Intuitively, $\overset{*d}{\vdash}$ is a sequence of moves that cannot proceed without reading some more input symbol.

Definition 1.14
A PDA A is *loop free* if and only if for any $x \in I^*$, $\langle q_0, x, Z_0 \rangle \overset{*d}{\vdash} \langle q, \epsilon, \gamma \rangle$ for some q and γ.   □

Thus a loop-free PDA always reads all its input, whatever it is, and eventually halts.

Theorem 1.11

For any PDA A there exists an equivalent loop-free PDA A_L.

Outline of the proof

First notice that any PDA can be augmented in such a way that in any configuration of the type $\langle q, ix, Z\gamma \rangle$, $\delta(q, i, Z)$ or $\delta(q, \epsilon, Z)$ is always defined. Such a modification can be done, of course, without affecting the language accepted by the automaton.

Second, observe that a PDA of this type can fail to behave in the way $\langle q_0, x, Z_0 \rangle \overset{*d}{\vdash} \langle q, \epsilon, \gamma \rangle$ only if, for some state $\bar{q}$, and $\gamma = \bar{Z}\xi$, it can perform an infinity of ϵ-moves without erasing $\bar{Z}$, that is, there exists a state $\bar{p}$ such that $\langle \bar{q}, \epsilon, \bar{\gamma} \rangle \overset{*}{\vdash} \langle \bar{p}, \epsilon, \bar{\alpha}\bar{\gamma} \rangle \overset{*}{\vdash} \langle \bar{p}, \epsilon, \bar{\beta}\bar{\alpha}\bar{\gamma} \rangle \overset{*}{\vdash} \langle \bar{p}, \epsilon, \bar{\beta}''\bar{\alpha}\bar{\gamma} \rangle$ for some $\bar{\alpha}, \bar{\beta} \in \Gamma^*$ (i.e., A enters a loop). In such a case, A can be modified into an equivalent A_L by letting

$$\delta(\bar{q}, \epsilon, \bar{Z}) = \langle q_E, \bar{Z} \rangle \quad \text{if during} \quad \langle \bar{q}, \epsilon, \bar{\gamma} \rangle \overset{*}{\vdash} \langle \bar{p}, \epsilon, \bar{\beta}\bar{\alpha}\bar{\gamma} \rangle$$

a final state is never entered; otherwise we let

$$\delta(\bar{q}, \epsilon, \bar{Z}) = \langle \bar{q}_F, \bar{Z} \rangle, \, \delta(\bar{q}_F, \epsilon, \bar{Z}) = \langle q_E, \bar{Z} \rangle,$$

$\bar{q}_F$ being a *new* final state. In both cases q_E is an error state suitable to consume all remaining input.

The details of the construction are left to the reader as an exercise. ∎

The relevance of Theorem 1.11 will be further enlightened in Section 1.4.1. Here it can be used as a technical lemma to show some relevant properties of PDAs.

Exercise

1.27* Prove that the class of languages accepted by PDAs is closed under complement.

Hint: Consider, without loss of generality, a loop-free PDA A accepting a given language L. This guarantees that all input strings are completely scanned. In order to build a PDA $\bar{A}$ accepting $\bar{L}$, first split any state q of the automaton into three states $\langle q, 1 \rangle, \langle q, 2 \rangle, \langle q, 3 \rangle$ and let all states of the type $\langle q, 3 \rangle$ be the accepting states. The purpose of this splitting is to record whether A has ever entered an accepting state or not during a sequence of ϵ-moves. In the former case $\bar{A}$ reaches states of the type $\langle q, 1 \rangle$. In the latter case, $\bar{A}$ reaches states of the type $\langle q, 2 \rangle$ from which the corresponding states $\langle q, 3 \rangle$ are reachable through suitable ϵ-moves.

The following theorem shows an important limitation in the recognition power of PDAs due to the constraints (last-in-first-out policy) on the use of the pushdown store.

Theorem 1.12

No PDA can recognize the language $L = \{a^n b^m | m = 2n \text{ or } m = n, n \geq 1\}$.

The theorem is substantiated in intuitive terms, since the formal proof requires several technicalities that are typical of a more advanced stage of formal language theory.

Example 1.10 and Exercises 1.18 and 1.20 have shown that a PDA can "count" an unbounded number of a only by means of its stack and can "compare" the counted value with an other integer only by popping elements off the stack, which implies destroying the information stored in the stack about the value of n. Thus, in the case of Example 1.10, after reading $a^n b^n$, a PDA will lose the information about n. This does not necessarily imply that the stack must be empty, but rather that its contents cannot have any more relation to the integer n.

On the other hand, for any PDA, if

$$\langle q_0, a^n b^n, Z_0 \rangle \overset{*}{\vdash} \langle q, \epsilon, \gamma \rangle, \quad \text{then } \langle q_0, a^n b^{n+k}, Z_0 \rangle \overset{*}{\vdash} \langle q, b^k, \gamma \rangle$$

In order to accept L, the behavior of the automaton must be such that

$$\langle q, b^k, \gamma \rangle \overset{*}{\vdash} (q', \epsilon, \gamma'), q' \in F \quad \text{only if } k = n$$

But this is impossible because the PDA has lost information about n. ■

Exercise

1.28 Show that no PDA can recognize the language $L = \{a^n b^n a^n | n \geq 1\}$, by using an informal reasoning similar to the previous explanation of Theorem 1.11.

1.4 Turing Machines

PDAs are more powerful than FAs in that they can solve all problems FAs can solve and also some problems FAs cannot solve. However, they have their own limitations. Such limitations are essentially due to the strict last-in-first-out (LIFO) policy under which their pushdown memory is managed. For instance, this policy forces the previously mentioned robot assembling dishes and cups to couple a new cup with the most recently received dish, which happens to be on top of the stack.

Suppose now that the robot has to assemble sets consisting of one large dish, one small dish, and one cup, where the cup must be put on top of a small dish that, in turn, must be put on top of the large dish. It is easy to realize that a stack storage based on a LIFO policy is now useless. Denote a large dish, a small dish, and a cup, by symbols l, s and c, respectively. If the robot stores all incoming items into a sequential storage and follows a LIFO policy, it will be unable to handle the sequence of items *lllssscccc*. In fact, no complete set is available until cups are received. Thus all items received before cups must be put aside. Notice that some of them could be kept in the robot's hands, but only in a finite number; therefore for sequences of the type $l^n s^n c^n$ with n sufficiently large, the items should be ultimately put aside in a secondary storage. If the secondary storage is a pushdown store, after receiving the first cup the robot can get to the small dish, but not to the large one.

This example shows in an intuitive way the limitations of a stack-managed storage and provides a motivation for looking for more general and powerful devices.

We now introduce another classical model of computer science, namely *Turing machines* (TMs), named after Alan Turing, a pioneer of the theory of computation who first proposed and studied the model. Following the usual style, we first informally introduce the model, then we provide formal definitions and explanatory examples, and finally we investigate its main properties.

Informally, a Turing machine (TM) consists of

- An input tape $\mathbf{T}_I$.
- An output tape $\mathbf{T}_O$.
- k memory tapes $\mathbf{T}_1, \ldots, \mathbf{T}_k$.
  Each tape is a sequence of cells and is infinite to the right. Each cell holds one of a finite number of tape symbols, one of which is the *blank*, denoted by $\not{b}$. Each tape is scanned by a tape head that can read, write, move right, move left, and remain stationary. The head of $\mathbf{T}_I$ cannot write. The head of $\mathbf{T}_O$ cannot read nor move left.
- A control device that has a finite number of states.

Figure 1.25 gives a pictorial description of a TM. Such a machine is usually called *multitape* or *k-tape TM*.

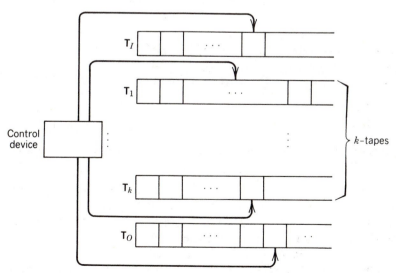

FIGURE 1.25 A Turing machine.

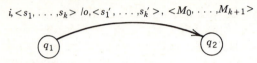

$$i,<s_1,\ldots,s_k> / o,<s_1',\ldots,s_k'>, <M_0,\ldots,M_{k+1}>$$

q_1 q_2

FIGURE 1.26 A TM transition.

One computational step of a multitape TM consists of the following. Depending on the current state of the finite control and the tape symbols that are under each tape head, the machine performs the following operations.

1. Changes the state of the control device.
2. Prints new tape symbols over the current symbols in the cells under tape heads (except for the head of T_I).
3. Moves any or all of the tape heads, independently from one another, one cell left (L), or right (R), or keeps them stationary (S), except for the head of T_O, which cannot move left.

Alternatively, the machine does not perform any operation at all and definitely halts.

A *configuration* of a k-tape TM consists of the state of the control unit, the configuration of the $k + 2$ tapes and the position of the $k + 2$ heads. The *initial configuration* corresponds to the initial state of the control unit; the input tape contains a finite number of nonblank symbols; memory tapes contain a special nonblank symbol Z_0 in their first cell and no other nonblank symbol; the output tape is all blank; the heads are all positioned on the first cell of their tapes. Thus at any step only a finite number of nonblank symbols will always exist in any tape.

A TM can be described by a graph: As usual, states are denoted by graph nodes and transitions, or computational steps, are denoted by labeled edges. For instance, Figure 1.26 represents the fact that starting from state q_1 and reading i from T_I, $s_1, \ldots, s_k$ from $T_1, \ldots, T_k$, the machine performs a transition to state q_2, writes o onto T_O, replaces $s_1, \ldots, s_k$ with $s_1', \ldots, s_k'$, and moves its $k + 2$ heads according to the tuple $\langle M_0, \ldots, M_{k+1} \rangle$. Each M_i can be L, R, or S. M_0 denotes the move of T_I; M_{k+1} denotes the move of T_O, and must be different from L.

Example 1.13

A robot assembling a sequence of large dishes (l), small dishes (s) and cups (c) can operate as follows:

- It receives all items on a moving tape and pushes each item onto one of three different stacks, one for l, one for s, and one for c.
- After having received all items, it pops one l, one s and one c off each stack and produces an assembled set (a) (see Figure 1.27).
- At the end of its operations it verifies that all stacks are empty. This guarantees that an equal number of items of the three types has been received.

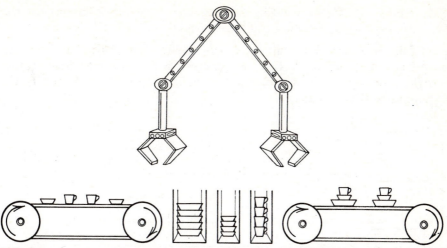

FIGURE 1.27 A robot assembling large dishes, small dishes, and cups.

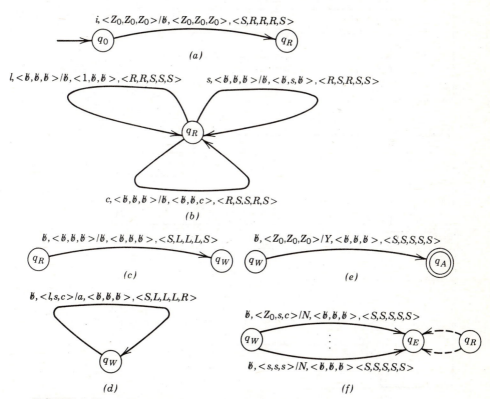

FIGURE 1.28 A TM modeling a robot. *i* denotes either *l*, *s*, or *c*.
(*a*) Initialisation. (*b*) Reading. (*c*) Commuting to a writing state.
(*d*) Writing. (*e*) Accepting. (*f*) Rejecting.

A description of a TM M modeling the foregoing robot follows. The machine has five states—q_0, q_R, q_W, q_A, q_E—and three memory tapes—T_1, T_2 and T_3.

- Initially M is in q_0. It commutes to q_R (a reading state), leaves unaffected the special symbol Z_0 in T_1, T_2, T_3 and moves the corresponding heads to the right, no matter which symbol is read from T_I. Both heads of T_I and T_O are not moved (Figure 1.28a).

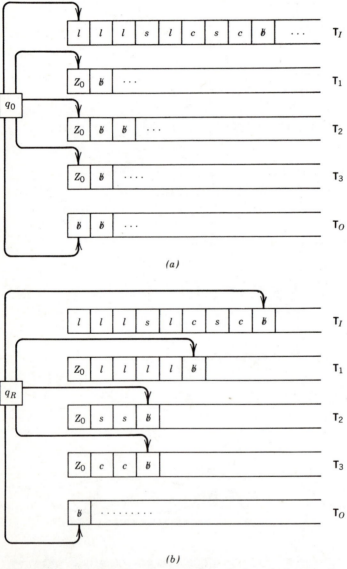

(a)

(b)

FIGURE 1.29   Sample configurations of the TM of Figure 1.28 (a) Initial configuration. (b) End of reading. (c) Start of writing. (d) Writing. (e) Detection of the failure.

- When M is in q_R and reads either l, s, or c from $\mathbf{T}_I$, it remains in q_R and writes the input symbol into $\mathbf{T}_j$, where $j = 1$ if $i = l$, $j = 2$ if $i = s$, and $j = 3$ if $i = c$. The heads of $\mathbf{T}_I$ and $\mathbf{T}_j$ are moved right, while other heads are not moved (see Figure 1.28b).
- When M is in q_R and reads a blank from $\mathbf{T}_I$, this means that all items have been read. From now on, the head of $\mathbf{T}_I$ will not move. M commutes to q_W (a

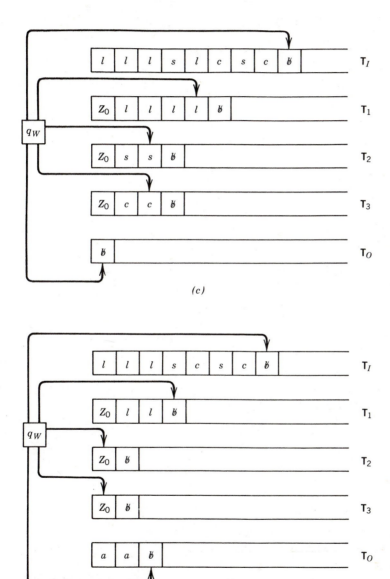

FIGURE 1.29   Continued.

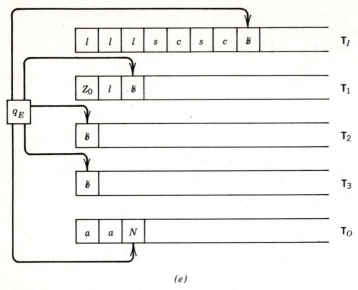

(e)

FIGURE 1.29   Continued.

writing state), moves left the heads of T_1, T_2, T_3 and does not write anything on T_O (see Figure 1.28c).

- When M is in q_W and reads the symbols l, s, c and T_1, T_2, T_3, it remains in q_W, writes a blank in place of the read symbols, and moves the heads left. Also, it writes an a on T_O and moves its head right (see Figure 1.28d).
- When M is in q_W and reads Z_0 from all of T_1, T_2, and T_3, this means that an equal number of l, s, c has been input and that all of them have been assembled. Thus, it commutes to q_A, an accepting state, writes a blank in place of Z_0, writes character Y (for *Yes*) on T_O and halts (see Figure 1.28e).
- In all other cases, M enters the error state q_E, then writes character N (for *No*) on T_O and halts (see Figure 1.28f).

Figure 1.29 displays five relevant configurations of M when operating on the input *lllslcsc*.

Exercises

1.29   Following the spirit of Example 1.13, build a TM modeling a robot assembling sets consisting of one dish, one cup, two forks, two knives, and one spoon.

1.30   Build a TM modeling a robot assembling large dishes, small dishes and cups, as in Example 1.13, with the difference that an assembled item is output as soon as each of the three stacks contains at least one element.

1.31 Build a TM that solves problem of Example 1.13 by using only one memory tape.

Let us go now into a more formal description and analysis of the TMs.

Definition 1.15
A *k-tape TM* is a 9-tuple $M = \langle Q, I, \Gamma, O, \delta, \eta, q_0, Z_0, F \rangle$ where

- Q is a finite set of *states*
- I is a finite *input alphabet*
- Γ is a finite *memory alphabet*
- O is a finite *output alphabet*
- $F \subseteq Q$ is the set of *final states*
- $q_0 \in Q$ is the *initial state*
- $Z_0 \in \Gamma$ is the *initial symbol* of the memory alphabet
- I, Γ, and O contain a special symbol called *blank* and denoted as $\cancel{b}$
- δ is the—possibly partial—*transition mapping*
  $\delta: (Q - F) \times I \times \Gamma^k \to Q \times \Gamma^k \times \{R, L, S\}^{k+1}$
- η is the—possibly partial—*output mapping*
  $\eta: (Q - F) \times I \times \Gamma^k \to O \times \{R, S\}$, defined whenever δ is defined.

When k is not specified, the TM is just called a *multitape TM*. $\qquad \square$

Definition 1.16
A *configuration* c of a k-tape TM M is a $k + 3$-tuple

$$c = \langle q, xiy, \alpha_1 \uparrow A_1\beta_1, \ldots, \alpha_k \uparrow A_k\beta_k, u \uparrow o \rangle$$

where $q \in Q$, x and $y \in I^*$, $i \in I$, α_r and $\beta_r \in \Gamma^*$, $A_r \in \Gamma$, for $1 \le r \le k$, $u \in O^*$, $o \in O$, $\uparrow \notin I \cup \Gamma \cup O$. $\qquad \square$

Intuitively, q denotes the current state of M, xiy, $\alpha_r A_r \beta_r$, uo, denote the contents of the input tape, memory tapes, and output tape, such that the remaining portions are all blank. The heads of each tape are positioned on the cell that stores the first symbol of the string following $\uparrow$.

Definition 1.17
An *initial configuration* c_0 of M is of the type

$$c_0 = \langle q_0, \uparrow iy, \uparrow Z_0, \ldots, \uparrow Z_0, \uparrow \cancel{b} \rangle$$

that is, $x = \epsilon$, $A_r = Z_0$, $\alpha_r = \beta_r = \epsilon$, $u = \epsilon$, $o = \cancel{b}$. $\qquad \square$

Definition 1.18

The *transition* relation $\underset{M}{\vdash}$ (also called *move* or *computation step*) between two configurations c and c' of M is defined as follows.

Let $c = \langle q, x \uparrow iy, \alpha_1 \uparrow A_1\beta_1, \dots, \alpha_k \uparrow A_k\beta_k, u \uparrow o \rangle$ with $x = \bar{x}\bar{i}$, $y = \bar{j}\bar{y}$, $\alpha_r = \bar{\alpha}_r\bar{A}_r, \beta_r = B_r\bar{\beta}_r$.

Let $c' = \langle q', x' \uparrow i'y', \alpha'_1 \uparrow A'_1\beta'_1, \dots, \alpha'_k \uparrow A'_k\beta'_k, u' \uparrow o' \rangle$, let

$$\delta(q, i, A_1 \dots A_k) = \langle p, C_1, \dots, C_k, N, N_1, \dots, N_k \rangle \qquad .$$

with $p \in Q$, $N \in \{R, L, S\}$, $C_r \in \Gamma$, $N_r \in \{R, L, S\}$ for $1 \le r \le k$, and let

$$\eta(q, i, A_1, \dots, A_k) = \langle v, M \rangle \quad \text{with } v \in O, M \in \{R, S\}.$$

Then $c \underset{M}{\vdash} c'$ if and only if

1. $p = q'$

and one of the following, mutually exclusive, cases 2.1, 2.2, or 2.3 holds:

2.1 $x = x'$, $i = i'$, $y = y'$ and $N = S$
2.2 $x' = xi$, $i' = \bar{j}$, $y' = \bar{y}$ and $N = R$
    (if $y = \epsilon$, then $i' = \not{b}$ and $y' = \epsilon$)
2.3 $x' = \bar{x}$, $i' = \bar{i}$, $y' = iy$ and $N = L$

and, for $1 \le r \le k$, one of the following, mutually exclusive, cases 3.1, 3.2, or 3.3 holds:

3.1 $\alpha'_r = \alpha_r$, $A'_r = C_r$, $\beta'_r = \beta_r$ and $N_r = S$
3.2 $\alpha'_r = \alpha_r C_r$, $A'_r = B_r$, $\beta'_r = \bar{\beta}_r$ and $N_r = R$
    (if $\beta_r = \epsilon$ then $A'_r = \not{b}$ and $\beta'_r = \epsilon$)
3.3 $\alpha'_r = \bar{\alpha}_r$, $A'_r = \bar{A}_r$, $\beta'_r = C_r\beta_r$ and $N_r = L$

and one of the following, mutually exclusive, cases 4.1 or 4.2 holds:

4.1 $u' = u$ and $o' = v$, $M = S$
4.2 $u' = uv$ and $o' = \not{b}$, $M = R$

If, in cases 2.3, and 3.3 $x = \epsilon$ or $\alpha_r = \epsilon$ (i.e., the reading head is positioned on the leftmost cell of the tape) there is no c' such that $c \underset{M}{\vdash} c'$ and M *halts*.
The same occurs if δ and η are not defined in $\langle q, i, A_1, \dots, A_k \rangle$. In such cases c is called a *halting configuration*. $\qquad\qquad \square$

Notice that, as usual, for any configuration c the transition relation holds at most for one c'. Also, if the state q of a configuration c belongs to F, then c is a halting configuration, that is, M always halts when it reaches a final state, but the converse does not necessarily hold.

    As usual, the symbol M will be dropped from $\underset{M}{\vdash}$ when no ambiguity arises from the context.

1.4.1 Turing Machines as Language Acceptors

When TMs are used to define languages as recognizing devices, the output tape is not considered, as it happens for FAs and PDAs. Thus we will consider here TMs as 7-tuples obtained by elimination O and η from Definition 1.15. The definition of a TM configuration is modified accordingly.

Informally a TM M accepts a string x stored in its input tape if it reaches a halting configuration whose state is final. This is formally defined as follows.

Definition 1.19

Let M be a multitape TM. A string $x \in I^*$ is *accepted* by M if and only if

$$c_0 = \langle q_0, \uparrow x, \uparrow Z_0, \ldots, \uparrow Z_0 \rangle \overset{*}{\underset{M}{\vdash}} \langle q, x' \uparrow iy, \alpha_1 \uparrow A_1\beta_1, \ldots, \alpha_k \uparrow A_k\beta_k \rangle$$

with $q \in F$.

The language *accepted* by M is defined as $L(M) = \{ x | x \in I^*$ and x is accepted by $M \}$.   □

Example 1.14

Consider the language $L = \{ a^n b^n c^n | n \geq 1 \}$. It is easy to realize that the 1-tape TM M sketched below accepts it.

Intuitively, M operates as follows.

Step 1:   On reading a, M switches to state q_1 and moves the head of its memory tape to the right.

Step 2: M scans all a's until the first b is reached (if any). In doing so, M writes as many $*$'s to the right of Z_0 in its memory tape as there are a's in the input tape.

Step 3: M scans all b's. In doing so it moves left the head of its memory tape by as many positions as there are b's in the input tape. Thus, after scanning all b's the head is positioned over Z_0 if and only if the number of b's equals the number of a's.

Step 4: M scans all c's (if any). In doing so, it moves the head of its memory tape for each c read from input to the right. Thus, when reaching the first ∮ to the right of the rightmost c, the memory tape head reaches the first ∮ to the right of $*$'s if and only if the number of c's equals the number of b's. In such a case M enters a final state and halts.

In all other cases M halts in a nonfinal state.

The state diagram of Figure 1.30 gives a more detailed description of M. As usual final states are double circled and the lack of an outgoing arc means that δ is not defined for those values.

We give below the full computation sequence of M in correspondence of the input *aabbcc*. The reader is invited to check the behavior of M both on other

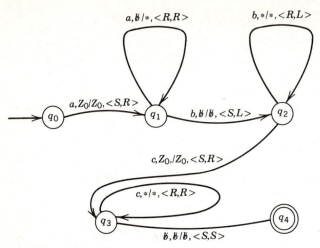

FIGURE 1.30 A TM accepting $\{a^n b^n c^n | n \geq 1\}$.

strings of the type $a^n b^n c^n$ and on strings not belonging to L, verifying that M actually accepts L.

$\langle q_0, \uparrow aabbcc, \uparrow Z_0 \rangle \vdash \langle q_1, \uparrow aabbcc, Z_0 \uparrow \not b \rangle \vdash \langle q_1, a \uparrow abbcc, Z_0 * \uparrow \not b \rangle$
$\vdash \langle q_1, aa \uparrow bbcc, Z_0 * * \uparrow \not b \rangle \vdash \langle q_2, aa \uparrow bbcc, Z_0 * \uparrow * \not b \rangle$
$\vdash \langle q_2, aab \uparrow bcc, Z_0 \uparrow * * \not b \rangle \vdash \langle q_2, aabb \uparrow cc, \uparrow Z_0 * * \not b \rangle$
$\vdash \langle q_3, aabb \uparrow cc, Z_0 \uparrow * * \not b \rangle \vdash \langle q_3, aabbc \uparrow c, Z_0 * \uparrow * \not b \rangle$
$\vdash \langle q_3, aabbcc \uparrow \not b, Z_0 \uparrow * * \not b \rangle \vdash \langle q_4, aabbcc \uparrow \not b, Z_0 * * \uparrow \not b \rangle$

Example 1.15

Consider the language $L = \{a^n b^n | n \geq 1\} \cup \{a^n b^{2n} | n \geq 1\}$. The 2-tape TM M sketched below accepts L.

After a trivial initialization step,

Step 1: M scans all a's and writes as many $*$'s to the right of Z_0 on $\mathbf{T}_1$ as there are a's on the input tape. Similarly, at the same time, it writes pairs of $*$'s on $\mathbf{T}_2$.

Step 2: While scanning the b's, M moves one step left both heads of $\mathbf{T}_1$ and $\mathbf{T}_2$.

Step 3: If all b's are scanned and the head of $\mathbf{T}_1$ is positioned onto Z_0, M enters a final state and halts.

Step 4: Otherwise, M scans all remaining b's and in doing so continues moving the head of $\mathbf{T}_2$ one step left for each scanned b.

Step 5: If all b's are scanned and the head of $\mathbf{T}_2$ is positioned on Z_0, M enters a final state and halts.

In all other cases, the input string is rejected.

As an exercise, the reader is invited to provide a detailed formal description of M and to verify that M actually accepts L.

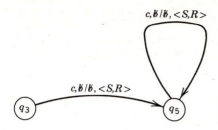

FIGURE 1.31 A modification of the TM of Figure 1.30.

Exercises

1.32 Build multitape TMs accepting the languages

$L_1 = \{wcw | w \in \{a, b\}^+\}$
$L_2 = \{wcw^R | w \in \{a, b\}^+\}^3$
$L_3 = \{a^n b^{n^2} | n \geq 1\}$
$L_4 = \{x \in \{a, b, c\}^*$ such that the number of occurrences of a in x equals the number of occurrences of b or the number of $c\}$.

1.33 Build a 1-tape TM accepting $L = \{a^n b^n\} \cup \{a^n b^{2n}\}$.

An important remark is now in order. All TMs used so far as language recognizers have the property that they always reach a halting configuration for any given input. In such a configuration if the state is final they accept it, otherwise they reject the input string. Observe, however, that this fact is not strictly required by Definition 1.19. According to it, if $x \notin L$, then M may never reach a halting configuration, that is, it may continue to operate indefinitely.

For instance, we could modify the TM of Example 1.14 by adding state q_5 and the transitions of Figure 1.31 (the rest of the graph remains unaffected). If the modified machine M' were supplied with input $a^n b^n c^{n+1}$, it would eventually enter state q_5 and then it would indefinitely loop. Notice however that, according to Definition 1.19, M' still accepts $L = \{a^n b^n c^n | n \geq 1\}$.

The reader should notice that something similar happens with PDAs, which may enter an infinite loop of ϵ-moves. However, we have been able to prove (Theorem 1.11) that this inconvenience can always be eliminated, thanks to the construction of loop-free PDAs. In Chapter 2 we show that this result does not hold for TMs and we investigate the enormous impact of this fact.

For the moment, we just warn the reader that *acceptance*, as defined in Definition 1.19, is a weaker concept than *decision*, where the latter term means the ability to state both relations $x \in L$ and $x \notin L$. A TM accepting L is able to state $x \in L$ when this is the case but not necessarily the opposite, since it may never halt for a given input. Again, the conceptual difference between the two terms are thoroughly investigated in Chapter 2.

---

[3]As it is customary, w^R denotes the reverse of string w.

1.4.2 Turing Machines as Language Translators

When TMs are defined with output tape and output function, they are *transducers*, that is, they can be used to *translate* strings of I^* into strings of O^*.

Definition 1.20

Let M be a multitape TM. M defines a *translation* $\tau_M \colon I^* \to O^*$ according to the following rule.

$$\tau_M(x) = y \quad \text{if and only if} \quad \langle q_0, \uparrow x, \uparrow Z_0, \ldots, \uparrow Z_0, \uparrow \not{b} \rangle \overset{*}{\underset{M}{\vdash}}$$

$$\langle q, x' \uparrow iy, \alpha_1 \uparrow A_1 \beta_1, \ldots, \alpha_k \uparrow A_k \beta_k, y \uparrow \not{b} \rangle$$

with $q \in F$.   □

As usual, M will be omitted in $\underset{M}{\vdash}$ and $\overset{*}{\underset{M}{\vdash}}$ when no ambiguity arises.

    Notice that, in general, a TM M defines a *partial translation*, that is, a partial function $\tau_M \colon I^* \to O^*$. In fact τ_M is undefined both if M reaches a halting configuration whose state is not in F and if M never halts when operating on x. This is illustrated by the following examples.

Example 1.16

The 1-tape TM M sketched below duplicates any input string in $\{a, b\}^+$. Precisely, $\tau_M(x) = xx$ for any $x \in \{a, b\}^+$.

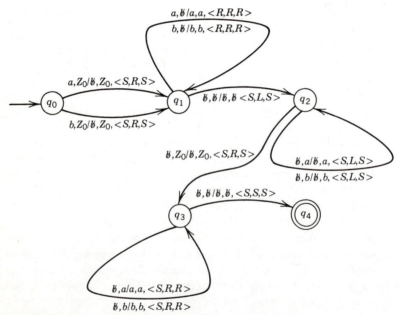

FIGURE 1.32 A TM that duplicates input strings. A double label for a single edge is a short notation for two parallel edges.

Step 1: M scans x from left to right, and copies it character by character, both in T_1 and in T_O.

Step 2: When the end of x is reached in T_I, M stops writing and moves back T_1's head until Z_0 is reached.

Step 3: At this point, M scans T_1 copying it character by character onto T_O. Thus a new copy of x in appended to T_O.

Step 4: When the first blank in T_1 is reached, M enters a final state and halts.

The diagram of Figure 1.32 gives a detailed description of M. The reader is invited to simulate M's behavior by hand on input *abb*.

Example 1.17

The 2-tape TM M sketched below performs the following translation:

$$\tau_M(a^n b^n) = *^n \qquad \tau_M(a^n b^{2n}) = *^{2n} \qquad n \geq 1$$

$\tau_M(x)$ is undefined if $x \notin \{ a^n b^n | n \geq 1 \} \cup \{ a^n b^{2n} | n \geq 1 \}$

Step 1: M scans all a's. For each a, it writes a single $*$ in T_1 and a pair of $*$ in T_2.

Step 2: M scans all b's and moves left the heads of T_1 and T_2 for each input b.

Step 3: If all b's have been scanned and the head of T_1 is positioned onto Z_0, M outputs as many $*$ as there are $*$ in T_1, then enters a final state and halts.

Step 4: Otherwise, if more b's remain to be scanned, M does so and moves left the head of T_2 for each input b.

Step 5: If all b's have been scanned and the head of T_2 is positioned onto Z_0, M outputs as many $*$ as there are $*$ in T_2, then enters a final state and halts.

In all other cases, M enters an error state $q_E \notin F$ and halts.

Example 1.18

The input tape T_I of a TM M contains a sequence of English words $w_0, w_1, \ldots, w_n$, organized as follows.

$$w_0 \$ w_1 \cent w_2 \cent \ldots w_n *$$

Symbols $, $\cent$, and $*$ act as delimiters and cannot appear inside words. M deletes from the sequence $w_1 \cent w_2 \cent \ldots w_n *$ all occurrences of strings equal to w_0 and prints the resulting sequence on the output tape T_O.

M is a 2-tape TM and operates as follows.

Step 1: w_0 is copied onto T_1.

Step 2: M scans the text word by word (the end of the list is marked by $*$). For each word w_i

    2.1 w_i is first copied onto T_2. In doing so, M compares w_i with w_0 character by character. The end of the word is denoted by $\cent$ or $*$.

2.2 M changes state if w_i and w_0 are found different but continues copying w_i onto $\mathbf{T}_2$.

2.3 The contents of $\mathbf{T}_2$ is copied onto $\mathbf{T}_O$ if M has changed state in 2.2.

2.4 The state is reset if there has been a state change in 2.2 and the heads of $\mathbf{T}_1$ and $\mathbf{T}_2$ are positioned on the first tape cell.

Exercises

1.34 Give a detailed formal description of the TM of Example 1.17.

1.35 Provide a 1-tape TM realizing the same translation as the TM of Example 1.17.

1.36 Give multitape TMs realizing the following translations.

- $\tau_1(x) = xx^R$
- $\tau_2(x) = xx$ if the first and the last characters of x is a a, xx^R otherwise.
- $\tau_3(x) = x^{|x|}$
- $\tau_4(a^n) = b^{n^2}$ if n is even, b^{n^3} if n is odd.

1.37 Give a detailed description of the TM outlined in Example 1.18.

1.38 Build a TM that substitutes each occurrence of a given word in an English text by another given word. *Hint*: Take inspiration from Example 1.18.

1.39 Build a TM that receives as input an English text containing an arbitrary number of blanks between each pair of words and outputs the text by using only one blank as a separator.

1.40 Build a TM that receives as input a sequence of English words separated by $\not b$ and outputs the input sequence with no repeated strings.

1.4.3 Turing Machines as Function Evaluators

So far, TMs and other automata have been considered mainly as language processors. Observe, however, that strings are also a medium to represent numbers. For example, 101 denotes *"one hundred and one"* if interpreted as a decimal number and *"five"* if interpreted as a binary number. Thus automata, and TMs in particular, if used to translate strings of digits in other strings of digits, can also be viewed as functions with numeric domain and range. For instance, one can build a TM that receives as input a string of decimal digits coding the natural number n and produces as output the string of decimal digits coding n^2, thus implementing function "square" via a TM. Once again, note that it may happen that the function $f_M: D \to R$ computed by some TM M is partial. In fact, f_M is undefined for some $x \in D$, if the computation of M on the input coding x halts in a nonfinal state or—even more important!—if M never halts.

Let us give some examples of TMs used as function computers.

Example 1.19

The 2-tape TM M outlined below receives as input a natural number n coded in decimal notation and produces as output its successor $n + 1$.

Step 1: M copies all digits of n onto $\mathbf{T}_1$, to the right of Z_0. In doing so, it moves the head of $\mathbf{T}_2$ by the same number of tape positions.

Step 2: M scans the digits stored in $\mathbf{T}_1$ from right to left. Tape $\mathbf{T}_2$ is also written from right to left as we describe shortly.

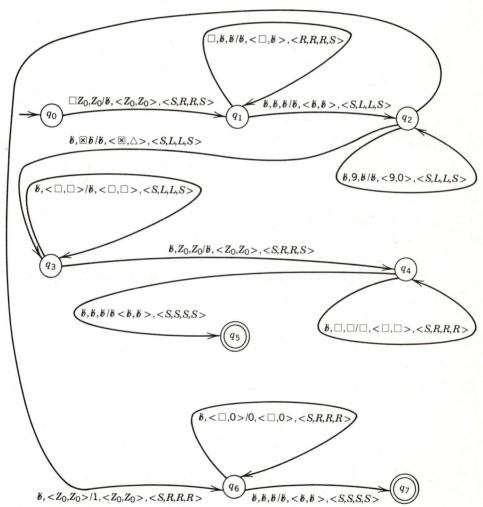

FIGURE 1.33 A TM computing the successor of a decimal number. □ denotes any decimal digit. When two or more □ occur in the same arc label, they denote the same digit. ⊠ denotes any digit other than 9. △ denotes the successor of the digit denoted by ⊠.

2.1 For each digit d found on T_1, if it is a 9, it writes 0 in the corresponding cell of T_2.

2.2 If d is other than 9, it writes the digit representing $d + 1$ in the corresponding cell of T_2. If the "read" symbol is a not a digit (it is Z_0), it writes 1 in the first cell of tape T_O.

2.3 All remaining digits of T_1 (if any) are copied identically into T_2.

Step 3:   The string of digits that has been produced in tape T_2 is copied into T_O.

Figure 1.33 gives a detailed description of M.

Exercise

1.41   Simulate the behavior of the TM of Example 1.19 with inputs 99, 12899, and 312.

Example 1.20

Let us build a TM M that adds two binary-coded natural numbers. The two numbers n and m are written in the input tape separated by a \$. M has three memory tapes T_1, T_2, and T_3 and operates as follows.

Step 1: M copies n into T_1 to the right of Z_0. In doing so, the heads of T_2 and T_3 are not moved.

TABLE 1.2   Rules for the Addition of Binary-coded Numbers

				n_i	
				0	1
r_i	0	m_i	0	0 / 0	1 / 0
			1	1 / 0	0 / 1
	1	m_i	0	1 / 0	0 / 1
			1	0 / 1	1 / 1

Legend: $\begin{array}{|c|}\hline a_i\ \diagdown\ \\ \diagdown\ r_{i+1}\\\hline\end{array}$

Step 2:   After reading the $ separating n and m, M copies m onto $\mathbf{T}_2$, keeping the heads of $\mathbf{T}_1$ and $\mathbf{T}_3$ stationary.

Step 3:   After reading m, the heads of $\mathbf{T}_1$ and $\mathbf{T}_2$ are positioned on the rightmost characters of n and m. Thus, M starts adding n and m, digit by digit according to the rule described by Table 1.2 where n_i, m_i, and a_i denote the ith digit of n, m and $a = n + m$, respectively. r_i represents the ith carry; initially (i.e., for $i = 1$) $r_i = 0$.

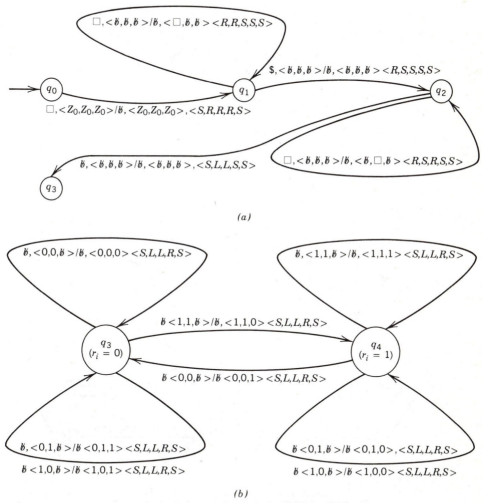

(a)

(b)

FIGURE 1.34 A TM performing binary addition. (*a*) Reading phase, corresponding to Steps 1, 2. (*b*) Step 3. (*c*) Step 4, when $r_i = 0$. (*d*) Steps 4 and 5, when $r_i = 1$. (*e*) Step 6. □ denotes either 0 or 1. Several occurrences of □ in the label of the same edge denote the same digit. Multiple labels on a single edge are a short notation for several labeled edges. When necessary, nodes enclose a brief comment on the meaning of the state.

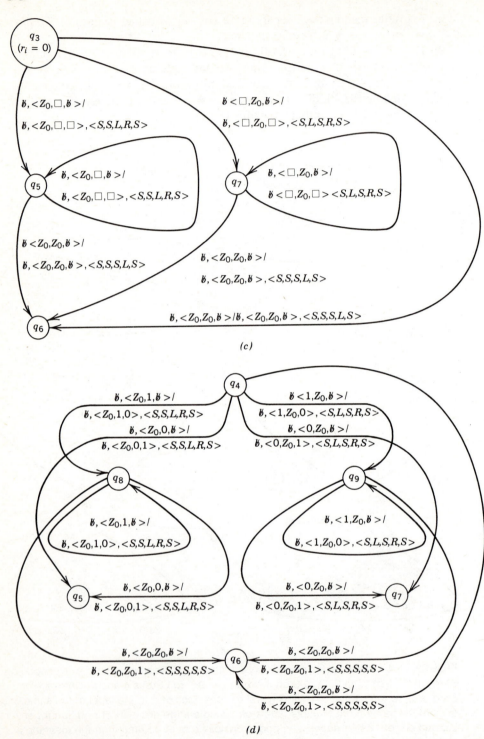

(c)

(d)

FIGURE 1.34 Continued.

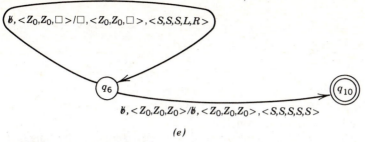

$$\text{b},<Z_0,Z_0,\square>/\square,<Z_0,Z_0,\square>,<S,S,S,L,R>$$

$q_6 \qquad q_{10}$

$$\text{b},<Z_0,Z_0,Z_0>/\text{b},<Z_0,Z_0,Z_0>,<S,S,S,S,S>$$

(e)

FIGURE 1.34 Continued.

The digits of a are written on $\mathbf{T}_3$ from left to right (i.e., a_1 is stored in the cell to the right of Z_0). At each step, given the values for n_i, m_i, and r_i, Table 1.2 shows how to evaluate a_i and r_{i+1}. The latter is used at the next step along with n_{i+1} and m_{i+1} to evaluate a_{i+1}.

Step 4: When the head of $\mathbf{T}_1$ ($\mathbf{T}_2$) reads Z_0 the computation continues as if the remaining digits in $\mathbf{T}_1$ ($\mathbf{T}_2$) were all 0's, until also the head of $\mathbf{T}_2$ ($\mathbf{T}_1$) reaches Z_0.

Step 5: When both heads of $\mathbf{T}_1$ and $\mathbf{T}_2$ reach Z_0, if r_{i+1} is 1, a 1 is appended to $\mathbf{T}_3$.

Step 6: Finally, string a is copied onto $\mathbf{T}_O$ in reverse order; that is, string a is copied from right to left.

Figure 1.34 gives a detailed description of M.

Exercises

1.42 Simulate by hands the behavior of M on some examples.

1.43 Show that q_5, q_7, q_8, and q_9 could be eliminated in the construction of M, that is, an equivalent TM M' can be built without those states.

1.44 Build (or at least sketch) a TM executing the sum of two decimal numbers.

1.45 Sketch a TM executing the multiplication of two numbers coded in any base.

1.46 Sketch a TM *deciding* whether a given number is prime or not. The machine must eventually halt for any given input with a positive or negative answer.

1.4.4 Properties of Turing Machines

In this section, we briefly review some relevant properties of TMs in order to familiarize the reader with the model, which will be extensively used in this text. First, we show that TMs are more powerful than PDAs, and hence FAs.

Theorem 1.13

The class of languages recognized by TMs strictly includes the class of languages recognized by PDAs.

Proof

Proving weak inclusion is an easy exercise once one realizes that, for any given PDA A, a 1-tape TM M can be constructed that acts exactly as A by using its memory tape exactly as A's pushdown store.

To prove strict inclusion, observe that a TM can recognize the language $\{a^n b^n\} \cup \{a^n b^{2n}\}$, as shown in Example 1.15, while a PDA cannot, as shown by Theorem 1.12. ∎

The following theorem is given without its proof, which is left as an exercise.

Theorem 1.14

TMs are more powerful translators than PDTs, that is, all translations performed by some PDT can be performed by some TM, but not conversely. ∎

Exercise

1.47 Prove Theorem 1.14. *Hint*: The translation defined in Example 1.17 requires the ability to recognize $L = \{a^n b^n\} \cup \{a^n b^{2n}\}$; but L cannot be recognized by any PDA (Theorem 1.12). This remark can be formalized by proving that the existence of a PDT realizing such a translation would lead to the existence of a PDA recognizing the foregoing language.

Definition 1.15 presents one of the many slightly different versions of the machine model that was named after Alan Turing. We present a sample of such a variety, anticipating that all versions have the same "power" as the previous model. In particular, the original Turing's model is slightly different from the one we have presented. Informally, the difference consists of having only one tape, which is used both as input, memory, and output device (see Figure 1.35).

The tape is infinite in both directions. As usual, the control unit can perform moves depending on the symbol under its head and on its internal state.

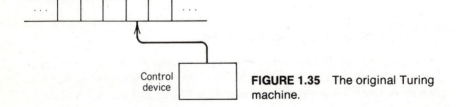

Control device

FIGURE 1.35 The original Turing machine.

A move consists of

- Changing the internal state.
- Rewriting the symbol under the head.
- Moving the head left (L), or right (R), or keeping it stationary (S).

Conventionally, the input of the machine is the tape contents at the beginning of its computation. The head is positioned on the leftmost nonblank character and the control unit is in q_0. If and when the machine halts a suitable convention defines which portion of the tape is considered to be the machine output. Formally, a single-tape TM can be defined as follows.

Definition 1.21
A *single-tape* TM is a 5-tuple $\langle Q, A, \delta, q_0, F \rangle$ where

- Q is a finite set of *states*.
- A is a finite *tape alphabet*, including a special blank symbol $\not{b}$.
- $q_0 \in Q$ is the initial state.
- $F \subseteq Q$ is the set of *final states*.
- δ is the—possibly partial—*transition function*

$$\delta: (Q - F) \times A \to Q \times A \times \{R, L, S\} \qquad \square$$

Exercise

1.48 Formalize the notions of configuration, initial configuration, transition, language recognition, and language translation for single-tape TMs.

Notice that 1-tape TMs are a different model than single-tape TMs, since T_I and T_O are always distinct from memory tapes in multitape TMs. In order to avoid confusion, the term 1-tape TM will denote a multitape TM with just one memory tape, while single-tape TM is reserved for the model of Definition 1.21. The acronym TM is used for any version of the Turing formalism.

Theorem 1.15
Multitape TMs and single-tape TMs are equivalent formalisms, that is, they accept the same class of languages and they realize the same class of translations.

Sketch of the proof
Clearly, simulating a single-tape TM via a multitape TM is not a problem. Simply add steps to copy the contents of the input onto a memory tape at the beginning of computation and from the memory tape onto the output tape at the end of computation. Let us briefly consider the opposite case.

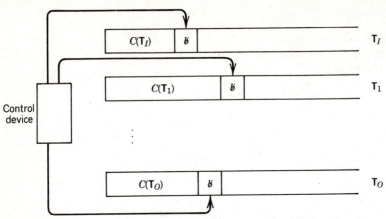

FIGURE 1.36 Configuration of the k-tape TM M. $c(T)$ denotes the nonblank portion of the contents of tape **T**.

Suppose that a generic configuration of a k-tape TM M looks like the one in Figure 1.36. We can represent such a configuration with a configuration of a single tape TM M' as shown in Figure 1.37.

A single transition of M is simulated by a suitable sequence of transitions of M'. Precisely, M' must "visit" $\bar{q}$ and the characters to the right of all $*$, except for the rightmost $*$, in order to get the information needed to select the move. Then M' simulates the move of M by suitably modifying the characters to the right of $*$'s and possibly changing positions of $*$.

If some tape of M, $\mathbf{T}_x$, requires one extra cell, this is provided by suitably shifting all characters to the right of the $\$$ marking the end of $c(\mathbf{T}_x)$. For instance, suppose that $c(\mathbf{T}_x)''$ contains one only character and $\mathbf{T}_x$'s head has to move right. M' first shifts all characters to the right of $c(\mathbf{T}_x)''$ including the $\$$ by one cell, then exchanges $c(\mathbf{T}_x)''$ with $*$ and writes a b in the remaining "hole."

The details of the construction are left to the reader as an exercise. ∎

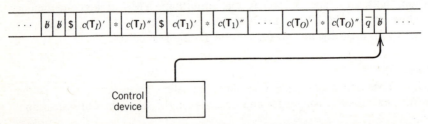

FIGURE 1.37 Configuration of the single-tape TM M'. $c(\mathbf{T}_x)'$ represents the nonblank contents of tape $\mathbf{T}_x$ of M to the left of $\mathbf{T}_x$'s head; $c(\mathbf{T}_x)''$ represents the contents of the same tape to the right of the head, including the character under the head. $\$$ and $*$ are symbols not belonging to $I \cup \Gamma \cup 0$ and are used to mark the boundary between the contents of different tapes and head positions, respectively. $\bar{q}$ is a suitable encoding of the state of M.

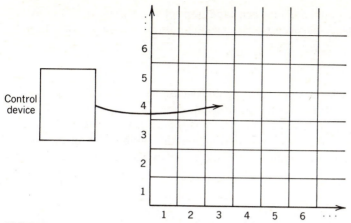

FIGURE 1.38 A multidimensional TM.

Both multitape and single-tape TMs may be equipped with multidimensional tapes: the resulting model is the *multidimensional tape TM*. A k-dimensional tape is such that each tape cell is uniquely determined by a k-tuple of positive integers. Figure 1.38 illustrates the case of a 2-dimensional tape (a planar tape). A 2-dimensional tape TM can move its head(s) in four directions up, down, left, right, or it can remain stationary.

The equivalence with the original model can be easily proved once a suitable bijective correspondence is stated between $\mathbb{N} - \{0\}$ and $(\mathbb{N} - \{0\})^k$, which denote the set of head positions for linear tapes and the set of head positions for multidimensional tapes, respectively. For instance, one can enumerate the squares of a 2-dimensional tape by following a diagonal method as shown in Figure 1.39, where for each pair $\langle x, y \rangle$,

$$d(x, y) = x + \frac{(x + y - 1) \cdot (x + y - 2)}{2}$$

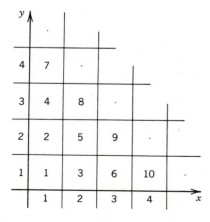

FIGURE 1.39 A bijection between positive integers and pairs of positive integers.

Once a correspondence between tape positions is established, it is easy to state a correspondence between machine configurations and sequences of moves.

Exercises

1.49 Give a formal definition of a multidimensional tape TM and prove its equivalence with respect to our original model.

1.50 A multihead TM is like a multitape TM, but it can have several heads on each tape and the move can depend on the symbols being read by all heads. Formally define this device and prove its equivalence with multitape TMs.

When dealing with formal models, one often faces the problem of transforming one formal model into another more concise, or even "minimal," equivalent form. This happens with computer programs, which may be transformed into equivalent versions that reduce the amount of used storage or execution time. The problem has been discussed also in the case of FAs. Given a FA A that recognizes a given language, we have shown that one can try to reduce the number of states up to the point where we reach the minimum number (Theorem 1.4). Does a similar result hold for TM? The following theorem provides an answer.

Theorem 1.16
Every TM is equivalent to some TM having only two nonfinal states and one final state (and possibly an increased number of symbols). ■

The proof of Theorem 1.16 is highly technical and can be skipped by most readers. The advanced reader can try it as a challenging exercise with a little help. A sketchy solution is also given at the end of the chapter.

Exercise

1.51* Prove Theorem 1.16.

Hint: Without any loss of generality, you can consider a single-tape TM M and a single move of M consisting of the transition, say,

$$\langle q_7, \ldots a_5 \uparrow a_3 a_{13} \ldots \rangle \underset{M}{\vdash} \langle q_3, \ldots a_5 a_8 \uparrow a_{13} \ldots \rangle$$

Build a single-tape TM $\overline{M}$ with only two nonfinal states, q_α, q_β, which simulates the above M's move through the following sequence of moves.

$$\langle q_\alpha, \ldots \bar{a}_5 \uparrow \langle q_7, a_3, -, * \rangle \bar{a}_{13} \ldots \rangle \underset{\overline{M}}{\vdash^4}$$
$$\langle q_\beta, \ldots \bar{a}_5 \langle q_3, a_8, +, R \rangle \uparrow \bar{a}_{13} \ldots \rangle \vdash$$

---

[4] $*$ denotes either L or R depending on $\overline{M}$ previous move but does not affect further behavior.

$$\langle q_\alpha, \ldots \bar{a}_5 \uparrow \langle q_3, a_8, +, R \rangle \langle q_0, a_{13}, -, R \rangle \ldots \rangle \vdash$$
$$\langle q_\beta, \ldots \bar{a}_5 \langle q_2, a_8, +, R \rangle \uparrow \langle q_0, a_{13}, -, L \rangle \ldots \rangle \vdash$$
$$\langle q_\alpha, \ldots \bar{a}_5 \uparrow \langle q_2, a_8, +, R \rangle \langle q_1, a_{13}, -, L \rangle \ldots \rangle \vdash$$
$$\langle q_\beta, \ldots \bar{a}_5 \langle q_1, a_8, +, R \rangle \uparrow \langle q_1, a_{13}, -, L \rangle \ldots \rangle \vdash$$
$$\langle q_\alpha, \ldots \bar{a}_5 \uparrow \langle q_1, a_8, +, R \rangle \langle q_2, a_{13}, -, L \rangle \ldots \rangle \vdash$$
$$\langle q_\beta, \ldots \bar{a}_5 \langle q_0, a_8, +, R \rangle \uparrow \langle q_3, a_{13}, -, L \rangle \ldots \rangle \vdash$$
$$\langle q_\alpha, \ldots \bar{a}_5 \uparrow \langle q_0, a_8, +, R \rangle \langle q_3, a_{13}, -, L \rangle \ldots \rangle \vdash$$
$$\langle q_\alpha, \ldots \bar{a}_5 \bar{a}_8 \uparrow \langle q_3, a_{13}, -, L \rangle \ldots \rangle$$

We have previously been able to build TMs computing the sum of two natural numbers both for binary and decimal coding. The general problem we wish to address is whether the power of TMs is affected by the way a problem is coded. The following theorem answers this question.

Theorem 1.17
Every TM is equivalent to some TM having a two-symbol alphabet (and possibly an increased number of states). ∎

The proof of Theorem 1.17 is left as an exercise to the reader after noticing that two symbols are sufficient to code any finite alphabet. For instance, let $A = \{ \not{b}, a_1, \ldots a_m \}$, $\bar{A} = \{ \not{b}, \bar{a} \}$. One may represent the string

$$\ldots \not{b} a_2 a_5 a_1 \not{b} a_3 \not{b} \ldots$$

as

$$\ldots \not{b} \not{b} \overline{aa} \not{b} \overline{aaaaa} \not{b} \overline{a} \not{b} \not{b} \overline{aaa} \not{b} \not{b} \ldots$$

That is, symbol a_i is coded by i occurrences of $\bar{a}$, $\not{b}$ is used as a separator between each coded a_i, and a double $\not{b}$ is used to code the original $\not{b}$.

Unlike TMs, FAs may be sensitive to the choice of coding. For instance, a FT can easily compute the successor of a natural number, if coded in unary base (i.e., n is represented by a sequence of n identical symbols—say $\bar{a}$). The FT simply copies its input on the output tape and then appends one extra $\bar{a}$. The same computation cannot be performed by a FT if n is written in any other base, as the following theorem states.

Theorem 1.18
No FT can compute the successor of a natural number coded in any base $k > 1$.

Proof
The proof is given for $k = 10$, but clearly applies as well to any $k > 1$.
Suppose by contradiction, that there exists a FT T computing the successor of any natural number coded as a string of decimal digits. Consider numbers represented by strings of the type 9^x that is, $n = 99 \ldots 9$ (9 is repeated x times).

Let $\eta^*(q_0, 9^x) = z (z \neq \epsilon$ by assumption).

Thus $\eta^*(q_0, 9^x \cdot 9) = z \cdot y_1, \eta^*(q_0, 9^x \cdot 8) = z \cdot y_2$. But the successor of $9^x \cdot 9$ is $1 \cdot 0^{x+1}$, whereas the successor of $9^x \cdot 8$ is 9^{x+1}, which do not have any common proper prefix z.   ∎

Exercises

1.52 Prove the following stronger version of Theorem 1.18. No FT can compute the translation $\tau: I^*\$ \rightarrow O^*\$$ such that $\tau(x\$) = y\$$, where y is the coding of the successor of the number coded by x.

1.53 Show that there exists a PDT computing the reverse string of the decimal coding of the successor of a given natural number coded in decimal base.

1.54 Formally define the following variations of TMs and prove their equivalence with the multitape model:

1. *Nonstationary TM*: at each step the tape heads must move either right or left and cannot remain stationary.
2. The machine can perform one of the following two actions:
   a. Rewriting, without moving the head.
   b. Moving the head without writing any symbol.
3. *Semiinfinite single-tape TM*: the tape of the machine is infinite only to the right.

1.55 Prove that the set of languages accepted by TMs is closed with respect to union and intersection.

1.5 Grammars: A Formalism to Generate Languages

Very often automata are used as abstract models in language recognition problems. One can even say that a recognizer is a formal device that can be used for defining a language: the set of all strings accepted by the recognizer. If A is a recognizer and I is its input alphabet, we have introduced the notation

$$L(A) = \{ x | x \in I^*, x \text{ is accepted by } A \}$$

to denote the language defined by A. According to this viewpoint, a recognizer is an operational device that defines a language by providing a mechanical way of stating whether a string belongs to the language being defined.

In this section we define another formal device that can be used to define languages: formal grammars. A formal grammar defines a language by showing how any strings belonging to language can be derived: As such, it is a generative device. In the sequel, we give a formal definition of a grammar, we define various classes of grammars, and we give examples. The next section studies some properties of grammars and, in particular, compares them with automata.

Definition 1.22

An *unrestricted grammar* (or, shortly, a *grammar*) G is a quadruple $G = \langle V_T, V_N, P, S \rangle$ where

- V_T is a finite set of *terminal symbols*, called *terminal alphabet*.
- V_N is a finite set of *nonterminal symbols* such that $V_T \cap V_N = \varnothing$, called *nonterminal alphabet*. V denotes $V_T \cup V_N$.
- P is a finite subset of $V_N^+ \times V^*$, called the set of *productions* of G. An element $p = \langle \alpha, \beta \rangle$ of P will be denoted by $\alpha \to \beta$. String α is the *left-hand side* of p; string β is its *right-hand side*.
- S is a distinguished element of V_N called the *axiom*. $\qquad \square$

Definition 1.23

For a given grammar G, a binary relation called *immediate derivation*, denoted by $\underset{G}{\Rightarrow}$, is defined on V^*: $\alpha \underset{G}{\Rightarrow} \beta$ if and only if $\alpha = \alpha_1 \gamma \alpha_2$, $\beta = \alpha_1 \delta \alpha_2$, with α_1, α_2, and $\delta \in V^*$, $\gamma \in V_N^+$ and $\gamma \to \delta \in P$. As usual, $\underset{G}{\overset{*}{\Rightarrow}}$, $\underset{G}{\overset{+}{\Rightarrow}}$, $\underset{G}{\overset{k}{\Rightarrow}}$ denote the reflexive and transitive closure, the transitive closure, and chain of length k of $\underset{G}{\Rightarrow}$, respectively. The symbol G will be omitted in $\underset{G}{\Rightarrow}$ when obvious. $\qquad \square$

Definition 1.24

For a given grammar G, *the language $L(G)$ generated by G* is defined as $L(G) = \{ x \mid S \underset{G}{\overset{*}{\Rightarrow}} x, \, x \in V_T^* \}$. $\qquad \square$

Example 1.21

Consider the following grammar.

$G_1 = \langle \{0, 1\}, \{S\}, P_1, S \rangle$
where

$P_1 = \{ S \to 0S, \, S \to 1S, \, S \to 1 \}$

Sample derivations of G_1 are

$S \Rightarrow 1$
$S \Rightarrow 0S \Rightarrow 01$
$S \Rightarrow 1S \Rightarrow 11$
$S \Rightarrow 0S \Rightarrow 00S \Rightarrow 001$
$S \Rightarrow 0S \Rightarrow 01S \Rightarrow 011$
$S \Rightarrow 1S \Rightarrow 10S \Rightarrow 101$
$S \Rightarrow 1S \Rightarrow 11S \Rightarrow 111$

It is now immediate to generalize from these sample derivations and notice that

$$L(G_1) = \{0, 1\}^* \cdot 1$$

that is, the language generated by G_1 is the set of bit sequences that represent an odd integer number. $L(G)$ coincides with the language recognized by the automaton discussed by Example 1.4. In order to prove this, note that the first two productions provide a mechanism to generate any sequence of $\{0, 1\}^*$, while the third forces the rightmost character of the string to be a 1.

Example 1.22

Consider the following grammar.

$G_2 = \langle \{a, b\}, \{S\}, P_2, S \rangle$
where

$P_2 = \{S \rightarrow aSb, S \rightarrow ab\}$

Sample derivations of G_2 are

$S \Rightarrow ab$
$S \Rightarrow aSb \Rightarrow aabb$
$S \Rightarrow aSb \Rightarrow aaSbb \Rightarrow aaabbb$

Any string belonging to $L(G_2)$ can be derived through some sequence of applications of the first production (which generates $a^m Sb^m$, $m \geq 0$), followed by the application of the second production (which generates $a^m abb^m$, $m \geq 0$). Thus:

$$L(G_2) = \{a^n b^n | n \geq 1\}$$

We invite the reader to observe that the language generated by G_2 coincides with the language recognized by the automaton of Example 1.10. In other words, the two formalisms define the same language.

Example 1.23

Consider the following grammar.

$G_3 = \langle \{a, b, c\}, \{S, A, B, C, D\}, P_3, S \rangle$
where

$P_3 = \{S \rightarrow aACD, A \rightarrow aAC, A \rightarrow \epsilon, B \rightarrow b, CD \rightarrow BDc, CB \rightarrow BC, D \rightarrow \epsilon\}$

Some sample derivations of G_3 are

$S \Rightarrow aACD \Rightarrow aCD \Rightarrow aBDc \Rightarrow abDc \Rightarrow abc$
$S \Rightarrow aACD \Rightarrow aaACCD \Rightarrow aaCCD \Rightarrow aaCBDc \Rightarrow aaBCDc \Rightarrow$
$\quad aabCDc \Rightarrow aabBDcc \Rightarrow aabbDcc \Rightarrow aabbcc$
$S \stackrel{*}{\Rightarrow} aaaACCCD \stackrel{*}{\Rightarrow} aaaCCC$

A straightforward generalization shows that $L(G_3) = \{a^n b^n c^n | n \geq 1\}$, that is, the same language recognized by the TM of Example 1.14.

The previous examples have made it clear why grammars are a generative formalism to define languages. Grammars describe the generation of all strings in a language by a sequence of derivation steps starting from the axiom. Each derivation step uses a production $\alpha \rightarrow \beta$ as a rewriting rule, that is, a rule specifying how a substring α within a string is to be replaced with another substring β.

Two subclasses of grammars are particularly relevant in practice: context-free grammars and regular grammars.

Definition 1.25

Let $G = \langle V_T, V_N, P, S \rangle$ be an unrestricted grammar. Suppose that for every production $\alpha \to \beta$ in P, $|\alpha| = 1$ (i.e., $\alpha \in V_N$). Then G is a *context-free* (*CF*) *grammar*. A language L is *context free* if and only if it is generated by some context-free grammar. □

Definition 1.26

Let $G = \langle V_T, V_N, P, S \rangle$ be an unrestricted grammar. Suppose that for every production $\alpha \to \beta$ in P

- $|\alpha| = 1$ (i.e., $\alpha \in V_N$).
- β is either of the form aB or a, with $B \in V_N$, $a \in V_T$, or it is ϵ.

Then G is a *regular* (*R*) *grammar*. A language L is *regular* if and only if it is generated by some regular grammar. □

According to the previous examples, $L = \{0, 1\}^* \cdot 1$ is regular, whereas $L = \{a^n b^n | n \geq 1\}$ is context free. Obviously, every R-grammar (language) is also a CF-grammar (language).

R-grammars and CF-grammars have important practical applications in the definition of programming languages and in the theory that underlies compiler design. In fact, the lexical structure of a language is usually defined by an R-grammar, while its syntactic structure is defined by a CF-grammar. For example, the reader is invited to show that the lexical structure of Pascal identifiers (see also Figure 1.7) can be described by an R-grammar. Similarly, the syntactic nesting of Pascal structures (see Example 1.9) can be described by a CF-grammar.

Exercises

1.56 Write an R-grammar generating the language recognized by the FA of Figure 1.7.

1.57 Write a CF-grammar generating the language described by Example 1.9.

1.58 Write a CF-grammar generating the language

$$L = \{a^n b^m a^m b^n | n, m \geq 1\}$$

1.59 Write grammars generating the following languages.

$$L_1 = \{a^n b^{n^2} | n \geq 1\}$$
$$L_2 = L_1^*$$
$$L_3 = \{a^n b^{n^2} a^n b^{n^3} | n \text{ even and } \geq 1\}$$

1.5.1 Properties of Grammars

In Section 1.5 we have given examples of grammars. In particular Example 1.21 has shown an R-grammar G_1 that generates exactly the same language that is recognized by the *FA* of Example 1.4. Similarly, Example 1.22 has shown a *CF*-grammar G_2 that generates exactly the same language that is recognized by the PDA of Example 1.10. As these examples show, an important question arises about the relation between various types of recognizers and various types of grammars in terms of the classes of languages accepted and generated, respectively. Some relevant facts on this topic are now stated. A more complete treatment is provided in Section 1.8.

Theorem 1.19

Let A be a FA. An equivalent R-grammar G can be found constructively: G generates exactly the same language that is recognized by A.

Proof

Let $A = \langle Q, I, \delta, q_0, F \rangle$. Define $G = \langle I, Q, P, q_0 \rangle$, where elements of P have the following form.

- $B \to bC$ if $\delta(B, b) = C$
- $B \to \epsilon$ if $B \in F$

It is easy to show that $L(A) = L(G)$. In fact, suppose that $x \in L(G)$. Then, a suitable derivation exists such that

$$q_0 \underset{G}{\Rightarrow} a_1 A_1 \underset{G}{\Rightarrow} a_1 a_2 A_2 \underset{G}{\Rightarrow} \cdots \underset{G}{\Rightarrow} a_1 a_2 \ldots a_n A_n \underset{G}{\Rightarrow} a_1 a_2 \ldots a_n = x$$

for $A_1, \ldots, A_n \in Q, a_1, a_2 \ldots a_n \in I$.

Note that, in general, the number of derivation steps is $|x| + 1$ (thus, it is 1 if $x = \epsilon$). By definition of G, the first $|x|$ derivation steps correspond to a sequence of moves that let A enter state A_n starting from q_0. The last derivation step simply states that $A_n \in F$. Consequently, x is in $L(A)$.

     Conversely, suppose that $x \in L(A)$. Then a suitable sequence of moves is performed by A before reaching a state $q_n \in F$ on reading x. Let $q_0, q_1, \ldots, q_n$ be the sequence of states, where $n = |x|$. Each move of the automaton corresponds to a step of the derivation $q_0 \overset{*}{\underset{G}{\Rightarrow}} x q_n$. Since $q_n \in F$, $q_n \to \epsilon$ is in P. Thus $x \in L(G)$.   ∎

The converse of Theorem 1.19 holds as well. It will be proved in Section 1.8.

Exercise

1.60   Theorem 1.8 has proved that the class of regular languages is closed with respect to union, intersection, and complement. Prove the same results using R-grammars.

Theorem 1.20

Unrestricted grammars are equivalent to TMs used as language acceptors, that is, for any unrestricted grammar G there exists a TM M such that the language accepted by M is the same as the language generated by G and conversely.

Outline of the proof

We first outline the proof that for any single-tape TM M, whose tape is infinite only to the right, an equivalent grammar G can be built. Since single-tape TMs whose tape is infinite only to the right are equivalent to the other classes of TMs (see Exercise 1.54.3), there will be no loss of generality.

Let Q be the set of states, A the set of symbols ($V_T \subseteq A$, $\not b \in (A - V_T)$), $F \subseteq Q$ the set of final states, and δ the transition function. Thus, $L(M)$ is defined as

$$L(M) = \left\{ x | x \in V_T^* \wedge \langle q_0, \uparrow x \rangle \overset{*}{\underset{M}{\vdash}} \langle q, \alpha_1 \uparrow \alpha_2 \rangle, \alpha_1, \alpha_2 \in A^*, q \in F \right\}$$

The grammar G such that $L(G) = L(M)$ is built along the following lines. Productions are such that G generates two copies of any string x in V_T^* separated by the special symbol \$ and by the initial state of M. Then it simulates the sequence of moves of the TM on the second copy of x. If such a sequence eventually enters a final state, then all symbols to the right of \$ are erased, \$ included. Thus x is generated. Otherwise, either a string $\alpha \in (V^* - V_T^*)$ is generated such that for no β, $\alpha \underset{G}{\Rightarrow} \beta$, or nonterminating derivations (corresponding to nonterminating computations of the TM) are produced.

Let us outline now the construction of a TM M accepting $L(G)$ for any given grammar $G = \langle V_T, V_N, P, S \rangle$.

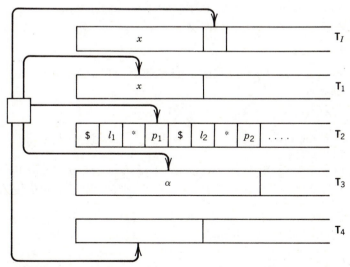

FIGURE 1.40 A TM accepting the language generated by an unrestricted grammar.

First, we label all productions of G with labels $l_1, \ldots, l_k$, with $k = |P|$. M can be derived as a four-tape TM, without output tape, organized as follows (see Figure 1.40).

- $\mathbf{T}_1$ is used to store the input string $x \in V_T^*$ originally recorded in $\mathbf{T}_I$.
- $\mathbf{T}_2$ is used to store sequences of pairs $\langle l_i, p_i \rangle$ with $l_i \in \{l_1, \ldots, l_k\}$, $p_i \in \mathbb{N}$.
- $\mathbf{T}_3$ is used to store strings α in V^* such that $S \overset{*}{\underset{G}{\Rightarrow}} \alpha$.
- $\mathbf{T}_4$ is a scratch tape used for intermediate computations.

Let E be any enumeration of all elements of $(\{l_1, \ldots, l_k\} \times \mathbb{N})^*$, that is, of all finite sequences of the type $\langle l_1, p_1 \rangle \langle l_2, p_2 \rangle \ldots \langle l_r, p_r \rangle$ with $l_i \in \{l_1, \ldots, l_k\}$, $p_i \in \mathbb{N}$. It is clear that there exist enumerations of this type that can be provided by some TM. For instance, if naturals are coded in binary notation, the following sequence

$$E' = \langle 0 \rangle, \langle 1 \rangle,$$
$$\langle 0, 0 \rangle, \langle 0, 1 \rangle, \langle 1, 0 \rangle, \langle 1, 1 \rangle, \langle 00 \rangle, \langle 01 \rangle, \langle 10 \rangle, \langle 11 \rangle,$$
$$\langle 0, 0, 0 \rangle, \langle 0, 0, 1 \rangle, \ldots \langle 1, 1, 1 \rangle, \langle 000 \rangle, \langle 001 \rangle, \ldots \langle 111 \rangle, \langle 0, 00 \rangle, \langle 0, 01 \rangle,$$
$$\langle 0, 10 \rangle, \ldots \langle 1, 11 \rangle, \ldots$$

is an enumeration of $\mathbb{N}^*$, which can be provided by a TM. (Notice that the tuple $\langle 1, 0 \rangle$ represents the set of the two numbers 1 and 0, whereas the tuple $\langle 10 \rangle$ represents the set consisting of the single number 10.) The enumeration E specified above can be easily obtained as a slight modification of E'.

M operates as follows.

1. First the input string x is copied into $\mathbf{T}_1$.
2. Then the first element of E is built and stored into $\mathbf{T}_2$.
3. Let $\langle \langle l_{i_1}, p_1 \rangle, \ldots, \langle l_{i_r}, p_r \rangle \rangle$ be any element of E. M checks whether, for some $\alpha \in V^*$, $S \overset{*}{\underset{G}{\Rightarrow}} \alpha$ via a sequence of immediate derivations of the type

$$S = \alpha_0 \underset{G}{\Rightarrow} \alpha_1 = X_{11} X_{12} \ldots X_{1n_1} \underset{G}{\Rightarrow} \alpha_2 = X_{21} X_{22} \ldots X_{2n_2} \underset{G}{\Rightarrow}$$
$$\cdots \underset{G}{\Rightarrow} \alpha_r = X_{r1} \ldots X_{rn_r}$$

with $\alpha_j \underset{G}{\Rightarrow} \alpha_{j+1}$ by applying the production labeled l_{i_j} whose lefthand side starts with X_{j, p_j}, that is,

$$\alpha_j = X_{j1} \ldots X_{j, p_j - 1} X_{jp_j} \ldots X_{jn_j} \underset{G}{\Rightarrow} X_{j1} \ldots X_{j, p_j - 1} Y_1 \ldots X_{jn_j},$$

l_{i_j} being the label of the production $X_{jp_j} \ldots \to Y_1 \ldots$. Clearly such a check can be performed by a TM.
4. If M succeeds in verifying that the sequence $\langle l_{i_1}, p_1 \rangle \ldots \langle l_{i_r}, p_r \rangle$ actually derives some α according to the above rule, α is subsequently checked for equality with x.
5. In the positive case M halts with success, that is, accepts x. In the negative case M builds in $\mathbf{T}_2$ the next element of E and starts again from point 3.

Clearly if M accepts x, then $S \overset{*}{\underset{G}{\Rightarrow}} x$.
On the other side if a derivation $S \overset{*}{\underset{G}{\Rightarrow}} x$ exists, sooner or later M will produce the corresponding sequence $\langle l_{i_1}, p_1 \rangle \ldots \langle l_{i_r}, p_r \rangle$ in E and will therefore accept it. Thus M accepts exactly $L(G)$.

Notice, however, that if $x \notin L(G)$, M will never halt since it will continue to enumerate all elements of E—which is infinite—always failing the test for $S \underset{G}{\overset{*}{\Rightarrow}} x$. In Chapter 2 we will realize that this drawback cannot be avoided. ∎

Exercises

1.61 Complete the proof the Theorem 1.20 formally.

1.62 (Elimination of ϵ-productions in CF-grammars).

Let G be a CF-grammar. Prove that an equivalent CF-grammar G' can be built such that

- If $\epsilon \notin L(G)$ then G' has no productions of the type $A \to \epsilon$.
- If $\epsilon \in L(G)$ then $S \to \epsilon$ is the only production of G that generates the empty string and S does not occur in the right-hand side of any other production.

Hints:

- Find a procedure that states, for any nonterminal A of G, whether $A \underset{G}{\overset{*}{\Rightarrow}} \epsilon$.
- Observe that if $A \underset{G}{\overset{*}{\Rightarrow}} \epsilon$ and $B \to \alpha_1 A \alpha_2$, with $\alpha_1 \alpha_2 \neq \epsilon$, is a production of G, $L(G)$ is not altered by adding the production $B \to \alpha_1 \alpha_2$.

1.63* Prove that the following extension of Pumping Lemma holds for context-free languages.

Let L be a context-free language. There exists an integer n such that for any x in L, if $|x| \geq n$ then x can be decomposed as $uywzv$ with

- $|yz| \geq 1$.
- $|ywz| \leq n$.
- for all integers $i \geq 0$, $uy^i wz^i v$ is in L.

Notice that the above statement reduces to the already known version when L is accepted by a FA.

Hint: Consider any CF-grammar G generating L and observe that if a derivation $S \overset{*}{\Rightarrow} x$ is sufficiently long, then it must be of the type $S \underset{G}{\overset{*}{\Rightarrow}} uAv \underset{G}{\overset{*}{\Rightarrow}} uyAzv \underset{G}{\overset{*}{\Rightarrow}} uywzv$. In other words, an *autoinclusion* $A \underset{G}{\overset{*}{\Rightarrow}} yAz$ must necessarily occur in sufficiently long derivations.

1.64 Use the theorem proven by Exercise 1.63 to prove that $L = \{ a^n b^n c^n | n \geq 1 \}$ is not a context-free language.

Hint: See Exercise 1.25.

1.6 Denotational Language Definitions

So far in this chapter we have devoted a great deal of attention to automata and grammars as two formalisms that enable us to describe languages. In this section we discuss two other formalisms: equations in language spaces and regular expressions. The reason why we have chosen to cover these subjects here, besides their mathematical elegance, is that they will give us an opportunity to assess and compare two styles of formal modeling: denotational versus operational models. The deep impact of the two styles goes far beyond the present subject: for example, they are discussed in Chapter 4 in a more general context. In the sequel, we first present the models and then we compare their style with previous models.

1.6.1   Equations in Language Spaces

Let V_T be a terminal alphabet. As we have seen in Section 0.1.5, the family of languages over V_T, $\mathcal{P}(V_T^*)$, is provided with some algebraic operations such as Boolean operations, concatenation, etc. As for more conventional algebras, one can define equations in language variables. For example, a general system of equations has the following form.

$$f_1(X_1, \ldots, X_m) = \varnothing$$
$$f_2(X_1, \ldots, X_m) = \varnothing$$
$$\vdots$$
$$f_n(X_1, \ldots, X_m) = \varnothing$$

where f_i, $i = 1, \ldots, n$ are functions $f_i \colon \mathcal{P}(V_T^*)^m \to \mathcal{P}(V_T^*)$, and X_j, $j = 1, \ldots, m$ are variables ranging over $\mathcal{P}(V_T^*)$.

As usual, a *solution* of a system of equations is an m-tuple of languages such that all equations are verified. In the following, we restrict our attention to equations of the form $X = F(X)$ where $X = \langle X_1, \ldots, X_n \rangle$ is a vector of variables, $F = \langle f_1, \ldots, f_n \rangle$ is a vector of functions, and each f_i is obtained as a composition of unions "$\cup$" and concatenations "$\cdot$". Since "$\cdot$" is distributive with respect to "$\cup$" (see Exercise 0.6), each f_i may be expressed—in a normal form—as a union of concatenations of variables (and constants). For example, $f(X_1, X_2, X_3) = X_1 \cdot A \cdot X_2 \cup X_2 \cdot X_3 \cdot B$ where X_1, X_2, and X_3 are language variables and A and B are language constants. Furthermore, language constants are assumed as finite languages.

A solution X of a system of the type $X = F(X)$ is also called a *fixed point* of F, as the mapping $F \colon \mathcal{P}(V_T^*)^n \to (V_T^*)^n$ transforms X into itself.

We extend the vector notation by stating the following conventions.

- The n-tuple $\langle \varnothing, \ldots, \varnothing \rangle$ will still be denoted by the symbol $\varnothing$ as this will not cause confusion.
- The relation $X \subseteq X'$ is the natural extension of the inclusion relation to n-tuples of languages, that is, $X \subseteq X'$ if and only if $X_1 \subseteq X_1', \ldots, X_n \subseteq X_n'$.

Example 1.24

Consider the following system of one equation in one language variable X:

$$X = A \cdot X \cdot B \cup A \cdot B$$

where $A = \{a\}$ and $B = \{b\}$

The language $L = \{a^n b^n | n \geq 1\}$ is clearly a fixed-point for the above equation, since $\{a\} \cdot L \cdot \{b\} = \{a^n b^n | n \geq 2\}$ and $\{a\} \cdot L \cdot \{b\} \cup \{a\} \cdot \{b\} = \{a^n b^n | n \geq 2\} \cup \{a\} \cdot \{b\} = \{a^n b^n | n \geq 1\} = L$.

In general, a system of equations of the form $X = F(X)$ does not have a unique fixed-point. This property is illustrated by the following example.

Example 1.25

Consider the following equation in one language variable X:

$$X = X \cdot X \cup \{aa\}$$

This equation has infinite fixed points of the type

$L_k = L_0 \cup L_{1k}$ for any $k \geq 0$ with

$L_0 = \{a^{2n} | n \geq 0\}, L_{1k} = \{a^{2n+k} | n \geq 0\}$

In fact, for any $k \geq 0$, we obtain

$$
\begin{aligned}
L_k \cdot L_k &= (L_0 \cup L_{1k}) \cdot (L_0 \cup L_{1k}) \\
&= L_0 \cdot L_0 \cup L_{1k} \cdot L_0 \cup L_0 \cdot L_{1k} \cup L_{1k} \cdot L_{1k} \\
&= \{a^{2n} | n \geq 0\} \cup \{a^{2n+k} \cdot a^{2m} | n, m \geq 0\} \\
&\quad \cup \{a^{2m} \cdot a^{2n+k} | n, m \geq 0\} \cup \{a^{2k} \cdot a^{2n} \cdot a^{2m} | n, m \geq 0\} \\
&= \{a^{2n} | n \geq 0\} \cup \{a^{2r+k} | r \geq 0\} \cup \{a^{2(k+r)} | r \geq 0\} \\
&= \{a^{2n} | n \geq 0\} \cup \{a^{2n+k} | n \geq 0\}
\end{aligned}
$$

Thus $L_k \cdot L_k \cup \{aa\} = \{a^{2n} | n \geq 0\} \cup \{a^{2n} | n = 1\} \cup \{a^{2n+k} | n \geq 0\} = L_k$.

One question that arises quite naturally is whether a minimal fixed point exists for any vector equation $X = F(X)$. By minimal fixed point we mean an n-tuple of languages L such that $L = F(L)$ and for any L' such that $L' = F(L')$, $L \subseteq L'$. Obviously, a minimal fixed point, if it exists, must be unique. In fact, if L_1 and L_2 are two minimal fixed points, by definition we must have both $L_1 \subseteq L_2$ and $L_2 \subseteq L_1$. Hence, $L_1 = L_2$.

For equations of the type $X = F(X)$, where F is a vector function whose elements are unions of concatenations of language variables and constants, a minimal fixed point always exists. Such minimal fixed point L is given by the following formula:

$$L = \bigcup_{i=1}^{\infty} F^i(\varnothing)$$

that is, $L = \varnothing \cup F(\varnothing) \cup F(F(\varnothing)) \ldots$.

This statement is a particular case of a more general theorem presented in Chapter 4.

Therefore, equations of the previous type can be used to denote their *unique* minimal fixed point. Since a one-to-one correspondence exists between this special class of equations in language space and their unique minimal fixed point, we say that equations *denote* a language: their minimal fixed point.

Now, let us go back to context-free grammars. Observe that the production set of a *CF*-grammar $G = \langle V_T, V_N, P, S \rangle$ can be written as

$$X_1 \to \alpha_{11} | \alpha_{12} \ldots | \alpha_{1h_1}$$
$$X_2 \to \alpha_{21} | \alpha_{22} \ldots | \alpha_{2h_2}$$
$$\ldots$$
$$X_n \to \alpha_{n1} | \alpha_{n2} \ldots | \alpha_{nh_n}$$

where $V_N = \{ X_i | i = 1, \ldots, n \}$, $V = V_N \cup V_T$, $\alpha_{ij} \in V^*$, and where

$$X_j \to \alpha_{j1} | \alpha_{j2} | \ldots \alpha_{jh_j}$$

is a short notation for

$$X \to \alpha_{j1}, X \to \alpha_{j2}, \ldots, X \to \alpha_{jh_j}, 1 \le j \le n.$$

Now, if we interpret nonterminals of a context-free grammar as language variables, the grammar can also be viewed as a system of equations in language variables.

$$X_1 = \alpha'_{11} \cup \alpha'_{12} \cup \cdots \cup \alpha'_{1h_1} = f_1(X_1, \ldots, X_n)$$
$$X_2 = \alpha'_{21} \cup \alpha'_{22} \cup \cdots \cup \alpha'_{2h_2} = f_2(X_1, \ldots, X_n)$$
$$\ldots$$
$$X_n = \alpha'_{n1} \cup \alpha'_{n2} \cup \cdots \cup \alpha'_{nh_n} = f_n(X_1, \ldots, X_n)$$

where if

$$\alpha_{ij} = w_{ij}^0 W_{ij}^1 w_{ij}^1 W_{ij}^2 \ldots W_{ij}^m w_{ij}^m$$
$$w_{ij}^k \in V_T^* \qquad W_{ij}^k \in V_N$$

then

$$\alpha'_{ij} = \left\{ w_{ij}^0 \right\} \cdot W_{ij}^1 \cdot \left\{ w_{ij}^1 \right\} \cdot W_{ij}^2 \cdot \cdots \cdot W_{ij}^m \cdot \left\{ w_{ij}^m \right\}.$$

The foregoing system of equations is called the *system of equations associated to grammar G*. If we set $X = \langle X_1, \ldots, X_n \rangle$, the system of equations can be written as a vector equation $X = F(X)$.

Theorem 1.21

Let $G = \langle V_T, V_N, P, S \rangle$ be a context-free grammar where $V_N = \{ X_1, X_2, \ldots, X_n \}$ and let S be X_1. Let $X = F(X)$ be the system of equations associated to G. Then the n-tuple of languages $L = \langle L_1, \ldots, L_n \rangle$, with $L_i = \{ x_i \in V_T^* | X_i \overset{*}{\underset{G}{\Rightarrow}} x_i \}$, $i = 1, \ldots, n$, is the minimal fixed point of the system of equations. In particular, $L(G) = L_1$.

Proof

We already know that a unique minimal fixed point for vector equation $X = F(X)$ exists. Let $\tilde{X}$ be such minimal fixed point. It is easy to realize that $\tilde{X}$ is exactly the intersection of all fixed points of equation $X = F(X)$. $\tilde{X}$ is given by

$$\tilde{X} = \cap \overline{X} | \overline{X} = F(\overline{X})$$

The proof of this statement is left to the reader as an exercise.

Let $\tilde{X}_i$ be the ith component of vector $\tilde{X}$.

We have seen before that $\tilde{X} = \bigcup_{j=1}^{\infty} F^j(\varnothing)$. We now prove that for all integers k and i, with $k \geq 1$, $1 \leq i \leq n$, $X_i \overset{k}{\underset{G}{\Rightarrow}} x$ if and only if x belongs to the ith component of $\bigcup_{j=1}^{k} F^j(\varnothing)$. This allows us to conclude that, for each $x \in V_T^*$, $X_i \overset{*}{\underset{G}{\Rightarrow}} x$ if and only if $x \in \tilde{X}_i$, which implies the theorem.

The proof is done by induction on the value of k.

i. *Basis of the induction:*

   $X_i \Rightarrow x$ if and only if $x \in f_i(\varnothing)$.

   If $X_i \Rightarrow x$ then the ith equation of the system will have the form $X_i = f_i(X) = \{x\} \cup \cdots \cup \cdots$. Consequently, $x \in f_i(\varnothing)$.

   Conversely, let $x \in f_i(\varnothing)$. $f_i(\varnothing)$ is the union of language constants, because the concatenation of any language with $\varnothing$ is $\varnothing$. Thus $X_i = f_i(X) = \{x\} \cup \cdots \cup \cdots$.

   Thus $X_i \rightarrow x$ is in G's production set.

ii. *Induction step:*

   Assume that for any X_i, $X_i \overset{h}{\Rightarrow} x$ with $h \leq k$, if and only if x belongs to the ith component of $\bigcup_{j=1}^{k} F^j(\varnothing)$.

   Suppose now $X_i \overset{k+1}{\Rightarrow} x$, that is, $X_i \Rightarrow \xi_i \overset{k}{\Rightarrow} x$ with $\xi_i = x_0 Y_1 x_1 Y_2 \ldots Y_m x_m$, $x_i \in V_T^*$, $Y_i \in V_N$.

   But $X_i \Rightarrow \xi_i$ if and only if the ith equation of $X = F(X)$ is of the type $X_i = \xi_i \cup \cdots$.

   Furthermore, $Y_r \overset{h_r}{\Rightarrow} z_r$, with $h_r \leq k$, for any r, with $1 \leq r \leq m$, and $x_0 z_1 x_1 \ldots z_m x_m = x$.

   By the induction hypothesis z_r belongs to the rth component of $\bigcup_{j=1}^{k} F^j(\varnothing)$ for any r, with $1 \leq r \leq n$.

   Thus x belongs to the ith component of $F\left(\bigcup_{j=1}^{k} F^j(\varnothing)\right) \subseteq \bigcup_{j=1}^{k+1} F^j(\varnothing)$. In a similar way it can be proved the converse statement that if x belongs to the ith component of $F^{k+1}(\varnothing)$, then $X_i \overset{h}{\Rightarrow} x$, $h \leq k + 1$. ∎

Exercise

1.65 Complete the proof of Theorem 1.21 by showing that $\tilde{X} = \cap \overline{X}|\overline{X} = F(\overline{X})$.

Example 1.26

Consider the grammar

$$G = \langle \{a, b\}, \{S\}, S \rightarrow aSb, S \rightarrow ab, S \rangle$$

G is transformed into the following equation

$$S = \{a\} \cdot S \cdot \{b\} \cup \{ab\}$$

We know that $L = \{a^n b^n | n \geq 1\}$ is the language generated by G and a fixed point for the corresponding equation. According to the previous theorem, L is the minimal fixed point.

L can also be obtained as $\bigcup\limits_{j=1}^{\infty} F^j(\varnothing) = \{ab\} \cup \{aabb\} \cup \cdots$. It is immediate to verify in this example that the process of constructing L as $\bigcup\limits_{i=1}^{\infty} F^i(\varnothing)$ yields strings whose grammar derivations have an increasing length. This is a general property of the construction.

Exercise

1.66 Compute the minimal fixed point of the following equations and verify that they coincide with the languages generated by the corresponding grammars. Check also whether there exists some nonminimal fixed points for the same equations and compare them with the minimal ones.

S_1: $X = aX$

S_2: $X = aX \cup a$

S_3: $\begin{cases} X = aY \\ Y = bX \cup b \end{cases}$

S_4: $X = X \cup a$

S_5: $X = X^2 \cup a \cup b$

S_6: $\begin{cases} X = a \cup XY \\ \cdot Y = b \cup XY \end{cases}$

1.6.2 Regular Expressions

A regular expression (RE) is an expression that can be used to denote a language. We first define REs and the languages denoted by them. Then we prove that the class of such languages is exactly the class of regular languages.

Definition 1.27
Let V_T be an alphabet. A *regular expression* over V_T and the language it denotes are defined by the following rules.

1. **Ø** is a regular expression which denotes the empty language.
2. For all $a \in V_T$, *a* is a regular expression. The language denoted by *a* consists of the single string *a*.
3. If $\mathbf{R}_1$ and $\mathbf{R}_2$ are regular expressions, $(\mathbf{R}_1 \cup \mathbf{R}_2)$ is a regular expression. The language denoted by $(\mathbf{R}_1 \cup \mathbf{R}_2)$ is the union of the languages denoted by $\mathbf{R}_1$ and $\mathbf{R}_2$.
4. If $\mathbf{R}_1$ and $\mathbf{R}_2$ are regular expressions, $(\mathbf{R}_1 \cdot \mathbf{R}_2)$ is a regular expression. The language denoted by $(\mathbf{R}_1 \cdot \mathbf{R}_2)$ is the concatenation of the languages denoted by $\mathbf{R}_1$ and $\mathbf{R}_2$.
5. If $\mathbf{R}$ is a regular expression, $\mathbf{R}*$ is a regular expression. The language denoted by $\mathbf{R}*$ is the result of the Kleene star applied to the language denoted by $\mathbf{R}$.
6. Nothing else is a regular expression. □

There are a few important points to observe in Definition 1.27. First, symbols $\cup$, $\cdot$ and $*$ used in REs have the same lexical appearance as the union, concatenation, and Kleene star operators, but they appear in boldface. They must be interpreted as RE operators representing the union, concatenation, and Kleene star of the languages denoted by the corresponding RE operands.

Also, in practice, parentheses introduced in rules 3 and 4 can be omitted if no ambiguity arises in the interpretation of a RE.

Example 1.27

Let $V_T = \{a, b\}$. Then $\mathbf{R} = (a \cup b)*$ is a RE according to rules 3 and 5. The language L denoted by $\mathbf{R}$ is

$$L = \{\epsilon, a, b, aa, ab, ba, bb, \dots\} = V_T^*$$

Exercises

1.67 What is the language defined by the following REs over *a* and *b*?
- $(a* \cup b*)*$
- $a* \cdot b*$

1.68   Find REs denoting $L_1 = \{a^n b \mid n \geq 0\}$ and $L_2 = \{x \mid x$ contains at least two consecutive a's$\}$.

Theorem 1.22

The class of languages denoted by regular expressions coincides with the class of regular languages.

The proof of Theorem 1.22 is left to the reader as an exercise.

Hint: First prove that any language denoted by a RE is regular by observing that

- The empty language and all elements of V_T are regular languages.
- Regular languages are closed with respect to union, concatenation, and Kleene star operation. (For instance, if G is an R-grammar, $L(G)^*$ is generated by the R-grammar obtained from G by adding to its production set the rule $A \to aS$, S being G's axiom, for each rule of the type $A \to a$).

In order to prove the converse statement, observe that the language generated by the R-grammar whose production set is

$$S \to aA,\ A \to bB,\ B \to aA,\ A \to aC,\ C \to bC,\ C \to a$$

is denoted by the RE $a \cdot (ba)^* \cdot a \cdot (b)^* \cdot a$ and try to generalize this fact.   ∎

Both equations in language spaces and regular expressions are formal models for language definition. Apart from questions concerning the power of formalisms, grammars and automata can be used for exactly the same purpose. How can we compare them? How are the specification styles different in these cases from a philosophical viewpoint?

Equations and expressions on one side and automata on the other belong to two different classes of conceptual models: *denotational* (or *denotationary*) and *evolutionary* (or *operational*) models, respectively. Evolutionary models simulate the behavior of the entity being modeled by describing the sequence of states entered during its dynamic evolution, starting from some initial state.[5] For example, automata define a language through a set of transitions that lead from the initial configuration to a final configuration on reading strings in the language. Thus, automata can be viewed as abstract processors and transitions as computational steps performed by the processor during recognition of strings in the language. Conversely, both equations and regular expressions are static formalisms. Equations in language spaces denote their solution—a language—without specifying how the solution is actually computed. Similarly, regular expressions denote languages via a suitable set-theoretic interpretation of

---

[5] We warn the reader that the term "state" has been used here informally, in a more comprehensive way than in the case of the state of the control unit of automata. Such informal colloquial use of the term "state" is very common, but, speaking formally, the intuitive concept of state is actually formalized by the notion of configuration.

their operators. One might say that both are a purely abstract formalism to define a language, whereas automata are more concrete, "implementation oriented," in that they suggest a mechanical way to accepting strings in the language. These viewpoints, however, are rather controversial, as we show in depth in Chapter 4.

How do we classify grammars in this discussion? On one hand, we have shown that grammars can be viewed as a set of equations. On the other hand, grammars can be viewed as a way to compute the solution of a set of equations: $L = F(\emptyset) \cup F(F(\emptyset)) \cup \dots$. In conclusion, we may view grammars as an ideal bridge between purely denotational and purely evolutionary models.

1.7   Nondeterministic Models

All evolutionary models considered so far are *deterministic* in the sense that, once their state and input are given, their evolution is uniquely determined; in other terms, the transition relation is single valued. It is often the case, however, that the system to be modeled cannot be described in such deterministic way: that is, the knowledge an observer has of its behavior is not sufficiently accurate to predict its exact evolution, as a consequence of the present state and of the given input.

For instance, consider a game defined by the following rules. A player can stay in any of a finite set of sites, each site having a name. He or she receives an input from another player consisting of a letter. Accordingly, he or she must move to a site whose name begins with the input letter. If more than one site has a name beginning with that letter an arbitrary choice is taken.

Such a game could be described by a graph of the type of Figure 1.41, which looks quite like a FA but exhibits more than one arrow labeled g starting from any node.

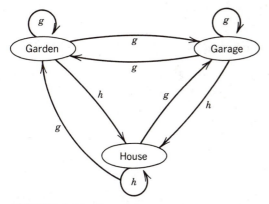

FIGURE 1.41 A graph representation of a game.

In other cases, a *nondeterministic* model is chosen because it provides a more "abstract" description of some actual phenomenon. For example, the self-explaining notation:

$$a \geq b \Rightarrow max := a$$
$$a \leq b \Rightarrow max := b$$

defines the maximum of two numbers, a and b. One may view it as a nondeterministic specification of how a machine may evaluate such maximum. Nondeterminism arises when $a = b$, since anyone of the two rules may be chosen. Here, nondeterminism favors abstraction of the specification since any of the branches that may be chosen during interpretation gives an acceptable result.

All evolutionary models previously described have their nondeterministic counterpart. We describe them in the following way. Then we introduce a new formalism: Petri nets. Finally, we will end with some general considerations on nondeterminism.

1.7.1 Nondeterministic finite-state automata

The following definition rephrases all basic definitions given for FAs in the nondeterministic case.

Definition 1.28

A *nondeterministic finite-state automaton* (NFA) is defined as in Definition 1.1 with the only difference that the transition function is

$$\delta: Q \times I \to \mathscr{P}(Q)$$

Let δ be the transition function of a NFA. Then $\delta^*: Q \times I^* \to \mathscr{P}(Q)$ is defined by

$$\delta^*(q, \epsilon) = \{q\} \text{ for all } q \qquad \delta^*(q, xi) = \bigcup_{q' \in \delta^*(q, x)} \delta(q', i)$$

In the case of acceptors, $x \in I^*$ is *accepted* by a NFA $\langle Q, i, \delta, q_0, F \rangle$ if and only if $\delta^*(q_0, x) \cap F \neq \varnothing$ □

The above definition states that

- A NFA can exhibit several different transition sequences for a given state and a given input sequence.
- An input sequence is accepted if and only if *at least one* of the possible transition sequences leads to a final state.

This means that if we "simulate" the behavior of the acceptor and we find one sequence of moves leading to an accepting state, then we can conclude that the

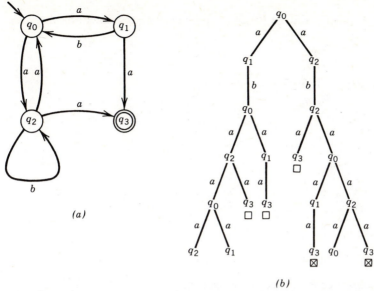

FIGURE 1.42 A NFA (*a*) and the tree of choices (*b*) performed during recognition. ⊠ denotes acceptance. □ denotes a state from which computation cannot proceed. The tree represents all paths traversed during recognition of *abaaa*.

input sequence is accepted. But we cannot reach the opposite conclusion until we have verified that all sequences do not lead to a state of *F*.

Exercise

1.69 Write a computer program that simulates a NFA. The program takes as input a description of the acceptor and a string to be analyzed and gives as output acceptance or rejection of the string.

Hint: A tree data structure can be built to represent all possible paths traversed by the acceptor during recognition (Figure 1.42). When a path cannot be explored further, the program must backtrack, that is, it must try another unexplored path starting from the most recently encountered state whose output transitions have not been all explored yet.

Nondeterministic automata are not more powerful than their deterministic counterpart as far as language recognition is concerned. This property is proven by the following theorem.

Theorem 1.23

For any NFA A, a deterministic FA A_D can be constructed accepting the same language.

Proof

Let $A = \langle Q, I, \delta, q_0, F \rangle$, $\delta \colon Q \times I \to \mathscr{P}(Q)$

Define A_D as $\langle Q_D, I, \delta_D, q_{0D}, F_D \rangle$ with

$$Q_D = \mathscr{P}(Q)$$

$$\delta_D(q_D, i) = q'_D = \bigcup_{q \in q_D} \delta(q, i)$$

$$F_D = \{ q_D | F \cap q_D \neq \varnothing \}$$

$$q_{0D} = \{ q_0 \}$$

In order to prove that $L(A_D) = L(A)$ we have to show that

$$\delta_D^*(q_{0D}, x) \in F_D \quad \text{if and only if} \quad \delta^*(q_0, x) \cap F \neq \varnothing$$

This is an immediate consequence of the fact that

$$\delta_D^*(q_{0D}, x) = \delta^*(q_0, x) \quad \text{for any } x$$

This last statement in turn can be proved by means of an easy induction. In fact,

$$\delta_D^*(q_{0D}, \epsilon) = \delta^*(q_0, \epsilon) \quad \text{because} \quad q_{0D} = \{ q_0 \}$$

$$\delta_D(\delta_D^*(q_{0D}, y), i) = \bigcup_{q \in \delta_D^*(q_{0D}, y)} \delta(q, i)$$

$$= \bigcup_{q \in \delta^*(q_0, y)} \delta(q, i) \quad \text{by the induction hypothesis} \qquad \blacksquare$$

NFAs are not more powerful language acceptors than FAs. However, they are very often more convenient to use. In many cases, the most direct formalization of a problem is in terms of a NFA. Also, many mathematical proofs are more straightforward in the case of NFAs. The following examples and exercises illustrate these points.

Example 1.28

The NFA in Figure 1.43 recognizes some lexical units of a toy programming language: numbers, identifiers, arithmetic operators, and comments. Lexical units are separated by one or more blank ($\not b$). Comments start with $/*$ and terminate by $*/$. The acceptor of Figure 1.43 is nondeterministic. For example, after reading a $/$ in state q_0, the acceptor can enter either q_3 or q_4. Similarly, after reading a $*$ in state q_5 it can enter q_6 or stay in q_5.

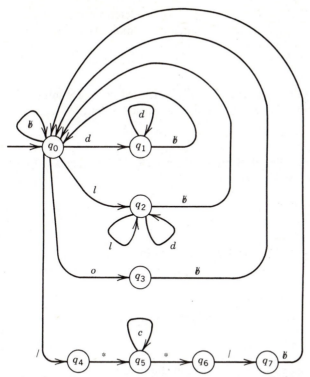

FIGURE 1.43 A NFA recognizing lexical units of a toy programming language. b = blank; d = digit; l = letter; o = operator ($+$, $-$, $*$, $/$); c = any character.

Exercises

1.70 Transform the NFA of Figure 1.42 into an equivalent deterministic FA using the construction of Theorem 1.22.

1.71 Transform the NFA of Figure 1.43 into an equivalent deterministic FA using the construction of Theorem 1.22.

1.72 Prove that the class of languages accepted by FAs is closed under union. (This result has been proven—Theorem 1.8—as a consequence of the closure with respect to complement and intersection. Notice how easier it is to find a direct proof of the statement by means of NFAs than of FAs.)

1.73 Prove that the class of languages accepted by FAs is closed with respect to concatenation and Kleene star. You can prove this result using R-grammars or NFAs. (Note that the proof is not as easy in the case of deterministic FAs.)

1.74 Prove Theorem 1.22 by using NFAs and the result of Exercise 1.73 instead of R-grammars.

It is now interesting to introduce and briefly discuss nondeterministic, finite-state transducers. As we see, the introduction of nondeterminism here has a deep effect on the behavior of the formal device.

Definition 1.29

A *nondeterministic finite-state transducer* (NFT) is defined as in Definition 1.4, the only difference being that functions δ and η constitute a pair.

$$\langle \delta, \eta \rangle: Q \times I \to \mathscr{P}_F(Q \times O^*)$$

where $\mathscr{P}_F(Q \times O^*)$ denotes the set of finite subsets of $Q \times O^*$. δ and η are the projection of $\langle \delta, \eta \rangle$ on Q and O^*, respectively:

$$\delta(q, i) = \{ q' | \langle q', w \rangle \in \langle \delta, \eta \rangle(q, i) \quad \text{for some} \quad w \in O^* \}$$

$$\eta(q, i) = \{ w | \langle q', w \rangle \in \langle \delta, \eta \rangle(q, i) \quad \text{for some} \quad q \in Q \}$$

$\langle \delta, \eta \rangle^*: Q \times I^* \to \mathscr{P}_F(Q \times O^*)$ is defined as usual inductively by

$$\langle \delta, \eta \rangle^*(q, \epsilon) = \langle q, \epsilon \rangle$$

$$\langle \delta, \eta \rangle^*(q, xi) = \{ \langle q', y \rangle | \exists q'', u, v \quad \text{such that}$$

$$y = uv \quad \text{and} \quad \langle q'', u \rangle \in \langle \delta, \eta \rangle^*(q, x) \text{ and}$$

$$\langle q', v \rangle \in \langle \delta, \eta \rangle(q'', i) \}$$

A NFT defines a translation $\tau: I^* \to \mathscr{P}_F(O^*)$ in the following way.

$$\tau(x) = \{ y | \exists q \in F \text{ such that } \langle q, y \rangle \in \langle \delta, \eta \rangle^*(q_0, x) \}. \qquad \square$$

Observe that FTs and NFTs are quite different models, and it does not make much sense to compare their translation power. In fact, FTs define single-valued translations $\tau: I^* \to O^*$, whereas NFTs define multivalued translations $\tau: I^* \to \mathscr{P}_F(O^*)$.

Exercise

1.75 Write a program that simulates a NFT. Note that in order to compute $\tau(x)$, the simulation requires the construction of all possible sequences of moves leading to final states.

1.7.2 Nondeterministic Pushdown Automata and Nondeterministic Turing Machines

The definitions of nondeterministic pushdown automata and nondeterministic Turing machines derive quite naturally from their deterministic counterparts. First, we refer to nondeterministic pushdown automata as language acceptors.

Definition 1.30

A *nondeterministic pushdown acceptor* (NPDA) is a 7-tuple $\langle Q, I, \Gamma, \delta, q_0, Z_0, F \rangle$ where all symbols have the same meaning as in Definition 1.8, except for δ, which is defined as follows.

$$\delta: Q \times (I \cup \{\epsilon\}) \times \Gamma \to \mathscr{P}_F(Q \times \Gamma^*)$$

(where $\mathscr{P}_F(Q \times \Gamma^*)$ denotes the finite subsets of $Q \times \Gamma^*$). The relation $\vdash$ on $Q \times I^* \times \Gamma^*$ is defined by $\langle q, x, \gamma \rangle \vdash \langle q', x', \gamma' \rangle$ if and only if

1. $x = ay, x' = y, \gamma = A\beta, \gamma' = \alpha\beta, \langle q', \alpha \rangle \in \delta(q, a, A)$

or

2. $x = x', \gamma = A\beta, \gamma' = \alpha\beta, \langle q', \alpha \rangle \in \delta(q, \epsilon, A)$.

$x \in I^*$ is accepted by the automaton if and only if

$$\langle q_0, x, Z_0 \rangle \overset{*}{\vdash} \langle q, \epsilon, \gamma \rangle, q \in F, \gamma \in \Gamma^* \qquad \square$$

Nondeterminism does not increase the power of finite-state automata as language recognizers. The same result does not hold in the case of pushdown automata.

Theorem 1.24

The language $L = \{a^n b^n | n \geq 1\} \cup \{a^n b^{2n} | n \geq 1\}$ is accepted by a NPDA but no deterministic PDA can accept it.

Proof

The second part of the theorem coincides with Theorem 1.12. Thus we only need to give a NPDA A accepting L. Such automaton is given in Figure 1.44.

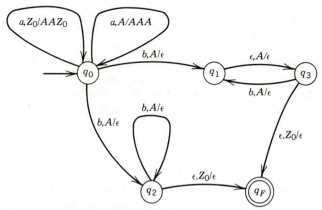

FIGURE 1.44 A NPDA accepting $L = \{a^n b^n | n \geq 1\} \cup \{a^n b^{2n} | n \geq 1\}$. ∎

Exercise

1.76 Design a NPDA recognizing the language

$$L = \left\{ ww^R | w \in \{ a, b \}^* \right\}.$$

Definition 1.31

Nondeterministic Turing machines (NTM) are defined as their deterministic counterparts, the only difference being that for a multitape TM the transition and output functions are defined as

$$\langle \delta, \eta \rangle : (Q - F) \times I \times \Gamma^k \rightarrow \mathscr{P}\left(Q \times \Gamma^k \times \{ R, L, S \}^{k+1} \times \{ R, S \}\right)$$

and for a single-tape TM δ is defined as

$$\delta : (Q - F) \times A \rightarrow \mathscr{P}(Q \times A \times \{ R, L, S \}) \qquad \qquad \square$$

Exercise

1.77 Formalize the behavior of NTMs both as language acceptors, language translators, and function evaluators. As in the case of other automata, a NTM accepts a string if there exists at least one sequence of moves leading to a final state. It defines a multivalued function of the input as the set of all possible output values obtained by any legal sequence of moves.

Theorem 1.25

Nondeterministic Turing machines are not more powerful than deterministic Turing machines as language recognizers.

Informal Proof

Theorem 1.20 has proven unrestricted grammars equivalent to deterministic Turing machines. Proving NTMs equivalent to unrestricted grammars is straightforward. In fact, the proof that given a NTM one can find an equivalent unrestricted grammar exactly follows the proof of Theorem 1.20. The opposite is a trivial consequence of Theorem 1.20. ∎

Exercise

1.78* Show that deterministic TMs can simulate NTMs as language translators and therefore also as function evaluators by suitable encoding of the set $\tau(x)$. For instance let $\tau(x) = \{ u_1, u_2, \ldots, u_n \} \subseteq O^*$. Then, one may define a translation $\tau_D(x) = u_1 \$ u_2 \ldots \$ u_n$, with $\$ \notin O$. However, you should realize that such a simulation works properly only if all computations of the original NTM terminate (i.e., reach a halting configuration). Otherwise the set $\tau(x)$ could even be infinite, in which case $\tau_D(x)$ could not even be defined.

You are invited to go back to this exercise after reading Chapters 2 and 3.

1.7.3* An Intrinsically Nondeterministic Evolutionary Model: Petri Nets

Nondeterministic evolutionary models discussed in the previous sections have been defined as an extension of an original deterministic version. In this section we introduce yet another evolutionary model that is intrinsically nondeterministic: Petri nets. Petri nets cannot be considered as basic as the models discussed so far. However, they are presented here for the following reasons.

- Petri nets are increasingly used in practice to model complex systems, for example, computer systems or even human organizations. They are a useful formal specification tool that can be used in the requirements phase of software development.
- Petri nets have been widely studied both in theoretical and in applied computer science as models for concurrency. This fact is taken up in Chapter 6.

Definition 1.32

A *Petri net* (PN) is a 4-tuple $\langle P, T, IF, OF \rangle$ where

- $P = \{ p_1, \ldots, p_n \}$ is a finite set of *places*
- $T = \{ t_1, \ldots, t_m \}$ is a finite set of *transitions*
- $IF: P \times T \rightarrow \mathbb{N}$ is the *transition–input function*
- $OF: T \times P \rightarrow \mathbb{N}$ is the *transition–output function*   □

A Petri net can be graphically described by means of a bipartite graph (more properly, a multigraph) where a set of nodes is associated to P and a disjoint set of nodes is associated to T. Usually, places are denoted by circles and transitions by bars. For any pair $\langle p, t \rangle$ $IF(p, t)$ edges connect p to t and for any pair $\langle t, p \rangle$, $OF(t, p)$ edges connect t to p.

Example 1.29

The Petri net $\langle P, T, IF, OF \rangle$, with

- $P = \{ p_1, \ldots, p_5 \}$
- $T = \{ t_1, \ldots, t_5)$

TABLE 1.3   Transition – Input Function

T \ P	p_1	p_2	p_3	p_4	p_5
t_1	1	0	2	0	0
t_2	1	1	0	0	0
t_3	0	0	0	1	0
t_4	0	0	0	0	0
t_5	0	0	0	0	1

TABLE 1.4   Transition – Output Function

P \ T	t_1	t_2	t_3	t_4	t_5
p_1	0	0	0	1	0
p_2	0	0	2	0	0
p_3	0	0	0	0	1
p_4	0	2	0	0	0
p_5	1	0	0	0	0

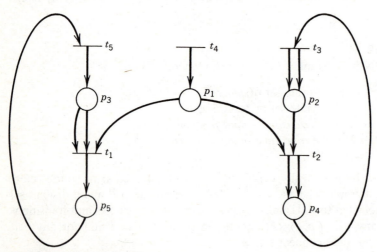

FIGURE 1.45   A Petri net.

- *IF* given by Table 1.3
- *OF* given by Table 1.4

is described in Figure 1.45

Definition 1.33

A *marking* of a Petri net is a mapping $M: P \to \mathbb{N}$. ☐

A marking M of a PN is the PN counterpart of the general notion of state. It is described graphically by a number $M(p)$ of *tokens* (dots) in the node representing p.

Intuitively the behavior of a PN is described as follows. If in a given marking M of P all input places of a transition t, that is, all places p for which $IF(p, t) > 0$, have a number of tokens greater than or equal to the number of arcs connecting p to t, then t is *enabled* by M (we also say that t *can fire*). If an enabled transition t *fires* a new marking, M' is obtained from M by subtracting exactly $IF(p, t)$ tokens from all input places of t, and by adding exactly $OF(t, p)$ tokens to all output places of t. A formalization of the above description is given as follows.

Definition 1.34

For a given marking M of a PN, a transition $t \in T$ is enabled by M if and only if for any place p, $M(p) \geq IF(p, t)$. ☐

Definition 1.35

The transition relation $\vdash$ is defined on the space of possible markings, that is, on the set of functions $\{ M | M: P \to \mathbb{N} \}$, by $M \vdash M'$ if and only if there exists a t enabled by M and for any p, $M'(p) = M(p) - IF(p, t) + OF(t, p)$. ☐

Example 1.30

The marking M shown in Figure 1.46a allows the Petri net to reach both marking M_1 shown in Figure 1.46b (by firing t_1) and M_2 shown in Figure 1.46c (by firing t_2). M_2, in turn, can produce M_3, where $M_3(p_1) = M_3(p_3) = 1$, $M_3(p_2) = M_3(p_5) = 0$, $M_3(p_6) = 2$, by successively firing either t_3 and t_4 or t_4 and t_3. Notice, however, that $M \vdash M_1$ and $M \vdash M_2$ but neither $M_1 \overset{*}{\vdash} M_2$ nor $M_2 \overset{*}{\vdash} M_1$. M_1 and M_2 can both be reached from M by choosing to fire either t_1 or t_2 in a nondeterministic fashion. However, once a choice is made, the subsequent behavior of the system follows different paths. Thus M_1 and M_2 are *mutually exclusive*.

Example 1.31

Suppose a computer system consists of one CPU and two video terminals (VT_1 and VT_2). Each terminal inputs one task at a time into the system. The CPU can only run one task at a time from either terminal.

If we do not know about the operating system scheduling policy that assigns the CPU to tasks, the external system behavior can be described by the PN of Figure 1.47. Clearly, such PN allows the system always to choose t_1, thus leaving VT_2 in "starvation." This could happen, for example, if the operating system always gives higher priority to tasks originated from VT_1.

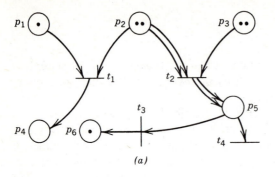

(a)

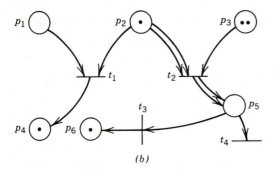

(b)

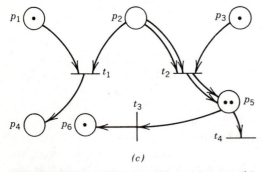

(c)

FIGURE 1.46   A Petri net (a) and its possible evolution (b or c).

Suppose, instead, we know that the operating system uses an alternate policy between terminals VT_1 and VT_2. In order to simplify the discussion, suppose also that there is always some user sitting at each terminal, who is ready to generate a new task whenever possible. In this case the system can be modeled by the new net of Figure 1.48 that enforces an alternate choice t_1 and t_2. Also, note that here the system behavior is deterministic.

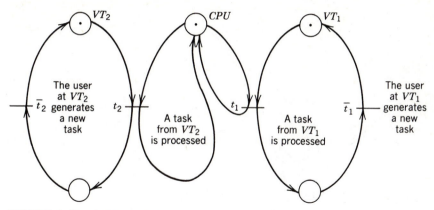

FIGURE 1.47 A PN modeling a computer system.

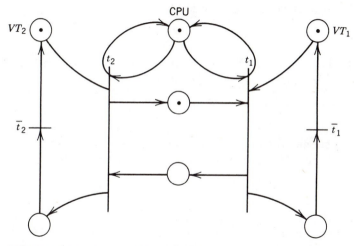

FIGURE 1.48 Another PN model for the computer system of Figure 1.47.

Exercises

1.79 For the PN of Figure 1.45, find all markings M reachable from the following initial markings M_0, that is, all M such that $M_0 \overset{*}{\vdash} M$.
1. $M_0(p_4) = 1$, $M_0(p_i) = 0$ for $i \neq 4$
2. $M_0(p_5) = 1$, $M_0(p_i) = 0$ for $i \neq 5$
3. $M_0(p_5) = 2$, $M_0(p_2) = 1$, $M_0(p_i) = 0$ for $i \neq 2, 5$

1.80 The evaluation of arithmetic expressions can be described by PNs, as illustrated by Figure 1.49 for the expression $(a + b)*(c + d)$. Places denote operands, transitions denote operators, and a token in a place denotes availability of the operand's value.

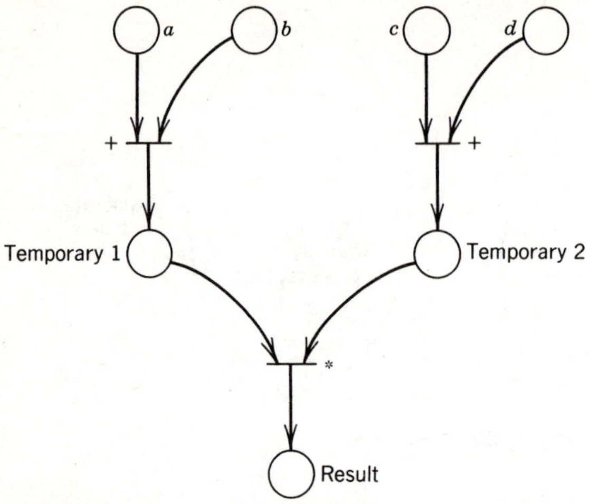

FIGURE 1.49 A PN representing an arithmetic expression.

Give formal rules to derive a PN for Pascal expressions. Discuss how the PN shows possible parallel evaluation of subexpressions.

Petri nets are a nondeterministic evolutionary model because in general it may happen that $M \vdash_T TM'$ and $M \vdash_T M''$ (with the obvious meaning of the notation $\vdash_T$). Furthermore, it may happen that $M \vdash_{t_1} M_1 \vdash_{t_2} M_3$ and $M \vdash_{t_2} M_2 \vdash_{t_1} M_3$, in which case t_1 and t_2 are *concurrent* for M, as they can both occur starting from M in any order. Instead, if M_1 does not enable t_2 and M_2 does not enable t_1, but t_1 and t_2 are both enabled by M, they are in *conflict* as the choice of one of them prevents the other from firing.

1.7.3.1 Petri Nets as Language Recognizers

Petri nets can be used in several ways as language recognizers. A natural and classical way is to see them as recognizers of sets of *firing sequences* defined as follows.

Definition 1.35

A *Petri net acceptor* PNA is a 6-tuple $\langle P, T, IF, OF, M_0, M_F \rangle$ where P, T, IF, OF are defined as in Definition 1.31, M_0 and M_F are markings, called the *initial and final marking*, respectively. A firing sequence s for a given PNA, P, is an element of T^*. $s = t_{i_1} t_{i_2} \ldots t_{i_n}$ is accepted by P if and only if there exist $n - 1$ markings $M_1, \ldots, M_{n-1}$ of P such that

$$M_0 \vdash_{t_{i_1}} M_1 \vdash_{t_{i_2}} M_2 \ldots M_{n-1} \vdash_{t_{i_n}} M_F.$$

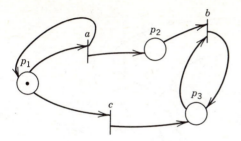

FIGURE 1.50 A PN accepting the language $\{a^n cb^n | n \geq 0\}$.

The language of firing sequences of P is $L(P) = \{s | s \in T^* \text{ and } s \text{ is accepted by } P\}$. $\square$

Example 1.32

1. Consider the PN of Figure 1.47 and assume as $M_0 = M_F$, the marking of the figure.

   A sample of firing sequences accepted by the PNA is

   $$t_1 \bar{t}_1, t_2 \bar{t}_2, t_1 t_2 \bar{t}_1 \bar{t}_2, t_1 \bar{t}_1 t_2 \bar{t}_2, t_2 t_1 \bar{t}_1 \bar{t}_2, \ldots$$

   which is easily generalized to the language

   $$\left\{ t_1 \bar{t}_1, t_2 \bar{t}_2, t_1 t_2 \bar{t}_1 \bar{t}_2, t_1 t_2 \bar{t}_2 \bar{t}_1, t_2 t_1 \bar{t}_2 \bar{t}_1, t_2 t_1 \bar{t}_1 \bar{t}_2 \right\}^*$$

2. The language of firing sequences of the PN of Figure 1.48 with initial and final markings as in figure is

   $$\left\{ t_1 \bar{t}_1 t_2 \bar{t}_2, t_1 t_2 \bar{t}_1 \bar{t}_2, t_1 t_2 \bar{t}_2 \bar{t}_1 \right\}^*$$

3. Consider the PN of Figure 1.50 with M_0 consisting of one token in p_1 and no token in other places, M_F consisting of one token in p_3 and no token in other places.

   In M_0 a and c are enabled; a can fire any number $n \geq 0$ of times producing n tokens in p_2 and one in p_1. If and when c eventually fires a and c are definitely disabled and b is enabled. It can fire at most n times. If it fires exactly n times the marking M_F is produced. Thus the accepted language is

   $$L = \{ a^n cb^n | n \geq 0 \}$$

Exercises

1.81 Give PNAs accepting the following languages.

$$L_1 = \{ a^n cb^n de^n | n \geq 0 \}$$
$$L_2 = \{ a^n cb^{2n} | n \geq 0 \}$$
$$L_3 = \{ a, b \}^* \cdot \{ c^n de^n | n \geq 0 \}$$

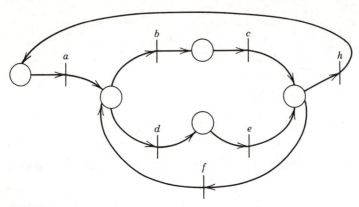

FIGURE 1.51   A PN.

1.82   Determine the language accepted by the PN of Figure 1.51 with $M_0(p_1) = M_F(p_1) = 1$, $M_0(p_i) = M_F(p_i) = 0$ for all other places. Also, determine the language accepted if $M_0(p_1) = M_F(p_1) = 2$, $M_0(p_i) = M_F(p_i) = 0$ for all other places.

1.83   Write (possibly regular) grammars generating the languages accepted by the PN of Figure 1.51 with the initial and final markings of Exercise 1.82.

1.84   Show that, if we allow the same identifier to be used to denote several transitions of a PN, then the class of languages accepted by PNAs properly includes the class of languages accepted by FAs.

A thorough investigation of the formal properties of PN languages and their relations with other families of languages is beyond the scope of this text. The interested reader is therefore urged to refer the references given in the bibliographic remarks for further study of the topic.

1.7.4   Some Remarks on Nondeterministic versus Stochastic Models

Nondeterministic models are not to be confused with *probabilistic* or *stochastic models*. Roughly speaking, in the framework of evolutionary formalisms, stochastic systems are such that the transition from one state to another occurs with a given probability. Many stochastic models exist in the literature that are applied both within and outside computer science. Some of them are derived from deterministic formalisms in the very same way as nondeterministic ones.

A typical example is given by *Markov chains* that are finite-state automata where each transition is associated with a given probability distribution. In such a context, the fragment of automaton given in Figure 1.52 states that if the system

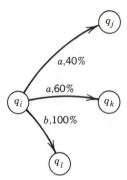

FIGURE 1.52 A Markov chain.

reaches state q_i and input a is supplied, then it will reach either q_k or q_j with probabilities 60% and 40%, respectively; if the input is b it will certainly reach q_l.

In some sense, nondeterministic models describe a higher degree of "uncertainty" than probabilistic ones. In fact, a probabilistic distribution on transitions is a sort of knowledge on how the system behaves.

Stochastic models are well suited to answering questions such as "Which is the most likely state the system will reach if supplied with a given input sequence?" or "what is the average service time of a system that receives customers with a given incoming probabilistic distribution?"

Although stochastic models are extensively used in some areas of computer science, such as performance evaluation, we decided not to study them here because their use is more specialized compared with the other models presented in this text.

1.8 On the Power Relations among Formalisms

Several times we compared formalisms from the point of view of their ability to solve problems, such as defining languages or translating them. We realized that PDAs are more powerful than FAs both as language recognizers and as language translators, that unrestricted grammars can define exactly the same languages TMs can recognize, that any language recognized by a FA is generated by some R-grammar, and so on. Let us now summarize and complete, through Table 1.5, the display of power relations between formalisms. In this section, we give the proof of two relations that have not yet been stated. The remaining ones are left as nontrivial exercises to the reader.

Theorem 1.26
For each R-grammar G, a FA A can be constructed, such that $L(G) = L(A)$.

TABLE 1.5   Power Relations Among Formalisms

	FA	PDA	NPDA	TM	NTM	$\mathscr{G}_R$	$\mathscr{G}_{CF}$	$\mathscr{G}$	EQ
FA	▨	⊂	⊂	⊂	⊂	=	⊂	⊂	⊂
PDA	▨	▨	⊂	⊂	⊂	⊃	⊂	⊂	⊂
NPDA	▨	▨	▨	⊂	⊂	⊃	=	⊂	=
TM	▨	▨	▨	▨	=	⊃	⊃	=	⊃
NTM	▨	▨	▨	▨	▨	⊃	⊃	=	⊃
$\mathscr{G}_R$	▨	▨	▨	▨	▨	▨	⊂	⊂	⊂
$\mathscr{G}_{CF}$	▨	▨	▨	▨	▨	▨	▨	⊂	=
$\mathscr{G}$	▨	▨	▨	▨	▨	▨	▨	▨	⊃
EQ	▨	▨	▨	▨	▨	▨	▨	▨	▨

        FA = Finite-state acceptors
       PDA = Deterministic pushdown acceptors
      NPDA = Nondeterministic pushdown acceptors
        TM = Deterministic Turing acceptors
       NTM = Nondeterministic Turing acceptors
    $\mathscr{G}_R$ = R-grammars
   $\mathscr{G}_{CF}$ = Context-free grammars
     $\mathscr{G}$ = Unrestricted grammars
        EQ = Language equations of the type X = F(X), F being a vector of unions of
             concatenation of variable and finite constant languages

Proof

Let $G = \langle V_T, V_N, P, S \rangle$. We build an NFA A equivalent to G. Thanks to Theorem 1.23, this implies that a deterministic FA equivalent to G can also be found. A is defined as $\langle V_N \cup \{q_F\}, V_T, \delta, S, F \rangle$ where

- $q_F \notin V_N$ is a final state
- $\delta(A, a)$ contains B if and only if $A \to aB$ is in P
- $\delta(A, a)$ contains q_F if and only if $A \to a$ is in P
- $F = \{q_F\} \cup \{A | A \to \epsilon \in P\}$

The proof that $L(A) = L(G)$, (i.e., $S \overset{*}{\Rightarrow} x$ if and only if $\delta^*(S, x) \cap F \neq \varnothing$) is quite similar to the corresponding proof in Theorem 1.19 and is therefore omitted.   ∎

The foregoing theorem, together with Theorems 1.19 and 1.23, provides a formal statement of the equivalence relation between FAs and R-grammars.

Theorem 1.27

For each context-free grammar G, an equivalent NPDA A can be obtained.

Proof*

Let $G = \langle V_T, V_N, P, S \rangle$. $A = \langle Q, \Gamma, V_T, \delta, q_0, Z_0, F \rangle$ is built as follows.

- $Q = \{q_0, q_1, q_F\}$
- $\Gamma = \{Z_0\} \cup V_N \cup \{\bar{a} | a \in V_T\}$ that is, elements of Γ are exactly the elements of V, provided that elements of V_T are marked in some way to avoid confusion with input alphabet, plus the distinguished symbol Z_0.
- $\delta(q_0, \epsilon, Z_0) = \{\langle q_1, SZ_0 \rangle\}$;
  $\delta(q_1, \epsilon, A)$ contains $\langle q_1, \bar{\alpha} \rangle$ if and only if $A \to \alpha$ is in P and $\bar{\alpha}$ is obtained from α by substituting each element $a \in V_T$ with its corresponding $\bar{a}$;
  $\delta(q_1, a, \bar{a}) = \{\langle q_1, \epsilon \rangle\}$ for each $a \in V_T$
  $\delta(q_1, \epsilon, Z_0) = \{\langle q_F, \epsilon \rangle\}$
- $F = \{q_F\}$

In order to show that A is equivalent to G, we need to prove the following lemma.

Lemma 1.28

Let G be a context-free grammar. If $S \underset{G}{\overset{*}{\Rightarrow}} x$, then there exists a derivation $S \underset{G}{\Rightarrow} \gamma_1 \underset{G}{\Rightarrow} \gamma_2 \ldots \Rightarrow \gamma_n = x$ such that for all i, with $1 \le i \le n - 1$, $\gamma_i = x_i A_i \beta_i$, $\gamma_{i+1} = x_i \alpha_i \beta_i$ with $x_i \in V_T^*$. $\qquad\Box$

Intuitively, Lemma 1.28 states that any string of $L(G)$ can be derived by rewriting the leftmost nonterminal at each derivation step. A derivation of this type is called a *leftmost derivation* and is denoted as $S \overset{l*}{\Rightarrow} x$. The proof of the lemma is trivial and therefore omitted.

Thanks to Lemma 1.28, A is proved equivalent to G once we prove that $S \underset{G}{\overset{l*}{\Rightarrow}} x$ if and only if $\langle q_0, x, Z_0 \rangle \underset{A}{\overset{*}{\vdash}} \langle q_F, \epsilon, \gamma \rangle$ for some γ in Γ^*.
We prove this claim by a double induction.

i. $S \overset{l*}{\Rightarrow} x$ implies
   i.1 $\langle q_0, x, Z_0 \rangle \overset{*}{\vdash} \langle q_1, \epsilon, Z_0 \rangle$ and
   i.2 $\langle q_1, \epsilon, Z_0 \rangle \vdash \langle q_F, \epsilon, \epsilon \rangle$

   i.1 is proved using induction on the length of derivation to show that if $S \overset{l*}{\Rightarrow} x$, then $\langle q_0, x, Z_0 \rangle \overset{*}{\vdash} \langle q_1, \epsilon, \bar{\gamma} Z_0 \rangle$, where $\bar{\gamma}$ is obtained from γ in the same way as we did in the construction of A.
   The basis of the induction is obvious since $S \overset{l*}{\Rightarrow} S$ and $\langle q_0, \epsilon, Z_0 \rangle \vdash \langle q_1, \epsilon, SZ_0 \rangle$
   Assume now that $S \overset{lk}{\Rightarrow} x$ implies $\langle q_0, x, Z_0 \rangle \overset{*}{\vdash} \langle q_1, \epsilon, \bar{\gamma} Z_0 \rangle$ and consider any leftmost derivation of length $k + 1$ (i.e., $S \overset{lk}{\Rightarrow} xA\gamma \Rightarrow x\alpha\gamma$).
   Let $\alpha = y\eta$ with $y \in V_T^*$, $\eta \in V^* - V_T V^*$, (i.e., the first character of η, if any, is a nonterminal.)
   By the inductive hypothesis $\langle q_0, x, Z_0 \rangle \overset{*}{\vdash} \langle q_1, \epsilon, A\bar{\gamma} Z_0 \rangle$.
   Since $\langle q_1, \alpha \rangle$ is in $\delta(q_1, \epsilon, A)$, $\langle q_0, x, Z_0 \rangle \overset{*}{\vdash} \langle q_1, \epsilon, \bar{\alpha}\bar{\gamma} Z_0 \rangle$.
   Furthermore, since for any a in V_T, $\delta(q_1, a, \bar{a}) = \langle q_1, \epsilon \rangle$, $\langle q_1, y, \overline{\alpha}\bar{\gamma} Z_0 \rangle \overset{*}{\vdash} \langle q_1, \epsilon, \bar{\eta}\bar{\gamma} Z_0 \rangle$ and the induction is complete.

   i.2 is immediate from the construction of A.

ii. $\langle q_0, x, Z_0 \rangle \overset{*}{\vdash} \langle q_F, \epsilon, \gamma \rangle$ implies
$\langle q_0, x, Z_0 \rangle \overset{*}{\vdash} \langle q_1, \epsilon, Z_0 \rangle \vdash \langle q_F, \epsilon, \epsilon \rangle$
because a transition to q_F can occur in A only if Z_0 is on top of the stack. But Z_0 can only be the bottom of the stack because it is not a symbol of V.
Let us show, by induction on the length of the transition sequence, that if

$$\langle q_0, x, Z_0 \rangle \overset{*}{\vdash} \langle q_1, \epsilon, \bar{\gamma} Z_0 \rangle,$$

then $S \overset{l*}{\Rightarrow} x\gamma$. This will complete the proof.
The basis of the induction is obvious since the first transition of A is necessarily $\langle q_0, x, Z_0 \rangle \vdash \langle q_1, x, S Z_0 \rangle$ and $S \overset{*}{\Rightarrow} S$.
Assume now that $\langle q_0, x, Z_0 \rangle \overset{k}{\vdash} \langle q_1, \epsilon, \bar{\gamma} Z_0 \rangle$ implies $S \overset{l*}{\Rightarrow} x\gamma$ and consider a transition sequence of $k + 1$ steps. This can be either of the type

$$\langle q_0, x, Z_0 \rangle \overset{k}{\vdash} \langle q_1, \epsilon, A\bar{\gamma} Z_0 \rangle \vdash \langle q_1, \epsilon, \bar{\alpha}\bar{\gamma} Z_0 \rangle$$

or of the type

$$\langle q_0, xa, Z_0 \rangle \overset{k}{\vdash} \langle q_1, a, \bar{a}\bar{\gamma} Z_0 \rangle \vdash \langle q_1, \epsilon, \bar{\gamma} Z_0 \rangle$$

In the former case we have $S \overset{l*}{\Rightarrow} xA\gamma$ by the induction hypothesis and $A \to \alpha$ in P by construction, thus $S \overset{l*}{\Rightarrow} x\alpha\gamma$.
In the latter case $\langle q_0, x, Z_0 \rangle \overset{k}{\vdash} \langle q_1, \epsilon, \bar{a}\bar{\gamma} Z_0 \rangle$.[6]
Thus $S \overset{l*}{\Rightarrow} xa\gamma$ by the induction hypothesis.   ∎

Exercises

1.85 * Prove that for any NPDA we can build an equivalent context-free grammar.

1.86 * Prove that context-free languages are properly included in the class of languages recognized by TMs. For a hint, see Exercise 1.64.

Chapter Summary

This chapter has been devoted to introducing and discussing several classical formalisms of computer science. At this point, we expect the reader to be able not only to understand, choose, and use the models presented so far, but also to extend them or adapt them if the need should arise.

The presented formalisms have been classified as evolutionary (operational, dynamical) models and denotational (denotationary, statical) ones. Finite-state automata, pushdown automata, Turing machines, and Petri nets are examples of

---

[6] In general, $\langle q, xy, \alpha \rangle \overset{*}{\vdash} \langle q', y, \alpha' \rangle$ if and only if $\langle q, x, \alpha \rangle \overset{*}{\vdash} \langle q', \epsilon, \alpha' \rangle$.

the former class. Equations in language spaces and regular expressions are examples of the latter. Grammars have been viewed as somewhat in the middle between the two classes.

It has been shown that a model can help formalize and solve practical problems. A problem to be solved can be formalized (coded) as a language recognition, a language translation problem, or as the computation of a function.

We have emphasized the usefulness of nondeterministic models and we have both extended deterministic models (automata) to behave nondeterministically and introduced an intrinsically nondeterministic model (Petri nets).

Models have been compared to each other from the point of view of their power, that is, their relative ability to solve a wider (or less wide) class of problems. We have realized that TMs and unrestricted grammars are *maximal formalisms* because they can define any language defined through any other model.

Many of the proposed exercises, the appendix, and the bibliographic remarks are additional sources of inspiration and urge on the reader towards further investigations into more advanced topics.

Further Exercises

1.87 Build a FA modeling the algebra of integers modulo k, provided with the operations $Succ$: $[N]_k \to [N]_k$ defined by $Succ\ ([n]_k) = [(n + 1)]_k$, $Pred$: $[N]_k \to [N]_k$ defined by $Pred\ ([n]_k) = [n - 1]_k$.

1.88 What is the language accepted by the NFA shown in Figure 1.53? Derive a R-grammar that generates the same language. Transform the automaton into an equivalent deterministic FA.

1.89 Prove that the set of context-free languages is closed with respect to union, concatenation, and Kleene star.

1.90 * Prove that the intersection of a context-free language with a regular language is a context-free language.
Hint: Use a FA and a NPDA.

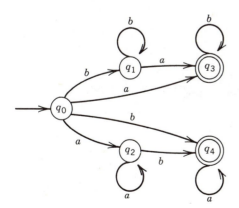

FIGURE 1.53 A NFA.

1.91   Give a context-free grammar G that generates the set of wfs of propositional calculus.
Hint: The infinite set of statement letters $\{A_i\}$ can be represented by
strings of the type Ai, where the index i is coded as a sequence of, say,
decimal digits.

1.92   Formalize double-pushdown automata. They are the same as PDAs but
are provided with two stacks instead of one. A single move depends on
the top values of both stacks, besides current state and input value, and
operates on both stacks at the same time. Provide both a deterministic
and a nondeterministic version of such automata.

1.93   Prove that double-pushdown automata, (both deterministic and nondeterministic) are equivalent to TMs.

Sketchy Solutions to Selected Exercises

1.11,   The minimal FT equivalent to the FT of Figure 1.10 is given in Figure
1.14   1.54. Its subjacent FA is the minimal FA equivalent to the FA subjacent
the FT of Figure 1.10. Notice that this fact does not hold in general.

1.51   Let M have $A = \{a_1, \ldots, a_m\}$, $Q = \{q_0, \ldots, q_n\}$, $F \subseteq Q$.
$\overline{M}$ is defined by
  i. $\overline{Q} = \{q_\alpha, q_\beta, q_F\}$
  ii. $\overline{I}$ consisting of
      1. $\{\bar{a}_1, \ldots, \bar{a}_m | a_k \in A\}$
      2. $\{\langle q, a, x, y \rangle | q \in Q, a \in A, x \in \{+, -\}, y \in \{R, L\}$
 iii. $\overline{\delta}$ defined by
      1.   for $\delta(q, a) = \langle q', a', S \rangle$
           define

$$\overline{\delta}(q_\alpha, \langle q, a, -, R \rangle) = \langle q_\alpha, \langle q', a', -, R \rangle, S \rangle$$
$$\overline{\delta}(q_\alpha, \langle q, a, -, L \rangle) = \langle q_\alpha, \langle q', a', -, L \rangle, S \rangle$$

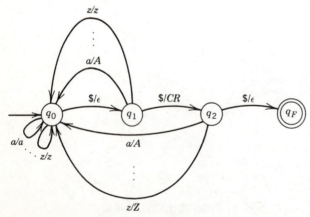

FIGURE 1.54   A FT.

2. for $\delta(q, a) = \langle q', a', R' \rangle$
   define, for $* = R$ and $* = L$

   $$\bar{\delta}(q_\alpha, \langle q, a, -, * \rangle) = \langle q_\beta, \langle q', a', +, R \rangle, R \rangle$$

3. for $\delta(q, a) = \langle q', a', L \rangle$
   define, for $* = R$ and $* = L$

   $$\bar{\delta}(q_\alpha, \langle q, a, -, * \rangle) = \langle q_\beta, \langle q', a', +, L \rangle, L \rangle$$

4.a $\bar{\delta}(q_\alpha, \bar{a}) = \langle q_\alpha, \langle q_0, a, -, R \rangle, R \rangle$, for every $a \in A$

4.b $\bar{\delta}(q_\beta, \bar{a}) = \langle q_\alpha, \langle q_0, a, -, L \rangle, L \rangle$, for every $a \in A$
   for $\square = q_\alpha$ and q_β, and $* = R$ and L:

4.c $\bar{\delta}(\square, \langle q_j, a, +, * \rangle) = \langle q_\beta, \langle q_{j-1}, a, +, * \rangle, * \rangle$
   For all $a \in A$, $j = 1, \ldots, n$.

4.d $\bar{\delta}(q_\beta, \langle q_j, a, -, * \rangle) = \langle q_\alpha, \langle q_{j+1}, a, -, * \rangle, * \rangle$
   for all $a \in A$, $j = 0, \ldots, n-1$

4.e $\bar{\delta}(\square, \langle q_0, a, +, * \rangle) = \langle q_\alpha, \bar{a}, * \rangle$
   for all $a \in A$

5. $\bar{\delta}(q_\alpha, \langle q, a, -, * \rangle) = \langle q_F, \bar{a}, S \rangle$
   for all $q \in F$, $a \in A$

1.55 Let M_1 be a k_1-tape TM accepting L_1 and let M_2 be a k_2-tape TM accepting L_2. A $(k_1 + k_2)$-tape TM M accepting $L_1 \cup L_2$ (respectively, $L_1 \cap L_2$) can be easily built along the following lines. M's state set Q is $Q_1 \times Q_2$ plus a unique final state q_F. Given an input x, M simulates M_1's moves by means of its first k_1 tapes and of the first component of its states; M_2 is simulated in a similar way. If M ever reaches a state $\langle q_1, q_2 \rangle$ with $q_1 \in F_1$ or (respectively, and) $q_2 \in F_2$ it enters q_F and halts.

1.61 Construction of G such that $L(G) = L(M)$. G is defined as follows

$G = \langle V_T, V_N, P, S \rangle$, with
$V_N = \bar{A} \cup \hat{V}_T \cup \tilde{V}_T \cup Q \cup \{S, V, Y, Z, E, \$, D, H, F_1, F_2\}$,

where $\bar{A} = \{\bar{a} | a \in A\}$, $\hat{V}_T = \{\hat{x} | x \in V_T\}$, $\tilde{V}_T = \{\tilde{x} | x \in V_T\}$. We assume that $b \in A$; $S, V, Y, Z, E, \$, D, H \notin A$.
P contains the following groups of rules.

1. • $S \to V\$YE$,
   • $S \to \$q_0E$,
   • for each $a \in V_T$:
     $V \to aZ\hat{a}$
     $Y \to aZ$,
     $\hat{a}\$ \to \$\hat{a}$,
     $\hat{a}b \to b\hat{a}$ for all $b \in \bar{V}_T$
     $\hat{a}\tilde{a}Z \to D\bar{a}Y$
     $\hat{a}\tilde{a}Z \to H\bar{a}$
   • for each $b \in \bar{V}_T$:
     $bD \to Db$
     $bH \to Hb$
   • $Z\$D \to V\$$
   • $Z\$H \to \$q_0$

2. • for each $q \in Q - F$, a, a', $b \in A$:

$\quad q\underline{a} \to q'\overline{a}'$,   if $\delta(q, a) = \langle q', a', S \rangle$,

$\quad b q\underline{a} \to \overline{q}'ba'$,   if $\delta(q, a) = \langle q', a', L \rangle$,

$\quad q\underline{a}b \to \overline{a}'q'\underline{b}$,   if $\delta(q, a) = \langle q', a', R \rangle$,

$\quad q\underline{a}E \to \overline{a}'q'E$,   if $\delta(q, a) = \langle q', a', R \rangle$;

 • $E \to \not{b}E$

3. • for each $q \in F$:

$\quad q \to F_1$

$\quad F_1\overline{a} \to F_1$ for all $\overline{a} \in \overline{A}$

$\quad F_1 E \to F_2$

$\quad \overline{a}F_2 \to F_2$ for all $\overline{a} \in \overline{A}$

$\quad \$F_2 \to \epsilon$

1.85 Let $A' = \langle Q', I, \Gamma', \delta', q_0', Z_0', F' \rangle$ be a NPDA.
Build an equivalent A such that $\langle q_0, x, Z_0 \rangle \overset{*}{\underset{}{\vdash}} \langle q, \epsilon, \epsilon \rangle$ with $q \in F$, if and
only if $\langle q_0', x, Z_0' \rangle \overset{*}{\underset{A'}{\vdash}} \langle q', \epsilon, \gamma \rangle$ with $\gamma' \in \Gamma'^*$, $q' \in F'$, that is, A accepts
its input if and only if A' does so, but, besides, A accepts by entering a
configuration where the stack is empty.
An equivalent CFG is $\langle V_N, I, P, S \rangle$ where

$$V_N = \{S\} \cup \{\langle q, C, q' \rangle | q, q' \in Q, C \in \Gamma\}$$

P contains:

• $S \to \langle q_0, Z_0, q \rangle$ for each $q \in F$.
• $\langle q, C, q_{n+1} \rangle \to a \langle q_1, B_1, q_2 \rangle \langle q_2, B_2, q_3 \rangle \ldots \langle q_n, B_n, q_{n+1} \rangle$ for each
$q, q_1, \ldots, q_{n+1}$ in Q, a in $I \cup \{\epsilon\}$, $C, B_1, \ldots B_n$ in Γ such that
$\langle q_1, B_1 \ldots B_n \rangle$ is in $\delta(q, a, C)$.

The proof of equivalence between G and A is by induction on the lengths
of derivations and transition sequences.

Appendix

1.A. The Equivalence between TMs and Partial Recursive Functions

TMs and unrestricted grammars are "maximal formalisms" among those examined so far, because they are more powerful than any other model. The
number of maximal formalisms from the point of view of computational power is
large. It is certainly useless here—and even impossible—to be exhaustive in the
listing of such formalisms and in equivalence proofs. The ones presented so far
should be sufficient to give the reader an intuitive view of the essential properties
of maximal formalisms and the ability to work out equivalence proofs by him or
herself, at least in the simplest cases. However, it seems worth adding one more
element to this general picture.

Partial recursive functions, as defined in Section 0.2.4.2 are another classical maximal formalism, usually related to the domain of natural numbers. We now sketch how partial recursive functions can define any function computable by TMs. The vice-versa is easier to prove and its construction is left to the reader as an exercise.

For the sake of simplicity we make the following assumptions, which do not affect the generality of the statement.

- We consider single-tape TMs.
- A has just two elements, $A = \{\emptyset, 1\}$ herewith denoted as $\{0, 1\}$ (see Theorem 1.17).
- The machine halts if and only if it enters a certain, specific final state. It is left as an exercise for the reader to prove that for any TM M, whether used as language recognizer or as function computer, an equivalent TM M' can be easily built, satisfying this assumption.
- TMs are used to compute functions on naturals. This does not cause loss of generality since suitable bijective correspondence can be stated between $\mathbb{N}$ and $\mathbb{N}*$, which can be computed both by a TM and as a primitive recursive function. One such correspondence is $g: \mathbb{N}* \to \mathbb{N}$, where

$$g(n_1, \ldots, n_k) = 2^{n_1} . 3^{n_2} \ldots p_k^{n_k}$$

where p_i is the ith prime number.

Both x and $f(x)$ are stored in the machine tape in unary base according to the following rule.
The initial configuration is $\langle q_0, \uparrow A_1 \ldots A_x \rangle$ with $A_1 = A_2 \ldots = A_{x-1} = 0$, $A_x = 1$; the final configuration, if any, is $\langle q_F, \uparrow B_1 \ldots B_{f(x)} \rangle$ with $B_1 = B_2 = \ldots = B_{f(x)-1} = 0$, $B_{f(x)} = 1$.
The following points explain how to build a partial recursive function RF_M denoting the function computed by the TM M.

1. Coding M's state.
   Let M's configuration be $c = \langle q, \alpha_1 \uparrow \alpha_2 \rangle$ with $\alpha_1 = X_1 \ldots X_r$, $\alpha_2 = Y_1 \ldots Y_s$. It can be represented by a 4-tuple of natural numbers $\bar{c} = \langle \bar{q}, a, m, n \rangle$ where

   - $\bar{q}$ is the number coding state q ($\overline{Q}$ is the set of numbers coding the states of Q);
   - $a \in \{0, 1\} = Y_1$, that is, the current symbol scanned by M's head.
   - $m = \sum_{k=0}^{r} X_{r-k} . 2^k$ represents the tape configuration to the left of M's head.
     It is interpreted as a binary number, whose least relevant digit is the one to the left of the reading head.
   - $n = \sum_{k=2}^{s} Y_k . 2^{k-2}$ represents the tape configuration to the right of the head.
     It is interpreted as a binary number read from left to right.

   Notice that m, a, and n represent the tape configuration.

2. Coding M's move.

Let $c \underset{M}{\vdash} c'$. $\bar{c}'$ is obtained as a primitive recursive function of $\bar{c}$.

Let $\bar{c} = \langle \bar{q}, a, m, n \rangle$ and $\delta(q, a) = \langle p, s, y \rangle$. Let $D(n)$ and $R(n)$ be defined by the equations $n = 2 \cdot D(n) + R(n)$, and $0 \le R(n) \le 1$. Define $\bar{c}'$ as $\bar{c}' = \langle \bar{q}', a', m', n' \rangle$, where

- $\bar{q}'$ is the number coding p
- if $y = R$ then
  - $a' = R(n)$
  - $m' = 2m + s$
  - $n' = D(n)$
- if $y = L$ then
  - $a' = R(m)$
  - $m' = D(m)$
  - $n' = 2n + s$
- if $y = S$ then
  - $a' = s$
  - $m' = m$
  - $n' = n$

Let us define function $\bar{Y}_R : \bar{Q} \times A \to \{0,1\}$ by $\bar{Y}_R(\bar{q}, a) = $ **if** $y = R$ **then** 1 **else** 0. Functions $\bar{Y}_L$ and $\bar{Y}_S$ are defined accordingly, by substituting L and S to R. We obtain

- $\bar{q}' = \bar{p}$
- $a' = R(n) \cdot \bar{Y}_R(\bar{q}, a) + R(m) \cdot \bar{Y}_L(\bar{q}, a) + s \cdot \bar{Y}_S(\bar{q}, a)$
- $m' = (2m + s) \cdot \bar{Y}_R(\bar{q}, a) + D(m) \cdot \bar{Y}_L(\bar{q}, a) + m \cdot \bar{Y}_S(\bar{q}, a)$
- $n' = D(n) \cdot \bar{Y}_R(\bar{q}, a) + (2n + s) \cdot \bar{Y}_L(\bar{q}, a) + n \cdot \bar{Y}_S(\bar{q}, a)$

Thus, by denoting $\bar{c}' = \langle Z_q(\bar{c}), Z_a(\bar{c}), Z_m(\bar{c}), Z_n(\bar{c}) \rangle$, it is immediate to verify that Z_q, Z_a, Z_m, Z_n are all primitive recursive functions.

3. Coding M-computations.

Consider now a sequence of transitions $c_0 \underset{M}{\vdash} c_1 \vdash \ldots c_t$. It is easy to realize that $\bar{c}_t$ can be obtained as a 4-tuple

$$\bar{c}_t = \langle \varphi_q(t, \bar{c}_0), \varphi_a(t, \bar{c}_0), \varphi_m(t, \bar{c}_0), \varphi_n(t, \bar{c}_0) \rangle$$

where $\varphi_q, \varphi_a, \varphi_m, \varphi_n$ are primitive recursive functions. In fact,

$$\varphi_q(0, \bar{q}, a, m, n) = \bar{q}, \text{ for every } a, m, n,$$

$$\varphi_q(t + 1, \bar{q}, a, m, n) = \varphi_q(t, Z_q(\bar{q}, a, m, n), Z_a(\bar{q}, a, m, n),$$

$$Z_m(\bar{q}, a, m, n), Z_n(\bar{q}, a, m, n))$$

(for all a, m, n and for all $t \ge 0$ φ_q can be easily proved to be primitive recursive provided that Z_q, Z_a, Z_m and Z_n are also primitive recursive).

(Notice, however, that φ_q is *not* defined by immediate application of primitive recursion.)

Similarly functions $\varphi_a, \varphi_m, \varphi_n$ can be defined and proved primitive recursive.

4. Defining TM-computable functions as partial recursive functions.

Let f_M denote the function on naturals computed by M according to previous conventions.

M halts at time t_f (if any) such that $\varphi_q(t_f, \bar{q}_0, a_0, m_0, n_0) = \bar{q}_f$; that is,

$$t_f = \mu_t(\varphi_q(t, \bar{q}_0, a_0, m_0, n_0) - \bar{q}_f) = 0$$

Notice that t_f is defined if and only if M halts.

Finally, let the primitive recursive function $C: \mathbb{N} \to \mathbb{N}$ be defined by

$$C(x) = \text{if } x = 2^{x_1} \cdot 3^{x_2} \ldots p_n^{x_n}, \ p_i \text{ being the } i\text{th prime number, } \textbf{then } x_1,$$

that is, $C(x)$ is the exponent of prime number 2 in the factorization of x into the product of powers of prime numbers.

Then

$$f_M(x) = C\Big(\varphi_n\big(\mu_t\big(\varphi_q(t, \bar{q}_0, 0, 0, 2^x) - \bar{q}_f\big) = 0\big), \bar{q}_0, 0, 0, 2^x\Big)$$

This concludes the proof of the following theorem.

Theorem 1.29
Every TM-computable function is a partial recursive function. ∎

Corollary 1.30
Every partial recursive function can be defined by means of one only application of minimalization. □

Bibliographic Remarks

All models presented in this chapter are extensively used in computer science. Finite-state automata, pushdown automata, and Turing machines are described practically in any book on computation theory. Similarly, grammars are a universal concept of formal language theory. Some classic texts covering these topics are Ginsburg (1966), Hopcroft and Ullman (1969), Hopcroft and Ullman (1979), Harrison (1978), and Lewis and Papadimitriou (1981). These texts have been a major source for the material presented here. They are also suggested for further reading in the field of automata, languages, and computation theory.

The most relevant papers that originated the results presented here are by Bar-Hillel, Perles, and Shamir (1961), (Pumping Lemma), Myhill (1957), Nerode (1958), (Myhill–Nerode theorem), Chomsky (1956, 1959, 1963), Schützenberger (1963), (grammars and pushdown automata), and Turing (1936) (Turing machines).

The proof of Theorem 1.11 is by Ginsburg and Greibach (1966) and is reported in Harrison (1978). Ginsburg and Greibach's proof has been revised and corrected by Citrini, Crespi-Reghizzi and Mandrioli (1986). Theorem 1.16 is due to Shannon (1956). The sketchy proof given here is adapted from Brady (1977).

Equations in language spaces are maybe less widely used and their study is in general of more special interest. They have been treated, for example, in Gross and Lentin (1967). This formalism has been presented here just as a simple introductory example of a denotationary model. In Chapter 4 this kind of models is thoroughly exploited to assign a meaning to programming languages.

Regular expressions have been studied by McNaughton and Yamada (1960).

It is worth mentioning the recent applications of denotationary models based on equations on heterogeneous algebras to the description, implementation, and correctness of abstract data types (ADJ (1975) and Guttag (1977).)

Petri nets are not yet a "classical" model for computer science, but in the recent past they have been deeply analyzed in their mathematical properties and widely applied to practical problems. The interested reader can find an extensive and easy to read description of the model in Peterson (1977, 1981). Other relevant, original literature on Petri nets and applications is Petri (1962) and Holt and Commoner (1970).

Many other relevant formalisms have not been included here in order to make the exposition easier to follow. It is worth mentioning Church's lambda calculus (Church (1941)) and Markov's rewriting systems, which are quite similar to grammars (Markov (1954)).

Some insight on the use of stochastic models and their application to computer science can be obtained from Kleinrock (1976).

CHAPTER TWO

Solvable and Unsolvable Problems

2.1 On the Ability of a Mechanism to Solve a Problem

Let us recall some relevant facts we learned in Chapter 1.

1. Automata, grammars, and other formalisms can be viewed as "mechanical" devices to solve mathematical problems. Often, the mathematical problem is a formalization of some practical, nonmathematical problem. A typical example is the language membership problem: Does a given string belong to a given language? This mathematical problem is just a formal restatement of such practical problems as the recognition of commands of an operating system job control language or the recognition of statements in programs written in some programming language.
2. Some formalisms are more powerful than others; that is, they can recognize languages that cannot be accepted by another formalism or implement translations that cannot be performed by other formalisms, etc.
3. No formalism, among those considered in Chapter 1, is more powerful than TMs, whether they are seen as language recognizers, language translators, or

147

function computers. However, some formalisms are as powerful as TMs. We call these formalisms *maximal formalisms*.

These facts naturally generate some related questions.

a. Are the formalisms examined so far really adequate to capture the deep essence of a mechanical problem solver? Even if we restrict our attention to well-formalized problems, there are many problems that do not appear to fall into the class of previous examples. Solving a differential equation, finding a path in a graph, updating a database through a transaction, finding the optimal allocation of goods among several stores, etc. have nothing to do with the membership of a word in a language, at a first glance.

b. Does the ability of a mechanism to solve a given problem depend on the way the problem is formalized? We have already observed this fact at least in one case, and the answer to this question has been positive. In fact, a FT can compute the successor of a natural number coded in unary base, but it cannot if the number is coded in a base k with $k > 1$ (see Theorem 1.18).

c. Do there exist computing formalisms more powerful then TMs? For example, can some existing (or future) supercomputer perform computations that cannot be performed by a TM?

d. Once a problem has been suitably formalized, can we *always* solve it by means of some "mechanical" device?

This chapter is devoted to discussing questions of this nature. First, we realize that our present formal tools are adequate to describing any particular problem to be solved mechanically. Then we show that TMs and other equivalent formalisms allow us to derive some general statements on the power of any theoretical, or practical, computing device. Finally, we investigate the limits of mechanical problem solving.

2.2 On the Formalization of the Notion of a Problem

We have seen that several problems can be suitably described as language recognition, or as language translation, or as function computation problems. Notice now that any mathematically formalized problem can be described in one of the above ways. Formally, it suffices that its domain be denumerable. In fact, in such a case its elements can be put in a bijective correspondence with elements of $\mathbb{N}$, or with the elements of V^*, V being some alphabet. Consequently, the original problem can be restated as the problem of computing a function $f: \mathbb{N} \to \mathbb{N}$, or performing a translation, or as recognizing a language in V^*.

For instance, finding the solutions of a system of equations of the type

$$a_1 x_1 + a_2 x_2 = c_1$$
$$b_1 x_1 + b_2 x_2 = c_2$$

can be described as computing the function f from $\mathbb{Z}^6$ to $\mathbb{R}^2$, where $\mathbb{Z}$ denotes the set of integers and $\mathbb{R}$ the set of rational numbers, defined as

$$f(a_1, a_2, b_1, b_2, c_1, c_2) = \langle r_1, r_2 \rangle$$

r_1, r_2 being the rational numbers, if any, solving the above system. Notice then that $\mathbb{Z}$, and therefore $\mathbb{Z}^6$, can be mapped bijectively onto $\mathbb{N}$. The same holds for $\mathbb{R}^2$, since a rational number can be described as a pair of integers: for any $r \in \mathbb{R}$, $r = m/n$ for some $m, n \in \mathbb{Z}$. Thus the foregoing problem can be reduced to the problem of computing a suitable $f \colon \mathbb{N} \to \mathbb{N}$.

Exercises

2.1 Describe the following problems as functions from $\mathbb{N}$ to $\mathbb{N}$.
  1. Find the maximum among a sequence of integer numbers.
  2. Find a path connecting two nodes of a given graph, if there is one.
  3. Sort an array of n integers.
  4. Sort an array of any number of integers.
2.2 Describe the following problems as language recognition problems.
  1. Check whether or not a formula of propositional calculus is a tautology.
  2. State whether or not a given graph is cyclic.
  3. State whether or not any three points in an integer-squared Cartesian plane lie on the same straight line.

An important remark is now in order. All mathematical formalisms examined so far are discrete; more precisely, they have denumerable mathematical domains, defined in a finite way. Several considerations could be based on this remark. For the moment, let us simply observe that this is certainly in agreement with the digital technology of today's computers. Furthermore, let us recall that continuous formalisms, such as real numbers, historically follow—and are *based on*—natural numbers. One may even say that human thinking and the behavior of the machines invented by humans is essentially based on discrete models and the concept of "continuous" models is only a powerful abstraction, which has to be approximated by discrete models in order to be dominated.

We can conclude that any problem can always be coded in terms of some of the previous schemes. Furthermore, we have already seen in Section 1.4.3 that language translation and function computing are easily reducible to one another. Notice now that even language recognition can be described as a language translation problem, and conversely. In fact, the problem of stating whether or not $x \in L$ for given string x and language L can also be stated as the translation τ_L, where $\tau_L(x) = 1$ if $x \in L$, $\tau_L(x) = 0$ if $x \notin L$. Conversely, given the translation $\tau \colon V_1^* \to V_2^*$, one can define the language

$$L_\tau = \{ z \mid z = x\$y, \text{ with } x \in V_1^*, \, y \in V_2^*, \$ \notin (V_1 \cup V_2) \quad \text{and} \quad y = \tau(x) \}$$

A device recognizing L_τ can be used as a translator to compute τ. In fact, for any x, one can enumerate all $y \in V_2^*$, and verify whether $x\$y \in L$ or not. If this is the case, one concludes that $\tau(x) = y$. Notice that this process terminates if and only if $\tau(x)$ is defined.

Exercises

2.3 The previous process of representing translation as language acceptance is easily implemented by TMs *deciding* L_τ, that is, such that they always halt providing a positive or negative answer to the question: does z belong to L_τ? Show that it can be extended to TMs only *accepting* L_τ.
Warning. This exercise may be rather difficult at present. If you are not able to solve it now, you are invited to go back to it after reading Section 2.8.

2.4 Show that if there exists a TM computing τ_L as defined above, then L can be decided. Instead, if τ_L is defined only as $\tau_L(x) = 1$ if and only if $x \in L$, leaving open the possibility that τ_L be undefined for $x \notin L$, then L can only be accepted.

As a final remark, let us recall from Theorem 1.17 that, unlike other automata, the class of problems that can be solved by TMs is independent of the alphabet chosen to represent them provided that it contains at least two elements.

All the remarks discussed so far lead to the following major conclusion: TMs, and formalisms equivalent to TMs, are the most powerful mechanical problem solvers among those considered so far, no matter how a problem is coded. This fact allows us to concentrate in the following on TMs as problem solvers without bothering on the chosen formalization of the notion of problem.

Exercises

2.5 Consider grammars as function computing formalisms by means of the following convention:

$f \colon \mathbb{N} \to \mathbb{N}$ is "computed" by a grammar G if and only if
$L(G) = \{ a^n b^{f(n)} | n \in \mathbb{N} \}$

Prove that
a. A context-free grammar can compute $f(n) = 2n$.
b.* A context-free grammar cannot compute $f(n) = n^2$.
c. An unrestricted grammar can compute any function computed by some TM.

2.6* Change the convention of Exercise 2.5 into the following: $f \colon \mathbb{N} \to \mathbb{N}$ is computed by G if and only if $L(G) = \{ x\$y | x = $ decimal coding of n, $y = $ decimal coding of $f(n) \}$.
Show that the identity function cannot be computed by context-free grammars.

2.7 Show that if a context-free grammar can compute $f(n)$ according to the convention of Exercise 2.5, then a TM can compute $f(n)$ according to the convention of Exercise 2.6.

2.8 Show that TMs can transform natural numbers coded in unary base into any base $k > 1$ and conversely, whereas FTs cannot.

2.9 Solve Exercise 2.8 by considering PDTs instead of FTs.

2.3 Turing Machines, Programming Languages, and Church's Thesis (Part 1)

So far, we considered TMs and other automata as abstract computing devices. Apparently, real computers and their programming languages do not look very much like abstract automata. However, a little insight shows that the computation of, say, a Pascal program can be realized by a suitable TM. In fact, it suffices to arrange the tapes of the TM in order to store the data on which the program operates and to simulate the execution of any Pascal statement through a sequence of TM moves. It is not difficult to verify that assignments, conditional statements, etc. can be implemented by lengthy sequences of TM moves. Conversely, it is an easy programming exercise to build a Pascal program simulating any given TM provided that the finiteness of memory of the machine can be ignored. These facts are summarized by the following statements.

Statement 2.1
Given any TM M it is possible to build a Pascal program (or a FORTRAN program, a C program, or the like), which simulates M provided that the computer actually running the program has an arbitrarily large amount of storage. □

Statement 2.2
Given any Pascal program (or a FORTRAN program, a C program, etc.) it is possible to build a TM computing the same function computed by the program. □

The details of the proofs are left to the reader as an exercise.

In conclusion, we have discovered that TMs have the same power not only as grammars and as partial recursive functions but also as the more familiar programs we can write in usual high-level languages. It is even possible to formulate the following stronger and more general statement.

Statement 2.3
All known formalisms to model discrete computing devices have at most the power of TMs. □

The foregoing statement, a thorough analysis of the capabilities of TMs, and of mechanical computation in general, led Alonso Church to formulating his landmark thesis:

Church's Thesis (Part 1)
There is no formalism to model any mechanical calculus that is more powerful than TMs and equivalent formalisms.   □

Church's thesis is intrinsically nonprovable because it is based on the intuitive notion of what "mechanical calculus" is: It is supported only by previous experience and by intuitive evidence. On its basis, if we have shown that a problem can (or cannot) be solved by any TM, we can deduce that the same problem can (or cannot) be solved by any existing mathematical computation model nor by any conceivable computing mechanism. The lesson is: Do not try to solve mechanically what cannot be solved by TMs!

2.4 Algorithms and Church's Thesis (Part 2)

"Algorithm" is probably the fundamental concept in computer science. Intuitively, by algorithm we mean a procedure to solve a problem by means of an automatic computing device, such as a digital computer. Algorithms are also intended as an abstract way to describing computer programs: A computer program—be it coded in assembly language or in a high-level language—is a sequence of commands that once executed by the computer, can solve a given problem. These commands, however, depend on the particular chosen computer or high-level language. Consequently, the commands to compute $\sqrt{x^2 + y^2}$ with an error less than 0.01 by means of a mainframe will probably differ from those to compute the same result on a personal computer. Also, a program to sort an array in FORTRAN differs from a program to sort an array in Pascal. However, there is some intuitive evidence that different programs coded in different languages may actually implement the "same solution," independent of the differences of code. This is exactly the case of the two programs given in Figure 2.1a and in Figure 2.1b. One program (*P1SORT*) is written in Pascal and the other (*P2SORT*) is written in FORTRAN.

In conclusion, the notion of algorithm is intended to capture the notion of the abstract sequence of commands to solve a problem in a mechanical way, independent of the particular chosen processor, i.e., the particular language chosen to code it. Thus, we intuitively claim that both programs *P1SORT* and *P2SORT* above implement the same algorithm, which can be more abstractly (and informally) described as follows:

Algorithm "Sort by Straight Insertion"

Step 1: Read the array a to be sorted (n is the number of its elements)
Step 2: Let i denote a variable which takes all values in the range 2 to n. For each of these values repeat the following procedure.

```
Program P1SORT (input, output);
                const n = 20;
                var  i, j, x: integer;
                    a: array [0..n] of integer;
        begin for i := 1 to n do read (a[i]);
            for i := 2 to n do
                begin x := a[i]; a[0] := x; j := i − 1;
                while x < a[j] do
                        begin a[j + 1] := a[j]; j := j − 1;
                        end;
                    a[j + 1] := x;
                end;
            for i := 1 to n do write (a[i])
        end P1SORT.
```

(a)

```
C  P2 SORT
   PARAMETER (N = 20)
   INTEGER X
   INTEGER A(21)
C  IN THE FORTRAN IMPLEMENTATION INDEXES VARY BETWEEN 1 AND 21
   DO 73 I = 2, N + 1
   READ (5,75)A(I)
73 CONTINUE
   DO 77 I = 3, N + 1
   X = A(I)
   A(1) = X
   J = I − 1
78 IF(X.GE.A(J)) GO TO 79
   A(J + 1) = A(J)
   J = J − 1
   GO TO 78
79 A(J + 1) = X
77 CONTINUE
75 FORMAT (I5)
   DO 74 J = 2, N + 1
   WRITE (6,75) A(J)
74 CONTINUE
   STOP
   END
```

(b)

FIGURE 2.1   Two programs to sort arrays. (a) Pascal version. (b) FORTRAN version.

2.1. Split a into two subsequences $s_1 = a_1, \ldots, a_{i-1}$ and $s_2 = a_i, \ldots, a_n$ in such a way that s_1 always happens to be ordered. (Note that at the initial step this is trivially true since $i = 2$.)

2.2. Insert a_i in its appropriate place within s_1.
   This is performed by

2.2.1. Storing a_i into a temporary variable x.

2.2.2. Shifting all elements a_j greater than x one step rightwards in such a way that an array position is left free and later loaded with the value stored in x.

This step can be specified in further detail as

2.2.2.1. Temporarily store x into a_0.

2.2.2.2. Let j denote a current variable starting from $j = i - 1$.

2.2.2.3. Compare x with a_j and if $x < a_j$ shift a_j one step rightwards, that is, assign a_j to a_{j+1}. Decrement j by 1.

2.2.2.4. Repeat 2.2.2.3 until $x \geq a_j$.
(Note that step 2.2.2.3 will be repeated at most i times since $x = a_0$.)

2.2.2.5. Insert x in position $j + 1$.   □

The advantages of describing problem solutions in a way that abstracts away from the specific details of a programming language (in particular, see the case of *P2SORT*) should be evident, especially from the point of view of understandability. Unfortunately, the concept of an algorithm is necessarily informal, and any attempt to describe it formally would result in the definition of a new, abstract (mathematical) or physical processor and of its language. FAs, TMs, PDAs, machine languages, and higher-level languages all provide different notations for translating informally described algorithms into formally defined and executable codes. The main difference between automata and programming languages is that automata are more suitable to mathematically proving properties whereas computer languages are more supportive of efficient implementations.

Even though the concept of an algorithm is an informal one, it is possible to state several (informal) properties that capture its deepest essence.

1. An algorithm must consist of a finite sequence of statements.
2. Any statement must be immediately executable by some mechanical computing processor, that is, there must exist an agent who is able to understand statements univocally and to execute them by producing precise and predictable results.
3. The computing processor is provided with memory devices where intermediate results can be saved.
4. Computation is discrete, that is, the information is coded in digital form and computation proceeds through discrete steps.

The previous four features correspond to our experience with modern digital computers. Further general assumptions on algorithms are

5. Algorithms are executed deterministically. For our present purposes, stochastic and nondeterministic computation models, of the type discussed in Section 1.7, are not considered for at least two reasons. First, our everyday experience shows that in practice mechanical computations are performed deterministi-

cally. Second, we have learned that the power of TMs cannot be further increased by the introduction of nondeterminism (see Theorem 1.25).

6. There is no finite bound on input and output data. This corresponds to the fact that a computer can input and output arbitrarily long streams of characters via a terminal. Correspondingly, all abstract automata have unbounded input and output tapes.

7. There is no bound on the available amount of storage required to perform computations. This is a crucial point: We all know that any physical computer has a limited number of registers of limited size and a bounded, though large, main memory. Even if we add mass storage, the total amount of available memory can never be infinite. On the other hand, we have seen in Section 1.3.3 that in order to recognize the simple language $\{a^n b^n | n \geq 1\}$ the bounded memory of a finite state automaton is not sufficient. The maximal computation power of TMs is achieved thanks to its unbounded memory. However, this remark should not lead to the conclusion that the finite state automaton is the only realistic computation model. Insofar as physical memory devices are not saturated they can be considered as unbounded. If the main memory of a computer is never completely filled up during a computation, we can assume that it is unbounded with respect to that particular computation. The problem is that it is not always possible to foresee the needed amount of storage to perform any computation: For this reason all real computation machines are provided with overflow mechanisms. Such mechanisms warn the user that in a particular case the computation performed by the computer does not correspond to the ideal computation that would be performed by an abstract automaton modeling the actual computer and without memory limitations.

Although we can assume that we can always implement any abstract automaton, including a TM, by adding new storage whenever required by the computation, we see in the next chapter that there are several other reasons why many computations that can be performed by some abstract automaton cannot be implemented in practice.

8. There is no bound on the number of discrete steps required to perform a computation: Even infinite computations may occur.[1] This fact perfectly agrees with the fact that TM computations may never stop (see also the discussion of Section 2.6).

Exercise

2.10 Write a computer program simulating a PDA that recognizes $L = \{a^n b^n | n \geq 1\}$. The program must also recognize when it does not properly simulate the automaton and warn the user accordingly.

---

[1] Other authors require algorithms to terminate after a finite number of discrete steps for any value of input data.

We can now review Church's thesis from a more complete point of view: Its relevance is not just that all existing formalisms are not more powerful than TMs: It states that no algorithm can solve a problem that cannot be solved by TM. In fact, it is now clear that if we are able to describe an algorithm to solve a problem in a precise—though informal—way, we would be able also to design a TM to solve the same problem, even if this process happens to be quite lengthy and tedious in most cases. Therefore we can restate Church's thesis in a more general way.

Church's Thesis (Part 2)
Any algorithm can be coded in terms of a TM (or an equivalent formalism).   □

Thus, in the following the terms "algorithmic," "mechanic," "effective," and "computable" will be used interchangeably.

The second formulation of Church's thesis allows us to address the question d raised in Section 2.1 in quite a general way. That is, we can investigate the limits of mechanical computation independent of problem formalization and of the particular computation model. This is exactly the main purpose of the rest of this chapter.

2.5 Turing Machine Enumeration and Universal Turing Machines

So far, we have been studying TMs as devices that can solve a given, predefined problem. The specific problem a TM can solve is defined by function δ, and therefore it is built into the structure of the machine. As such, TMs can be viewed as abstract special purpose nonprogrammable computers. Once a program is loaded into the read-only memory (ROM) of the special-purpose computer, the machine can execute just that program.

An obvious question arises at this point: Can TMs model programmable computers? That is, can TMs model general problem solving devices where the problem to be solved is not encoded into the structure of the device but rather is provided as input to the device? We will see that this problem leads to the concept of a universal TM.

Another fundamental issue discussed in the next section is whether TMs can compute all functions from $\mathbb{N}$ to $\mathbb{N}$. Since the answer is negative, we will investigate the notion of "unsolvable problem" and we will discuss several important concepts of the theory of computation.

In order to go deep into these fundamental issues, we need to equip ourselves with some background results concerning the enumeration of TMs. Section 2.5.1 is devoted to this point. Subsequently, Section 2.5.2 discusses universal TMs and Section 2.6 addresses the issue of unsolvable problems.

2.5.1 Turing Machine Enumeration

For any given alphabet A, the set $\{TM_A\}$ of TMs having A as a set of symbols can be enumerated (i.e., a bijection $\mathscr{E}: \mathbb{N} \to \{TM_A\}$ can be stated). Let us analyze in some detail this fundamental fact of the theory of computation.

In order to simplify the notation , we restrict our attention to the case of single-tape TMs. However, it will be clear that the same reasoning can be applied as well to any class of TMs.

For a given number k, there exists a finite number of TMs with A as set of symbols and exactly k states because the number of different ways to define the transition function δ is finite as δ has finite domain and range. Precisely, since for any finite D, R there are exactly $|R|^{|D|}$ different total functions f, where $f: D \to R$, there are exactly $(1 + 3 \cdot |Q| \cdot |A|)^{|Q| \cdot |A|}$ TMs with symbol set A and state space Q. In fact δ can take any value in $Q \times A \times \{R, L, S\}$, or it can be undefined, in which case we write $\delta(q, i) = \perp$. Thus, if h denotes A's cardinality there are $(1 + 3 \cdot h \cdot k)^{h \cdot k}$ TMs with k states.

Now, let us order the $(1 + 3 \cdot h \cdot k)^{h \cdot k}$ TMs with k states in some systematic way, for example, in *lexicographic order*: Impose any order on $Q, A, \{R, L, S\}$, for example.

$$q_0 < q_1 \ldots < q_{k-1}, \not{b} = a_0 < a_1 \ldots < a_{h-1}, R < L < S$$

Then, for $q, q' \in Q$, $a, a' \in A$, $m, m' \in \{R, L, S\}$, define

- $\langle q, a \rangle < \langle q', a' \rangle$ if and only if $(q < q') \vee ((q = q') \wedge (a < a'))$, that is, $\langle q_0, \not{b} \rangle < \langle q_1, a_1 \rangle$, $\langle q_0, a_2 \rangle < \langle q_1, \not{b} \rangle$, $\langle q_1, \not{b} \rangle < \langle q_1, a_1 \rangle$, etc.
- $\perp < \langle q, a, m \rangle$
- $\langle q, a, m \rangle < \langle q', a', m' \rangle$ if and only if

$$(q < q') \vee ((q = q') \wedge (a < a')) \vee ((q = q') \wedge (a = a') \wedge (m < m'))$$

Figure 2.2 explains the rationale of lexicographic ordering.

Finally, define $M < M'$, M and M' being two k-states single-tape TMs, if and only if there exists a pair $\langle q, a \rangle$ such that $\delta(q, a) < \delta'(q, a)$ and for any

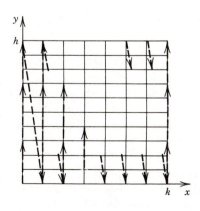

FIGURE 2.2 The rationale of lexicographic ordering. $\langle x, y \rangle < \langle x', y' \rangle$ with $0 \le x, x' \le k$, $0 \le y, y' \le h$ if and only if the dotted line goes from $\langle x, y \rangle$ to $\langle x', y' \rangle$.

$(q', a') < (q, a)$, $\delta(q', a') = \delta'(q', a')$. In other words, M precedes M' in the lexicographic order if, in the first pair $\langle q, a \rangle$ where their transition functions differ, the value of δ is less than the value of δ'. On the basis of this ordering we can *effectively build* for any k, the first, the second, ... the $(1 + 3 \cdot h \cdot k)^{h \cdot k}$-th TM with k states.

At this point, an enumeration of all TMs can be obtained as follows. First, enumerate all one-state TMs according to the given order. Then enumerate all two-state TMs, and so on. As a result, we obtain a bijection

$$\mathscr{E}: \mathbb{N} \rightarrow \{\mathrm{TM}_A\}$$

The foregoing construction can be easily implemented by an algorithm. In other words it is easy to build a program, in any programming language, that outputs all elements of $\{\mathrm{TM}_A\}$ in their lexicographic order. Such a program would necessarily never terminate because the set $\{\mathrm{TM}_A\}$ is infinite. However, it can be easily transformed into an (always terminating) program computing $\mathscr{E}$, that is, a program that receives as input a natural number, n, and produces as output a description of the nth TM.

Exercises

2.11 Write two Pascal programs which, for any A contained in the set of Pascal characters, compute the following functions.

$$\mathscr{E}: \mathbb{N} \rightarrow \{\mathrm{TM}_A\}$$
$$\mathscr{E}^{-1}: \{\mathrm{TM}_A\} \rightarrow \mathbb{N}$$

2.12 Outline the definition of a TM that enumerates all members of $\{\mathrm{TM}_A\}$, for any fixed alphabet A. It is not necessary to specify all the details of the construction of such machine, but you must show that you actually know how it can be done.

2.13 Outline an effective enumeration of all multitape TMs with given input, memory (output) alphabets I, $\Gamma(O)$. Notice that the number of memory tapes is not fixed a priori.

Often, an enumeration that can be computed by some TM is called *Gödelization*, in honor of K. Gödel, the mathematician who first applied this technique to derive fundamental results of mathematical logic and computation theory. (Remember that in Section 0.2.4.3 we gave the original Gödelization of arithmetic entities.) The natural number bijectively associated by such enumeration to a formal object, here a TM, is called the *Gödel number* of the object. Thus, in the above enumeration $\mathscr{E}$, any TM is bijectively identified by its Gödel number.

We know that a TM M, be it single-tape or multitape, can be used to compute a function $f_M: D \rightarrow R$, where D and R are suitably coded into M's alphabet, or to recognize a language L_M over an alphabet suitably coded into

M's alphabet, provided that M's alphabet has a cardinality ≥ 2. Thus, from the foregoing enumeration of TMs we can deduce an effective enumeration of all computable functions from any given domain to any given range, and an effective enumeration of all acceptable languages over a given alphabet. To summarize, we have obtained the following fundamental statement.

Statement 2.4

1. For any alphabet A, the set $\{TM_A\}$ of TMs over alphabet A can be enumerated algorithmically, that is, an algorithmic bijection $\mathscr{E}: \mathbb{N} \rightarrow \{TM_A\}$ can always be stated.
2. All algorithmically computable functions can be algorithmically enumerated.
3. All algorithmically recognizable languages can be algorithmically enumerated.

$\square$

Notice that, although $\mathscr{E}$ is a bijective function, enumerations of computable functions and of recognizable languages are not bijective functions, as it happens that several (actually an infinite number of) TMs compute the same function.

For convenience, in the following of this chapter we mainly refer to TMs as devices computing functions from $\mathbb{N}$ to $\mathbb{N}$. For any function f, with $f: D \rightarrow R$, where D and R are other than $\mathbb{N}$, we will implicitly assume a coding of D and R in terms of $\mathbb{N}$. Furthermore, M_y will denote the yth TM in the above enumeration, that is, $M_y = \mathscr{E}(y)$, and f_y will denote the function computed by M_y.

Exercise

2.14 Show that, for any given x, y, the function g defined as the composition $f_x \circ f_y$, that is, $g(w) = f_x(f_y(w))$, is computable, that is, there exists an index z such that g is f_z.

Also, show that not only g is computable, but also there exists a *computable function h*: $\mathbb{N} \times \mathbb{N} \rightarrow \mathbb{N}$ such that, for any x, y, the value $z = h(x, y)$ is such that $g = f_z$. In other words, given the (Gödel numbers of) TMs computing two given functions, one can effectively build (the Gödel number of) a TM computing their composition.

Finally, notice that $g(w)$ is defined if and only if $f_y(w)$ is defined and $f_x(f_y(w))$ is defined, that is, both the computation of M_y with input w *and* the computation of M_x with input $f_y(w)$ must terminate in order to ensure termination of M_z.

Hint: Outline an algorithm that receives as input a description of M_y and M_x and produces as output the description of a TM, M, which "concatenates" their computations. M first simulates M_y on any input. Then, if and when M_y terminates its computation, M simulates the behavior of M_x on the result produced by M_y's simulation. Then compute M's Gödel number, z. Because all this is performed by an algorithm, the function h is computable by some TM.

2.5.2 Universal Turing Machines

Consider the enumeration discussed in Section 2.5.1: $\mathscr{E}: \mathbb{N} \to \{TM_A\}$. Define a new function $g: \mathbb{N} \times \mathbb{N} \to \mathbb{N}$ where $g(x, y) = f_y(x)$. $g(x, y)$ is the integer value, if any, computed by the yth TM as a consequence of the input value x. Function $g(x, y)$ can also be seen as a function $\tilde{g}: \mathbb{N} \to \mathbb{N}$, provided that a suitable TM-computable bijection from $\mathbb{N} \times \mathbb{N}$ to $\mathbb{N}$ is defined. In order to simplify the notation let us use the same symbol g for $\tilde{g}$ too.

Now, the question naturally arises whether g is a TM-computable function, that is, there exists $i \in \mathbb{N}$, such that $f_i = g$. The answer to this question is positive. In fact, we can organize the computation of $g(n)$ into the following steps.

Step 1: Choose a finite alphabet A to code natural numbers and any other possible information needed for the computation.
We already know that any A, with $|A| \geq 2$, will work.

Step 2: Translate the representation of n into a suitable representation of the pair $\langle x, y \rangle$ represented by n. The decimal representation of n may be translated into the two decimal representation of x and y, separated by a marker \$. If we choose the bijection $d: \mathbb{N} \times \mathbb{N} \to \mathbb{N}$ defined by $d(x, y) = [(x + y + 1)(x + y)]/2 + x$ (see Section 1.4.4), then $n = 18$ is translated into "3\$2".

Step 3: Translate number y into a suitable encoding of the yth TM in the $\mathscr{E}$ enumeration (i.e., M_y).

Step 4: Simulate the computation of M_y on x.

We already know how steps 1 and 2 can be done. Let us examine here more closely how M_y can be encoded. Figure 2.3a illustrates the portion of tape that encodes the transition defined by

$$\delta(p, a) = \langle q, b, m \rangle$$

Figure 2.3b illustrates the case where $\delta(q, a)$ is undefined. In Figure 2.3, overscored symbols (such as $\bar{p}, \bar{q}, \ldots$) stand for the encoding of the corresponding TM entity (i.e., $p, q, \ldots$). Special symbols \$ and \# are used only as

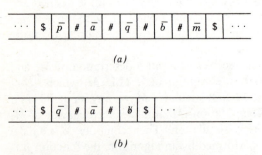

(a)

(b)

FIGURE 2.3 Encoding of M_y (a) $\delta(p, a) = \langle q, b, m \rangle$. (b) $\delta(q, a)$ is undefined.

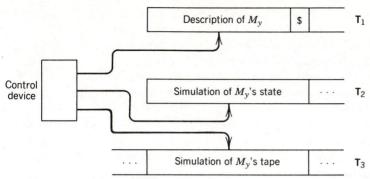

FIGURE 2.4 A TM simulating M_y.

separators and cannot appear elsewhere. In particular, a pair of $ enclose the tape portion that encodes each value of δ. Values of δ are given for all elements of $Q \times A$, Q and A being the set of states and the input set of M_y, respectively.

It is clear that step 3 is TM computable too, that is, there exists a TM able to translate the (coding of the) natural number y into the above description of M_y.

Finally, step 4 can also be performed by a TM, as outlined as follows in the case of a multitape TM. Our TM uses one tape to store the description of M_y as shown in Figure 2.3, one tape to simulate the current state of M_y at each computation step, and one tape to simulate the contents of M_y's tape at each computation step. The third tape is infinite on both sides, as M_y's tape is (see Figure 2.4).

The computation of our "simulator" TM (STM) consists of a sequence of *macrosteps*. Each macrostep simulates the execution of one computation step of M_y and is organized as the following sequence of actions $m1$ through $m4$.

$m1$. Initialization of the macrostep:
- The heads of T_1 and T_2 are positioned on the first cells of the tapes. Let $\bar{q}_c$ be the contents of T_2.
- T_3's head is positioned on the first location of the tape portion corresponding to the location where the M_y's head would be positioned in the real case.
- q_{INIT} is the current state of STM.

$m2$. STM looks within T_1 for a portion of tape bracketed by two consecutive $, such that the first element is $\bar{q}_c$ and the second element is $\bar{a}_c$, $\bar{a}_c$ being the coding of the symbol that would be read by M_y. It must eventually find such a portion of tape. When it does, it enters a new state q_{FOUND}.

$m3$. When STM enters q_{FOUND} if the retrieved portion of T_1 denotes an undefined transition, then STM enters a new state q_{HALT} and halts, as M_y would do. Otherwise, STM performs the following actions.
- Substitute $\bar{q}_c$ in T_2 with the third element of the retrieved portion of T_1, that is, with the description of the new state of M_y, say $\bar{q}_N$.

- Substitute $\bar{a}_c$ in $\mathbf{T}_3$ with the fourth element of the retrieved portion of $\mathbf{T}_1$; that is, rewrite $\mathbf{T}_3$ as M_y would do with its input tape.
- Move $\mathbf{T}_3$'s head as specified by the fifth element of the retrieved portion of $\mathbf{T}_1$; that is, simulate the movement of M_y's head.

Notice that, if the coding an any single symbol of M_y is a string longer than a single character, then $\mathbf{T}_3$'s head could move, during any macrostep, through several cells.

m4. After *m3*, if STM did not enter state q_{HALT}, it goes back to the same situation as described in *m1*. At this point, the move of M_y has been completely simulated and the macrostep is completed; STM is ready to perform a new macrostep.

Exercise

2.15 Detail the macrosteps of STM into a complete formal description of the machine.

Let us go back to our starting problem: Is g a TM-computable function? We have used a constructive approach to solve the problem. Each step (1 through 4) of the construction can be performed by a TM; thus we can define a single TM that performs all of them. In conclusion, we have proved the following statement.

Statement 2.5
There exists a TM that is able to compute $g(x, y) = f_y(x)$. □

Such a TM is called a *universal Turing machine* (UTM), because it is able to simulate the behavior of any other TM. The UTM built by the above construction has a larger alphabet than the machines it simulates. However, this simplifying assumption can be easily removed. Thus we obtain that, in $\{TM_A\}$ there are infinitely many UTMs.

Exercise

2.16 Show how a UTM can simulate itself.

Statement 2.5 gives a positive answer to the question raised at the beginning of Section 2.5. Indeed, the TM formalism can model general purpose computers via UTMs. The encoding of M_y in tape $\mathbf{T}_1$ of the UTM of Figure 2.4 corresponds to the computer program that is executed by the machine. Also note that the issues discussed here in the case of TMs can be extended to any formalism equivalent to TMs. Pascal programs can be enumerated much like TMs. Also, one can write a Pascal program (an interpreter) that simulates the execution of any other Pascal program, and so on.

2.6 Unsolvable Problems

All computable functions $f: \mathbb{N} \to \mathbb{N}$ can be enumerated; this statement has been investigated in Section 2.5.1. On the other hand, it is well known that the cardinality of the class $\mathscr{F}$ of functions on $\mathbb{N}$, where $\mathscr{F} = \{ f | f: \mathbb{N} \to \mathbb{N} \}$, is a $2^{\aleph_0}$: it is the so called cardinality of continuum, as it is the same as the cardinality of the set of real numbers (see Section 0.1.1). Therefore, roughly speaking, a vast majority of functions on $\mathbb{N}$ cannot be computed.

This fact should not be considered as a disaster by itself. In fact, it is true that the class of all functions $f: \mathbb{N} \to \mathbb{N}$ has the cardinality of continuum, but—intuitively—we are only interested in computing the functions we can in some way "define." But what does "define" mean exactly?

Whatever it means (whether formal or informal) when we choose to define a function, we will ultimately use a language to express it (i.e., a set of strings on some alphabet). For example, we can use predicate calculus or English, but ultimately a function will be denoted by some sentence of some denumerable language. So, a function could be expressed by the string $f(x) = (2x) + x^2$ as well as by the sentence "Multiply x by 2, then compute x square and finally add the two results." But both English and the set of arithmetic expressions are denumerable sets, as they are subsets of some free monoid on some finite alphabet. As a result, the class $\mathscr{FD}$ of functions denotable by a language is still denumerable.

$\mathscr{FD}$ contains exactly all practically interesting functions. Thus, we can still hope that the class $\mathscr{FD}$ coincides with the class of *computable functions*. Unfortunately, this hope too will be frustrated, by virtue of the following fundamental theorem. As usual, let M_y denote the yth TM according to the $\mathscr{E}$ enumeration of Section 2.5.1 and let f_y denote the function computed by M_y.

Theorem 2.6
No TM can compute the total function $g: \mathbb{N} \times \mathbb{N} \to \{0, 1\}$ defined as

$g(x, y) = $ **if** $f_y(x) \neq \perp$ (i.e., M_y comes to a halt in a final state on reading x so that $f_y(x)$ is defined)

   then 1 **else** 0

Proof
By contradiction, suppose that g is computable. Thus the partial function h defined as

$h(x) = $ **if** $g(x, x) = 0$ **then** 1 **else** $\perp$

is computable. In fact, once we have a TM M that computes g, it is quite easy to modify it to compute h: It is sufficient to transform the result 0 into 1 and to force the new machine never to halt whenever M would produce the result 1.

Let x_0 be the Gödel number of some TM M_{x_0} computing h: i.e., $f_{x_0} = h$. Thus, by definition of h, if $h(x_0) = f_{x_0}(x_0)$ is defined, $h(x_0) = 1$ and $g(x_0, x_0) = 0$. But, by definition of $g(x, y)$, this implies $f_{x_0}(x_0)$ to be undefined.

Otherwise, if $h(x_0)$ is undefined, $g(x_0, x_0) = 1$ which, in turn, means that $f_{x_0}(x_0) = h(x_0)$ is defined.

In both cases we obtain a contradiction; thus g is not computable. ∎

In other words, Theorem 2.6 states that no TM can decide whether any TM will halt for any input value.[2] Before commenting and analyzing the profound consequences of this result, let us list some other negative statements on the power of TMs which are strictly related to Theorem 2.6.

Corollary 2.7
No TM can compute the total function k defined by

$$k(x) = \textbf{if } f_x(x) \neq \perp \textbf{ then } 1 \textbf{ else } 0$$

Proof
The proof follows the previous proof of Theorem 2.6. First define

$$h(x) = \textbf{if } k(x) = 0 \textbf{ then } 1 \textbf{ else } \perp$$

Then observe that h is computable if k is computable. Let x_0 be the Gödel number of some TM, M_{x_0}, computing h: that is, $h = f_{x_0}$. But $h(x_0) = 1$ would imply $f_{x_0}(x_0) = h(x_0) = \perp$ and $h(x_0) = \perp$ would imply $h(x_0) = 1$, that is, $f_{x_0}(x_0) = h(x_0) = 1$. In both cases, we obtain a contradiction. ∎

The following theorem shows that no mechanical computation can verify whether the function computed by any TM is totally defined or not over (the input domain) $\mathbb{N}$.

Theorem 2.8
There is no TM computing the function k given by

$$k(x) = \textbf{if } f_x \text{ is total (i.e., it is defined for all naturals)}$$
$$\textbf{then } 1 \textbf{ else } 0$$

Proof
Once again, the proof is by contradiction. Suppose k is total and computable. Thus function $g: \mathbb{N} \to \mathbb{N}$, such that $g(x) = w$, w being the Gödel number of the xth TM in the $\mathscr{E}$ enumeration computing a total function f_w is total and computable too. In fact, we can enumerate all TMs by means of a TM. For each of them, we check whether it computes a total function or not, and thus we

---

[2] Notice that Theorem 2.6 states that no TM can decide whether any TM will halt *in a final state* for any input. But each TM can always be built in such a way that it eventually halts if and only if it reaches a final state.

obtain an effective enumeration of all TMs computing total functions. Since, for each z, there exists a $z' > z$ such that $f_{z'}$ is total, $g(x)$ is total too.

Consider now the function h defined by

$$h(x) = f_{g(x)}(x) + 1 = f_w(x) + 1$$

Since for every x, $f_{g(x)}$ is total and computable, so is h. Since g is total and strictly monotonic (i.e., $x' > x$ implies $g(x') > g(x)$), g^{-1} is a function defined on $W = \{$Gödel numbers of TMs computing total functions$\}$ and clearly is computable if g is computable.

Let w_0 be the Gödel number of a TM computing h. Since h is total, $g^{-1}(w_0)$ is defined: Let $x_0 = g^{-1}(w_0)$. Thus, by definition of h:

$$h(x_0) = f_{g(x_0)}(x_0) + 1 = f_{w_0}(x_0) + 1$$

But h is f_{w_0} and thus $h(x_0) = f_{w_0}(x_0)$: a contradiction. ∎

Exercises

2.17 Following the lines of the previous proofs by contradiction, prove that there is no TM computing the function g defined by:

$$g(x, y, z) = \text{if } f_x(y) = z \text{ then } 1 \text{ else } 0.$$

2.18* Prove that there is no TM deciding whether, for any x, the function computed by M_x is constant or not. That is, show that the function g defined by

$$g(x) = \text{if } f_x \text{ is constant then } 1 \text{ else } 0$$

cannot be computed by any TM.

2.19* Show that there is no TM computing any of the functions defined in the following way.

$-\ g_1(x, y) = \text{if } y \in I_{f_x} \text{ then } 1 \text{ else } 0$

   (Recall from Section 0.1.1 that I_f denotes the image of f.)

$-\ g_2(x, y) = \text{if } f_x \text{ coincides with } f_y$ (i.e., M_x and M_y compute

                             the same function)

      then 1 **else** 0

$-\ g_3(x) = \text{if } I_{f_x} \text{ is finite then } 1 \text{ else } 0$

2.20 Show that, for any fixed z_0, there is no TM computing the function g defined by

$$g(x) = \text{if } z_0 \in I_{f_x} \text{ then } 1 \text{ else } 0$$

2.21 For any fixed x_0, discuss whether the function g defined by

$$g(z) = \text{if } z \in D_{f_{x_0}} \text{ then } 1 \text{ else } 0$$

is computable by a TM or not. (Recall that D_f denotes the definition domain of function f.)

2.22   Answer the same question as in Exercise 2.21 by replacing $D_{f_{x_0}}$ with $I_{f_{x_0}}$. *Warning*: If you have not been able to solve some of the above exercises, we advise you to go back to them after reading Sections 2.7, 2.8, and 2.9.

Let us evaluate the impact of the previous statements in their own perspective. First, we now definitely know that there are problems that cannot be solved mechanically (or algorithmically). This fact does not prevent the possibility to find a solution for such problems: If a problem cannot be solved by TMs (i.e., by any algorithm), one can always hope to solve it by means of human ingenuity.

Second, the scope of the statements and of the used proof techniques goes far beyond the strict mathematical results we have proved. In fact, Theorem 2.6 can be restated in a more general framework as the impossibility to decide mechanically whether a given algorithm, no matter the language in which it is coded, will ultimately halt for a given input. Similarly, Theorem 2.8 ensures that no algorithm can decide whether a given program will halt for all possible inputs. Notice also that the used proof techniques are not strictly related to the TM formalism. They could be directly applied to, say, Pascal programs, given an algorithmic enumeration thereof and a convention to state which problem is solved by the xth program of the enumeration.

Finally, we like to comment on the consequences of the fact that TMs define *partial functions*. In fact, function g used in the proof of Theorem 2.6 is uncomputable just because it is total. If we restrict it to the following function g' given by

$$g'(x, y) = \textbf{if } f_y(x) \neq \perp \textbf{ then } 1 \textbf{ else } \perp$$

it is easy to verify that g' is computable. In fact, it is just a slight modification of the function computed by a UTM. All these remarks are thoroughly discussed in the following sections.

2.7   More on Solvable and Unsolvable Problems

We now know that there exist unsolvable problems or, equivalently, uncomputable functions. To go deeper into these computability issues, we must be aware that there are problems for which there is no proof of their unsolvability. This rather intricate sentence, on the other hand, by no means provides a way to solve such problems. An example should clarify these statements.

We have proved that there is no TM that can decide whether or not any TM will eventually halt for any input. Suppose now we have to deal with a particular TM, say $M_{\bar{y}}$, to which we wish to supply a particular input, say $\bar{x}$. Let $f_{\bar{y}}$ be the function computed by $M_{\bar{y}}$. Of course, it may happen that we are not able to state whether or not $M_{\bar{y}}$ will eventually halt when supplied with input $\bar{x}$. Can we prove that, actually, this problem is unsolvable, as well as the more general problem of stating whether or not $f_y(x)$ is defined for any $\langle x, y \rangle$? Well, it is useless to look for *such a proof* because it simply *does not exist*. In fact, suppose by contradiction that the proof exists. Now, either $f_{\bar{y}}(\bar{x})$ is defined or not. If it is defined, $M_{\bar{y}}$ would halt when supplied with $\bar{x}$, but in this case $M_{\bar{y}}$ itself would contradict the claim that there does not exist any TM solving the problem. To avoid the contradiction, we must conclude that $f_{\bar{y}}(\bar{x})$ is not defined; but again we would have solved the above problem. In conclusion: Assuming the existence of a proof of unsolvability leads to a solution for our problem, but this does not imply that the problem can be solved!

To state it in another way, the foregoing problem can be also formulated as the function h given by

$$h(w) = \textbf{if } f_{\bar{y}}(\bar{x}) \neq \perp \textbf{ then } 1 \textbf{ else } 0$$

The above definition shows that h is either the constant function 1, or it is the constant function 0. Predicate "$f_{\bar{y}}(\bar{x})$ is defined" does not contain any variable (i.e., it is a closed wf (see Section 0.2.3)); thus it is either true or false. Consequently, function h is computable, because it is either the constant function 0 or the constant function 1, each of which is computable. However, we do not know how to compute h, even if we know it is computable.

In order to clarify this rather intricate and subtle point, let us consider this further example: The well-known Fermat's Last Theorem. The theorem states that one cannot find four integer values x, y, z, n, with $n > 2$, such that $x^n + y^n = z^n$. It is just folklore that this theorem has not yet been proved nor disproved.

Now, the function h given by

$$h(w) = \textbf{if } \text{Fermat's Last Theorem is true } \textbf{then } 1 \textbf{ else } 0$$

is certainly computable because it is either the constant function 1 ($h(w) = 1$ for all w), or the constant function 0 ($f(w) = 0$ for all w). Both of them are computable. However, we do not know, at present, which one it is, therefore we are not able to compute it even if we know that it is computable.

This fact has a quite general scope. Whenever a problem has either a positive or a negative answer it cannot be undecidable, because it is equivalent either to computing the constant function 1 or to computing the constant function 0. However, this does not imply that the solution can actually be found.

Algorithmic problem unsolvability may occur only in the case where infinitely many cases (arguments of a function, strings of a language) are to be considered.

Let us consider one more example.

Example 2.1

Consider the function $g: \mathbb{N} \to \{0, 1, \ldots, 9\}$ defined as $g(x) = x$th digit in the decimal representation of real number π. One might wonder whether g is computable, since π is not a rational number. However, numerical analysis provides algorithms to compute an approximation of π for any chosen value $\epsilon > 0$ of the error bound. Thus, we have algorithms to compute a decimal approximation of π such that the xth digit is exact, for any integer x. So $g(x)$ is computable: There exists a TM M_y that computes a function f_y such that $g = f_y$. Furthermore, we can actually find such a y.

Now, let us consider a new function g_1:

$g_1(x) = $ **if** there exists a sequence of exactly x consecutive 5 in the decimal
expansion of π
then 1 **else** 0

Here the foregoing numerical methods do not allow us to conclude that g_1 is computable. In fact, for any given x we might start a computation of the never-ending decimal expansion of π. Two cases might occur at any given time: Either a sequence of exactly x consecutive 5 has been found or not. In the former case we might conclude that $g_1(x) = 1$ and stop our computation, but in the latter case no conclusion could be drawn. On the other hand, this does not allow us to conclude that g_1 is not computable. An algorithm to compute g_1 could still be invented by some ingenious scientist. It could even happen that a theorem of the type "For any given x there exist x consecutive 5 in the expansion of π" will be proved: in this case $g_1(x)$ would be identically equal to 1.

A long time ago, the same kind of uncertainty existed for the function h defined by

$h(x) = $ **if** there exists a sequence of x consecutive 5
in the expansion of $741/2339$
then 1 **else** 0

which we now know to be computable.

Let us modify our problem slightly by considering the following function g_2.

$g_2(x) = $ **if** there exists a sequence of *at least*
x consecutive 5 in the decimal expansion of π
then 1 **else** 0

In this case g_2 is certainly computable, as it is necessarily of one of the two types that follow.

a. There exists k such that

$g_2(x) = $ **if** $x < k$ **then** 1 **else** 0

b. $g_2(x) = 1$ (i.e., g_2 is identically equal to 1)

In case (b), g_2 is a constant function and therefore it is clearly computable. In case (a) it is computable too, whichever the value of k is. The problem is that we do not know neither if we are in case (a) or (b), nor, when g_2 is of type 1, which is the actual value of k. Thus we know that there exists a y such that $g_2 = f_y$, but we do not know which one it is. Again, it might happen that at some future time such a y will be actually found. As far as this does not happen, we should not try to prove that the problem of finding such a y is mechanically unsolvable.

Exercises

2.23 Are the following functions computable?

1. $h_1(x) =$ **if** the decimal coding of x occurs within the decimal expansion of π
    then 1 **else** 0.
2. $h_2(x) =$ **if** 5 occurs after the xth digit of π's expansion
    then 1 **else** 0.
3. $h_3(x) =$ **if** 5 occurs before the xth digit of π's expansion
    then 1 **else** 0.
4.* $h_4(x, y) =$ **if** in π's expansion there is a sequence of $h \geq x$ digits repeated y times
    then 1 **else** 0

In the positive case, can you actually find an algorithm to compute them?

2.8 Fundamental Statements of Computability Theory

The topics treated in this chapter usually fall under the terms "theory of computation" or "computability theory." Our purpose is to present the most relevant results of the theory and to show their practical impact on computer science. We have already discussed several of these results; others are examined in Sections 2.8.1 and 2.8.2.

2.8.1 Recursive and Recursively Enumerable Sets

We observed several times that the intuitive notion of problem can be formalized by means of several different mathematical concepts, depending on the particular point of view one wishes to emphasize in the formalization.

We focus now on the problem of *set decidability*. Intuitively, it consists of solving the membership problem for a given element and a given set. For example, stating whether or not a given string belongs to a language is a typical set membership problem. In the rest of this section we concentrate on subsets of $\mathbb{N}$; the symbol S denotes any such subset.

Definition 2.1

The *characteristic function* c_S: $\mathbb{N} \to \{0,1\}$ of a set S, is defined by

$c_S(x)$ = **if** $x \in S$ **then** 1 **else** 0 □

Definition 2.2

A set S is *recursive* (or *decidable*) if and only if its characteristic function is computable. □

Notice that, for any S, c_S is total.

Definition 2.3

A set S is *recursively enumerable* (or *semidecidable*) if and only if it is either empty or it is the image of a total and computable function g_S, that is,

$$S = I_{g_S} = \{x \mid x = g_S(y), \ y \in \mathbb{N}\} \qquad \square$$

Decidable sets owe their name to the fact that the membership problem can be solved mechanically for them. In fact, a TM or whatever algorithm implementing their characteristic function will eventually give an answer to the question $x \in S$, for any x. The alternative term "recursive" is clearly due to the formalism of recursive functions. In the case of recursively enumerable sets, we are only able to enumerate their elements by means of an algorithm. So, for any recursively enumerable set S, we can build a sequence

$$x_0 = g_S(0), \ x_1 = g_S(1), \ldots$$

such that if $x \in S$, then there exists an i, such that $x = g_S(i)$. In this case, by following the sequence $\{x_i\}$, we would eventually find x and therefore conclude $x \in S$. If $x \notin S$, we would never find x in $\{x_i\}$. However if, given any i, $x \notin \{g_S(i) \mid 0 \le i \le i\}$ then we could neither conclude that $x \in S$ nor that $x \notin S$. For this reason, S is also called semidecidable.

Here are the essential properties of recursive and recursively enumerable sets.

Theorem 2.9

a. If S is recursive, it is also recursively enumerable.
b. S is recursive if and only if both S and $\bar{S} = \mathbb{N} - S$ are recursively enumerable.

Proof of Part a

Let c_S be the characteristic function of S. If S is empty, then it is recursively enumerable by definition. Otherwise, let $k \in S$: thus the function

$g_S(x)$ = **if** $c_S(x) = 1$ **then** x **else** k

is clearly total, computable, and such that $I_{g_S} = S$.
Notice that, in order to state the existence of g_S, the proof does not require

neither the existence of an algorithm to state whether $S = \varnothing$, nor the existence of an algorithm to find out an actual $k \in S$.

Proof of Part b

i. We prove that if both S and $\bar{S}$ are recursively enumerable, then S is recursive. If S is empty or S is $\mathbb{N}$ the statement is obvious. Otherwise, since neither S nor $\bar{S}$ are empty, there exist two total computable functions g_S, $\bar{g}_S$ such that $S = I_{g_S}$, $\bar{S} = I_{\bar{g}_S}$. Consider the consequence:

$$\mathcal{S} = \{ g_S(0), \bar{g}_S(0), g_S(1), \bar{g}_S(1), \dots \}$$
$$\mathcal{S} = \mathbb{N} \text{ because } \mathbb{N} = I_{g_S} \cup I_{\bar{g}_S}; \text{ furthermore, } I_{g_S} \cap I_{\bar{g}_S} = \varnothing.$$

Thus for every $x \in \mathbb{N}$, x occurs in $\mathcal{S}$ just once.
Define c_S as

$$c_S(x) = \text{if } x = s_i \in \mathcal{S} \text{ with } i \text{ odd then } 1 \text{ else } 0$$

Clearly, c_S is well defined because s_i occurs in $\mathcal{S}$ only once.
It is total and computable since the enumeration $\mathcal{S}$ is effective (i.e., can be performed by some TM). Finally, c_S is the characteristic function of S.

ii. If S is recursive then $\bar{S}$ is also recursive.
In fact,

$$c_{\bar{S}}(x) = \text{if } c_S(x) = 0 \text{ then } 1 \text{ else } 0$$

So, by virtue of Part (a) of Theorem 2.9 both S and $\bar{S}$ are recursively enumerable. ∎

For each recursively enumerable set S, there exists a computable function g_S such that $S = I_{g_S}$. Thus the cardinality of the class of recursively enumerable sets does not exceed the cardinality of the class of computable functions, which we have seen to be $\aleph_0$. As in the case of computable functions, most of the subsets of $\mathbb{N}$ are not recursively enumerable as the cardinality of $\mathscr{P}(\mathbb{N})$ is $2^{\aleph_0}$. The reasoning perfectly parallels the analysis of computable and uncomputable functions. Here we describe some nonrecursively enumerable sets.

Theorem 2.10

For any S if

1. $i \in S$ implies that f_i is total, and
2. For any total and computable function f there exists an $i \in S$ such that $f = f_i$, then S is not recursively enumerable.

Proof

Suppose, by contradiction, that there exists a total computable function g_S such that $S = I_{g_S}$. Thus we can effectively enumerate $i_0 = g_S(0)$, $i_1 = g_S(1), \dots$ and therefore $M_{i_0}, M_{i_1}, \dots$ and $ft_{i_0}, ft_{i_1}, \dots$ (ft_{i_k} is the total function computed by TM M_{i_k}). By hypothesis, the sequence $\{ ft_{i_0}, ft_{i_1}, \dots \}$ contains all total computable functions.

Now define the function h by

$$h(x) = ft_x(x) + 1$$

Clearly $h(x)$ is computable and total as for any x, $ft_x(x)$ is defined and computable. Thus there exists $i \in S$ such that $ft_i = h$ (i.e., ft_i is identical to h). But this implies $ft_i(i) = h(i)$ and $h(i) = ft_i(i) + 1$ by definition: a contradiction. ∎

Intuitively, Theorem 2.10 states that total computable functions are not recursively enumerable (whereas partial computable functions are). Notice that the set $S_{tot} = \{x | f_x$ is total$\}$ satisfies the hypothesis of Theorem 2.10; thus it is not recursively enumerable. However, a set satisfies such hypothesis if it contains at least one index for each total computable function. S_{tot} is the maximum set among all such sets.

Theorem 2.10 has a strong negative impact on the goal of defining formalisms comprising all (and only) total computable functions. In fact, a formalism permitting an effective enumeration of algorithms computing all total computable functions would permit also an effective enumeration of TMs defining all total computable functions. But this contradicts Theorem 2.10.

Corollary 2.11

Primitive recursive functions are a *proper* subset of total computable functions.

□

The proof of this statement is a trivial exercise.

We present now another negative result on total computable functions. A function h is called an *extension* of another function g if, whenever $g(x)$ is defined, so is $h(x)$ and $h(x) = g(x)$.

Theorem 2.12

There is no total computable function h that is an extension of the following function

$$g(x) = \textbf{if } f_x(x) \neq \bot \textbf{ then } f_x(x) + 1 \textbf{ else } \bot$$

Proof

As usual, suppose the theorem does not hold. Thus $h = f_i$ for some i. But if h is total, $h(i)$ is defined. So $h(i) = f_i(i)$ and $h(i) = g(i) = f_i(i) + 1$: a contradiction. ∎

As a consequence we cannot take advantage of a "trick" to extend a partial function into a total function. The extension may have a harmful side effect: A computable function may become uncomputable.

We know that the set of total computable functions is properly included in the set of computable functions that in turn is properly included in the set of all functions. Similarly, recursive sets are included in recursively enumerable sets that are properly included in the powerset of $\mathbb{N}$. (Theorem 2.10 provides an example of a nonrecursively enumerable set.) We investigate now whether recursive sets are *properly* included into recursively enumerable sets. We answer this question thanks to the following theorem, which provides further insights into recursively enumerable sets.

Theorem 2.13

A set S is recursively enumerable if and only if

a. $S = D_h$ for some computable partial function h; that is, $S = \{x | h(x) \neq \perp\}$, or

b. $S = I_g$ for some computable partial function g.

Proof of (a)

i. *If part*
   If $h(x)$ is undefined for every x, then $S = \varnothing$ and thus it is recursively enumerable. Otherwise, let k be a value such that $h(k)$ is defined and let i be such that $h = f_i$. Define the function $\tilde{h}$ by means of the following procedure.
   1. State the (effective) bijection $d: (\mathbb{N} - \{0\}) \times \mathbb{N} \to \mathbb{N}$ defined by

   $$d(x, y) = \frac{(x + y)(x + y - 1)}{2} + x - 1$$

   2. For a given n, first compute the unique pair $\langle x, y \rangle$ such that $n = d(x, y)$. Then simulate no more than y moves of M_i with input x. If the computation terminates within $s \leq y$ moves, then let $\tilde{h}(n) = x$, otherwise let $\tilde{h}(n) = k$.
   By virtue of this definition, $\tilde{h}$ is clearly computable, as the above procedure is effective, and total. Furthermore $I_{\tilde{h}} = D_h$ by definition of $\tilde{h}$.

ii. *Only if part*
   If $S = \varnothing$ then let $h(x)$ be undefined for any x. Otherwise, $S = I_g$, where g is a total computable function.
   Define h by means of the following procedure. For any x, enumerate $g(0), g(1), \ldots, g(i), \ldots$. If an i is found such that $g(i) = x$ then let $h(x) = 0$. Clearly h is computable but the above procedure may never terminate, thus h is partial. Furthermore $D_h = I_g$.

Proof of (b)

j. *If part*
   It is similar to the *if part* of (a) and thus it is left to the reader as an exercise.
jj. *Only if part*
   Obvious, as a total function is a particular case of a partial function. ∎

Thanks to Theorem 2.13 we can attach a "semicharacteristic" function c_S to any recursively enumerable set S. Function c_s is defined as

$c_S(x) = $ **if** $x \in S$ **then** 1 **else** 0 or $\perp$

Strictly speaking, the foregoing formula is not a definition of the semicharacteristic function, but rather a constraint. $c_S(x)$ must be 1 if x is in S, but if $x \notin S$, c_S can be either 0 or undefined. Thus, recursively enumerable or semidecidable sets have a computable semicharacteristic function.

At this point, we are able to show a semidecidable set that is not decidable:

$$K = \{ x | f_x(x) \neq \perp \}$$

In fact, the function h defined by $h(x) = f_x(x)$ is clearly computable, thus $K = D_h$ is semidecidable.

On the other hand, the characteristic function of S is

$$c_S(x) = \textbf{if } f_x(x) \neq \perp \textbf{ then } 1 \textbf{ else } 0$$

which we know to be uncomputable from Corollary 2.7.

Exercises

2.24 Show that the languages accepted by TMs are recursively enumerable sets but, in general, they are not recursive. For a hint, see Theorem 2.17.

2.25 Show that if $S = I_g$ for some computable, total, and monotonic function g, then S is recursive (g is monotonic if $x < y$ implies $g(x) < g(y)$).

2.26 Does the above statement of Exercise 2.25 hold if g is weakly monotonic (i.e., $x < y$ implies $g(x) \leq g(y)$)?

2.27 Does the statement of Exercise 2.25 hold if g is monotonic but not total (i.e., $x < y$ and g defined for both x, y imply $g(x) < g(y)$)?

2.8.2 Kleene's and Rice's Theorems

In this section we introduce two fundamental theorems of the theory of computation: Kleene's Theorem and Rice's Theorem. We discuss the intuitive meaning and the impact of the former later on in Chapter 4. For the present, let us simply consider it as a lemma in the proof of the latter and as useful exercise for the reader.

Theorem 2.14 (Kleene's Fixed-Point Theorem)
Let t be any total computable function. Then it is always possible to find an integer p such that

$$f_p = f_{t(p)}$$

Function f_p is called a *fixed point* of t.

Proof*
Let u be any integer. Define a TM realizing the following procedure applied to the value x.

1. Compute $z = f_u(u)$
2. If and when the computation of $f_u(u)$ terminates, then compute $f_z(x)$.

Since the foregoing procedure is effective, there exists a TM realizing it. Furthermore we can actually build it and compute its index $g(u)$ for every u. Thus we have defined a function that is total (such a TM exists for any u even if $f_u(u)$ is not defined) and computable (we can actually build it). Consequently, we have obtained a function $f_{g(u)}$ defined by

$$f_{g(u)}(x) = \text{if } f_u(u) \neq \bot \text{ then } f_{f_u(u)}(x) \text{ else } \bot$$

Notice that g is total while $f_{g(u)}$ is not necessarily total. Now, let t be any total computable function: the composition $t \circ g$ is total and computable too (see Exercise 2.14).

Let v be such that $f_v = t \circ g$ and let $u = v$ in the previous construction. We obtain $f_{g(v)} = f_{f_v(v)}$ because $f_v(v) = t \circ g(v)$ is defined. Thus, $f_{g(v)}(x) = f_{f_v(v)}(x)$ for every x. But $f_{f_v(v)} = f_{t \circ g(v)}$. Thus $f_{g(v)} = f_{t \circ g(v)}$ and $g(v)$ is a fixed point of t. ∎

Theorem 2.15 (Rice's Decision Theorem)
Let F be any set of computable functions. The set $S = \{x | f_x \in F\}$ is recursive if and only if $F = \emptyset$ or F is the set of all computable functions.

Proof
By contradiction, suppose that S is recursive, $F \neq \emptyset$, and F is not the set of all computable functions. By effectively enumerating all TMs M_i we can find the first $i \in S$ such that (α): $f_i \in F$, and the first $j \notin S$ such that (β): $f_j \notin F$.

Let us consider now the characteristic function c_S of S.

$$c_S(x) = \text{if } f_x \in F \text{ then } 1 \text{ else } 0$$

By hypothesis, c_S is computable. But the following function $\bar{c}_S$ is also computable.

$$(\gamma): \bar{c}_S(x) = \text{if } f_x \notin F \text{ then } i \text{ else } j$$

Now, by Kleene's Theorem there exists an $\bar{x}$ such that

$$(\delta): f_{\bar{c}_S(\bar{x})} = f_{\bar{x}}.$$

Suppose $\bar{c}_S(\bar{x}) = i$; then, by (γ), $f_{\bar{x}} \notin F$. But, by (δ), $f_{\bar{x}} = f_i$ and, by (α), $f_i \in F$: a contradiction. Suppose, instead, $\bar{c}_S(\bar{x}) = j$; then, by (γ), $f_{\bar{x}} \in F$. But, by (δ), $f_{\bar{x}} = f_j$ and, by (β), $f_j \notin F$; again a contradiction. ∎

Rice's Theorem has a strong negative practical impact. For example, choose $F = \{g\}$, that is, F consists of a single function g. Because of Rice's Theorem, it is not decidable whether any given TM computes g or not. But because of Church's Thesis the result is not restricted to the TM and function formalisms. So we cannot state by means of an algorithm whether any given algorithm solves any given problem, nor whether two programs are equivalent (i.e., they compute the same function). Notice that this latter fact coincides with the result of Exercise 2.19 (function g_2 is uncomputable). Such a result was not easy to prove without the help of Rice's Theorem but is straightforward here.

As a further example to show the power of Rice's Theorem as a tool for proving problem unsolvability, consider Exercise 2.18. The set of constant functions clearly satisfies the hypothesis of Theorem 2.15. Thus the set of their indexes is not recursive, which means that function g defined in Exercise 2.18 is uncomputable. The reader is invited to compare this very simple proof with his or her proof and with the sketchy solution provided at the end of the chapter.

Exercises

2.28 Prove the unsolvability of the problem of stating whether a given program (TM, etc.) computes a primitive recursive function or not.

2.29 Prove the unsolvability of the problem of stating whether the definition domain of any computable function is finite or not.

2.9 Reasoning on Problem Unsolvability

The first and very basic education in computer science concerns the invention of algorithms for simple problems: A student learns the art of algorithm design by trying to find computer solutions to simple numerical and symbolic computations.

However, we should realize that the job of inventing algorithms may become a never-ending task. As far as a programmer is facing such problems as array sorting or searching we know (but the programmer might not know!) that if no algorithmic solution is found, this is only because the unexperienced programmer has not been able to find it. But if the programmer were facing the problem of finding an algorithm to state whether any two Pascal programs compute the same function, we know (but the programmer might not know!) that his or her job would be hopeless.

Now, if we are in the position where we already know whether a problem is solvable or not, we can decide whether it is a reasonable goal to find an algorithm to solve it. But if we are facing a new problem (i.e., we are in the same situation as the unexperienced programmer), we might become engaged in a hopeless job trying to find an algorithmic solution for an undecidable problem. In these cases, it is essential to state whether the problem is solvable or not. This, in turn, is an unsolvable problem (i.e., we will never be able to state *mechanically* whether a problem is decidable or not.) We must rely on our ingenuity. In conclusion, problem solving goes through the following iterative mental process.

a. Try to find an algorithm to solve the given problem.
b. After some time if you do not succeed in finding an algorithm ask yourself whether you suspect that such an algorithm does not exist.
c. In such a case try to prove its unsolvability.

Performs steps (a) through (c) repeatedly, until either you find an algorithm, or you prove the problem is unsolvable, or you are exhausted and decide to give up. (Note that the last alternative is essential in order to survive!)

The experienced programmer is often able to find an algorithm to solve a problem if such an algorithm exists and if the problem is not too difficult, on the basis of previous experience. Similarly, there are some general, widely applicable proof schemes that can be used to prove problem unsolvability.

The careful reader has probably already identified a number of general proof schemes we have used extensively in the undecidability proofs given in the previous sections. We already commented on the power of Rice's Theorem as a tool to prove unsolvability. Other classical proof schemes may be classified as *diagonal proofs* (both the method and the terminology are borrowed from more classic mathematics). If there are problems in the computation of a function $g(x, y)$, problems are likely to appear in the diagonal (i.e., when $x = y$). For instance, we have seen diagonal proofs for Theorem 2.6, Corollary 2.7, Theorem 2.8, etc.

Diagonal proof methods are the most classical way of proving unsolvability in a direct fashion. The proof is always a *reductio ad absurdum*: If the problem were solvable, some contradiction would arise and this is likely to occur in the diagonal. However, proving unsolvability of unsolvable problems in a direct way would be a terrible job because the literature and the practice show an incredibly large number of unsolvable problems.

We have already seen that checking termination of any program in a mechanical way is impossible; but we based this result on the fact that any TM can be simulated by a computer program and conversely. The proof method used in this case was not based on *reductio ad absurdum*, but on another important and powerful principle: We simply realized that the existence of a solution for the problem being studied would imply solvability of another problem that was already proved unsolvable. More generally, the technique of *problem reduction* tries to reduce a problem solution to the solution of yet another problem whose solvability or unsolvability is already known. If we can find an algorithmic way to build a solution of a problem P starting from a solution of a problem P', we can deduce that

1. If P' is solvable, so is P.
2. If P is unsolvable, so is P'.

A few examples, as usual, will help clarify the problem reduction technique.

Example 2.2

Consider Theorem 2.6 and Corollary 2.7. They state, by means of independent though very similar proofs, that the two functions g, k, respectively defined by $g(x, y) = $ **if** $f_y(x) \neq \perp$ **then** 1 **else** 0 and by $k(x) = $ **if** $f_x(x) \neq \perp$ **then** 1 **else** 0, are not computable. Intuitively, the former statement looks more general than the latter. Thus it cannot be the case that we are able to solve the general problem if we fail to solve the particular one. Formally, this means that we could quite easily derive an algorithm to compute k starting from an algorithm computing g (i.e., k is *reduced* to g by simply letting $y = x$.)

This fact makes the proof of the former theorem a trivial consequence of the latter. We just need to prove Corollary 2.7; then Theorem 2.6 follows by observing that g's computability would imply k's computability. In some sense, Corollary 2.7 becomes the main theorem.

Our next example shows the undecidability of the problem of stating whether the image of f_x, for any x, is empty. This is accomplished by reducing it to the problem of stating, for a given fixed z_0, whether, for any x, $z_0 \in I_{f_x}$. This, in turn, is already known as an undecidable problem (see Exercise 2.20).

Theorem 2.16
The problem of stating whether or not $I_{f_x} = \emptyset$, for any x, is undecidable.

Proof
Choose any fixed value z_0. For any x, compute y such that $f_x(z) \neq z_0$ implies $f_y(z) = \perp$, $f_x(z) = z_0$ implies $f_y(z) = z_0$. It is clear that f_y is computable and y can be effectively computed on the basis of a TM computing f_x. Thus $I_{f_y} = \emptyset$ if and only if $z_0 \in I_{f_x}$: If we were able to solve the former problem we could also solve the latter.   ∎

Notice that Theorem 2.16 could also be derived as a simple consequence of Rice's Theorem (Theorem 2.15). In fact, the set of totally undefined computable functions is neither empty nor coincides with the set of all computable functions.

To summarize, we are now equipped with a powerful set of tools to prove problem unsolvability, namely diagonal proofs, problem reduction, and a set of fundamental statements such as Rice's Theorem.

Exercise

2.30 Prove the unsolvability of problems given in Exercises 2.17 through 2.22 by using the *problem reduction* technique and/or by applying Rice's Theorem.

An important remark is now in order. So far, we have collected a sample of negative results on the limits of mechanical problem solving. For instance, there is no algorithmic way to state whether or not *any* program for *any* input ultimately halts. Note, however, that if we restrict our attention to the class of Pascal programs that do not use **go to**, **while**, and **repeat** statements, nor recursive procedure calls, then such programs are guaranteed to terminate for any input. Programs that satisfy this constraint can be built to solve many nontrivial and useful problems: For example, several numerical problems can be solved by algorithms which use only **for** loops. Similarly, primitive recursive functions are guaranteed a priori to be total.

In general, an unsolvable problem may become solvable in a more or less trivial way if restricted to suitable particular cases. The language recognition problem provides some interesting examples of such cases. We review them in the next section.

2.10 Solvable and Unsolvable Language Problems

In this section we discuss several solvable and unsolvable language problems. Let us first consider TMs as language recognizer. It is immediate to derive the following theorem.

Theorem 2.17
For any TM M and any string $x \in V_T^*$ it is undecidable whether or not $x \in L(M)$.

Proof
The proof of Theorem 2.17 is immediate once one recalls the initial remarks on problem coding. In fact, suppose that the problem $x \in L(M)$ is decidable. Let $\{M_i\}$ be an effective enumeration of TMs recognizing languages in V_T^* and let $\{x_i\}$ be an effective enumeration of strings of V_T^*. Observe that there is no loss of generality in assuming that each M_i halts on input x only if $x \in L(M_i)$. In fact, it is easy to restrict the enumeration $\{M_i\}$ to TMs that never halt if $x \notin L(M_i)$. Thus, deciding whether or not $x_i \in L(M_j)$ is the same as deciding whether or not M_j halts on input string x_i. However, this cannot be decided by any TM. ∎

Exercises

2.31 Give a direct diagonal proof of Theorem 2.17 by considering the language $L = \{x_i | x_i \notin L(M_i)\}$

2.32 Show that the following problems are undecidable.
  1. For any TM M, $L(M) = \emptyset$?
  2. For any TM, M, $L(M) = V_T^*$?
  3. For any grammar G and string $x \in V_T^*$, $x \in L(G)$?
  4. For any grammar G, $L(G) = \emptyset$?
  5. For any pair of grammars G_1, G_2, $L(G_1) \subseteq L(G_2)$?

Observe now that languages recognized by FAs are recursive. In fact, for any string x and for any FA it is trivially decidable if $\delta^*(q, x) \in F$. It suffices to run

A until either δ is not defined (case (a)) or x is completely read (case (b)). The decision procedure halts giving an answer "yes" in case (b), if A is in a final state. Otherwise, the answer is "no." Thus, we have the following statement.

Statement 2.18
The languages accepted by FAs are recursive (i.e., the membership problem is decidable for them). $\qquad\square$

Exercise

2.33 Show that the languages recognized by PDAs are recursive. *Hint*: Use Theorem 1.11.

We have also seen that the *emptiness problem* (i.e., the problem of stating whether or not a given language is empty) is undecidable for languages accepted by any TM (Exercise 2.32.1). However this problem becomes decidable when restricted to regular languages.

Theorem 2.19
It is decidable whether or not for a given FA A, $L(A) = \varnothing$. $\qquad\blacksquare$

The proof of the theorem is a trivial consequence of Theorem 1.1.
    Let us now introduce an unsolvable language problem through a nontrivial example of a problem reduction technique.

Theorem 2.20*
Let G_1 and G_2 be two context-free grammars. It is undecidable whether or not

$$L(G_1) \cap L(G_2) = \varnothing$$

for any pair G_1, G_2.

Theorem 2.20 will be proved by showing that if an algorithm exists to solve the foregoing problem, then an algorithm can be derived to solve the problem of stating whether or not $L(M) = \varnothing$ for any TM M. But this problem, in turn, is unsolvable (see Exercise 2.32.1). We need some background definitions and results in order to prove the theorem.

Definition 2.4
Let M be a single-tape TM accepting a language $L(M) \subseteq V_T^*$. A *valid computation* of M is a string $w_1\$w_2^R\$w_3\$w_4^R\$\dots$ where

- w_i^R denotes the reversal of the string w_i.
- $\$ \notin A$, where A is the alphabet of M and $V_T \subseteq A$, such that

- for any i, w_i is a suitable encoding of a configuration of M, defined in the following way: If $c_i = \langle q, x_1 \uparrow x_2 \rangle$ then $w_i = x_1 q x_2$. In short, w_i are called configurations.
- w_1 is an initial configuration (i.e., $w_1 = q_0 x$, $x \in V_T^*$).
- w_n is an accepting configuration (i.e., $w_n \in A^* \cdot F \cdot A^*$).
- $w_i \underset{M}{\vdash} w_{i+1}$ for all i, with $1 \leq i < n$. □

The proof of Theorem 2.20 basically relies on the following lemma, which intuitively states that the transition relation between two TM configurations can be described by a context-free grammar.

Lemma 2.21
For any single-tape TM M the languages

$$L = \left\{ x | x = y\$z^R, \; y \underset{M}{\vdash} z \right\}, \; L_R = \left\{ x | x = y^R \$z, \; y \underset{M}{\vdash} z \right\}$$

are context-free.

Proof
We describe a context-free grammar G generating L. The grammar for L_R is obtained by a trivial modification of G.

G is the 4-tuple $\langle A \cup Q \cup \{\$\}, \{S, T\}, P, S \rangle$, where P is built as follows.

- For each $a \in A$, $S \to aSa$, $T \to aTa$ are in P.
- For each $q \in Q$ and $a \in A$,
  - if $\delta(q, a) = \langle q', a', R \rangle$ then $S \to qaTq'a'$ is in P.
  - if $\delta(q, a) = \langle q', a', S \rangle$ then $S \to qaTa'q'$ is in P.
  - if $\delta(q, a) = \langle q', a', L \rangle$ then for any $b \in A$, $S \to bqaTa'bq'$ is in P.
- $T \to \$$ is in P.

For instance, if a move of M consists of $\langle q, ab \uparrow \phi \rangle \underset{M}{\vdash} \langle q', a \uparrow bc \rangle$, G has the following derivation.

$$S \underset{G}{\Rightarrow} aSa \underset{G}{\Rightarrow} abq\phi Tcbq'a \underset{G}{\Rightarrow} abq\phi \$cbq'a.$$

The foregoing sample derivation should suffice to convince that $L(G) = L$ without further explanation. ∎

Proof of Theorem 2.20
Define the following languages $L_1, L_2 \subseteq (A^* \cdot Q \cdot A^*\$)^*$ as follows. A string $x = x_1\$x_2 \ldots x_m\$$, $x_i \in A^* \cdot Q \cdot A^*$ is in L_1 (respectively, L_2) if and only if

- $x_i \underset{M}{\vdash} x_{i+1}^R$ for odd values of i, $1 \leq i < m$
- $x_i^R \underset{M}{\vdash} x_{i+1}$ for even values of i, $1 < i < m$
- x is in L_2 only if x_1 is an initial configuration of M (i.e., $x_1 = q_0 u$, $u \in V^*_T$).
- if m is odd (even, respectively) x is in L_1 (L_2, respectively) only if x_m is an accepting configuration (i.e., $x_m \in A^* \cdot F \cdot A^*$).

Clearly $L_1 \cap L_2$ is the set of valid computations of M as $x = x_1\$x_2 \ldots x_m\$$ is in

TABLE 2.1   A Display of Classical Decidability Problems in Formal Language Theory

Language Class \ Problem	$x \in L$	$L = \emptyset$	$L_1 = L_2$	$L_1 \cap L_2 = \emptyset$
Accepted by TM	U	U	U	U
Regular	D	D	D	D
Context free	D*	D*	U*	U
Accepted by PDA	D	D*	Open problem	U

Legend:
D: decidable.
U: undecidable.

$L_1 \cap L_2$ if and only if $x_1 \underset{M}{\vdash} x_2^R \underset{M}{\vdash} x_3 \dots$. Notice now that $L_1 = (L\$)^* \cdot (\{\epsilon\} \cup A^* \cdot F \cdot A^* \cdot \$)$ and $L_2 = q_0 \cdot V_T^* \cdot \$ \cdot (L_R\$)^* \cdot (\{\epsilon\} \cup A^* \cdot F \cdot A^* \cdot \$)$, where L and L_R are the languages of Lemma 2.21. Once one has context-free grammars to generate L and L_R, it is an easy exercise to build two context-free grammars G_1, G_2 generating L_1 and L_2, respectively.

In conclusion, we obtained an algorithm, which, for any TM M, builds two context-free grammars G_1, G_2 such that $L(G_1) \cap L(G_2)$ is the set of valid computations of M. But $L(M) = \emptyset$ if and only if M's set of valid computations is empty. Thus, if the problem of stating whether $L(G_1) \cap L(G_2) = \emptyset$ were decidable, so would be the problem of stating whether $L(M) = \emptyset$: a contradiction. ∎

Exercise

2.34 Give the construction of PDAs recognizing L and L_R as defined in Lemma 2.21.

Table 2.1 summarizes and somewhat completes the decidability results for formal languages explored in this section. The results listed here that have not been proved before are left to the reader as exercises, with the warning that a * marks exercises that require some specialized knowledge in language theory.

2.11*   Problem Reducibility and Degrees of Unsolvability

We have seen that problem reduction is a powerful technique to state whether a given problem P is solvable or not. Furthermore, whenever the answer is positive, the method provides an actual solution method, at least in principle. In this section we investigate this technique in more depth. We realize later in Chapter 3 that the same technique can provide interesting results even outside the scope of problem solvability.

Among the several possible formalizations of the notion of problem, here we choose the one based on sets of integers. A problem P will be represented as a set S_p: thus P solvable will mean S_p recursive, P partially solvable will mean S_p recursively enumerable, and P unsolvable will mean S_p nonrecursively enumerable.

Before going into a formal treatment of the notion of problem reducibility, let us consider the following examples in an intuitive way. For simplicity, in what follows we use the short notation D_x and I_x for D_{f_x} and I_{f_x}, respectively, that is, to denote the definition domain and the image of the function computed by the xth TM.

Example 2.3

Consider the two sets

$S_1 = \{ x \mid D_x \text{ is infinite} \}$
$S_2 = \{ x \mid D_x = \mathbb{N} \text{ (i.e., } f_x \text{ is total)} \}$

We know from Theorem 2.10 that S_2 is not recursively enumerable. We can realize that in some sense they are reducible each other. In fact, suppose there exists an algorithm to test whether for any x, f_x is total—that is, suppose S_2 is recursive. Then, in order to test whether D_x is infinite, proceed as follows: Define a computable and total function h such that, for $y = h(x)$, $I_y = D_x$ and $z_1 \neq z_2$ implies $f_y(z_1) \neq f_y(z_2)$. This can be done by means of a construction based on the construction of $\tilde{h}$ in the proof of Theorem 2.13. Thus D_x is finite if and only if f_y is total.

On the other hand, assume there exists an algorithm to test if D_x is finite, for any x. Then, to test if f_x is total, define a computable and total function h such that, for $y = h(x)$.

$f_y(z) = \text{ if } f_x(w) \neq \perp \text{ for any } w \leq z$
    then 1 **else** $\perp$

Thus f_x is total if and only if D_y is infinite. Since such total and computable function h can be effectively obtained, we have derived a procedure to decide if f_x is total.

The foregoing construction provides a proof of the undecidability of S_1 once the undecidability of S_2 has been stated, and conversely. The proof is by *reductio ad absurdum*.

There is another interesting point of view to interpret this fact. Imagine to augment a TM with a nonalgorithmic device that is able to decide membership for S_1. Let us call such a device an *oracle*. Then you could use an augmented TM of this type to solve the membership problem for S_2 too. In fact, such a TM could answer the question "$x \in S_2$?" in the following way: First, it could compute y according to the previous procedure; then, it would ask the oracle whether $y \in S_1$ and would use the answer to solve the original problem. Conversely, an oracle able to decide membership for S_2 could be used to decide it for S_1 too. Therefore, we can claim that the same oracle can be used for deciding both S_1 and S_2.

Example 2.4

Consider the two sets

$$\overline{S}_1 = \{x \mid D_x \text{ is finite}\}$$

$$K = \{x \mid f_x(x) \neq \bot\}$$

We can reduce K to $\overline{S}_1$. In fact suppose an oracle is able to decide the membership problem for $\overline{S}_1$. The membership problem for K can be solved by means of the following procedure. Define, as usual, a total and computable function h such that, for $y = h(x)$

$f_y(w) = $ **if** M_x with input x does not halt in less than w moves

        then 1 **else** $\bot$

Thus $f_x(x)$ is defined if and only if D_y is finite.

We will see later that in this case problem reduction cannot be applied in the other direction: This leads to some intuitive notion that the membership problem for K is "more solvable" than the membership problem for $\overline{S}_1$. In short: K is "more solvable" than $\overline{S}_1$. Equivalently we may say that $\overline{S}_1$ is "less solvable" than K. In fact, note that K is recursively enumerable, although not recursive, whereas $\overline{S}_1$ is not (prove this fact as an exercise). To state it in another way, an oracle deciding membership for $\overline{S}_1$ could be used also for deciding membership for K but not conversely.

The previous example suggests the need for defining some measure of "degree of (un)solvability." We formally introduce this notion here in just one of the several possible ways, with no ambition for completeness. Let A, B denote subsets of $\mathbb{N}$ and define $\overline{A} = \mathbb{N} - A$, $\overline{B} = \mathbb{N} - B$.

Definition 2.5
A is *reducible* to B (denoted as $A \leq_r B$) if and only if there exists a total computable function t such that for any x, $x \in A$ if and only if $t(x) \in B$. $\qquad \square$

Here are some properties of relation $\leq_r$.

Theorem 2.22

1. $\leq_r$ is reflexive and transitive.
2. $A \leq_r B$ implies $\bar{A} \leq_r \bar{B}$.
3. If $A \leq_r B$ and B is recursive, then A is recursive
4. If $A \leq_r B$ and B is recursively enumerable, then A is recursively enumerable.

Proof

1. and 2. are trivial exercises.
3. Let t be a computable and total function such that $x \in A$ if and only if $t(x) \in B$, (i.e., $A = t^{-1}(B)$). Let c_A and c_B be the characteristic functions of A, B. Thus $c_A = c_B \circ t$. Thus if B is recursive so is c_A.
4. Again, $A \leq_r B$ means $A = t^{-1}(B)$ with t computable and total. Now if B is recursively enumerable, it is the definition domain of some computable function f_x (i.e., $B = D_x$). But $A = t^{-1}(B)$ is the definition domain of $f_x \circ t$, which is computable. ∎

Exercise

2.35 Re-examine Examples 2.3 and 2.4 in the light of Theorem 2.22. In the case of Example 2.3, prove that $S_1 \leq_r S_2$ and $S_2 \leq_r S_1$. In the case of Example 2.4, prove that $K \leq_r \bar{S_1}$, but $S_1 \not\leq_r K$. In both cases, use h to define $\leq_r$.

Definition 2.6
$A =_r B$ means that $A \leq_r B$ and $B \leq_r A$. □

Obviously $=_r$ is an equivalence relation. Thus we can define the equivalence classes of $=_r$ as *unsolvability degrees*. Notice that any degree containing a recursive set contains all and only recursive sets. Thus we can speak of "the recursive degree." Also, any degree containing a recursively enumerable set contains only recursively enumerable sets. Thus we can speak of recursively enumerable degrees (it can be shown that there are several recursively enumerable degrees).

Several questions naturally arise when a partial ordering is introduced in any mathematical structure. For example,

- Is the ordering a total ordering?
- Is the ordering a lattice?
- If $A \leq_r B$ and $A \neq_r B$, does there exist one or more C "between A and B", such that $A <_r C <_r B$? (As usual, $<_r$ means $\leq_r \wedge \neq_r$).

These and other questions do not have a purely mathematical interest. For example, if $\leq_r$ were a total ordering this would imply that, given any two problems P_1, P_2, either P_2 is more difficult than P_2, or conversely, or they are equally difficult. A complete algebraic treatment of these issues is out of the scope of this text. We simply list a few statements here, trying to choose among those that describe the simplest but most relevant properties.

Theorem 2.23

1. There exist nonrecursive sets A and B that are noncomparable with respect to $\leq_r$.
2. $\leq_r$ defines an upper semilattice (i.e., any two sets have a least upperbound). Furthermore, if such sets are recursively enumerable their least upperbound is recursively enumerable.

Proof of 1
The set K of Example 2.4 and its complement $\overline{K}$ are noncomparable. In general, note that for any A either $A =_r \overline{A}$ or A and $\overline{A}$ are noncomparable. In fact, by Theorem 2.22.2 $A \leq_r \overline{A}$ would imply $\overline{A} \leq_r A$. Since K is recursively enumerable, whereas $\overline{K}$ is not (otherwise both of them would be recursive), $\overline{K} \leq_r K$ is false (see Theorem 2.22.4). This excludes $K =_r \overline{K}$. Therefore K and $\overline{K}$ are noncomparable.

Proof of 2
For any A, B define $A \sqcup B$ as

$$\{x|(x = 2z, z \in A) \vee (x = 2z + 1, z \in B)\}.$$

Now, $A \leq_r A \sqcup B$ by means of $f(x) = 2x$ and $B \leq_r A \sqcup B$ by means of $t(x) = 2x + 1$. Furthermore, if $A \leq_r C$ by means of f and $B \leq_r C$ by means of g then $A \sqcup B \leq_r C$ by means of function h defined by $h(2x) = f(x)$, $h(2x + 1) = g(x)$. Thus $\sqcup$ satisfies the axioms of the operation in a lattice.

Furthermore let $A = I_{g_A}$, $B = I_{g_B}$, with g_A, g_B total computable functions (the case A and/or B are empty is left to the reader as an exercise). Then $A \sqcup B = I_g$, where

$$g(x) = \text{if } x \text{ is even then } 2g_A(x/2) \text{ else } 2g_B(x/2 + 1) + 1. \qquad \blacksquare$$

Of course Theorem 2.23 applies as well to unsolvability degrees, i.e., equivalence classes of $=_r$.

Definition 2.7 (Complete Sets)
A set S is *complete* with respect to $\leq_r$ (S is r-complete) if and only if

a. S is recursively enumerable, and
b. A recursively enumerable implies $A \leq_r S$. $\qquad\qquad\qquad\qquad\qquad$ □

Thus a possible r-complete set C is maximal with respect to $\leq_r$ among recursively enumerable sets. Intuitively, such a set could be claimed as the "most difficult semidecidable problem" since, once C's solution were obtained—say, by an oracle machine—the solution of any other semidecidable problem could be obtained by mechanical reduction to C's solution. Notice also that if C_1 and C_2 are two r-complete sets, then $C_1 =_r C_2$. Thus there would exist a unique maximum unsolvability degree, if any, namely $[C]_{=_r}$.

In Chapter 3 we realize that the notion of completeness has quite a general scope and can be applied to other relevant topics of computation theory.

The next theorem states the existence of r-complete sets.

Theorem 2.24
The set $H = \{\langle x, y \rangle \mid x \in D_y\}$ is r-complete.[3]

Proof
H is the set $\{\langle x, y \rangle \mid \exists z \text{ such that } M_y \text{ with input } x \text{ halts in less than } z \text{ moves}\}$. H can be proved recursively enumerable by means of a reasoning of the type used in the proof of Theorem 2.13.

Let A be any recursively enumerable set. Then $A = D_{y_0}$ for some y_0. Thus $x \in A$ if and only if $\langle x, y_0 \rangle \in H$ and $A \leq_r H$ by means of function f defined by $f(x) = \langle x, y_0 \rangle$. ∎

Since it can also be shown $H \leq_r K$, we have $K =_r H$ and K is r-complete too.

Exercises

2.36 Are $A = \{x \mid D_x \text{ is finite}\}$ and $B = \{x \mid I_x \text{ is finite}\}$ comparable?
2.37 Show that $C = \{x \mid D_x \neq \varnothing\}$ is r-complete.
2.38 If A is recursive while B is not, are A and B comparable?

Chapter Summary

This chapter has been devoted to investigating the notion of mechanical problem solvability.

First, we have recalled from Chapter 1 that, no matter how the notion of problem is formalized, TMs, unrestricted grammars, recursive functions, and

---

[3] Obviously H can be coded as a subset of $\mathbb{N}$ in the usual way.

other formalisms are at least as powerful as any other known computation model. This fact, along with a thorough analysis of the intuitive notion of algorithm, allowed us to derive Church's Thesis, which states that TMs, as any other equivalent formalism, are an adequate formalization of the notion of a mechanical computational device.

Then we have introduced the notion of the universal TM: a machine that is able to simulate the computation of any other TM, including itself. The existence of mechanically unsolvable problems has been shown first by using direct diagonal proofs, then by reducing the solution of a problem to the solution of another one that was already proved as unsolvable.

Sections 2.6 through 2.10 have shown a variety of solvable and unsolvable problems and should have helped the reader develop the skill required to understand by him or herself whether a problem is mechanically solvable or not. We have introduced two fundamental theorems: Kleene's and Rice's Theorems. The latter has been investigated as a very powerful tool for proving problem unsolvability.

Section 2.11, which is restricted to a more advanced readership, introduced the notions of problem reducibility, unsolvability degrees, and completeness.

Further Exercises

2.39 Show that it is undecidable whether or not for any given Pascal program P and for any given statement S within P, there exist some input data such that P's execution flow eventually reaches statement S.

2.40 Sometimes in the literature the class of *total recursive functions* is defined as the class of functions defined by means of base functions, composition, recursion, and the *total μ-operator*, that is, operator μ defined as in Section 0.2.4.2 ($\mu_y(g(x_1 \ldots x_n, y) = 0)$), with the constraint that a y satisfying μ always exists.

It can be shown, in a nontrivial way, that the class of total recursive functions coincides with the class of partial recursive functions that are total. On the other hand, the class of partial recursive functions coincides with the class of functions computable by a TM (see Appendix 1.A). Does this result contradict Theorem 2.10? Why? Why not? Recall that primitive recursive functions are total and computable, but they do not cover the entire class of total and computable functions.

2.41* Show that the set of theorems of $\mathscr{A}$ (the axiomatization of arithmetic given in Section 0.2.4) is recursively enumerable but not recursive.

2.42 *Post Correspondence Problem (PCP)*
Let $S_1 = \{x_1, \ldots, x_k\}$, $S_2 = \{y_1, \ldots, y_j\}$ be any two finite sets of strings over an alphabet V_T. PCP asks whether there exists a finite sequence of integers $\{i_1, i_2, \ldots, i_m\}$ such that $x_{i_1} x_{i_2} \ldots x_{i_m} = y_{i_1} y_{i_2} \ldots y_{i_m}$.
For example, with $S_1 = \{x_1 = 1, x_2 = 1011, x_3 = 110\}$ and $S_2 = \{y_1 = 111, y_2 = 10, y_3 = 0\}$, the sequence $2, 1, 1, 3$ provides a solution to PCP

as

$$x_2 x_1 x_1 x_3 = y_2 y_1 y_1 y_3 = 101111110.$$

Show that PCP is unsolvable.

2.43 *Hilbert's tenth problem* (for the reader who knows some history of mathematics) asks the following question.

"Let $P(x_1, \ldots, x_n)$ be a polynomial with variables $x_1, \ldots, x_n$ and integer coefficients. Is it decidable whether any given polynomial P has integer roots (i.e., solutions of $P(x_1, \ldots, x_n) = 0$)?"

What can you say now about decidability of Hilbert's problem? What could you say 40 years ago about decidability of the same problem?

Notice that decidability of Hilbert's tenth problem is *not* decidability of the existence of integer roots for any polynomial P, but *decidability of the decidability* of the existence of such solutions.

Sketchy Solutions to Selected Exercises

2.17 Define the function h by
$h(x) = $ **if** $f_x(x) = x$ **then** $x + 1$ **else** x.
If g is computable, so is h. Let h be f_{x_0}. Consider the case $h(x_0) = $ **if** $f_{x_0}(x_0) = x_0$ **then** $x_0 + 1$ **else** x_0 and find the usual contradiction.

2.18 Follow the following path.
a. Consider the usual function k defined by $k(x) = f_x(x)$. Add the "dummy variable y" and define k' by $k'(x, y) = $ **if** $f_x(x) \neq \perp$ **then** 1 **else** $\perp$ for every y.
b. For any x consider the function f_w given by
$f_w(y) = k'(x, y)$
where $w = h(x)$, h being a computable function, because so is k'. f_w is a constant function if and only if $f_x(x)$ is defined.
c. Assume, by contradiction that the function g given by $g(x) = $ **if** f_x is constant **then** 1 **else** 0, is computable. Thus $g(w) = g(h(x)) = $ **if** $f_x(x)$ is defined **then** 1 **else** 0; that is, the composition $g \circ h$ defined by $g \circ h(x) = g(h(x))$ is a computable function of x.
d. At this point the proof proceeds as in Corollary 2.7.

2.21 Clearly for some value of x_0 the answer is "yes." In fact, if x_0 is the Gödel number of the constant function h, $h(x) = i$ for every x, then g is the constant function $g(z) = 1$ for every z. On the other hand, let x_0 be the Gödel number of the function h defined by $h(x) = $ **if** $f_x(x) \neq \perp$ **then** $f_x(x) + 1$ **else** $\perp$. In such case g is not computable. In fact, suppose by contradiction that g is computable. Then function $\tilde{g}$ defined by $\tilde{g}(z) = $ **if** $z \in D_{f_{x_0}}$ **then** $f_{x_0}(z)$ **else** 0, would also be computable.

But $\tilde{g}$ is the same as **if** $h(z) \neq \perp$ **then** $h(z)$ **else** 0. Thus $\tilde{g}$ is a total extension of h, which contradicts Theorem 2.12.

2.23 Function h_4 is the same function as $f(x, y) = 1$ for all x, y. In fact, in a sequence of $10^{x \cdot y}$ digits there must exist a string of at least x digits repeated at least y times.

-Proof of the decidability of the problem $L = \varnothing$ for CF-languages (see Table 2.1).

-Consider a context-free grammar $G \cdot L(G) \neq \varnothing$ means that there exists a derivation $S \overset{*}{\underset{G}{\Rightarrow}}$ to x, $x \in V_T^*$. But, if such a derivation exists, then there exists also a derivation with no *autoinclusion* (i.e., which is not decompasable as $S \overset{*}{\Rightarrow} uAv \overset{*}{\Rightarrow} uyAzv \overset{*}{\Rightarrow} uywzv$) (see Exercise 1.63). Derivations without autoinclusion are of length not greater than $l = k^{|V_N|+1}$ where V_N is the nonterminal alphabet of G and k is the maximum length of righthand sides of G's productions. Thus $L(G) \neq \varnothing$ if and only if $S \overset{h}{\underset{G}{\Rightarrow}} x$ for some, $h \leq l$, $x \in V_T^*$. Clearly an algorithm can enumerate all G's derivation of length not greater than l and this completes the proof.

2.40 The apparent contradiction is solved by remarking that the total μ-operator is not necessarily computable. In other words, the constraint that a y satisfying μ always exists is not decidable.

2.41 It is fairly easy to give an algorithm which enumerates all theorems of $\mathscr{A}$. In order to show that the set of $\mathscr{A}$'s theorems is not recursive it suffices to realize that the wf V: $\exists y(f(x) = y)$, represents the fact that function f is defined in x. By Statement 0.9, if f is a partial recursive function, V is a theorem of $\mathscr{A}$ if and only if the above fact is true. If $\mathscr{A}$'s theorems were a recursive set, we could effectively check whether or not any partial recursive function f is defined for any value x. But this is absurd because partial recursive functions coincide with computable functions (see Appendix 1.A).

2.43 Hilbert's tenth problem. We now know that the answer to the problem is "No," (i.e., it is unsolvable to state whether a given polynomial P has integer roots or not). The original Matijasevic's proof is reported by Davis and Hersh (1973). However, in 1940 the situation was the same as for Fermat's last theorem (i.e., it was known that the answer was either "Yes" or "No," but no human being nor machine was able to give it).

Bibliographic Remarks

The power of formalisms and undecidability results are the basis of textbooks on automata and computation theory. Thus the theory treated in this chapter can be found also in other texts on automata, formal languages, and computation theory. In particular we mention Hopcroft and Ullman (1969, 1979), Rogers (1963), Harrison (1978), Minsky (1967), and Lewis and Papadimitriou (1981).

The originators of the main results on solvability and unsolvability are Gödel (1930, 1934), Church (1936), Turing (1936, 1937), Markov (1954), Shannon (1938, 1956), Kleene (1952, 1967), Post (1936, 1947) and Rice (1953).

The first inspection of unsolvability issues in formal language theory is due to Bar-Hillel, Perles, and Shamir (1961).

Some key papers on unsolvability degrees are Dekker (1955), Dekker and Myhill (1958) and Kleene and Post (1954).

The exposition of fundamental statements of computation theory given here, including Example 2.1, has been mostly based on Rogers (1963), Knuth (1969), and Minsky (1967). Among these texts, Rogers' is particularly suitable for the reader interested in a more advanced and deeper understanding of computability.

CHAPTER THREE

The Complexity of Computing

3.1   Problem Solving in Practice: Some Difficulties

In the previous chapter we have learned that if a problem can be solved by some TM, then we can write a computer program to solve it, and conversely. Unfortunately computations, as well as any other services, must be paid for. Even if we had free access to the most powerful computer in the world there is a price we would pay for, namely *time*. If it is not possible to obtain a problem solution within a "reasonable" amount of time, the problem becomes intractable in practice, even though it is solvable according to theory. For example, the problem of stating the result of a "perfect" chess match, that is, a match where both players play at best, is certainly decidable: In fact, there is only a finite number of different states of the chess board. Thus, from the initial configuration of the board, an ideal algorithm could enumerate all reachable configurations and state the sequence that would be chosen by two "perfect" players. However, it can be shown that the fastest existing computers would not complete execution of this algorithm in the estimated lifetime of the universe. Consequently, the solvable

193

problem of the "perfect chess match" is intractable; that is, it is unsolvable in practice using the previous algorithm.

In the previous chapter we have seen that many problems are unsolvable. Unsolvability, however, is not the only obstacle we can find along the path of problem solving. Intractability is equally important in practice. Indeed, unfortunately, there are many important problems that are solvable, but intractable in practice.

This chapter is devoted to intractability. Before embarking in a rigorous analysis of the subject it is necessary to lay down the foundations of this new concept and illustrate its background motivations further.

The concept "intractability" is obviously related to "complexity": A problem is intractable whenever its complexity is too high. By *complexity* we mean some kind of measure for the price we have to pay in order to solve our problem. Thus, our ultimate goal is to define complexity in a formal way and to show how complexity analysis can be performed.

Intuitively, complexity can be split into two factors: space complexity and time complexity. The former accounts for the amount of storage that is needed by an algorithm to solve a problem, whereas, the latter accounts for the time required to deliver the solution.

Example 3.1

The following Pascal procedure solves the set membership problem. Parameters of the procedure are x—a set represented by an array—and y—the element to be checked for membership.

```
procedure search (var x: int__set; y: integer; var found: boolean);
    {int__set is globally defined as array [1 .. n] of integer;
    where n is a constant. The procedure sets found to true if y is found in the
    array; otherwise found is set to false}
var i: integer;
begin
    i := 1;
    found := false;
    while i ≤ n and not found do
        if x[i] = y
        then found := true
        else i := i + 1
end {search}
```

Let us try intuitively to analyze both space and time complexity of procedure search. First, we note that both the number of seconds and the number of memory cells required to run the procedure depend on set x. In the case of space complexity, we can say that the total number of required cells $\mathscr{S}$ is given by

$$\mathscr{S} = |x| + k$$

where $|x|$ is the cardinality of set x (i.e., n) and k is a constant that does not depend on the cardinality of x. Intuitively, k accounts for the cells used to store all other variables and the object code.

The analysis of time complexity is slightly more elaborate. The total number of seconds $\mathscr{T}$ required to execute procedure *search* can be written as:

$$\mathscr{T} = \mathscr{T}_1 + \mathscr{T}_2$$

where $\mathscr{T}_1$ is the time spent outside the **while** loop and $\mathscr{T}_2$ is the time spent inside it. Observe that $\mathscr{T}_1$ is a constant value (say, h) which does not depend on set x, whereas $\mathscr{T}_2$ does depend on it; thus we can write

$$\mathscr{T} = h + \mathscr{T}_2(x)$$

Note that the time required by procedure *search* is highly variable. In the *best case*, the procedure finds an element equal to y in the first array position: Thus the loop is executed only once. In the *worst case*, the procedure scans the entire array before coming to a conclusion on set membership: Thus the loop is executed $|x|$ times.

What can we say about the *average case*? Here we need some statistical knowledge on input data distribution. Let p be the probability that procedure search is called with a value y that is in the set. Also, suppose that all such values are equally likely to occur in procedure calls. Thus $(1 - p)$ is the probability that y is not in the set, while $p/|x|$ is the probability that the loop be executed i times, for all i with $1 \le i \le |x|$, coming to the conclusion that y is in the set in position i.

If we assume that the time spent in the loop by each iteration is a constant r, we can derive the following formulas for time complexity.

Best case: $\mathscr{T}_b = h + r$
Worst case: $\mathscr{T}_w = h + r \cdot |x|$

Average case: $\mathscr{T}_a = (1 - p) \cdot r \cdot |x| + \dfrac{p}{|x|} \cdot r \cdot \sum_{i=1}^{x} i$

$$= (1 - p) \cdot r \cdot |x| + \frac{1}{2} \cdot p \cdot r \cdot (|x| + 1)$$

$$= s \cdot |x| + \frac{1}{2} \cdot p \cdot r$$

where $s = r - \dfrac{1}{2} \cdot p \cdot r$

Example 3.2

Suppose you are asked to solve the membership problem for an ordered set, represented by an array sorted in ascending order. Procedure *search* described above can be used to solve the problem but, of course, it does not take advantage of the additional information that the set is ordered. Another solution that can be applied in this case is as well known as a *binary__search*.

procedure *binary__search* (**var** *x*: *int__set*; *y*: *integer*; **var** *found*: *boolean*);
    var *i, j, k*: 1 .. *n*;
      {same comments as for *search* of Example 3.1}
    begin
      i := 1; *j* := *n*;
      found := *false*;
      while *i* < *j* **and not** *found* **do**
        begin {set of candidates is *x*[*i*] through *x*[*j*];
               pick-up middle element}
            k := (*i* + *j*) **div** 2;
            if *y* = *x* [*k*]
            then *found* := *true*
            else {halve the set of candidates}
                if *y* < *x* [*k*]
                then *j* := *k* − 1
                else *i* := *k* + 1
      end
      {*i* > *j* here means that no candidates remain to be checked for membership; it implies *found* = *false*}
    end { *binary__search* }

Why is *binary__search* better than *search* if *x* is sorted? The difference is in the average and in the worst-case behavior of the algorithm. Let us discuss here the worst-case behavior.

Each iteration of *binary__search* checks one element of *x* for membership and, at each iteration, the set of candidates in *x* is halved. In the worst case, the loop terminates when we are left with an empty set of candidates. Thus, the loop can be repeated at most $\lfloor \log|x| \rfloor + 1$ times. Thus, assuming that each iteration takes the same amount of time *u* and that *v* is the time spent before entering the loop, we obtain:

(Worst case) $\mathcal{T}_w' = v + u \cdot (\lfloor \log|x| \rfloor + 1)$ $|x| \geq 1$

Now, in order to compare $\mathcal{T}_w'$ and $\mathcal{T}_w$ in the case of a sorted set, one should analyze what happens when the size of the set to be searched ($|x|$) gets larger and larger. Because *u* and *v* (in the case of $\mathcal{T}_w'$), *h* and *r* (in the case of $\mathcal{T}_w$) are constants that do not depend on $|x|$, one can always find a value *c* such that $\mathcal{T}_w'(x) < \mathcal{T}_w(x)$ for all sets *x* such that $|x| > c$. More precisely, there is an order of magnitude between $\mathcal{T}_w(|x|)$ and $\mathcal{T}_w'(|x|)$ as $|x|$ goes to infinity:

$$\lim_{|x| \to \infty} \frac{\mathcal{T}_w(|x|)}{\mathcal{T}_w'(|x|)} = \infty$$

In conclusion, *binary __search* has a better time complexity than *search* in most cases, that is, in all but a finite number of cases. Unless we know a priori that the membership problem will mostly be solved for a set of size less then *c*, *binary __search* is definitely preferable.

Exercise

3.1 Analyze the time complexity of the *binary __search* procedure for the average case, under the same probability assumptions as we saw for the *search* procedure.

Hint: Notice that, if $y \in x$, the probability of finding y at the first loop iteration is $1/|x|$. The probability of finding y at the second iteration is $(1 - 1/|x|) \cdot 1/\lfloor |x| \text{ } \mathbf{div} \text{ } 2 \rfloor$ and so on. Also, notice that for a sufficiently large x even the worst case time complexity of *binary __search* is far better than the average case of search.

3.1.1   How to Define Complexity Precisely

We have presented Examples 3.1 and 3.2 informally and in several places we have been deliberately vague. We learn how to be more rigorous—and even formal—in the rest of this chapter. However, the examples have risen several important issues that are taken up here.

1. There are two kinds of complexity: time complexity and space complexity. We anticipate here that time complexity is by far the more critical. Thus, most of our discussion in this chapter addresses the issues of time complexity.
2. It is necessary to define the unit of measure to be used in complexity analysis. In our previous examples, we have been quite informal on this point. However, to be rigorous, one should specify the exact values of constants in the complexity formulas we have presented, and this requires a precise notion of the cost of each program instruction.
3. In the previous examples—and in most practical cases—complexity depends on the "size" of the input. Very often, it depends also on the specific input values. Thus, for any input size ($|x|$ in the previous examples), we can derive a best-, worst-, or average-case complexity analysis.
4. Complexity depends on the algorithm chosen to solve a given problem. We have seen in Example 3.2 that the same problem (searching a sorted set) can be solved with different complexities by two different algorithms (*search* and *binary __search*).

There are other aspects that must be investigated in order to derive a theory of complexity.

5. We have seen in Chapter 2 that, as far as solvability is concerned, a problem of a given type (e.g., a translation problem) can be formulated as an equivalent problem of another type (e.g., language recognition). For example, the translation $y = \tau(x)$ can be coded as the recognition of $x \$ y$ ($\$ \notin x, \$ \notin y$). The same equivalence does not hold in general for time complexity. In fact, suppose that a deterministic computation performs the translation $y = \tau(x)$ in time $t(x)$. Then it can be decided whether $x \$ y \in L_\tau = \{z_1 \$ z_2 | z_2 = \tau(z_1)\}$ in the same time $t(x)$. However, the same does not hold on the other side. If the problem $x \$ y \in L_\tau$ can be decided in time $t(x \$ y)$ and the algorithm that recognizes L is used to compute $y = \tau(x)$, then we need to enumerate all possible $\{y_i\}$, say by increasing length. For each y_i a time $t(x \$ y_i)$ is needed to decide $x \$ y_i \in L_\tau$. Thus the total time to compute $\tau(x)$, in the worst case, is

$$\sum_{|y_i| \leq |\tau(x)|} t(x \$ y_i)$$

This reasoning, of course, does not prevent the possibility that a more "clever" algorithm computes $\tau(x)$ in less time.

In this chapter we mainly refer to the complexity of decision problems. However, in several cases, other types of problems will also be considered.

6. As we saw in point 3, complexity depends on the "size" of the problem. However, the size (and thus complexity) depends on the coding of the input. For instance, n symbols are needed to code integer n in unary base, whereas $\lfloor \log_k n \rfloor + 1$ are needed to code it in base k ($k > 1$).

7. Complexity estimates depend on the choice of the model of computation. This is shown in the rest of this chapter, where we consider Turing machines and both lower- and higher-level machines roughly corresponding to an assembly-level language and Pascal.

3.1.2 Asymptotic Behavior

In our discussion of searching for an ordered set, we have come to the conclusion that in the worst case *binary__search* has a better time complexity than *search*. The basic argument was that, apart from values of $|x|$ less than a constant c that does not depend on $|x|$, the number of seconds needed to execute *binary__search* is always less than the number of seconds needed to execute *search*. Also, there is an order of magnitude between the two, as demonstrated by the following limit:

$$\lim_{|x| \to \infty} \frac{\mathscr{T}_w(|x|)}{\mathscr{T}_w'(|x|)} = \infty$$

This is because the asymptotic behavior of $\mathscr{T}_w$ has an order $\log_2(|x|)$, whereas $\mathscr{T}_w'$ has an order $|x|$.

The order notation, referred to as *big-theta-notation*, enlightens the dominant factors that affect the growth of complexity as a function of the size of input (say n).

Definition 3.1
Let g, f be two functions from natural numbers to real numbers. Function g is $\Theta(f)$ if and only if we can find a real constant $c > 0$, such that

$$\lim_{n \to \infty} \frac{g(n)}{f(n)} = c \qquad \square$$

For example, $5n^2 + 7n + 9$ is $\Theta(n^2)$; $27n + 258 \cdot \log_2 n$ is $\Theta(n)$; $n^2 + 356n \cdot \log_{10}(n)$ is $\Theta(n^2)$[1].

The reader should notice that Θ is a binary relation between functions on natural numbers. For compatibility with the current literature, we use the notation

g is $\Theta(f)$

instead of the standard notation for relations

$g \Theta f$

An immediate consequence of Definition 3.1 is given by the following properties whose proof is left to the reader as an exercise.

Statement 3.1
Relation Θ is an equivalence relation. $\qquad \square$

Statement 3.2
If g is $\Theta(f)$ there are positive constants c and $\bar{n}$ such that $g(n) \le c \cdot f(n)$ for all $n \ge \bar{n}$[2]. $\qquad \square$

For each equivalence class defined by relation Θ over the set of functions on naturals, it is customary to select a function with a simple formula as a representative of its order. For example, we refer to $\Theta(n^k)$ rather than $\Theta(a_k n^k + a_{k-1} n^{k-1} + \cdots + a_0)$.

Definition 3.2
Let g and f be two functions on naturals. $\Theta(g) < \Theta(f)$ if and only if $\lim_{n \to \infty} g(n)/f(n) = 0$. Similarly, $\Theta(g) > \Theta(f)$ if and only if $\lim_{n \to \infty} g(n)/f(n) = \infty$. $\qquad \square$

Exercises

3.2 Let $f_i, i = 1, \ldots, 5$ be defined as $f_1(n) = n^2$, $f_2(n) = n^2 \cdot \log_2 n$, $f_3(n) = n^2 \cdot \log_{10}(n)$, $f_4(n) = n^2 \cdot \sqrt{n}$, $f_5(n) = |\sin(n) \cdot n^6|$. State whether f_i is $\Theta(f_j)$ or $\Theta(f_i) < \Theta(f_j)$ for all $i, j = 1, \ldots, 5$.

---

[1] Note that the notations $5n^2 + 7n + 9$, n^2, etc. denote *functions*, not their values.

[2] Whenever there are positive constants c and $\bar{n}$ such that $g(n) \le c \cdot f(n)$ for all $n \ge \bar{n}$, g is said $O(f)$. Relations O—called the big-oh relation—is used by many authors instead of the big-theta as order notation for complexity measure. Notice that if g is $\Theta(f)$ then g is also $O(f)$ but the converse does not hold. For example, if g is $O(n^k)$ it is also $O(n^{k+1})$ but not conversely. Thus, Statement 3.1 does not hold for the big-oh relation. For a thorough discussion of several alternative definitions of complexity order notations see Knuth (1975), Vitanyi and Maertens (1985), and Brassard (1985).

3.3 Prove that the relations $<$, $>$ are *partial* orders over the set of functions on natural numbers. As a consequence we obtain an ordering on equivalence classes $[f]_\Theta$.

Big-theta accounts for the dominant factors that affect the growth of complexity. For example, we can say that an algorithm with time complexity $\Theta(n^2)$ is worse than an algorithm with time complexity $\Theta(n \cdot \log n)$: The asymptotic behavior of the latter is definitely better than that of the former. Notice however that, since big-theta is not a total ordering, it may happen that two algorithms have uncomparable complexities.

Big-theta does not discriminate between two functions in the same complexity class. But what about $\Theta(n^2)$ and $\Theta(10^6 n^2)$? How can we put them in the same equivalence class if we know that the latter is always 10^6 times better than the former? The reader will find a rigorous answer to this question later in this chapter, when we will present the linear Speed-Up Theorem (Theorem 3.12). The theorem ensures that computations can always be speeded up by a constant factor. For instance, we can start from a machine solving a problem in time $10^6 n^2$ and derive, at least in principle, an equivalent machine running in time n^2. The new machine will obviously require more "resources" than the previous one. Thus, the dominant factor of complexity is the functional rate of growth, whereas constant factors can be ignored. As a further consequence, we can also talk about logarithmic complexity factors without bothering with the base of the logarithm. In fact, notice that for any $b_1, b_2 > 1$, and for any function f,

$$\left[\log_{b_1} \circ f \right]_\Theta = \left[\log_{b_2} \circ f \right]_\Theta.$$

3.1.3 Other Sources of Complexity

So far, we have decomposed the cost of a program into two components: time and space complexity. However, these are not the only costs of a program: They capture the run-time behavior of the program but ignore the costs due to the development and maintenance of software.

There are several factors—both technical and nontechnical—that influence the costs of software development and maintenance. Also, a number of sound software engineering principles have been discovered that help reduce the costs involved in software development and in maintenance. However, here things are more elusive than for time and space complexity. Precise definitions of the software qualities to measure and of quantitative measuring methods are still lacking, and the presently proposed metrics are highly controversial. Thus, despite the dramatic relevance of these software complexity problems, we have decided to ignore them in this text. The reader interested in them can find an overview of them in most textbooks on software engineering.

3.2 Complexity Analysis by Means of Automata

In what follows we will discuss complexity analysis using various models of computation. We start our discussion from automata in this section. Then we will define models which more closely reflect the behavior of real computers, and we will evaluate complexity using these more realistic models.

3.2.1 The complexity of problem solving by Turing machines

In Chapters 1 and 2 we have presented TMs as our principal computational model; thus it seems reasonable to start our formal analysis of computational complexity from this model.

Let us define time complexity. The time a TM spends to solve a problem is clearly related to the number of steps (transitions) performed during its computation. Each transition implies entering a new state, printing tape symbols, and moving tape heads; we can assume that transitions require a constant time for execution. Thus we can assume the single transition of the TM as our unit of measure and we can evaluate time complexity as the total number of transitions performed by the machine before reaching a halt condition.

Definition 3.3

Let M be a deterministic k-tape TM and let $x \in I^*$. Let $c_0 \underset{M}{\vdash} c_1 \underset{M}{\vdash} c_2 \vdash \cdots \underset{M}{\vdash}$ c_r be a *computation*, that is, a sequence of transitions of M such that

$$c_0 = \langle q_0, \uparrow x, \uparrow Z_0, \ldots \uparrow Z_0 \rangle$$
$$c_i = \langle q_i, x_i \uparrow y_i, \alpha_{i1} \uparrow \beta_{i1}, \ldots, \alpha_{ik} \uparrow \beta_{ik} \rangle$$

c_r is a halting configuration of M, *if any*.
Then the time complexity function T_M of M is defined as

$$T_M(x) = \textbf{if} \text{ the computation is finite } \textbf{then } r \textbf{ else } \infty$$

The definition holds also in the case of a k-tape TM with output, with only a few minor formal differences. □

Time complexity is defined above as a function that gives the exact number of steps required by a TM to reach a halt for every input string x. In the same spirit, we can define space complexity, as the maximum amount of used tape cells.

Definition 3.4

Let $M, x, c_0, \ldots, c_r$ be defined as in Definition 3.3. Then the space complexity function S_M of M is defined as

$$S_M(x) = \sum_{j=1}^{k} \max \left\{ |\alpha_{ij}| + 1 | i = 1, \ldots, r \right\}$$ □

Notice that the definition of $S_M(x)$ ignores both $\mathbf{T}_I$ and $\mathbf{T}_O$. Furthermore, $S_M(x)$ may be finite even if the computation of M never halts.

Example 3.3

Let us define a TM M recognizing the language $L = \{wcw^R | w \in \{a, b\}^*\}$. M recognizes the language by checking for equality the ith and the $(n - i + 1)$th element of the input string, n being the length of the string and $i = 1, 2, \ldots$. If all equality checks give a positive answer the string is accepted when $i = n - i + 1$ and the ith element is a c.

Apart from the read-only input tape (tape $\mathbf{T}_I$), there are four other tapes, organized as follows.

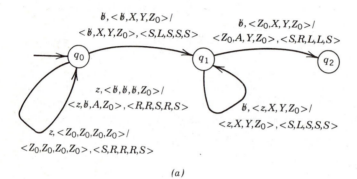

(a)

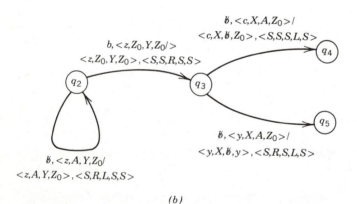

(b)

FIGURE 3.1 A TM accepting $L = \{wcw^R | w \in \{a, b\}^*\}$. (a) Steps 1, 2. (b) Steps 3.1 to 3.4. (c) Steps 3.5 to 3.6. (d) Steps 3.7 to 3.9. (e) Step 4. z stands for a, b, or c. y stands for a or b. X, Y, Z stand for A, Z_0, or $\cancel{b}$.

Tape T_1: Contains a copy of the input string.
Tape T_2: Contains the value of i, coded in unary form.
Tape T_3: Contains the number of unexamined cells of the input tape.
Tape T_4: Contains a copy of the ith element of the input string.

Figure 3.1 gives a formal description of M using a condensed graph representation. As we did in Chapter 1, we use a short notation that allows us to

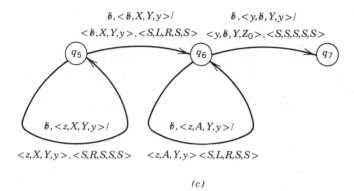

(c)

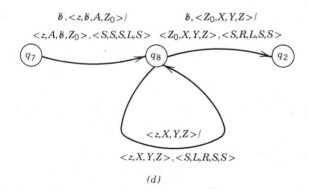

(d)

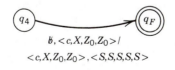

(e)

FIGURE 3.1 Continued.

represent multiple arcs with a single labeled arc. The following detailed description of M's behavior follows exactly the formal description shown in Figure 3.1.

Step 1: The initial configuration is $c_0 = \langle q_0, \uparrow x, \uparrow Z_0, \uparrow Z_0, \uparrow Z_0, \uparrow Z_0 \rangle$ where x is the input string to be recognized.

Step 2: Set the contents of tapes T_1 to x, T_2 to 1, and T_3 to n by scanning the input string from left to right. Then return to the first position of the string that has been copied on tape T_1 in order to start the actual recognition process. Symbol A is used for unary coding on tapes T_2 and T_3. After this step M is in state q_2.

Step 3: Repeat the following actions 3.1 through 3.9.

    3.1 Perform i moves—i is the contents of T_2—on T_1 from left to right (M enters state q_3).

    3.2 If the value being read on T_1 is a c, exit the loop (M enters state q_4).

    3.3 Decrement the value coded in T_3 (if T_3 is empty M halts without accepting);

    3.4 Store the current input value into T_4 (M enters state q_5).

    3.5 Move the head of T_1 from left to right, up to the first blank that follows the input string.

    3.6 Perform i right to left moves on tape T_1; on checking that the current input symbol equals the symbol stored in T_4, the machine enters state q_7.

    3.7 Decrement the value coded in T_3 (if T_3 is empty, M halts without accepting).

    3.8 Increment the value coded in T_2.

    3.9 Move the head of T_1 from right to left up to the symbol Z_0 that precedes the input string.

Step 4: The string is accepted if the current input symbol is a c and the contents of T_3 is zero.

What is the time complexity of recognizing $L = \{ wcw^R | w \in \{ a, b \}^* \}$? Let us first try to derive an answer by applying informal arguments. M does an initial double scan of the input string x of length n to set tape T_1 and T_2. Then it does a double scan for each pair of symbols in position $\langle 1, n \rangle$, $\langle 2, n - 1 \rangle, \ldots$ until it reaches the middle c. Thus, the number of moves is about $2 \cdot n + 2 \cdot n \cdot (n - 1)/2$, n being the length of x.

Let us derive this conclusion more formally by examining the graph that represents M. The number of moves performed to enter state q_2, starting from q_0, is $2 \cdot n + 3$. The number of moves performed on the chain of states q_2, q_3, q_5, q_6, q_7, q_8, q_2 is $2 \cdot n + 5$ (no matter which is i's value). Moreover, this chain is executed $m = (n - 1)/2$ times. In fact, at the $(m + 1)$th iteration the chain from q_2 becomes q_2, q_3, q_4, q_F, which corresponds to $m + 3$ moves. In conclusion, if $x = wcw^R$ for some $w \in \{ a, b \}^*$ and $n = |x|$, then we obtain

$$T_M(x) = 2 \cdot n + 3 + (2 \cdot n + 5) \cdot (n - 1)/2 + (n - 1)/2 + 3$$

$$= (2 \cdot n + 6) \cdot (n + 1)/2$$

It remains to consider what happens when the input string $x \notin L$.

Case 1. $x = \epsilon$. Here we have $T_M(x) = 0$.

Case 2. $|x| = 1$ and $x \neq c$. Here we have $T_M(x) = 7$.

Case 3. $x = w_1 w' w_2 w'' w_1^R$ for some $w_1 \in \{a, b\}^*$, $w' \in \{a, b\}$, $w'' \in \{a, b, c\}$, $w' \neq w''$. Here we have

$$T_M(x) = 2 \cdot n + 3 + (|w_1| - 1) \cdot (2 \cdot n + 5) + n + 2 + |w_1|$$

Case 4. $x = w_1 c w_2$ for some $w_1, w_2 \in \{a, b\}^*$, and $|w_1| < |w_2|$. Here we have

$$T_M(x) = 2 \cdot n + 3 + (|w_1| - 1) \cdot (2 \cdot n + 5) + |w_1| + 2$$

Finally, we turn to the simpler problem of space complexity. The number of cells used on tape $\mathbf{T}_1$ and $\mathbf{T}_3$ is $n + 2$. This is a bound also for the number of cells used on $\mathbf{T}_2$. Tape $\mathbf{T}_4$ only uses one cell. In conclusion, $S_M(x)$ is bounded by $3 \cdot (|x| + 2) + 1$ for any x.

Let us draw some conclusions from the previous example. According to Definitions 3.3 and 3.4, both T_M and S_M are functions on I^*. The example has shown that T_M depends both on the length of the string and on its value. This is true in general for time and space complexity and, in fact, in Section 3.1 we have captured dependency on the values by introducing the concepts of best-, average-, and worst-case complexity. In practice, however, dealing with complexity as a function over I^* leads to unnecessary intricacies in the analysis of algorithms. In addition, average-case complexity is heavily dependent on statistical information on input data, whereas best-case complexity is not so useful in practice. Thus, for simplicity, the rest of this chapter implicitly refers to worst-case complexity unless otherwise explicitly stated. Consequently, we decide to base our definitions of time and space complexity on the length of the string (i.e., their domain is $\mathbb{N}$ instead of I^*). For simplicity, we use the same function names T_M and S_M to denote time and space complexity both when the domain is $\mathbb{N}$ and when it is I^*. In doing so, we are trading readability for formality. The context will always make clear which domain is implied. Also, in the sequel we will mostly refer to complexity in terms of the length of the string.

Definition 3.5

Let M be a TM. The time complexity function T_M with domain $\mathbb{N}$ is defined as

$$T_M(n) = \max \{ T_M(x) \mid |x| = n \}$$

Similarly, the space complexity function S_M with domain $\mathbb{N}$ is defined as

$$S_M(n) = \max \{ S_M(x) \mid |x| = n \} \qquad \square$$

Definition 3.5 relates time and space complexities to the length of the input. The asymptotic behavior can thus be described by means of the big-theta notation that was introduced in Section 3.1.2. In the case discussed in Example 3.3, we can conclude that T_M is $\Theta(n^2)$ and S_M is $\Theta(n)$.

Exercises

3.4 Consider a different TM M_2 that recognizes $L = \{wcw^R | w \in \{a, b\}^*\}$. M_2 copies the contents of tape $\mathbf{T}_I$ onto tape $\mathbf{T}_1$ until c is encountered. Then it scans backwards $\mathbf{T}_1$ as it reads from $\mathbf{T}_I$ and checks the symbols it reads for equality. Note that, in this case, tape $\mathbf{T}_1$ simulates the behavior of a stack, and the entire recognition process resembles the recognition with a pushdown automaton (see Exercise 1.20 and Example 3.5). Design M_2 and describe T_{M_2} and S_{M_2}, in every detail, both in the case where the domain is I^* and when the domain is $\mathbb{N}$. Prove that T_{M_2}, the time complexity function with domain $\mathbb{N}$, is $\Theta(n)$.

3.5 Design a TM M_3 that recognizes $L = \{ww^R | w \in \{a, b\}^*\}$. M_3 should be based on the definition of M given in Example 3.3. If x is an input string, n is its length and x_j denotes the jth symbol of x, M should apply an equality check to all pairs $\langle x_i, x_{n-i+1} \rangle$, for $i < n - i + 1$. Prove that T_{M_3} is $\Theta(n^2)$.

3.6* Design a TM M_4 to recognize $L = \{wcw^R | w \in \{a, b\}^*\}$, which has space complexity $\Theta(\log n)$. Essentially, M_4 is derived from the original machine M of Example 3.3 by coding the counters in binary base instead of unary base. However, two nontrivial modifications are necessary in order to carry over the construction of M_4 with the desired space complexity. First the initial copy of the input string into $\mathbf{T}_1$ must be avoided because this would immediately produce a $\Theta(n)$ space complexity. Since, after Step 2, $\mathbf{T}_1$ is used as a read-only tape, we can use directly $\mathbf{T}_I$ instead of $\mathbf{T}_1$. Although this use of $\mathbf{T}_I$ perfectly agrees with the formal definition of TMs, the reader might prefer to view $\mathbf{T}_I$ as a pure input channel, as we did in Example 3.3. However, this little "trick" is needed if we wish to achieve the required complexity. Second, it is necessary that, at every loop iteration, $\mathbf{T}_I$'s head reaches positions i and $n - i + 1$ without requiring that any other head scans more cells than a number bounded by a $\Theta(\log n)$ function.

Once you have completely designed M_4, analyze its time complexity too.

3.7* Design a TM M that recognizes the language

$$L = \{a^{n_1}ba^{n_2}b \cdots a^{n_k}c | k \geq 2, n_1 \leq n_2 \cdots \leq n_k\}$$

such that T_M is $\Theta(n)$.

Having realized that a problem P—say, recognizing a language L—can be solved by different machines with different complexities, one might wonder whether it makes any sense to define some complexity measure for the problem itself. In the case of language recognition, one might try to define it as the "best" complexity among those achieved by the machines recognizing L. Unfortunately, this definition does not make sense, because we know that, in general, different solutions may not be comparable even from the point of view of their big-theta complexity. However, we shall see in Section 3.3 that interesting comparisons can be obtained on complexity of language recognition without explicit reference to particular machines.

Example 3.4

Let us define a TM M that solves the membership problem (see Example 3.1) for a set of characters of alphabet I. The input string is $x = ay$ where y is a string representation of the set and a is a single character. M accepts x whenever $a \in \{c \mid c$ is a character of $y\}$.

Besides input tape $\mathbf{T}_I$, M has another tape $\mathbf{T}_1$ where we keep the first character of x. The solution is shown in Figure 3.2 in the usual condensed graph form.

What is time complexity in this case? It is not difficult to derive the following formula

$$T_M(x) = \textbf{if } x = aw_1aw_2, w_1 \in (I - \{a\})^*, w_2 \in I^*$$
$$\textbf{then } |aw_1a| \textbf{ else } |x|$$

Thus $T_M(n) = n$.

We obtain here the same results we discussed in Section 3.1 using Pascal as computation model. The main difference, however, is that the linear search algorithm is the best we can do with TMs: It is not possible here to obtain a better time complexity by applying binary search. In fact, the tape of a TM is a sequential access device and therefore it does not provide random access in one time unit. The reader is invited to verify that the execution of binary search on a

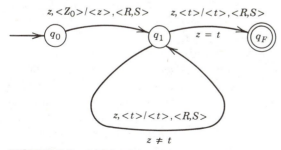

FIGURE 3.2 A TM solving the membership problem. z, t denote any symbol of I.

TM would actually lead to a worse time complexity than in the case of linear search.

Exercises

3.8 The TM of Example 3.4 solves a slightly different problem than the procedures of Examples 3.1 and 3.2. In fact, in this case a single character is searched, whereas previously an integer was searched. Modify the TM M of Example 3.4 in order to search binary coded integers. Precisely, the new machine M_2 must recognize the language $L = \{ x | x = z \$ y_1 \$ \cdots \$ y_m, z, y_i \in \{0, 1\}^*$ and $\exists i, 1 \le i \le m$, such that $z = y_i \}$.

For simplicity, assume that z and y_i all have the same length and compute T_{M_2} both as a function of x and as a function of the number of elements m of the set to be searched.

3.9* Remove the simplifying assumption in the previous exercise and solve it again.

Example 3.4 and the related exercises confirm an important fact that was mentioned before in Section 3.1.1: Problem complexity depends on the computational model. Worst-case complexity of the searching problem is $\Theta(\log n)$ if we choose Pascal as our computational model; it is $\Theta(n)$ if we refer to TMs.

This remark should be contrasted with Church's Thesis, which refers to problem solvability. We know that if a problem can be solved in Pascal, then it can be solved by some TM, and conversely. Instead, if a problem is solved by a Pascal program with complexity function T, this does not guarantee that a TM can solve the same problem with the same complexity function. However, we realize in Sections 3.2.2 and 3.5 that computational complexities that refer to different computational models can at least be related to each other in a fairly systematic way.

In Section 3.1.1 we mentioned yet another factor that may affect our complexity measures: data encoding. In fact, we related complexity to the length of the input string; but the input string is used to represent input data in some coded form. If the coding changes, we may get a different complexity for the same algorithm. An example of this is provided by the machine described in Example 3.3 and by its modification outlined in Exercise 3.6, which dramatically affects its space complexity. The influence of data encoding on complexity is clearly disturbing. However, we ignore the problem here and continue our discussion by examining TMs that recognize languages, without any further assumption on whether the input strings do indeed represent some other entities in coded form.

Exercise

3.10 Give TMs solving the problems below and analyze the complexity of their computations. Try to understand if the results you have obtained can be improved and to what extent.
1. Subtract two integers coded in base 2.
2. Subtract two integers coded in unary base.
3. Recognize the language $L = \{ a^n b^n c^n | n \geq 1 \}$.
4. Recognize the language $L = \{ a^n b^{n^2} | n \geq 1 \}$.
5. Recognize the language $L = \{ a^n b^n | n \geq 1 \} \cup \{ a^n b^{2n} | n \geq 1 \}$

3.2.2 The Complexity of Problem Solving by Other Automata

So far we have analyzed the complexity of solving a few simple problems by means of multitape TMs. How general are the results we have obtained? Are complexity formulas likely to change if we change the abstract machine that computes the solution of a problem? If the answer to this question is "Yes," can we expect any dramatic changes? Somehow, these questions try to find a counterpart of Church's Thesis for computational complexity. Since we discovered results of general validity in the field of problem solvability, and since complexity can be seen as a refinement of decidability there is hope to answer these questions. To do so, let us start analyzing the complexity of problem solving by means of some other formalisms among those presented in Chapter 1.

3.2.2.1 Complexity of Finite-State Automata Computations

Let A be a finite-state automaton. We naturally define $T_A(x)$ as the integer i such that $\delta^i(q_0, x) = q$ for some q, if any. If $\delta^*(q_0, x)$ is undefined, we conventionally set $T_A(x) = |x|$. Clearly $T_A(x)$ denotes the number of moves (state transitions) of A during recognition. Going back to Definition 1.1 and realizing that FAs perform exactly one move for each input symbol, we can state time complexity as follows.

Statement 3.3
For any FA A and for any x, $T_A(x) = |x|$. □

It is worth pointing out the relevance of Statement 3.3. Unlike previous examples, here a whole class of models has a fixed—and very simple—complexity formula independent of the particular problem to be solved.

Notice also that it is straightforward to simulate FAs by means of suitable PDAs or TMs in such a way that the same time complexity formula still holds. More precisely, a TM simulating a FA may take $|x| + 1$ moves to decide $x \in L$, since a TM can accept only in a halting configuration, whereas a FA does not require a final state to be a halting state. Thus we obtain the following general statement.

Statement 3.4
Regular languages can be recognized by FAs, PDAs, and TMs in a number of moves equal to $|x|$ or $|x| + 1$, x being the input string to recognize.   □

Space complexity for FAs is quite a simple matter. Just consider that a FA is a k-tape TM with $k = 0$. Thus we obtain that $S_A(x) = 0$ for any FA A and for any input string x. This fact is only apparently striking. In fact, FAs are truly finite-memory devices, whereas $S(x)$ gives a measure of the unbounded memory that is needed to process a string (apart from the finite memory of the control unit).

3.2.2.2 Complexity of Pushdown Automata Computations

For a given PDA A, let us first define $T_A(x)$ and consequently $T_A(n)$.

Definition 3.6
Let A be a PDA. For any $x \in I^*$, let $c_0 = \langle q_0, x, Z_0 \rangle$ be an initial configuration and let $c_0 \vdash c_1 \vdash \cdots \vdash c_r$ be the sequence of transitions starting from c_0; let c_r be a halting configuration, either accepting or rejecting x, if there is one. If A halts, let $T_A(x) = r$. Otherwise, let $T_A(x) = \infty$ if there is no halting configuration.

$$T_A(n) = \max \{ T_A(x) | \; |x| = n \}$$ □

Definition 3.7
Let $c_0 = \langle q_0, x, Z_0 \rangle \vdash \cdots \vdash c_i = \langle q_i, x_i, \gamma_i \rangle \cdots \vdash c_r$ be the sequence of transitions performed by a PDA A when operating on input $x \in I^*$ (the sequence can be infinite if the PDA does not halt). Then

$$S_A(x) = \max \{ |\gamma_i| \; | i = 1, \ldots, r \}$$
$$S_A(n) = \max \{ S_A(x) | \; |x| = n \}$$ □

Thus, space complexity of PDA is the amount of stack necessary to perform a computation. As for FAs and TMs, the finite memory of the control unit is not considered.

Let us go back to a previous example from the point of view of PDA complexity.

Example 3.5

The PDA described in Figure 3.3 (see also Exercise 1.20) recognizes the language $L = \{ wcw^R | w \in \{ a, b \}^* \}$, which has been examined also in Example 3.3.

Determining the values $T_A(x)$ (and $T_A(n)$) is quite an easy job, because A does not make any ϵ-move except for the last one. Thus $T_A(x) = |x| + 1$ if

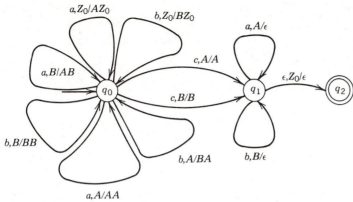

FIGURE 3.3 A PDA accepting $\{wcw^R\}$.

$x \in L(A)$ and, in general, $T_A(n) = n + 1$. $S_A(n)$ is also quite easy to obtain. Input symbols are stacked until c is encountered; then they are popped off (if $x \in L$). Thus $S_A(x) = (|x| - 1)/2$ if $x \in L$ and, in general, $S_A(n) = n$

These results are not surprising at all. In general, it is easy to prove that for any PDA A a 1-tape TM can be built that simulates it and has the same time and space complexity formulas[3].

Unlike FAs, PDAs can perform ϵ-moves. Thus the simple time complexity formula of FAs does not hold in general for PDAs. However, we will realize that a simple complexity formula holds for PDAs as well. First, notice that if we restrict our attention to loop-free PDAs, without any loss of generality (thanks to Theorem 1.11), then we may assume $T_A(n)$ finite for any PDA A and for any n. Furthermore, the following theorem holds.

Theorem 3.5
Any deterministic context-free language L can be recognized by some PDA A with time complexity $T_A(n) = k_A \cdot n$, where n is the length of the input string and k_A is a suitable constant.

Proof
We already stated that we can assume A to be loop-free without any loss of generality. For $q \in Q$, $z \in \Gamma$, let C_{qz} be the maximum number of moves in A's transition sequences of the type $\langle q, \epsilon, Z \rangle \overset{*}{\vdash} \langle p, \epsilon, \alpha Z \rangle$, $\alpha \in \Gamma^*$. Because A is loop-free, C_{qz} is finite for any q and Z.

Let $C = \max \{ C_{qz} | q \in Q, Z \in \Gamma \}$

---

[3]As it happens for FAs, a TM simulating a PDA may require one extra step to enter a final state.

Let $h = \max\{|\alpha| \,|\, \delta(q, a, Z) = \langle q', \alpha \rangle \lor \delta(q, \epsilon, Z) = \langle q', \alpha \rangle$, for $q \in Q$, $Z \in \Gamma\}$, that is, the maximum length of strings that can be pushed onto the stack in one move. Notice that both C and h can be effectively computed.

Now observe that in the sequence

$$\langle q_0, x, Z_0 \rangle \overset{*d}{\underset{A}{\vdash}} \langle q, \epsilon, \gamma \rangle$$

there are exactly $|x|$ transitions of the type

$$\langle p, ay, \gamma \rangle \vdash \langle p', y, \gamma' \rangle$$

and at most $C \cdot |x|$ transitions of the type

$$\langle p, y, Z\gamma_1 \rangle \vdash \langle p', y, \gamma_2\gamma_1 \rangle$$

All other transitions are of the type

$$\langle p, y, Z\gamma_1 \rangle \vdash \langle p', y, \gamma_1 \rangle$$

Thus transitions of the latter type cannot be more than $h \cdot |x| + h \cdot C \cdot |x|$. So the total length of the transition sequence is bounded by $(1 + h + h \cdot C + C) \cdot |x|$. ∎

Corollary 3.6
Any deterministic context-free language L can be recognized with a $\Theta(n)$ space complexity. □

The trivial proof is left to the reader as an exercise.

3.2.2.3 Complexity of Single-Tape TMs

Now let us consider the complexity of computations performed by single-tape TMs. We will derive some interesting and somewhat surprising remarks. Time and space complexity are obviously defined for single tape TMs as for multitape TMs. A surprising consequence can be derived from our definition of space complexity. In fact, $S_M(x)$—the number of tape cells visited by M during computation on input x—can never be less than $|x|$. The same does not hold for multitape TMs, FAs, and PDAs. The reason is that single-tape TMs use their unique tape both as input, output, and memory device. Other surprising facts can be derived for time complexity, as we will show in the sequel.

Consider again the familiar example of the language

$$L = \{wcw^R \,|\, w \in \{a, b\}^*\}$$

A simple single-tape TM M recognizing L performs the following steps.

Step 1: M reaches character c of the input string x, if any.
Step 2: Let z be the position of the cell storing c. M alternatively checks for equality the characters stored in positions $z - 1$ and $z + 1$, $z - 2$ and

$z + 2$, and so on. After the check, M writes a special character in the cell.

Step 3: M recognizes x if all equality checks succeed and blanks are found in positions $z + m$, $z - m$ where $m = (|x| + 1)/2$.

Exercise

3.11 Detail the construction of M and prove that T_M is $\Theta(n^2)$.

The result proven in Exercise 3.11 shows that a single-tape TM recognizing L has the same big-theta complexity as the multitape machine of Example 3.3.

It is not as easy to simulate the behavior of M_2 described in Exercise 3.4 while maintaining its linear complexity formula. Even worse, the following theorem shows that such goal cannot be reached.

Theorem 3.7

No single-tape TM M can recognize $L = \{wcw^R | w \in \{a, b\}^*\}$ with $\Theta(T_M) < \Theta(n^2)$.

Proof *

The proof of this theorem is not trivial and is based on the notion of *crossing sequence*, which has been useful in the proof of several results of computation

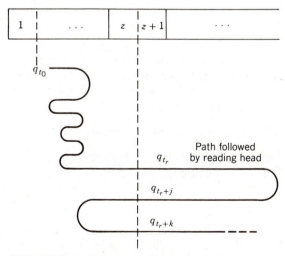

FIGURE 3.4 Crossing sequences.

theory. Intuitively, a crossing sequence of a TM computation is the sequence of states in which the machine crosses the boundary between two consecutive cells during its computation. This is illustrated intuitively in Figure 3.4. Figure 3.4 shows the tape, the path followed by the head, and the state each time the boundary between cells z and $z + 1$ is crossed. In the case of Figure 3.4, the sequence of states $q_{t_r}, q_{t_r+j}, q_{t_r+k}$, is the crossing sequence of the boundary between cell z and $z + 1$. Formally, a crossing sequence is defined as follows.

Definition 3.8 (Crossing Sequence)

Let $c_0 \vdash c_1 \vdash \cdots c_t \vdash \ldots$ be a transition sequence of a single-tape TM M. Let $\{q(t)|t = 0, 1, \ldots\}$ be the sequence of states entered by M and let $\{z(t)|t = 0, 1, \ldots\}$ be the sequence of head positions at times $0, 1, \ldots t$ (by convention, assume that $z(0) = 1$).

The crossing sequence $CS(z)$, associated to position z is the subsequence $\{q(t_k)\}$ of $\{q(t)\}$ such that either

a. $z(t_k) = z$ and $z(t_k + 1) = z + 1$, or
b. $z(t_k) = z + 1$ and $z(t_k + 1) = z$ □

Before going into the proof of Theorem 3.7, we need the following technical lemmas.

Lemma 3.8

If a single-tape and deterministic TM M has no move where $\delta(q, i) = \langle q', i', S \rangle$ for some q' and i', then the time taken by M on input string w is the sum of the lengths of the crossing sequences over all z's. In the general case, M's computation time is bounded by a linear function of such a sum, provided that M cannot perform an unbounded sequence of moves such that the head remains stationary (S-moves).

Outline of the Proof

The first part of the statement can be immediately obtained by looking at Figure 3.4. In fact, if M cannot perform S-moves, each state belongs to just one $CS(z)$.

The second part of the statement follows from the fact that M can perform a number of consecutive S-moves that is bound by some integer k. Thus, if $\sum_{z=-\infty}^{+\infty} CS(z)$ is r, the number of M's moves is at most $k \cdot r$. Notice that, for each TM M, one can easily build an equivalent M' that performs only a bounded number of consecutive S-moves, such that $T_M(n) \geq T_{M'}(n)$ for every n.   □

Lemma 3.9

Let M be a single-tape and deterministic TM. When M terminates its computation, suppose it always halts to the right of the cells on which its input was originally written. Then, if M accepts $w_1 w_2$ and $CS(|w_1|) = CS(|x_1|)$, when M

M is given input $x_1 x_2$ (i.e., the crossing sequence on the boundary between w_1 and w_2 is the same as between x_1 and x_2), then M accepts $x_1 w_2$.

Outline of the Proof

Let $|w_1| = z$ and $|x_1| = y$. Also, let $CS(z) = \{q_{i_1}, \ldots, q_{i_k}\}$ when M operates with input $w_1 w_2$ and let $CS(y) = \{q_{i_1}, \ldots, q_{i_k}\}$ when M operates with input $x_1 x_2$.

Consider now M's behavior on $x_1 w_2$. The first time M crosses the boundary between position y and $y + 1$ it enters a state q_{i_1}. Thus its subsequent move is the same as after the first time it crosses the boundary between cells z and $z + 1$ when operating on $w_1 w_2$. The same occurs the *third* time it crosses the same boundary (the second time it crosses the boundary in the reverse direction), the *fifth* time, and so on. Notice that k must be odd because M halts to the right of $w_1 w_2$. Thus every time M reaches the portion of tape occupied by w_2 its moves are the same as for $w_1 w_2$ and the thesis follows. Notice that every TM can be modified to meet the hypothesis of the lemma by increasing its T_M by a term which is $\Theta(n)$. □

Proof of Main Theorem

First assume that the hypothesis of both Lemmas 3.8 and 3.9 hold, that is, M does not have any transition such that $\delta(q, i) = \langle q', i', S \rangle$ and, if it accepts its input, does so with its head to the right of the cells on which the input was originally written. These assumptions do not cause any loss of generality. In fact, we have shown in the proofs of the above lemmas that, if a TM M has time complexity T_M, then an equivalent M' can be built, satisfying the hypothesis of the lemmas and with $\Theta(T_{M'}) \leq \Theta(T_M)$.

Consider any string wcw^R and let $|wcw^R| = n$, so that $|w| = m = (n - 1)/2$. Let $l_{w, z} = |CS(z)|$, $1 \leq z \leq m$ where $CS(z)$ refers to a computation of a TM M recognizing wcw^R.

Let $a(z)$ be the average of $l_{w, z}$ over all strings w with $|w| = m$, that is,

$$a(z) = \frac{\sum\limits_{|w| = m} l_{w, z}}{2^m}$$

Notice that for at least half of all words w, $l_{w, z} \leq 2 \cdot a(z)$ for any z. In fact, if for more than half of such words, $l_{w, z}$ were greater than $2 \cdot a(z)$, even in the case where the remaining $l_{w, z}$ were 0, we would have

$$a(z) > \frac{\frac{1}{2} \cdot 2 \cdot a(z) \cdot 2^m}{2^m} = a(z)$$

But this would be a contradiction. Thus, since there are exactly 2^m different words w, there are at least 2^{m-1} such words where $l_{w, z} \leq 2 \cdot a(z)$.

For any i, the number of different crossing sequences of length i is $|Q|^i$, where Q is the set of M's states. Thus the number of different crossing sequences not longer than $2 \cdot a(z)$ is

$$\sum_{i=1}^{2 \cdot a(z)} |Q|^i$$

Notice now that for any $k \geq 1$ and $n \geq 2$,

$$\sum_{i=1}^{k} n^i \leq n^{k+1}$$

This can be easily proved by induction on k since, for $k = 1$, $n \leq n^2$ and $\sum_{i=1}^{k} n^k \leq n^{k+1}$ implies

$$\sum_{i=1}^{k+1} n^i = \sum_{i=1}^{k} n^i + n^{k+1} \leq n^{k+1} + n^{k+1} \leq n^{k+2}$$

Since $|Q|$ is necessarily greater than or equal to 2 (otherwise M could not accept L) the number of different crossing sequences whose length does not exceed $2 \cdot a(z)$ is less than or equal to $|Q|^{2 \cdot a(z)+1}$. Thus there are at least

$$\frac{2^{m-1}}{|Q|^{2 \cdot a(z)+1}}$$

words w with the same $CS(z)$ for any z. Consider the partitioning $w = w_z \hat{w}_z$ with $|w_z| = z, |\hat{w}_z| = m - z$. For any z, the number of different words $\hat{w}_z$ is 2^{m-z}.

Now, either

$$\frac{2^{m-1}}{|Q|^{2 \cdot a(z)+1}} > 2^{m-z}$$

or not. In the former case, there would be more different words w with the same $CS(z)$ than different words $\hat{w}_z$. Thus at least two of them must differ in the part w_z, say $w' = w_z'\hat{w}_z'$, $w'' = w_z''\hat{w}_z''$ with $w_z' \neq w_z''$. Then by Lemma 3.9, since M accepts $w'cw'^R$, it must also accept $w_z''\hat{w}_z'cw'^R$: a contradiction.
Therefore it must be

$$\frac{2^{m-1}}{|Q|^{2 \cdot a(z)+1}} \leq 2^{m-z}$$

that is,

$$a(z) \geq \frac{(z-1)}{2 \cdot \log_2 (|Q|)} - \frac{1}{2}$$

By virtue of Lemma 3.8, the time spent by M when recognizing $x = wcw^R$ is

$$T_M(x) = \sum_{z=-\infty}^{+\infty} l_{w,z} \geq \sum_{z=1}^{m} l_{w,z}$$

Thus the average time spent by M to recognize all strings $x = wcw^R$, with $|x| = n$ is

$$\sum_{|w|=m} \frac{T_M(x)}{2^m} \geq \frac{\sum\limits_{|w|=m} \sum\limits_{z=1}^{m} l_{w,z}}{2^m}$$

$$= \frac{\sum\limits_{z=1}^{m} \sum\limits_{|w|=m} l_{w,z}}{2^m} = \sum_{z=1}^{m} a(z) \geq \sum_{z=1}^{m} \frac{z-1}{2\log|Q|} - \frac{m}{2}$$

$$= \frac{1}{2\log|Q|} \sum_{z=1}^{m} z - \frac{m}{2\log|Q|} - \frac{m}{2}$$

$$= \frac{m(m-1)}{4\log|Q|} + \frac{m}{2}\left(1 - \frac{1}{2\log|Q|}\right)$$

Clearly, the longest computation on strings of length n cannot be shorter than the average one. Thus T_M is $\Theta(n^2)$ and the thesis is finally proved. ∎

Theorem 3.7 shows a somewhat surprising fact. Although single-tape TMs have maximal computational power as far as the class of problems they can solve is concerned, sometimes they may be slower than less powerful formalisms. The reason is in the way single-tape TMs use their tape. Since the tape serves both as input, output, and auxiliary memory, several back and forth movements of the machine are only due to the need for reaching the auxiliary information. For instance, in the case of $L = \{wcw^R\}$, the pushdown automaton must simply compare the input symbols after c with the top symbols of the stack (and pop them). On the contrary, a single-tape TM while reading w^R must look for a corresponding symbol stored somewhere else in the tape, possibly not so close.

Notice that the same inconvenience does not hold for multitape TMs which we already know to be more powerful than other automata even from the viewpoint of computational complexity. Therefore, it is worth investigating some general complexity properties of the multitape model. Section 3.3 presents some relevant ones that should shed some light on the problems of computational complexity without trying to provide a complete overview of the field.

Exercises

3.12 Prove that no single-tape TM can recognize $L = \{ww^R\}$ with time complexity less than $\Theta(n^2)$.

3.13 Build single-tape TMs solving the problems listed in Exercise 3.10 and check whether their asymptotic behavior has changed with respect to multitape TMs or not.

3.3 Some General Properties of Multitape TM Complexity

The results presented in this section should enlighten the use of formal models in understanding computational complexity issues. We will turn to more practical, programming-oriented topics in later sections. As a first step, let us generalize complexity definitions to nondeterministic computations.

Definition 3.9

Let M be a nondeterministic multitape TM accepting language L. M has time complexity T_M (respectively, space complexity S_M) with domain I^* if for any input string x, $x \in L$ if and only if there exists at least one computation of M accepting x in $T_M(x)$ moves (respectively, using $S_M(x)$ memory tape cells) and no other computation accepts x in less than $T_M(x)$ moves (respectively, using less than $S_M(x)$ memory tape cells). $T_M(n)$ (respectively, $S_M(n)$) is defined as the maximum of $T_M(x)$ (respectively, $S_M(x)$) over all $x \in L$ of length n. □

Warning *

The careful reader probably did not miss a few critical points in the foregoing definition. First, the definition refers to TMs used as language acceptors, that is, a restriction with respect to all their potential uses. The definition is consistent with the usual way nondeterministic devices are used as language recognizers. Among the many possible computations we are interested in the existence of *at least* one leading to acceptance. Therefore, it seems natural centering complexity definition on that computation.

Instead, in case we were interested in TMs as language translators (i.e., in computing *all* values of a multivalued translation $\tau(x)$ computed by the nondeterministic TM), the "worst-case" philosophy should lead to the choice of the longest computation among those due to input x. This choice, however, would lead to some intricacy in the case where some computations on x were non-terminating. However, here we focus our attention on the language recognition framework, which is generally adopted in the literature on TM complexity.

Another unpleasant consequence of Definition 3.9 is that it does not reduce to Definition 3.3 in the particular case where M is deterministic. In fact, if $x \notin L$ the definition is satisfied by any value of T_M. For instance, if $T_M(n) = n^2$, for some $x \notin L$ M can take more than $|x|^2$ moves and even enter nonterminating computations according to Definition 3.9. This is not permitted according to Definition 3.3.

Alternatively, one could adopt the following definition.

Definition 3.9a

Let M be a nondeterministic TM. $T_M(x)$ is such that no computation performed on input x takes more than $T_M(x)$ moves and at least one takes exactly $T_M(x)$ moves. $S_M(x)$, $T_M(n)$, and $S_M(n)$ are defined accordingly. □

Such definition would somewhat contrast with the above remarks. Therefore, Definition 3.9 is generally preferred. However, in most interesting cases the difference between the two definitions is not dramatic. First, notice that if T_M is a total computable function, the language accepted by M is recursive. In fact, in order to state if $x \in L(M)$, we just need to consider all computations with length less than or equal to $T_M(n)$, where $n = |x|$. There is only a finite number of such computations. Thus we can assume, without any loss of generality, that M always halts. The same holds if $T_M(n) \leq f(n)$ for same total computable function f. Second, all of the results presented in this text concerning the computational complexity of nondeterministic TMs hold as well for both definitions. This can be verified by the reader statement by statement. Third, we will realize that in many interesting cases the two definitions are in some sense equivalent. This will be shown later in this section as a corollary of the Linear Speed-up Theorem (Corollary 3.14). ■

Once a complexity function has been associated to a machine, it is natural to consider the class of problems solved within some predefined complexity bounds. In terms of language recognition this leads to the following definition.

Definition 3.10
Let f be a total function on naturals. DTIME(f) is the family of languages recognized by some deterministic multitape TM with time complexity bounded by f, that is, such that $T_M(n) \leq f(n)$ for every n.

Similarly, DSPACE(f) is the family of languages accepted by some deterministic multitape TM with space complexity bounded by f.

NTIME(f) and NSPACE(f) are defined similarly for languages accepted by nondeterministic TMs. □

As an example $L = \{wcw^R\}$ is in DTIME(n) and in DSPACE ($\log_2 n$) as shown in Exercises 3.4 and 3.6. Notice, however, that this does not mean that L can be recognized by the same TM in both time n and space $\log n$. Very often, in general, one must trade time efficiency for space efficiency, and vice versa.

Exercises

3.14 Prove that if $f_1(n) \leq f_2(n)$ for every n, then DTIME(f_1) $\subseteq$ DTIME(f_2) and similarly for NTIME, DSPACE, and NSPACE.

3.15 Find deterministic and nondeterministic time and space complexity classes as small as you can containing the following languages.

$$L_1 = \{ww | w \in \{a, b\}^*\}$$

$$L_2 = \{a^{n_1} b a^{n_2} \cdots a^{n_k} | \exists i, j, 1 \leq i \neq j \leq k \text{ such that } n_i = n_j\}$$

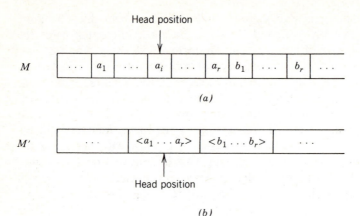

FIGURE 3.5 *(a)* A tape of *M*. *(b)* The corresponding tape of *M'*.

In Sections 3.1 and 3.2 we have noticed that the complexity of a problem solution can be improved by a suitable change in the solution algorithm. How much can complexity be improved? We will show that linear improvements can be obtained both for time and space complexity in a systematic way.

Theorem 3.10
If *L* is accepted by a multitape—whether deterministic or not—TM with space complexity *S* then, for any real constant $c > 0$, *L* is accepted by some TM with space complexity $c \cdot S$ ($c \cdot S$ denotes the function S' such that $S'(n) = c \cdot S(n)$ for every n).

Outline of the Proof
Let *r* be an integer such that $r \cdot c \geq 2$. We can collapse *r* adjacent cells of any tape of TM *M* into a single cell and still have an equivalent TM *M'*, by means of a suitable coding and a modification of Γ, *Q*, δ. Clearly, the new TM has the desired space complexity. Figure 3.5 gives an intuitive sketch of the construction. In order to code the position of *M*'s head within the r-tuple $\langle a_1, \ldots, a_r \rangle$, the state of *M'* is a pair $\langle q, i \rangle$, with $1 \leq i \leq r$, in the case of a single-tape TM; a $(k + 1)$-tuple in the case of a *k*-tape TM. ∎

Theorem 3.11
If *L* is accepted by some *k*-tape TM *M* with space complexity *S*, then it is accepted also by some 1-tape TM *M'* with the same complexity *S*.

The proof is left as an exercise to the reader. As a hint, in Figure 3.6 it is suggested that mutually disjoint alphabets can be used for each memory tape. The "meaningful" portions of each memory tape of *M* (i.e., a portion including all nonblank cells and the head position) are stored consecutively in the only

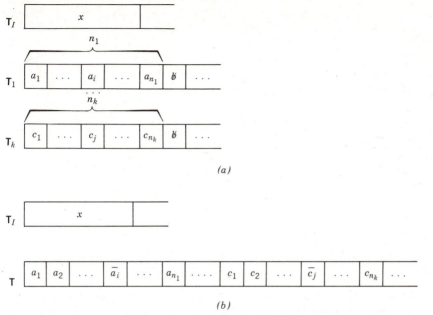

FIGURE 3.6 (a) A k-tape TM, M. (b) An equivalent 1-tape TM, M', with the same space complexity.

memory tape of M'. The positions of the k heads of M are recorded by using suitable special symbols. ∎

Exercise

3.16 Prove that if a language L is accepted by a TM with space complexity such that $S(n) \geq n$ for each n, then it is accepted by a single-tape TM with space complexity S.

Similar results do not hold for time complexity in general. For example, the counterpart of Exercise 3.16 does not hold for time complexity, since $L = \{ wcw^R \}$ can be recognized with time complexity that is $\Theta(n)$ by a 1-tape TM, but no single-tape TM can have the same complexity (see Theorem 3.7).

However, we will be able to state a suitable counterpart of Theorem 3.10 for time complexity. First, let us give a new definition.

Definition 3.11

Let f be any function on natural numbers. We define $\displaystyle\sup_{n \to \infty} f(n)$ (respectively, $\displaystyle\inf_{n \to \infty} f(n)$) as the limit of the least upper bound (respectively, greatest lower bound) of the sequence $\{ f(n), f(n + 1)\dots \}$ as $n \to \infty$. □

Obviously, if $\lim_{n \to \infty} f(n)$ exists, then $\lim_{n \to \infty} f(n) = \inf_{n \to \infty} f(n) = \sup_{n \to \infty} f(n)$. For instance,

$$\sup_{n \to \infty} n \cdot (\sin(n) + 1) = \infty, \quad \inf_{n \to \infty} n \cdot (\sin(n) + 1) = 0,$$

$$\sup_{n \to \infty} (\sin(n) + 1) = 2, \quad \inf_{n \to \infty} (\sin(n) + 1) = 0,$$

$$\sup_{n \to \infty} \frac{n + \log n}{n} = \inf_{n \to \infty} \frac{n + \log n}{n} = 1.$$

Theorem 3.12 (Linear Speed-Up Theorem)

Let L be accepted by a k-tape TM M with time complexity T_M such that

$$\inf_{n \to \infty} \frac{T(n)}{n} = \infty$$

Then, for any real constant $c > 0$, a $k + 1$-tape TM M' can be built that accepts L with time complexity $T_{M'}$, such that $T_{M'}(n) = \max\{n + 1, c \cdot T(n)\}$.

Proof

The main idea of the proof is similar to the case of space complexity linear reduction (Theorem 3.10), because it consists of collapsing r adjacent cells of M into one cell of M', for a suitable value of r (see Figure 3.7). However some more care to the details of the construction is definitely needed in order to derive time complexity for M'.

In a preliminary phase M' copies the contents of input tape $\mathbf{T}_I$ into its extra storage tape $\mathbf{T}_{k+1}$ by collapsing r adjacent cells of $\mathbf{T}_I$ into one cell of $\mathbf{T}_{k+1}$. Furthermore, it positions the head of $\mathbf{T}_{k+1}$ back onto the first tape cell.

This preliminary phase takes a time $n + \lceil n/r \rceil$, where n is as usual the length of the input string. From now on, M' simulates M by using $\mathbf{T}_{k+1}$ as its input tape. The computation of M' consists of a sequence of *macro moves*. Each macro move, in turn, consists of two groups of at most four and two elementary moves, respectively.

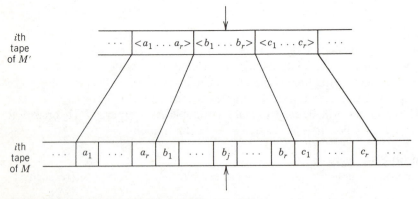

FIGURE 3.7 Construction to speed up a TM.

The former group is organized as follows. For each tape T_i, $1 \le i \le k + 1$, M' visits the two cells to the right and to the left of the previously scanned cell and goes back to it. For instance, M' shown in Figure 3.7 visits cells $\langle a_1 \ldots a_r \rangle$ by one step left, $\langle c_1 \ldots c_r \rangle$ by two steps right and goes back to $\langle b_1 \ldots b_r \rangle$ by one step left.

At this point M' "knows" the contents of the $3 \cdot r$ cells of M, $a_1 \ldots a_r$, $b_1 \ldots b_r$, $c_1 \ldots c_r$. Since such contents may consist of $|\Gamma|^{3r}$ different values, they can be recorded by M' through its state set. Notice that, when M operates on the portion of T_i consisting of the $3 \cdot r$ above cells it may

1. Halt, either accepting or not.
2. Never leave the above portion of tape *for all tapes* T_i. In this case, it must eventually enter a loop of configurations repeated infinitely many times because of the finitely many possible different configurations.
3. Perform a sequence of *at least* $r + 1$ moves such that for some T_i the corresponding head eventually leaves the above portion of $3 \cdot r$ cells.

Cases 1 and 2 can be decided by M' with no move, by only inspecting its state. In fact they correspond to finitely many possible alternatives.

In case 1, M' halts as well as M. In case 2, M' halts rejecting the string or, equivalently, enters a loop, as M does. In case 3, M' simulates r moves of M for each T_i, through the latter group of at most two moves. This is organized as follows.

M' modifies the contents of the current cell and (possibly) of one adjacent cell as M would do in the corresponding portion of tape and leaves the head positioned on the cell corresponding to the group of cells where the head of M would be after r moves. For instance, suppose that r moves of M consist of visiting $b_j \cdots b_s \ldots b_1 a_r \ldots a_m$ changing their values to $b'_j \ldots b'_s \ldots a'_m$ and going back to b'_s. Note that if one element of $a_1 \ldots a_r$ is visited by M, no element of $c_1 \ldots c_r$ can be visited in a sequence of r moves. This can be simulated by M' through two moves substituting $\langle a_1 \ldots a_r \rangle$ with $\langle a_1 \ldots a'_m \ldots a'_r \rangle$ and $\langle b_1 \ldots b_r \rangle$ with $\langle b'_1 \ldots b'_s \ldots b_r \rangle$ and leaving the head on $\langle b'_1 \ldots b_r \rangle$ in a state recording position s for tape T_i.

Thus, r moves of M have been simulated by, at most, six moves of M'. This implies that if M takes $T_M(n)$ moves to perform its computation, M' does not take more than

$$n + \left\lceil \frac{n}{r} \right\rceil + 6 \left\lceil \frac{T_M(n)}{r} \right\rceil < n + n/r + 6T_M(n)/r + 2$$

Now recall that $\inf_{n \to \infty} T_M(n)/n = \infty$, which means that for any real constant δ there is an n_δ such that for all $n \ge n_\delta$, $T(n)/n \ge \delta$. Therefore, it is easy to verify that for all $n \ge n_\delta$ and $n \ge 2$, where $n + 2 \le 2n$,

$$\left(n + \frac{n}{r} + \frac{6T(n)}{r} + 2 \right) \le T(n) \cdot \left(\frac{6}{r} + \frac{2}{\delta} + \frac{1}{r \cdot \delta} \right)$$

Clearly, for any given $c > 0$, an integer r and a δ can be found such that

$$\left(\frac{6}{r} + \frac{2}{\delta} + \frac{1}{r \cdot \delta} \right) < c$$

It remains to consider the finite set of words whose length is less than $\max \{2, n_\delta\}$. But this is not a problem since a finite set of words can always be recognized by a FA and therefore by a TM in $n + 1$ moves (recall that a TM needs at most one extra move after reading the end of the input string to enter a halting state).   ∎

On the basis of Theorem 3.12 the proof of the following corollary is a trivial exercise for the reader.

Corollary 3.13

1. If

$$\inf_{n \to \infty} \frac{f(n)}{n} = \infty$$

   and $c > 0$, then $\text{DTIME}(f) = \text{DTIME}(c \cdot f)$,
   $\text{NTIME}(f) = \text{NTIME}(c \cdot f)$.
2. If $f(n) = c \cdot n$ for some $c > 1$ and $g(n) = (1 + \epsilon) \cdot n$ for any ϵ, with $\epsilon > 0$
   then $\text{DTIME}(f) = \text{DTIME}(g)$, $\text{NTIME}(f) = \text{NTIME}(g)$.   □

Both the statement and the proof of Theorem 3.12 have a strong conceptual and practical impact. First, observe that the linear speed-up property further supports the relevance of the big-theta notion. In fact, thanks to Theorem 3.12, we know that whenever two languages are recognized by machines having complexity functions that satisfy the hypothesis of the theorem and belong in the same big-theta class, they can then be recognized by machines bounded by the very same function.

Furthermore, notice that the construction of the proof shows that we can always gain in execution speed provided that we pay more in computation resources (e.g., by making several computations in parallel). This is exactly what happens when more powerful computers are used to speed up the solution of practical problems. However, according to Theorem 3.12, such a gain is constrained to be linear. This fact has a striking consequence. Suppose you run an algorithm with time complexity $\Theta(n^2)$ to solve a problem P on a small, personal computer. The execution speed you may gain commuting to a supercomputer running the same algorithm—for sufficiently "large" instances of P—is far less than the gain provided by commuting to a $\Theta(n^{1.9})$ algorithm running on the same personal computer. In other words, ingenuity in inventing clever algorithms gives better results than brute-force-based computation.

As another consequence of Theorem 3.12, we can fill up the gap between complexity Definitions 3.9 and 3.9a for nondeterministic computations.

Corollary 3.14 *

Let f be a total function such that

a. $\displaystyle\inf_{n\to\infty} \frac{f(n)}{n} = \infty.$

b. For any n, the value of $f(n)$ is computable by a deterministic TM in time t, with $t \le f(n)$.

If a nondeterministic TM M has time complexity f according to Definition 3.9, an equivalent M' can be built with complexity f according to Definition 3.9a. Thus, for any f satisfying the hypothesis, NTIME(f) does not depend on which of the two definitions is chosen.

Proof

M' can be easily built along the following lines.

For any given input x of length n, M' first computes $f(n)$ in time t, with $t \le f(n)$. There is no loss of generality in assuming that $f(n)$ is coded in unary base in some tape of M', since the conversion of any number m from unary base to base k with $k > 1$, and conversely, can be made in time $\Theta(m)$.

M' simulates M by decrementing $f(n)$ by one at each move; if it does not accept x before $f(n)$ moves, it halts rejecting it. Clearly there is some computation of M' accepting x if and only if the same happens for M. Furthermore, the time bound for *all* computations of M' on strings of length n is $2 \cdot f(n)$. By virtue of Theorem 3.12, such computations can be speeded up in such a way that they are performed in a time bounded exactly by $f(n)$. $\qquad\square$

Exercises

3.17 Show that if a language is recognized by a multitape TM M with time complexity T_M, then it is recognized by a single-tape TM with time complexity that is $\Theta(T_M^2)$.[4]

3.18 Show that Corollary 3.14 holds as well if $f(n) = c \cdot n$, with $c > 1$ or $f(n) = n + c$, with $c \ge 1$.

3.19 Prove that Corollary 3.14 holds as well for space complexity.

3.20 Prove that functions n^k, for fixed k, $n^k \cdot \log^h(n)$ for fixed k, h, $n\sqrt{n}$, satisfy the hypothesis of Corollary 3.14.

3.4 Complexity Analysis of Real Computer Programs

The examples considered so far are purely theoretical: They belong in the realm of formal language recognition and the used computation models are in the class of abstract automata. How general are the results obtained so far? Supposing we

---

[4]T_M^2 is an obvious short notation for the function T' defined by $T'(n) = (T_M(n))^2$.

have been able to prove that a problem can be solved by a TM with time complexity that is $\Theta(f)$, does the same result hold for a Pascal solution of the same problem? We have already given comments on this point where we have shown that the membership problem for a sorted set can be solved in time $\Theta(n)$[5] on a TM, whereas it can be solved in $\Theta(\log n)$ by a Pascal program implementing binary search. Similarly, consider the problem of adding two natural numbers. It is a trivial exercise to prove the following statement (see also Example 1.20).

Statement 3.15
A 2-tape TM can perform the sum of two natural numbers n_1 and n_2 for any base k, where $k > 1$, with a time complexity function that is $\Theta(n)$, where $n = \max\{\lfloor log_k n_1 \rfloor + 1, \lfloor log_k n_2 \rfloor + 1\}$. No multitape TM M can perform this operation with $\Theta(T_M) < \Theta(n)$.   □

On the other hand, we all know that any digital computer is provided with some ADD instruction that executes—in one time unit (machine cycle)—the sum of two integers whose values may be stored either in some register or in main memory and leaves the result either in a register or in some memory cell.

This motivates the need for studying more practical computation models, so that complexity results proved on those models have an immediate, practical applicability. In this section, we study two such models: the RAM machine—an abstraction of a conventional computer—and SMALG—a higher-level Algol-like programming language. We will then compare complexity analyses obtained on different computational models in rigorous terms in Section 3.5.

3.4.1 The RAM Machine

The RAM machine is an abstraction of a conventional von Neumann computer architecture. The machine has one input and one output tape, and one random-access memory. All devices are composed of an unlimited number of cells, each of which can hold an integer of any value. The input and output tapes can only be accessed sequentially: Any read (write) operation implicitly advances the tape head one cell to the right. Memory cells are addressed by natural numbers: $M[i]$ denotes the ith cell of the memory. $M[0]$ refers to a special register—the accumulator—which is used to hold the value of one of the two operands of binary arithmetic operations.

Our RAM is a fixed-program cabled machine, whose structure is sketched in Figure 3.8. The instructions repertoire is a highly simplified set of what is possible to find in real computers: input/output instructions, assignments, arithmetic, and branching instructions. Addressing modes can be immediate, direct, and indirect.

---

[5] The above notation is a "slang" for "time bounded by a $\Theta(n)$ function." In the following, it will be used for simplicity, whenever this will not cause confusion.

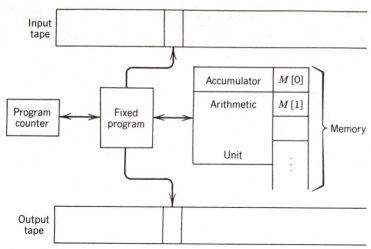

FIGURE 3.8 The RAM machine.

RAM instructions and their semantics are described in Table 3.1 using a self-explanatory Pascal-like notation, under the assumption that M can be viewed as an unbounded array of integers. The program counter can be viewed as an integer variable PC, whose value is in the subrange $1..m$, m being the size of the program. All instructions 1 through 8 in Table 3.1 implicitly increment the value of PC as a side effect. The machine halts in a correct state on reaching the HALT instruction. It halts in an incorrect state when values are out of range or syntactically meaningless instructions (e.g., READ = x) are encountered during execution.

Unlike data, which are referenced by means of their memory address, instructions are referenced symbolically, by means of a label. No two instructions can have the same label, and labels are uniquely bound to values of PC. The description of semantics of jumps (instructions 9 through 11 in Table 3.1) makes use of a function b that uniquely binds labels to integers in the subrange $1..m$. Precisely $b(lab) = y$ means that the statement labeled by lab is the yth statement of the program.

RAM programs can be interpreted as functions. A program P that reads n integer input values and produces m integer output values before halting can be viewed as a function $p: \mathbb{Z}^n \to \mathbb{Z}^m$. Because RAM programs are not guaranteed to halt, the corresponding functions are partial. From a formal viewpoint, it can be proved quite easily that RAMs, like any other reasonable model of a computer, can compute exactly all TM computable functions.

RAM programs can also be interpreted as language recognizers. Because we assumed that the RAM can only manipulate integer values, the interpretation as a recognizer requires a coding of characters via integers. If V_T is the alphabet of a language L and $k = |V_T|$, each symbol $a \in V_T$ can be represented by an integer i_a such that $1 \le i_a \le k$. Every string $x \in V_T^*$ can be represented by a

TABLE 3.1   Instruction Set of the RAM Machine

Operation Code	Instruction Formats		Instruction Semantics
1 LOAD	LOAD =	x	$M[0] := x$
	LOAD	x	$M[0] := M[x]$
	LOAD*	x	$M[0] := M[M[x]]$
2 STORE	STORE	x	$M[x] := M[0]$
	STORE*	x	$M[M[x]] := M[0]$
3 ADD	ADD =	x	$M[0] := M[0] + x$
	ADD	x	$M[0] := M[0] + M[x]$
	ADD*	x	$M[0] := M[0] + M[M[x]]$
4 SUB	SUB =	x	$M[0] := M[0] - x$
	SUB	x	$M[0] := M[0] - M[x]$
	SUB*	x	$M[0] := M[0] - M[M[x]]$
5 MULT	MULT =	x	$M[0] := M[0] * x$
	MULT	x	$M[0] := M[0] * M[x]$
	MULT*	x	$M[0] := M[0] * M[M[x]]$
6 DIV	DIV =	x	$M[0] := M[0] \, \mathbf{div} \, x^6$
	DIV	x	$M[0] := M[0] \, \mathbf{div} \, M[x]$
	DIV*	x	$M[0] := M[0] \, \mathbf{div} \, M[M[x]]$
7 READ	READ	x	$M[x] :=$ current input value
	READ*	x	$M[M[x]] :=$ current input value
8 WRITE	WRITE =	x	output x
	WRITE	x	output $M[x]$
	WRITE*	x	output $M[M[x]]$
9 JUMP	JUMP	lab	$PC := b(lab)$
10 JGZ	JGZ	lab	$PC :=$ **if** $M[0] > 0$ **then** $PC := b(lab)$ **else** $PC := PC + 1$
11 JZ	JZ	lab	$PC :=$ **if** $M[0] = 0$ **then** $PC := b(lab)$ **else** $PC := PC + 1$
12 HALT	HALT		computation terminates

[6] The Pascal integer division **div** truncates the result of division of two integers.

suitable sequence of integers, followed by a 0, which acts as a terminator. Strings belonging to L are accepted by a RAM program if, on reading the entire input string (up to the rightmost 0), the machine prints an "ok value" (say, 1) and halts. For strings not in L, the machine may halt and print any value other than 1, or it may not halt. From a formal viewpoint, it can be proved quite easily that a language is accepted by a RAM if and only if it is recursively enumerable. A language is accepted by a RAM that halts on all inputs if and only if it is recursive.

We give the two following examples illustrating a RAM program interpreted as a function (Example 3.6) and a RAM program interpreted as a language recognizer (Example 3.7).

Example 3.6

Let *is__prime* be the function on positive integers defined as

is__prime $(n) = $ **if** n is prime **then** 1 **else** 0

RAM Program			Comment
	READ	1	The input value n is stored into $M[1]$
	LOAD =	1	If $n = 1$ then it is trivially
	SUB	1	prime and the rest of the program
	JZ	YES	is skipped
	LOAD =	2	$M[2]$ is initialized
	STORE	2	to 2
LOOP:	LOAD	1	If $M[1] = M[2]$, this
	SUB	2	will imply that
	JZ	YES	n is prime
	LOAD	1	If $M[1] = (M[1]$ **div** $M[2]) * M[2]$
	DIV	2	$M[2]$ divides $M[1]$;
	MULT	2	thus $M[1]$ is not
	SUB	1	prime
	JZ	NO	
	LOAD	2	$M[2]$ is incremented by 1 and the
	ADD =	1	sequence of statements starting
	STORE	2	from LOOP is
	JUMP	LOOP	repeated
YES:	WRITE = 1		
	HALT		
NO:	WRITE = 0		
	HALT		

FIGURE 3.9 A RAM program computing *is-prime*.

RAM Program			Comment
	LOAD =	4	$M[2]$—the stack pointer—is initialized
	STORE	2	to 4.
	LOAD =	0	$M[4]$ is initialized to 0, which represents
	STORE	4	the initial stack symbol.
	LOAD =	0	$M[3]$—the PDA's state—is initialized
	STORE	3	to 0, representing q_0.
LOOP:	READ	1	If the current input symbol is
	LOAD	1	0 the string is terminated and it
	JZ	ENDTEST	must be either accepted or rejected.
	LOAD	3	If the current state is 1,
	JGZ	POP	jump to the instruction labeled POP.
	LOAD	1	If the current input symbol is not c,
	SUB =	2	push it onto the stack. Otherwise
	JGZ	CHANGE	change state.
	LOAD	2	The stack pointer $M[2]$ is incremented by 1
	ADD =	1	and the current input symbol is stored into
	STORE	2	$M[M[2]]$ (i.e., it is pushed onto the stack).
	LOAD	1	The sequence of statements starting from
	STORE*	2	LOOP is then repeated.
	JUMP	LOOP	
CHANGE:	LOAD =	1	The new state is q_1.
	STORE	3	
POP:	LOAD	1	Verify that the current input
	SUB*	2	symbol equals the topmost stack symbol.
	JZ	CONTINUE	In such a case, proceed from CONTINUE;
	JUMP	NO	otherwise reject the string.
CONTINUE:	LOAD	2	Pop a value off
	SUB =	1	the stack and check it for
	STORE	2	emptiness. If this is the case, proceed from
	SUB =	4	ENDTEST; otherwise repeat
	JZ	ENDTEST	from LOOP.
	JUMP	LOOP	
ENDTEST:	LOAD	1	To accept the input string, we check that
	JGZ	· NO	a. The input has been completely scanned.
	LOAD	3	b. The state is q_1.
	JZ	NO	
	LOAD	2	c. The stack is empty.
	SUB =	4	
	JZ	YES	
NO:	WRITE =	0	
	HALT		
YES:	WRITE =	1	
	HALT		

FIGURE 3.10 A RAM program deciding $L = \{wcw^R\}$.

230

A RAM program implementing function *is__prime* can enumerate all values from 2 to n until either the value equals n, or it divides n. In the former case the program outputs a 1; in the latter the output value is a 0. A solution is shown in Figure 3.9.

Example 3.7

The RAM program in Figure 3.10 recognizes the familiar language $L = \{wcw^R | w \in \{a, b\}^*\}$ under the following coding conventions.

- a is coded by 1.
- b is coded by 2.
- c is coded by 3.
- 0 is used as an endmarker in the input tape.

For all input sequences representing strings of L, the program prints a 1 and then the machine halts. For all sequences representing strings to reject, the program prints a 0 and then the machine halts.

The RAM program simulates a PDA recognizing L, as described in Exercise 1.20 and Example 3.5. Memory locations $M[4]$, $M[5], \ldots$ represent the contents of the PDA's stack. $M[4]$ is initialized to the initial stack symbol (coded by 0). Other stack values are 1 and 2, which are pushed onto the stack on reading an a and a b, respectively, during the analysis of w. $M[1]$ stores the currently read input symbol. $M[2]$ stores the address of the topmost stack symbol. $M[3]$ stores the code for the state of the PDA. 0 represents state q_0 (where the PDA remains until it reads the c), 1 represents state q_1 (where the PDA remains during the analysis of w^R).

Exercises

3.21 Write RAM programs computing the functions defined as follows.
1. *prime* $(n) = k$, where $n > 0$ and k is the nth prime number starting from 2.
2. *all-primes* $(n) = \{x | x$ is a prime number and $x \leq n\}$.
3. $f(n_1, n_2, \ldots, n_k) = 2^{n_1} \cdot 3^{n_2} \ldots p_k^{n_k}$, p_i being the ith prime number. Assume that the input stream contains first the number k followed by $n_1, n_2 \ldots n_k$.
4. f^{-1}, where f is the function of above point 3.
5. *sorted* $(n_1, \ldots, n_k) = 1$ **if** $n_1 \leq n_2 \ldots \leq n_k$, **else** 0. The input stream is arranged as in the above point 3.

3.22 Write RAM programs recognizing the following languages:
1. $L_1 = \{ww^R | w \in \{a, b\}^*\}$.
2. $L_2 = \{ww | w \in \{a, b\}^*\}$.
3. $L_3 = \{a^n b^n | n \geq 0\}$.

In particular, write two RAM programs, P_1 and P_2, recognizing L_3. P_1 is obtained as a straightforward simulation of the PDA recognizing L_3. P_2 counts the occurrences of a, instead of storing them in the stack.

Let us try now to use the RAM model to estimate the complexity of computations performed by real computers. The RAM model of computation is very similar to the behavior of conventional computers. The most notable difference is that conventional computers are programmable: Programs are stored in memory and can modify themselves. Other differences are in the instruction repertoire, since our RAM is a simplified version of what one can find in the real world of computers. For example, most computers provide an INC instruction to increment a value by one. An "INC i" instruction must be simulated by a sequence of RAM instructions.

LOAD	i
ADD =	1
STORE	i

On the other hand, our RAM does have primitive MULT and DIV instructions, which may be unavailable on a very simple computer. To execute them on such machine, one must provide a suitable sequence of instructions containing a loop, which requires a time that depends on the value of the operands. Furthermore, machines that provide an integer division very often provide the remainder (**mod** in Pascal) as side effect in some register of the arithmetic unit.

In such a case, the following test in the RAM program of Figure 3.9.

$$M[1] = (M[1] \operatorname{\mathbf{div}} M[2]) * M[2]$$

that is

$$M[1] \operatorname{\mathbf{mod}} M[2] = 0$$

would be implemented by a single machine instruction.

Apart from these problems, we can assume that our RAM is a reasonable approximation of real computers. The results of formal reasonings on RAM programs (e.g., computational complexity) should be immediately transferable to our computer programs.

The question we address now is how to evaluate computational complexity for RAM programs. First, we must define the time required for executing each RAM instruction and the space needed for each memory location and the accumulator (remember that the program is not stored in memory). One way of defining these quantities is called the *uniform cost criterion*. According to it, the execution of each instruction requires one time unit; each memory location and the accumulator require one space unit. How realistic is the uniform cost criterion?

In practice, input/output instructions are certainly slower than other kinds of instructions; operand evaluation is slower for indirect addressing than for direct addressing, and direct addressing is slower than immediate addressing. To take these facts into account, one could slightly change the uniform cost criterion by assuming that execution of each RAM instruction i takes k_i time units, where k_i is a constant. However, it is easy to realize that this assumption does not change the results of complexity analysis in terms of the order notation (big-theta).

More serious problems with the uniform cost criterion are due to the fact that integer values stored in memory cells of the RAM can be arbitrarily large. Also, the RAM storage device is unlimited, and addresses can be arbitrarily large. As a consequence, we can safely assume that the time needed to execute any RAM instruction is fixed and independent on the values of the operands, provided that operands can be kept in one memory cell. For example, an ADD of two very large integers would require more than one time unit for its execution. The same holds for MULT and DIV. Whether they are directly provided by hardware or not, we can still safely assume that the time required to execute them is bounded only if the value of operands and the result can be stored in single cells of the memory. Similarly, access to memory locations can be assumed as performed in bounded time only if the memory size itself is bounded.

These points lead to another cost criterion: the *logarithmic cost criterion*. This criterion is based on the assumption that the time required to execute an instruction is proportional to the length of the operands. In binary code, an operand of value v is represented by $\lfloor \log_2 |v| \rfloor + 1$ bits (1 bit if $v = 0$). Consequently, if l is the following function on integers:

$$l(i) = \textbf{if } i \neq 0 \textbf{ then } \lfloor \log_2 |i| \rfloor + 1 \textbf{ else } 1$$

we can define the *logarithmic time complexity* of the various RAM instructions as in Table 3.2. Note that STORE instructions and arithmetic instructions have an implicit operand: The accumulator ($M[0]$). This is explicitly taken into account in the expressions that give the logarithmic cost.

The same philosophy applies to space costs. Let m be the largest address of memory cell accessed during execution of a RAM program, and let M_i be the largest absolute value stored in $M[i]$ during execution. Then we define the *logarithmic space complexity* of the program as the sum.

$$\sum_0^m l(M_i)$$

Obviously, the results of complexity analysis are quite different depending on whether we use the fixed cost criterion or the logarithmic cost criterion. The uniform cost criterion is simpler to apply; it can be applied safely if we can anticipate that each value arising during computation can be stored in one memory cell. Otherwise, we must refer to the logarithmic cost criterion. For instance, the uniform cost criterion would be inappropriate for analyzing complexity of a program computing the factorial function for very large input values.

TABLE 3.2 The Logarithmic Cost of RAM Instructions.

Instruction Format		Logarithmic Cost
LOAD =	x	$l(x)$
LOAD	x	$l(x) + l(M[x])$
LOAD*	x	$l(x) + l(M[x]) + l(M[M[x]])$
STORE	x	$l(M[0]) + l(x)$
STORE*	x	$l(M[0]) + l(x) + l(M[x])$.
ADD =	x	$l(M[0]) + l(x)$
ADD	x	$l(M[0]) + l(x) + l(M[x])$
ADD*	x	$l(M[0]) + l(x) + l(M[x]) + l(M[M[x]])$
	SUB, MULT, DIV are defined exactly as for ADD	
READ	x	$l(\text{current input value}) + l(x)$
READ*	x	$l(\text{current input value}) + l(x) + l(M[x])$
WRITE =	x	$l(x)$
WRITE	x	$l(x) + l(M[x])$
WRITE*	x	$l(x) + l(M[x]) + l(M[M[x]])$
JUMP	*lab*	1
JGZ	*lab*	$l(M[0])$
JZ	*lab*	$l(M[0])$
HALT		1

In practice, one could take both criteria into account in the following way. Let k be the word length of the used computer (usually k is 8, 16, 32, or 64). For any positive integer i, let s be the integer defined by the following inequality:

$$2^{k \cdot s - 1} \leq i < 2^{k(s+1)-1}$$

Then redefine $l(i)$ as $s + 1$. Intuitively, $l(i)$ denotes the number of words needed to store i. It reduces to the uniform cost criterion if $i < 2^{k-1}$. However, for simplicity reasons we choose not to use the foregoing formula.

Let us analyze the complexity of previous examples under the above criteria. The symbols T and S denote the time and space complexity functions under both cost criteria.

Example 3.8

Consider the RAM program shown in Figure 3.9. To evaluate its (worst case) time complexity T under the uniform cost criterion, we simply count the maximum number of instruction executions.

It is immediate to realize that

a. The first six instructions are executed once at most.
b. Two out of the last four instructions are executed once.

c. The instructions between "LOOP: LOAD 1" and "JUMP LOOP" are repeated at most $M[1] - 2$ times, where $M[1] = n$ (n is the input value).

d. The sequence of three instructions starting from LOOP is executed one more time.

Thus, assuming $n \geq 2$, $T(n) = 6 + 2 + 12(n - 2) + 3 = 12 \cdot n - 13$ (if $n \geq 2$) (i.e., T is $\Theta(n)$).

In order to obtain $T(n)$ under the logarithmic cost criterion, we can rephrase the above analysis by substituting the appropriate logarithmic cost to the unitary cost of single statements. Referring to the above components of the total cost (a through d), we perform a detailed costs analysis.

Cost of a:

Instruction		Cost
READ	1	$1 + l(n)$
LOAD =	1	1
SUB	1	$1 + 1 + l(n)$
JZ	YES	$l(n - 1) \leq l(n)$
LOAD =	2	2
STORE	2	$2 + 2$
Rounded off subtotal:		$10 + 3 \cdot l(n)$

Cost of b: 2

Cost of c:

Instruction			Cost
LOOP:	LOAD	1	$1 + l(n)$
	SUB	2	$l(n) + 2 + l(M[2])$
α:	JZ	YES	$l(M[0])$
	LOAD	1	$1 + l(n)$
	DIV	2	$l(n) + 2 + l(M[2])$
	MULT	2	$l(n/M[2]) + 2 + 1(M[2]) < l(n) + 3$[7]
	SUB	1	$l(M[0]) + 1 + l(n) < 2 \cdot l(n) + 1$
	JZ	NO	$l(M[0]) \leq l(n)$
	LOAD	2	$2 + l(M[2])$
	ADD =	1	$l(M[2]) + 1$
	STORE	2	$l(M[2] + 1) + 2 \leq l(M[2]) + 3$
	JUMP	LOOP	1
Rounded off subtotal:			$17 + 8 \cdot l(n) + 5 \cdot l(M[2]) + l(M[0])$

Note that $M[2]$ assumes the values $2, 3, \ldots, n - 1$; $M[0]$, at α, assumes the values $n - 2, n - 3, \ldots, 1$. Thus, the subtotal due to $n - 2$ iterations is

$$17 \cdot (n - 2) + 8 \cdot (n - 2) \cdot l(n) + 5 \cdot \sum_{i=2}^{n-1} l(i) + \sum_{i=1}^{n-2} l(i)$$

Cost of d: $1 + l(n) + l(n) + 2 + l(n) + 1 = 3 \cdot l(n) + 4$

[7]Remember that $\log(a/b) = \log a - \log b$.

Putting all four terms together, and going straight to the essentials, we easily see that time complexity is $\Theta(n \cdot \log n)$.

We could have come directly to this conclusion by considering that time complexity of the program is dominated by the loop and, within the loop, by the MULT and DIV operations (see the detailed evaluation of the cost of c). A total of $(n - 2)$ MULT and DIV operations are executed. Thus, time complexity in $\Theta(n \cdot \log n)$ under the logarithmic cost criterion. Under the uniform cost criterion, each operation in the loop costs one time unit: Thus the resulting time complexity is $\Theta(n)$.

Exercises

3.23 Evaluate space complexity of the RAM program shown in Figure 3.9. Use both the uniform cost criterion and the logarithmic cost criterion.

3.24 Evaluate time and space complexities of the RAM program shown in Figure 3.10. Use both the uniform cost criterion and the logarithmic cost criterion.

3.25 Write a RAM program to evaluate n^n through a loop of n multiplications. Prove that, under the uniform cost criterion, T is $\Theta(n)$ and S is a constant. Under the logarithmic cost criterion, T is $\Theta(n^2 \cdot \log n)$ and S is $\Theta(n \cdot \log n)$.

Hint: Time complexity is dominated by the loop of multiplications, which is executed n times. Each multiplication (as any other instruction) costs one time unit under the uniform cost criterion. It costs $\Theta(l(n^i))$ under the logarithmic cost criterion since, at each step $1, 2, \ldots, i, \ldots n - 1$, the partial result n^i is multiplied by n. But

$$\sum_{i=1}^{n-1} l(n^i) \text{ is } \Theta(n^2 \cdot \log n)$$

As for space complexity, $\Theta(n \cdot \log n)$ in the case of the logarithmic cost unit stems from the fact that the largest value stored in memory cells during execution is n^n, which requires a storage cell of $\Theta(n \cdot \log n)$ bits.

3.26 Even under the logarithmic cost criterion, assuming the cost of MULT and DIV equal to the cost of ADD and SUB could be inadequate. Write a RAM program computing n^n without MULT operations and check its complexity.

Hint: You may assume as elementary a "times 2" operation, which can be easily implemented through a register shift.

3.27 Design k-tape TMs (with suitable values of k) and RAM programs to solve the following problems and compare their complexities by applying

—for the programs—the two cost criteria.

1. Recognize the language $L = \{ a^n b^{kn} | n, k \geq 1 \}$.
2. Recognize the language $L_k = \{ a^n b^{in} | n \geq 1, 1 \leq i \leq k \}$.
3. Recognize the language $L = \{ w_1 c w_2 c \ldots w_k | k \geq 2, \ w_1 \in \{ a, b \}^+,$ $\exists i, j, i \neq j$ such that $w_i = w_j \}$.
4. Compute the factorial of n.
5. For given $a_0, a_1 \ldots a_n, x$. Compute the polynomial

$$a_n x^n + a_{n-1} x^{n-1} \cdots + a_0$$

In some cases, we suggest not to carry over the design to full details but just to reach a point where the complexity degree of the computation can be determined safely.

3.4.2   Higher-Level Programming Languages

Two different and contrasting needs arise in the analysis of computational complexity. On the one side, our models of computation must be close enough to real computers if we expect to get realistic results from complexity analysis. In fact, we observed that the results obtained by analyzing abstract machines may not adequately reflect the properties of computations performed by real machines. On the other hand, we would like to be able to perform algorithm analysis without bothering about too many details that depend on the particular language and processor used to actually perform computations.

The models of computation analyzed so far are too low level to be used in practice. After having struggled with the RAM in the solution of simple programming exercises, the reader will agree that a higher-level language is desirable, especially if we wish to solve larger programming assignments in an easy, safe, and understandable way.

In what follows, we define a new computational model that exhibits the essential features of higher-level programming languages. This model is progressively enriched throughout this text in order to cope with new exigencies; however, it will remain a "toy language," that is, a simplification of a real programming language. The concepts we learn here, however, will enable us to address the issues of complexity of programs written in real programming languages in a safe way. For example, we will be able to take up the Pascal procedures introduced in Section 3.1 (*search* and *binary__search*) and redo their analysis on a firmer ground.

The language we study here is called SMALG (small Algol) in honor of Algol-60, the common ancestor of most modern high-level programming languages. The machine supporting execution of SMALG programs is called SMALM (Small-Algol Machine). SMALG is generated by the context-free grammar given in Figure 3.11.

$G = \langle V_T, V_N, P, \langle \text{Program} \rangle \rangle$

$V_T = \{$**begin, end, if, then, else, fi,** ; , **while, do, od,**
      $a, b, c, \ldots, z, A, B, \ldots, Z,$:= , $0, 1, \ldots 9,$ +, $-$, $*$, **div, mod**
      $[,],$ = , $\neq$, $<$, $>$, $\leq$, $\geq$, **read, write**$\}$

$V_N = \{\langle \text{Program} \rangle, \langle \text{StatList} \rangle, \langle \text{Stat} \rangle, \langle \text{AssStat} \rangle, \langle \text{CondStat} \rangle, \langle \text{WhileStat} \rangle,$
      $\langle \text{InputStat} \rangle, \langle \text{OutputStat} \rangle, \langle \text{Var} \rangle, \langle \text{Exp} \rangle, \langle \text{Term} \rangle, \langle \text{SimpleVar} \rangle,$
      $\langle \text{IndexedVar} \rangle, \langle \text{Ident} \rangle, \langle \text{ArrayVarId} \rangle, \langle \text{Index} \rangle, \langle \text{Constant} \rangle, \langle \text{Digit} \rangle,$
      $\langle \text{Letter} \rangle, \langle \text{Cond} \rangle, \langle \text{RelOp} \rangle\}$

$P = \{\langle \text{Program} \rangle \rightarrow$ **begin** $\langle \text{StatList} \rangle$ **end**
      $\langle \text{StatList} \rangle \rightarrow \langle \text{Stat} \rangle$; $\langle \text{StatList} \rangle | \epsilon$
      $\langle \text{Stat} \rangle \rightarrow \langle \text{AssStat} \rangle | \langle \text{CondStat} \rangle | \langle \text{WhileStat} \rangle | \langle \text{InputStat} \rangle | \langle \text{OutputStat} \rangle$
      $\langle \text{AssStat} \rangle \rightarrow \langle \text{Var} \rangle$:= $\langle \text{Exp} \rangle$
      $\langle \text{Var} \rangle \rightarrow \langle \text{SimpleVar} \rangle | \langle \text{IndexedVar} \rangle$
      $\langle \text{SimpleVar} \rangle \rightarrow \langle \text{Ident} \rangle$
      $\langle \text{IndexedVar} \rangle \rightarrow \langle \text{ArrayVarId} \rangle [\langle \text{Index} \rangle]$
      $\langle \text{ArrayVarId} \rangle \rightarrow \langle \text{Ident} \rangle$
      $\langle \text{Index} \rangle \rightarrow \langle \text{Constant} \rangle | \langle \text{SimpleVar} \rangle$
      $\langle \text{Exp} \rangle \rightarrow \langle \text{Term} \rangle + \langle \text{Term} \rangle | \langle \text{Term} \rangle - \langle \text{Term} \rangle | \langle \text{Term} \rangle * \langle \text{Term} \rangle |$
                $\langle \text{Term} \rangle$ **div** $\langle \text{Term} \rangle | \langle \text{Term} \rangle$ **mod** $\langle \text{Term} \rangle | \langle \text{Term} \rangle$
      $\langle \text{Term} \rangle \rightarrow \langle \text{Var} \rangle | \langle \text{Constant} \rangle$
      $\langle \text{Constant} \rangle \rightarrow \langle \text{Digit} \rangle | \langle \text{Digit} \rangle \langle \text{Constant} \rangle$
      $\langle \text{Digit} \rangle \rightarrow 0 | 1 | 2 | \cdots | 9$
      $\langle \text{Ident} \rangle \rightarrow \langle \text{Letter} \rangle | \langle \text{Letter} \rangle \langle \text{Ident} \rangle$
      $\langle \text{Letter} \rangle \rightarrow a | b | c | \cdots | z | A | B | \cdots | Z$
      $\langle \text{CondStat} \rangle \rightarrow$ **if** $\langle \text{Cond} \rangle$ **then** $\langle \text{StatList} \rangle$**else**$\langle \text{StatList} \rangle$ **fi** $|$
                    if $\langle \text{Cond} \rangle$ **then** $\langle \text{StatList} \rangle$ **fi**
      $\langle \text{WhileStat} \rangle \rightarrow$ **while** $\langle \text{Cond} \rangle$ **do** $\langle \text{StatList} \rangle$ **od**
      $\langle \text{Cond} \rangle \rightarrow \langle \text{Exp} \rangle \langle \text{RelOp} \rangle \langle \text{Exp} \rangle$
      $\langle \text{RelOp} \rangle \rightarrow$ = $| \neq | < | \leq | > | \geq$
      $\langle \text{InputStat} \rangle \rightarrow$ **read** $\langle \text{Var} \rangle$
      $\langle \text{OutputStat} \rangle \rightarrow$ **write** $\langle \text{Var} \rangle\}$

FIGURE 3.11 SMALG's grammar. $\langle N_1 \rangle \rightarrow \beta_1 | \beta_2$ is a short notation for
$\langle N_1 \rangle \rightarrow \beta_1, \langle N_1 \rangle \rightarrow \beta_2$.

SMALG has structured control statements: sequences (StatList), conditionals (CondStat), and loops (WhileStat). Elementary data are of type integer.
Structured data are one-dimensional arrays. Relational (Cond) and arithmetic
(Exp) expressions are a simplified version of their counterpart in real programming languages.

Figure 3.12 shows a few examples of (not very useful) SMALG programs,
which should have an obvious, self-explaining meaning. However, in order to
perform rigorous reasonings on SMALG programs (in particular, on computational complexity) we should go deeper into the analysis of SMALG. In particular, we should equip ourselves with rigorous notions that will enable us to
perform complexity analysis on a sound, theoretical basis.

1. **begin** $i := 5$; $j := 10$; $x := 3$
    if $i \neq j$ **then** $a[2] := x + i$ **else** $a[j] := 6$ **fi**
   end
2. **begin while** $5 = 5$ **do** $x := 3$;
                         if $x < 3$
                         then $x := x + 1$
                         else $x := x - 1$
                         fi
                 od
   end
3. **begin read** n;
        if $n \leq 0$
        then write n
        else $z := n$;
            $c := n - 1$;
            while $c > 0$ **do** $z := z * n$;
                             $c := c - 1$
                     od;
            write z
        fi
   end

FIGURE 3.12 Sample SMALG programs.

The reader has probably already realized during the analysis of FAs, TMs, RAMs, etc. that the problem of rigorously defining state transformations (i.e., computations) operated by abstract machines or, more generally and informally, of defining the "meaning" of their "programs" becomes more difficult as more powerful and abstract are the machines. FA transition functions are immediately described by means of a simple table; TM transitions require more detail in their formal definition; state transformations of the RAM are somewhat more intricate (e.g., when dealing with indirect addressing). When we reach the expressive power of higher-level languages, a number of difficult problems arise. We thoroughly investigate this crucial point in Chapter 4. For our present purposes, we first define the state space of SMALM and the transformations operated by SMALG programs rather informally. Then we briefly discuss their complexity.

The state space of SMALM consists of

1. One memory location containing an integer value for each simple variable. The location associated to the simple variable x will be denoted by M_x.
2. An unbounded sequence of memory locations containing integer values for each array variable.
   An indexed variable $a[i]$ is associated with
   2.1 The ith location in the sequence associated with a if i is a constant integer value greater than zero.
   2.2 The jth location in the sequence associated with a, with $j > 0$, if i is a simple variable and j is the value stored in location M_i.

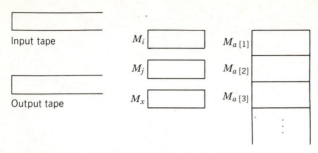

FIGURE 3.13 SMALM's state space for the SMALG
program 1 of Figure 3.12.

2.3 In all other cases $a[i]$ is undefined.
3. One Input and one Output tape, as in the case of the RAM.

Figure 3.13 gives a pictorial description of SMALM state space for the SMALG
program 1 of Figure 3.12.

State transformations and their time complexities are defined below for
every SMALG statement.

1. ***Assignment statement (\<AssStat\>)***
   1a. First the value of the expression is evaluated by accessing the values
       stored in the locations corresponding to the identifiers occurring in $\langle Exp \rangle$.
   1b. The result is stored into the location corresponding to the identifier
       denoted by $\langle Var \rangle$.
   Both time and space complexity of this statement obviously depend on how
   SMALM actually carries over its operations. By assuming—as it is usually the
   case—that SMALM operations are decomposable into sequences of simpler
   RAM-like operations, we can derive the time complexity expression computed
   according to the rules specified in Table 3.3. The table uses a self-explanatory
   Pascal-like notation to show how the total time complexity of an assignment
   statement results from the time complexities of its syntactical components.
   Function l used in the logarithmic cost expressions is exactly the same
   function we used for the RAM.

   Once again we emphasize that the definitions of Table 3.3 involve some
arbitrary choices. For example, as in the RAM case, we have chosen to assign the
same cost to any arithmetic operator both under the uniform and the logarithmic
cost criterion. This assumption is clearly not always realistic. We have also stated
that the cost of accessing an array element whose index is known before
executing the program is always 1. For this reason it turns out that accessing $a[5]$
takes 1 even under the logarithmic cost criterion, while accessing $a[x]$ takes a
variable amount of time. This is a reasonable, but not a necessary, assumption.
Finally, note that, according to the given rules, any assignment statement can be
performed in a bounded amount of time by SMALM under the uniform cost
criterion. Thus, as far as big-theta is concerned, we do not need to care much

TABLE 3.3 Time Complexity of an Assignment Statement in Terms of Time Complexities of its Constituents.

	Uniform Cost	Logarithmic Cost
$T'_{\langle AssStat\rangle}$ $T_{\langle Exp\rangle}$	$T'_{\langle Var\rangle} + T_{\langle Exp\rangle} + 1$ **if** $\langle Exp\rangle$ is of type $\quad\langle Term1\rangle$operator$\langle Term2\rangle$ **then** $T_{\langle Term1\rangle} + T_{\langle Term2\rangle} + 1$ **else** {it is of type $\langle Term\rangle$} $T_{\langle Term\rangle}$	$T'_{\langle Var\rangle} + T_{\langle Exp\rangle} + l(\text{value of }\langle Exp\rangle)$ **if** $\langle Exp\rangle$ is of type $\quad\langle Term1\rangle$operator$\langle Term2\rangle$ **then** $T_{\langle Term1\rangle} + T_{\langle Term2\rangle} +$ $\quad l(\text{value of }\langle Term1\rangle) +$ $\quad l(\text{value of }\langle Term2\rangle)$ **else** $T_{\langle Term\rangle}$
$T_{\langle Term\rangle}$	**if** $\langle Term\rangle$ is a $\langle Var\rangle$ **then** $T_{\langle Var\rangle}$ **else** {it is a $\langle Constant\rangle$} $\quad 1$	**if** $\langle Term\rangle$ is a $\langle Var\rangle$ **then** $T_{\langle Var\rangle}$ **else** {it is a $\langle Constant\rangle$} $\quad l(\text{value of }\langle Constant\rangle)$
$T'_{\langle Var\rangle}$ {is the time needed to access the location associated with the variable)	**if** $\langle Var\rangle$ is a $\langle Simple\ Var\rangle$ **then** 1 **else if** $\langle Var\rangle$ is an $\langle IndexedVar\rangle$ $\quad$ and $\langle Index\rangle$ is a $\langle Constant\rangle$ $\quad$ **then** 1 $\quad$ **else** {$\langle Var\rangle$ is an $\langle IndexedVar\rangle$ $\quad\quad$ and $\langle Index\rangle$ is a $\langle Var\rangle$} $\quad\quad 2$	**if** $\langle Var\rangle$ is a $\langle SimpleVar\rangle$ **then** 1 **else if** $\langle Var\rangle$ is an $\langle IndexedVar\rangle$ $\quad$ and $\langle Index\rangle$ is a $\langle Constant\rangle$ $\quad$ **then** 1 $\quad$ **else** {$\langle Var\rangle$ is an $\langle IndexedVar\rangle$ $\quad\quad$ and $\langle Index\rangle$ is a $\langle Var\rangle$} $\quad\quad 1 + l(\text{value of }\langle Index\rangle)$
$T_{\langle Var\rangle}$ {is the time needed to access the value associated with the variable)	**if** $\langle Var\rangle$ is a $\langle SimpleVar\rangle$ **then** 1 **else if** $\langle Var\rangle$ is an $\langle IndexedVar\rangle$ $\quad$ and $\langle Index\rangle$ is a $\langle Constant\rangle$ $\quad$ **then** 1 $\quad$ **else** 2	**if** $\langle Var\rangle$ is a $\langle SimpleVar\rangle$ **then** $1 + l(\text{value of }\langle Var\rangle)$ **else if** $\langle Var\rangle$ is an $\langle IndexedVar\rangle$ $\quad$ and $\langle Index\rangle$ is a $\langle Constant\rangle$ $\quad$ **then** $1 + l(\text{value of }\langle Var\rangle)$ $\quad$ **else** $1 + l(\text{value of }\langle Var\rangle) +$ $\quad\quad l(\text{value of }\langle Index\rangle)$

about the exact constants denoting the time complexities of individual assignment statements.

2. **Statement list (<StatList>)**
   2.1 If $\langle StatList\rangle$ is the empty list of statements, then SMALM performs no operation and $T_{\langle StatList\rangle} = 0$.
   2.2 If $\langle StatList\rangle$ is a $\langle Stat\rangle$ followed by a $\langle StatList\rangle$ then SMALM executes the statement according to rules 1 through 5 and then executes the statement list according to the present rule 2. In this case, $T_{\langle StatList\rangle} = T_{\langle Stat\rangle} + T_{\langle StatList\rangle'}$ where $T_{\langle StatList\rangle'}$ denotes the time required to execute the statement list in the right-hand side of the production.

3. **Conditional statement (<CondStat>)**
   SMALM evaluates the boolean condition derived from $\langle Cond\rangle$. If the result is true, it executes the statement list that follows the keyword **then** according to rule 2. Otherwise, if there is an **else** part, it executes the statement list that follows the **else**, according to rule 2. If there is no else part, the effect is the same as if there were an **else** part with an empty list of statements. Under this convention, if $T_{\langle StatList\rangle'}$ and $T_{\langle StatList\rangle''}$ are the times needed to execute the

then part and the **else** part, respectively,

$$T_{\langle CondStat \rangle} = T_{\langle Cond \rangle} + \text{\textbf{if} the value of } \langle Cond \rangle \text{ is true}$$
$$\text{\textbf{then} } T_{\langle StatList \rangle'}$$
$$\text{\textbf{else} } T_{\langle StatList \rangle''}$$

The rules to evaluate $T_{\langle Cond \rangle}$ are similar to those given in Table 3.3 for $T_{\langle Expr \rangle}$. An upperbound for $T_{\langle CondStat \rangle}$ is given by

$$T_{\langle Cond \rangle} + \max \left\{ T_{\langle StatList \rangle''}, T_{\langle StatList \rangle''} \right\}.$$

4. ***While statement* (<WhileStat>)**
   SMALM evaluates the boolean condition derived from $\langle Cond \rangle$. If the result is false, the execution of the while statement terminates. Otherwise, SMALM executes the statement list and repeats this step.
   Time complexity for the while statement is

$$T_{\langle WhileStat \rangle} = T_{\langle Cond \rangle} + \text{\textbf{if} value of } \langle Cond \rangle \text{ is false}$$
$$\text{\textbf{then} } 0$$
$$\text{\textbf{else} } T_{\langle StatList \rangle} + \bar{T}_{\langle WhileStat \rangle}$$

   where $\bar{T}_{\langle WhileStat \rangle}$ is the time needed to compute the same while statement after execution of the statement list.

5. ***I / O Statements* (<InputStat>, <OutputStat>)**
   5.1 When executing an input statement, SMALM reads the datum under the head of its input file, stores it into the denoted variable, and moves the head one cell rightwards.
       Thus $T_{\langle InputStat \rangle} = 1$ under the uniform cost criterion, whereas under the logarithmic cost criterion it can be defined as follows:

$$T_{\langle InputStat \rangle} = l(\text{read value}) +$$
$$\text{\textbf{if} } \langle Var \rangle \text{ is a } \langle SimpleVar \rangle$$
$$\text{\textbf{then} } 1$$
$$\text{\textbf{else} \{in this case } \langle Var \rangle \text{ is } \langle ArrayVarId \rangle \, [\langle Index \rangle]\}}$$
$$1 + l(\text{value of } \langle Index \rangle)$$

   5.2 The operations performed to execute an output statement are dual and

$$T_{\langle OutputStat \rangle} = T_{\langle Var \rangle}$$

   where $T_{\langle Var \rangle}$ is computed according to the rule given before in Table 3.3.

6. Finally the *global time complexity* of a SMALG program P is defined as follows. Let X be the stream of values stored in the input tape. $T_P(X) = T_{\langle StatList \rangle}$, where StatList is the list of program statements bracketed by the pair **begin end** and computed according to the above rules 1 through 5 in correspondence of input data X.

Space complexity of a SMALG program P is defined by the following rule in the case of uniform cost criterion. Let X be the stream of values stored in the input tape;

$$S_P(X) = NSV + \sum_{a \in A} N_a$$

where

- NSV is the total number of simple variables referenced by P.
- A is the collection of array variables referenced by P.
- for any $a \in A$, N_a is the maximum value assumed by index variables referencing array components.

Example 3.9

Let us apply the above rules to the very simple programs of Figure 3.12.

1. The execution of SMALG program 1, under the uniform cost criterium, takes a time

$$T_1 = (1 + 1 + 1) + (1 + 1 + 1) + (1 + 1 + 1)$$
$$+ (1 + 1 + 1) + (1 + 1 + 1 + 1 + 1)$$

Under the logarithmic cost criterium, it takes a time

$$T_1' \le (1 + l(5) + l(5)) + (1 + ((l(10) + l(10)) + (1 + l(3) + l(3)))$$
$$+ (1 + l(5) + 1 + l(10)$$
$$+ \max\{(1 + (1 + l(3)) + (1 + l(5)) + 1(8)),$$
$$((1 + l(10)) + l(6) + l(6))\}$$

In both cases, the program is $\Theta(1)$.
2. The execution of program 2 clearly takes a time $T_2 = \infty$ under any cost criterion, as it will never halt. In fact,

$$T_{\langle \text{WhileStat} \rangle} = T_{\langle \text{Cond} \rangle} + T_{\langle \text{StatList} \rangle} + \overline{T}_{\langle \text{WhileStat} \rangle}$$
$$= 2\left(T_{\langle \text{Cond} \rangle} + T_{\langle \text{Stat.List} \rangle}\right) + \overline{T}_{\langle \text{WhileStat} \rangle} = \cdots$$
$$= \infty$$

3. Program 3 is clearly the SMALG counterpart of the RAM program of Exercise 3.25 computing n^n.
   Without going into the useless details of computing all constants involved in the function T_3, it is immediate to realize that the same reasoning as for the RAM program apply as well to its SMALG counterpart.

It is not surprising that the complexities computed for the foregoing SMALG programs are nothing else than the complexities of suitable RAM programs that can be seen as their translation. The difference between the two is not in execution efficiency but in program understandability.

Exercise

3.28 Code the SMALG programs of Figure 3.12 as RAM programs and do the converse for the RAM Program of Examples 3.6 and 3.7 and Exercises 3.27.

Let P_R be the RAM program corresponding to the SMALG program P. Verify that if P has time complexity T_P, then T_{P_R} is $\Theta(T_P)$ and conversely.

3.5 Putting Things Together

Complexity results depend on the model we choose to formalize our algorithms. Also, they depend on the specific encoding of the problem being solved. This has been summarized elsewhere by saying that Church's Thesis cannot be transferred from the realm of decidability to the realm of complexity. We have discussed these concepts at length and we have given examples to substantiate them. The reader might suspect that no general results on problem complexity can ever be found. Fortunately, this is not true because a fairly general framework can be given to evaluate and compare complexity results obtained on different formal models.

First, let us discuss how we can relate complexity results obtained on the RAM and (deterministic) TM models. To do so, let us discuss first how a RAM can simulate a multitape TM. The most natural way (see Figure 3.14) is to use a block—block 0—of RAM memory cells to store the state and the positions of the k memory tape heads of our TM. Successive blocks of k RAM memory cells —block 1, block 2, etc.—are used to hold the values stored in positions 1, 2, etc. of each of the k TM memory tapes. Thus, the value represented in the ith cell of the jth tape of the TM is kept into location $c + k \cdot j + i$, c being a suitable constant, of the RAM memory. Also, in order to access the value currently under the head of the mth tape, one should perform one more indirect access through block 0 to find the value of the current position of the mth head. Finally, execution of the transition function $\delta(q, s_0, s_1 \ldots s_k)$ and the output function $\eta(q, s_0, s_1 \ldots s_k)$ require a fixed number of accesses to the RAM memory to access $q, s_1, s_2 \ldots s_k$, one read operation to access s_0, and a finite number of tests on these values to determine the values of δ and η. This leads to the following theorem in a straightforward way.

Statement 3.16

A multitape TM with time complexity T can be simulated by a RAM machine with time complexity that is $\Theta(T)$ under the uniform cost criterion and $\Theta(T \cdot \log T)$ under the logarithmic cost criterion. □

The simulation of a RAM on a TM is slightly more complex to analyze. We will show how this can be done in the case of the logarithmic cost criterion, which is

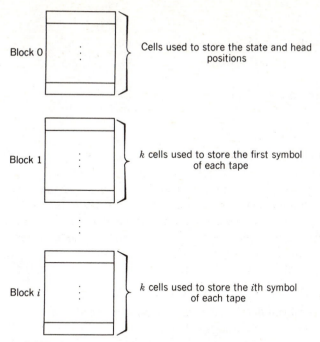

FIGURE 3.14 How a RAM can simulate a TM.

more broadly applicable than the uniform cost criterion, as we have seen in Section 3.4.1. Further comments on the uniform cost criterion will be given later after Theorem 3.17.

Theorem 3.17
Let L be a language accepted by a RAM with time complexity T under the logarithmic cost criterion. If the RAM program does not use MULT and DIV instructions, then L can be recognized in time bounded by a $\Theta(T^2)$ function by some multitape TM.

Proof
Let us map a RAM into a TM in the following way.

a. Input tapes of the two machines are isomorphic. In fact, the RAM input tape contains a sequence of integers in a bounded set since—by assumption—the machine works as language recognizer. Thus the corresponding TM input tape contains a sequence of symbols in a finite input set.

b. Because we are considering the machines as language recognizers we do not care about output tapes.

| $\cdots$ | $\$$ | $\$$ | i_1 | $\$$ | $M[i_1]$ | $\$$ | $\$$ | $\cdots$ | i_k | $\$$ | $M[i_k]$ | $\$$ | $\$$ | b | $\cdots$ |

FIGURE 3.15   Tape encoding the values kept in a RAM memory.

c. The TM has three tapes (besides $\mathbf{T}_I$).

   c.1 The first tape, $\mathbf{T}_1$, encodes the values kept in the RAM memory according to the following convention:

   Let $\{i_j | j = 1, \ldots, k\}$ be the set of indexes such that, at any given time, $M[i_j]$ has been explicitly initialized. The layout of tape $\mathbf{T}_1$ of the TM is shown in Figure 3.15. A cell is represented in tape $\mathbf{T}_1$ (see the simulation described as follows) only if a value was stored in it at some previous time. We use '$\$$' as a delimiter and code i_j and $M[i_j]$ in binary notation with the constraint that $i_j < i_{j+1}$. Note that, even if the RAM is used as a language recognizer it may happen that $M[i]$ is an unbounded integer (e.g., a temporary value) during computation.

   c.2 The second tape, $\mathbf{T}_2$, contains $M[0]$ in binary notation.

   c.3 The third tape, $\mathbf{T}_3$, is used as a temporary storage.

Let us show how the TM can simulate a meaningful sample of RAM instructions. We leave the remaining ones to the reader as an exercise.

1. LOAD h

   1.1 Search tape $\mathbf{T}_1$ for the sequence $\$\$ h \$ M[h] \$\$$.

   The search can be done sequentially starting from the left end of the tape and comparing h with i_j, $j = 1, \ldots, k$ until $i_j = h$ for some j. If the search fails, the TM enters an error state and halts.

   1.2 Copy the value $M[h]$ onto the second tape.

2. STORE h

   2.1 Search tape $\mathbf{T}_1$ for the sequence $\$\$ h \$ M[h] \$\$$

   2.1.a If the search fails, this means that either

   2.1.a.a $i_k < h$. In this case, store the sequence $h \$ M[0] \$\$$ at the right end of $\mathbf{T}_1$, where $M[0]$ (the value held in the accumulator of the RAM) is represented by the contents of $\mathbf{T}_2$.

   2.1.a.b There exists $j < k$ such that $i_j < h < i_{j+1}$.
   In this case:

   - Copy the portion of $\mathbf{T}_1$ to the right of $i_j \$ M[i_j] \$\$$ into $\mathbf{T}_3$.
   - Store the sequence $h \$ M[0] \$\$$ to the right of $i_j \$ M[i_j] \$\$$.
   - Store the contents of $\mathbf{T}_3$ into $\mathbf{T}_1$ to the right of $h \$ M[0] \$\$$.

   2.1.b If one j has been found such that $i_j = h$ then

   - Copy the portion of $\mathbf{T}_1$ to the right of $h \$ M[h] \$\$$ into $\mathbf{T}_3$.
   - Store $M[0] \$\$$ to the right of $h \$$ in $\mathbf{T}_1$.
   - Copy the contents of $\mathbf{T}_3$ to the right of $h \$ M[0] \$\$$.

3. ADD *h
   3.1 Search $\mathbf{T}_1$ for the sequence $\$\$ h \$ M[h]$.
       If the sequence is not found, enter an error state and halt.
   3.2 Copy $M[h]$ into $\mathbf{T}_3$
   3.3 Search for the sequence $\$\$ M[h] \$ M[M[h]]$ in $\mathbf{T}_1$. If the sequence is not found, enter an error state and halt.
   3.4 Perform the sum $M[0] + M[M[h]]$, where $M[0]$ (the value held in the accumulator) is represented by the contents of $\mathbf{T}_2$.
       Possibly use the scratch portion of $\mathbf{T}_3$ to perform the sum.
       Leave the result in $\mathbf{T}_2$.

   . . .

It is fairly obvious that such a TM actually simulates the RAM. We must show now that, if the RAM does not use MULT and DIV instructions and has a time complexity T—under the logarithmic cost criterion—the TM has a $\Theta(T^2)$ time complexity.

The key of the proof is in the following lemma.

Lemma 3.18
The length of the nonblank portion of tape $\mathbf{T}_1$ of the TM is bounded by a $\Theta(T)$ function.

Proof
First notice that at the beginning of computation both the RAM memory and the TM memory tapes are all blank.

     Each RAM instruction modifies at most one memory cell, say $M[h]$, and the cost of doing this is at least $l(h) + l(M[h])$ (see Table 3.2; it can be higher in the case of an indirect store). Also, the string $\$\$ h \$ M[h] \$\$$ appears in tape $\mathbf{T}_1$ of the TM only if at least one value has been explicitly stored into the hth cell of the RAM memory. The length of such string is equal to $l(h) + l(M[h]) + 5$, and is less than $c_x \cdot t_h$, t_h being the time required by the RAM to store a value into $M[h]$ and c_x being a suitable constant. In conclusion, the length L_1 of the nonblank portion of tape $\mathbf{T}_1$ is less then $c \cdot \sum_{j=1}^{k} t_{i_j}$, t_{i_j} being the time required to store a value into $M[i_j]$ (see Figure 3.15) and c being a suitable constant. But $\sum_{j=1}^{k} t_{i_j}$ is less than or equal to $T(n)$, n being the length of the input string, and this proves the lemma. $\square$

In order to complete the proof of Theorem 3.17, observe that any RAM instruction is simulated by a TM through a sequence of moves whose length is bounded by $d \cdot L_1$, L_1 being the length of the nonblank portion of tape $\mathbf{T}_1$ and d being a suitable constant. This is due to the fact that one must possibly search the entire tape in order to simulate any RAM instruction.

Because one RAM instruction costs at least one time unit, if T is the RAM time complexity, the number of RAM instructions to simulate is not greater than $T(n)$. Thus the total time complexity of simulation is bounded by a $\Theta(T^2)$ function.   ∎

Why have we proven Theorem 3.17—the converse of Theorem 3.16—in the special case where a logarithmic cost criterion is used for the RAM? As we mentioned, the logarithmic cost criterion has a more broadly applicable validity than the uniform cost criterion. Most important, the theorem does hold *only* under the logarithmic cost case. In fact, under the uniform cost criterion, a RAM can compute numbers such as 2^{2^n}, for all $n \geq 0$, in time $\Theta(n)$. A TM requires 2^n cells just to store and read them and therefore perform the computation in at least $\Theta(2^n)$ steps. Thus, no polynomial relationship exists in general between complexities of the RAM and the TM in the case of the uniform cost criterion.

To summarize and generalize the previous reasoning we give the following statement.

Statement 3.19
The RAM machine, under the logarithmic cost criterion, and the multitape TM are polynomially related (i.e., if the time complexity of the one model is $\Theta(T)$, the complexity of the other is $\Theta(P \circ T)$), P being a polynomial function.[8]

The proof is left to the reader as an exercise.

Hint: First, generalize Theorem 3.17 to the computation of any integer function. Then design TM subroutines that implement MULT and DIV instructions by using the subroutines for ADD and SUB. Verify that their complexity is polynomially related to the logarithmic cost of MULT and DIV.   □

A similar result holds for space complexity and is left to the reader as an exercise.

Now let us relate the complexity functions of the SMALM model with RAM and TM models. Let P_S be a SMALG program. It can be translated into an equivalent RAM program P_R according to the following procedure.

First, we define a bijection between the SMALM memory and the RAM memory. For the sake of simplicity, suppose we know a priori that no array index will ever exceed a value $\overline{N}$ during execution. Then we can associate one RAM memory cell with each simple variable of P_S and a sequence of $\overline{N}$ cells with each array variable of P_S. Three more cells ($M[1]$, $M[2]$, and $M[3]$) are used as temporaries, as we see shortly. We will denote by i the address of the cell corresponding to the SMALG simple variable i. We will denote by $\overline{a}$ the address of the first cell of the sequence associated to array a. Thus, if the two arrays a and b, respectively, are stored consecutively, then $\overline{b} = \overline{a} + \overline{N}$. Thus for each P_S variable x, $\overline{x}$ is an a priori known integer.

---

[8]Recall that $P \circ T$ denotes the composition of P and T.

Then, we give a set of rules to build a RAM program P_R equivalent to any SMALG program P_S. Let X be a nonterminal of the SMALG grammar and let P_S^X be a program fragment such that $X \overset{*}{\Rightarrow} P_S^X$. The corresponding fragment of P_R is obtained by applying the following rules.

1. Expression evaluation.
   1.1 If $\langle \text{Exp} \rangle \overset{*}{\Rightarrow} \langle \text{Simple Var} \rangle \overset{*}{\Rightarrow} x$, where x is a simple variable identifier, then generate the sequence

   LOAD $\quad \bar{x}$
   STORE $\ 1$

   1.2 If $\langle \text{Exp} \rangle \overset{*}{\Rightarrow} \langle \text{Constant} \rangle \overset{*}{\Rightarrow} k$, where k is a constant, then generate the sequence

   LOAD = $\quad k$
   STORE $\qquad 1$

   1.3 If $\langle \text{Exp} \rangle \overset{*}{\Rightarrow} \langle \text{ArrayVarId} \rangle [\langle \text{Constant} \rangle] \overset{*}{\Rightarrow} a[k]$, where a is an array identifier and k is a constant, then generate the sequence

   LOAD $\quad h$
   STORE $\ 1$

   where h is the integer $\bar{a} + k - 1$.
   1.4 If $\langle \text{Exp} \rangle \overset{*}{\Rightarrow} \langle \text{ArrayVarId} \rangle [\langle \text{simple var} \rangle] op \langle \text{ArrayVarId} \rangle [\langle \text{constant} \rangle]$ $\overset{*}{\Rightarrow} a[i] \ op \ b[k]$, where op is an arithmetic operator ($+$, $-$, $*$, **div**, or **mod**), a, b are the array identifiers, i is a simple variable identifier, k is a constant, then (assuming, e.g., $op = +$, and $c = \bar{b} + k - 1$) generate the following sequence

   LOAD = $\quad \bar{a}$
   ADD $\qquad\ \bar{i}$
   SUB = $\quad\ \ 1$
   STORE $\quad\ 1$
   LOAD = $\quad c$
   STORE $\quad\ 2$
   LOAD $*$ $\quad 1$
   ADD $*$ $\qquad 2$
   STORE $\quad\ 1$

   The translation associated with all other possible derivations of $\langle \text{Exp} \rangle$ are left to the reader as an exercise. Notice that the only requirement is that the value of the expression be stored into $M[1]$ at the end of the execution of the generated sequence.
2. Translation of assignment statements.
   If $\langle \text{AssStat} \rangle \overset{*}{\Rightarrow} \langle \text{Simple Var} \rangle := \langle \text{Exp} \rangle \overset{*}{\Rightarrow} x := \langle \text{Exp} \rangle$ then generate the sequence of statements needed to evaluate the expression according to the above

rule 1 and follow them by:

LOAD   1
STORE $\bar{x}$

Again, the treatment of other cases for ⟨AssStat⟩ is left to the reader as an exercise.

3. Translation of conditional statements.
   If

   ⟨CondStat⟩ ⇒ **if** ⟨Cond⟩ **then** ⟨StatList⟩^{1} **else** ⟨StatList⟩^{2} **fi**

   then generate the sequence

   $\tilde{P}_{\langle \text{Cond} \rangle}$
   JZERO F
   $\tilde{P}^1_{\langle \text{StatList} \rangle}$
   JUMP C
   F: $\tilde{P}^2_{\langle \text{StatList} \rangle}$
   C:

   where

   - $\tilde{P}_{\langle \text{Cond} \rangle}$, $\tilde{P}^1_{\langle \text{StatList} \rangle}$, $\tilde{P}^2_{\langle \text{StatList} \rangle}$ denote the translations of the condition, of the statement list in the **then** branch, and of the statement list in the **else** branch, respectively.
   - F, C are labels not used elsewhere in the RAM program, C being the label of the first statement following the above sequence of statements.

   The treatment of the **if** statement without an **else** part can be described accordingly.

4. Translation of the while statement.
   Let ⟨WhileStat⟩ ⇒ **while** ⟨Cond⟩ **do** ⟨StatList⟩ **od**
   then generate the sequence

   LOOP: $\tilde{P}_{\langle \text{Cond} \rangle}$
   JZERO   EXIT
   $\tilde{P}_{\langle \text{StatList} \rangle}$
   JUMP   LOOP
   EXIT:

   with the same meaning of the notation as in case 3.

5. The translation of the remaining statements (I/O, statement lists, etc.) is left to the reader as a simple exercise.

Exercises

3.29 Modify the above construction by removing the assumption that the size of arrays be bounded statically.

Hint: If a SMALG program uses j arrays, blocks of j consecutive RAM cells are used to store the array elements having the same index.

3.30 Translate the SMALG programs of Figure 3.12 into the corresponding RAM programs.

3.31* (The solution of this exercise requires some previous experience on compilation techniques.) Transform the foregoing rules for translating P_S into P_R into a computer program.

A brief inspection into the complexity rules given for SMALG and the preceding translation rules will convince the reader of the following statements.

Statement 3.20

If a problem can be solved by a SMALG program with time complexity T, then there exists a RAM program solving it with time complexity that is $\Theta(T)$. □

Statement 3.20 clearly holds under both cost criteria.

The converse result (i.e., a simulation of RAM programs by a SMALM) would be straightforward if SMALG were augmented by a low-level **go to** statement. Without such a statement, which has been avoided in honor of the principles of structured programming, the result stems from the construction given by Böhm and Jacopini in their proof that sequence, selection (**if-then-else**) and iteration (**while**) are sufficient to code any program control flow. Thus, we conclude our discussion with the following general statement.

Statement 3.21

All computation models, under reasonable assumptions of cost measures, have polynomially related time and space complexity functions. □

In other words, any problem that can be solved by some computation model with time complexity T can be solved by any other computation model with time complexity that is $\Theta(P \circ T)$, P being a polynomial function. This is true, of course, only if "reasonable" cost assumptions are made: We have already seen that, in the general case, the uniform cost criterion is not reasonable as it assumes that an unbounded piece of information can be accessed in a fixed time.

In some sense, Statement 3.21 is the complexity counterpart of Church's Thesis. Even if we cannot refer to a single computation model to obtain complexity measures of absolute validity, we can at least argue whether a problem has a polynomial complexity, an exponential complexity or even worse. Furthermore, the boundary between polynomial and higher than polynomial complexity is usually conventionally assumed as the boundary between practically tractable and intractable problems.

As usual, this statement must be taken cautiously. A polynomial complexity of type n^k where k is very large can hardly be viewed as practically tractable. On the other hand, there are cases where, within the practical range of values for n, $T_1(n) = k \cdot n^2$ may be better than $T_2(n) = h \cdot n$ if $h \gg k$. We return to this topic in the concluding discussion of Section 3.10.

Before closing this section, let us warn the reader in order to facilitate an understanding of the deep meaning of Statement 3.21.

- Pay attention to the used complexity parameter. In Exercise 3.25, you have derived a RAM program computing n^n in time $\Theta(n^2 \cdot \log n)$. If you translate the RAM program into an equivalent TM that receives as input a binary coding of n (say, $\bar{n}$) you obtain an exponential time complexity (why?). This does not contradict the previous statement, because here we have been changing the parameter used to measure complexity in a subtle way. In fact, here exponential time complexity uses as input dimension the length of the input string, as we usually do with TMs. But, in this case the length of the input string is $|\bar{n}|$ (i.e., $l(n)$), not the original value n.

  Similarly, after reading Example 3.8, which proves a $\Theta(n \cdot \log n)$ complexity for computing whether n is prime, the reader could find somewhere in the literature that it is not known whether primeness can be computed by a TM in polynomial time, which seems to contradict Statement 3.21. The "trick" is the same as before: we must remember that the size of the string coding n is $\Theta(\log n)$, unless a unary coding of n is assumed.

- If we eliminate MULT and DIV from the RAM repertoire of statements, then Theorem 3.17 holds under the uniform cost criterion too by substituting $\Theta(T^3)$ in place of $\Theta(T^2)$. This can be proved by following the same proof path as in Theorem 3.17 and by realizing that Lemma 3.18 holds as well after replacing $\Theta(T^2)$ for $\Theta(T)$. This remark suggests that MULT and DIV can hardly be viewed as elementary operations, at least if we are looking for results of general mathematical validity.

- The previous results (in particular Theorem 3.17 and its consequences) have been derived by considering full computations (i.e., computations starting from an initial configuration of the computing machine where the memory is empty). Obviously, for such computations T is at least $\Theta(n)$ since, apart from trivial cases, the entire input must be read. This reasonable assumption, however, rules out some interesting cases as the following example illustrates. The SMALG fragment of Figure 3.16 solves the membership problem for a sorted array of the length n (see Example 3.2). We use i and j to delimitate the portion of array x that is currently searched. The result of the search is $z = 1$ if there is an array element equal to y; $z = 0$ otherwise. Complexity of the SMALG fragment under the uniform cost criterion can be derived in a straightforward fashion and, obviously, it coincides with the result informally derived for Pascal in Example 3.2 (it is $\Theta(\log n)$). Let us analyze the

```
i := 1; j := n;
while i ≤ j do k := i + j;
                k := k div 2;
                if y = x[k]
                then i := k; j := k − 1
                else if y < x[k]
                        then j := k − 1
                        else i := k + 1
                        fi
                fi
        od;
if x = a[k]
then z := 1
else z := 0
fi
```

FIGURE 3.16 *Binary – search* in SMALG.

complexity of the foregoing fragment using the logarithmic cost criterion and under the assumption that, for any i, $l(x[i]) \le m$, $l(y) \le m$, for some integer constant m. Note that execution of k **div** 2 can be assumed as a truly elementary operation because the underlying SMALM can execute it by a shift of the bit string representing k one position to its right. The time needed to execute the loop body is $\Theta(l(n))$, because i, j, and k are in $\{1, \ldots, n\}$ and we assume m as a constant. The loop is iterated at most $l(n)$ times. Thus time complexity is $\Theta(\log^2(n))$ under the logarithmic cost criterion.

If you consider a TM working on the same problem, following the comments given at the end of Example 3.4 and Exercise 3.8, you can easily prove that the time needed to access a generic array element is $\Theta(n)$, not $\Theta(\log n)$. So there is no way to make the TM work in $\Theta(P(\log^2(n)))$ time, P being some polynomial function. Fortunately, the foregoing contradiction disappears when fragments are embedded in full programs, which have at least linear time complexity.

3.6* Advanced Complexity Concepts: Hierarchies, Reducibility, and Completeness

In Section 2.11, we introduced the notion of problem reducibility in order to prove several undecidability results. Furthermore, we were able to classify problems according to a difficulty measure based on the notion of unsolvability degree. Much of this philosophy can also be applied to problem classification in terms of the complexity of their solution. In this section, we move some preliminary steps along this way. This is a typical topic on the border between basic and advanced theory: There are several important open questions, and yet there are already several highly relevant results. Here we present a sample of such results, with no ambition of providing a broad and comprehensive coverage of the topic.

We will restrict our attention to solvable problems—formulated as recursive languages—because complexity becomes a rather elusive notion if non terminating computations are allowed. Furthermore, we rely on the multitape TM computation model used as language recognizer, which has been proved to be the most abstract and thus the most suitable to obtaining general results. Thanks to Statement 3.21 many of the results we give here can be rephrased in a way that is independent of the used computation model.

Many questions naturally arise when looking at the definitions and statements of Section 3.3. For example,

- Can the Speed-Up Theorem be pushed beyond a linear speedup?
- Does there exist a complexity function T such that DTIME(T) covers all recursive languages?
- If $T_1(n) < T_2(n)$, for each $n \geq \bar{n}$, is DTIME(T_1) $\subset$ DTIME(T_2)?
- Does nondeterminism affect computation complexity? (Recall Theorem 1.25, which states that nondeterministic TMs are not more powerful than deterministic TMs.)

  In other words, for any given T, or family $\mathscr{T} = \{T_i\}$ is DTIME(T) = NTIME(T), DTIME($\mathscr{T}$) = NTIME($\mathscr{T}$), where DTIME($\mathscr{T}$) obviously means $\bigcup_{T_i \in \mathscr{T}} \{\text{DTIME}(T_i)\}$?

All of the foregoing questions have an intuitive impact on possible applications, as well as their counterparts in terms of space complexity. Let us start by answering the second question by means of a theorem which can be seen as the complexity theory counterpart of Theorem 2.6 (undecidability of the halting problem for TMs).

Theorem 3.22

For any given total computable function T, there exists a recursive language L not in DTIME(T).

Proof

Even the proof of this theorem resembles the proof of Theorem 2.6: It is a classical diagonal proof.

First define any effective enumeration of multitape TMs, say $\{M_i, i = 1, 2 \ldots\}$. This can obviously be obtained by extending the enumeration technique proposed in Section 2.5.1. Similarly consider in effective enumeration of strings of V_T^*.

Now define $L = \{x_i | M_i$ does not accept x_i within $T(|x_i|)$ moves$\}$. Clearly L is recursive. In fact, to state whether $x_i \in L$ it is sufficient to simulate all possible M_i computation sequences whose length is not greater than $T(|x_i|)$; and such computations are finite.

Suppose now, by contradiction, that L is in DTIME(T). Thus, there exists an i_0 such that $L = L(M_{i_0})$, M_{i_0} having a time complexity bounded by T. Now, if $x_{i_0} \in L$ then M_{i_0} accepts x_{i_0} within $T(n_0)$ steps, where $n_0 = |x_{i_0}|$. Thus, by definition of L, x_{i_0} is not in L: a contradiction. On the other hand, if $x_{i_0} \notin L$, then M_{i_0} does not accept x_{i_0}. Thus, by definition of L, x_{i_0} is in L: again a contradiction. Both assumptions lead to contradictions, and thus complexity of M_{i_0} cannot be bounded by T. ■

Exercises

3.32 Prove that Theorem 3.22 holds as well for NTIME, DSPACE, and NSPACE.

3.33 Prove that for any f, DTIME(f) $\subseteq$ DSPACE(f)

3.34 Prove that for any L in DSPACE(f), with $f(n) \geq \log n$, or in NTIME(f) there exists a constant c such that L is in DTIME($c^{f(n)}$).

An immediate consequence of Theorem 3.22 is that deterministic time complexity (as well as nondeterministic time complexity, deterministic, and nondeterministic space complexity) provides an infinite hierarchy of languages. Consider, in fact, any function T. By Theorem 3.22, there exists a recursive language $L \notin$ DTIME(T). Let T_L be the time complexity function of a TM recognizing L. Define $T'(n) = \max\{T(n), T_L(n)\}$ for any n. Then obviously DTIME(T) $\subset$ DTIME(T'). Thus, recursive languages can be ordered in an infinite hierarchy according to their time or space complexity, both using deterministic and nondeterministic recognizing devices. In much the same spirit, in Section 2.11 we ordered recursively enumerable sets according to their degree of unsolvability.

The notion of hierarchy is a powerful tool towards classifying problems according to some difficulty parameter. Here is another example of a hierarchy.

Theorem 3.23

Regular languages are an infinite hierarchy with respect to the number of states of their accepting FAs. More precisely, for any n, there exists a language accepted by a FA having n states but by no FA with less than n states. ■

The proof of Theorem 3.23 is left as an exercise to the reader.

Let us now address the third of the foregoing questions. First notice that if for some $c > 0$, $T_2(n) \leq c \cdot T_1(n)$, then by Theorem 3.12 DTIME(T_1) = DTIME(T_2). We do not go deep into this topic. We just inform the interested reader that for some T it may happen that DTIME(T^2) = DTIME(T), but "in general" DTIME(T) $\subset$ DTIME($T \cdot \log T$). The advanced literature referenced in the bibliographic remarks can be used for more information on this topic.

Finally, let us address the last question we raised at the beginning of this section. We will address it in a specific, but fundamental framework. We claimed that polynomial time complexity has been conventionally—but realistically—

defined as the boundary between tractable and intractable problems. Let us define

$$\mathscr{P} = \bigcup_{i=1}^{\infty} \text{DTIME}(n^i)$$

and, similarly,

$$\mathscr{NP} = \bigcup_{i=1}^{\infty} \text{NTIME}(n^i)$$

The natural question whether $\mathscr{P} = \mathscr{NP}$ has a dramatic impact on the theory of problem solving. In fact, a large number of practically relevant problems are known to be in $\mathscr{NP}$. We provide a sample as follows.

Propositional formulas satisfiability (SAT)
Let $W(A_1, A_2, \ldots, A_m)$ be a propositional formula involving the logical variables $A_1, \ldots, A_m$. Does there exist an assignment of logical values $\{T, F\}$ to $A_1, \ldots, A_m$ such that $W(A_1, \ldots, A_m)$ is true?

In order to show that the above problem is in $\mathscr{NP}$, we first formulate it as a language recognition problem. The natural way is to encode propositional formulas into suitable strings in such a way that a language is defined consisting of exactly those strings which code satisfiable formulas.

Clearly, we can use an alphabet including all logical connectives, namely $\neg$, $\vee$, $\wedge$, $\supset$, $\equiv$, and parentheses $($, $)$. However, propositional formulas may contain an arbitrary number of *different* logical variable symbols. Thus we must solve the problem of representing an infinite set of possible symbols through a finite alphabet. The natural solution is to represent variable A_i by a coding (say, binary coding) of natural number i. Thus, $l(i)$ bits will be necessary to represent A_i. Since a wf W containing n *occurrences* of logical variables (the number of variable occurrences may be much larger than the number of distinct variables) may contain a $\Theta(n)$ number of logical connectives and parentheses, we conclude that the length of the string x representing W is $\Theta(n \cdot \log n)$. We can now state the following theorem.

Theorem 3.24
The language L consisting of the strings representing satisfiable wfs of $\mathscr{PC}$ is in $\mathscr{NP}$. In short, we say that SAT is in $\mathscr{NP}$.

Proof
Let W be any propositional formula involving n occurrences of m logical variables. Therefore, $m \leq n$.

Nondeterministically generate a sequence of m logical values. This can be performed in time $\Theta(m) \leq \Theta(n)$ by a nondeterministic TM. Then substitute any occurrence of A_i with its value. This can be done in time $\Theta(n \cdot \log n)$ since the original string must be scanned. However, we may assume that the resulting string involving only symbols $T, F, \neg, \ldots$) has length $\Theta(n)$.

At this point the truth of the resulting formula is checked by traversing it several times and by performing reductions $(\neg F) \rightarrow T, (\neg T) \rightarrow F, (F \wedge T) \rightarrow F$, etc. It is obvious that such a check can be performed in polynomial time with respect to n (actually, it is possible to devise $\Theta(n)$ algorithm). ∎

Hamiltonian Circuit Problem (HC)

Let G be a graph. Does G have a path that visits all vertices of the graph exactly once and returns to its starting vertex?

As an exercise, the reader is invited both to code HC as a language recognition problem and to prove it is in $\mathcal{NP}$. ☐

Traveling Salesman Problem (TS)

Let G_c be a graph where a cost $c \in \mathbb{N}$ is associated to each arc. Can we find a Hamiltonian circuit, if any, for which the sum of the costs associated to the arcs of the circuit is minimum?

This problem is harder to formulate as a language recognition problem. In fact, it is more naturally formulated as a function to be computed, rather than as a set to be decided. Thus, we must face the problem of switching from translation to decision: a nontrivial job when a discussion of complexity is involved, as we remarked in Section 3.1.

Consider the following *traveling salesman decision problem*, which is strictly related to the previous one. Let G_c be defined as before. Does there exist a Hamiltonian circuit whose total cost is not greater than a given bound B?

Clearly, the two versions are reducible to one another. Furthermore, as far as *complexity* is concerned, we can claim that the original problem is certainly not less costly than the new one, because once a solution for the original problem has been found, the solution for the latter is immediately obtained by comparing the cost of the optimal circuit with B. The opposite is not guaranteed. In conclusion, we can attack the decision problem by having in mind that the optimization problem is at least as difficult. Therefore, we refer in the following to the traveling salesman problem, meaning the decision version. ☐

Clique Problem (CP)

A *clique* of an undirected graph is a complete subgraph; that is, a subset of its nodes such that for every pair of vertices of the subgraph there is a connecting arc. The number of nodes of the clique is its *size*. A maximal clique is a clique such that no other clique has greater size. The problem is to find a maximal clique[9] in an undirected graph G.

This is another problem formulated as an optimization problem. Let us consider again the corresponding decision problem. For any undirected graph G, does G have a clique of size greater than, or equal to k?

Notice that in this case the optimization problem and its decision version are reducible to one another by linearly related complexities. In fact, solving the decision problem on the basis of the optimization problem requires a trivial

---

[9]Notice that a maximal clique may not be unique.

comparison, whereas the optimization problem can be solved by solving the decision version for $k = 1, \ldots, n$. Thus if the former can be solved in time $\Theta(f)$, the latter can be solved in $\Theta(f)$, whereas if the latter can be solved in $\Theta(f)$, the former can be solved in $\Theta(n \cdot f)$.

Consequently, we can claim that CP is in $\mathcal{NP}$ and wonder whether it is in $\mathcal{P}$ or not without specifying which version is intended. □

If $\mathcal{P} = \mathcal{NP}$ all these problems and many other oens could be classified as "tractable," and the hope to find for them really efficient algorithms would be strengthened. Unfortunately, the question is still open, but the fact that all attempts to find polynomial solutions to such problems have so far failed suggests a negative answer to the general question. Also, Exercise 3.34 suggests, but does not prove, that commuting from nondeterministic to deterministic computations, may require, in general, an exponential number of "tries." The relevance of the question is further emphasized by applying to it the concept of problem reducibility as shown below.

Definition 3.12
A language L_1 is polynomial-time reducible to a language L_2 if and only if there exists a polynomial-time bounded deterministic TM with output—that is, a TM whose time complexity T, is bounded by some polynomial p—which for any x produces an output $\tau(x)$ such that $\tau(x) \in L_2$ if and only if $x \in L_1$. □

Exercise

3.35 Show that polynomial-time reducibility is a transitive relation.

Warning: If L_1 is reducible to L_2 in $p_1(n)$ and L_2 is reducible to L_3 in $p_2(n)$, then L_1 is not reducible to L_3 in $p_1(n) + p_2(n)$!

Intuitively, the above definition states that a problem P_1 is polynomial-time reducible to P_2 if there exists an algorithm, which can be executed in polynomial time, able to compute the solution of any given instance of P_1 (stating whether $x \in L_1$) in terms of the solution of a suitable instance of P_2 (stating whether $\tau(x) \in L_2$). The notion of problem reducibility can be enriched with the notion of a complete problem in the same way as we did in Section 2.11 for recursively enumerable sets.

Definition 3.13
Let $\mathcal{L}$ be a class of languages. A language L—not necessarily in $\mathcal{L}$—is $\mathcal{L}$-hard with respect to polynomial-time reductions if and only if, for any $L' \in \mathcal{L}$, L' is polynomial-time reducible to L. A language L is *complete in* $\mathcal{L}$, or $\mathcal{L}$-complete (with respect to polynomial-time reductions) if and only if it is in $\mathcal{L}$ and it is $\mathcal{L}$-hard. □

The reader is invited to compare the present definition of completeness with Definition 2.7. The notion of completeness—in our case, polynomial-time completeness—becomes extremely relevant when applied to the class $\mathcal{NP}$. In fact, it would be sufficient to find a polynomial time algorithm for just one $\mathcal{NP}$-complete problem, in order to conclude that $\mathcal{P} = \mathcal{NP}$. Conversely, a proof of non-polynomial-time solvability for one of them would imply non-polynomial-time solvability for all of them. The exciting and challenging fact is that, despite being the question $\mathcal{P} = \mathcal{NP}$ still open, an incredible number of different $\mathcal{NP}$-complete problems is known and several scientific journals try to keep such a list always updated! In the next section, we present some classical $\mathcal{NP}$-complete problems. For all such problems, it is neither known a polynomial-time algorithm, nor it has been proved that such an algorithm does not exist!

3.7* Some Classical $\mathcal{NP}$-Complete Problems

SAT is the first historical example of a $\mathcal{NP}$-complete problem. We have already checked in an easy way that this problem is in $\mathcal{NP}$. It remains therefore to be proved that it is also $\mathcal{NP}$-hard.

Theorem 3.25
SAT is $\mathcal{NP}$-hard.

Proof
The goal of the proof is to provide a deterministic computation which, for every nondeterministic TM M with polynomial-time complexity p and for every string x on M's alphabet such that $|x| = n$ produces as output a propositional formula W in polynomial time $p'(n)$, such that W is satisfiable if and only if $x \in L(M)$.

The main idea originates from the fact that if $x \in L(M)$, then there exists a sequence of moves whose length does not exceed $p(n)$ leading M to an accepting state. Thus, at most $p(n) + 1$ memory cells can be used by M during such computation. Once we realize that a TM configuration has a bound space, it can be described by a suitable propositional formula. For instance, a logical variable $-Q_{t, k}$—can state whether at time t, M's state is q_k. Another variable—$C_{t, i, k}$—can state whether at time t the ith cell contains symbol a_k and so on. Furthermore, suitable logical connections may impose that at time $t = 0$ the formula describes an initial configuration, that the configuration at time $t + 1$ derives from the configuration at time t, and that at time $t = p(n)$, M is in an accepting state.

Let us proceed now with the details of the proof. First let us assume that M is a single-tape TM. As usual, this assumption is made only to simplify the notation. It is immediate to verify that it does not cause any loss of generality. In fact, from the construction of Theorem 1.15 we immediately come to the conclusion that if a k-tape TM has time complexity $p(n)$, then an equivalent single-tape TM has time complexity $p'(n)$, for a suitable polynomial p', even in the nondeterministic case (see also Exercise 3.17). As a side remark, observe that the construction of the single-tape TM is effective and can be carried over in a time that depends on the size of the machine (in terms of number of states and symbols), but independent of the length of the input string. We also assume that M's tape is infinite only to the right.

The formula W is built as the conjunction (logical $\wedge$) of several subformulas, or *clauses*, according to the following rules. Let t denote the time variable, $0 \le t \le p(n)$, and let i denote the position of a tape cell, $0 \le i \le p(n)$.

1. M's configuration description.
   We define the following sets of logical variables.
   - $\{Q_{t,k} | 0 \le t \le p(n), 0 \le k \le |Q| - 1\}$
     $Q_{t,k}$ will be true if and only if M will be in state q_k at time t.
   - $\{H_{t,i} | 0 \le t \le p(n), 0 \le i \le p(n)\}$
     $H_{t,i}$ will be true if and only if M's head will be in position i at time t.
   - $\{C_{t,i,h} | 0 \le t \le p(n), 0 \le i \le p(n), 0 \le h \le |A| - 1$, where A is M's full alphabet$\}$
     $C_{t,i,h}$ will be true if and only if at time t the ith cell will contain symbol a_h.

   Therefore, we have defined a number

   $$g(n) = (p(n) + 1) \cdot |Q| + (p(n) + 1)^2 + (p(n) + 1)^2 \cdot |A|$$

   of logical variables, g being a $\Theta(p^2)$ function. In short, we will say that we have defined $\Theta(p^2(n))$ variables.

   Clearly, at any time M must be in exactly one state, its head must be on exactly one cell, and each cell must contain exactly one symbol. Thus we obtain a first group of clauses (*configuration clauses*, CC) that logical variables must satisfy in order to describe M's configurations.

   Configuration clauses (CC):

   $$\bigwedge_{0 \le t \le p(n)} \left(\bigvee_{0 \le k \le |Q| - 1} Q_{t,k} \right)^{10}$$

   $\{M$ must be in at least one state at each time.$\}$

   $$\wedge$$

   $$\bigwedge_{\substack{0 \le t \le p(n) \\ 0 \le k_1 \ne k_2 \le |Q| - 1}} (Q_{t,k_1} \vee Q_{t,k_2})$$

   $\{$At each time M cannot be in two different states.$\}$

---

[10] This is an obvious short notation for

$(Q_{0,0} \vee Q_{0,1} \ldots \vee Q_{0,|Q|-1}) \wedge (Q_{1,0} \vee \ldots) \wedge \ldots (\ldots Q_{p(n),|Q|-1})$

$$\bigwedge$$
$$\bigwedge_{0 \le t \le p(n)} \left(\bigvee_{0 \le i \le p(n)} H_{t,i} \right)$$
$$\bigwedge$$
$$\bigwedge_{\substack{0 \le t \le p(n), \\ 0 \le i, j \le p(n), \\ i \ne j}} (\neg H_{t,i} \vee \neg H_{t,j})$$

{ M's head is on just one cell at each time.}

$$\bigwedge$$
$$\bigwedge_{\substack{0 \le t \le p(n), \\ 0 \le i \le p(n)}} \left(\bigvee_{0 \le h \le |A|-1} C_{t,i,h} \right)$$
$$\bigwedge$$
$$\bigwedge_{\substack{0 \le t \le p(n), \\ 0 \le i \le p(n), \\ 0 \le h, k, \le |A|-1, \\ h \ne k}} (\neg C_{t,i,h} \vee \neg C_{t,i,k})$$

{At each time each cell contains exactly one symbol.}
In summary, CC contains the following number of clauses:

$$(p(n) + 1) \cdot |Q| + (p(n) + 1) \cdot |Q| \cdot (|Q| - 1)$$
$$+ (p(n) + 1)^2 + (p(n) + 1)^2 \cdot p(n)$$
$$+ (p(n) + 1)^2 \cdot |A| + (p(n) + 1)^2 \cdot |A| \cdot (|A| - 1)$$

each clause being the logical 'or' of some *literals*, each literal being either a logical variable or its negation. Thus, CC contains $\Theta(p^3(n))$ clauses and $\Theta(p^3(n))$ literals (recall that $|Q|$ and $|A|$ are constants).

2. Initial configuration description.
   At $t = 0$, M must be in q_0, its head must be in position 0 and $x = a_{k_0} a_{k_1} \ldots a_{k_{n-1}}$, must be stored in the first n cells of the tape. All remaining cells must be blank. This yields a second group of clauses (*Initial Configuration Clauses*, IC), listed here.
   Initial configuration clauses (IC).

$$Q_{0,0} \wedge H_{0,0}$$
$$\wedge C_{0,0,k_0} \wedge C_{0,1,k_1} \ldots \wedge C_{0,n-1,k_{n-1}}$$
$$\bigwedge_{n \le i \le p(n)} C_{0,i,0}$$

   (we assume that $\flat$ is a_0)
   IC has $\Theta(p(n))$ literals.

3. Accepting configuration description.
   Assume the convention that if M halts at time $t_H < p(n)$, it will maintain the final configuration for all t, $t_H \le t \le p(n)$. This convention has an impact on

the machine transitions to be described next, but allows us to state that at time $t = p(n)$ M must be in an accepting state. This yields another clause (*Accepting Clause*, AC), which is described as follows:

$$Q_{p(n), i_1} \lor \cdots \lor Q_{p(n), i_s}$$

where $\{ q_{i_1}, \ldots, q_{i_s} \} = F$.
AC has $\Theta(1)$ literals.

4. Transition relation description.

Finally, we must give clauses describing the configuration transition from time t to time $t + 1$. Let the transition function be of the type $\delta(q_k, s_h) = \langle q_{k'}, s_{h'}, N \rangle$ with the convention that whenever M's original δ is undefined for some q_k, s_h, we set $\delta(q_k, s_h) = \langle q_k, s_h, S \rangle$.

Such clauses must impose

4.1 For each t and for each i, if M is in state q_k, its head is in position i and reading s_h, then at time $t + 1$ M is in $q_{k'}$, position i stores $s_{h'}$ and the head is either on position i or $i + 1$, or $i - 1$, depending on N. This is described by the logical formula:

$$\bigwedge_{\substack{0 \le t \le p(n), \\ 0 \le i \le p(n), \\ 0 \le k \le |Q|-1, \\ 0 \le h \le |A|-1}} ((Q_{t, k} \land H_{t, i} \land C_{t, i, h}) \supset (Q_{t+1, k'} \land H_{t+1, i'} \land C_{t+1, i, h'}))$$

where $i' = i$ (respectively, $i + 1$, $i - 1$) if $N = S$ (respectively, R, L).[11] The preceding formulation is quite intuitive. However, for future developments, we prefer the following equivalent formulation (see Section 0.2.2), which is expressed as the conjunction of clauses as well as the previous ones.

$$\bigwedge_{\substack{0 \le t \le p(n), \\ 0 \le i \le p(n), \\ 0 \le k \le |Q|-1, \\ 0 \le h \le |A|-1}} (\neg Q_{t, k} \lor \neg H_{t, i} \lor \neg C_{t, i, h} \lor Q_{t+1, k'}) \land$$

$$(\neg Q_{t, k} \lor \neg H_{t, i} \lor \neg C_{t, i, h} \lor H_{t+1, i'}) \land$$
$$(\neg Q_{t, k} \lor \neg H_{t, i} \lor \neg C_{t, i, h} \lor C_{t+1, i, h'})$$

4.2 If at time t the head is in position i, then at time $t + 1$ all cells except the ith have the same contents as at t.

$$\bigwedge_{\substack{0 \le t < p(n), \\ 0 \le i \le p(n), \\ 0 \le h \le |A|-1}} (\neg H_{t, i} \land C_{t, i, h}) \supset C_{t+1, i, h}$$

which again is reformatted as
$$H_{t, i} \lor \neg C_{t, i, h} \lor C_{t+1, i, h}$$

The set TC of transition clauses is defined as the conjunction of formulas derived in 4.1 and 4.2. TC has $\Theta(p^2(n))$ literals.

---

[11] If $i = 0$ and $N = L$ the formula is the same as in the case where δ is undefined, since M must halt.

Finally, we define $W = CC \wedge IC \wedge AC \wedge TC$, which means that W is the conjunction of all clauses belonging to the above sets. Therefore, W has $\Theta(p^3(n))$ literals.

At this point the core of the proof is complete. However, before formally closing it, it is worth pointing out some fairly obvious details.

a. A careful inspection into the construction of W should leave no doubt that $C_0 \overset{p(n)}{\underset{M}{\vdash}} C_A$, C_0 being the initial configuration and C_A being an accepting configuration, if and only if W is satisfiable. For instance, any truth assignment satisfying W must be such that $Q_{0,0}$ is true.

b. We have described a deterministic procedure that builds a W containing $\Theta(p^3(n))$ literals, starting from x. In order to show that the formal requirement of Definition 3.13 and hence of Definition 3.12 are fulfilled, we need to encode SAT as a language recognition problem. As we noted in Theorem 3.24, a propositional formula containing n occurrences of logical variables can be encoded as a string of length $\Theta(n \cdot \log n)$. Thus, for any x of length n, its translation $\tau(x)$ into a string encoding W is certainly not longer than $\Theta(p^4(n))$. Once you realize that the translation τ can be executed by a deterministic (may be multitape) TM in time $\Theta(|\tau(x)|)$, the polynomial-time reducibility is completely proved.

c. Notice that we do not need to actually know a TM M solving the original problem. The *existence* of such a machine guarantees the *existence* of a polynomial-time deterministic reducing machine. However, if such an M is actually known *and* a polynomial bound p for its nondeterministic computations is known, then the proof allows to effectively build the reducing machine.

∎

Notice that during the proof of Theorem 3.25 we devoted some effort towards maintaining W in conjunctive form. That effort was not necessary for the proof but now allows us to obtain—for free—an important corollary stating that even a subproblem of the original problem of propositional formulas satisfiability is $\mathcal{NP}$-complete. This corollary, in turn, will be a useful lemma for future developments.

Corollary 3.26
The problem of stating the satisfiability of propositional formulas in conjunctive normal form is $\mathcal{NP}$-complete.

Proof
If a problem is in $\mathcal{NP}$, obviously a subproblem thereof is in $\mathcal{NP}$ as well. Since the formula W built in the proof of Theorem 3.25 is in conjunctive normal form, the corollary is already proved. □

Propositional formulas satisfiability is a landmark result in the world of $\mathcal{NP}$-complete problems. It turns out that $\mathcal{NP}$-completeness of many of such problems can be naturally proved by reducing SAT to them, either directly or indirectly. Let us discuss another classical example.

Theorem 3.27
HC is $\mathcal{NP}$-complete.

Proof
Since we already stated that HC is in $\mathcal{NP}$, we only need to show that it is $\mathcal{NP}$-hard. This will be obtained by showing that SAT in conjunctive normal

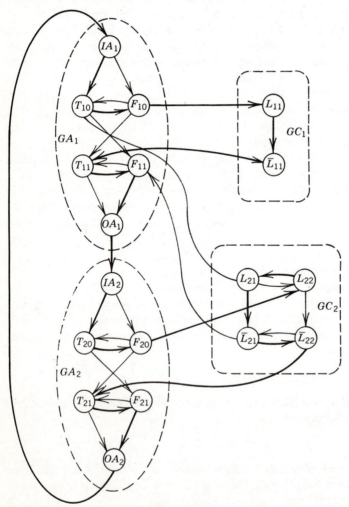

FIGURE 3.17 The graph associated to the wf *W*:
$A_1 \wedge (\neg A_1 \vee A_2)$. Solid edges identify the Hamiltonian circuit.
Dotted lines enclose the constituent "pieces."

form is polynomial-time reducible to HC. By the transitivity of polynomial-time reducibility, every problem in $\mathcal{NP}$ will be reducible to HC. Of course, the reduction will be obtained by a procedure which, for any propositional formula in conjunctive normal form W, builds a graph G such that a HC exists for G if and only if W is satisfiable.

The philosophy of the construction consists of building G as an aggregation of two classes of "pieces." Pieces of the first type will be associated to each logical variable in W and will in some sense display all occurrences thereof. Pieces of the second type will be associated to each clause of W and bound to nodes belonging to pieces of the former type in such a way that their traversal guarantees the truth of the associated clause.

Before going into the formal details of the proof, let us explain the idea of the construction through a simple example. Consider the wf W: $A_1 \wedge (\neg A_1 \vee A_2)$ and the graph G of Figure 3.17.

Subgraphs GA_1, GA_2 are associated to A_1 and A_2, respectively. GC_1 and GC_2 are associated to the clauses C_1: A_1, C_2: $\neg A_1 \vee A_2$. Clearly, W is satisfied only by $A_1 = T$, $A_2 = T$. Consider now G. A possible HC for G must necessarily go through IA_1. Notice that GC_1 prevents HC from choosing F_{10} as the next node after visiting IA_1. In fact, after F_{10} HC must reach L_{11} (otherwise it would become inaccessible) and then $\overline{L}_{11}$. But this clearly makes T_{10} inaccessible. Thus, T_{10} must necessarily follow IA_1. Intuitively this corresponds to the fact that C_1 imposes A_1 to be true.

After the choice of T_{10}, the path $F_{10}, L_{11}, \overline{L}_{11}, T_{11}, F_{11}, OA_1, IA_2$ is chosen because this guarantees the inclusion of F_{10}, F_{11} in HC. Once IA_2 is reached, consider the alternative between T_{20} and F_{20} (i.e., assigning A_2 a true or false value). Choosing F_{20} would force to follow the path L_{22} (otherwise the whole GC_2 would not be included into HC), L_{21} (otherwise L_{21} would become inaccessible), $\overline{L}_{21}, \overline{L}_{22}, T_{21}$. At this point T_{20} would be inaccessible. Thus, T_{20} must be chosen as successor of IA_2. In fact, GC_2 and $A_1 = T$ impose $A_2 = T$. At this point HC is completed.

Before going into the rest of the proof, the reader is invited to go through the following exercise.

Exercise

3.36 Build graphs G_i corresponding to the following W_i such that G_i has an HC if and only if W_i is satisfiable.

W_1: $(A_1 \vee A_2) \wedge (A_1 \vee \neg A_2)$
W_2: $(A_1 \vee A_2 \vee A_3) \wedge (\neg A_1 \vee A_2) \wedge (\neg A_2 \vee A_3)$
W_3: $(A_1 \vee \neg A_2) \wedge (\neg A_1 \vee A_2) \wedge (\neg A_1 \vee \neg A_2) \wedge (A_1 \vee A_2)$

In the case of success, the reader is probably able to complete the proof without our guidance. Otherwise, the reader is invited to study the following construction and then go back to the exercise.

Let W be $C_1 \wedge C_2 \ldots \wedge C_h$, where clauses contain logical variables $A_1, \ldots A_m$. For each A_i build a graph GA_i of the type of Figure 3.18a where p_i is the greater value between the number of occurrences of A_i and $\neg A_i$ in W. Observe that each GA_i has exactly two paths from IA_i to OA_i visitng all its nodes, one starting from T_{i0} and one starting from F_{i0}.

Now connect OA_i to IA_{i+1} (modulo m) (see Figure 3.18b).

Next, for each clause $C_j = L_{j1} \vee L_{j2} \ldots L_{jk_j}$, L_{jr} being either A_{j_r} or $\neg A_{j_r}$ for some variable A_{j_r}, build a graph GC_j of the type of Figure 3.18c.

Connect GC_j to the rest of the graph according to the following rule. For each r, if L_{jr} is A_{j_r} then connect the first node $F_{j_r, s}$ of GA_{j_r} having only two outgoing arcs to L_{jr} and $\overline{L}_{jr}$ to $T_{j_r, s+1}$; if L_{jr} is $\neg A_{j_r}$, then connect the first node $T_{j_r, s}$ of GA_{j_r} having only two outgoing arcs to L_{jr} and $\overline{L}_{jr}$ to $F_{j_r, s+1}$. Notice that such connections are certainly possible because p_i is greater than or equal to the number of occurrences of A_i in W.

Consider now the full graph G obtained from the foregoing construction and observe that

1. If GC_j are ignored, there are exactly 2^m HCs in the remaining graph, $\overline{G}$. This corresponds to the fact that if W is empty any assignment of truth values trivially satisfies it.

2. A possible HC entering some GC_j at L_{jr} must leave it at $\overline{L}_{jr}$. For instance, a path entering GC_j at L_{j2}, visiting $\overline{L}_{j2}$, $\overline{L}_{j1}$ and then leaving GC_j would make L_{j1} inaccessible. The generalization to all possible cases is straightforward. This fact does not imply that a possible HC must visit all nodes of each GC_j consecutively.

3. Any possible HC must be obtained from an HC of $\overline{G}$ by substituting some arc of the type $\langle F_{i,s}, T_{i,s+1} \rangle$ with a path going through some GC_j, if HC contains the arc $\langle IA_i, T_{i0} \rangle$. Conversely, if HC contains the arc $\langle IA_i, F_{i0} \rangle$, it must be obtained from an HC of $\overline{G}$, by substituting some arc of the type $\langle T_{i,s}, F_{i,s+1} \rangle$ with a path going through some GC_j.

4. The previous point implies that any GC_j can be entered through some L_{jr} by an HC only from some $T_{j_r, s}$ if $\langle IA_j, F_{j_r, 0} \rangle$ is in HC and only from some $F_{j_r, s}$ if $\langle IA_j, T_{j_r, 0} \rangle$ is in HC. This corresponds to the intuitive fact that entering GC_j from some $F_{j_r, s}$ means satisfying it by assuming $A_{j_r} = T$.

Suppose now that W is satisfied by some truth assignment to $A_1 \ldots A_m$. An HC can be built for G in the following way. First build an HC for $\overline{G}$ by choosing edge $\langle IA_i, T_{i0} \rangle$ if and only if A_i is true in the preceding assignment. Then, whenever such an HC has an arc $\langle T_{i,s}, F_{i,s+1} \rangle$ ($\langle F_{i,s}, T_{i,s+1} \rangle$, respectively) and an arc connecting $T_{i,s}$ ($F_{i,s}$, respectively) to some GC_j not yet entered, visit the *whole* GC_j entering it from $T_{i,s}$ ($F_{i,s}$, respectively) and reentering $\overline{G}$ at $F_{i,s+1}$ ($T_{i,s+1}$, respectively). Since for each GA_i there are at least as many $T_{i,s}, F_{i,s}$ as there are occurrences of $A_i, \neg A_i$ in W, it cannot happen that at the end of this procedure some GC_j has not been traversed because this fact would imply that all its L_{jr} can be accessed only from the "wrong nodes" of each GA_i (i.e., from $T_{j_r, s}$ if A_{j_r} is true and conversely). But this would mean that the above assignment does not satisfy W.

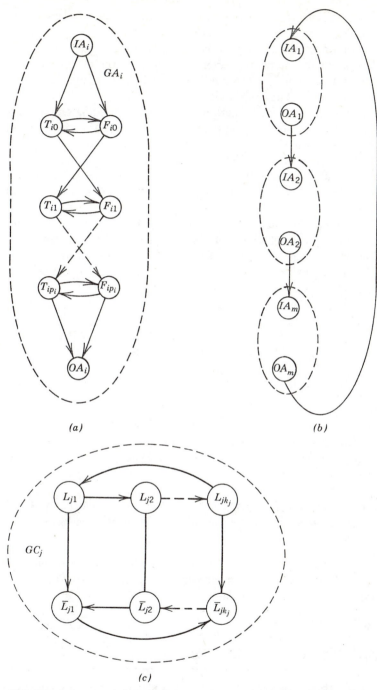

FIGURE 3.18 The construction of the graph associated to a wf. (*a*) The part associated to logical variable A_i. (*b*) The connection of parts $\{GA_i\}$ (*c*) The part GC_j associated to clause C_j.

The converse statement that the existence of an HC for G implies W satisfiability should now be an easy exercise for the reader.

In order to complete the proof, we must consider the complexity of the construction. Let n be the number of literals in W. Clearly $\overline{G}$ has at most $2(n + 1) + 2m$ nodes. Since $m \leq n$ $\overline{G}$'s size is $\Theta(n)$. The total number of nodes of $\{GC_j | j = 1, \ldots, h\}$ is $2n$. Thus G's nodes are $\Theta(n)$.

Similarly to Theorem 3.25, we remark that the fact that coding graphs with $\Theta(n)$ nodes may require strings of length that is $\Theta((n \cdot \log n)^2)$ (there are at most n^2 arcs in a graph with n nodes) causes no problem from the point of view of polynomial-time reducibility. Furthermore, it is fairly obvious that a trivial algorithm with $\Theta(n)$ complexity can build $\overline{G}$ and GC_j and an algorithm with $\Theta(n^2)$ complexity can easily complete the connections between $\overline{G}$ and GC. ∎

The problem reduction philosophy is widely applicable. For instance, in Chapter 2 we were able to prove the unsolvability of some language problems by encoding TM computations into strings belonging to suitable languages. Then the unsolvability of other language problems was derived by reducing them to the original one. Similarly, now we showed $\mathcal{NP}$-completeness of SAT by reducing the computations of polynomial-time-bounded nondeterministic TMs to suitable SAT. Then the $\mathcal{NP}$-completeness of HC has been shown by reducing SAT to it. The reader is invited to consider how much more difficult it would have been directly attacking the HC problem. Furthermore, the reader is invited to check his/her ability in applying reduction techniques by looking for proofs of $\mathcal{NP}$-completeness of the following problems.

- The traveling salesman problem.
- The Hamiltonian circuit problem for undirected graphs.
- The k-colorability problem, (i.e., can the nodes of an undirected graph be colored by using k-different colors in such a way that no two nodes connected by an edge have the same color?)
- The clique problem.
- Integer linear programming (i.e., let A be an $n \times m$ integer matrix and let B be an array of n integers. Does there exist an array X of m integers such that $AX \geq B$?)

This problem does not follow the usual pattern of $\mathcal{NP}$-complete problems. In fact, it is usually easy to show a that problem is in $\mathcal{NP}$ and it is more difficult to show it is $\mathcal{NP}$-hard. In this case, just the opposite happens.

3.8   Complexity Lower Bounds

Once an algorithm A has been discovered to solve a problem P whose complexity is T, we have an *upper bound* for the complexity of solving P. We know that, *at least* it can be solved within a time $T(n)$. Of course, one can always hope to find a new algorithm A' to solve P with better complexity T'. Our previous experience shows that this is often the case. Besides the mechanical application of the Speed-Up Theorem, which can arbitrarily improve time efficiency without changing $\Theta(T)$, one can use ingenuity to redesign new algorithms that may even improve the asymptotic behavior.

Therefore, a natural question is how much can be the efficiency of problem solution be improved. For instance, once an algorithm for P has been found with complexity T, can one hope to achieve a $\sqrt{T}$ or even a $\log(T)$ complexity by inventing new algorithms? In other words, we are interested in stating *complexity lower bounds* for problems, in such a way that one should not waste time attempting to achieve impossible goals.

Let us recall some previously observed facts. By Theorem 3.22, for any total function T, one can construct a language not in DTIME(T). By definition, T is a lower bound for the complexity of recognizing such a language. Notice that if T is a lower bound for recognizing a language by means of a deterministic multitape TM, then $\sqrt{T}$ is a lower bound for recognizing the same language by means of a RAM (see Theorem 3.17).

However, the languages constructed in the proof of Theorem 3.22 are typical "diagonal languages," so that they cannot help much to determine complexity lower bounds in the recognition of languages of the type $\{a^n b^n c^{n^2}\}$ or to sort an array, and so on. Therefore, we should look for some tools suitable to derive lower bounds for more concrete problems.

A first trivial remark is the following. In most worst cases, in order to decide whether a string is in a language or not it is necessary to scan it completely. For instance, consider the recognition of $L = \{a^n b^n\}$. When analyzing the string $abaaabaaab$ one can decide it is not in L just at the third character. However, when a string is of the type $a^n b^m$, $m \le n$, one can decide if $m = n$ only after scanning the whole string. Thus, the recognition of L has a $\Theta(n)$ lower bound. Since we already realized that L can actually be recognized in $\Theta(n)$ time, we have completely solved the problem of time complexity for L. Thus, for most problems there exists a trivial lower bound for time complexity, namely $\Theta(n)$.

Unfortunately, obtaining less trivial lower bounds for significant problems is not as easy. For instance, consider the problem of recognizing context-free languages. The complexity upper bound presently known is $\Theta(n^{2.49})$[12], but no lower bound larger than $\Theta(n)$ is known although one suspects that some context-free languages are not recognizable in linear time.

A major tool in deriving complexity lower bounds is $\mathcal{NP}$-completeness, at least under the conjecture that $\mathcal{P} \ne \mathcal{NP}$. In fact, if this statements holds, any $\mathcal{NP}$-complete problem must have a nonpolynomial complexity; and this is generally considered as a synonym of intractability.

Besides $\mathcal{NP}$-completeness, some problems have been proved to have exponential lower bounds so that they are certainly intractable. An example is the *reachability problem for Petri nets*. Given a PN N and two markings m_1, m_2

---

[12] This result has been obtained by reducing the problem to the problem of matrix multiplication.

deciding whether $m_1 \overset{*}{\underset{N}{\vdash}} m_2$ requires *at least* a space and a time that are $\Theta(2^{cn})$, where n is the number of places of N. However, we do not go through an analysis of this type of intractability results because the technicalities involved are out of the scope of this text. The interested reader is referred to the specialized literature.

The most difficult problems occur in general when we look for nontrivial lower bounds within $\mathscr{P}$. Suppose you know that a language is in $\mathscr{P}$ (for instance, context-free languages are in $\mathscr{P}$). Clearly, there is lot of difference between lower bounds $\Theta(n)$ and, say, $\Theta(n^{1000})$. Unfortunately, in this field the state of the art does not exhibit a powerful set of systematic tools. Only single facts can be proved, and general results are still lacking.

A noticeable exception is provided by Theorem 3.7 where the notion of crossing sequence was introduced to prove a $\Theta(n^2)$ lower bound for recognizing $\{wcw^R\}$ by a single-tape TM. Unfortunately, that statement and its proof are strictly related to the used model. In fact, a multitape TM can recognize the same language in time $\Theta(n)$. Indeed, crossing sequences are a powerful tool for proving complexity lower bounds, but their generalization to multitape TMs must take into account all possible configurations of memory tapes so that they become more suitable for exponential lower bounds.

Before closing this section let us mention another problem of high practical interest.

Theorem 3.28
Sorting a sequence of n unordered elements requires in the worst case at least $\Theta(n \cdot \log n)$ pairwise comparisons.

Proof
Let $A = \{a_1, \ldots, a_n\}$ be the sequence to be ordered. A sorting algorithm must produce an ordered permutation of A, say $A_o = \{a_{i_1}, \ldots, a_{i_n}\}$, by performing some number of comparisons. For instance if A is already ordered $n - 1$ comparisons are sufficient, namely it is sufficient to state $a_1 < a_2$, $a_2 < a_3, \ldots, a_{n-1} < a_n$.

The set of all possible executions of an ordering algorithm can be naturally represented by a *decision tree*, where each internal node represents a comparison, its left (respectively, right) son represents the consequence of the positive (respectively, negative) result, each leaf represents the permutation of A obtained as a result of the comparisons. Thus a path from the root to a leaf represents all comparisons performed by the algorithm to obtain the leaf as a result. Figure 3.19 represents a decision tree for sorting 3 elements by applying the algorithm *Sort-by-straight-insertion* given in Section 2.4.

The *height of the decision tree* (i.e., the length of the longest path from root to leaves) is the number of comparisons performed by the algorithm in the worst case.

Notice now that the number of leaves for such a tree is $n!$ since this is the number of possible different results of the algorithm. The decision tree is a binary

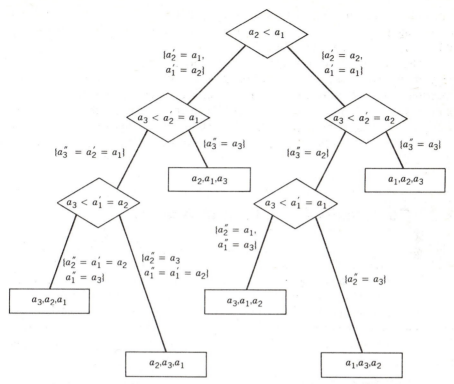

FIGURE 3.19 The decision tree to sort three elements by algorithm *sort-by-straight insertion*. Apices denote the new values assumed by elements a_i as a consequence of assignments. Comparisons with the dummy element $a[0]$ have been skipped.

tree. A binary tree of height h has at most 2^h leaves (verify this claim as an exercise). Therefore, the height of a binary tree with m leaves is at least equal to $\log_2 m$. In conclusion, the height of a decision tree corresponding to the execution of a sorting algorithm must be at least $\log(n!)$.

Finally $\Theta(\log n!)$ is at least $\Theta(n \cdot \log n)$ since, for $n > 1$.

$$n! \geq n(n-1)(n-2)\dots\left(\frac{n}{2}\right) \geq \left(\frac{n}{2}\right)^{n/2}$$

and thus $\log(n!) \geq n/2 \cdot \log\left(\dfrac{n}{2}\right)$, which is $\Theta(n \cdot \log n)$.

On the other hand, $\log(n!) = \log n + \log(n-1) + \dots$, so that $n \cdot \log n \geq \log(n!)$ ◼

Thus we need at least $\Theta(n \cdot \log n)$ comparisons to sort n elements. If we assume that the time required to perform a comparison is constant and that the total amount of time spent by a sorting algorithm is proportional to the number of performed comparisons, then we may state a $\Theta(n \cdot \log n)$ lower bound for sorting algorithms. Note that considering multiple—yet finite—comparisons only affects the base of the logarithm.

The skeptical reader might object to our assumption that a sorting algorithm must necessarily go through a sequence of comparisons. After all, ordering a list of elements that are in reverse order can be done with no comparison at all. We do acknowledge that there is only an intuitive evidence that a sorting algorithm must necessarily be based on a comparison mechanism. However, this justifies the assumption that, in practice, sorting requires at least a $\Theta(n \cdot \log n)$ time.

3.9 Complexity Evaluation in Action

This section does not introduce any new concept on computational complexity. Rather, it gives further examples of the concepts introduced elsewhere. Its purpose is mainly to consolidate the reader's practical attitude towards evaluating computational complexity. The outline of the section is the following: First, we discuss complexity of a sorting program. Second, we discuss complexity of an algorithm on graphs computing the reachability set and we draw some general considerations on graph algorithms. Third, we close the section with some practical advice.

3.9.1 A Sorting Example

Let us go back to the sorting algorithm known as *sort-by straight-insertion*, which was given in Pascal in Section 2.4. The SMALG version is illustrated in Figure 3.20.

We wish to evaluate time complexity of the SMALG program shown in Figure 3.20. We do not care about space complexity, which is clearly a rather trivial problem.

As a preliminary remark, we must keep in mind that all examined cost units are "abstract" because they do not refer to any specific, real machine cycle. Thus, if we wish to determine the absolute execution time, we need more information about the implementation of single instructions and the physical speed of our computer. However, we have already learned that the order notation provided useful results of general validity on complexity; in particular, it enlightens the asymptotic behavior of the algorithm. Thus, let us first look for an order notation to describe a first approximation of T. In a second step, we might decide to refine our analysis in order to obtain at least a bound to the actual constants involved in T. Let us base our analysis of the algorithm on its SMALG description illustrated in Figure 3.20 and let us refer to SMALM as a computation model.

The next step is the choice of a cost criterion. A brief look at the program shows that data are not going to increase dramatically in size during its

```
begin read n;
    i := 1;
    while i ≤ n do read a[i];
                i := i + 1
            od;
    i := 2;
    while i ≤ n do x := a[i]; a[0] := x; j := i − 1;
                while x < a[j] do k := j + 1;
                                a[k] := a[j];
                                j := j − 1
                        od
            k := j + 1;
            a[k] := x;
            i := i + 1
        od;
    i := 1;
    while i ≤ n do write a[i];
                i := i + 1
            od;
end
```

FIGURE 3.20 *Sort-by-straight-insertion* in SMALG.

execution. Let $m = \max \{n, a[1], \ldots, a[n]\}$; if memory cells can store m, then they will be able to store any other program variable during execution. Furthermore, the program does not involve any multiplication. Thus the uniform cost criterion seems to be a quite reasonable assumption.

We are now ready to start the true complexity analysis. First, observe that, under the uniform cost criterion, all assignment statements, read statements, write statements, and condition evaluations can be executed in a time bounded by some constant value: Thus we can set up Table 3.4.

Now let us follow the path of program execution.

1. Time $t_1 = c_1$ is spent before entering the first loop.
2. The first loop is executed exactly n times and requires a time

$$t_2 - t_1 = n \cdot (c_2 + c_3) + c_2$$

3. The second loop starts at time $t_3 = t_2 + c_4$.
4. The second loop is executed exactly $n - 1$ times.
   Thus, at the exit of the second loop, time is

$$t_4 = t_3 + \sum_{i=2}^{n} \left(c_2 + c_5 + t_i^I + c_8 \right) + c_2$$

$$= t_3 + (n - 1)(c_2 + c_5 + c_8) + c_2 + \sum_{i=2}^{n} t_i^I$$

where t_i^I is the time required to execute the inner loop at the ith iteration of the outer loop.

TABLE 3.4   Time Bounds for the Program of Figure 3.20.

Execution of Statements	Time Bound
read n; $i := 1$	c_1
$i \leq n$	c_2
read $a[i]$; $i := i + 1$	c_3
$i := 2$	c_4
$x := a[i]$; $a[0] := x$; $j := i - 1$	c_5
$x < a[j]$	c_6
$k := j + 1$; $a[k] := a[j]$; $j := j - 1$	c_7
$k := j + 1$; $a[k] := x$; $i := i + 1$	c_8
$i := 1$	c_4
$i \leq n$	c_2
write $a[i]$; $i := i + 1$	c_9

In order to evaluate t_i^I, note that the condition of the inner loop can be true at most i times as j is initialized to $i - 1$ and is decreased at each iteration until it reaches 0. At that point $x = a[0]$ and the condition will be false. Thus, for all i, we obtain

$$t_i^I \leq i \cdot (c_6 + c_7) + c_6$$

so that

$$\sum_{i=2}^{n} t_i^I \leq c_6 \cdot (n - 1) + (c_6 + c_7) \cdot \left(\frac{(n + 1)}{2} \cdot n - 1 \right)$$

5. The last portion of the program requires a time

$$t_5 - t_4 = c_4 + n \cdot (c_2 + c_9) + c_2$$

Putting it all together, we obtain $t_5 \leq \bar{c}_1 + \bar{c}_2 n + \bar{c}_3 n^2$ for some constants $\bar{c}_1$, $\bar{c}_2$, and $\bar{c}_3$. Therefore, T is $\Theta(n^2)$.

A few remarks are now in order.

r1. Under the uniform cost criterion, time complexity is a function only of n, the number of items to be sorted. If we apply the logarithmic cost criterion, it would depend also on the values stored in the array. If we assume $m = \max \{n, a[i] | i = 1, \ldots, n\}$, we easily obtain a $\Theta(\log m \cdot n^2)$ time complexity. In general, m is not related to n. In some sense, this is a verification that the uniform cost criterion was an appropriate choice.

r2. In most cases, the big-theta notation provides exactly what we ask from complexity analysis. However, we must be conscious that, if needed, we could compute the real value of constants c_i and $\bar{c}_i$, provided that full information is supplied on implementation details, such as exact sequence of machine instructions, single instruction execution speed, and so on.

r3. It is clear that the two nested loops are the core of the program. They are responsible for the $\Theta(n^2)$ complexity. It might be the case, however, that in practice c_1 and c_9, which contain the execution time of the **read** and **write** statements, are much greater than other c_i's and thus $\bar{c}_2 \gg \bar{c}_3$. As a consequence, in many practical cases, if the value of n is small enough, program time complexity would be "dominated" by $\bar{c}_2$ (the linear constant) instead of $\bar{c}_3$ (the quadratic constant). This remark emphasizes that during algorithm performance analysis, one should concentrate on the "real" sources of complexity. For instance, in many applicative programs it may be even useful to forget completely about CPU time and just concentrate on I/O statements.

r4. We should always keep in mind that T as studied here is defined as the "worst case complexity measure." It is obviously quite relevant, but certainly it is not the only meaningful time complexity measure. In many cases, it could happen that an algorithm, say A_1, solving problem P has worst case time complexity T_1 that is $\Theta(f_1)$ better than another algorithm A_2. Yet A_2 might be preferable to A_1 on the basis of its average performances.

Sorting is just an example of such a case. In fact, a very famous sorting algorithm, called Quicksort, has a $\Theta(n^2)$ worst-case time complexity but a $\Theta(n \cdot \log n)$ average time complexity with good proportionality constants (constants are sometimes relevant after all) that make it preferable over other algorithms with $\Theta(n \cdot \log n)$ worst case time complexity.

Exercises

3.37   Sketch a multitape TM implementing the *sort-by-straight-insertion* algorithm. What is its complexity order?

3.38   Could you obtain a better complexity order with some other TM solving the sort problem (without necessarily following the spirit of the above algorithm)?

3.39*   The example of Section 3.9.1 assumed that n (the length of the array to be sorted) and m (the maximum of the values stored in the array) were independent values. Similarly, Example 3.1 assumed n (the length of the array to be searched) and m (as before) as independent values. Give comments on the validity of this assumption as $n \to \infty$ and compare it with the treatment of SAT given in Sections 3.6 and 3.7.

3.9.2   An Algorithm on Graphs

Graphs are a powerful mathematical structure that can be used to model and solve many different problems. Therefore, algorithms on graphs have been widely studied. (Elements of graph theory have been briefly recalled in Section 0.1.4.)

Graphs can be represented by different data structures, such as

a. A binary matrix $\{G[i, j]|$ for $1 \leq i, j \leq n$, **if** there is an edge connecting v_i and v_j **then** $G[i, j] = 1$ **else** $G[i, j] = 0\}$.
b. A set of pairs $\{\langle v_i, v_j \rangle|$ there is an edge connecting v_i and $v_j\}$.

Both structures can be used to represent both directed and undirected graphs.

Using SMALG, we might decide to augment it with multidimensional arrays in order to implement the above encoding of graphs as matrices. However, it is also possible to represent a graph in the second way as a pair of arrays, say $SV[k], TV[k]$, such that $\langle v_i, v_j \rangle$ is an edge of the graph if and only if there exists a k such that $SV[k] = i$, $TV[k] = j$ (SV and TV stand for "source vertex" and "target vertex," respectively). Notice that the former representation always requires n^2 cells to store a graph, n being the number of vertices, while the latter requires $2m$ cells, m being the number of edges. In general, $m \ll n^2$.

Consider now the following problem on graphs. Let $G = \langle V, E \rangle$ be a directed graph. For each vertex $v_i \in V$, we wish to compute its *reachability set* (i.e., the set of vertices $\overline{V}_i = \{v_j|$ there exists a path from v_i to $v_j\}$). It is easy to give an elegant algorithm to solve this problem, based on the transitivity of the reachability relation: If v_j is reachable from v_i and v_k is reachable from v_j, then v_k is reachable from v_i.

Algorithm computing the reachability set of each vertex of a directed graph

Step 1: For each vertex $v_i \in V$, initialize $\overline{V}_i$ as $\{v_i\}$, which states that a vertex is reachable from itself.
Step 2: For each $v_j \in \overline{V}_i$, if there exists an edge $\langle v_j, v_k \rangle$ in E, then insert v_k into $\overline{V}_i$. Using a Pascal notation, we write $\overline{V}_i := \overline{V}_i \cup \{v_k\}$.
Step 3: Repeat step 2 exactly $n - 1$ times, n being $|V|$.   □

The preceding algorithm has been given in an abstract way, not using any particular computation model. Based on this abstract formulation, we can draw some conclusions that do not depend on any specific implementation.

1. The given algorithm can be easily transformed into a suitable TM, RAM program, or SMALG program.
2. It always halts as step 2 is repeated exactly $n - 1$ times.
3. It is correct (i.e., when it halts, $\overline{V}_i$ is exactly the reachability set of v_i). In fact, it is clear that if $v_j \in \overline{V}_i$, then v_j is reachable from v_i. On the other hand, notice that at the hth iteration of step 2, the algorithm inserts into $\overline{V}_i$ all those vertices v_k such that there exists a path of length h from v_i to v_k. This claim can be immediately verified inductively. Finally, it is clear that if v_k is reachable from v_i, then it is reachable by means of a path of length less than n. Thus, we have completely proved correctness.

Now let us try to analyze complexity. Intuitively, we can observe that, step 1 may require n "elementary operations." Furthermore, step 2 is repeated $n - 1$

```
j := 1;
while j ≤ n do if j ≠ i
              then if R[i, j] = 1
                   then k := 1
                        while k ≤ n do if G[j, k] = 1
                                       then R[i, k] := 1
                                       fi;
                                       k := k + 1
                                   od
                   fi
              fi;
              j := j + 1
          od
```

FIGURE 3.21 A SMALG fragment implementing Step 2 of the algorithm computing the reachability set.

times on each $\overline{V}_i$. Consequently, the following operation

$$\forall v_j \in \overline{V}_i, \text{ if } \exists \langle v_j, v_k \rangle \in E, \text{ then } \overline{V}_i := \overline{V}_i \cup \{ v_k \} \qquad (*)$$

must be repeated $n \cdot (n - 1)$ times. Is this an "elementary" operation? Can it be performed in a bounded time? Probably not. Its execution time is likely to depend on the size of the graph.

At this point, we realize that our analysis cannot go deeper on the basis of the previous abstract formulation. We need to look closer at the implementation, say a SMALG implementation.

Suppose that G has been stored into the SMALM memory as a matrix $\{G[i, j] | i, j = 1, \dots, n\}$. Similarly, we can decide to represent the reachability sets by means of another $n \times n$ matrix R. Namely, we set $R[i, j] = 1$ if $v_j \in \overline{V}_i$, 0 otherwise. Thus step 1 of the algorithm consists of initializing $R[i, i] = 1$, for $i = 1, \dots, n$. The first iteration of step 2 results in copying $G[i, j]$ into $R[i, j]$ for all $i \neq j$. In general, any subsequent iteration of step 2 can be implemented by repeating the SMALG fragment shown in Figure 3.21 for all i.

It is clear that the program fragment of Figure 3.21 actually implements the above operation $(*)$. Time complexity of the fragment is $\Theta(n^2)$. Therefore, without going into further coding details, we can conclude that the preceding algorithm can be implemented by using a matrix representation for G in time $\Theta(n^4)$.

Suppose now that G is represented by means of two arrays $SV[r]$, $TV[r]$, $r = 1, \dots, m$. Accordingly, let us represent the reachability sets by means of two arrays $SP[t]$, $TP[t]$, $t = 1, \dots, mm$, by assuming that there exists a path from v_i to v_j if and only if there exists a t such that $SP[t] = i$, $TP[t] = j$. Notice that $mm \leq n^2$.

Again, the first iteration of step 2 consists of copying SV into SP and TV into TP. Any subsequent iteration can be implemented by the fragment of Figure 3.22.

```
t := 1;
while t ≤ mm do  i := SP[t];  j := TP[t];
                 h := 1;
                 while h ≤ mm do if SP[h] = j
                                 then k := TP[h];
                                      "insert ⟨v_i, v_k⟩
                                       into arrays SP and TP"
                                 fi;
                                 h := h + 1
                 od;
                 t := t + 1
         od
```

FIGURE 3.22 An alternative implementation of Step 2.

The preceding fragment is not complete yet, as we did not specify how to "insert $\langle v_i, v_k \rangle$ into arrays SP and TP." Several choices are possible. We could simply add a new element to the list (i.e., setting $mm := mm + 1$; $SP[mm] := i$, $TP[mm] := k$). This operation would be quite simple but would introduce the risk of duplications. Thus, we could not rely anymore on the bound $mm \leq n^2$. Thus, before making the insertion, we decide to check whether $\langle v_i, v_k \rangle$ is already in the list. This results into the fragment shown in Figure 3.23 (notice that we use integers 0 and 1 to code a logical condition since SMALG does not provide booleans).

We observe that "insert $\langle v_i, v_k \rangle$ into arrays SP and TP" requires a $\Theta(mm)$ time. Consequently, step 2 of the algorithm is $\Theta(mm^3)$ and the complete algorithm is $\Theta(n \cdot mm^3)$. Since $mm \leq n^2$, we conclude that time complexity is, at worst, $\Theta(n^7)$.

Let us analyze these results more critically. We have implicitly assumed n, the number of nodes of the graph, as our measure of the "size" of the input. This is certainly reasonable and simple to deal with but somehow arbitrary. For example, the number of edges can be expressed in terms of n as $\Theta(n^2)$, but this may lead to very pessimistic results in many practical cases.

As we anticipated in Section 3.1, the practical use of complexity analysis requires a definition of what is the "size" of the input we wish to relate to

```
r := 1; found := 0;
while r ≤ mm do if SP[r] = i
                then if TP[r] = k
                     then found := 1
                     fi
                fi;
                r := r + 1
        od;
if found = 0
then mm := mm + 1;
     SP[mm] := i; TP[mm] := k
fi
```

FIGURE 3.23 A further detailed implementation of Step 2.

execution time. This is perfectly clear for TMs used in language recognition problems, but it becomes more elusive when we move towards higher-level computation models. Another definition for the "size" of the input in graph algorithms can be given in terms of two parameters: the number of nodes and the number of edges. But this would make formal complexity analysis more intricate. The choice of the particular notion of "size" to be used in the analysis depends on the practical problem that is being studied.

Exercises

3.40 Consider the implementation of the reachability set problem where we use arrays SV, TV, SP, and TP. Suppose that operation "insert $\langle v_i, v_k \rangle$ into arrays SP and TP" is implemented without checking whether $\langle v_i, v_k \rangle$ is already present. Evaluate complexity of this implementation.

3.41 Try to obtain more efficient algorithms (and SMALG implementations) for the problem of computing reachability sets.

3.42 Formulate the graph reachability problem as a language translation problem. Outline a TM solving it and compute its time complexity as a function of the input length.

3.43 Find an algorithm to evaluate the height of a tree and evaluate its complexity.

3.44 Try to find a sorting algorithm which is more efficient than *sort-by-straight-insertion* and evaluate its complexity (for hints, see Sections 5.5 and 5.7).

3.45 A weighted graph is a graph where a nonnegative integer weight (cost) is associated to edges. Find an algorithm to evaluate the path of minimum total cost between any two nodes. Evaluate the complexity of your solution.

3.46 Given two strings x_1 and x_2, consider the problem of computing the longest substring of both x_1 and x_2. (y is a substring of x if and only if $x = zyw$ for some z and w). Solve this problem both by means of a TM and SMALG. Compare their complexities.

3.47 Given a sequence of integers $S = \{i_1, i_2, \ldots, i_n\}$ and an integer k, find whether there is a subsequence of s whose sum is k. This is known as the *knapsack problem*. Solve the knapsack problem and derive the complexity of your solution.

3.10 Some Advice and Conclusions

In this chapter, we have emphasized the need for complexity analysis during algorithm design. However, we have seen that the validity of several results is limited by the dependency on many implementation choices, which are unknown at the design stage. Nevertheless, the theoretical models we have discussed do have a strong impact on practical algorithm design. The situation is somewhat similar to what happens in other engineering fields. During design of a bridge, mathematical formalisms do not allow us to reach an absolutely detailed knowledge about whether or not the bridge will collapse under certain conditions. However, their use—integrated with practical experience—will highly enhance the reliability of the resulting design.

Similarly, suppose we have to design an algorithm to solve a problem P under the constraint that such an algorithm should run on a machine equipped with a small-sized main memory. Many theoretical results can help us during design. First, it may be the case that theoreticians have already proved an exponential lower bound for the complexity of P's solution. In this case, we should either give up (as if P were undecidable) or look for some more favorable particular cases of P for which a better solution exists. Conversely, suppose we have been able to understand that computing P by means of multitape TMs requires a complexity T with

$$\Theta(p_1) \leq \Theta(T) \leq \Theta(p_2)$$

p_1, p_2 being two polynomials.

In such a case, P's solution is likely to be computable in an acceptable time. Thus, we may start designing an algorithm solving P (certainly not on the basis of TMs, but in terms of a higher-level language). After such an algorithm has been designed, we can start an actual complexity analysis on the basis of reasonable cost assumptions. For example, if we know that the values involved in the computation normally will not exceed the word size of our computer, we can use the uniform cost criterion for access to variables and arithmetic operations. On the contrary, we might attach a higher price to memory consuming operations and I/O since the possible overflow of memory size could require time-consuming swapping operations. As a result, we obtain a reasonable estimate of the expected cost of running our algorithm on our machine.

In some cases, it might even happen that a quadratic time algorithm runs better than a linear one. This is the case of some assemblers and compilers that can run in a single pass on main memory, whereas others adopt a multipass strategy where intermediate results are written on auxiliary files. Very often, the former solution has quadratic complexity, whereas the latter has linear complexity but uses many more time consuming I/O instructions.

As we observed at the beginning of this chapter, computational complexity is only one partial attack to the problem of estimating the cost of a computer program. The only components of cost taken into account by computational complexity are due to the usage of computers (i.e., execution time and required storage). In practice, people costs are —by far—the dominant factor. This includes both the human effort needed to derive the program in the first place and the effort needed to test, debug, and—most important—maintain it.

Unfortunately, these factors are not fully understood yet and no satisfactory theory has been developed to formalize them. Thus they are outside the scope of this text and should be addressed in the study of software engineering principles.

Chapter Summary

Computational complexity is a measure of the cost to be paid for mechanical problem solving. Several kinds of complexities can be considered and several factors may affect complexity measures. In this chapter, attention has been mainly focused on time and space complexity, on worst case analysis, and on language recognition problems.

Our study of computational complexity started from automata-like formalisms, namely TMs, FAs, and PDAs. Some general concepts have been derived within this framework such as complexity classes, the possibility of linearly improving complexity measures, and complexity hierarchies. Then, we turned our attention to other computational models, closer to practical computing devices. We have shown that complexity measures may differ from model to model, but they are at least polynomially related.

Also, nondeterministic computations have been considered and the two major classes of problems, $\mathscr{P}$—the class of languages recognizable in polynomial time by deterministic devices—and $\mathscr{NP}$—the class of languages recognizable in polynomial time by nondeterministic devices—have been investigated in some detail. The notion of problem reducibility has been applied to complexity classes and this has lead us to the central concept of $\mathscr{NP}$-completeness. A few classical $\mathscr{NP}$-complete problems have been described.

Some hints have been given to afford the difficult problem of proving nontrivial complexity lower bounds.

Finally, a few examples of complexity analysis for problems of more practical interest have been given and commented.

Further Exercises

3.48 Let L_1 and L_2 be recursive languages in DTIME(f_1) and DTIME(f_2), respectively. In which class are $L_1 \cup L_2$, $L_1 \cap L_2$, $\bar{L}_1$?
What happens if we replace DTIME by NTIME?

3.49 Consider the UTM M_U built in Section 2.5.2 or any other UTM. For any given TM M with time complexity $T_M(n)$, state the complexity $T_U(M, n)$ of M_U simulating M. Notice that T_U depends both on n and on the size of M's description.

3.50 The RASP (*R*andom *A*ccess *S*tored *P*rogram) machine is a modification of the RAM machine where the program is stored in the main memory of the machine in much the same way as in the classical von Neumann architecture. In some sense, the RASP machine can be considered as a universal RAM machine.

a. Give a rigorous definition of the RASP machine.

b. Show that in the RASP machine indirect addressing is superfluous.

c. State time complexity relations between RAM and RASP machines.

3.51 Modify the SMALG grammar given in Figure 3.11 in order to allow the use of multidimensional arrays and of arbitrarily complex arithmetic expressions (as in Pascal). Accordingly, modify the rules given in Table 3.3 to evaluate the time complexity of SMALG programs.

Sketchy Solutions to Selected Exercises

3.2 $\Theta(f_1) < \Theta(f_2) = \Theta(f_3)$ (i.e., f_2 is $\Theta(f_3)$) $< \Theta(f_4)$, f_5 is uncomparable with each f_i, $i = 1, \ldots, 4$.

3.17 Consider the construction outlined in Figure 3.6. A single-tape TM M' simulating the 1-tape TM M sketched in Figure 3.6*b* can have its only tape arranged as in Figure 3.24. The length of the nonblank portion of its tape does not exceed $n + S_M(n)$, with $S_M(n) \leq T_M(n)$.

Thus, the simulation of a single move of M by M' requires at most $n + S_M(n)$ steps by M' with $\Theta(n + S_M(n)) \leq \Theta(T_M(n))$ if $T_M(n) \geq n$. Thus $T_{M'}$ is $\Theta(T_M^2)$.

3.40 If we implement the operation "insert $\langle v_i, v_k \rangle$ into SP and TP" by the $\Theta(1)$ code "$mm := mm + 1$; $SP[mm] := i$, $TP[mm] := k$", the resulting program may even never terminate. In fact, suppose there exists a cycle of length, say, 1, on vertex v. When execution reaches a state such that $i = j$ and $h = t$, the path—consisting of a single edge—$\langle v, v \rangle$ is indefinitely added to the existing list of paths.

3.48 $\overline{L}_1$ is in DTIME(f_1) since the same TM *deciding* L_1 can be used to decide $\overline{L}_1$ with minor modifications that do not affect complexity function.

$L_1 \cup L_2$ and $L_1 \cap L_2$ are in DTIME($f_1 + f_2$), which is the same as DTIME(f), where $f(n) = \max \{ f_1(n), f_2(n) \}$.

In the nondeterministic case, the answer is the same for $L_1 \cup L_2$ and $L_2 \cap L_2$, because a machine deciding the union or the intersection of two languages needs only the simulation of the two machines deciding L_1 and L_2.

In the case of $\overline{L}_1$, one can prove that, if L_1 is in NTIME(f_1), then $\overline{L}_1$ is in DTIME(c^{f_1}), for a suitable c, by building a TM that enumerates all possible computations of the nondeterministic machine recognizing L_1.

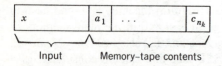

Input   Memory–tape contents

FIGURE 3.24 The display of the single tape of M'.

3.50   b. In a RASP machine, an instruction is the contents of some memory cell. Thus, it can be modified as any other value contained in a cell. For instance, if cell 10 contains the statement ADD 13, the result of executing the statements

LOAD 10
ADD = 1
STORE 10

is that the above statement is modified into ADD 14. This clearly makes indirect addressing superfluous, at least from the point of view of computational power.

c. If a RASP machine has a time complexity function T, then an equivalent RAM can be built with a time complexity that is $\Theta(T)$, and conversely. This holds for both cost criteria. In fact, it is easy to simulate execution of a single RAM statement by means of a bounded sequence of RASP statements and conversely. Notice that even if a RASP machine must first *read* the program for simulating any RAM machine, this always requires a time bounded by a $\Theta(1)$ function.

Bibliographic Remarks

Computational complexity is a relatively young branch of theoretical computer science and has not been adequately formalized yet in a coherent and systematic framework. Several crucial links are still missing and some mathematical results lack absolute validity and need some careful interpretation.

Landmark results in this area are presented in the papers by Hartmanis and Stearns (1965) (Speed-Up Theorem), Cook (1973) (the hierarchy DTIME), Cook and Reckhow (1973) (the RAM model), and Cook (1971) and Karp (1972) ($\mathcal{NP}$-completeness). The notion of crossing sequence and its application to derive complexity lower bounds is due to Hennie (1965). The equivalence between RAM and SMALG control structures can be derived from Böhm and Jacopini (1966). The exponential complexity of the reachability problem for Petri nets has been proved by Lipton (1976).

More recently, some interesting results have been obtained in the field of computational complexity by applying the concept of probabilistic algorithms and machines. As already stated in Chapter 1, we do not go into this topic. Some suggested references for the interested reader are Luecker (1981), Rabin (1976, 1977), and Hopcroft (1981).

Karp (1986a, 1986b) provides an interesting historical survey and examines the state of the art of the field.

Several texts have been published on computational complexity: They can be recommended for a more advanced reading. Let us mention Savage (1976) Lewis and Papadimitriou (1981), Hopcroft and Ullman (1978), and Garey and Johnson (1978). The application of computational complexity tools to the analysis of computer algorithms is best illustrated in Aho, Hopcroft, and Ullman (1974). Harrison (1978) is specialized to formal languages, and to context-free languages in particular. Kolence (1985) faces many complexity issues that have not been considered here because of their lack of appropriate formalization.

The presentation of this chapter has been influenced by several of the above references. In particular, we should mention Hopcroft and Ullman (1979) for Sections 3.4 and 3.7.

CHAPTER FOUR

Formal Semantics

4.1 Notation and Meaning

Very often, humans use symbols to denote objects, concepts, etc., and, conversely, they assign meanings to notations. For example, the English sentence "This is a square table" denotes a particular form of a particular object whose position is probably close to the speaker. Similarly, sequences of digits are used to denote numbers. Actually, by changing the base, different sequences of digits may denote the same number and the same sequence of digits may denote different numbers. Thus, 10 denotes "ten" in the usual decimal notation and "two" in binary notation; also, "two" may be represented by the unary sequence 11.

Our need for communication requires an encoding to represent our intents and a decoding to understand the meaning of a notation. Some time ago, sailors used to communicate from one ship to another by means of a predefined language based on the use of flags. A suitable convention—a translation rule—associated a message to flag movements; the same rule was used by the receiver to decode the message—to understand the intended meaning of flag movements.

Mathematicians emphasize the formal (i.e., precise and rigorous) way of stating a correspondence between a notation and its meaning(s). Going a little bit further in the preceding numeric example, we realize that arithmetics not only provides a method to represent numbers but also to compute operations. For any two numbers x and y we have a rule to denote them in a simple and precise way, say $d(x)$ and $d(y)$ in decimal form, and a mechanical way to compute $d(x + y)$, which denotes their sum. Mathematical logic provides yet another example of a formal notation and of its meaning. A formal theory defines a set of well-formed formulas and a set of theorems; an interpretation of a theory is an assignment of meaning to its formulas and theorems. Roughly speaking, the interpretation becomes a model of the theory if it properly "fits" the theory; that is, interpretations of theorems are valid formulas.

A theory can have several models and several theories can be developed to formalize more or less intuitive concepts. For example, this is the case of naive set theory and of its axiomatizations.

Quite often, the rules defining the denotation of a set of concepts are called the *syntax*, as they specify how individual symbols of a certain vocabulary can be put together to form legal patterns. The related set of concepts—the meanings of the set of patterns defined by the syntax—are called its *semantics*. Thus, the English grammar specifies how to form correct English sentences, each having one (or more) associated meaning or semantics.

Computer science, as any other discipline, needs both syntactic rules to correctly form its "sentences" and semantic rules to assign them a meaning. For example, consider a RAM program: It is a sequence of statements formed according to some very simple rules. The set of RAM programs is a language whose syntax can be formally described by the context-free grammar G shown in Figure 4.1. The semantics of this language has been defined in an informal but rigorous way in Section 3.4.1. Each RAM instruction has been assigned a meaning in such a way that the meaning of a RAM program can be defined as the function mapping any input tape into the output tape produced by the machine after reaching a halt condition (if ever), assuming that initially the program counter contains a 1 and all memory cells contain 0.

Similarly, we might define a simple syntax to define TM programs. For example, we could denote a TM by means of tables specifying functions δ and η. Accordingly, the semantics of a TM is the set of rules that define how to operate on the control unit and on the tapes.

We have already noticed that defining semantics of SMALG, whose syntax may be described by a context-free grammar, is considerably more complex than in the previous cases. In general, the difficulties encountered in providing a precise definition of semantics increase as the language level becomes higher. Syntactic difficulties arise as well, but to a much lesser extent.

In order to substantiate this claim suppose we wish to extend SMALG by adding procedures—a very useful feature provided by all higher-level languages. Figure 4.2*a* defines a simplified syntax of procedure declarations; Figure 4.2*b* defines the syntax of procedure calls.

$G = \langle V_T, V_N, P, \langle \text{Program} \rangle \rangle$, where:

$V_T = \{\text{LOAD,STORE,ADD,SUB,MULT,DIV,READ,WRITE,}$
$\quad \text{JUMP,JGZ,JZ,HALT,0,1,2,} \ldots, 9, \text{A,B,} \ldots, \text{Z}, = , * \}$

$V_N = \{\langle \text{Program} \rangle, \langle \text{StatList} \rangle, \langle \text{Stat} \rangle, \langle \text{UnlabStat} \rangle \langle \text{JumpStat} \rangle$
$\quad \langle \text{JumpOpCode} \rangle, \langle \text{OpStat} \rangle, \langle \text{OpCode} \rangle, \langle \text{HaltStat} \rangle, \langle \text{Label} \rangle, \langle \text{Suffix} \rangle,$
$\quad \langle \text{Letter} \rangle, \langle \text{Digit} \rangle \}$

$P = \{\langle \text{Program} \rangle \rightarrow \langle \text{StatList} \rangle$
$\quad \langle \text{StatList} \rangle \rightarrow \langle \text{Stat} \rangle \langle \text{StatList} \rangle | \epsilon$
$\quad \langle \text{Stat} \rangle \rightarrow \langle \text{UnlabStat} \rangle | \langle \text{Label} \rangle : \langle \text{UnlabStat} \rangle$
$\quad \langle \text{UnlabStat} \rangle \rightarrow \langle \text{JumpStat} \rangle | \langle \text{OpStat} \rangle | \langle \text{HaltStat} \rangle$
$\quad \langle \text{JumpStat} \rangle \rightarrow \langle \text{JumpOpCode} \rangle \langle \text{Label} \rangle$
$\quad \langle \text{JumpOpCode} \rangle \rightarrow \text{JUMP} | \text{JGZ} | \text{JZ}$
$\quad \langle \text{OpStat} \rangle \rightarrow \langle \text{OpCode} \rangle \langle \text{Operand} \rangle$
$\quad \langle \text{OpCode} \rangle \rightarrow \text{LOAD} | \text{STORE} | \text{ADD} | \text{SUB} | \text{MULT} | \text{DIV} | \text{READ} | \text{WRITE} |$
$\quad\quad\quad\quad\quad \text{LOAD} = | \text{ADD} = | \text{SUB} = | \text{MULT} = | \text{DIV} = | \text{WRITE} = |$
$\quad\quad\quad\quad\quad \text{LOAD}_* | \text{STORE}_* | \text{ADD}_* | \text{SUB}_* | \text{MULT}_* | \text{DIV}_* | \text{READ}_* | \text{WRITE}_*$
$\quad \langle \text{HaltStat} \rangle \rightarrow \text{HALT}$
$\quad \langle \text{Label} \rangle \rightarrow \langle \text{Letter} \rangle \langle \text{Suffix} \rangle$
$\quad \langle \text{Suffix} \rangle \rightarrow \langle \text{Letter} \rangle \langle \text{Suffix} \rangle | \langle \text{Digit} \rangle \langle \text{Suffix} \rangle | \epsilon$
$\quad \langle \text{Letter} \rangle \rightarrow \text{A} | \text{B} | \ldots | \text{Z}$
$\quad \langle \text{Digit} \rangle \rightarrow 0 | 1 | \ldots | 9$
$\quad \langle \text{Operand} \rangle \rightarrow \langle \text{DigitSequence} \rangle$
$\quad \langle \text{DigitSequence} \rangle \rightarrow \langle \text{Digit} \rangle | \langle \text{Digit} \rangle \langle \text{DigitSequence} \rangle \}$

FIGURE 4.1 A grammar generating the RAM language.

$\langle \text{ProcDecl} \rangle \rightarrow$ **procedure** $\langle \text{ProcIdent} \rangle (\langle \text{FormalParList} \rangle);$
$\quad\quad\quad\quad \langle \text{LocalVarDecl} \rangle ; \langle \text{ProcBody} \rangle$
$\langle \text{ProcIdent} \rangle \rightarrow \langle \text{Ident} \rangle$
$\langle \text{FormalParList} \rangle \rightarrow \langle \text{FormalPar} \rangle, \langle \text{FormalParList} \rangle | \epsilon$
$\langle \text{LocalVarDecl} \rangle \rightarrow$ **var**: $\langle \text{LocalVarList} \rangle | \epsilon$
$\langle \text{FormalPar} \rangle \rightarrow \langle \text{Ident} \rangle$
$\langle \text{LocalVarList} \rangle \rightarrow \langle \text{Ident} \rangle, \langle \text{LocalVarList} \rangle | \epsilon$
$\langle \text{ProcBody} \rangle \rightarrow$ **begin** $\langle \text{StatList} \rangle$ **end**

(a)

$\langle \text{ProcCall} \rangle \rightarrow$ **call** $\langle \text{ProcIdent} \rangle (\langle \text{ActualParList} \rangle)$
$\langle \text{ActualParList} \rangle \rightarrow \langle \text{ActualPar} \rangle \langle \text{ActualParList} \rangle | \epsilon$
$\langle \text{ActualPar} \rangle \rightarrow \langle \text{Ident} \rangle$

(b)

FIGURE 4.2 A grammar fragment describing the syntax of procedure declaration (a) and call (b) in SMALG.

In order to give a rigorous, complete, and consistent syntactic description of the language, one should integrate the grammar fragments shown in Figure 4.2 into the SMALG grammar of Figure 3.11. We leave this as an exercise to the reader under the following assumptions on integration.

- Procedures are defined externally to the main program (i.e., there is no Pascal-like nesting).
- Procedure calls are a particular type of statement.[1]

Let us turn to semantic issues. First, we may assume that procedures can access their local variables and parameters, and also variables declared in the main program. Second, all variable names must be disjoint (i.e., no renaming of variables is allowed in procedures). Things become somewhat more intricate when we wish to define the semantics of procedure calls. Very often, semantics is informally defined by rules of the following type.

1. The correspondence between actual and formal parameters is established according to their position.
2. Corresponding actual and formal parameters must have compatible types.
3. Actual parameters are substituted for formal parameters.
4. The procedure body is executed as if it were inserted within the text of the program at the point of call.

The reader with a minimum of experience in programming is certainly aware that the above semantic rules are quite unsatisfactory as they do not address several important questions. Two of them are discussed as follows.

Question 1. How are actual parameters substituted for formal parameters?
  Several choices are possible:
  a. The value of actual parameters is computed and then used to initialize local variables corresponding to formal parameters (*call-by-value*). As an example, consider the following procedure.

Procedure *sum* (x, y);
  begin $x := x + y$;
      $z := x$
  end

Suppose that z is a global variable and procedure *sum* is called by the program below:

begin $z := 0$;
      $a := 5$;
      $b := 3$;
      call *sum* (a, b);
      write a;
      write z
end

---

[1]A solution is illustrated in Figure 4.4. In fact, the whole issue of procedures in SMALG is taken up in full detail in Section 4.5.

Following the call-by-value rule, the values of a and z output by the program would be 5 and 8, respectively.

b. Let a be an actual parameter, let $\bar{a}$ be the memory location where the value of a is kept, and let f be the corresponding formal parameter. During execution of the procedure body, any reference to f is treated as an access to $\bar{a}$ (*call-by-reference*).

Following the call-by-reference rule, the values of a and z output by the above program would both be equal to 8.

c. The value of actual parameters at the point of call is used to initialize local variables corresponding to formal parameters (as in call-by-value). On procedure termination, the value of formal parameters are copied back into the corresponding actual parameters. This is usually defined *call-by-value result*. Under this assumption, the value of a and z output by the program would both be equal to 8. Call-by reference and call-by-value result may produce different results. For example, the reader can prove that this happens if statement $z := x$ of procedure *sum* is changed to $z := a$.

As a consequence, rules a, b, and c assign different semantics to procedure call.

Question 2. What happens to local variables at any new procedure call? Do they maintain their previous value? Are they reinitialized at each call? For example, consider the following procedure *counter*

```
procedure counter (x);
        var: c;
        begin if x ≠ 0 then c := c + 1
                       else c := 0
            fi;
            z := c
        end
```

and the program below using *counter*:

```
begin x := 0;
      call counter (x);
      x := x + 1;
      call counter (x);
      write z
end
```

If c maintains its previous value at each new call, the program would output "2." Under the other hypothesis, the second call of procedure counter would probably generate a run-time error since the value of c would be undefined.

This short and sketchy discussion of a single issue in programming language semantics should have shown how difficult it is to give a precise and safe, yet informal, semantics of a real high-level language. On the basis of the preceding discussion, the next section introduces and motivates the notion of formal semantics of programming languages. A detailed formalization of SMALG procedures is delayed to Section 4.5.

4.2 The Need for a Formal Definition of Semantics

Quite often, the meaning of a given notation is not precisely defined. This occurs in human communications, where a certain amount of ambiguity is often present. In some cases, this is because the context where communication takes place allows one to resolve ambiguity quite easily. As an example, consider the sentence: "Give me that book" where the intended book may be identified either because the two speakers where already talking about a particular book or by means of a gesture of the speaker.

In other cases, ambiguity may be tolerated as it does not affect the effectiveness of communication. For example, if somebody tells you "John told me this story: ...", and you don't realize who the particular John is, you might decide not to interrupt the speaker to inquire about John as this detail might not add to the meaning of the conversation. In still other cases, ambiguity may be explicitly desired as in the famous title *The Importance of Being Earnest* of a play by Oscar Wilde. Furthermore, quite often ambiguous communication is less tedious and time consuming than a communication where all details are stated precisely.

However, in many other cases, a lack of precision is an unfortunate circumstance, or even a fatal disaster. For example, undesirable or unforeseen ambiguity may cause dangerous misunderstandings between interlocutors during mission-critical operations. Ambiguity, that is, imprecise meaning of a notation, is almost never desired in science.

In the previous section, we have already discussed some possible ambiguities arising from an informal and vague definition of procedure called semantics. It is just folklore that there are cases where compilers of the "same" language have been found inconsistent; that is, they provided different semantics for the same language. As a consequence, the same program may produce different results if compiled by different compilers. This is due to the lack of a rigorous semantic definition of the language, which allowed several implementors to give different interpretations to the same language features. Had language semantics been defined in a rigorous way, language implementation could be checked against it; that is, it could be *proved* (or disproved) *correct*.

At this point, a subtle philosophical question arises. Didn't we introduce a formal notation exactly to denote any concept or meaning in a formal way? For example, arithmetic is the formal notation introduced to capture in a precise way the notions of numbers and operations. Similarly, TMs have been introduced to formalize the notion of computable functions. Therefore, the request to formally define the meaning of a formal notation might seem to be a little extravagant, if not a nonsense.

All this is somewhat similar to the notion of *models* in mathematical logic. After having built a formal theory—axiomatic set theory—we "interpret" it on the basis of a more intuitive mathematical concept—naive set theory—whose inadequacy from a rigorous viewpoint (see the case of paradoxes) was exactly the starting point that motivated the definition of a formal theory.

Here, we will not go deep into the philosophical question of meaning. Rather, we will assume a more pragmatic point of view that at least should shed the appropriate light on the problem, as far as its application to computer science issues is concerned. Once again, let us go back to TMs. The relevance of this formalism stems from the fact that it is based on elementary operations that are simple enough to convince anybody that they can be easily realized by some mechanical device and, most important, they are universally understood. The formal notation used to describe TM computations can be assumed as an unambiguous and simple way to define semantics of TMs. Unfortunately, TMs are not usable in practical problem solving because they are too low-level.

High-level programming languages support a much simpler description of algorithms by providing more powerful basic data types and operations. However, the more powerful a basic operation is (e.g., a procedure call), the more difficult it is explaining its semantics. That is why one is tempted to rely on the reader's intuition. In the case of TMs it is easy to define machine computations, but we must rely on the reader's imagination to extrapolate that the machine does indeed solve a given problem (e.g., matrix inversion). On the contrary, it is pretty easy to write a program that solves this problem in a high-level language such as Pascal, but it is not so immediate to explain exactly what happens when executing a procedure call.

This reasoning might lead to the following conclusion: The semantics of TMs is rigorously defined, whereas Pascal semantics is not. However, this cannot be the case as both TMs and Pascal are just formal notations suited to describing computing activities. The point is that the concepts of state and computation of a TM are so simple that their meaning can be immediately captured by simple mathematical notations such as strings and string operations. In other terms, the formalization of TM computations is given in terms of another formal notation whose ultimate meaning is left (necessarily) to the reader's intuition. For example, consider a TM performing additions of natural numbers. The formal definition of its computation consists of a sequence of transformations on strings denoting natural numbers. Thus the semantics of the formalism is given in terms of yet another formal notation. In conclusion, formal semantics of a formal notation, such as the definition of state transformations of a TM, is nothing else than a *translation* between different formalisms. In our case a table *denoting* the pair $\langle \delta, \eta \rangle$ of TM functions is *translated* into the set of all possible sequences *denoting* TM computations.

Unfortunately, the meaning of more complex and powerful Pascal statements is not immediately expressible in terms of simple mathematical objects and simple operations: There is a large "semantic gap" between the operations implied by a statement and its syntactic denotation (the string representing it). Consequently, one is tempted to avoid the cumbersome process of filling the gap with a lot of mathematical details and to rely on the reader's intuition, by using more intuitive (but less rigorous) natural language descriptions. Notice, however, that even in this case semantics of a language construct is defined by means of a translation. The only difference is the chosen target language, which may be the safe but tedious mathematical notation used to denote elementary operations, or even the more expressive but informal and ambiguous natural language used to denote more intricate meanings.

The need for mathematical concepts suitable to defining language semantics formally can thus be rephrased as the need for formal translation mechanisms suitable to describing the meaning of complex formal objects in terms of simpler ones, which should be closer to the reader's intuition.

A first example of giving semantics of one formalism in terms of another has already been seen in the case of SMALG. The meaning of SMALG instructions—SMALM operations—was given in terms of RAM-like statements which, in turn, had been previously defined by means of a (supposedly) well understood Pascal-like notation. This style of describing semantics is taken up in detail in Section 4.5.

4.3   The Use of Formal Semantics

In the previous sections, we have given some arguments in favor of formal descriptions of programming language semantics. More arguments are raised in this section to substantiate our thesis.

The first important point we discuss here is that formal semantics of a language L supports formal reasonings on programs written in L; in particular, it supports mathematical proofs of properties of L programs. We illustrate this concept in the case of SMALG.

Example 4.1

Prove that the following SMALG fragment F computes $x = \sum_{j=1}^{n} a[j]$.

```
F: x := 0;
   i := 1;
   while i ≤ n
       do x := x + a[i];
          i := i + 1
       od
```

The intended semantics of fragment F can be expressed by the following predicate α that must be true after execution of F.

$$\alpha: x = \sum_{j=1}^{n} a[j]$$

Let variables x and i be associated in SMALM to memory locations M_x and M_i, respectively, and array a to the sequence of locations $M_{a[1]}, M_{a[2]}, \dots$. We must prove that, at the end of F's execution,

$$M[M_x] = \sum_{j=1}^{n} M[M_{a[j]}]$$

For this purpose, let us observe that

1. after execution of

    $x := 0; \; i := 1$

    the following relation holds:

$$\beta: \; M[M_x] = \sum_{j=1}^{M[M_i]-1} M[M_{a[j]}]$$

   In fact, $M[M_x] = 0$, $M[M_i] = 1$, and the sum of no elements is obviously 0.

2. as long as $i \leq n$, β holds after execution of the pair of statements enclosed by **do, od**. This is because $x := x + a[i]$ results in

$$M[M_x] := M[M_x] + M[M_{a[i]}]$$

   and $i := i + 1$ results in

$$M[M_i] := M[M_i] + 1$$

   As a consequence, both the upper limit of the summation and its expected result change consistently.

3. at the exit from the **while** body, β still holds and $M[M_i] = n + 1$; thus it is

$$M[M_x] = \sum_{j=1}^{n} M[M_{a[j]}]$$

   Therefore, the contents of M_x, which represents x, equals the sum of the contents of all cells associated to a.

Let us draw a few conclusions from the preceding simple example. Suppose we have a formal tool to express the semantics of a programming language by means of, say, first-order formulas involving program variables (as in Example 4.1), that is, a tool that allows one to "translate" a program into a relation involving input and output variables of the program. This tool could be used to prove program properties. For example, if our problem is finding the maximum of n integers stored into an array a, we could write a program P intended to find such a maximum max and then we could try to prove that the semantics of P is such that predicate

PR: $max \in \{ a[i] | i = 1, \dots, n \} \land \forall i (1 \leq i \leq n \supset max \geq a[i])$

holds after P's execution.

The foregoing predicate PR can be assumed as a formal requirement for P. If SEM is the semantics of program P expressed as a first-order formula and we can prove that $SEM \supset PR$, then we conclude that P is correct with respect to PR. Notice, however, that if we fail to capture the right requirements for P by means of a predicate PR and yet we come to the conclusion that $SEM \supset PR$, the program is correct with respect to its stated requirements, but nevertheless it is wrong. In other terms, formal semantics allow us to translate one formal description—a program—into another formal description—its meaning. Whether this meaning matches the concepts we have in our mind requires a two-step verification procedure. First, we must express such concepts into a formal description—the requirements. Second, we must prove that our formal requirements derive from the program's meaning. The first step cannot be mechanized, whereas all other aspects involved in this process can, at least partially. That is, there is no way to verify that the concepts we have in our mind are adequately captured by formal requirements.

For example, if a is an array, and n is its size, the formal statement

$$a[i] \le a[i + 1] \qquad \forall i, 1 \le i < n$$

does not reflect adequately the informal requirement that the program sorts array a. In fact, it does not specify that the values stored in array a at the end of the program must be a permutation of the values initially stored in it. A program that satisfies the formal requirement, such as one that stores the sequence $1, 2, \ldots, n$ into a, does not necessarily sort a, according to the intuitive notion of "sort" we have in our mind.

Another major result can be obtained by formal definition of programming language semantics, that is, automatic implementation tools. We have already noticed that the definition of SMALG semantics given in Chapter 3 is exactly a translation scheme from SMALG into a RAM-like notation. The exercise of transforming the informal description of the translation illustrated in Section 3.5, into an effective algorithm is left to the reader. In addition, one can imagine a tool that translates RAM programs into equivalent machine programs for real computers. As a result we could associate to SMALG semantics an actual translation tool, that is, a compiler, to translate SMALG programs into executable code. To state it in another way we used a sort of abstract compiler to define SMALG semantics in terms of RAM-like statements. The same abstract compiler can be used to drive the process of building an actual compiler. Even if the topic of automatic compiler design based on formal semantic definitions of programming languages is far beyond the scope of this text, the following sections should convince the reader that the abstract approach can be made into a practical one.

4.4   Main Approaches to Giving Formal Semantics of Programming Languages

Several approaches have been proposed in the literature to formally defining language semantics. All of them share some common aspects and choosing among them can depend on several factors, such as the particular purposes to be achieved, the characteristics of the language to be defined, the personal taste and experience, etc. We now briefly introduce and comment on two major categories of formal semantics definitions—*operational* and *denotational semantics*—which are based on evolutionary and denotationary models, respectively. Each of the two approaches are analyzed in more detail in Sections 4.5 and 4.6, respectively. A further approach, which exploits the spirit of Example 4.1, is illustrated in Chapter 5.

4.4.1 The Operational Approach to Semantics

Operational semantics is certainly the more traditional of the two approaches. Basically, it consists of associating a language with an abstract machine—or processor—and specifying the meaning of language constructs in terms of the computations—or operations—performed by the machine when executing the construct. A first, rather informal, example of operational semantics is the aforementioned definition of SMALM in terms of RAM-like operations. Thanks to such semantics, the reader can understand the meaning of a SMALG program by imagining—or even simulating—the sequence of moves SMALM would perform to execute it. Let us examine a simple example in more detail (this example is used to illustrate denotational semantics too).

Consider the following simple SMALG program P.

begin read x;
      read y;
      $x := f(x, y)$;
      write x
end

where f denotes any expression (or function) on x and y (for example, a sum).

Suppose we wish to express the semantics of the above program by means of a TM. Let us define a multitape TM M with one memory tape, T_M. T_I and T_O are arranged as sequential files of decimal integers as shown in Figure 4.3a. Each integer is represented by a string of digits and symbol $ is used as a separator between integers. T_M is a sequence of pairs $\langle$symbolic identifier, integer value$\rangle$, whose layout is shown in Figure 4.3b. T_M and T_O are initially empty. M operates as follows.

1. For each instruction **read** $\langle$identifier$\rangle$, M looks for the identifier in T_M. If the identifier is found, a value is read from T_I and stored into the value field associated with the identifier in T_M. This copy operation may require some action to match the length of the field in T_M and the length of the value read from T_I. If the identifier is not found in T_M, a new pair $\langle$symbolic identifier, integer value$\rangle$ is appended to the sequence stored in T_M. The symbolic identifier field is set to contain the identifier named by the read instruction. The integer value field is set to contain the value read from T_I.
2. For each instruction **write** $\langle$identifier$\rangle$, M looks for the identifier in T_M. If finds it, the associated value is copied into T_O. If it does not find it, it enters an error state (or writes an error message in T_O).

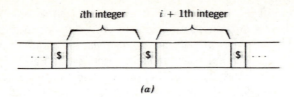

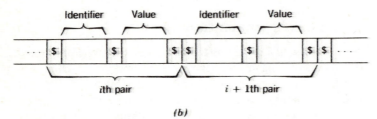

FIGURE 4.3   A TM. (a) Structure of T_I and T_O. (b) Structure of T_M.

3. For each assignment instruction, say $x := f(y, z)$, M searches tape T_M to find the values associated with arguments y and z. If no value is found, it enters an error state (or outputs an error message). Otherwise, M computes f by using the free portion of T_M when necessary to store intermediate results. Finally, if a pair for identifier x already exists in T_M, M replaces the contents of the value field with the computed value. Otherwise, a new pair for x and the computed value is appended to the sequence stored in T_M.

By following the preceding rules, we can prove that if M starts in an initial configuration of T_I containing the sequence v_1, v_2 then on reaching a halt configuration, T_O will contain $v = f(v_1, v_2)$. This is a way of stating P's semantics.

The reader has probably noticed the similarity between the above construction of a TM and the simulation of a RAM by a TM as described in Section 3.5. In fact, in both cases we are dealing with the translation from a von Neumann-like architecture into a TM architecture. The simplicity of the chosen example may give the impression that such a translation is a useless and time-consuming game used to explain well-understood concepts. However, the reader should keep in mind that real programs are definitely more complex than P and that we are developing some tools whose ultimate goal is to define the meaning of any program in a rigorous and formal way.

4.4.2   The Denotational Approach to Semantics

Suppose you ignore the meaning of the SMALG operations **read**, **write**, and $:=$. In order to understand the semantics of P defined in terms of M you should go through all computation steps to finally deduce the relation $v = f(v_1, v_2)$ between input and output. Even if a TM is substituted by a more suitable abstract machine, understanding P's semantics in terms of computation steps of the abstract machine might require a rather detailed and intricated analysis.

A different approach consists of trying to *denote* the meaning of P by means of some mathematical object without going into the details of how P is actually executed. After all, we are interested in the ultimate result of the relation between input and output values. Thus, the semantics of a program P could be simply defined as the function relating input and output values. In the case of our oversimplified example, this does not seem to be a hard job. However, a solution of this problem in the general case requires a considerable amount of new mathematical background that is developed in Section 4.6.

In order to get a first insight into the denotational approach, here we proceed in the discussion of the previous example. So far, we did not pay too much attention to the particular function denoted by f in the instruction $x := f(x, y)$. Whichever computable function f denotes, we know that a suitable M exists to compute exactly that function. However, if we abandon the approach based on abstract machines, we need an alternative formalism to denote functions. As far as pure SMALG is concerned, we know that f can denote only simple arithmetic operations. But in a real programming language, f could denote an arbitrarily complex function thanks to the use of procedures. Thus its denotation by means of a mathematical formalism is not a trivial task.

A very first step towards the goal of defining complete rules to denote the semantics of a program is the following. Consider the new SMALG program P' listed below.

begin
    read x;
    read y;
    $x := f_1(x, y); \ x := f_2(x, y); \ldots x := f_n(x, y);$
    write x
end

where f_i, $i = 1, \ldots, n$ denote simple arithmetic functions that can be written in SMALG (i.e., arithmetic operations). The input/output relation established by P' can be defined as

$$v = f_n\big(\ldots f_3\big(f_2\big(f_1(v_1, v_2), v_2\big), v_2\big), \ldots v_2\big)$$

What we actually did was to give a translation rule from the SMALG notation into a functional notation intended to denote its meaning. The sequence of two assignment statements of the type $x := f_i(x, y); \ x := f_{i+1}(x, y)$ is translated into the composition of the two functions f_i and f_{i+1}. Function f_i, in turn, can be expressed in terms of any mathematical notation. If we do not consider arithmetic symbols as sufficiently elementary denotations, we could denote the meaning of f_i by means of the formalism of primitive recursive functions, by using only the "successor" function, composition, and primitive recursion (See Section 0.2.4.2.)

On the basis of the foregoing preliminary remarks, we may claim that denotational semantics is more abstract than operational semantics, since it does not take care of the language implementation. Remember, however, that in operational semantics the term "implementation" refers to an abstract machine rather than an actual computer. On the other hand, the function associated with a program by denotational semantics, must be denoted by means of some mathematical notation. Such a notation is ultimately a string that must be built (i.e., computed) in some mechanical way. For example, given the sequence of two statements "$x := f_i(x, y);\ x := f_{i+1}(x, y)$" we have used the composition rule to denote its semantics. In some sense, we may view the rule that led to the notation $f_{i+1}(f_i(x, y), y)$ as a computation rule. In the general case, of course, we must be able to give rules to build a notation representing functions to be attached to any program. This will turn out not to be an easy job.

Operational semantics and denotational semantics are now discussed separately in detail in Sections 4.5 and 4.6, respectively. We return to an assessment of the two styles in the conclusions (Section 4.7).

4.5   Operational Semantics

In this section, we explore operational semantics by means of a detailed example. The example is based on an enriched version of SMALG, which is closer to an actual programming language, but remains simple enough to be useful as a teaching vehicle.

First, we present the augmented version of SMALG, called SMALG$^+$, by means of an enrichment of the original syntax and an informal description of its semantics. The essential new feature of SMALG$^+$ is the possibility of defining and calling procedures, as we informally anticipated in Section 4.1. Then we formally define an abstract machine for SMALG$^+$, called SMALM$^+$. SMALM$^+$ is a highly simplified version of the abstract machines used in practice to define operational semantics of real programming languages. A typical example of such machines is the P-code machine that has been used to define and implement Pascal. Finally, we give rules to translate SMALG$^+$ programs into sequences of SMALM$^+$ instructions (i.e., we define the meaning of SMALG$^+$ programs in terms of SMALM$^+$ operations). The latter two steps necessarily involve many details that may be skipped by the reader in a first reading.

4.5.1   SMALG$^+$: Syntax and Informal Semantics

A SMALG$^+$ program consists of a *main* section and a list of procedures. Both the main section and the procedures may contain a declarative part, where local variables must be declared, and a statement part. For simplicity, variables can be only integer scalars. The case of integer arrays is discussed later in Exercises 4.1 and 4.6. The statement part may contain any SMALG statements and procedure calls.

For the sake of simplicity, the same identifier cannot be declared more than once in the whole program; that is, if x is declared in the declarative part of procedure P, it cannot be declared elsewhere, neither in the main section nor in any other procedure. The variable identifiers used in the statement part of any procedure must have been defined either in the declarative part of that procedure or in the declarative part of the main section. The statement part of the main section can obviously refer only to its own identifiers. Any procedure can be invoked by any other procedure, or by itself (direct recursion), or by the main section. The number of actual and formal parameters must be equal and parameter passing convention is call-by-value–result.

The grammar of SMALG$^+$ is reported in Figure 4.4. It is an extension of the grammar given for SMALG in Section 3.4.2 but presents a slight restriction, since arrays are left out for simplicity. The grammar specifies several of the requirements we have just given informally. Other requirements, such as those on the legal use of identifiers, cannot be expressed by means of a context-free grammar. Many authors and language manuals refer to them as the *static semantics* of a language, the term "static" emphasizing that such rules are not related to the execution of the program and thus can be checked before run-time.[2]

We give a formal definition of static semantics as an extension of context-free grammars:

1. Let ID_M and ID_{P_i} denote the set of identifiers declared in the declarative part of the main section and of procedure P_i, respectively.
   Formally, if

   $$\langle\text{ProcDecl}\rangle \overset{*}{\Rightarrow} \textbf{procedure } P_i(id_1, id_2, \ldots, id_k);$$
   $$\textbf{var } id_{k+1}, \ldots, id_n;$$
   $$\langle\text{Body}\rangle$$

   then $id_j = id_i$, with $1 \leq i, \ j \leq n, \ i \neq j$, makes the terminal string an illegal SMALG$^+$ program; otherwise ID_{P_i} is the set $\{id_h | 1 \leq h \leq n\}$. ID_M is defined similarly, the only difference being that there are no parameters ($k = 0$).

2. If $ID_{Z_1} \cap ID_{Z_2} \neq \varnothing$ for $Z_1, Z_2 \in \{P_1, \ldots, P_n, M\}$ then the terminal string is an illegal SMALG$^+$ program.

3. A little bit less formally (full formalization is left to the reader), if an identifier id occurs in the body of procedure P_i then id must belong to $ID_{P_i} \cup ID_M$. Similarly, if an identifier id occurs in the body of the main section, then id must belong to ID_M. If there exists an identifier id that does not satisfy such property, then the terminal string is an illegal SMALG$^+$ program.

---

[2]We warn the reader that this statement is widely, but not universally, valid. In fact, there are languages where the rules on the use of identifiers must be checked at run-time.

⟨Program⟩ → ⟨MainSection⟩⟨ProcDeclList⟩
⟨MainSection⟩ → ⟨LocalVarDecl⟩;⟨Body⟩
⟨ProcDeclList⟩ → ⟨ProcDecl⟩⟨ProcDeclList⟩|ε
⟨ProcDecl⟩ → **procedure** ⟨ProcIdent⟩ ((⟨FormalParList⟩));
           ⟨LocalVarDecl⟩; ⟨Body⟩
⟨ProcIdent⟩ → ⟨Ident⟩
⟨FormalParList⟩ → ⟨FormalPar⟩,⟨FormalParList⟩|ε
⟨FormalPar⟩ → ⟨Ident⟩
⟨LocalVarDecl⟩ → **var** :⟨LocalVarList⟩|ε
⟨LocalVarList⟩ → ⟨Ident⟩,⟨LocalVarList⟩|⟨Ident⟩
⟨Body⟩ → **begin** ⟨StatList⟩ **end**
⟨StatList⟩ → ⟨Stat⟩⟨StatList⟩|ε
⟨Stat⟩ → ⟨AssStat⟩|⟨CondStat⟩|⟨WhileStat⟩|⟨InputStat⟩|
     ⟨OutputStat⟩|⟨ProcCall⟩
⟨AssStat⟩ → ⟨Ident⟩ := ⟨Exp⟩
⟨Exp⟩ → ⟨Term⟩⟨AritOp⟩⟨Term⟩|⟨Term⟩
⟨AritOp⟩ → +| − |*|**div**|**mod**
⟨Term⟩ → ⟨Ident⟩ ⟨Constant⟩
⟨CondStat⟩ → **if** ⟨Cond⟩ **then** ⟨StatList⟩ **else** ⟨StatList⟩ **fi**|
       if ⟨Cond⟩ **then** ⟨StatList⟩ **fi**
⟨WhileStat⟩ → **while** ⟨Cond⟩ **do** ⟨StatList⟩ **od**
⟨Cond⟩ → ⟨Term⟩⟨RelOp⟩⟨Term⟩
⟨RelOp⟩ → = | ≠ | < | ≤ | > | ≥
⟨InputStat⟩ → **read** ⟨Ident⟩
⟨WriteStat⟩ → **write** ⟨Term⟩
⟨Constant⟩ → ⟨Digit⟩⟨Constant⟩|⟨Digit⟩
⟨Ident⟩ → ⟨Letter⟩⟨DigitsOrLetters⟩
⟨DigitsOrLetters⟩ → ⟨Digit⟩⟨DigitsOrLetters⟩|⟨Letter⟩⟨DigitsOrLetters⟩
⟨Digit⟩ → 0|1|2| ... |9
⟨Letter⟩ → a|b|c| ... z|A|B| ... |Z

FIGURE 4.4 SMALG$^+$ grammar.

4. Legality of procedure calls is specified slightly informally as follows.
Let **call** P $(a_1, a_2, ..., a_k)$ be any procedure call appearing in the program.
Then
  a. There must be exactly one declaration for procedure P.
  b. The number of formal parameters in the declaration must be equal to k.

Example 4.2

Figures 4.5*a* through 4.5*d* illustrate examples of correct SMALG$^+$ programs, both from a syntactic and from a static semantics viewpoint. Note that correctness in the foregoing sense does not mean that no errors will ever arise at run-time (as in the case of Figure 4.5*b*, when the input value of *y* is zero), or that

```
var: x,y,z;
begin read x; read y;
        call sum (x,y,z);
        write z
end
procedure sum (a,b,c);
begin c := a + b
end
```

(a)

```
var: x,y,div,rem;
begin read x;
        read y;
        call division (x,y,div,rem);
        write div;
        write rem
end
procedure division (a,b,c,d);
var: temp;
begin c := a div b;
        temp := c * b;
        d := a − temp
end
```

(b)

```
var: x, abs;
begin read x;
        if x > 0
        then abs := x
        else abs := − x
        fi
end
procedure foo (z);
begin z := −z
end
```

(c)

```
var: x;
begin call p(x)
end
procedure p(y);
begin call q(y)
end
procedure q(z);
begin call p(z)
end
```

(d) **FIGURE 4.5**   A sample of SMALG$^+$ programs.

var: *a*: **array** [1..10], *i*, *integral*;
begin *i* := 1;
        while *i* ≤ 10
            do read *a*[*i*];
                i := *i* + 1
            od;
        i := 1; *integral* := 0;
        call *sum* (*a*);
        write *integral*
end
procedure *sum* (*fa*: **array** [1..10]);
begin if *i* ≤ 10
        then *integral* := *integral* + *fa*[*i*];
            i := *i* + 1;
            call *sum* (*fa*)
        fi
end

FIGURE 4.6 A SMALG⁺ program using arrays.

the program is meaningful (Figure 4.5*c*: what is the purpose of procedure *foo* since the program does not use it?), or that program execution terminates (Figure 4.5*d*).

Exercise

4.1 Add arrays to the formal description of the syntax and static semantics of SMALG⁺. Syntactic extensions include variable declarations and formal parameters, which must specify the type of identifiers (i.e., whether an identifier is a scalar or an array). Rules for static semantics given before must be modified accordingly. Figure 4.6 shows an example of a SMALG⁺ program using arrays.

4.5.2 Description of SMALM⁺

SMALM⁺ is the machine architecture intended to support execution of SMALG⁺ programs in a straightforward manner. We describe SMALM⁺ in this section; a description of how SMALG⁺ instructions are executed by SMALM⁺ is given in Section 4.5.3.

SMALM⁺ is a stack machine. This means that its data storage is managed according to a last-in-first-out (LIFO) policy. The reader who knows a bit about run-time management of a recursive programming language (such as Pascal) will recognize that a LIFO policy is required to manage allocation and deallocation of the block of locations needed to store local variables and parameters of procedure activations. We discuss this point in detail in Section 4.5.3. The stack memory $STACK$ of SMALM$^+$ is a sequence of *cells* $STACK[i]$, $i = 1, 2, \ldots$. A special register TOP is used to store an integer value that represents the address of the most recently allocated stack cell, $STACK[TOP]$. The stack is empty if $TOP = 0$. Each cell $STACK[i]$ stores a pair $\langle Id[i], V[i] \rangle$ where $Id[i]$ is a symbolic identifier and $V[i]$ is an integer value. This will enable us to represent a SMALM$^+$ variable via a cell containing the pair $\langle x, y \rangle$, where x is the variable name and y is its current value. The identifier part of the ith cell of $STACK$ is denoted by the dot notation $STACK[i].Id$; similarly, the value part will be denoted by $STACK[i].V$.

In addition, SMALM$^+$ has a read-only random-access storage area $PROG$, which contains the program to be executed, a read-only input tape $INPUT$, and a write-only output tape $OUTPUT$ that can store sequences of integer values. Register PC (Program Counter) contains the address of the instruction of $PROG$ that is currently being executed. Registers IH (Input Head) and OH (Output Head) denote a sequential position of the input and output tapes, respectively. Precisely, IH denotes the position where the next value will be input and OH denotes the position where the next value will be output. Register ACC is the

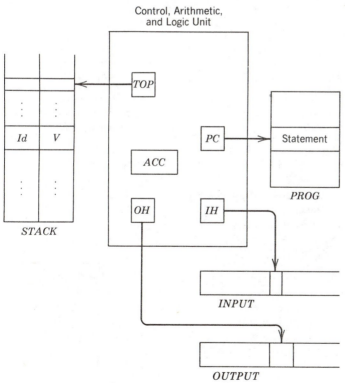

FIGURE 4.7 The architecture of SMALM$^+$.

TABLE 4.1 SMALM$^+$ Instructions

Statement	Semiformal Definition	Comment
PUSH x x may be omitted; in this case PUSH is equivalent to PUSH \$, \$ being a reserved name	$TOP := TOP + 1$ $STACK[TOP].Id := \text{“}x\text{”}$ $STACK[TOP].V := \bot$ $PC := PC + 1$	One cell is pushed on top of $STACK$. “x” stands for the same literal string occurring in the PUSH instruction. The value field of the cell is undefined.
POP n n may be omitted; in this case POP is equivalent to POP 1	$TOP := TOP - n$ $PC := PC + 1$	n cells are popped off $STACK$
LOAD x x may be omitted	$ACC := STACK[source] \cdot V$ $PC := PC + 1$ where $source = TOP$ if x is omitted; otherwise, $source$ is such that $STACK[source].Id = \text{“}x\text{”}$ $\land \nexists j,\ source < j \leq TOP,$ $STACK[j].Id = \text{“}x\text{”}$	The value of the topmost cell (whose identifier field contains “x”) is copied into the accumulator
LOAD $= n$ n is a constant	$ACC := n$ $PC := PC + 1$	“Immediate load” ACC is set to constant n
LOAD @ PC	$ACC := PC$ $PC := PC + 1$	ACC is set to the current value of the program counter
STORE x x may be omitted	$STACK[target].V := ACC$ $PC := PC + 1$ where $target = TOP$ if x is omitted; otherwise, target is such that $STACK[target].Id = \text{“}x\text{”} \land$ $\nexists j,\ target < j \leq TOP,$ $STACK[j].Id = \text{“}x\text{”}$	It is the obvious counterpart of LOAD
ADD x x may be omitted	$ACC := ACC + STACK[operand].V$ $PC := PC + 1$ where $operand = TOP$ if x is omitted; otherwise, $operand$ is such that $STACK[operand].Id = \text{“}x\text{”}$ $\land$ $\nexists j,\ operand < j \leq TOP,$ $STACK[j].Id = \text{“}x\text{”}$	The value of the topmost cell (whose identifier field contains “x”) is added into the accumulator

TABLE 4.1   Continued

Statement	Semiformal Definition	Comment
ADD = n n is a constant	$ACC := ACC + n$ $PC := PC + 1$	"Immediate" add; constant n is added to the accumulator
SUB x, SUB = n MULT x, MULT = n DIV x, DIV = n	These are similar to the case of ADD	
READ	$ACC := INPUT[IH]$ $IH := IH + 1$ $PC := PC + 1$	
WRITE	$OUTPUT[OH] := ACC$ $OH := OH + 1$ $PC := PC + 1$	
JUMP n n is a constant	$PC := n$	Unconditional jump
JUMP @ ACC	$PC := ACC$	The target address of jump is the value stored in ACC
JZ n	**if** $ACC = 0$ **then** $PC := n$ **else** $PC := PC + 1$	Conditional jump ("jump on zero")
JGZ n	**if** $ACC > 0$ **then** $PC := n$ **else** $PC := PC + 1$	Conditional jump (jump on greater than zero)
HALT	Execution terminates	

accumulator. It is used as a target of the LOAD instruction and as a source of the STORE instruction. Also, it is used to hold one of the operands in arithmetic operations.

In conclusion, the *state* of SMALM$^+$ is represented by a 9-tuple $\langle STACK, PROG, INPUT, OUTPUT, TOP, PC, IH, OH, ACC \rangle$, and is illustrated as in Figure 4.7. Initially, $TOP = 0$, $PC = 1$, $IH = 1$, $OH = 1$, $ACC = \bot$. The machine state then changes as instructions stored in $PROG$ are executed. SMALM$^+$ instructions are listed in Table 4.1 along with a self-explaining semiformal Pascal-like description and a few comments, where necessary. We implicitly assume that any access to an undefined value results in a run-time error of SMALM$^+$.

Exercises

4.2   Write a SMALM$^+$ program that reads a positive integer n and evaluates the sum of the first n integers in the input tape that follow n.

4.3   Write a computer program that simulates SMALM$^+$.

4.4   Write a report comparing SMALG$^+$ and your favorite programming language.

4.5.3   Semantics of SMALG$^+$ Defined via SMALM$^+$

Before giving a complete, formal description of how SMALG$^+$ programs are translated into SMALM$^+$ sequences of statements, let us provide an informal overview. For simplicity, here and in what follows we restrict our attention to the SMALG$^+$ definition shown in Figure 4.4. The case of arrays and other extensions will be sketched in Exercises 4.6 and 4.8.

1. At the beginning of execution, SMALM$^+$ allocates into *STACK* (i.e., it pushes) the amount of cells required to store the variables declared in the main section.
2. When executing a procedure call, SMALM$^+$ performs the following actions.
   a. It pushes onto *STACK* one cell that is reserved to store the address of the instruction to be executed after the procedure terminates. Such cell is named *retadd*.
   b. It pushes onto *STACK* the cells required to store formal parameters and local variables.
   c. It copies the values of actual parameters into the value-fields of corresponding formal parameters.
   d. It evaluates the address of the instruction to be executed after procedure termination, and stores it in the *value* field of the stack cell whose *Id* field is *retadd*.
   e. It starts execution of the procedure body.
3. At the end of execution of a procedure, SMALM$^+$ returns to the address that was saved at Step 2.d.
4. After execution of a procedure, SMALM$^+$ performs the following actions.
   a. It copies the values of the formal parameters back into the value-fields of the corresponding actual parameters.
   b. It deallocates from *STACK* (i.e., it pops) all of the cells that had been allocated when executing the call.
5. Execution of other SMALG$^+$ statements is rather straightforward. In particular, the value of a variable whose identifier is *id* can be retrieved by means of a LOAD *id* instruction, which puts the value into the accumulator. Similarly, the value of *id* can be altered by means of a STORE *id* instruction.

Now, let us provide a complete and rigorous operational semantics for SMALG$^+$. The description is given in terms of the SMALG$^+$ grammar. In particular, for any nonterminal of the SMALG$^+$ grammar and for any production we use to rewrite the nonterminal in the derivation of a SMALG$^+$ source program P_S, we give rules to generate the corresponding object SMALM$^+$ program P_O. The evolution of the SMALM$^+$ state during execution of P_O is defined as the operational semantics of P_S.

Initialization
Generate a sequence of SMALM$^+$ statements of the form PUSH x for all $x \in ID_M$.

Statement list
If the statement list is empty (i.e., it is obtained by the rule $\langle \text{StatList} \rangle \to \epsilon$), no SMALG$^+$ statement is generated. Otherwise (i.e., $\langle \text{StatList} \rangle^1 \Rightarrow \langle \text{Stat} \rangle$ $\langle \text{StatList} \rangle^2$), generate the sequence of SMALM$^+$ statements corresponding to $\langle \text{Stat} \rangle$ and follow it by the sequence of SMALM$^+$ statements corresponding to $\langle \text{StatList} \rangle^2$ (superscripts are used only for notational convenience).

Assignment statement
Case a.

$\langle \text{AssStat} \rangle \overset{*}{\Rightarrow} \langle \text{Ident} \rangle := \langle \text{Ident} \rangle \overset{*}{\Rightarrow} id1 := id2$

The corresponding SMALM$^+$ fragment is

LOAD   *id1*
STORE *id2*

Case b.

$\langle \text{AssStat} \rangle \overset{*}{\Rightarrow} \langle \text{Ident} \rangle := \langle \text{Constant} \rangle \overset{*}{\Rightarrow} id := c$

The corresponding SMALM$^+$ fragment is

LOAD =   *c*
STORE   *id*

Case c.

$\langle \text{AssStat} \rangle \overset{*}{\Rightarrow} \langle \text{Ident} \rangle := \langle \text{Term} \rangle + \langle \text{Term} \rangle$
$\qquad \overset{*}{\Rightarrow} \langle \text{Ident} \rangle := \langle \text{Constant} \rangle + \langle \text{Constant} \rangle \overset{*}{\Rightarrow} id := c1 + c2.$

The corresponding SMALM$^+$ fragment is

LOAD =   *c1*
ADD =   *c2*
STORE   *id*

Case d.

$\langle \text{AssStat} \rangle \overset{*}{\Rightarrow} \langle \text{Ident} \rangle := \langle \text{Term} \rangle + \langle \text{Term} \rangle$
$\qquad \overset{*}{\Rightarrow} \langle \text{Ident} \rangle := \langle \text{Ident} \rangle + \langle \text{Ident} \rangle \overset{*}{\Rightarrow} id1 := id2 + id3$

The corresponding SMALM$^+$ fragment is

LOAD   *id2*
ADD   *id3*
STORE *id1*

The cases where one of the operands of the addition is the constant, whereas the other is a variable is handled in a similar way. We leave this and the case of other arithmetic expressions as an exercise for the reader.

Condition

The SMALM$^+$ code generated to evaluate a condition produces a value in the accumulator, which is interpreted according to the following convention: If the condition evaluates to false, the value stored in the accumulator is a zero. Otherwise, it is a one. Formally, consider the following case.

$\langle \text{Cond} \rangle \Rightarrow \langle \text{Term} \rangle \langle \text{RelOp} \rangle \langle \text{Term} \rangle \overset{.}{\Rightarrow} id1 \leq id2$

The corresponding SMALM$^+$ fragment is

```
LOAD    id1
SUB     id2
JGZ     n₁
LOAD  = 1
JUMP    n₂
LOAD  = 0
```

where n_1 is the location of *PROG* that stores instruction LOAD = 0, and n_2 is the location of *PROG* that stores the first instruction that follows the foregoing fragment.

Other cases, where one of the operands (or both) are a constant and where the relational operator is different are handled in a similar way. We leave the details as an exercise for the reader.

Conditional statement

Case a.

$\langle \text{CondStat} \rangle \Rightarrow$ **if** $\langle \text{Cond} \rangle$ **then** $\langle \text{StatList} \rangle$ **else** $\langle \text{StatList} \rangle$ **fi**
$\overset{.}{\Rightarrow}$ **if** C **then** *List1* **else** *List2*

Let $\mathscr{C}$ be the sequence of SMALM$^+$ statements generated to evaluate C (see above); let $\mathscr{L}_1$ and $\mathscr{L}_2$ be the sequences of SMALM$^+$ statements corresponding to *List1* and *List2*, respectively. The SMALM$^+$ fragment corresponding to the above SMALG$^+$ fragment is

```
𝒞
JZ      n₁
𝓛₁
JUMP  n₂
𝓛₂
```

where n_1 is the location of *PROG* that stores the first SMALM$^+$ instruction of list $\mathscr{L}_2$, and n_2 is the location of *PROG* that stores the first instruction that follows list $\mathscr{L}_2$.

Case b.

$\langle \text{CondStat} \rangle \Rightarrow$ **if** $\langle \text{Cond} \rangle$ **then** $\langle \text{StatList} \rangle$ **fi** $\overset{.}{\Rightarrow}$ **if** C **then** *List1* **fi**

This can be handled as in case a assuming *List2* (and $\mathscr{L}_2$) as empty. Using the same conventions as in case a and performing an obvious simplification, we come to the following SMALM$^+$ fragment

$\mathscr{C}$
JZ $\quad n_1$
$\mathscr{L}_1$

where n_1 is the location of *PROG* that stores the first instruction that follows list $\mathscr{L}_1$.

While statement
Let $\langle$WhileStat$\rangle \stackrel{*}{\Rightarrow}$ **while** C **do** *List* **od**

Let $\mathscr{C}$ be the sequence of SMALM$^+$ statements needed to evaluate C (see above); let $\mathscr{L}$ be the sequence of SMALM$^+$ statements corresponding to *List*. The SMALM$^+$ fragment corresponding to the above SMALG$^+$ fragment is

$\mathscr{C}$
JZ $\quad n_1$
$\mathscr{L}$
JUMP n_2

where n_1 is the location of *PROG* that stores the first SMALM$^+$ instruction that follows JUMP n_2 and n_2 is the location of *PROG* that stores the first SMALM$^+$ instruction of $\mathscr{C}$.

Input statement
Let $\langle$InputStat$\rangle \stackrel{*}{\Rightarrow}$ **read** *id*. The corresponding SMALM$^+$ fragment is

READ
STORE $\quad$ *id*

Output statement
If $\langle$OutputStat$\rangle \stackrel{*}{\Rightarrow}$ **write** $\langle$Ident$\rangle \stackrel{*}{\Rightarrow}$ **write** *id*, the corresponding SMALM$^+$ fragment is

LOAD $\quad$ *id*
WRITE

Otherwise, if $\langle$OutputStat$\rangle \stackrel{*}{\Rightarrow}$ **write** $\langle$Constant$\rangle \stackrel{*}{\Rightarrow}$ **write** c, the corresponding SMALM$^+$ fragment is

LOAD $=$ $\quad c$
WRITE

Procedure call
Let $\langle$ProcCall$\rangle \stackrel{*}{\Rightarrow}$ **call** $p(a1, a2, \ldots, an)$.

Let $f1, f2, \ldots, fn$ be the formal parameters corresponding to $a1, a2, \ldots, an$, respectively. Let $t1, t2, \ldots, tm$ be the local variables declared in procedure p. The

SMALM$^+$ fragment corresponding to the call is

PUSH	retadd	one cell, named *retadd*, is reserved to store the address of return instruction. *retadd* is a reserved identified.

PUSH	f1	
LOAD	a1	
STORE	f1	
PUSH	f2	
LOAD	a2	parameter passing
STORE	f2	
:		
PUSH	fn	
LOAD	an	
STORE	fn	

PUSH	t1	
PUSH	t2	allocation of local
:		variables
PUSH	tm	

LOAD@	PC	
ADD =	4	address of return instruction is saved
STORE	retadd	

Before p's execution

JUMP	ap	ap is the address of the location of *PROG* which stores the first SMALM$^+$ instruction of p's body. Thus, control is transferred to p

POP	m	deallocation of local variables

LOAD		
STORE	an	
POP		
:		parameter passing and deallocation
LOAD		
STORE	a2	
POP		
LOAD		
STORE	a1	
POP		

after p's execution

POP		*retadd* is deallocated

Procedure declaration

The SMALM$^+$ fragment associated with a SMALG$^+$ procedure is the code associated with the procedure body, which is generated according to the previous rules, followed by

LOAD	*retadd*	return address is copied into the accumulator
JUMP@	ACC	control is returned to the caller

End of program

The SMALM$^+$ statements corresponding to the end of the main section have the purpose of undoing the effect of initialization (see foregoing). These statements are simply a sequence of POPs, one for each $x \in ID_M$, followed by HALT.

To fully understand the operational semantics we have given above, we advise the reader to follow the state changes of SMALM$^+$ in correspondence of sample SMALG$^+$ programs.

Example 4.3

According to the operational semantics of SMALG$^+$, the program of Figure 4.5a is translated into the SMALM$^+$ program given as follows with some comments. The reader is invited to sketch snapshots of the SMALM$^+$ state during execution.

PUSH	*x*	
PUSH	*y*	initialization
PUSH	*z*	
READ		
STORE	*x*	**read** *x*
READ		
STORE	*y*	**read** *y*
PUSH	*retadd*	push return-address cell
PUSH	*a*	
LOAD	*x*	
STORE	*a*	
PUSH	*b*	parameter passing at the point
LOAD	*y*	of call of *sum*
STORE	*b*	
PUSH	*c*	
LOAD	*z*	
STORE	*c*	

LOAD@	PC	⎫ address of return instruction
ADD =	4	⎬ is saved in *STACK*
STORE	*retadd*	⎭

JUMP   38   ⎫ transfer to procedure *sum*; 38 is the
⎬ address of its first instruction (LOAD *a*)

LOAD		⎫
STORE	z	
POP		
LOAD		formal parameters are
STORE	y	copied back into actual
POP		parameters
LOAD		
STORE	x	
POP		⎭

POP   ⎫ return-address cell is
⎬ deallocated

LOAD	z	⎫
WRITE		⎬ **write** z

POP	⎫
POP	⎬ end of program
POP	
HALT	⎭

LOAD	a	⎫	
ADD	b	⎬ c := a + b	
STORE	c	⎭	code for
LOAD	*retadd*	⎫ return-address	procedure *sum*
		⎬ is copied into *ACC*	
JUMP@	*ACC*	} return to caller	

Exercises

4.5   Give an operational definition for assignments of the type $x := a \bmod b$.

4.6   We wish to define the operational semantics of SMALG$^+$ with arrays, as outlined in Exercise 4.1. First, it is necessary to design suitable extensions to SMALM$^+$ to cope with array indexing. In particular, we extend operation PUSH as follows.

PUSH $x + n$

where n is a positive constant. The portion "$+n$" may be omitted, in which case we fall under the usual case. The meaning is

$STACK[TOP + 1] \cdot Id := \text{`}x\text{'}$
$STACK[TOP + 1] \cdot V := \perp$
for $k := 2$ **to** n **do**
    $STACK[TOP + k] \cdot Id := \text{`\$'}$
    $STACK[TOP + k] \cdot V := \perp$
$TOP := TOP + n$
$PC := PC + 1$

Thus, only the first of the n cells pushed onto $STACK$ contains the array name in field Id.

Similarly, we extend the addressing mode of operations LOAD, STORE, ADD, SUB, MULT, DIV, READ, and WRITE as illustrated by the following example

LOAD $x + n$

where n is a positive constant. The meaning is

$ACC := STACK[source + n - 1] \cdot V$
$PC := PC + 1$

where $source = TOP$ if x is omitted; otherwise, $source$ is such that

$STACK[source] \cdot Id = x$ and $\nexists j$, $source < j \leq TOP$, such that $STACK[j] \cdot Id = x$

The reader can define all other SMALM$^+$ statements accordingly. After doing so, the reader should extend the definition of operational semantics of SMALG$^+$ in the spirit of the definition we have described in Section 4.5.3.

4.7 Following the operational semantics defined in Exercise 4.6, generate the SMALM$^+$ program corresponding to the SMALG$^+$ program of Figure 4.6. Sketch snapshots of the SMALM$^+$ state during execution of the program.

4.8 We wish to extend SMALG$^+$ to handle arithmetic expressions in full generality, as illustrated by the following grammar fragment:

$\langle Exp \rangle \rightarrow \langle Exp \rangle + \langle Term \rangle | \langle Exp \rangle - \langle Term \rangle | \langle Term \rangle$
$\langle Term \rangle \rightarrow \langle Term \rangle * \langle Factor \rangle | \langle Term \rangle$ **div** $\langle Factor \rangle |$
            $\langle Term \rangle$ **mod** $\langle Factor \rangle | \langle Factor \rangle$
$\langle Factor \rangle \rightarrow (\langle Exp \rangle) | \langle Var \rangle | \langle Constant \rangle$

Similarly, we extend conditions as follows:

$\langle Cond \rangle \rightarrow \langle Exp \rangle \langle RelOp \rangle \langle Exp \rangle$

Define a complete grammar for SMALG$^+$ incorporating these extensions. Then, provide an operational semantics for the SMALG$^+$ extension.

To do so, it is necessary to define an extension of SMALM$^+$. In fact, consider the following example of an arithmetic expression e.

$$e1 * (e2 * (e3 + x) + y)$$

where $e1$, $e2$, and $e3$ are arithmetic (sub)expressions and x, y, are either constants or variables. The SMALM$^+$ code generated to evaluate $e1$ must produce the result in a temporary location. The same is true for the code generated to evaluate $e2$ and $e3$. In general, for a complex expression, the number of temporaries needed to hold the value of subexpressions evaluated in a left-to-right scan of the originary expression can become arbitrarily large if the length of the expression is unbounded. However, it is well known that the temporaries needed to hold such values can be taken from a stack of cells. Thus, instead of a single cell (the accumulator) as in the case of our original SMALM$^+$, here we need a stack of accumulators. In practice, we can use *STACK* for this purpose, and thus we can change the instruction repertoire of SMALM$^+$ by eliminating the accumulator and using the free part of *STACK* to hold temporary values.

The reader is urged to implement these ideas into a SMALM$^+$ extended architecture and to define how each SMALG$^+$ instruction is mapped into fragments of extended SMALM$^+$ instructions.

4.9   Consider the program of Figure 4.8 written in extended SMALG$^+$ using general expressions introduced in Exercise 4.8.

Evaluate the corresponding extended SMALM$^+$ program using the operational semantics defined in Exercise 4.8 and describe snapshots of the extended SMALM$^+$ state during execution of the program.

4.10*   Implement a compiler that translates SMALG$^+$ programs into SMALM$^+$ programs. Use the simulator implemented in Exercise 4.3 to execute the translated programs.

4.11*   Modify the SMALG$^+$ parameter passing convention from call-by-value result to call-by reference. How can you define formally operational semantics? Do SMALG$^+$ programs always produce the same results under the two conventions?

```
var: i,n,x,y,b;
begin
      read n; i := 1;
      while i ≤ n
            do read x,y;
                call even (x,y,b);
                write b
            od
end
procedure even (u,v,d);
begin
      d := u - (u div v)*v
end
```

FIGURE 4.8   A SMALG$^+$ program using general expressions.

4.12 Suppose you allow procedures to redeclare identifiers with the same name as those declared in the main. Also, suppose you assume that procedures can access an identifier that is not locally declared only if it is declared in the main. Is the operational semantics given in Section 4.5.3 still correct in this case? Why?

4.13* Modify SMALM$^+$ by eliminating the symbolic name of identifiers in the *Id* field of *STACK* locations. How can you modify the addressing mechanisms of SMALM$^+$ to support execution of SMALG$^+$ programs?

4.6 Denotational Semantics

The operational semantics as examplified in Section 4.5 is, in some sense, the "natural" semantics for languages like SMALG$^+$ (or, more practically, Pascal, FORTRAN, Ada,...) as these languages are tightly connected to the notion of state and state transformations caused by execution of the statements. The I/O function associated to a SMALG$^+$ program, as well as to a TM, is—by definition —the function computed by the program.

If we wish to emphasize the I/O function as the semantics of a language, we need a tool for denoting such a function independent of the state transformations involved during computation. In the simple case of the example presented in Section 4.4.2 we were able to associate a sequence of assignments with the composition of functions appearing in right hand sides. In the general case, however, providing complete rules suitable to describing any SMALG$^+$ program is not an immediate job.

Conventional programming languages are based on the concepts of the underlying traditional von Neumann computer architecture. Computer programs described by such languages represent computations, whose effect is a step-by-step change of the machine state. If we wish to describe the function associated to a program written in such languages, we must be able to abstract away from the step-by-step state transformation.

On the other hand, there exist other programming languages which are based on a *functional programming* style. LISP has been the first of this family of languages. Functional languages are not based on the von Neumann computational model but rather on more classical mathematical objects, namely functions. Functional languages are intended to denote functions rather than defining their computation steps: Consequently they provide a descriptive style which is entirely different from that of conventional languages. In addition, the functional style makes these unconventional languages amenable to a formal description given by means of denotational semantics.

In order to make all this more precise, we will follow this path: We will first introduce a new formal notation, known as *McCarthy's formalism*, which is an abstract version of a functional programming language. Then we discuss its semantics both from an operational and a denotational point of view. Afterwards, we try to give a denotational description of ALGOL-like languages. Finally we contrast the two approaches by discussing both their common aspects and the peculiar aspects of each one.

4.6.1 McCarthy's Formalism and Its Semantics

Let us introduce the syntax of McCarthy's formalism.

Definition 4.1

Let $X = \{x_1, x_2, \ldots\}$ be an infinite set of *variable symbols*.

Let $f = \{f_1, \ldots, f_k\}$ be finite a set of *base function symbols*.

Let n_i be the *arity* of each function symbol f_i (i.e., the number of arguments of f_i). If $n_i = 0$, f_i is said to be a *constant symbol*.

Let $F = \{F_1, F_2, \ldots\}$ be an infinite set of *variable function symbols*.

A *recursive program* P over $\langle X, f, F \rangle$ is a finite set of pairs.

$$\langle F_1, t_1 \rangle$$
$$\vdots$$
$$\langle F_n, t_n \rangle$$

where $F_1, \ldots, F_n \in F$, $t_1, \ldots, t_n$ are *terms*[3] involving elements of X, f, and F. In order to simplify the notation, we assume that all function symbols F_i, $i = 1, \ldots, n$, have the same arity k so that $F_i(x_1, \ldots, x_k)$ is a term for every F_i. This, of course, does not cause any loss of generality, since a term $F_i(x)$ can also be considered as a term $F_i(x, y)$. P is denoted as $P: F(x) \Leftarrow \tau[F](x)$ where F denotes the vector $\langle F_1, \ldots, F_n \rangle$ and $\tau[F](x) = \langle \tau_1[F], \ldots, \tau_n[F] \rangle(x)$ denotes the n-tuple of terms involving F and $x = \langle x_1, \ldots, x_k \rangle$, $x_i \in X$ (f is dropped from the notation as a priori fixed). □

Example 4.4

Let $f = \{0, 1 \text{ (with arity 0)}, =, +, -, *, \textbf{div} \text{ (with arity 2)}, \textbf{if-then-else} \text{ (with arity 3)}\}$. Let $F = \{\text{FACT}, \ldots\}$. A recursive program P is

$\text{FACT}(x) \Leftarrow \textbf{if-then-else} \, (= (x, 0), 1, *(x, \text{FACT}(-(x, 1))))$

By associating the usual *infix notation*, instead of the *prefix notation* used above, P is rewritten in the more understandable notation

$\text{FACT}(x) \Leftarrow \textbf{if } x = 0 \textbf{ then } 1 \textbf{ else } x * \text{FACT}(x - 1)$

Thus far, the preceding example shows only a *syntactic notation*. However, the used symbols immediately suggest the intended meaning of the program; in Example 4.4 it is clearly an implementation of the factorial function. Before going into a rigorous definition of semantics for recursive programs, let us

---

[3] For the definition of *term* see Section 0.2.3.

intuitively discuss the "meaning" of P. Let us interpret the symbols x as an integer variable and $0, 1, =$, **if-then-else**, $-$, $*$ according to their usual meaning. We can "rewrite" P as a Pascal function definition.

function $FACT(x: integer): integer;$
      begin if $x = 0$ **then** $FACT := 1$
                    else $FACT := x * FACT(x - 1)$
    end

Our informal knowledge of the Pascal semantics tells us that $FACT$ defines the *recursive computation* of the function "factorial of x."

Going back to P, we immediately understand it realizes the same definition of "factorial of x" by abstracting away from the fact that $FACT$ is ultimately a computer memory cell to be loaded with some computed value. To put it in another way, the reader can realize the similarity between recursive programs and the formalism of recursive functions (see Section 0.2.4.2). In fact, still relying on the intuitive evidence of the above example, we can reformulate the $FACT$ function in yet another way by means of the formalism of primitive recursive functions in the following way.

$$FACT(0) = 0'$$
$$FACT(x') = x' \cdot FACT(x)$$

where the recursive definition of multiplication is omitted as it is obvious. The three formulations of $FACT$ by means of McCarthy's formalism, Pascal, and recursive functions share a common view of defining and computing the "factorial" function. Consequently, McCarthy's formalism can be seen as a reformulation of the formalism of recursive functions made closer to a (recursive) programming style.

Now let us get into the problem of giving a formal semantics to recursive programs. We first define an operational semantics and successively a pure denotational semantics; the two styles are then compared. Consider again the foregoing factorial example and suppose you wish to simulate the computation of $FACT(3)$ by means of P. You would perform the following sequence of steps.

- Is $3 = 0$? No. Then I must compute $FACT(2)$ and multiply it by 3
- Is $2 = 0$? No. Then . . .

   . . .

- Is $0 = 0$? Yes. Thus $FACT(0) = 1$
- Thus $FACT(1) = 1 * 1 = 1$

   . . .

- Thus $FACT(3) = 3 * 2 * 1 * 1 = 6$

Formally, the computation of a recursive program can be defined as follows.

Definition 4.2

Let P be a recursive program over $\langle X, f, F \rangle$. An *interpretation* of P is a 4-tuple $\langle \{ S_j \}, \mathscr{I}_x, \mathscr{I}_f, \mathscr{I}_F \rangle$, where

- $\{ S_j \}$ is a finite set of sets.

- $\mathscr{I}_x$ is the *type assignment* to $x = \langle x_1, \cdots, x_k \rangle$, x_i being the variable symbols occurring in P. Precisely $\mathscr{I}_x$ assigns a set of values in $\{S_j\}$ to each x_i.
- $\mathscr{I}_f$ is the *interpretation of f*, that is, a mapping that assigns to each symbol f_i of f a function

$$\tilde{f}_i : D_{i1} \times \ldots \times D_{ik_i} \to R_i$$

where $D_{ir}, R_i \in \{S_j\}$ and k_i is the arity of f_i. If $k_i = 0$ then $\tilde{f}_i$ is an element (constant) of R_i.

- $\mathscr{I}_F$ is the *range assignment* to F, that is, a mapping assigning a range $R_i \in \{S_j\}$ to each variable function symbol F_i. For simplicity, in the notation we assume that the domain of each F_i is $D = D_1 \times \ldots \times D_k$, $D_r \in \{S_j\}$. Clearly, this assumption does not cause any loss of generality.

A 4-tuple $\langle \{S_i\}, \mathscr{I}_x, \mathscr{I}_f, \mathscr{I}_F \rangle$ assigns a *type* to each term t over X, f, and F according to the following rules.

- If $t = c_j$, c_j being a constant element of S_j, then t is of type S_j.
- If $t = x_j$, x_j being a variable symbol, then t is of type $\mathscr{I}_x(x_j)$.
- If $t = f_i(t_{i1}, \ldots, t_{ik_i})$, with $\mathscr{I}_f(f_i): D_{i1} \times \ldots \times D_{ik_i} \to R_i$, then t_{ir} must be of type D_{ir} for $r = 1, \ldots, k_i$, and t is of type R_i.
- If $t = F_i(t_{i1}, \ldots, t_{ik})$, then t_{ir} must be of type D_{ir} for $r = 1, \ldots, k$ and t is of type $R_i = \mathscr{I}_F(F_i)$.
- In a recursive program $P: \langle F_1, t_1 \rangle, \ldots \langle F_n, t_n \rangle$, each t_i must be of type $\mathscr{I}_F(F_i)$. $\square$

Intuitively, an interpretation of P assigns a set of values, or type, to each term of P and an actual function to each base function symbol. In particular, we will always include into f the symbols $= , + , - , * , / , \mathbf{div},$[4] with their usual interpretation, whenever they are meaningful for a particular choice of $\{S_i\}$. For example, if D is $\mathbb{N}$ (or $\mathbb{Z}$, $\mathbb{R}$, etc.)

$$= \; : D \times D \to \{\mathrm{T}, \mathrm{F}\}$$
$$+ \; : D \times D \to D$$
$$\vdots$$

Furthermore, **if-then-else** will always be in f with the following interpretation. For any D, **if-then-else** $: \{\mathrm{T}, \mathrm{F}\} \times D \times D \to D$; **if** x **then** y **else** z is defined by

- if $x = \mathrm{T}$ then y, for all z
- if $x = \mathrm{F}$ then z, for all y

Definition 4.3

Let $P: F(x) \Leftarrow \tau[F](x)$ be a recursive program over $\langle X, f, F \rangle$ with an interpretation $\langle \{S_j\}, \mathscr{I}_x, \mathscr{I}_f, \mathscr{I}_F \rangle$. Let $v = \langle v_1, \ldots, v_k \rangle$ be a k-tuple of values in

---

[4] $/$ denotes rational division, whereas **div** denotes integer division.

$D = D_1 \times \ldots \times D_k$, the domain of all F_i. Let $F(v)$ denote $\langle F_1(v_1, \ldots, v_k), \ldots, F_n(v_1, \ldots, v_k) \rangle$ each v_r being an element of D_r, $r = 1, \ldots, k$.

A *computation* of $F(v)$ is a sequence of terms t_0, t_1, and $t_2 \ldots$ involving elements of S_j, f, F—but not involving variable symbols in X—such that

1. $t_0 = F(v)$.
2. For every $s \geq 0$, t_{s+1} is obtained from t_s by the following sequential steps.
   a. *Substitution*: Some occurrences of terms of the type $F_i(t')$ where t' is a k-tuple of terms of type D, are replaced, in each component of t_s, by $\tau_i[F](t')$. The occurrences of $F_i(t')$ to be substituted are selected according to suitable *computation rules* to be detailed below.
   b. *Simplification*: Terms of the type $f_i(t_1, \ldots, t_r)$ are replaced by the value $\tilde{f}_i(v_1, \ldots, v_r)$ *whenever possible* until no further simplification can be made. The term "whenever possible" involves semantic knowledge of functions $\tilde{f}_i$: so $1 = 1$ is replaced by T, $1 + 1$ is replaced by $2, \ldots$ etc. In particular, **if** T **then** t_1 **else** t_2 is replaced by t_1 no matter what t_2 is (denotes)[5] and, similarly, **if** F **then** t_1 **else** t_2 is replaced by t_2.

Let t_{si} denote the ith component of the sth term of the computation of $F(v)$. For each i two cases are possible.

α. There exists an $\bar{s}$ such that $t_{\bar{s}i}$ does not contain any occurrence of variable function symbols. In such a case, $t_{\bar{s}i}$ is a value of the range of F_i and, for all $s \geq \bar{s}$, $t_{si} = t_{\bar{s}i}$. Thus $F_i(v)$ is defined as $t_{\bar{s}i}$.
β. Otherwise, the sequence $t_0, t_1, \ldots$ is infinite. Then $F_i(v)$ is undefined and we conventionally write $F_i(v) = \perp$.

If for all i, $F_i(v)$ is defined, then the computation of $F(v)$ is finite.

- $F(v)$ is defined as $\langle F_1(v), \cdots, F_n(v) \rangle$ whether $F_i(v) = \perp$ or not.
- $F(v) = \perp$ is a short notation for $F_i(v) = \perp$ for each i.

The resulting partial function $f^P : D_1 \times \ldots \times D_k \to R_1 \times \ldots \times R_n$ is called the *function computed* by P. □

Example 4.5

Consider the recursive program of Example 4.4 with its usual interpretation consisting of

- The two sets $\{T, F\}$ and $\mathbb{N}$.
- The usual meaning of $=: \mathbb{N} \times \mathbb{N} \to \{T, F\}$

  if-then-else : $\{T, F\} \times \mathbb{N} \times \mathbb{N} \to \mathbb{N}$, etc.

- $\mathbb{N}$ as domain and range of FACT.

---

[5] However, $F(t) = F(t)$ should not be replaced by T because the value of $F(t)$ could be undefined.

The computation of $FACT(3)$, which was previously introduced in an intuitive way, is the following sequence of terms:

$t_0 = FACT(3)$;
$t_1 = $ **if** $3 = 0$ **then** 1 **else** $3 * FACT(3 - 1) = 3 * FACT(2)$,
$t_2 = 3 * ($**if** $2 = 0$ **then** 1 **else** $2 * FACT(2 - 1)) = 6 * FACT(1)$
$t_3 = 6 * ($**if** $1 = 0$ **then** 1 **else** $1 * FACT(1 - 1)) = 6 * FACT(0)$;
$t_4 = 6 * ($**if** $0 = 0$ **then** 1 **else** $FACT(0 - 1)) = 6 * 1 = 6$.
Thus, $FACT(3) = 6$.

Notice that we have applied the simplification of the **if-then-else** expression *whenever possible* in such a way that "**if** $0 = 0$ **then** 1 **else** $FACT(0 - 1)$" is evaluated to 1 even if one of its arguments, namely $FACT(-1)$ is undefined. From a rigorous point of view this requires to extend the **if-then-else** function[6] as well as any other function, to the case where some of its arguments are undefined, as we will see formally in the sequel. We will return later to this crucial point of evaluation of recursive programs.

The preceding example did not cause any problem in the application of the substitution mechanism because the only variable function symbol $FACT$ occurs only once in the term $\tau[F](x)$. In the general case, however, τ is a n-tuple $\langle \tau_1, \ldots, \tau_n \rangle$ of terms, each containing several occurrences of variable function symbols $F_1, \ldots, F_n$: so the problem arises of which occurrences of which terms $F_i(t)$ should be substituted by $\tau_i[F](t)$. It turns out that *computation rules* (i.e., the rules regulating such a rewriting) do affect the semantics of recursive programs. It may happen that computations performed according to different rules may produce different results.

We give below some widely known computation rules. Each rule is ex-amplified through the following recursive program $P : F(x, y) \Leftarrow \tau[F](x, y)$ where F is $\langle F_1, F_2 \rangle$, τ is the pair $\langle \tau_1, \tau_2 \rangle$ defined as

$\tau_1[F_1, F_2](x, y) : $ **if** $y = F_2(x - 1, y - 1)$ **then** 0 **else** $F_1(x - 1, y - 1)$
$\tau_2[F_1, F_2](x, y) : $ **if** $x = y$ **then** x **else** $F_1(F_2(x - 1, y - 1), F_2(x - 1, y - 1))$

with the obvious interpretation.
Consider the computation of $F(3, 2)$. For each computation rule we obtain the following terms.

$t_0 = \langle F_1(3, 2), F_2(3, 2) \rangle$
$t_1 = \langle$**if** $2 = F_2(3 - 1, 2 - 1)$ **then** 0 **else** $F_1(3 - 1, 2 - 1)$,
　　　if $3 = 2$ **then** 3 **else** $F_1(F_2(3 - 1, 2 - 1), F_2(3 - 1, 2 - 1)))\rangle$
　　$= \langle$**if** $2 = F_2(2, 1)$ **then** 0 **else** $F_1(2, 1), F_1(F_2(2, 1), F_2(2, 1)))\rangle$

---

[6]More properly, the function associated by $\mathcal{J}_f$ to the symbol **if-then-else**.

The computation of term t_2 may vary by using different computation rules, as we show now. For each of the computation rules given below we use an arrow to mark the occurrences of F_1 and F_2 to be replaced by $\tau_1[F]$ and $\tau_2[F]$, respectively, and for some of them we display the result of the substitution.

1. Leftmost innermost (LI) rule (call-by value)

In any component t_{s_j} of t_s, replace the leftmost occurrence of a term of the type $F_i(t')$, such that t' does not contain any variable function symbol, by $\tau_i[F](t')$. In our example we have

$$\langle \textbf{if } 2 = F_2(2,1) \textbf{ then } 0 \textbf{ else } F_1(2,1),\ F_1\Big(F_2(2,1),\ F_2(2,1)\Big)\rangle$$
$$\uparrow \qquad\qquad\qquad\qquad\qquad\qquad\qquad \uparrow$$

Thus the result is

$$t_2 = \Big\langle \textbf{if } 2 = \big(\textbf{if } 2 = 1 \textbf{ then } 2 \textbf{ else } F_1(F_2(2-1,1-1),\ F_2(2-1,1-1))\big) \textbf{ then } 0$$
$$\textbf{else } F_1(2,1),$$
$$F_1\big(\textbf{if } 2 = 1 \textbf{ then } 2 \textbf{ else } F_1(F_2(2-1,1-1),\ F_2(2-1,1-1)),\ F_2(2,1))\Big\rangle$$
$$= \Big\langle \textbf{if } 2 = F_1(F_2(1,0),\ F_2(1,0)) \textbf{ then } 0 \textbf{ else } F_1(2,1),$$
$$F_1(F_1(F_2(1,0),\ F_2(1,0)),\ F_2(2,1))\Big\rangle$$

2. Leftmost (L) rule (call-by name)

Replace the term $F_i(t')$ containing the leftmost occurrence of a variable function symbol by $\tau_i[F](t')$. In our example,

$$\langle \textbf{if } 2 = F_2(2,1) \textbf{ then } 0 \textbf{ else } F_1(2,1),\ F_1(F_2(2,1), F_2(2,1))\rangle$$
$$\uparrow \qquad\qquad\qquad\qquad \uparrow \qquad\quad \uparrow$$

The result of the substitution is

$$t_2 = \Big\langle \textbf{if } 2 = F_1(F_2(1,0),\ F_2(1,0)) \textbf{ then } 0 \textbf{ else } F_1(2,1),$$
$$\textbf{if } F_2(2,1) = F_2(F_2(2,1)-1,\ F_2(2,1)-1)$$
$$\textbf{then } 0 \textbf{ else } F_1(F_2(2,1)-1,\ F_2(2,1)-1)\Big\rangle$$

3. Parallel innermost (PI) rule

Simultaneously replace by $\tau_i[F](t')$ all terms of the type $F_i(t')$, such that t' does not contain any variable function symbol. In the example

$$\langle \textbf{if } 2 = F_2(2,1) \textbf{ then } 0 \textbf{ else } F_1(2,1),\ F_1(F_2(2,1), F_2(2,1))\rangle$$
$$\uparrow \qquad\qquad\qquad\qquad \uparrow \qquad\quad \uparrow$$

The computation of the result of the substitution is left to the reader as an exercise.

4. Parallel outermost (PO) rule

Simultaneously replace all terms of the type $F_i(t')$ such that F_i is the outermost occurrence of variable function symbols, by $\tau_i[F]\,(t')$.

In the example

$$\langle \mathbf{if}\ 2 = F_2(2,1)\ \mathbf{then}\ 0\ \mathbf{else}\ F_1(2,1),\ F_1(F_2(2,1),F_2(2,1))\rangle$$
$$\uparrow \qquad\qquad\qquad\qquad \uparrow \qquad\quad \uparrow$$

5. Full substitution (FS) rule

Simultaneously replace all variable function symbols F_i by the corresponding $\tau_i[F]$. Here some caution is needed because the simultaneous substitution of $\tau_i[F]$ in $F_i(t')$ may affect the composition of t'. The application of the rule to the example should make things clear.

$$
\begin{aligned}
t_2 = \big\langle &\mathbf{if}\ 2 = F_1\big(F_2(1,0),\ F_2(1,0)\big)\ \mathbf{then}\ 0\ \mathbf{else}\\
&\quad \mathbf{if}\ 1 = F_2(1,0)\ \mathbf{then}\ 0\ \mathbf{else}\ F_1(1,0),\\
&\mathbf{if}\ \big(\mathbf{if}\ 2 = 1\ \mathbf{then}\ 2\ \mathbf{else}\ F_1\big(F_2(1,0),\ F_2(1,0)\big)\big) =\\
&\quad F_2\big(\big(\mathbf{if}\ 2 = 1\ \mathbf{then}\ 2\ \mathbf{else}\ F_1\big(F_2(1,0),\ F_2(1,0)\big)\big) - 1,\\
&\qquad \big(\mathbf{if}\ 2 = 1\ \mathbf{then}\ 2\ \mathbf{else}\ F_1\big(F_2(1,0),\ F_2(1,0)\big)\big) - 1\big)\\
&\quad \mathbf{then}\ 0\ \mathbf{else}\ F_1\big(\big(\mathbf{if}\ 2 = 1\ \mathbf{then}\ 2\ \mathbf{else}\ F_1\big(F_2(1,0),\ F_2(1,0)\big)\big),\\
&\qquad\qquad \big(\mathbf{if}\ 2 = 1\ \mathbf{then}\ 2\ \mathbf{else}\ F_1\big(F_2(1,0),\ F_2(1,0)\big)\big)\big)\big\rangle\\
= \big\langle &\mathbf{if}\ 2 = F_1\big(F_2(1,0),\ F_2(1,0)\big)\ \mathbf{then}\ 0\ \mathbf{else}\\
&\quad \mathbf{if}\ 1 = F_2(1,0)\ \mathbf{then}\ 0\ \mathbf{else}\ F_1(1,0),\\
&\mathbf{if}\ F_1\big(F_2(1,0),\ F_2(1,0)\big) = F_2\big(F_1\big(F_2(1,0),\ F_2(1,0)\big) - 1,\\
&\quad F_1\big(F_2(1,0),\ F_2(1,0)\big) - 1\big)\\
&\quad \mathbf{then}\ 0\ \mathbf{else}\ F_1\big(F_1\big(F_2(1,0),\ F_2(1,0)\big),\ F_1\big(F_2(1,0),\ F_2(1,0)\big)\big)\big\rangle
\end{aligned}
$$

For each computation rule C, the function $f_C^P : D_1 \times \ldots \times D_k \to R_1 \times \ldots \times R_n$ computed by C for the recursive program P is called the *operational semantics* of P according to C.

The preceding rules have been given in the hypothesis that the computation of $\langle F_1(v),\ldots, F_n(v)\rangle$ is carried over for all F_i in parallel. However, they could be similarly defined for the computation of, say, $F_i(v)$. In this case, clearly $t_0 = F_i(v)$, t_{s+1} is obtained from t_s by applying any one of the above computation rules to t_s. Notice that at each step different $\tau_j(t')$ may be used according to the chosen $F_j(t')$ to be substituted.

Example 4.6

Consider the following recursive program P.

$$F_1(x) \Leftarrow \mathbf{if}\ x = 0\ \mathbf{then}\ 1\ \mathbf{else}\ F_1(x - 1) - F_2(x)$$
$$F_2(x) \Leftarrow \mathbf{if}\ x = 0\ \mathbf{then}\ 0\ \mathbf{else}\ F_2(x + F_1(x - 1) - 2)$$

with x ranging over $\mathbb{N}$ and the usual interpretation of $=$, $+$, $-$, **if-then-else**. Let us first compute $\langle F_1(1), F_2(1)\rangle$ by means of the leftmost innermost rule. We obtain

$$t_0 = \langle F_1(1), F_2(1)\rangle$$
$$\qquad\quad \uparrow \qquad \uparrow$$
$$t_1 = \langle \text{if } 1 = 0 \text{ then } 1 \text{ else } \big(F_1(1-1) - F_2(1)\big),$$
$$\qquad \text{if } 1 = 0 \text{ then } 0 \text{ else } F_2\big(1 + F_1(1-1) - 2\big)\rangle$$
$$\quad = \langle F_1(0) - F_2(1), F_2\Big(F_1(0) - 1\Big)\rangle$$
$$\qquad\quad \uparrow \qquad\qquad\quad \uparrow$$
$$t_2 = \langle \text{if } 0 = 0 \text{ then } 1 \text{ else } \big(F_1(-1) - F_2(0)\big) - F_2(1),$$
$$\qquad F_2\big((\text{if } 0 = 0 \text{ then } 1 \text{ else } (F_1(-1) - F_2(0))) - 1\big)\rangle =$$
$$\quad = \langle 1 - F_2(1), F_2(0)\rangle$$
$$\qquad\quad\quad \uparrow \qquad \uparrow$$
$$t_3 = \langle 1 - F_2\Big(F_1(0) - 1\Big), (0)\rangle$$
$$\qquad\qquad\qquad \uparrow$$
$$t_4 = \langle 1 - F_2(1-1), 0)\rangle = \langle 1 - F_2(0), 0\rangle$$
$$\qquad\qquad\qquad\qquad\qquad\qquad \uparrow$$
$$t_5 = \langle 1, 0\rangle$$

Thus $f_{LI}^P(1) = \langle 1, 0\rangle$
Let us now compute $F_2(1)$ by means of the *FS* rule.

$$t_0 = F_2(1)$$
$$t_1 = \text{if } 1 = 0 \text{ then } 0 \text{ else } F_2(1 + F_1(0) - 2) = F_2\Big(F_1(0) - 1\Big)$$
$$\qquad\qquad\qquad\qquad\qquad\qquad\qquad\qquad\qquad\qquad \uparrow \quad \uparrow$$
$$t_2 = \text{if } \big(\text{if } 0 = 0 \text{ then } 1 \text{ else } (F_1(0-1) - F_2(0))\big) - 1 = 0 \text{ then } 0$$
$$\qquad \text{else } F_2\big((\text{if } 0 = 0 \text{ then } 1 \text{ else } (F_1(0-1) - F_2(0))) - 1$$
$$\qquad\quad + F_1((\text{if } 0 = 0 \text{ then } 1 \text{ else } (F_1(-1) - F_2(0))) - 1 - 1) - 2\big)$$
$$\quad = \text{if } 1 - 1 = 0 \text{ then } 0 \text{ else } F_2(1 - 1 + F_1(1 - 1 - 1) - 2)$$
$$\quad = 0$$

Finally, let us compute $F_1(2)$ by the leftmost rule.

$$t_0 = F_1(2)$$
$$t_1 = F_1(1) - F_2(2)$$
$$\qquad \uparrow$$
$$t_2 = F_1(0) - F_2(1) - F_2(2)$$
$$\qquad \uparrow$$
$$t_3 = 1 - F_2(1) - F_2(2)$$
$$\qquad\quad \uparrow$$

$$t_4 = 1 - F_2\big(1 + F_1(0) - 2\big) - F_2(2)$$
$$\uparrow$$

$$t_5 = 1 - \big(\mathbf{if}(1 + F_1(0) - 2) = 0 \textbf{ then } 0$$
$$\qquad \textbf{else } F_2(1 + F_1(0) - 2 + F_1(1 + F_1(0) - 2 - 1) - 2)\big) - F_2(2)$$
$$= 1 - \left(\mathbf{if}\Big(F_1(0) - 1\Big) = 0 \textbf{ then } 0\right.$$
$$\qquad\qquad\qquad \uparrow$$
$$\left.\textbf{else } F_2\big(F_1(0) - 1 + F_1(F_1(0) - 2) - 2\big)\right) - F_2(2)$$

$$t_6 = 1 - 0 - F_2(2) = 1 - F_2(2)$$
$$\qquad\qquad\qquad\qquad \uparrow$$

$$t_7 = 1 - F_2\big(2 + F_1(1) - 2\big) = 1 - F_2\big(F_1(1)\big)$$
$$\qquad\qquad\qquad\qquad\qquad\qquad \uparrow$$

$$t_8 = 1 - \mathbf{if}\, F_1(1) = 0 \textbf{ then } 0 \textbf{ else } F_2\big(F_1(1) + F_1(F_1(1) - 1) - 2\big)$$
$$\qquad \uparrow$$

After skipping the repetition of some steps we obtain

$$t_9 = 1 - \mathbf{if}\, 1 = 0 \textbf{ then } 0 \textbf{ else } F_2\big(F_1(1) + F_1(F_1(1) - 1) - 2\big))$$
$$\quad = 1 - F_2\big(F_1(1) + F_1(F_1(1) - 1) - 2\big))$$
$$\qquad\qquad \uparrow$$

$$t_{10} = 1 - \mathbf{if}\left(F_1(1) + F_1(F_1(1) - 1) - 2\right) = 0 \textbf{ then } 0 \textbf{ else}$$
$$\qquad\qquad\qquad \uparrow$$
$$\qquad\qquad F_2\big(F_1(1) + F_1(F_1(1) - 1) - 2$$
$$\qquad\qquad\quad + F_1(F_1(1) + F_1(F_1(1) - 1) - 2 - 1) - 2\big)$$

$$\cdots$$

$$t_{11} = 1 - \mathbf{if}\left(1 + F_1(F_1(1) - 1) - 2\right) = 0 \textbf{ then } 0 \textbf{ else}\ldots$$
$$\qquad\qquad\qquad \uparrow$$

$$t_{12} = 1 - \mathbf{if}\left(1 + \mathbf{if}\Big(F_1(1) - 1\Big) = 0 \textbf{ then } 1 \textbf{ else}\ldots -2\right) = 0 \textbf{ then } 0 \textbf{ else}\ldots$$
$$\qquad\qquad\qquad\qquad \uparrow$$

$$t_{13} = 1 - \mathbf{if}(1 + 1 - 2) = 0 \textbf{ then } 0 \textbf{ else}\ldots$$
$$\quad = 1 - 0 = 1$$

Exercises

4.14 Compute $F_1(2)$ by using the *LI* rule and verify that you get the same result as if the *L* rule were used, but with a shorter computation.

4.15 What is the value of $f_L^P(2)$?
Hint: There is no need to compute $\langle F_1(2), F_2(2)\rangle$.

4.16 For the following P:

$$F_1(x) \Leftarrow \text{if } x = 0 \text{ then } 1 \text{ else } F_1(x - 1) + F_2(x - 1)$$

$$F_2(x) \Leftarrow \text{if } x = 0 \text{ then } 0 \text{ else } F_2(x + F_1(x))$$

compute $F(1)$ and $F(2)$ by using all computation rules.

Example 4.7

Consider the following recursive program P.

$$F(x, y) \Leftarrow \text{if } x = 0 \text{ then } 0 \text{ else } F(x - 1, G(x, y))$$
$$G(x, y) \Leftarrow \text{if } y = 0 \text{ then } 1 \text{ else } G(x, y), y - 1)$$

Let us compute $f_L^P(1, 1)$. We have

$$t_0 = \langle F(1, 1), G(1, 1) \rangle$$
$$t_1 = \langle F(0, G(1, 1)), G(F(1, 1), 0) \rangle$$
$$\qquad\quad\uparrow \qquad\qquad\qquad \uparrow$$
$$t_2 = \langle 0, 1 \rangle$$

Instead, if we compute $f_{LI}^P(1, 1)$, we obtain

$$t_0 = \langle F(1, 1), G(1, 1) \rangle$$
$$t_1 = \langle F(0, G(1, 1)), G(F(1, 1), 0) \rangle$$
$$\qquad\qquad\uparrow \qquad\qquad\quad \uparrow$$
$$t_2 = \langle F(0, G(F(1, 1), 0)), G(F(0, G(1, 1)), 0) \rangle$$
$$\cdots$$

Clearly, $f_{LI}^P(1, 1) = \perp \neq f_L^P(1, 1)$.

Thus, we have seen that different computation rules may sometimes result in different operational semantics for the same recursive program. This is because one is allowed to simplify formulas (i.e., computing values of some function $\tilde{f}_i$) *whenever possible* (i.e., without necessarily waiting for all arguments of $\tilde{f}_i$). The effect of this is evident in the case of the **if-then-else**; for example, one does not need to evaluate the **else** branch if the condition is true.

Similarly a program of the type

$$F(x, y) \Leftarrow \text{if } x = 0 \text{ then } 0 \text{ else } F(x - 1, G(x, y)) * G(x, y)$$
$$G(x, y) \Leftarrow \text{if } x = y \text{ then } 1 \text{ else } G(x + 1, y + 1)$$

may produce different results by applying different computation rules if one assumes that $0 * G(x, y)$ is 0 even without computing $G(x, y)$. We leave the proof of this fact to the reader as an exercise.

However, the reader has probably realized that differences in the effects of computation rules occur only in rather "tricky" cases. In the following we support the claim that the various computation rules are, in fact, equivalent in nonpathological cases.

Exercises

4.17   Compute the values of the following recursive program for $F(1, 1)$, $F(2, 1)$, and $F(2, 2)$ by applying the aforementioned computation rules.

$$F(x, y) \Leftarrow \textbf{if } x = 0 \textbf{ then } 1$$
$$\textbf{else if } y = 0 \textbf{ then } 1$$
$$\textbf{else if } even(x) \textbf{ then } F(x - 2, F(x, y))$$
$$\textbf{else } F(x, F(x, y - 1))$$

where $even(x) = $ T if x is even, F otherwise.

4.18*   Provide examples that give different results under different computation rules. In particular, for any pair of comutation rules C, C' check whether there are P and v such that $f_C^P(v) \neq f_{C'}^P(v)$.

4.19*   There is an analogy between computation rules for McCarthy's formalism and parameter passing mechanisms for Pascal-like languages. The effect of a subprogram call may be different if call-by-value-result is used instead of call-by-reference. However, nonpathological programs have the same effect. Comment on this analogy and give the conditions under which call-by-reference and call-by-value result have the same effects.

Looking at McCarthy's formalism as a programming language, we see that any computation rule (i.e., operational semantics) results in an "abstract implementation" of the language. However, we are concerned with describing semantics of recursive programs by abstracting away from any particular implementation, in such a way that the meaning of the program does not depend on the mechanical details of computation rules, which may lead to different behaviors. Once semantics is described in an abstract way, particular implementations will be checked for correctness.

Once again, let us go back to the recursive program P computing the factorial function.

$FACT(x) \Leftarrow \tau[FACT](x)$
where $\tau[FACT](x)$ is
$\textbf{if } x = 0 \textbf{ then } 1 \textbf{ else } x * FACT(x - 1)$

Intuitively, we can interpret P as an equation, since τ can be seen as a transformation that maps a variable $FACT$ ranging over functions with domain $D = \mathbb{N}$ into another function $\tau[FACT]$ with the same domain. If we substitute in P the symbol "$\Leftarrow$" with the symbol "$=$", we obtain the equation

$$FACT(x) = \tau[FACT](x)$$

A solution of such an equation is a function f, with domain $\mathbb{N}$, such that $f(x) = \tau[f](x)$ for all x.

It is immediate to verify that the factorial function '!' is a solution of the above equation. In fact, $x!$ is

if $x = 0$ **then** 1 **else** $\displaystyle\prod_{i=1}^{x} i$

thus substituting $x!$ to $FACT(x)$ in the equation we obtain

if $x = 0$ **then** 1 **else** $\displaystyle\prod_{i=1}^{x} i = $ **if** $x = 0$ **then** 1

$$\textbf{else } x * \left(\textbf{if}(x - 1) = 0 \textbf{ then } 1 \textbf{ else } \prod_{i=1}^{x-1} i \right)$$

The first member of the equation can be decomposed as follows.

a. **if** $x = 0$ **then** 1

$\qquad\qquad\qquad\qquad\qquad b_1 :$ **if** $x = 1$ **then** 1

b. **if** $x > 0$ **then** $\displaystyle\prod_{i=1}^{x} i \ =$

$\qquad\qquad\qquad\qquad\qquad b_2 :$ **if** $x > 1$ **then** $\displaystyle\prod_{i=1}^{x} i$

The second member can be decomposed as follows

a′. **if** $x = 0$ **then** 1

$\qquad\qquad\qquad\qquad\qquad b_1' :$ **if** $x = 1$ **then** 1

b′. **if** $x > 0$ **then** $x *$

$\qquad\qquad\qquad\qquad\qquad b_2' :$ **if** $x > 1$ **then** $\displaystyle\prod_{i=1}^{x-1} i$

It is easy to verify that $a = a'$; simplification of $b'b_1'$ yields b_1, and simplification of $b'b_2'$ yields b_2. Thus '!' is a solution of the equation.

On the basis of this example it is quite tempting to define the semantics of a recursive program P in the following way.

1. Transform P into a system of equations S_P by simply substituting "$\Leftarrow$" with "$=$".
2. Define P's semantics as the solution (or *fixed point*) of S_P. The term "fixed point" is due to the fact that S_P has the form $F(x) = \tau[F](x)$ and f is a solution of S_P if and only if τ maps f into itself.

However, when dealing with equations, some care is always necessary in the use of terms like "the solution of the equation." We can talk about *the solution of S_P* only after proving that such solution *exists* and is *unique*. It is immediate to realize that, in general, this is not the case.

Example 4.8

1. Consider the following recursive program P.

$F(x, y) \Leftarrow \tau[F](x, y)$,
where $\tau[F](x, y)$ is defined as
if $x = y$ **then** 1 **else** $F(x - y, y)$

The associated S_P is

$F(x, y) =$ **if** $x = y$ **then** 1 **else** $F(x - y, y)$

As usual, assume that the unknown function has domain $\mathbb{N} \times \mathbb{N}$ and range $\mathbb{N}$. Any function of the type

$f_n(x, y) =$ **if** $\exists k(k \geq 1 \wedge x = k \cdot y)$ **then** 1 **else** n

is a solution of S_P. In fact,

$$\begin{aligned}
\tau[f_n](x, y) &= \textbf{if } x = y \textbf{ then } 1 \textbf{ else}\\
&\quad\quad \textbf{if } \exists k(k \geq 1 \wedge (x - y) = k \cdot y) \textbf{ then } 1 \textbf{ else } n\\
&= \textbf{if } x = y \textbf{ then } 1 \textbf{ else if } \exists k(k \geq 1 \wedge x = (k + 1)y) \textbf{ then } 1 \textbf{ else } n\\
&= \textbf{if } x = y \vee \exists k(k \geq 1 \wedge x = (k + 1)y) \textbf{ then } 1 \textbf{ else } n\\
&= \textbf{if } \exists k(k \geq 1 \wedge x = k \cdot y) \textbf{ then } 1 \textbf{ else } n\\
&= f_n(x, y)
\end{aligned}$$

Notice that computing the above P by means of any of the previous computation rules yields the function

$f(x, y) =$ **if** $\exists k(k \geq 1 \wedge x = k \cdot y)$ **then** 1 **else** $\perp$

which is a fixed point of S too (verify this claim as an exercise).

2. Let $\tau[F](x)$ be $F(x) + 1$ and $\rho[F](x)$ be $F(x)$. Then the equations

$F(x) = F(x) + 1 \quad$ and $\quad F(x) = F(x)$

have no solution and infinite solutions, respectively.

   However, observe that if we compute $F(x)$ by means of any computation rule, we obtain $F(x) = \perp$ for any $x \in \mathbb{N}$ in *both cases*. Thus, in some sense, we may conclude that the totally undefined function is a solution for both of them. This point will be made clear later.

3. Let $\tau[F_1, F_2](x)$ be defined as

$\tau_1[F_1, F_2](x) :$ **if** $\forall x(F_1(x) = F_2(x))$ **then** $F_2(x)$ **else** $F_2(x)$
$\tau_2[F_1, F_2](x) :$ **if** $\forall x(F_1(x) = F_2(x))$ **then** $F_1(x) + 1$ **else** $F_1(x)$

The corresponding S_P has no fixed point. In fact suppose by contradiction that a pair $\langle f_1(x), f_2(x) \rangle$ is a solution for it. If $f_1(x) = f_2(x)$ for all x then $f_1(x)$ is mapped by τ_1 into $f_2(x) = f_1(x)$ but $f_2(x)$ is mapped by τ_2 into $f_1(x) + 1 \neq f_1(x) = f_2(x)$. Thus f_2 is modified by τ_2. Instead, if f_1 and f_2 differ for some x, they are interchanged by τ_1, τ_2, that is, f_1 is transformed into f_2 (which differs from f_1) and conversely. Thus in no case a pair of functions is left unchanged by τ.

Exercise

4.20 Show that the equation

$F(x) = \tau[F](x)$ with
$\tau[F](x) :$ **if** $\forall x(F(x) = 1)$ **then** 0 **else** 1

has no fixed point. Instead, if $\tau[F](x)$ is defined as

if $\forall x(F(x) = 1)$ **then** 1 **else** 0

the equation has two fixed points, namely

$$f_1(x) = 1 \ \forall x \qquad \text{and} \qquad f_2(x) = 0 \ \forall x$$

The preceding examples show that, if we want to talk about fixed points as the semantics of recursive programs, some sound mathematical background must first be developed. The most classical and powerful tool to prove the existence and uniqueness of a solution for an equation in a given space is the concept of continuity, which has been used for centuries in the field of mathematical analysis. To be used here, however, the concept must be transferred from continuous to discrete spaces. In the next subsection we show how this can be done.

4.6.1.1 Mathematical Background

This section develops the necessary mathematical background that will enable the reader to understand how the semantics of a recursively defined program can be defined rigorously as the fixed point of a set of recursive equations. At a first reading, one may simply concentrate on the results of the theorems, without entering into the details of the proofs. Definitely, these must be studied later, in order to gain a deep and sound understanding of the concepts.

Definition 4.4
Let D_1, D_2 be two posets, with a reflexive relation $\subseteq$.
A function $f: D_1 \rightarrow D_2$ is said to be *monotonic* if and only if, for any $x, y \in D_1$, $x \subseteq y$ implies $f(x) \subseteq f(y)$. $\qquad \square$

Quite often, we deal with natural numbers. The usual order relation $\leq$ on $\mathbb{N}$, however, is not good for us. In fact, we realize that for our purposes it is crucial that all considered functions be monotonic. Therefore, if we assume the usual $\leq$ relation on $\mathbb{N}$ as $\subseteq$, we would rule out functions as

$$f(x) = 10 - 3x + x^2$$

Therefore, we will use a standard type of posets, as shown in the following definition.

Definition 4.5
Let D be any set $D\hat{}$ denotes the poset obtained as $D\hat{} = D \cup \{\bot\}$, $\bot \notin D$ being called the *undefined element*. $\subseteq$ is defined on $D\hat{}$ by

$\bot \subseteq x$ for all x
$x \subseteq x$ for all x
$x \not\subseteq y$ for all x with $x \neq \bot$, $x \neq y$

For $D = D_1 \times D_2$, $\subseteq$ is extended to $D\hat{}_1 \times D\hat{}_2$ by

$$\langle x_1, x_2 \rangle \subseteq \langle y_1, y_2 \rangle$$

if and only if $x_1 \subseteq y_1$ and $x_2 \subseteq y_2$. $\square$

Notice that $(D_1 \times D_2)\hat{} \neq D\hat{}_1 \times D\hat{}_2$

By the use of $D\hat{}$, most useful functions can be made monotonic, as we will see shortly. Also, any partial function $f: D \to R$ can be extended in a natural way to a total function

$$f\hat{} : D\hat{} \to R\hat{}$$

by letting $f\hat{}(\bot) = \bot$, $f\hat{}(x) = \bot$ whenever $f(x)$ is undefined. However, on the basis of the results of Chapter 2, recall that this extension can transform a computable partial function f into a noncomputable total function $f\hat{}$. In the following, we use the notation f instead of $f\hat{}$ in order to make formulas not too cumbersome. Furthermore, the notation $[D\hat{}_1 \times \cdots \times D\hat{}_k \to R\hat{}]$ will denote the set of all monotonic functions $f: D\hat{}_1 \times \cdots \times D\hat{}_k \to R\hat{}$.

Definition 4.6
A function $f: D\hat{}_1 \times D\hat{}_2 \times \cdots \times D\hat{}_k \to R\hat{}$ is said to be *naturally extended* (it is called a *natural extension*) if and only if $f(x_1, x_2, \ldots, x_k) = \bot$ if at least one x_i is $\bot$. $\square$

In the following, the notation $D\hat{}$ will be an abbreviation for $D\hat{}_1 \times D\hat{}_2 \cdots D\hat{}_k$; $x, y, z, \ldots$ will denote elements of $D\hat{}$. The following statement gives a first important and simple property of naturally extended functions.

Theorem 4.1
Every naturally extended function is monotonic.

Proof
Let $f : D_1^{\hat{}} \times \cdots \times D_n^{\hat{}} \to R^{\hat{}}$ be naturally extended and $\langle x_1, \ldots, x_n \rangle \subseteq \langle y_1 \cdots y_n \rangle$. Now, if $x_i \neq \perp$ for all i, then $x_i = y_i$, for all i, $\langle x_1, \ldots, x_n \rangle = \langle y_1, \ldots, y_n \rangle$, $f(x_1, \ldots, x_n) = f(y_1, \ldots, y_n)$ and thus $f(x_1, \ldots, x_n) \subseteq f(y_1, \ldots, y_n)$. If for some i, $x_i = \perp$, then $f(x_1, \ldots, x_n) = \perp \subseteq f(y_1, \ldots, y_n)$ whatever $f(y_1, \ldots, y_n)$ is. ∎

Example 4.9

1. $D_1 = D_2 = \mathbb{Z}$ (integer numbers), $R = \mathbb{R}$ (rational numbers), and let $f : \mathbb{Z} \times \mathbb{Z} \to \mathbb{R}$ be the quotient function. f can be made a total function: $\mathbb{Z}^{\hat{}} \times \mathbb{Z}^{\hat{}} \to \mathbb{R}^{\hat{}}$ by letting $(x/0) = \perp$, and monotonic by letting $\perp/y = x/\perp = \perp \; \forall x, y \in \mathbb{Z}$.
2. For any D, the usual equality $= : D \times D \to \{T, F\}$ is naturally extended by

   $x = y$ is T if $x \neq \perp$, $y \neq \perp$, and $x = y$
   $x = y$ is F if $x \neq \perp$, $y \neq \perp$, and $x \neq y$
   $x = y$ is $\perp$ if either x or y is $\perp$

   Such a natural extension is also called *weak equality*.
   Notice that the so called *strong equality* defined by
   $x \equiv y$ is T if $(x \neq \perp$, $y \neq \perp$, and $x = y)$ or $(x = \perp$ and $y = \perp)$
   $x \equiv y$ is F otherwise,
   is not monotonic since for $y \neq \perp$, $\langle \perp, y \rangle \subseteq \langle y, y \rangle$;
   but $\perp \equiv y$ is F, whereas $y \equiv y$ is T.
3. For $D_1 = \{T, F\}$, $D_2 = D_3 = R = \mathbb{R}$
   the usual **if-then-else** function is given by

   (if T then x **else** y**)** $= x$
   (if F then x **else** y**)** $= y$ for any x and y

   Its natural extension would make the function

   if $x = 0$ **then** 1 **else** $1/x$

   undefined for $x = 0$.

The previous example shows that the natural extension of the **if-then-else** function is almost useless, not only from a mathematical point of view (e.g., recall its use in Example 4.5 on McCarthy's formalism), but even in the practice of programming as it is often used just to discriminate between the usual (normal) case and the exceptional (anomalous) case. For example, consider the following fragment of a Pascal program

if $x \neq 0$ **then** $t := y/x$ **else** *write* 'division by 0'

The intended effect of this statement is to warn the programmer about an illegal division by zero; however it would have an undefined semantics if we assume the natural extension of **if-then-else**. Fortunately, the **if-then-else** function can be extended to $\{T, F\}^{\wedge} \times \mathbb{R}^{\wedge} \times \mathbb{R}^{\wedge} \to \mathbb{R}^{\wedge}$ in a more useful way, still preserving the critical property of being monotonic. In the following, for any D, the function **if-then-else**: $\{T, F\}^{\wedge} \times D^{\wedge} \times D^{\wedge} \to D^{\wedge}$ will be defined by

if T **then** x **else** $y = x$ for any x and y, whether defined or not
if F **then** x **else** $y = y$ for any x and y, whether defined or not
if $\perp$ **then** x **else** $y = \perp$ for any x and y

The above **if-then-else** function is monotonic. In fact,

$\langle \perp, x, y \rangle \subseteq \langle T, x, y \rangle$ for all x, y and **if** $\perp$ **then** x **else** $y = \perp \subseteq$
  if T **then** x **else** $y = x$ for all x, y

$\langle \perp, x, y \rangle \subseteq \langle F, x, y \rangle$ for all x, y and **if** $\perp$ **then** x **else** $y = \perp \subseteq$
  if F **then** x **else** $y = y$ for all x, y

$\langle T, \perp, y \rangle \subseteq \langle T, x, y \rangle$ for all x, y and **if** T **then** $\perp$ **else** $y = \perp \subseteq$
  if T **then** x **else** $y = x$ for all x, y

$\langle T, x, \perp \rangle \subseteq \langle T, x, y \rangle$ for all x, y and **if** T **then** x **else** $\perp = x \subseteq$
  if T **then** x **else** $y = x$ for all x, y

The verification of the remaining cases is left to the reader as an exercise.

From now on, unless otherwise explicitly stated, we implicitly assume that the **if-then-else** function is extended as above to a monotonic function; constant functions are extended to monotonic functions by letting $f(\perp) = k = f(x)$ for any x; all other functions are assumed as naturally extended. Monotonic functions exhibit several nice mathematical properties, as shown by the statements below.

Theorem 4.2
Let $f: D_1^{\wedge} \to D_2^{\wedge}$, $g: D_2^{\wedge} \to D_3^{\wedge}$ be two monotonic functions, then the *composite function* $g \circ f: D_1^{\wedge} \to D_3^{\wedge}$ given by $g \circ f(x) = g(f(x))$ is a monotonic function.

Proof
Since f is monotonic $x \subseteq y$ implies $f(x) \subseteq f(y)$, which in turn implies $g(f(x)) \subseteq g(f(y))$. ∎

The following theorem proves distributivity of monotonic functions over the **if-then-else** function.

Theorem 4.3
Let $p: D^{\wedge} \to \{T, F\}^{\wedge}$, $h, h_2: D^{\wedge} \to D_1^{\wedge}$ and $g: D_1^{\wedge} \to D_2^{\wedge}$ be monotonic functions. Then, for all x, with $x \in D^{\wedge}$

$g(\textbf{if } p(x) \textbf{ then } h_1(x) \textbf{ else } h_2(x)) \subseteq$
  if $p(x)$ **then** $g(h_1(x))$ **else** $g(h_2(x))$

Furthermore, if $g(\perp) = \perp$, the two preceding members are identical functions (i.e., the two functions give strongly equal values for all $x \in D^{\wedge}$). ∎

Exercises

4.21 Prove Theorem 4.3 ...

4.22 Let $f_1, f_2, h_1, h_2 : D^\wedge \to R^\wedge$ be monotonic functions. Are the functions g_1, g_2, g_3 defined by

$g_1(x)$: **if** $f_1(x) \equiv f_2(x)$ **then** $h_1(x)$ **else** $h_2(x)$
$g_2(x)$: **if** $f_1(x) \equiv f_2(x)$ **then** $f_1(x)$ **else** $f_2(x)$
$g_3(x)$: **if** $f_1(x) \equiv f_2(x)$ **then** $f_2(x)$ **else** $h_1(x)$

monotonic? (Recall that $\equiv$ denotes strong equality; also, recall footnote 5).

The next step towards the goal of defining a denotational semantics for recursive programs leads to the notion of the least upper bound of a chain of functions.

Definition 4.7
Let f and g be two functions in $[D^\wedge \to R^\wedge]$. $f \subseteq g$ (read "f is less defined than g") denotes that for any $x \in D^\wedge$, $f(x) \subseteq g(x)$. $f \equiv g$ denotes that $f \subseteq g$ and $g \subseteq f$. □

Obviously, $f \equiv g$ if and only if $f(x) \equiv g(x)$ for every $x \in D^\wedge$. Also, $f \equiv g$ if and only if $f = g$, that is they are the same function. For any D and R let us define by convention the *undefined function* $\Omega : D^\wedge \to R^\wedge$ as $\Omega(x) = \bot$ for all $x \in D^\wedge$. Obviously, Ω is monotonic and $\Omega \subseteq f$ for any $f \in [D^\wedge \to R^\wedge]$.

Definition 4.8
Let $\{ f_i | i = 0, 1, 2, \ldots \}$ be a sequence of functions in $[D^\wedge \to R^\wedge]$

1. $\{ f_i \}$ is called a *chain* if and only if for all i, $f_i \subseteq f_{i+1}$.
2. $f \in [D^\wedge \to R^\wedge]$ is called an *upper bound* (UB) of $\{ f_i \}$ if and only if for any i, $f_i \subseteq f$.
3. An upper bound f of a chain $\{ f_i \}$ is called *the least upper bound* denoted as LUB $\{ f_i \}$ if and only if for any UB g of $\{ f_i \}$, $f \subseteq g$. □

Obviously, if a LUB exists for a chain $\{ f_i \}$, it is unique.

Theorem 4.4
Every chain $\{ f_i \}$ has a least upper bound.

Proof
Let $x \in D^\wedge$. Consider the sequence $\{ f_i(x) | i = 0, 1, 2 \ldots \}$. It is true that $f_i(x) \subseteq f_{i+1}(x)$ for any i with $i \geq 0$. Thus either

a. $f_i(x) \equiv \bot$ for all i, or
b. there exist an integer $\bar{i}$ and a $y \in R^\wedge$ such that $f_i(x) \equiv y$ for all $i \geq \bar{i}$ and $y \neq \bot$ (i.e., $y \in R$).

Thus, let us define $f(x) = \perp$ in case a, $f(x) = y$ in case b. Clearly, $f \in [D^\wedge \to R^\wedge]$. In fact, let $x_1 \subseteq x_2$. If $f(x_1) \equiv \perp$, then obviously $f(x_1) \subseteq f(x_2)$. If $f(x_1) \equiv y \neq \perp$, then there exists an i such that $f_i(x_1) \equiv y$ for all $i \geq i$. Thus, $f_i(x_2) \equiv y$ for $i \geq i$ and $f(x_2) \equiv y$.

Note that f is an UB of $\{f_i\}$ since for all i and x, $f_i(x) \subseteq f(x)$. Also, f is the LUB of $\{f_i\}$. In fact, suppose that there exists a $g \in [D^\wedge \to R^\wedge]$ such that $f_i \subseteq g$ for all i. For any x if $f(x) \equiv \perp$, then clearly $f(x) \subseteq g(x)$. If $f(x) \equiv y \neq \perp$, then $f_i(x) \equiv y$ for some i. So $f(x) \equiv y \equiv f_i(x) \subseteq g(x)$. ∎

Example 4.10

1. Consider the set of functions $\{f_i\}$, $f_i \in [\mathbb{N}^\wedge \to \mathbb{N}^\wedge]$, defined by

   $f_i(x)$: **if** $x < i$ **then** $x!$ **else** $\perp$.

   Clearly, it is true that $f_i \subseteq f_{i+1}$; thus $\{f_i\}$ is a chain. The LUB of $\{f_i\}$ is the factorial function '!' In fact, for any i, $f_i(x) \subseteq x!$. On the other hand let $g : \mathbb{N}^\wedge \to \mathbb{N}^\wedge$ be such that $f_i \subseteq g$ for all i. For any x there is an i such that $x! = f_i(x) \subseteq g(x)$. Thus $! \subseteq g$.

2. Let $D = V_T^*$, $V_T = \{a, b\}$.
   Consider functions $f_i : (V_T^*)^\wedge \to \{T, F\}^\wedge$ defined as

   $f_i(x)$: **if** $|x| \leq 2i$ **then if** $\exists k\ (0 \leq k \leq i \wedge x = a^k b^k)$ **then** T **else** F
   $\qquad\qquad$ **else** $\perp$

   $\{f_i\}$ is a chain and LUB $\{f_i\}$ is the characteristic function of the language $L = \{a^n b^n | n \geq 0\}$.

Exercise

4.23 Let f_i be an n-tuple of functions $f_i = \langle f_{i1}, \ldots, f_{in} \rangle$. Prove that for a given chain $\{f_i\}$ if $\bar{f} = \text{LUB}\{f_i\}$ then $\bar{f} = \langle \bar{f}_1, \ldots, \bar{f}_n \rangle$, and $\bar{f}_h = \text{LUB}\{f_{ih}\}$, for $h = 1, \ldots, n$.

The LUB f of a chain $\{f_i\}$ can be seen as the *limit* of the sequence $\{f_i\}$, each f_i being an approximation of f. The function f_{i+1} is a better approximation than f_i, where "better" means it is more defined. Here is the peculiarity of fixed point theory: The measure we use to compare functions is their degree of definition, not the usual metrics of vector spaces used in mathematical analysis.

Notice that Theorem 4.4 does not state anything about computability of LUB $\{f_i\}$. Actually, it may be the case that

a. the functions f_i are computable for every i, and
b. the enumeration of $\{f_i\}$ is effective

but LUB $\{f_i\}$ is not computable since this would require a decision procedure to state whether or not $f_i(x)$ is defined for any i and x. This fact does not matter here, because presently we are concerned just with the existence of a solution of a set of equations, not on computability issues.

We now proceed to discussing function transformations.

Definition 4.9

An *operator*[7] τ is a mapping from a given family of monotonic functions $[D\hat{\ } \rightarrow R\hat{\ }]^n$ into itself.   □

Example 4.11

1. Consider the recursive program P of Example 4.8.1. It defines an operator $\tau : [\mathbb{N}\hat{\ } \times \mathbb{N}\hat{\ } \rightarrow \mathbb{N}\hat{\ }] \rightarrow [\mathbb{N}\hat{\ } \times \mathbb{N}\hat{\ } \rightarrow \mathbb{N}\hat{\ }]$, defined as

   $\tau[F](x, y)$: **if** $x = y$ **then** 1 **else** $F(x - y, y)$

   For instance, let $f(x, y)$ be $x * y$. Then $\tau[f](x, y)$ is

   if $x = y$ **then** 1 **else** $(x - y) * y$

2. The operators corresponding to τ and ρ of Example 4.8.2 are, respectively, "add 1" (i.e., $\tau[f](x)$ is $f(x) + 1$ and "identity" (i.e., $\rho[f]$ coincides with f for any f).
3. The operator τ of Example 4.8.3 transforms any pair of functions $\langle f_1, f_2 \rangle \in [\mathbb{N}\hat{\ } \rightarrow \mathbb{N}\hat{\ }]^2$ into the pair $\langle h_1, h_2 \rangle$ defined by $h_1(x) = f_2(x)$, $h_2(x) = f_1(x) + 1$, if f_1 and f_2 are identically equal. It exchanges the two functions if they differ. Notice that $\tau[f_1, f_2](x) \equiv \langle \perp, \perp \rangle$ whenever at least *one* of $f_1(x)$, $f_2(x)$ is undefined. If strong equality is used instead of weak equality, $\tau[f_1, f_2](x) \equiv \langle \perp, \perp \rangle$ if and only if both $f_1(x)$ and $f_2(x)$ are undefined.

Definition 4.10

1. An operator $\tau : [D\hat{\ } \rightarrow R\hat{\ }]^n \rightarrow [D\hat{\ } \rightarrow R\hat{\ }]^n$ is said to be *monotonic* if and only if $f \subseteq g$ implies $\tau[f] \subseteq \tau[g]$.[8]
2. A monotonic operator τ over $[D\hat{\ } \rightarrow R\hat{\ }]^n$ is said to be *continuous* if and only if for any chain $\{f_i\}$ in $[D\hat{\ } \rightarrow R\hat{\ }]^n$ $\tau[\text{LUB}\{f_i\}] \equiv \text{LUB}\{\tau[f_i]\}$.   □

Note that Definition 4.10.2 is well defined since $\{f_i\}$ is a chain.

---

[7]In the literature, this concept is often called a *functional*.
[8]The relation $\subseteq$ over $[D\hat{\ } \rightarrow R\hat{\ }]^n$ is the natural extension of $\subseteq$ over $[D\hat{\ } \rightarrow R\hat{\ }]$, that is, $f = \langle f_1, \ldots, f_n \rangle \subseteq g = \langle g_1, \ldots, g_n \rangle$ if and only if $f_1 \subseteq g_1, \ldots, f_n \subseteq g_n$.

Example 4.12

1. Let τ be the identity operator, that is, $\tau[F](x)$ is $F(x)$. τ is both monotonic and continuous. In fact, $f \subseteq g$ implies $\tau[f] = f \subseteq g \equiv \tau[g]$ and $\text{LUB}\{\tau[f_i]\} \equiv \text{LUB}\{f_i\} \equiv \tau[\text{LUB}\{f_i\}]$.

2. The constant operator $\tau[F]: h$, for any F, is both monotonic and continuous.

3. Let $\tau = \langle \tau_1, \tau_2 \rangle : [\mathbb{N}^{\wedge} \to \mathbb{N}^{\wedge}]^2 \to [\mathbb{N}^{\wedge} \to \mathbb{N}^{\wedge}]^2$ be defined by

   $\tau_1[F, G](x)$: **if** $x = 0$ **then** 1 **else** $F(x - 1) * G(x - 2)$
   $\tau_2[F, G](x)$: **if** $x = 1$ **then** 1 **else** $F(x - 2) * G(x - 1)$

   τ is monotonic. In fact, for $f_1 \subseteq f_2$, $g_1 \subseteq g_2$

   $\tau_1[f_1, g_1](x) \equiv$ **if** $x = 0$ **then** 1 **else** $f_1(x - 1) * g_1(x - 2) \subseteq$
   $\subseteq$ **if** $x = 0$ **then** 1 **else** $f_2(x - 1) * g_2(x - 2) \equiv \tau_1[f_2, g_2](x)$

   $\tau_2[f_1, g_1](x) \equiv$ **if** $x = 1$ **then** 1 **else** $f_1(x - 2) * g_1(x - 1) \subseteq$
   $\subseteq$ **if** $x = 1$ **then** 1 **else** $f_2(x - 2) * g_2(x - 1) \equiv \tau_2[f_2, g_2](x)$

   Observe now that

   3.1 $\text{LUB}\{\langle f_i, g_i \rangle\} \equiv \langle \text{LUB}\{f_i\}, \text{LUB}\{g_i\} \rangle$ (see Exercise 4.23).
   3.2 $\text{LUB}\{f_i * g_i\} \equiv \text{LUB}\{f_i\} * \text{LUB}\{g_i\}$.

   In fact, for any x, there exist i_1, i_2, and i_3 such that $\text{LUB}\{f_i * g_i\}(x) \equiv$
   $f_{i_1}(x) * g_{i_1}(x)$, $\text{LUB}\{f_i\}(x) \equiv f_{i_2}(x)$, and $\text{LUB}\{g_i\}(x) \equiv g_{i_3}(x)$.
   Let $i = \max\{i_1, i_2, i_3\}$. Thus
   $\text{LUB}\{f_i * g_i\}(x) \equiv f_i(x) * g_i(x) \equiv \text{LUB}\{f_i\}(x) * \text{LUB}\{g_i\}(x)$
   On the basis of 3.1 and 3.2, τ can be proved continuous. In fact
   $\text{LUB}\{\tau[\langle f_i, g_i \rangle]\}(x) \equiv \langle \text{LUB}\{\tau_1[\langle f_i, g_i \rangle]\}(x), \text{LUB}\{\tau_2[\langle f_i, g_i \rangle]\}(x) \rangle$

   $\equiv \langle$ **if** $x = 0$ **then** 1 **else** $\text{LUB}\{f_i(x - 1) * g_i(x - 2)\}$,[9]
   if $x = 1$ **then** 1 **else** $\text{LUB}\{f_i(x - 2) * g_i(x - 1)\}\rangle$

   $\equiv \langle$ **if** $x = 0$ **then** 1 **else** $\text{LUB}\{f_i(x - 1)\} * \text{LUB}(g_i(x - 2)\}$,
   if $x = 1$ **then** 1 **else** $\text{LUB}\{f_i(x - 2)\} * \text{LUB}\{g_i(x - 1)\rangle$

   $\equiv \langle$ **if** $x = 0$ **then** 1 **else** $\text{LUB}\{f_i\}(x - 1) * \text{LUB}\{g_i\}(x - 2)$,
   if $x = 1$ **then** 1 **else** $\text{LUB}\{f_i\}(x - 2) * \text{LUB}\{g_i\}(x - 1)\rangle$

   $\equiv \tau[\text{LUB}\{\langle f_i, g_i \rangle\}](x)$.

4. Let $\tau = \langle \tau_1, \tau_2 \rangle : [\mathbb{N}^{\wedge} \to \mathbb{N}^{\wedge}]^2 \to [\mathbb{N}^{\wedge} \to \mathbb{N}^{\wedge}]^2$ be defined by

   $\tau_1[F, G](x)$: **if** $F(x) \equiv G(x)$ **then** 1 **else** 0
   $\tau_2[F, G](x): 0$

   τ is not monotonic. In fact, let

   $f_1(x) \equiv g_1(x) \equiv \bot$, $f_2(x) \equiv a$, $g_2(x) \equiv b$, $a \neq b$, $a, b \neq \bot$

   Thus, $\langle f_1, g_1 \rangle(x) \subseteq \langle f_2, g_2 \rangle(x)$.
   However, $\tau_1[f_1, g_1](x) \equiv 1 \not\subseteq \tau_1[f_2, g_2](x) \equiv 0$.

---

[9] This is a short notation for "$\text{LUB}\{h_i\}(x)$, where h_i is defined by $h_i(x) = f_i(x - 1) * g_i(x - 2)$."

5. Let $\sigma : [\mathbb{N}^{\hat{}} \to \mathbb{N}^{\hat{}}] \to [\mathbb{N}^{\hat{}} \to \mathbb{N}^{\hat{}}]$ be defined by

$\sigma[F](x)$: **if** $\forall y \ (y \in \mathbb{N} \supset F(y) = 0)$ **then** 0 **else** $\perp$.

σ is monotonic but not continuous. In fact,

5.1 If $f(y) = 0$ for any $y \in \mathbb{N}$ and $f \subseteq g$, then
$g(y) = 0$ for any $y \in \mathbb{N}$ and thus
$\sigma[f](x) = 0 = \sigma[g](x)$ for every $x \in \mathbb{N}$; otherwise
$\sigma[f](x) = \perp \subseteq \sigma[g](x)$ for any x

5.2 Let $\{f_i\}$ be a sequence of functions, where f_i is defined as $f_i(x)$: **if** $x < i$ **then** 0 **else** $\perp$. Clearly LUB $\{f_i\}$ is the constant function 0 (naturally extended). But $\sigma[0](x) = 0$, while $\sigma[f_i] = \Omega$ for any i and LUB $\{\sigma[f_i]\} = \Omega$.

6. $\tau[F](x)$: **if** $F(x)$ is computable (i.e., there exists a TM computing $F(x)$ whenever $F(x) \neq \perp$) **then** 1 **else** 0, is not monotonic since there exist functions f and g, with $f \subseteq g$, f computable and g noncomputable.

Exercises

4.24 Discuss the case of Example 4.12.4 when strong equality is replaced by weak equality.

4.25 Consider the following operators.

$\tau_1[F](x)$: **if** $F(x) = 0$ **then** 1 **else** 0

$\tau_2[F](x)$: **if** $F(x) = 0$ **then** 0 **else** 1

State whether they are monotonic and continuous.

The previous examples could have given the wrong impression that operators are most likely to be noncontinuous and nonmonotonic. However, observe that all the examples we have given of noncontinuous or nonmonotonic operators used "heavy predicates" on the function variable F. Fortunately, we can show that a large class of operators of practical utility are continuous thanks to the following theorem.

Theorem 4.5
Any operator τ defined by composition of monotonic functions and function variables F_i is continuous.

Proof *
The proof is by induction on the structure of

$\tau[F] = \langle \tau_1[F], \ldots, \tau_n[F] \rangle$, where $F = \langle F_1, \ldots, F_n \rangle$

Basis

Let τ be $\langle \tau_1, \ldots, \tau_n \rangle$, τ_i being either a function $f_i \in [D^{\wedge} \to R^{\wedge}]$, or a variable function F_i ranging over $[D^{\wedge} \to R^{\wedge}]$. Then τ is clearly continuous (see Examples 4.12.1 and 4.12.2).

Induction step

Let $\tau = \langle \tau_1, \ldots, \tau_n \rangle$, with either

1. $\tau_i = f_i(\tau_{i1}[F], \ldots, \tau_{im}[F])$ or
2. $\tau_i = F_i(\tau_{i1}[F], \ldots, \tau_{im}[F])$

in both cases τ_{ij} being continuous operators

$$\tau_{ij} : [D^{\wedge} \to R^{\wedge}]^n \to [D^{\wedge} \to R^{\wedge}]$$

In order to prove the thesis we need to show that, in both cases, every τ_i is continuous.

First let us show that every τ_i is monotonic. Let $g \subseteq h$ and $g, h \in [D^{\wedge} \to R^{\wedge}]^n$. Thus, in case 1 we have $\tau_i[g] = f_i(\tau_{i1}[g], \ldots, \tau_{im}[g])$. Since all τ_{ij} are continuous $\tau_{ij}[g] \subseteq \tau_{ij}[h]$ for every i, and j. Since f_i is monotonic, $f_i(\tau_{i1}[g], \ldots, \tau_{im}[g]) \subseteq f_i(\tau_{i1}[h], \ldots, \tau_{im}[h]) = \tau_i[h]$. Thus $\tau_i[g] \subseteq \tau_i[h]$.
In case 2, we have $\tau_i[g] = g_i(\tau_{i1}[g], \ldots, \tau_{im}[g]) \subseteq g_i(\tau_{i1}[h], \ldots, \tau_{im}[h]) \subseteq h_i(\tau_{i1}[h], \ldots, \tau_{im}[h]) = \tau_i[h]$. Again, $\tau_i[g] \subseteq \tau_i[h]$.

Second, let us show that for every chain $\{h_r | h_r \in [D^{\wedge} \to R^{\wedge}]^n\}$, $\text{LUB}\{\tau_i[h_r]\} \subseteq \tau_i[\text{LUB}\{h_r\}]$. Since $h_r \subseteq \text{LUB}\{h_r\}$ for any r and τ_i is monotone, $\tau_i[h_r] \subseteq \tau_i[\text{LUB}\{h_r\}]$ for any r. Thus $\tau[\text{LUB}\{h_r\}]$ is an UB of $\{\tau_i[h_r]\}$ and therefore $\text{LUB}\{\tau_i[h_r]\} \subseteq \tau[\text{LUB}\{h_r\}]$.

Finally, let us show that for every chain $\{h_r\}$, $\tau_i[\text{LUB}\{h_r\}] \subseteq \text{LUB}\{\tau_i[h_r]\}$. Let $x \in D^{\wedge}$ and let $\bar{h}$ be $\text{LUB}\{h_r\} = \langle \bar{h}_1, \ldots, \bar{h}_n \rangle$. In case 1 we have $\tau_i[\bar{h}](x) \equiv f_i(\tau_{i1}[\bar{h}](x), \ldots, \tau_{im}[\bar{h}](x)) \equiv f_i(\text{LUB}\{\tau_{i1}[h_r]\}(x), \ldots, \text{LUB}\{\tau_{im}[h_r]\}(x))$ since all τ_{ij} are continuous.
In case 2 we have $\tau_i[\bar{h}](x) \equiv \bar{h}_i(\text{LUB}\{\tau_{i1}[h_r]\}(x), \ldots, \text{LUB}\{\tau_{im}[h_r]\}(x))$.
Since all τ_{ij} are continuous, $\{\tau_{ij}[h_r]\}$ is a chain for every j, thus there exists an $\bar{r}$ such that $\text{LUB}\{\tau_{ij}[h_r]\}(x) \equiv \tau_{ij}[h_{\bar{r}}](x)$ for every j. (See the proof of Theorem 4.4.)
Thus in case 1 we obtain

$$\tau_i[\bar{h}](x) \equiv f_i(\tau_{ij}[h_{\bar{r}}](x), \ldots, \tau_{im}[h_{\bar{r}}](x))$$
$$\equiv f_i(\tau_{ij}[h_{\bar{r}}], \ldots, \tau_{im}[h_{\bar{r}}])(x) \equiv \tau_i[h_{\bar{r}}](x) \subseteq \text{LUB}\{\tau_i[h_r]\}(x)$$

since $h_{\bar{r}} \subseteq h_r$ for every $r \geq \bar{r}$ and τ_i is monotonic.
In case 2 we obtain $\tau_i[\bar{h}](x) \equiv \bar{h}_i(\tau_{i1}[h_{\bar{r}}](x), \ldots, \tau_{im}[h_{\bar{r}}](x))$.
Now let y be $\langle \tau_{i1}[h_{\bar{r}}](x), \ldots, \tau_{im}[h_{\bar{r}}](x) \rangle$. There exists $\tilde{r} > \bar{r}$ such that $\bar{h}_i(y) \equiv h_{\tilde{r}, i}(y)$ (See Exercise 4.23.) So $\tau_i[\bar{h}](x) \equiv h_{\tilde{r}, i}(\tau_{i1}[h_{\bar{r}}](x), \ldots, \tau_{im}[h_{\bar{r}}](x)) \equiv \tau_i[h_{\bar{r}}](x) \subseteq \text{LUB}\{\tau_i[h_r]\}(x)$.
The proof is completed by the remark that the above relation holds in both cases 1 and 2 for any $x \in D^{\wedge}$. ∎

Corollary 4.6
Let P be a recursive program together with an interpretation $\langle \{ S_i \}, \mathscr{I}_x, \mathscr{I}_f, \mathscr{I}_F \rangle$. An operator τ is naturally associated to P by

a. Extending $\mathscr{I}_f(f_i)$ in the usual way (i.e., by defining a natural extension for all functions except for the **if-then-else** and the constant functions).
b. Composing functions $\tilde{f}_i$ and function variables F_i according to the terms τ_i.

Then τ is a continuous operator.

Proof
Only the composition is used to define τ. $\qquad\qquad\qquad\qquad\qquad\qquad$ □

At this point we are ready for the key statements of fixed point theory and their use to give a denotational semantics to McCarthy's formalism.

4.6.1.2 Denotational semantics of McCarthy's formalism

Definition 4.11

1. Let τ be an operator over $[D^\wedge \to R^\wedge]^n$. An n-tuple of functions $f = \langle f_1, \ldots, f_n \rangle$ in $[D^\wedge \to R^\wedge]^n$ is called a *fixed point* (FP) of τ if and only if $\tau[f] \equiv f$.
2. A fixed point f of operator τ is its *least fixed point* (LFP) if and only if for any g, $\tau[g] \equiv g$ implies $f \subseteq g$. $\qquad\qquad\qquad\qquad\qquad\qquad$ □

Obviously, if τ has a least fixed point f, then f is its *only* least fixed point.

Example 4.13

Consider the operators obtained from the recursive programs of Example 4.8.

1. All functions f_n are FP of τ.
   The LFP of τ is the function f given by
   $f(x, y)$: **if** $\exists k (k \geq 1 \wedge x = k \cdot y)$ **then** 1 **else** $\perp$.
   In fact, let g be a FP of τ. Then, consider $\tau[g](k \cdot y, y)$ for any $k \geq 1$. Since g is a FP of τ it must be
   $$\tau[g](k \cdot y, y) \equiv g((k-1)y, y) \equiv \ldots g((k-(k-1))y, y) \equiv g(y, y) \equiv 1.$$
   Thus, $f(x, y) \subseteq g(x, y)$ for any x and y.
2. The undefined function Ω given by $\Omega(x) \equiv \perp$ for any x is a FP of both τ and ρ defined by $\tau[F](x)$: $F(x) + 1$ and $\rho[F](x)$: $F(x)$. As a consequence, Ω is also their LFP. This confirms what we anticipated in Example 4.8.2.
3. The third operator of Example 4.8 has no fixed point, as we anticipated.
4. The operator τ given by $\tau[F](x)$: **if** $F(x) \equiv 0$ **then** 0 **else** 1 has two fixed points f_1 and f_2 where f_1 is the constant function 1 and f_2 is the constant function 0, but has no least fixed point. Notice that τ is not monotonic.

Exercise

4.26 Let F range over $[(\{a, b\}*)^\wedge \to \{0, 1\}^\wedge]$. Find the LFP, if any, of the operator τ given by

$\tau[F](x)$: **if** $x = ab$ **then** 1
 else if $\exists y\, (x = ayb)$ **then** $F(y)$
  else 0

The following theorem, which is known as *Kleene's Recursion Theorem*, is the central result of fixed-point theory.

Theorem 4.7

Every continuous operator τ has a unique least fixed point f_τ. $f_\tau \equiv \mathrm{LUB}\,\{\tau^i[\Omega]\}$. ($\tau^i[f]$ is defined as usual by: $\tau^0[f] \equiv f$, $\tau^{i+1}[f] \equiv \tau[\tau^i[f]]$).

Proof

First notice that f_τ is well defined since τ is continuous and therefore $\{\tau^i[\Omega]\}$ is a chain. Let us show that f_τ is a fixed point of τ.

$$\tau[f_\tau] \equiv \tau\big[\mathrm{LUB}\,\{\tau^i[\Omega]\}\big] \equiv \mathrm{LUB}\,\{\tau^{i+1}[\Omega]\} \equiv \mathrm{LUB}\,\{\tau^i[\Omega]\} \equiv f_\tau$$

We show that $f_\tau \subseteq g$, g being any fixed point of τ. $\tau^i[\Omega] \subseteq g$ for any i. In fact, $\Omega \subseteq g$ and if $\tau^i[\Omega] \subseteq g$, then $\tau[\tau^i[\Omega]] \subseteq \tau[g] \equiv g$. So g is an UB of $\{\tau^i[\Omega]\}$ and therefore $f_\tau \subseteq g$. ∎

Finally, we have a tool to attach a denotational semantics to McCarthy's formalism. Given a recursive program P, P uniquely defines an operator τ over a suitable function space. τ is guaranteed to have a unique least fixed point f_τ. Thus we may assume f_τ as P's semantics. P *denotes*, by means of τ, the function f_τ.[10]

Let us check our new semantic tool by means of some examples. The least fixed point (LFP) of τ given by

$\tau[F](x)$: **if** $x = 0$ **then** 1 **else** $x * F(x - 1)$

is $x!$. This is exactly the same function computed by

$P: F(x) \Leftarrow$ **if** $x = 0$ **then** 1 **else** $x * F(x - 1)$

through any computation rule.
The same holds for the following recursive programs, which are left to be verified as exercises.

---

[10] Obviously a standard choice of base functions f—and of their interpretation—guarantees that the set of obtainable f_τ coincides with the set of computable functions. (See Appendix 4.A.)

Exercise

4.27 Compute the LFP of the following operators:

1. $\tau[GCD](x, y)$: **if** $x = y$ **then** x

                    else $GCD(max\,(x,\, y) - min\,(x,\, y), min\,(x,\, y))$

Where *max* and *min* give the maximum and minimum of two elements. $max : \hat{\mathbb{N}} \times \hat{\mathbb{N}} \to \hat{\mathbb{N}}$ is defined by $max(x,\, y)$: **if** $x > y$ **then** x **else** y. Function *min* is defined accordingly.

2. The operator defined in Example 4.12.3.

However, we must recall that in some cases different computation rules may lead to different results (i.e., different functions f_C^P). Thus, it will certainly not happen, in the general case, that $f_\tau \equiv f_C^P$ for any C. Let us explore the relationship between operational and denotational semantics within McCarthy's formalism.

    Let P be a recursive program $P : F(x) \Leftarrow \tau[F](x)$. Let f_τ denote the LFP of τ, let C denote any computation rule, and let f_C^P denote the function computed by P with computation rule C. A first fundamental statement allows us to be sure that if $f_\tau(x)$ and $f_C^P(x)$ are both defined, then they coincide.

Theorem 4.8

For any computation rule C and any recursive program P, $f_C^P \subseteq f_\tau$.

Before going into the formal proof of this theorem, let us go back to Example 4.7. We realized that $f_L^P(1, 1) = \langle 0, 1 \rangle$, while $f_{LI}^P(1, 1) = \perp$.
Let us compute $f_\tau(1, 1)$.

$$f_\tau(1, 1) \equiv \text{LUB} \left\{ \tau^i[\Omega] \right\}(1, 1)$$

Thus, $\Omega(1, 1) \equiv \langle \perp, \perp \rangle$. $\tau[\Omega](1, 1)$
$\equiv \langle$ **if** $1 = 0$ **then** 0 **else** $\Omega(1 - 1, \Omega(1, 1)),$ **if** $1 = 0$ **then** 1 **else** $\Omega\ (\Omega(1, 1), 1, 1)\rangle$
$\equiv \langle \Omega(0, \Omega(1, 1)), \Omega(\Omega(1, 1), 0)\rangle \equiv \langle \perp, \perp \rangle$

$\tau^2[\Omega](1, 1) \equiv$ **if** $1 = 0$ **then** 0 **else** $\tau_1[\Omega](0, \tau_2[\Omega](1, 1)),$
              if $1 = 0$ **then** 1 **else** $\tau_2[\Omega](\tau_1[\Omega](1, 1), 0)\rangle$
        $\equiv \langle \tau_1[\Omega](0, \perp), \tau_2[\Omega](\perp, 0)\rangle$
        $\equiv \langle$ **if** $0 = 0$ **then** 0 **else** $\Omega(-1, \Omega(0, \perp)),$
              if $0 = 0$ **then** 1 **else** $\Omega(\Omega(\perp, 0), 0)\rangle \equiv \langle 0, 1\rangle$

Thus $f_{LI}^P(1, 1) \subseteq f_L^P(1, 1) \equiv f_\tau(1, 1)$.

Proof of Theorem 4.8

Let $t_0, t_1 \ldots t_s$ be a computation of $F(v)$.
Define $t_s[\Omega]$ as the result of substituting in t_s any occurrence of variable function symbol F_i by the undefined function Ω.
Two facts hold.

1. If for any C, $f_C^P(v)$ is defined and equal to t_s for some t_s, then $t_s[\Omega](v) \equiv t_s$ because if t_s has no occurrence of variable function symbols, then $t_s[\Omega](v)$ has no occurrence of Ω and they coincide.

2. For any s and v, $t_s[\Omega](v) \subseteq \tau^s[\Omega](v)$. This is easily proved by induction on s. In fact, $t_0[\Omega](v) \equiv \tau^0[\Omega](v) \equiv \Omega(v)$. t_{s+1} is obtained from t_s by substituting *some* occurrences of Ω by $\tau[\Omega]$, while $\tau^{s+1}[\Omega]$ is obtained from $\tau^s[\Omega]$ by substituting *all* occurrences of Ω by $\tau[\Omega]$. Now, since τ is monotonic, for any $f \subseteq g$, $\tau[f] \subseteq \tau[g]$ provided that f and g substitute the *same* occurrence of any variable function symbol. In particular, since $\Omega \subseteq \tau[\Omega]$, $t_s[\Omega] \subseteq \tau^s[\Omega]$ implies that $t_{s+1}[\Omega] \subseteq \tau^{s+1}[\Omega]$.

Thus, for any computation rule C, $f_C^P(v)$ either is undefined or equals t_s for some s. In both cases, $f_C^P(v) \subseteq \text{LUB}\{\tau^s[\Omega]\}(v) = f_\tau(v)$. ∎

Definition 4.12

A computation rule C is called a *fixed point computation rule* if and only if, for any P, $f_\tau \equiv f_C^P$. □

We already know from Example 4.7 that not all C's given above are fixed point computation rules since we discovered a case where $f_{LI}^P \neq f_C^P \subseteq f_\tau$. Thus, $f_{LI}^P \subset f_\tau$ because of Theorem 4.8. So the question naturally arises whether some C exists that is a fixed point computation rule. This question is answered by the following theorem.

Theorem 4.9

FS is a fixed point computation rule.

Proof

The proof of Theorem 4.9 is derived in a trivial way from the proof of Theorem 4.8. In fact, it suffices to realize that in the case of the FS rule $t_s[\Omega] = \tau^s[\Omega]$. ∎

Exercises

4.28* Show that PO is a fixed point computation rule.

4.29 Compute $f_\tau(x)$ for the following τ and x by means of the chain $\{\tau^s[\Omega]\}$.
1. $\langle f_\tau, g_\tau \rangle(2)$, $\langle f_\tau, g_\tau \rangle(3)$, $\langle f_\tau, g_\tau \rangle(7)$, $\langle f_\tau, g_\tau \rangle(8)$, for the operator of Example 4.12.3.
2. $f_\tau(2)$, $f_\tau(5)$, $f_\tau(6), \ldots, f_\tau(x), \ldots$ for
$\tau[F](x)$: **if** $x < 2$ **then** 1 **else** $(F(x - 1) + F(x - 2))$ (Fibonacci function)

Thus, we know that there exists an operational semantics for McCarthy's formalism equivalent to denotational semantics, but also that operational and denotational semantics do not coincide a priori. A typical process of language design and implementation based on the preceding semantic notions could be described as follows. First define the language and its semantics by means of a denotational formalism, then find an operational semantics, which is more implementation oriented, make sure they are equivalent, and then implement the language by using the above operational semantics. If you follow this procedure, you are guaranteed of a *correct implementation*.

However, the distinction between the previous phases is not as sharp as it might seem at a first glance. In fact, observe that the existence of f_τ for any continuous operator τ is proved in a constructive way (i.e., by building the chain $\{\tau^s[\Omega]\}$). Furthermore, if we use standard base functions (i.e., arithmetic functions, $=$, and **if-then-else**), the construction of $\tau^s[\Omega]$ is *effective*. Therefore, we have an effective way to compute $f_\tau(x)$ for any x (i.e., compute $\tau^s[\Omega]$ until $\tau^s[\Omega](x)$ is defined). Obviously, this procedure may never terminate ($f_\tau(x)$ is $\perp$), as it happens also for TM computations. Not surprisingly, this procedure looks much like the computation of the value $f(x)$, f being defined by means of the formalism of recursive functions. Not surprisingly, McCarthy's formalism is as powerful as partial recursive functions, TMs, unrestricted grammars, etc., whichever denotational or operational semantics is chosen.

In conclusion, the proof of the existence of the LFP of an operator τ is constructive and looks much like a computation rule. Thus, denotational semantics provides an effective procedure to compute the function denoted by an operator. This reminds us what we have seen in the case of formal languages that were defined both by means of evolutionary (i.e., operational) and denotational formalisms. In Chapter 1 we showed that (context-free) languages can be defined either by means of automata or by means of equations.

Equations for defining languages are a denotational formalism to which a *mechanism* to generate their solution is attached (i.e., grammars). Automata are an operational mechanism that models language compilation (i.e., implementation). The reader familiar with formal languages already knows that automata may be used as well to *define* languages, whereas equations (or grammars) may *canonically drive* the construction of a recognizing mechanism. This has strong analogies with what we have seen here in the case of semantic formalisms and makes, in the authors' opinion, the distinction between operational and denotational semantics less sharp than one usually believes.

Exercise

4.30 Prove the existence and uniqueness of a minimal solution (with respect to the set inclusion relation) of the language equations defined in Section 1.6.1. Also, prove that such a solution is the language generated by the context-free grammar canonically associated to the equation.

Hint: Verify that the fixed point theory here developed for monotonic functions can be rephrased, step by step, for languages ordered by the set inclusion relation. The critical point is showing the existence of a LUB of every chain.

4.6.2 McCarthy's Formalism as a Programming Language

We claimed that McCarthy's formalism can be considered as an abstract version of a non-conventional (non-von Neumann) programming language. McCarthy's formalism can be seen as an abstraction of functional languages (like LISP) in much the same way as the RAM is an abstraction of the von Neumann architecture and SMALG of Algol-like languages. There is no space in this text for a discussion on programming language concepts and techniques, and thus for a discussion of conventional versus functional languages. However, because our readers may be unacquainted with functional programming, we use McCarthy's formalism to give a few examples that show the peculiar aspects and the programming style promoted by a functional language.

Example 4.14

We are already familiar with the sorting problem: An array of n elements in a totally ordered set, say $\mathbb{N}$, must be arranged in such a way that $a[i] \leq a[i + 1]$, $i = 1, \ldots, n - 1$. Let us see here how the same problem can be solved by means of McCarthy's formalism. For the sake of simplicity, we assume that the array to be sorted has no repetitions (i.e., $i \neq j$ implies $a[i] \neq a[j]$).

First observe that an array of k elements can be seen as a function from $\{1, \ldots, k\}$ to $\mathbb{N}$. We use the set $A_n = \{a \mid a : \{1, \ldots, k\} \to \mathbb{N}, 1 \leq k \leq n\}$ to describe the collection of all arrays of k natural numbers, with $k \leq n$. We maintain the usual notation $a[i]$ to denote the application of function a to the object i and we keep in mind, thanks to the simplifying assumption, that all a's in A_n are one-to-one functions.

Now observe that, in order to sort an array, we can put its minimum value in the first position, followed by the result of sorting its remaining portion. This is a recursive solution: We are left with the same problem—sorting an array—but on a simpler object. So we can repeat the same procedure on smaller and smaller arrays until we obtain an array of size 1, which is trivially already sorted.

This can be translated into McCarthy's formal notation by applying the following steps.

Step 1: The new set $\overline{A}_n$ is defined on the basis of A_n by

$$\overline{A}_n = \{\,\overline{a}\,|\,\textbf{if } a \in A_n, a : \{1, \ldots, k\} \to \mathbb{N}, 1 \leq k \leq n$$
$$\textbf{then } \overline{a}[i] = a[i], 1 \leq i \leq k,$$
$$\overline{a}[j] = \bot\,,\, k < j \leq n\,\} \cup$$
$$\{\,\overline{\varnothing}, \text{defined by } \overline{\varnothing}[i] = \bot\,,\, i = 1, \ldots, n\,\}$$

Step 2: The function $SORT : \overline{A}_n \to \overline{A}_n$ is defined by the following recursive program

$$SORT(\overline{a}) \Leftarrow \textbf{if } CARD(\overline{a}) = 1 \textbf{ then } \overline{a} \textbf{ else } MIN(\overline{a}) \circ SORT(\overline{a} \dot{-} MIN(\overline{a}))$$

Step 3: In order to define *SORT* we need to give meaning to functions *CARD*, $\circ$, *MIN*, and $\dot{-}$ (notice that for $\circ$ and $\dot{-}$ an infix notation has been used).

3.1. $CARD : \bar{A}_n \to \mathbb{N}$ is defined by

$CARD(\bar{a}) \Leftarrow DEF(\bar{a}, 0)$ with
$DEF : \bar{A}_n \times \mathbb{N} \to \mathbb{N}^{11}$ defined by

$$DEF(\bar{a}, x) \Leftarrow \textbf{if } \bar{a}[x + 1]^{12} = \perp \textbf{ then } x \textbf{ else}$$
$$\textbf{if } x = n - 1 \textbf{ then } n \textbf{ else } DEF(\bar{a}, x + 1)$$

As an exercise verify that $CARD(\bar{a})$ defines the integer $k \leq n$ such that $\bar{a}[k] \in \mathbb{N}$ and $\bar{a}(k + 1) = \perp$.

3.2. $\circ : \mathbb{N} \times \bar{A}_n \to \bar{A}_n$ is defined by

$$(x \circ \bar{a})[i] \Leftarrow \textbf{if } i = 1 \textbf{ then } x \textbf{ else } \bar{a}[i - 1]$$

Notice that $x \circ \bar{a}$ (or, more properly, its restriction to the subdomain $\{1, \ldots, CARD(\bar{a})\}$) is one-to-one only if $x \notin \{\bar{a}[i], \; i = 1, \ldots, n - 1\}$.

3.3. $\dot{-} : \bar{A}_n \times \mathbb{N} \to \bar{A}_n$ is defined by

$$(a \dot{-} x) \Leftarrow \textbf{if } CARD(\bar{a}) = 1 \textbf{ then}$$
$$\textbf{if } x = \bar{a}[1] \textbf{ then } \overline{\varnothing} \textbf{ else } \bar{a}$$
$$\textbf{else if } x = a[1] \textbf{ then } TAIL(\bar{a})$$
$$\textbf{else } \bar{a}[1] \circ (TAIL(\bar{a}) \dot{-} x)$$

where $TAIL : \bar{A}_n \to \bar{A}_n$ is defined by

$$TAIL(\bar{a})[i] \Leftarrow \textbf{if } i = n \textbf{ then } \perp \textbf{ else } \bar{a}[i + 1]$$

Notice that (only) if a is one-to-one, then $x \notin \{(\bar{a} \dot{-} x)[i], \; i = 1, \ldots, n\}$.

3.4. $MIN : \bar{A}_n \to \mathbb{N}$ is defined by

$$MIN(\bar{a}) \Leftarrow \textbf{if } CARD(\bar{a}) = 1 \textbf{ then } \bar{a}[1]$$
$$\textbf{else } min(\bar{a}[1], MIN(TAIL(\bar{a}))),$$

where $min : \mathbb{N} \times \mathbb{N} \to \mathbb{N}$ is defined by

$$min(x, y) \Leftarrow \textbf{if } x < y \textbf{ then } x \textbf{ else } y$$

The reader is urged to verify that the recursive program defined above actually sorts any array $\bar{a} \in \bar{A}_n$, provided that $\bar{a}$ is a bijective function. Furthermore, since the foregoing recursive programs do not contain more than one occurrence of the function variable symbols in their right-hand sides, both operational and denotational semantics are guaranteed to coincide a priori.

---

[11] In this section we do not follow the assumption that all variable function symbols have the same domain.

[12] Notice that $\langle \bar{a}, x + 1 \rangle$ is an element of the domain $\bar{A}_n \times \mathbb{N}$. Thus, from a syntactic point of view, the notation $\bar{a}[x + 1]$ is not consistent with the definition of a term. The difficulty is easily overcome by considering $\bar{a}[x]$ as a short notation for *Eval* $(\bar{a}, x)$, where *Eval* is a base function from $\bar{A}_n \times \mathbb{N}$ to $\mathbb{N}$ whose result is the value of $\bar{a}$ for x.

Exercise

4.31 Modify the above recursive program in order to
   1. Remove the assumption that $\bar{a}$ is one-to-one.
   2. Cope with arrays of arbitrary size.

Before closing the example, a few remarks are in order.

1. The main control mechanism has been recursion, instead of the more familiar iteration. Most modern programming languages support the use of recursion. However, recursion is the most distinctive aspect of functional languages.
2. Some attention should be paid in the handling of arrays. In fact these objects are both *functions* and elements of the particular domain, $\overline{A}_n$. Thus, they can occur as arguments of other functions as *CARD* and *SORT*.
3. The most relevant property of functional languages is that function application generates *new* objects starting from the arguments. Thus, $SORT(\bar{a})$ is a new array obtained from $\bar{a}$. This is in sharp contrast with conventional programming languages whose execution modifies the state of the machine, by changing the value of some variables. For example, the sorting programs given in Sections 2.4 and 3.9.1 make *a* sorted by rearranging the values contained therein.

   A discussion of the impact of this fact on programming style is clearly out of our scope. Let us simply say that there are both advantages and disadvantages. For instance, the dangers of "side effects" are definitely ruled out by functional programming. On the other hand, being forced to forget about the execution state and to define new objects may be awkward in some cases, as the following example shows.

Example 4.15

We want to program the insertion of an element into a table, by means of McCarthy's formalism. A *table* is a finite but unbounded sequence of *elements*; each element is a finite but unbounded string of characters belonging to an alphabet V. As usual a table may be defined as an object $tab : \mathbb{N} \rightarrow V^* \cup \{\perp\}$, $\perp \notin V^*$ such that there exists an $\bar{n} \in \mathbb{N}$, such that $n \leq \bar{n}$ implies $tab(n) \in V^*$, $n > \bar{n}$ implies $tab(n) = \perp$. Notice that $\perp \neq \epsilon$.

   Therefore it is natural to define $TAB = \{tab \mid tab$ defined above$\}$ and $INSERT : TAB \times V^* \rightarrow TAB$.

   However we must keep in mind that whenever we apply $INSERT(tab, v)$, $tab \in TAB$, $v \in V^*$, we define a new table. This may contrast with our wish to simply *update* the table. For example, if we are handling the file of customers of a company, the result of inserting a new customer into the file is to produce a new file. It may be argued that this fact should not cause any trouble to the programmer: it is just a matter of programming style. Unfortunately, the same does not hold for language implementors, who are faced with the nontrivial problems of memory management. Again, there is no room for these issues in this text.

At this point, building the recursive program defining $INSERT(tab, v)$ is a rather simple exercise that is left to the reader. In finding a solution, suppose that the table does not contain repetitions, that is, $i \neq j$ implies $tab(i) \neq tab(j)$.

Exercises

4.32 Define an ordering on $V*$. Modify the insertion algorithm in order to cope with ordered tables, such that $i < j$ implies $\neg tab(j) > tab(i)$.

4.33 Build recursive programs to implement functions
$BELONGS : TAB \times V* \to \{T, F\}$
$DELETE : TAB \times V* \to TAB,$
$EQUAL : TAB \times TAB \to \{T, F\}$
with the obvious meaning of the notation.

Once again, the topic of this chapter is not to compare and assess real programming languages, nor to teach their use in practical problem solving. Rather, we have been discussing the formal tools that can help us describe and understand them rigorously. The next section discusses denotational techniques for conventional Algol-like programming languages.

4.6.3 Denotational Semantics for Algol-like Languages

As we anticipated in Section 4.4.2, formalizing conventional languages via denotational semantics is not an immediate job, as we have to translate into functional notation a behavior essentially based on the notion of a state.

Again, we refer to SMALG without concealing from the reader that, in this case, extensions to treat real programming languages are not only a matter of dealing with more details, but new mathematical difficulties must be tackled. We refer the reader to more specialized literature for a complete treatment of this topic.

In Chapter 3 we gave a rather informal operational semantics of SMALG by means of SMALM. This operational semantics has been made more precise and complete in Section 4.5 for SMALG$^+$ and SMALM$^+$. Any SMALM computation associates to a stream of input values stored in the input tape a stream of output values stored into the output tape. Because each cell of both tapes may contain integer values, SMALM associates to each SMALG program P a function $f_P : \mathbb{Z}^* \to \mathbb{Z}^*$. We now want to achieve the same result without bothering with the details of SMALM computations.

The main points of the construction leading to f_P will be

1. The state of SMALM will be "coded" by means of a functional representation.
2. The denotation of f_P is represented as a suitable aggregation of basic functions associated to elementary SMALG constructs. The syntax of SMALG plays a central role in this decomposition, as it was for operational semantics.

Before going into a full analysis of SMALG semantics let us consider the simplest case of an assignment statement of the type

$x := y + 5$

Intuitively, if we describe a SMALM state as a mapping m assigning integer values to x and y, we can say that the semantics of the above instruction consists essentially of two aspects.

- Expression evaluation: This is given by evaluating $m(y) + 5$ (in the operational framework, $m(y)$ was $M[y]$).
- Building a new state described by a new mapping m' defined on the basis of the previous m and of the above instruction

$$m'(z) = m(z) \quad \text{if } z \neq x$$
$$m'(x) = m(y) + 5$$

We now proceed to some mathematical technicalities that are needed to give a complete semantics to SMALG. For the sake of simplicity, we first refer to a further simplified version of SMALG, called SMALG$^-$, which does not include arrays. Precisely the syntax of SMALG$^-$ is obtained from that of SMALG by deleting the nonterminals $\langle$ArrayVarId$\rangle$ and $\langle$IndexedVar$\rangle$ and all productions involving such nonterminals. SMALG$^-$ expressions are allowed to contain any level of nesting as in Exercise 4.6. Later on we sketch how to cope with full SMALG and other typical features of high level programming languages.

Let us start by defining some *syntactic domains* in a way already used in previous cases.

Definition 4.13

For each nonterminal N belonging to the nonterminal set of SMALG$^-$, $\overline{N}$ denotes the set $\{x \mid N \stackrel{*}{\Rightarrow} x\}$.

In particular, $\langle \overline{\text{Program}} \rangle$ is the set of SMALG$^-$ programs. For each $P \in \langle \overline{\text{Program}} \rangle$ and for each $N \neq \langle \text{Program} \rangle$, N_P denotes the set $\{x \mid P = z_1 x z_2, z_1, z_2 \in V_T^* \wedge N \stackrel{*}{\Rightarrow} x\}$ (i.e., the set of legal "program fragments" that derive from N). $\qquad \square$

Thus, giving a denotational semantics of SMALG$^-$ is defining a function

$Sem: \langle \overline{\text{Program}} \rangle \to \left[(\mathbb{Z}^*)^{\hat{}} \to (\mathbb{Z}^*)^{\hat{}} \right]$

where the notation $[D^{\hat{}} \to R^{\hat{}}]$ is the same as in Section 4.6.1. For $P \in \langle \overline{\text{Program}} \rangle$ the function $f_P = Sem(P)$ will be obtained by means of a suitable aggregation of functions f_{N_p} associated to some N_p. As in the case of operational semantics, the semantics of a complex fragment of program is built on the basis of its simpler components.

The core of this process is in the functional definition of P's state.

Definition 4.14

For $P \in \langle \overline{\text{Program}} \rangle$, P's *state space* S_P is defined as

$$S_P = Mem_P \times Input \times Output$$

where

- P's *memory function* $Mem_P = [\langle \overline{\text{Ident}} \rangle_P \to \mathbb{Z} \cup \{ \perp \}]$, that is, $m \in Mem_P$ assigns an integer or an undefined value to any identifier of P.
- *Input* and *Output* are the set $\mathbb{Z}^*$ of finite strings over integers.   □

In the following, the subscript P is dropped from the notation when no ambiguity arises.

Following the same syntactic pattern as for operational semantics, we first consider the semantics of an assignment statement. Intuitively, we need to define a function $f_{\langle \text{AssStat} \rangle} : S \to S$. Let $s = \langle m, i, o \rangle$, $m \in Mem$, $i \in Input$, and $o \in Output$. Since an assignment does not affect input/output streams, clearly

$$f_{\langle \text{AssStat} \rangle}(s) = s' = \langle m', i', o' \rangle \qquad \text{with } i' = i, \, o' = o$$

Furthermore, let $ID \in \langle \overline{\text{Ident}} \rangle$ denote the identifier such that

$$\langle AssStat \rangle \overset{*}{\Rightarrow} ID := \langle Exp \rangle.$$

Then

$$\begin{cases} m'(Id) = m(Id) \text{ if } Id \neq ID \\ m'(Id) = \text{value associated to } \langle Exp \rangle \text{ if } Id = ID \end{cases}$$

Thus, we need a function that defines the value associated to $\langle Exp \rangle$ in order to define the semantics of the assignment statement (recall that something similar occurred when giving operational semantics too). Thus, let us turn to $f_{\langle Exp \rangle}$.

1. Definition of $f_{\langle Exp \rangle}$

Intuitively $f_{\langle Exp \rangle} : \langle Exp \rangle \times S \to \mathbb{Z}$ since the value of a SMALG$^-$ expression is an integer depending on the expression and on the value of the variables involved therein. However, an error can occur if we try to retrieve the value of an undefined variable, say x (i.e., $m(x) = \perp$). Thus, let us state

$$f_{\langle Exp \rangle} : \langle \overline{Exp} \rangle \times S \to \mathbb{Z} \cup \{ E_r \}$$

The rules to define $f_{\langle Exp \rangle}$ are simple.

1.1 If $\langle Exp \rangle \overset{*}{\Rightarrow} ID$, $ID \in \langle \overline{\text{Ident}} \rangle$, then $f_{\langle Exp \rangle}(ID, s)$, where $s = \langle m, i, o \rangle$, is given by

   if $m(ID) \in \mathbb{Z}$ **then** $m(ID)$
   if $m(ID) = \perp$ **then** E_r

1.2 If $\langle Exp \rangle \overset{*}{\Rightarrow} \langle Constant \rangle \overset{*}{\Rightarrow} \bar{n}$, $\bar{n}$ being the decimal representation of integer n, then $f_{\langle Exp \rangle}(\bar{n}, s) = n$

1.3 If $\langle \text{Exp} \rangle \Rightarrow \langle \text{Exp} \rangle' + \langle \text{Term} \rangle \overset{*}{\Rightarrow} x + y$, with $\langle \text{Exp} \rangle' \overset{*}{\Rightarrow} x$, $\langle \text{Term} \rangle \overset{*}{\Rightarrow} y$, then $f_{\langle \text{Exp} \rangle}(x + y, s) = f_{\langle \text{Exp} \rangle}(x, s) + f_{\langle \text{Term} \rangle}(y, s)$ where the definition of $f_{\langle \text{Term} \rangle} : \langle \text{Term} \rangle \times S \to \mathbb{Z} \cup \{ E_r \}$ is left to the reader as an exercise.

The remaining details in the definition of $f_{\langle \text{Exp} \rangle}$ are also left as an exercise.[13] We can now go back to the definition of $f_{\langle \text{AssStat} \rangle}$.

2. Definition of $f_{\langle AssStat \rangle}$

Refining a bit the previous definition, let us state that

$$f_{\langle \text{AssStat} \rangle} : \langle \overline{\text{AssStat}} \rangle \times S \to S \cup \{ E_r \}$$

Let $\langle \text{AssStat} \rangle \overset{*}{\Rightarrow} ID := x$, where $ID \in \langle \overline{\text{Ident}} \rangle$, $x \in \langle \overline{\text{Exp}} \rangle$, $ID := x \in \langle \overline{\text{AssStat}} \rangle$. Then we define $f_{\langle \text{AssStat} \rangle}$ as follows.

$f_{\langle \text{AssStat} \rangle}(ID := x, s) = $ **if** $f_{\langle \text{Exp} \rangle}(x, s) = E_r$
     then E_r
     else $s' = \langle m', i', o' \rangle$ with
      $i' = i, o' = o$
      $m'(Id) = m(Id)$ for $Id \neq ID$
      $m'(Id) = f_{\langle \text{Exp} \rangle}(x, s)$ for $Id = ID$

This gives a complete and precise semantics of the assignment statement.

3. Definition of $f_{\langle InputStat \rangle}$

$$f_{\langle \text{InputStat} \rangle} : \langle \overline{\text{InputStat}} \rangle \times S \to S \cup \{ E_r \}$$

Let $\langle \text{InputStat} \rangle \overset{*}{\Rightarrow}$ **read** ID, $ID \in \langle \overline{\text{Ident}} \rangle$, $s = \langle m, i, o \rangle$. Then we define $f_{\langle \text{InputStat} \rangle}$ as follows.

$f_{\langle \text{InputStat} \rangle}(ID, s) = $ **if** $i = \epsilon$
     then E_r
     else $s' = \langle m', i', o' \rangle$ with
     $o' = o$, $i' = tail(i)$, $m'(Id) = m(Id)$ for $Id \neq ID$,
     $m'(Id) = first(i)$ for $Id = ID$, with the obvious
     meaning of functions $tail$: $\mathbb{Z}^+ \to \mathbb{Z}^*$ and $first$:
     $\mathbb{Z}^+ \to \mathbb{Z}$.

4. Definition of $f_{\langle WriteStat \rangle}$

We leave it as an exercise.

  The pattern followed so far for semantic definition has been quite similar to the operational case and, perhaps, some reader wonders what was the purpose of all this. The next definitions show the essential difference between the denotational and the operational approach and in some sense support the claim that the former is more abstract.

5. Definition of $f_{\langle CondStat \rangle}$

$$f_{\langle \text{CondStat} \rangle} : \langle \overline{\text{CondStat}} \rangle \times S \to S \cup \{ E_r \}$$

First define $f_{\langle \text{Cond} \rangle} : \langle \overline{\text{Cond}} \rangle \times S \to \{ \text{T}, \text{F}, E_r \}$ in the obvious way (we leave it as an exercise).

---

[13] Recall that x **div** 0 must result in an error.

If $\langle$CondStat$\rangle \Rightarrow$ **if** $\langle$Cond$\rangle$ **then** $\langle$StatList$\rangle$ **else** $\langle$StatList$\rangle$ **fi** $\overset{*}{\Rightarrow}$ **if** x **then** y **else** z **fi** $= w$, then we define $f_{\langle\text{CondStat}\rangle}$ as follows.[14]

$$f_{\langle\text{CondStat}\rangle}(w, s) = \text{\textbf{if} } f_{\langle\text{Cond}\rangle}(x, s) = E_r \text{ \textbf{then} } E_r$$
$$\text{\textbf{if} } f_{\langle\text{Cond}\rangle}(x, s) = \text{T}$$
$$\text{\textbf{then} } f_{\langle\text{StatList}\rangle}(y, s)$$
$$\text{(including the case } f_{\langle\text{StatList}\rangle}(y, s) = E_r. \text{ For}$$
$$\text{the definition of } f_{\langle\text{StatList}\rangle} \text{ see point 7 following.)}$$
$$\text{\textbf{if} } f_{\langle\text{Cond}\rangle}(x, s) = \text{F \textbf{then} } f_{\langle\text{StatList}\rangle}(z, s)$$

Notice that $f_{\langle\text{CondStat}\rangle}(w, s)$ is well defined if $f_{\langle\text{Cond}\rangle}(x, s) = \text{T}$ even in the case where $f_{\langle\text{StatList}\rangle}(z, s) = E_r$ or it is undefined. This perfectly agrees with the semantics of the **if-then-else** construction as discussed in Section 4.6.1.

The case $\langle$CondStat$\rangle \Rightarrow$ **if** $\langle$Cond$\rangle$ **then** $\langle$StatList$\rangle$ **fi** is left as an exercise.

6.   Definition of $f_{\langle WhileStat\rangle}$

$$f_{\langle\text{WhileStat}\rangle} : \langle\overline{\text{WhileStat}}\rangle \times S \to S \cup \{E_r\}$$

Let $\langle$WhileStat$\rangle \Rightarrow$ **while** $\langle$Cond$\rangle$ **do** $\langle$StatList$\rangle$ **od** $\overset{*}{\Rightarrow}$ **while** x **do** y **od** $= w$. We can define $f_{\langle\text{WhileStat}\rangle}$ as follows.

$$f_{\langle\text{WhileStat}\rangle}(w, s) = \text{\textbf{if} } f_{\langle\text{Cond}\rangle}(x, s) = E_r \text{ \textbf{then} } E_r$$
$$\text{\textbf{if} } f_{\langle\text{Cond}\rangle}(x, s) = \text{F \textbf{then} } s$$
$$\text{\textbf{if} } f_{\langle\text{Cond}\rangle}(x, s) = \text{T \textbf{then}}$$
$$\text{\textbf{if} } f_{\langle\text{StatList}\rangle}(y, s) = E_r \text{ \textbf{then} } E_r$$
$$\text{\textbf{else} } f_{\langle\text{WhileStat}\rangle}(w, f_{\langle\text{StatList}\rangle}(y, s))$$

7.   Definition of $f_{\langle StatList\rangle}$

$f_{\langle\text{StatList}\rangle} : \langle\overline{\text{StatList}}\rangle \times S \to S \cup \{E_r\}$
If $\langle$StatList$\rangle \Rightarrow \epsilon$, then $f_{\langle\text{StatList}\rangle}(\epsilon, s) = s$
If $\langle$StatList$\rangle \Rightarrow \langle$Stat$\rangle$; $\langle$StatList$\rangle \Rightarrow x$; y
then $f_{\langle\text{StatList}\rangle}(x; y, \text{s}) = $ is defined as
if $f_{\langle\text{Stat}\rangle}(x, s) = E_r$
  then E_r
  else $f_{\langle\text{StatList}\rangle}(y, f_{\langle\text{Stat}\rangle}(x, s))$

where the definition of $f_{\langle\text{Stat}\rangle} : \langle\overline{\text{Stat}}\rangle \times S \to S \cup \{E_r\}$ is left as an exercise.

8.   Definition of $f_{\langle Program\rangle}$

$$f_{\langle\text{Program}\rangle} : \langle\overline{\text{Pogram}}\rangle \times Input \to Output$$

Let $\langle$Program$\rangle \Rightarrow$ **begin** $\langle$StatList$\rangle$ **end** $\overset{*}{\Rightarrow}$ **begin** x **end** $= y$

$$f_{\langle\text{Program}\rangle}(y, i) = f_{OUT}(f_{\langle\text{StatList}\rangle}(x, f_{INIT}(i)))$$

---

[14] The reader should be careful while reading the definition of $f_{\langle\text{CondStat}\rangle}$ since there are two types of **if-then-else**'s involved: the SMALG conditional and the functional notation used to define conditional functions.

where $f_{INIT}: Input \to S$ is defined by

$$f_{INIT}(i) = \langle m_0, i, \epsilon \rangle, \; m_0(Id) = \perp \text{ for each } Id \in \langle \overline{Ident} \rangle$$
$$f_{OUT}: S \cup \{E_r\} \to Output \cup \{E_r\}$$

is defined by

$$f_{OUT}(E_r) = E_r$$
$$f_{OUT}(\langle m, i, o \rangle) = o$$

The above rules 1 through 8 allow us to associate a *recursive definition* of f_P to each program $P \in \langle \overline{Program} \rangle$.

The theory developed in Section 4.6.1 allows us to conclude that for any $P \in \langle \overline{Program} \rangle$, $f_{\langle Program \rangle}(P, i) = o$ defines an operator τ on $[Input\hat{\ } \to Output\hat{\ }] = [(Z*)\hat{\ } \to (Z*)\hat{\ }]$, which has a least fixed point, f_P. Thus we *define Sem(P)* = f_P for any $P \in \langle \overline{Program} \rangle$.

Example 4.16

Consider the following SMALG$^-$ program P

begin read n; *fact* := 1; i := 1;
      while $i \le n$ **do** *fact* := *fact* $* i$;
                i := $i + 1$
            od
      write *fact*
end

Let us compute $f_P: (\mathbb{Z}*)\hat{\ } \to (\mathbb{Z}*)\hat{\ }$.

First we immediately realize that $f_P(\perp) = \perp$, $f_P(\epsilon) = E_r$.

Let us now consider $w = z\tilde{w}$ where $z \in \mathbb{Z}$ and $w \in \mathbb{Z}*$. S_P is $mem_P \times \mathbb{Z}* \times \mathbb{Z}*$, with $mem_P = [\{n, fact, i\} \to \mathbb{Z} \cup \{\perp\}]$

By skipping the obvious details, we have

$$f_P(z\tilde{w}) = f_{OUT}(f_{\langle StatList \rangle}(\textbf{read } n; \ldots \textbf{write } fact, \langle m_0, z\tilde{w}, \epsilon \rangle))$$
$$= f_{OUT}(f_{\langle StatList \rangle}(\textbf{while} \ldots \textbf{write } fact, \langle m_1, \tilde{w}, \epsilon \rangle))$$
$$\text{where } m_1(n) = z, \; m_1(fact) = 1, \; m_1(i) = 1$$
$$= f_{OUT}(f_{\langle WriteStat \rangle}(\textbf{write } fact, f_{\langle WhileStat \rangle}(\textbf{while} \ldots \textbf{od } \langle m_1, \tilde{w}, \epsilon \rangle)))$$

Let us now concentrate on $f_{\langle WhileStat \rangle}(\textbf{while} \ldots \textbf{od}, \langle m_1, \tilde{w}, \epsilon \rangle)$, the rest of f_P definition being fairly obvious. We have, by rule 6,

$$f_{\langle WhileStat \rangle}(\textbf{while} \ldots \textbf{od } \langle m_1, \tilde{w}, \epsilon \rangle)$$
$$= \textbf{if } f_{\langle Cond \rangle}(i \le n, s_1) = F \textbf{ then } s_1$$
$$\textbf{else } f_{\langle WhileStat \rangle}(\textbf{while} \ldots \textbf{od } f_{\langle StatList \rangle}(fact := \ldots i + 1, s_1))^{15}$$
$$= \textbf{if } (m_1(i) \le m_1(n)) \textbf{ then } s_1 \textbf{ else } f_{\langle WhileStat \rangle}(\textbf{while} \ldots \textbf{od}, s_2),$$
$$\text{where } s_2 = \langle m_2, \tilde{w}, \epsilon \rangle,$$
$$\text{with } m_2(n) = m_1(n), \; m_2(fact) = m_1(fact) * m_1(i), \; m_2(i) = m_1(i) + 1$$

---

[15] Let us forget about the error cases.

The foregoing equations define a recursive program on the function variable $f_{\langle \text{WhileStat} \rangle}(\textbf{while} \ldots \textbf{od}, s) : S_P \to S_P$. Let $f_{\langle \text{WhileStat} \rangle}(\textbf{while} \ldots \textbf{od}, \langle m, i, o \rangle) = s' = \langle m', i', o' \rangle$ (obviously $i' = i$ and $o' = o$). It is just an exercise to verify that $m'(fact) = m(n)!$. Thus $f_P(z\tilde{w}) = z!$ for any $\tilde{w} \in \mathbb{Z}^*$.

Notice that a nonterminating **while** loop gives rise to an undefined recursively defined $f_{\langle \text{WhileStat} \rangle}$. This further emphasizes the need for a universal computation formalism to be partial as remarked in Chapter 2. Observe also that $f_{\langle \text{Exp} \rangle}$ is recursively defined as $f_{\langle \text{WhileStat} \rangle}$. However, the convergence of $f_{\langle \text{Exp} \rangle}$ depends on a "compile-time" elaboration, namely the syntactic processing of $\langle \text{Exp} \rangle \overset{*}{\Rightarrow} x$; instead, the convergence of $f_{\langle \text{WhileStat} \rangle}$ depends on the state evolution.

Exercise

4.34 *Compute* the denotational semantics of the following SMALG⁻ programs.

$P1$: **begin read** x; **read** y;
        while $x \neq y$ **do if** $x > y$
                    then $x := x - y$
                    else $y := y - x$
                    fi
            od;
        write x
    end
$P2$: **begin read** x; $i := 1$;
        while $x = x$ **do** $i := i + 1$;
                write i;
            od
    end

SMALG⁻ is a simplified version of an already oversimplified toy language, namely SMALG. How long is the way towards a full denotational definition of a real programming language? We just claim that this is a long way, along which some critical mathematical difficulties arise. The reader willing to go further on this topic is referred to the specialized literature. Here, we will proceed for only a few more steps that will allow us to deal with full SMALG. In particular, we sketch a possible way of handling arrays in denotational semantics.

Because SMALG does not impose any bound to arrays (which are linear), it seems reasonable to claim that an array a is a function $a: (\mathbb{N} - \{0\}) \to \mathbb{Z} \cup \{\perp\}$ with the bound that there exists an $\bar{n} \in \mathbb{N}$ such that for $n > \bar{n}$, $a(n) = \perp$.

Accordingly, for every $P \in \langle \overline{\text{Program}} \rangle$, we could partition $\langle \overline{\text{Ident}} \rangle_P$ as $\langle \overline{\text{Ident}} \rangle_P$ $= \langle \overline{\text{IdS}} \rangle_P \cup \langle \overline{\text{IdA}} \rangle_P$ as the union of simple variable identifiers and array variable identifiers. We require that the two sets be disjoint. Thus Mem_P can be defined as

$$Mem_P : [\langle \overline{\text{IdS}} \rangle_P \to \mathbb{Z} \cup \{\bot\}] \times [\langle \overline{\text{IdA}} \rangle_P \to [(\mathbb{N} - \{0\} \to \mathbb{Z} \cup \{\bot\}]]$$

The completion of SMALG's denotational semantics is left as an exercise.

Exercise

4.35 Augment SMALG's denotational semantics in order to cope with the following features belonging to Pascal and to many other programming languages.
1. Variable declaration and the rules regulating the use of identifiers. (Assume only SMALG$^+$ types, including bounded arrays.)
    Hint: We suggest a set *Environment* contained in the set *Universe* of all possible identifiers. The effect of a declaration is to insert an element into *Environment*. The memory function *Mem*: *Universe* $\to \mathbb{Z}$ $\cup \{\bot\}$ (as far as it concerns only simple variables) does not need to depend on the particular program P but must be undefined for elements not belonging to *Environment*. However, this is not the only way to solve the exercise.
2.* Procedures (Allow the redefinition of variable identifiers but forbid procedure nesting. Also, allow recursive procedure calls.)
3. **Record** variables and **with** statements.
4. **case** and **repeat-until** control structures.

4.7 Concluding Remarks

Formal semantics can enhance the programmer's confidence in the programs he or she writes. The user can give a mathematical proof that a program behaves in a specified manner (see also Chapter 5) as well as a correctness proof of the implementation. Notice, however, that formally defining the meaning of a notation simply consists of translating it into another formal notation. Consequently, the very first and very last steps of the ideal chain leading from a problem to an actual solution, as depicted in Figure 4.9, will never be checkable in a mathematical way, since they are, *by definition*, informal.

Two main categories of formal tools for defining language semantics have been investigated. Operational semantics is based on the use of evolutionary models, that is, machines that can change their state; denotational semantics uses function equations to define the meaning of programs. The boundary between the two techniques is not as sharp as it might seem—and as some people claim. This

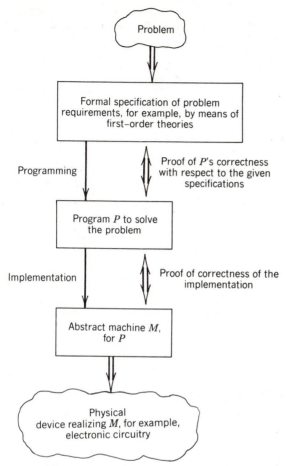

FIGURE 4.9   The ideal path leading from a
problem to its solution.

is just an instance of a general remark made in Chapter 1 on the use of
denotationary versus evolutionary models. If we emphasize the problem of
computing the solution of an equation, we have transformed the equation into an
algorithm producing a sequence converging towards its solution. This is the case
when we *compute* (by means of an effective procedure) the least fixed point of a
continuous operator.

Rather than insisting on an often useless and tedious debate on which style
for formal semantics definition is better, our opinion is that a semantic tool must
be evaluated on the basis of its usability. Such an evaluation must be performed
from several points of view. For example, even if one does not agree that
SMALG's denotational semantics does not suggest any implementation, there is

no doubt that proving correctness of a SMALG implementation is easier by checking it against its denotational definition rather than its operational definition (see Chapter 5). In general, however, choosing among one style of formal definition or another depends largely on a matter of personal taste, experience, and mathematical culture.

Chapter Summary

This chapter has been devoted to the issue of formal semantics of programming languages. We started by a motivation of formal semantics as a tool to enhance the programmer's confidence in program correctness, and to drive language implementation. Then we introduced the two main approaches to formal semantics—operational and denotational semantics—on the basis of an oversimplified example. The so-called axiomatic semantics, whose flavor has been given in Example 4.1, will be treated in Chapter 5, because its use is mainly applied in correctness proofs.

Sections 4.5 and 4.6 have been devoted to illustrate the two approaches in more detail. In the former, we gave the operational semantics of a toy Pascal-like language through an abstract stack-machine. In the first part of the latter, we introduced McCarthy's formalism as a toy functional programming language. A formal semantics has been given to McCarthy's formalism by means of computation rules (operational semantics) and of fixed-point theory (denotational semantics). Section 4.6.2 has shown how a denotational semantics can be given to Pascal-like languages.

Finally the two approaches have been contrasted and a few concluding remarks have been given.

Further Exercises

4.36* Augment SMALG$^+$ by introducing variables of type *record* and *variant records* as they are defined in Pascal. Formalize the rules regulating their use by means of a suitable modification of SMALM$^+$.

4.37 Give an implementation schema to compute primitive recursive functions by means of SMALG programs.

4.38 Solve Exercise 4.37 again with partial recursive functions replacing primitive recursive functions.

4.39 Give an operational semantics for SMALG by using TM as basic abstract machine. In other words give translation schemas from SMALG's constructs to sequence of moves of suitable TMs.

4.40* Give an operational semantics of McCarthy's formalism, provided with the "call by value" computation rule by means of SMALM$^+$. As a simplifying hypothesis, you may assume that each variable function symbol occurs at most once in each term.

Sketchy Solutions to Selected Exercises

4.13 A SMALM$^+$ without *Id* field in the stack locations can be derived from the original SMALM$^+$ in the following way.

1. Stack locations consist only of the *value* field.

2. A new register, named *base-address register*, is added to the state of SMALM$^+$.

3. The *operand* field of SMALM$^+$ statements is a natural number as in the case of RAM. However, the value i in the operand field does not refer to $STACK\ [i]$, but to $STACK\ [base\ address + i]$.

4. An *activation record* is associated to each SMALG$^+$ procedure. It consists of one memory cell for each formal parameter, one cell for each local variable of the procedure, plus one cell for storing the address of the return instruction, and one cell for saving the value of the *base address* at the moment of procedure call. The activation record is allocated on the top of the stack at procedure call and deallocated at procedure exit (with obvious initialization of its cells). Furthermore, at procedure call the *base-address* register is initialized to the previous value of *TOP* register.

5. Each reference to a symbolic identifier in the original SMALG program is translated into a natural number which is the *offset* of the (local) variable with respect to the *base address*. For instance, if the cell bound to the local variable x is the fifth in the activation record of the procedure where x is local, then instead of generating the statement LOAD x, LOAD 5 is generated.

Notice that the above implementation schema is closer to real implementations of ALGOL-like languages and is far more efficient than the original one.

4.19 Call-by reference and call-by value result have the same effect if there is no *aliasing* (i.e., if the same memory location is not accessed in the same procedure under two or more different names). See also Ghezzi and Jazayeri (1986).

4.22 For each g_i, g_i is nonmonotonic if and only if $g_i(\bot) = k \neq \bot$ and for same x, $g_i(x) \neq k$. This may happen for g_1 and g_3. Instead, g_2 is monotonic. In fact, $g_2(x) \neq \bot$ if and only if $(f_1(x) \neq \bot \wedge f_1(x) = f_2(x))$ $\vee\ (f_2(x) \neq \bot \wedge f_1(x) \neq f_2(x))$. Thus $g_2(\bot) \neq \bot$ implies that either $f_1(\bot) = f_2(\bot) \neq \bot$ or $f_2(\bot) \neq \bot$ and $f_1(\bot) \neq f_2(\bot)$. But a monotonic function h such that $h(\bot) = k \neq \bot$ is necessarily a constant function, such that $h(x) = k$ for every x. Thus, in the former case f_1 and f_2 are the same constant function and $g_2 = f_1 = f_2$. In the latter case, f_2 is a constant function and whenever $f_1(x) \neq f_2(x)$, $g_2(x) = f_2(x)$; whenever $f_1(x) = f_2(x)$, $g_2(x) = f_2(x) = f_1(x)$. Thus, $g_2 = f_2$ in any way.

4.37 1. Base functions are computed in a trivial way.

2. In order to compute functions obtained by composition, proceed as follows. Let $P_1, \ldots, P_k$ and Q be fragments of SMALG programs

computing functions $h_1, \ldots, h_k$ and g, respectively. Furthermore, assume that

a. The value of variables $x_1, \ldots, x_n$ are initially stored in SMALG variables having the same name.

b. No P_i affects variables $x_1, \ldots, x_n$.

c. Each P_i ends execution leaving the result $h_i(x_1, \ldots, x_n)$ in variable y_i.

d. Q accesses the arguments of function g in variables $y_1, \ldots, y_k$ and leaves the result in variable z.

Then the fragment $P_1; \ldots; P_k; Q$ computes

$$g(h_1(x_1, \ldots, x_n), \ldots, h_k(x_1, \ldots, x_n)).$$

Notice that assumptions a through d do not cause any loss of generality.

3. In order to compute the functions obtained by immediate recursion, proceed as follows (details concerning how to store function arguments and values into suitable SMALG variables are similar to the above point 2).

Let P and Q be two SMALG fragments computing, respectively, g and h (their results are given in variables p and q, respectively). Then f is computed by the following fragment

P;
$z := p$;
$i := 0$
while $i < y$ **do** $i := i + 1$;
$\qquad\qquad Q$; {the $(n + 1)$st and $(n + 2)$nd arguments
$\qquad\qquad\qquad$ of h are stored in i and z, respectively}
$\qquad\qquad z := q$
$\qquad$ **od**
$result := z$

Appendix

4.A. Equivalence between McCarthy's formalism, partial recursive functions, and Turing Machines

Consider the basic set $D = \mathbb{N}$ and the set $\{T, F\}$ and give the usual meaning to function symbols $=: D \times D \rightarrow \{T, F\}$, *Pred*: $\mathbb{N} \rightarrow \mathbb{N}$, and **if-then-else**

1. Every recursive function $f: \mathbb{N} \rightarrow \mathbb{N}$ can be expressed by means of McCarthy's formalism. To prove this, it suffices to notice that McCarthy's formalism trivially allows one to denote base functions and function compositions.

Furthermore primitive recursion:

$$\begin{cases} f(0, x_1, \ldots x_n) = h(x_1, \ldots, x_n) \\ f(y + 1, x_1, \ldots, x_n) = g(y, f(y, x_1, \ldots, x_n)) \end{cases}$$

can be denoted by

$$F(y, x_1, \ldots, x_n) \Leftarrow \textbf{if } y = 0 \textbf{ then } h(x_1, \ldots, x_n)$$
$$\textbf{else } g(Pred(y), F(Pred(y), x_1, \ldots, x_n))$$

The minimalization operator

$$\mu_y f(y, \ldots) = 0$$

can be defined as $\mu \_ F(0)$ where $\mu \_ F(y)$ is defined by

$$\mu \_ F(y) = \textbf{if } F(y, \ldots) = 0 \textbf{ then } y \textbf{ else } \mu \_ F(y + 1, \ldots)$$

Notice that there is no need to specify which semantics we attach to the above recursive programs because all of them exhibit only one occurrence of the function variable symbol. This natural construction further supports our claim that McCarthy's formalism is the programming counterpart of the formalism of recursive functions.

2. Every function computable by means of recursive programs—whichever semantic rule it is chosen—is computed by some TM. In fact, for any recursive program P it is easy to build a TM simulating the computation of f_C^P, for any chosen computation rule as well as to build a TM computing the least fixed point f_τ attached to P. □

Bibliographic Remarks

The need for a formal and sound basis for semantic definitions of programming languages was first stated by the pioneering works of McCarthy (1963a, b) and Floyd (1967a). The most significant case of operational semantics based on an abstract machine rather than on rough implementation choices is VDL (Lucas and Walk (1969)), which has been applied to give a full semantic definition of PL/1.

For a reference to Pascal semantics based on PCODE see Wirth (1981). For an informal, but comprehensive, operational view of the main semantic features of programming languages see Ghezzi and Jazayeri (1987).

McCarthy's formalism (McCarthy (1960)) is the theoretical foundation of the LISP programming language (McCarthy et al. (1965)).

The cornerstones of denotational semantics have been laid by the work of Tarski (1955), Strachey (1964), Scott (1970), and Scott and Strachey (1971).

Denotational semantics has been widely used in the development of Vienna Development Method (VDM), a methodology for formal specification that has been widely used to define and implement programming languages (see Bjorner and Jones (1982)). VDM has been successfully used for definition and implementation of large languages such as CHILL and Ada (see Gehani (1973)).

The treatment of McCarthy's formalism and its semantics given here is strongly based on Manna (1974). The exposition of denotational semantics of ALGOL-like languages somewhat follows the lines of Gordon (1979). Gordon (1979) is an excellent introductory textbook on denotational semantics: It goes in sufficient depth into technical problems and yet maintains a good level of understandability for the nonspecialized reader. Stoy (1977) is suggested for a more rigorous and detailed analysis of denotational semantics.

Another interesting approach to formal semantics is the so called *algebraic semantics* which, in a denotational style, exploits the use of category theory and isomorphisms of algebras. Significant original papers in this field are Burstall and Landin (1969), Burstall (1970), and ADJ (1977).

CHAPTER FIVE

Proving Program Properties

5.1 The Impact of Formal Techniques on Program Reliability

In Chapter 4 we saw that if we are given a formal tool to define the meaning of a formalism, then we can use such a tool to *mathematically prove* properties of an instance of the formalism. For example, we were able to prove that a given SMALG program computes the sum $\sum_{i=1}^{n} a[i]$.

It is worth repeating that "formally proving" is not the same as "automatically proving." In fact, from Chapter 2 we know that it is impossible to prove, by means of an algorithm, that any given TM recognizes a given language or that any given program computes a given function. However, by using human ingenuity, we were able to prove that a particular abstract machine can solve a particular problem. We could not have achieved the same result without relying on a safe and formal definition of what the machine was intended to do.

This chapter is about proving properties of computer programs written in a given programming language. In such a case, starting from the formal description of language semantics, we can state the desired behavior of a program as a tentative *theorem* that can either be proved or disproved (in such a case it is not a theorem; it was just a wrong conjecture) or never be neither proved nor disproved. This fact may have a tremendous practical impact. We must be conscious that, whenever programming tackles nontrivial, critical problems, the issue of program correctness and, more generally, of program reliability becomes a most critical one.

The traditional approach of practitioners to the problem of program correctness has been a—more or less systematic—activity of program testing and debugging. Once completely coded, the program is tested by means of sample data in order to check whether it behaves properly. If not, that is, if the results do not match the expected outputs, one must try to find the "bug" (i.e., the source of the error), then the program must be repaired, and finally the new version of the program must be retested. When the program is found to behave satisfactorily for a sufficiently large and meaningful number of input data, one comes to the conclusion that the program *is likely to be correct*.

This is not the place to discuss the methods and techniques of systematic program testing and debugging that can enhance one's confidence on program correctness—a typical software engineering topic. Let us simply point out the essential weakness of testing as a tool to assess program correctness. The only way to be absolutely sure of program correctness by means of testing is to test a program for *all possible input data*, which is clearly impossible whenever input domains are infinite. Furthermore, it is not always possible to anticipate what the *expected results* of a program are for any given input. For example, if we are given a program to sort arrays, we can easily test it by supplying input data according to some criterion, computing the corresponding result by hands, running the program, and then verifying that the two outputs coincide. But if we write a program to compute the nth decimal digit of π, we can hardly verify its correctness by hand-computing the result corresponding to, say, $n = 10^9$.

In principle, if we are able to prove program correctness by means of an appropriate mathematical reasoning on the basis of formal semantics, then we do not need to rely on testing any more. However, you should not come to the wrong conclusion that in the future formal correctness proofs will make program testing techniques obsolete or useless. Here are some reasons.

1. Formal proofs can be checked only against formal specifications. But very often we make mistakes in the process that leads from informal to formal problem descriptions, as we noticed in the previous chapter.
2. Formal program proofs can be as complex as program design and coding, and thus they are error prone as well.
3. Too much mathematical background is required of the programmer.

The purpose of this chapter is exactly to enable the reader to master the difficulties inherent in formal program verification. In doing so, we do not intend to fall into the—often meaningless—dispute on whether formal verification is better than testing or vice versa. In our opinion, program testing and correctness proofs are complementary tools, both useful in software engineering to enhance the designer's confidence in his or her product.

Proving programs correct is exactly like mathematical theorem proving, once we accept the view that programs are formal objects (i.e., they have a formally defined syntax and semantics). When facing a new, unsolved problem, the mathematician formulates a theorem and then tries to prove it. After a few unsuccessful attempts, the mathematician checks the validity of the theorem in some sample cases, trying to find possible *counterexamples* that would prove the statement to be wrong. Very often, in the unsuccessful process of finding counterexamples, the mathematician discovers new relevant facts that may inspire a new proof method, and so on. Eventually, it may happen that either a proof or a counterexample is found. Similarly, by alternating between correctness proof and testing, one may either prove a program to be correct or find some bug.

The reader will notice that in this procedure, testing is used with the explicit purpose of causing an error condition. This is in perfect agreement with a lucid statement by E. W. Dijkstra, who claimed that testing is useful to prove the presence of errors in a program, not their absence.

According to this viewpoint, program validation is an interplay between formal verification of correctness and testing. However, we will show that the formal tools required to prove programs correct are not only useful—a posteriori—to prove correctness of fully implemented programs. Rather, they can be used—a priori—to guide programmers in the derivation of programs that are guaranteed to be correct. This important point is discussed in Section 5.5.

Finally, we observe that formal tools for program analysis mainly concentrate on the correctness issue. Their scope, however, is far more general. Chapter 3 already showed that complexity analysis can be accomplished by means of suitable formal tools; we will come back to this point in Section 5.7 to show that correctness and complexity analysis can be developed jointly. In principle, we can hope to formally derive any property of a program once the semantics of the programming language is formally defined.

Before closing this introductory section, let us briefly discuss how program correctness relates to the more general (but informal) concept of *reliability*. Having proved the correctness of a program certainly improves our confidence on its behavior: Thus we can rely more on it. But correctness is only one aspect that contributes to what we informally classify under reliability. For example, suppose you have to design a program that computes the factorial of any integer $n \geq 0$. Also, suppose you find two different programs P and P' solving the problem and that both can be proven correct with respect to the above requirement. However, suppose that in the case $n < 0$, P indefinitely loops, whereas P' outputs a diagnostic message and halts. Clearly, you rely more on P' than on P.

In some cases, even an incorrect program could be more reliable than a correct one. In the previous example, suppose that both P and P' use approximate methods to compute the factorial of n when n becomes large. One may state the correctness requirement that the program output is an approximation of the real value of *fact*(n) within a bound of, say, $10n$. Suppose now that P is correct with respect to this requirement, whereas P' only guarantees an approximation bound of $10.001n$. Clearly, we could still consider P' as more reliable than P even if, strictly speaking, P is correct while P' is not.

Similarly, one can state that a compiler for a given language L is correct if

a. It properly translates any sentence $x \in L$ into a given machine language, according to L's semantics.
b. It outputs an error message if $x \notin L$.

Again, it may happen that a correct compiler C is considered more reliable than another correct compiler C' if, say, its diagnostic is better or in the presence of some frequently occurring error it is able to perform some recovery action, whereas C' does not, etc.

These examples show that typical—though not exclusive—program properties that fall under the concept of reliability are program correctness and the ability to react to abnormal or exceptional situations. We do not intend here to go further into the reliability issue as it is characterized by several informal aspects that naturally place it in the field of software engineering. Observe that, at least in principle, one may try to translate any property affecting program reliability into a suitable formal specification, which could be formally proved. However, the real problem here is that at present we do not know how to define all desirable properties of software in a formal way.

The rest of this chapter presents the simplest and most widely used techniques for formal program analysis. The accent is mainly on correctness, but also program complexity is reanalyzed in the same framework. More generally, the foregoing discussion should have convinced the reader that a more appropriate term to be used should be "formal analysis of program properties."

5.2   A Proof-Oriented Formal Semantics: The Axiomatic Approach

Let us return to the operational semantics of SMALG as defined in Chapter 4.[1] We already observed that such semantics is certainly useful to enlighten the issues underlying an implementation, but provides program descriptions that become cluttered with a lot of details that make the "real meaning" of the program rather obscure. The semiformal proof of Example 4.1, however, suggests a way to obtain a fairly simple method to derive *proofs* on program properties. Consider the execution of the statement

$$x := x + a[i]$$

---

[1] From now on, we decide to use the names SMALG and SMALM to denote any member of the language and machine families discussed in the previous chapters.

The SMALM machine performs the following steps.

Step 1: Evaluate the contents of M_x, say $M[M_x]$.
Step 2: Evaluate $M[M_i]$.
Step 3: Access the $M[M_i]$th cell in the sequence of cells associated to the array a, and evaluate its contents $M[M_{a[M[M_i]]}]$ (notice that in Example 4.1 the location $M_{a[M[M_i]]}$ was—less formally but more shortly—denoted as $M_{a[i]}$).
Step 4: Perform the sum $M[M_x] + M[M_{a[M[M_i]]}]$.
Step 5: Store the result into M_x.

Let P be any predicate that is supposed to hold immediately after execution of $x := x + a[i]$. A necessary and sufficient condition on SMALM's state before execution of the statement such that P holds afterwards, is the same predicate P where all occurrences of the term $M[M_x]$, if any, have been substituted by the term $M[M_x] + M[M_{a[M[M_i]]}]$. In fact, the execution of the above instruction has the effect of modifying the M_x component of machine state by substituting for its value the value denoted by the right-hand side expression. For example, after execution of the statement, if we wish $M[M_x]$ to be greater than or equal to 7, then before execution it must be $M[M_x] + M[M_{a[M[M_i]]}] \geq 7$.

Now let us abandon our low-level notation by using the same identifier to denote a variable, say x, and the contents of the associated cell, $M[M_x]$. The above rule associated to the statement

$$x := x + a[i]$$

is denoted by $\{P_x^{x+a[i]}\}\, x := x + a[i]\, \{P\}$ and is read as "Let P be any predicate. A necessary and sufficient condition in order for P to hold immediately after SMALM has executed $x := x + a[i]$ is that $P_x^{x+a[i]}$ holds immediately before, where $P_x^{x+a[i]}$ denotes the result of substituting $x + a[i]$ for any occurrence of x in P."

In general, it is immediate to realize that the semantics of SMALG's assignment statements of the type $x := f(x_1, \ldots, x_n)$, where f is any expression involving (possibly indexed) variables $x_1, \ldots, x_n$ is described by the rule

$$\left\{ P_x^{f(x_1, \ldots, x_n)} \right\} x := f(x_1, \ldots, x_n) \{ P \} \qquad (*)$$

The foregoing rule has been obtained as a consequence of the operational semantics of SMALG. However, it may be interpreted also as a *definition of SMALG's semantics* (often called *axiomatic semantics*). That is, we could forget about the previous operational definition of semantics and simply state that any implementation of SMALG must guarantee that rule (*) holds for any assignment statement. Under this new viewpoint, SMALM and the translator from SMALG into the SMALM language can be seen as a particular implementation of SMALG, and the above reasoning that lead to the derivation of (*) can be viewed as a proof of correctness of the implementation with respect to the given axiomatic semantics. In conclusion, (*) can be viewed both as a fragment of formal semantics for SMALG or, alternatively, as a fragment of a system of proof rules suitable to prove SMALG program properties, which can be derived from formal semantics.

Incidentally, notice that the foregoing style of formal semantics is still operational in nature since the rule (*) asserts a property of the program's state and of its evolution.

What we need now is to extend (*) to a full system of proof rules for SMALG to be derived from its operational semantics. By generalizing the above remarks that lead to the construction of (*), we derive notations of the type

$$\{ Pre \} S \{ Post \}$$

where S is a program (fragment), *Post* and *Pre* are predicates on S's variables. The intended meaning of this notation is: "If predicate *Pre* (*precondition*) holds on the program's state before S's execution and if execution terminates, then predicate *Post* (*postcondition*) holds after S's execution." If this can be proven, S is said to be correct with respect to precondition *Pre* and postcondition *Post*.

The system of rules leading to formulas of the type $\{ Pre \} S \{ Post \}$ is based on a formal theory containing *axioms* and *inference rules* in such a way that formulas are statements to be proved within the theory. This is the reason why the approach is often called *axiomatic*. It is also called Hoare-like, in honor of one of the pioneers of this approach to formal semantics and program verification.

We present the proof system as an augmented first-order theory. For the sake of simplicity, we refer to Peano's axiomatization of arithmetic as presented in Section 0.2.4.[2]

The well-formed formulas of Hoare's system are all well-formed formulas of arithmetic plus the strings of the type

$$\{ P \} S \{ Q \}$$

where

- P and Q are well-formed formulas of first-order arithmetic. They will also be called (*program*) *assertions*.
- S is a *program fragment*, that is, in the case of SMALG, a string derivable from the nonterminals ⟨Program⟩, ⟨Stat⟩, or ⟨StatList⟩ of the SMALG grammar.

For simplicity, in our treatment we rule out I/O statements. The discussion in Section 5.6 shows that this assumption can be removed quite easily. As a further simplification, we assume that both P and Q do not contain quantifiers and we ignore indexed variables. These latter assumptions are removed in the next section.

Besides the usual axioms and inference rules of first-order arithmetic the following axiom (schema) and rules are introduced.

---

[2]We must acknowledge that Peano's arithmetic deals with natural numbers, whereas SMALG deals with integers. However, this discrepancy has no conceptual relevance. Furthermore, most examples presented in this chapter are restricted to the domain of natural numbers.

Assignment axiom

For any well-formed formula P, for any term t and variable x that are derivable from nonterminals $\langle\text{Expression}\rangle$ and $\langle\text{Var}\rangle$ of the SMALG grammar the well-formed formula

$$A1 : \left\{ P_x^t \right\} x := t \left\{ P \right\}$$

is an axiom. P_x^t, is defined in Definition 0.9 in Section 0.2.3. In this context, the application of rule A1 to derive P_x^t from P is called *backwards substitution*. Notice that axiom A1 is just a restatement of (*).

Inference rules are defined by means of the classical Hoare's notation

$$I : \frac{f_1, f_2, \ldots, f_n}{f}$$

which stands for "statement f is a direct consequence of statement $f_1, \ldots, f_n$ by virtue of rule I."

Strictly speaking, any first-order theory should not have any inference rule besides *MP* and *Gen*. However, we can consider I as a reformulation of the *axiom* $f_1 \wedge \ldots \wedge f_n \supset f$, which allows us to derive f from $f_1, \ldots, f_n$ by *MP*. We call I an inference rule for consistency with the literature and with its intuitive meaning.

Composition rule

For any program fragments S_1, S_2, and $S = S_1; S_2$ and for any formulas P, R, Q

$$IR1 : \frac{\{P\}S_1\{R\}, \{R\}S_2\{Q\}}{\{P\}S_1; S_2\{Q\}}$$

Intuitively, the meaning of the composition rule is as follows: If P guarantees that R holds after execution of S_1, and R guarantees that Q holds after execution of S_2, then we may infer that P guarantees that Q holds after execution of the sequence $S_1; S_2$.

For example, let S_1 be $x := f_1(x)$ and S_2 be $x := f_2(x)$. The application of A1 allows us to obtain, for any P

$$\left\{ P_x^{f_2(x)} \right\} x := f_2(x)\{P\}$$

and

$$\left\{ P_x^{f_2(f_1(x))} \right\} x := f_1(x)\left\{ P_x^{f_2(x)} \right\}$$

Then, by applying *IR1*, we obtain

$$\left\{ P_x^{f_2(f_1(x))} \right\} x := f_1(x); \; x := f_2(x)\{P\}$$

which intuitively means that the foregoing program fragment results in the composition of the two functions f_2 and f_1. For example, if we want to prove that $x \geq 7$ after execution of the above fragment, it is sufficient to prove that $f_2(f_1(x)) \geq 7$ before its execution.

Consequence rule

The following rule is trivial and not strictly related to language semantics, but is helpful in deriving proofs.

$$IR2: \frac{P_1 \supset P, \{P\}S\{Q\}, Q \supset Q_1}{\{P_1\}S\{Q_1\}}$$

For example,

$$\frac{x \geq 3 \wedge y \geq 4 \supset x + y \geq 7, \{x + y \geq 7\}x := x + y\{x \geq 7\}, x \geq 7 \supset x \geq 5}{\{x \geq 3 \wedge y \geq 4\}x := x + y\{x \geq 5\}}$$

if-then-else *rule*

For any program fragments S_1 and S_2 derivable from $\langle StatList \rangle$, for any condition c derivable from $\langle Cond \rangle$, and for any assertions P and Q

$$IR3a: \frac{\{P \wedge c\}S_1\{Q\}, \{P \wedge \neg c\}S_2\{Q\}}{\{P\} \text{ if } c \text{ then } S_1 \text{ else } S_2 \text{ fi } \{Q\}}$$

$$IR3b: \frac{\{P \wedge c\}S_1\{Q\}, P \wedge \neg c \supset Q}{\{P\} \text{ if } c \text{ then } S_1 \text{ fi } \{Q\}}$$

The intuitive meanings of *IR3a* and *IR3b* are fairly obvious. When we enter the statement **if** c **then** S_1 **else** S_2 **fi** either c or $\neg c$ hold. Thus if we want to be sure that precondition P guarantees postcondition Q after execution, we need to state that

- If c holds (the **then** branch is chosen), precondition $P \wedge c$ guarantees Q after execution of S_1.
- If c does not hold (the **else** branch is chosen) precondition $P \wedge \neg c$ guarantees Q after execution of S_2.

Because we do not know a priori whether c holds or not, both alternatives must be proved. Note that *IR3b* can be seen as a particular case of *IR*3a when S_2 is the null statement.

For example, suppose we wish to prove that after the statement

if $x > y$ **then** $z := x$ **else** $z := y$ **fi**

the assertion $z \geq y \wedge z \geq x$ *always* holds.
This is specified by the formula

$$\{T\} \text{ if } x > y \text{ then } z := x \text{ else } z := y \text{ fi } \{z \geq y \wedge z \geq x\}^3$$

The foregoing theorem can be proven in the following way.

$$T \wedge x > y \supset (x \geq y \wedge x \geq x)$$
$$\{x \geq y \wedge x \geq x\}z := x\{z \geq y \wedge z \geq x\}$$

Thus, by *IR2*,

$$\{T \wedge x > y\}z := x\{z \geq y \wedge z \geq x\}$$

---

[3] Recall that predicate T means that no constraints are given on the machine state (i.e., any state satisfies predicate T).

Also,

$$T \wedge \neg(x > y) \supset (y \geq y \wedge y \geq x)$$
$$\{y \geq y \wedge y \geq x\}z := y\{z \geq y \wedge z \geq x\}$$

Thus, by *IR2*,

$$\{T \wedge \neg(x > y)\}z := y\{z \geq y \wedge z \geq x\}$$

Finally, by *IR3a*, we obtain the desired result.

while *rule*

For any program fragment S derivable from $\langle \text{StatList} \rangle$, for any condition c derivable from $\langle \text{Cond} \rangle$, and for any assertion I

$$IR4: \qquad \frac{\{I \wedge c\}S\{I\}}{\{I\} \text{ while } c \text{ do } S \text{ od } \{I \wedge \neg c\}}$$

Notice that in this case it is required that the assertion I, if true before entering the loop, continues to hold after execution of its body. In fact, if c holds, the body is executed, and $\{I \wedge c\}S\{I\}$ implies that I still holds after S. Thus, I will always hold after any iteration of the loop. For this reason, assertion I is called a *loop invariant*. At loop exit, *if this ever occurs*, $I \wedge \neg c$ will hold as $\neg c$ is the loop exit condition. The use of *IR4* will be clarified by the following example.

Example 5.1

Consider the following SMALG program (with no I/O)

```
P:   begin x := 1;
            j := 1;
            while y ≥ j
            do j := j + 1;
               x := x * z
            od
      end
```

The program is intended to perform the exponentiation z^y. The values of z and y are supposed to be already stored in memory. An obvious assertion capturing P's correctness is

$$PA: \{y > 0\}P\{x = z^y\}$$

In order to prove P correct (with respect to PA) we have to prove PA as a *theorem* within the above formal theory.

As a very first try we could apply our proof rules by attempting to use directly the output assertion $Q: x = z^y$ as the loop invariant. In this case, our job would become to prove

i: $\{Q \wedge (y \geq j)\}j := j + 1; \; x = x * z\{Q\}$.
ii: $\{y > 0\}x := 1; \; j := 1\{Q\}$.

By applying rule $IR4$ to i, we would have

$\{Q\}$ **while** $y \geq j$ **do** $j := j + 1$, $x := x * 7$ **od** $\{Q \wedge y < j\}$

and by the composition rule $IR1$ and ii the thesis would follow.

Unfortunately, it is immediate to realize that Q is not an invariant for the loop (i.e., i does not hold). In fact, backward substitution of Q through $x := x * z$ and $j := j + 1$ shows that

$\{x * z = z^y\} j := j + 1; x := x * z \{x = z^y\}$

And $x = z^y \wedge y \geq j$ by no means implies that $x * z = z^y$.

This failure brings up an important point: The loop invariant (i.e., the assertion to be used in order to apply $IR4$), must be carefully chosen by using *ingenuity* and our knowledge of the program's behavior. In our case, let us observe that every iteration of the loop increments a counter variable j and multiplies x by z. As a consequence, there must exist a relation between the values of x, z and j. Intuitively, let us postulate $I: x = z^j$ invariant and let us retry the previous procedure by using I instead of Q. It is immediate to verify that $I \wedge y < j$ (the exit assertion of the loop) does not imply $x = z^y$, which is our goal. Actually, $x = z^j$ and $y < j$ implies $x \neq z^y$.

This new failure suggests that at the exit of the loop x should be less than z^j; why not $x = z^{j-1}$? This new candidate is at least noncontradictory with predicates $y < j$ and $x = z^y$. But in order to prove our thesis, we need more information on the value of j: It is necessary to show that y is exactly equal to $j - 1$. This suggests enriching $x = z^{j-1}$ with another assertion: Let us try the most natural one, namely $y = j - 1$. If we can prove that the new predicate $I': x = z^{j-1} \wedge y = j - 1$ is a loop invariant we are almost done with our proof. Again, however, it is trivial to realize—through backwards substitution—that I' is not a loop invariant.

As a last try, let us make predicate I' a bit weaker and observe that by choosing a new candidate as loop invariant, namely $J: x = z^{j-1} \wedge y \geq j - 1$, we can complete the proof successfully. In fact, $J \wedge y < j$ implies $y = j - 1$ and thus the assertion $x = z^y$ at loop exit. Furthermore, J actually is a loop invariant, as backwards substitution through the loop body shows

$\{J \wedge y \geq j\} j := j + 1$, $x := x * z \{J\}$

(details of this proof are left to the reader as an exercise).

To complete the proof we need to show only that J holds at loop entry.

$\{y > 0\} x := 1; j := 1 \{J\}$

Again, the proof of this can be accomplished by simple backwards substitution and is left to the reader as an exercise.

Example 5.1 has been carried out in order to emphasize the key point of correctness proofs by using the axiomatic method, namely the *invention of loop invariants*. As we have shown, the loop invariant one looks for is not just *any* invariant (i.e., a predicate whose truth is preserved by the loop body): It must be such that through it we can prove the truth of the desired program's postcondition. If this process fails, either the program is incorrect or, simply, our proof has failed! Looking for appropriate loop invariants should not be a blind search, but rather should be driven by a deep knowledge of the program structure and of the axiomatic method itself. As it usually happens in such cases, practical experience is needed before one can attack correctness proofs of nontrivial programs. Therefore, the reader is invited to practice the method by carefully analyzing the proposed examples and by experimenting with a few exercises of increasing complexity. However, once again we warn the reader that the purpose of this chapter—and of the whole text—is to equip the reader with a sound set of theoretical tools that can be used in the practical world of software production. The practical skills needed to apply these concepts to real-life cases of software engineering are beyond the scope of this text.

Exercises

5.1 Prove program P of Example 5.1 correct with respect to the following assertion

$$\{ y \geq 0 \wedge z \neq 0 \} P \{ x = z^y \}$$

5.2 Can you prove program P of Example 5.1 correct with respect to the following assertion?

$$\{ y \geq 0 \} P \{ x = z^y \}$$

Why? Why not?

5.3 Prove the following theorem.

```
{n > 1}
begin i := 1;
      z := 1;
      while z ≤ n do
                  i := i + 1;
                  z := i * i
                  od;
         sqrt := i - 1
end
{sqrt² ≤ n ∧ n < (sqrt + 1)²}
```

Hint: Use the following predicate I as loop invariant.

$$I : z = i^2 \wedge (i - 1)^2 \leq n$$

What happens if you replace the precondition $n > 1$ with $n \geq 0$?

5.4 Disprove the correctness of the following program with respect to precondition $Pre : n \geq 0$ and postcondition $Post : sqrt^2 \leq n \wedge n < (sqrt + 1)^2$. Use failures in your proof to fix the program until you come to a version that can be proven correct.

```
begin  x := 0;  y := 1;  z := 1;
      while y < n do
                  x := x + 1;
                  z := z + 2;
                  y := y + z
                  od;
          sqrt := x
end
```

Hint: This program is based on the property that $(x + 1)^2 = x^2 + 2x + 1$. Variable y is intended to store the current value of x^2; variable z is intended to store the current value of $2x + 1$. Thus, each iteration evaluates the new value of z and the new value of y according to the above property.

5.2.1　Handling Quantified Assertions

In the previous section, we were able to prove the correctness of very simple programs, which do not deal with arrays, by using quantifier-free assertions. Let us now proceed a few steps further. This section enables us to deal with assertions using quantifiers. The next section discusses how to handle indexed variables.

　　　Notice that often the use of quantifiers in program assertions may be useful. For example, we might wish to assert that a program variable x is positive and even at a certain point of program execution. This could be expressed by the formula

$$\exists z(x = 2 \cdot z \land z > 0)$$

Unfortunately, axiom A1 cannot be applied as it is if P contains quantified variables. In fact, in our case it would yield the following axiom.

$$F \equiv \{\exists z(z = 2 \cdot z \land z > 0)\}\, x := z\, \{\exists z(x = 2 \cdot z \land z > 0)\}$$

Predicate F means that no machine state satisfies the precondition needed to establish the stated postcondition. This is clearly incorrect in the example.

　　　This problem is exactly the same problem we had with axiom A4 in Section 0.2.3. In fact, notice that the term z is not free for x in $\exists z\,(x = 2 \cdot z \land z > 0)$. Thus, we must restrict application of A1 to the case where *t is free for x in P*, as we did for A4 in Section 0.2.3. Following the suggestion of Section 0.2.3, we adopt a notation that avoids a priori the intricate verification that t be free for x in P, without any loss of generality. In the rest of this chapter quantified variables are overbarred. The previous case would be formulated as

$$\{\exists \bar{z}(z = 2 \cdot \bar{z} \land \bar{z} > 0)\}\, x := z\, \{\exists \bar{z}(x = 2 \cdot \bar{z} \land \bar{z} > 0)\}$$

which clearly works properly.

　　　Suppose now we wish to state that after the execution of a program fragment S, the variable z has the maximum value among all program variables. At a first glance, we might try to prove that, after S, $\forall \bar{y}(z \geq \bar{y})$ holds. In this case, the application of A1 would yield

$$\{\forall \bar{y}(z \geq \bar{y})\} x := z + 1\{\forall \bar{y}(z \geq \bar{y})\}$$

as x does not occur in the assertion. But this would mean that if z is greater than or equal to any $\bar{y}$ before execution of the statement then the same holds after execution, which is clearly false because the value of x becomes greater then the value of z. The problem here is due to an ambiguity in using variable identifiers within first-order wfs. In fact, the formula $\exists \bar{z}(x = 2 \cdot \bar{z} \wedge \bar{z} > 0)$ was intended to mean that there exist a positive integer $\bar{z}$ such that the integer value of program variable x equals $2 \cdot \bar{z}$. Instead, the formula $\forall \bar{y}(z \geq \bar{y})$ was intended to state that the value of program variable z is greater or equal to the value of any other program variable. So the same variable symbols of a first-order theory are used to denote different things. In order to avoid this problem, we stick to the assumption that overbarred variable symbols denote any value ranging over the set of integers. As a consequence, the quantifier $\forall \bar{x}$ will always mean "For every integer value $\bar{x}$." Instead, an occurrence of a program variable x should be read as "that particular integer value that is the value of program variable x." An immediate consequence of this point of view is that quantifying symbols denoting program variables is meaningless and should be avoided. Going back to our example, if we wish to state that z is greater or equal to any program variable, we should write

$$\forall \bar{y}((\bar{y} = x_1 \vee \bar{y} = x_2 \dots) \supset z \geq \bar{y})$$

where $\{x_i\}$ denotes the set of all variable symbols associated to program variables. At this point, axiom A1 is correct as we know—without loss of generality—that all occurrences of program variables in any assertion will be free. Now, if we apply backward substitution of the above axiom through $x := z + 1$, we obtain

$$\forall \bar{y}((\bar{y} = x_1 \vee \dots \bar{y} = z \vee \dots \bar{y} = z + 1) \supset z \geq \bar{y})$$

which is a contradiction.

Example 5.2

The following program is intended to compute the greatest common divisor (GCD) of two numbers.

PGCD: **begin**

```
        x := z;
        y := w;
        while x ≠ y do
                if x > y
                then x := x − y
                else y := y − x
                fi
                od
    end
```

We wish to prove

$$\{z > 0 \land w > 0\}\, PGCD\, \{x = GCD(z, w)\}$$

where $x = GCD(u, v)$ is a short notation for

$$\exists \bar{k}\big((\bar{k} = x) \land \exists \bar{u}_1, \bar{v}_1\big(u = \bar{u}_1 \cdot \bar{k} \land v = \bar{v}_1 \cdot \bar{k}\big)$$
$$\land\, \not\exists \bar{h}, \bar{u}_2, \bar{v}_2\big(u = \bar{u}_2 \cdot \bar{h} \land v = \bar{v}_2 \cdot \bar{h} \land \bar{h} > \bar{k}\big)\big)^4$$

A natural loop invariant is

$$I : GCD(x, y) = GCD(z, w)$$

which, again, must be intended as a short notation for

$$\exists \bar{k}\big((\exists \bar{x}_1, \bar{y}_1\big(x = \bar{x}_1 \cdot \bar{k} \land y = \bar{y}_1 \cdot \bar{k}\big)$$
$$\land\, \not\exists \bar{h}, \bar{x}_2, \bar{y}_2\big(x = \bar{x}_2 \cdot \bar{h} \land y = \bar{y}_2 \cdot \bar{h} \land \bar{h} > \bar{k}\big)\big) \land$$
$$\big(\exists \bar{z}_1, \bar{w}_1\big(z = \bar{z}_1 \cdot \bar{k} \land w = \bar{w}_1 \cdot \bar{k}\big)$$
$$\land\, \not\exists \bar{h}, \bar{z}_2, \bar{w}_2\big(z = \bar{z}_2 \cdot \bar{h} \land w = \bar{w}_2 \cdot \bar{h} \land \bar{h} > \bar{k}\big)\big)\big)$$

First, observe that I holds at loop entry.

$$\{z > 0 \land w > 0\}\, x := z;\; y := w\, \{I\}$$

In fact, backwards, substitution of I through $x := z;\; y := w$ yields $GCD(z, w) = GCD(z, w)$, which is clearly true.

Second, at loop exit the assertion $I \land x = y$ implies $x = GCD(z, w)$, which is the desired postcondition. Thus the proof will be completed if we prove that I is actually a loop invariant; i.e.

$$\{I \land x \neq y\}\ \textbf{if } x > y \textbf{ then } x := x - y \textbf{ else } y := y - x \textbf{ fi } \{I\}.$$

This is obtained by proving that

a. $I \land x > y \supset M$, where M is the predicate obtained by backwards substituting I through $x := x - y$, that is, $M : GCD(x - y, y) = GCD(z, w)$.

Notice that (a) states that, if $x > y$, the greatest common divisor of x and y equals the greatest common divisor of $x - y$ and y. The proof of (a) is left to the reader as an exercise. We suggest that the extended formulation for GCD be used.

b. $I \land y > x \supset GCD(x, y - x) = GCD(z, w)$, which is clearly proved in a similar way as (a).

Finally, since $x \neq y \supset (x > y \lor y > x)$ (and thus

$$(x \neq y \land \neg(x > y)) \supset y > x),$$

the proof is completed.

---

[4] The above notation is a slight, self-explanatory, modification of the pure syntax of first-order theories. It is introduced to make formulas more understandable.

Exercises

5.5 Prove point (a) of Example 5.2.

5.6 Write a SMALG program to check whether a given value x is prime and prove it correct with respect to precondition $Pre: x > 1$ and postcondition

Post: $prime = 0 \supset \exists y(1 < y < x \land x \bmod y = 0) \land$
          $prime = 1 \supset \forall y(1 < y < x \supset x \bmod y \neq 0)$

5.7 Write a program to evaluate the minimum common multiple of two positive integers x and y. Prove correctness of your program.

5.2.2 Handling Indexed Variables

Let us study now how to handle indexed variables. An array variable can be seen as a function mapping (positive) integers (indexes) into integers (array elements). Thus, there is no need for any syntactic enrichment of previous wfs (the use of square brackets instead of the usual round brackets used for functional notations is only a trivial extension).

We must realize that this decision slightly limits the set of allowed wfs since, e.g., wfs with quantified array identifiers are excluded. To cope with such formulas one should enrich Peano's axioms to cover interpretations whose domains contain array variables, in a similar way as we did in Example 4.14. However, because the cases considered in this chapter do not need the above type of formulas, we prefer to remain within the case of Peano's arithmetics.

As a first attempt we might try to apply A1 to subscripted variables as we did for simple variables. In fact, it is clear that the following statement is correct

$\{T\}\, a[x] := 5\{a[x] = 5\}.$

However, consider the following statement

$\{a[x] = 3\}\, a[k] := 5\{a[k] = 5 \land a[x] = 3\}$

The statement is clearly incorrect if k happens to be equal to x. In such a case, $a[k] = 3$ would be false after execution of the statement. Inconsistencies of this type become even more apparent in the following cases.

a. Let P be the predicate $\forall i(1 \le i \le 10 \supset a[i] = 5)$
   Using A1, backwards substitution of P through the statements $k := 3;$
   $a[k] := 6$ yields P. But the contradiction of $\{P\}k := 3;\ a[k] := 6\{P\}$ is obvious.

b. Let P be the following predicate $a[x] = 1 \land x = a[2]$. Using A1, backwards substitution of P through $x := a[2];\ a[x] := 1$ yields

   $\{T\}x := a[2];\ a[x] := 1\{P\}.$

   This is clearly incorrect if $a[2] = 2$ before execution of the two statements, since x would not be equal to $a[2]$ afterwards.

The previous examples show that application of A1 yields incorrect results whenever two variables used as indexes—say m and n—have the same value and thus an assignment to $a[m]$ results in a "hidden assignment" to $a[n]$. In such case, $a[n]$ and $a[m]$ are *aliases* for the same memory location. It is clear that A1 must be modified to take this fact into account. To do so, we prefix any occurrence of an indexed variable by a suitable **if-then-else** "mask." For instance, if P is $a[x] = z$, backwards substitution of P through $a[k] := 3$ should produce $\bar{P}$, where $\bar{P}$, is

(**if** $x = k$ **then** 3 **else** $a[x]) = z$

In general, for any assertion P, let $\bar{P}^t_{a[i]}$ denote the result of substituting any occurrence of $a[i]$ in P by t and any occurrence of $a[x]$ (x being either a variable or a constant[5]) by the term

if $x = i$ **then** t **else** $a[x]$

For example if P is $\forall \bar{p}((a[\bar{p}] \geq a[i]) \supset (\forall \bar{z}(a[\bar{z}] \neq a[j])))$, $\bar{P}^t_{a[i]}$ is

$\forall \bar{p}((\textbf{if } \bar{p} = i \textbf{ then } t \textbf{ else } a[\bar{p}]) \geq t \supset$
$\quad (\forall \bar{z}(\textbf{if } \bar{z} = i \textbf{ then } t \textbf{ else } a[\bar{z}]) \neq (\textbf{if } j = i \textbf{ then } t \textbf{ else } a[j])))$

Now we define the axiom $\overline{\text{A1}}$ for assignment statements whose left-hand side is an indexed variable as

$$\overline{\text{A1}} : \left\{ \bar{P}^t_{a[i]} \right\} a[i] := t \{ P \}$$

(where i is either a variable or a constant value).

Thanks to $\overline{\text{A1}}$ we are now ready to verify programs handling arrays. However, there is one more little detail to be fixed up. We focus on it in Example 5.4. In the meanwhile the reader is invited to discover by him or herself what the remaining detail is.

Example 5.3

Consider the following simple and self-explanatory SMALG program, which is intended to verify whether an array a is sorted or not. As usual, we forget about I/O, that is, we assume that the array is already stored in memory and we do not require to write the result.[6]

```
VERIFYSORT:  begin
                  sorted := 1; i := 2;
                  while i ≤ n
                      do k := i − 1;
                         if a[k] > a[i]
                         then sorted := 0
                         fi;
                         i := i + 1
                      od
             end
```

---

[5]$\bar{P}^t_{a[c]}$, c being a constant value, may be defined more simply as the result of substituting any occurrence of $a[c]$ by t and any occurrence of $a[x]$ by the term **if** $x = c$ **then** t **else** $a[x]$. In other words, terms of the type $a[c']$, c' being a constant other than c, need not be substituted.

[6]As it happended before, note that SMALG imposes a few minor adaptations with respect to coding in a real high-level language such as Pascal.

First, let us state suitable input and output assertions to capture the correctness of *VERIFYSORT*. It is clear that the program is designed with the purpose of assigning the values 1 and 0 to the variable *sorted* if the array a is sorted or not, respectively. This can be formalized by the following formula:

$$P_O : ((sorted = 1) \supset (\forall \bar{p}(1 \le \bar{p} \le n - 1) \supset a[\bar{p}] \le a[\bar{p} + 1])) \wedge$$
$$((sorted = 0) \supset \neg(\forall \bar{p}(1 \le \bar{p} \le n - 1) \supset a[\bar{p}] \le a[\bar{p} + 1]))$$

The input assertion simply states that a is not empty, that is, $P_I : n \ge 1$.

Let us now start our correctness proof; that is, the proof of

$$\{P_I\} VERIFYSORT \{P_O\}.$$

The main problem is finding a suitable invariant for program's loop, that is, an assertion I such that

1. $\{P_I\} sorted := 1; i := 2\{I\}$.
2. $\{I \wedge i \le n\} k := i - 1; \textbf{if} \ldots \textbf{fi}; i := i + 1\{I\}$
3. $\{I \wedge i > n\} \supset P_O$

An intuitive analysis of *VERIFYSORT* shows that it is designed in such a way that variable *sorted*, after initialization to 1, maintains this value until an element $a[i]$ is found such that $a[i - 1] > a[i]$, if any. This suggests the following predicate as a tentative invariant.

$$I : ((sorted = 1) \supset (\forall \bar{p}(1 \le \bar{p} \le i - 1) \supset a[\bar{p}] \le a[\bar{p} + 1])) \wedge$$
$$((sorted = 0) \supset \neg(\forall \bar{p}(1 \le \bar{p} \le i - 1) \supset a[\bar{p}] \le a[\bar{p} + 1]))$$

In other words, I states that *VERIFYSORT* has checked a for being sorted or not up to the ith element. However, we immediately notice that $I \wedge i > n$ does not imply P_O. In fact, $i > n$ does not give enough information on the relation between i and n at loop exit. We can augment I with $1 \le i \le n + 1$, which is clearly a loop invariant and, in such case, at loop exit we can deduce $i = n + 1$. However, $\{P_I\} sorted := 1; i := 2\{I\}$ does not hold.

In fact, backwards substitution of I through the two statements yields

$$((1 = 1) \supset (\forall \bar{p}(1 \le \bar{p} \le 1) \supset a[\bar{p}] \le a[\bar{p} + 1])) \wedge$$
$$((1 = 0) \supset \neg(\forall \bar{p}(1 \le \bar{p} \le 1) \supset a[\bar{p}] \le a[\bar{p} + 1]))$$

which is clearly equivalent to $a[1] \le a[2]$. This relation is by no means implied by P_I.

As a consequence of this failure, a deeper insight into the program shows that after every iteration of the loop, a has been checked up to the $(i - 1)$th element. Thus we must correct the loop invariant into

$$I : ((sorted = 1) \supset (\forall \bar{p}(1 \le \bar{p} < i - 1) \supset a[\bar{p}] \le a[\bar{p} + 1])) \wedge$$
$$((sorted = 0) \supset \neg(\forall \bar{p}(1 \le \bar{p} < i - 1) \supset a[\bar{p}] \le a[\bar{p} + 1])) \wedge 1 \le i \le n + 1$$

The proofs of points 1 and 3 above are now easy exercises. We outline here the proof of point 2.

Backwards substitution of I through $i := i + 1$ produces

$I_1 : ((sorted = 1) \supset (\forall \bar{p}(1 \leq \bar{p} < i) \supset a[\bar{p}] \leq a[\bar{p} + 1])) \wedge$

$\quad ((sorted = 0) \supset \neg(\forall \bar{p}(1 \leq \bar{p} < i) \supset a[\bar{p}] \supset a[\bar{p} + 1])) \wedge$

$\quad 1 \leq i + 1 \leq n + 1$

Let I_2 be the following predicate.

$I_2 : ((sorted = 1) \supset (\forall \bar{p}(1 \leq \bar{p} < i - 1) \supset a[\bar{p}] \leq a[\bar{p} + 1])) \wedge$

$\quad ((sorted = 0) \supset \neg(\forall \bar{p}(1 \leq \bar{p} < i - 1) \supset a[\bar{p}] \leq a[\bar{p} + 1])) \wedge$

$\quad 1 \leq i + 1 \leq n + 1 \wedge k = i - 1$

It is easy to verify that

- $I_2 \wedge a[k] > a[i] \supset I_1^*$, where I_1^* is the result of backwards substitution of I_1 through $sorted := 0$. In fact, I_1^*, is equivalent to

  $\neg(\forall \bar{p}(1 \leq \bar{p} < i) \supset a[\bar{p}] \leq a[\bar{p} + 1]) \wedge 0 \leq i \leq n,$

  which in turn is equivalent to

  $\exists \bar{p}(1 \leq \bar{p} < i) \wedge a[\bar{p}] > a[\bar{p} + 1] \wedge 0 \leq i \leq n.$

- $I_2 \wedge a[k] \leq a[i] \supset I_1$. In fact, if $sorted = 1$, $a[\bar{p}] \leq a[\bar{p} + 1]$ for any $\bar{p}$, with $1 \leq \bar{p} < i - 1$, and $a[i - 1] \leq a[i]$. Thus $a[\bar{p}] \leq a[\bar{p} + 1]$ for any $\bar{p}$, with $1 \leq \bar{p} < i$. If $sorted = 0$, then there is a value $\bar{p}$, with $1 \leq \bar{p} < i - 1$, such that $a[\bar{p}] > a[\bar{p} + 1]$ and, a fortiori, $1 \leq \bar{p} < i$. Thus, we derive $\{I_2\}$**if**$\ldots$**fi**$\{I_1\}$.

Finally, by backwards substitution of I_2 through $k := i - 1$, we obtain

$((sorted = 1) \supset (\forall \bar{p}(1 \leq \bar{p} < i - 1) \supset a[\bar{p}] \leq a[\bar{p} + 1])) \wedge$

$((sorted = 0) \supset \neg(\forall \bar{p}(1 \leq \bar{p} < i - 1) \supset a[\bar{p}] \leq a[\bar{p} + 1])) \wedge$

$1 \leq i + 1 \leq n + 1$

which is implied by $I \wedge i \leq n$.

The program *VERIFYSORT* of Example 5.3 is a very simple program, which does not involve subscripted variables as lefthandsides of assignment statements. The next example considers a more complex case.

Example 5.4

Consider the following SMALG program which is intended to sort array a. Again, suppose the array to be sorted is already stored in memory.

PSORT: **begin**
$\quad\quad i := 2;$
$\quad\quad$ **while** $i \le n$
$\quad\quad\quad$ **do**
$\quad\quad\quad\quad x := a[i]; \; a[0] := x; \; j := i - 1;$
$\quad\quad\quad\quad$ **while** $x < a[j]$
$\quad\quad\quad\quad\quad$ **do** $k := j + 1;$
$\quad\quad\quad\quad\quad\quad a[k] := a[j];$
$\quad\quad\quad\quad\quad\quad j := j - 1$
$\quad\quad\quad\quad\quad$ **od**
$\quad\quad\quad\quad k := j + 1; \; a[k] := x; \; i := i + 1$
$\quad\quad\quad$ **od**
$\quad\quad$ **end**

The intuitive explanation of the algorithm implemented by the above program has already been given in Section 2.4. Since the above program is intended as to sort array a, a natural output assertion is

$P_O : P_{O1} \wedge P_{O2}$

where

$P_{O1} : \forall \bar{p}(1 \le \bar{p} \le n - 1) \supset a[\bar{p}] \le a[\bar{p} + 1]$

states that at program exit a is sorted, while P_{O2} should state that at program exit a is a permutation of what it was before program starting. Here we run into problems because at program exit there is no variable whose value is the original value of array a. We can overcome this difficulty by means of a little trick. Let us modify *PSORT* into the following $\overline{PSORT}$ as

$\overline{PSORT}$: **begin** $i := 1$
$\quad\quad$ **while** $i \le n$ **do** $b[i] := a[i]; \; i := i + 1$ **od**;
$\quad\quad i := 2;$
$\quad\quad$ **while** $i \le n$
$\quad\quad\quad$ **do**
$\quad\quad\quad\quad x := a[i]; \; a[0] := x; \; j := i - 1;$
$\quad\quad\quad\quad$ **while** $x < a[j]$
$\quad\quad\quad\quad\quad$ **do** $k := j + 1;$
$\quad\quad\quad\quad\quad\quad a[k] := a[j];$
$\quad\quad\quad\quad\quad\quad j := j - 1$
$\quad\quad\quad\quad\quad$ **od**
$\quad\quad\quad\quad k := j + 1; \; a[k] := x; \; i := i + 1$
$\quad\quad\quad$ **od**
$\quad\quad$ **end**

In order to state that $\overline{PSORT}$ actually sorts array a we could use as output predicate $P_O : P_{O1} \wedge P_{O2}$ where P_{O1} is the same as above and P_{O2} is

$P_{O2} : (\forall \bar{p}(1 \le \bar{p} \le n) \supset (\exists \bar{r}(1 \le \bar{r} \le n) \wedge (a[\bar{p}] = b[\bar{r}]))) \wedge$
$\quad\quad (\forall \bar{r}(1 \le \bar{r} \le n) \supset (\exists \bar{p}(1 \le \bar{p} \le n) \wedge (a[\bar{p}] = b[\bar{r}])))$

Notice that P_{O2} is a correct specification of a permutation only if b does not contain multiple occurrences of the same value. In fact, a program transforming

$b = \{3, 4, 5, 4\}$ into $a = \{3, 3, 4, 5\}$ would satisfy P_O. However, for simplicity, we suppose, without formally specifying it, that the array does not contain multiple occurrences of the same element. Thus, P_{O2} becomes adequate.

Notice now that the new array variable b serves just for recording purposes but does not affect $\overline{PSORT}$, which is exactly the same as $PSORT$. Thus, in what follows we refer to $PSORT$ and we use b as a dummy array variable that contains the initial value of a. We also assume that initially the array is not empty (i.e., $n \geq 1$), so that the precondition for $PSORT$ is

$$P_I : 1 \leq n \wedge \forall \bar{p}(1 \leq \bar{p} \leq n) \supset a[\bar{p}] = b[\bar{p}])$$

Our goal is to prove the truth of

$$\{P_I\} PSORT \{P_O\}$$

which, rewritten in detail, is

$$\{1 \leq n \wedge \forall \bar{p}((1 \leq \bar{p} \leq n) \supset a[\bar{p}] = b[\bar{p}])\}$$
$$\quad PSORT$$
$$\{(\forall \bar{p}(1 \leq \bar{p} \leq n - 1 \supset (a[\bar{p}] \leq a[\bar{p} + 1]))) \wedge$$
$$(\forall \bar{p}(1 \leq \bar{r} \leq n) \supset (\exists \bar{r}(1 \leq \bar{r} \leq n) \wedge (a[\bar{p}] = b[\bar{r}]))) \wedge$$
$$(\forall \bar{r}(1 \leq \bar{r} \leq n) \supset (\exists \bar{p}(1 \leq \bar{p} \leq n) \wedge (a[\bar{p}] = b[\bar{r}])))\}$$

This looks like an intricate job. Before going into the details of the proof, consider that, for any program P, if we can prove

$$\{Pre1\} P \{Post1\}$$

and

$$\{Pre2\} P \{Post2\}$$

then we can deduce

$$\{Pre1 \wedge Pre2\} P \{Post1 \wedge Post2\}$$

without any need for further proof.
Thus, let us try to prove

1. $\{1 \leq n\} PSORT \{P_{O1}\}$
2. $\{P_I\} PSORT \{P_{O2}\}$

If we succeed in this, we will have the desired proof.

Proof of 1
We recall from the informal description given in Section 2.4 that the algorithm is such that at every iteration of the external loop the "lower" portion of the array $a[1..i - 1]$ is sorted while the "upper" portion is not. Because i goes from 2 to $n + 1$ during the iterations of the external loop, at the end of the process the array will be completely sorted. This suggests the following invariant assertion for the external loop

$$I_{\text{EXT}} : 1 \leq i \leq n + 1 \wedge \forall \bar{p}((1 \leq \bar{p} < i - 1) \supset a[\bar{p}] \leq a[\bar{p} + 1])$$

It is easy to prove that $(I_{\text{EXT}} \wedge i > n) \supset P_O$ and that $\{1 \leq n\} i := 2 \{I_{\text{EXT}}\}$.

It remains to prove that I_{EXT} is indeed invariant for the external, loop (i.e.,: $\{I_{\text{EXT}} \wedge i \leq n\}$ *external loop body* $\{I_{\text{EXT}}\}$).
Let us backwards substitute I_{EXT} through

$$k := j + 1; \ a[k] := x; \ i := i + 1$$

First, we obtain

$$\{0 \leq i \leq n \wedge \forall \bar{p}((1 \leq \bar{p} < i) \supset a[\bar{p}] \leq a[\bar{p} + 1])\} i := i + 1 \{I_{\text{EXT}}\}$$

Then we face the problem of backwards substitution through the assignment $a[k] := x$, where an indexed variable occurs in the lefthandside. When trying to apply $\overline{A1}$, we discover the detail to be fixed up that we anticipated. In fact, it may happen that indexes in program assertions are expressions, even if the languages of the SMALG family do not allow this. Here, we decide to treat the index expression in the very same way as we did in the case of simple variable indexes. However, we warn the reader that a subtle trap may occur in such a case (see the remark at the end of the example for a complete analysis of this case).

Backwards substitution of I_{EXT} through $k := j + 1; \ a[k] := x; \ i := i + 1$ by means of $\overline{A1}$ gives

$$I_{\text{EXT}}^* : (0 \leq i \leq n) \wedge \forall \bar{p}((1 \leq \bar{p} < i) \supset (\text{if } \bar{p} = j + 1 \text{ then } x \text{ else } a[\bar{p}]) \leq$$
$$(\text{if } \bar{p} + 1 = j + 1 \text{ then } x \text{ else } a[\bar{p} + 1]))$$

which can be rewritten into the equivalent more readable form.

$$(0 \leq i \leq n) \wedge$$
$$\forall \bar{p}((1 \leq \bar{p} < i) \supset$$
$$\quad \text{if } \bar{p} = j + 1 \text{ then if } \bar{p} + 1 = j + 1 \text{ then } x \leq x$$
$$\quad\quad\quad\quad\quad\quad\quad\quad\quad\quad\quad\quad\quad\quad\quad \text{else } x \leq a[\bar{p} + 1]$$
$$\quad\quad\quad\quad\quad\quad\quad \text{else if } \bar{p} + 1 = j + 1 \text{ then } a[\bar{p}] \leq x$$
$$\quad\quad\quad\quad\quad\quad\quad\quad\quad\quad\quad\quad\quad\quad \text{else } a[\bar{p}] \leq a[\bar{p} + 1])$$

and simplified into

$$I_{\text{EXT}}^* : 0 \leq i \leq n \wedge \forall \bar{p}(1 \leq \bar{p} < i) \supset$$
$$\quad\quad\quad\quad \text{if } \bar{p} = j + 1 \text{ then } x \leq a[\bar{p} + 1]$$
$$\quad\quad\quad\quad\quad\quad\quad \text{else if } \bar{p} = j \text{ then } a[\bar{p}] \leq x$$
$$\quad\quad\quad\quad\quad\quad\quad\quad\quad\quad \text{else } a[\bar{p}] \leq a[\bar{p} + 1])$$

since $\bar{p} = j + 1$ implies $\bar{p} + 1 \neq j + 1$.

Now we have to go through the inner loop; therefore, we must invent a new invariant. Going back to the informal explanation of the algorithm, we find that the purpose of the inner loop is to create a "hole," in the appropriate position of the ordered portion of the array where the first element of the unordered portion (namely, $a[i] = x = a[0]$) will be inserted. Informally, the invariant I_{IN} of the inner loop must state that index j, with $0 \leq j < i$, partitions the sorted subarray $a[1..i - 1]$ plus the element $a[i]$ into two sorted subarrays $a[1..j]$ and $a[j + 1..i]$ such that each element of the latter is greater than or equal to x which, in turn, is equal to $a[0]$. Furthermore $a[j] \leq a[j+1]$, except when $j = i - 1$. Formally,

$$I_{IN} : \forall \bar{p}(((1 \leq \bar{p} < j) \supset a[\bar{p}] \leq a[\bar{p}+1]) \land$$
$$((j+1 \leq \bar{p} < i) \supset a[\bar{p}] \leq a[\bar{p}+1])) \land$$
$$x \leq a[j+1] \land 0 \leq j < i \land x = a[0] \land (j < i - 1 \supset a[j] \leq a[j+1])$$

At this point, the proof of correctness of *PSORT* with respect to point 1 consists of the following steps.

Step 1: Prove the invariance of I_{IN} that is,

    1.1 Backwards substitute I_{IN} through

$$k := j + 1; \; a[k] := a[j]; \; j := j - 1$$

which yields

$$I_{IN}^* : \forall \bar{p}(((1 \leq \bar{p} < j - 1) \supset a[\bar{p}] \leq a[\bar{p}+1]) \land$$
$$((j \leq \bar{p} < i) \supset$$
$$(\textbf{if } \bar{p} = j + 1 \textbf{ then } a[j] \leq a[\bar{p}+1]$$
$$\textbf{else if } \bar{p} = j \textbf{ then } a[\bar{p}] \leq a[j]$$
$$\textbf{else } a[\bar{p}] \leq a[\bar{p}+1])) \land$$
$$x \leq a[j] \land 0 \leq j - 1 < i \land x = a[0] \land$$
$$(j < i \supset a[j-1] \leq a[j])$$

    1.2 Prove that $I_{IN} \land x < a[j] \supset I_{IN}^*$.

Step 2: Prove that $I_{IN} \land x \geq a[j] \supset I_{EXT}^*$.

Step 3: Prove that $I_{EXT} \land i \leq n \supset \bar{I}_{IN}$ where $\bar{I}_{IN}$ is the result of backwards propagating I_{IN} through $x := a[i]; \; a[0] := x; \; j := i - 1$.

The proofs of steps 1.2, 2, and 3 are left to the reader as an exercise.

    Let us turn now to the second part of the proof.

Proof of 2

We will prove part 2 by using $I_{EXT}' = P_{O2} \land i \geq 1$ as loop invariant for the external loop. In fact, each time the external loop is completed the array a is a permutation of its previous contents and thus of b. As invariant assertion for the internal loop we will use

$$I_{IN}' : a[0] = x \land 0 \leq j \leq i - 1 \land i \leq n \land$$
$$\forall \bar{p}(0 \leq \bar{p} \leq n) \supset (\exists \bar{r}((1 \leq \bar{r} \leq n) \land (a[\bar{p}] = b[\bar{r}]))) \land$$
$$\forall \bar{r}(1 \leq \bar{r} \leq n) \supset (\exists \bar{p}((0 \leq \bar{p} \leq n) \land \bar{p} \neq j + 1 \land a[\bar{p}] = b[\bar{r}]))$$

whose main part states that the elements of a of index $0, \ldots, j, j+2, \ldots, n$ are the same as the elements of b.

Let us first prove the invariance of I_{IN}' through the following steps.

Step 1': $a[0] = x \land i \leq n$ is obviously invariant since no element is affected within loop body (k is always positive).

Step 2': Backwards substitution of $0 \leq j \leq i - 1$ through the loop body yields $1 \leq j \leq i$. This is implied by $0 \leq j \leq i - 1 \land x < a[j] \land x = a[0]$ (a portion of $I_{IN}' \land x < a[j]$) because $x = a[0]$ and $x < a[j]$ imply $j \neq 0$.

Step 3': Backwards substitution of

$$\forall \bar{p}(0 \leq \bar{p} \leq n) \supset (\exists \bar{r}((1 \leq \bar{r} \leq n) \wedge (a[\bar{p}] = b[\bar{r}]))) \text{ gives}$$
$$\forall \bar{p}(0 \leq \bar{p} \leq n) \supset (\exists \bar{r}((1 \leq \bar{r} \leq n) \wedge$$
$$((\text{if } \bar{p} = j + 1 \text{ then } a[j] \text{ else } a[\bar{p}]) = b[\bar{r}])))$$

which is implied by the following portion of I'_{IN}:

$$\forall \bar{p}(0 \leq \bar{p} \leq n) \supset (\exists \bar{r}((1 \leq \bar{r} \leq n) \wedge (a[\bar{p}] = b[\bar{r}]))) \wedge j \leq i - 1 \leq n)$$

In fact, if all elements $a[\bar{p}]$, with $\bar{p} = 0, \ldots, n$ are in b, so happens for all elements $a[\bar{p}]$, with $\bar{p} = 0, \ldots, j$, and $\bar{p} = j + 2, \ldots, n$ and for $a[j]$, because $j \leq n$.

Step 4':   Backwards substitution of

$$\forall \bar{r}(1 \leq \bar{r} \leq n) \supset (\exists \bar{p}((0 \leq \bar{p} \leq n) \wedge \bar{p} \neq j + 1 \wedge a[\bar{p}] = b[\bar{r}]))$$

yields

$$\forall \bar{r}(1 \leq \bar{r} \leq n) \supset (\exists \bar{p}((0 \leq \bar{p} \leq n) \wedge \bar{p} \neq j \wedge$$
$$((\text{if } \bar{p} = j + 1 \text{ then } a[j] \text{ else } a[\bar{p}]) = b[\bar{r}]))$$

This predicate states that every element in b is equal either to some $a[\bar{p}]$, where $\bar{p} = 0, \ldots, j - 1$ or $\bar{p} = j + 2, \ldots, n$, or it is equal to $a[j]$; thus it is equal to some $a[\bar{p}]$, where $\bar{p} = 0, \ldots, j$, or $p = j + 2, \ldots, n$.
It is easy to verify that this predicate is implied by I'_{IN}.

Now we prove I'_{EXT} invariant through the following steps.

Step 1'': Backwards substitution of I'_{EXT} through

$$k := j + 1; \, a[k] := x; \, i := i + 1$$

yields
$$i \geq 0 \wedge$$
$$\forall p(1 \leq \bar{p} \leq n) \supset$$
$$\exists \bar{r}((1 \leq \bar{r} \leq n) \wedge (\text{if } \bar{p} = j + 1 \text{ then } x \text{ else } a[\bar{p}]) = b[\bar{r}]) \wedge$$
$$\forall \bar{r}(1 \leq \bar{r} \leq n) \supset$$
$$\exists \bar{p}((1 \leq \bar{p} \leq n) \wedge (\text{if } \bar{p} = j + 1 \text{ then } x \text{ else } a[\bar{p}]) = b[\bar{r}])$$

This is implied by I'_{IN} as the reader may prove as an exercise.

Step 2'': Backwards substitution of I'_{IN} through $x := a[i]; \, a[0] := x; \, j := i - 1$
yields

$$0 \leq i - 1 \wedge i \leq n \wedge$$
$$\forall \bar{p}(0 \leq \bar{p} \leq n) \supset$$
$$\exists \bar{r}((1 \leq \bar{r} \leq n) \wedge (\text{if } \bar{p} = 0 \text{ then } a[i] \text{ else } a[\bar{p}]) = b[\bar{r}]) \wedge$$
$$\forall \bar{r}(1 \leq \bar{r} \leq n) \supset$$
$$\exists \bar{p}((0 \leq \bar{p} \leq n) \wedge \bar{p} \neq i \wedge (\text{if } \bar{p} = 0 \text{ then } a[i] \text{ else } a[\bar{p}]) = b[\bar{r}]).$$

Clearly, the first two predicates of the conjunction are implied by I'_{EXT}.

The other two predicates of the conjunction state that

- All elements $a[\bar{p}]$, with $\bar{p} = 1, \ldots, n$ are in b.
- All elements $b[\bar{r}]$, with $\bar{r} = 1, \ldots, n$ coincide with some $a[\bar{p}]$ with $\bar{p} = 0, \ldots, i-1$, or $\bar{p} = i+1, \ldots, n$ where $a[0]$ is substituted by $a[i]$. This is a baroque way of saying that all elements of b are in $\{a[\bar{p}], \bar{p} = 1, \ldots, n\}$.

In conclusion, these two predicates are implied by I'_{EXT}, which is thus proven invariant.

Finally, the predicate obtained by backwards substitution of I'_{EXT} through $i := 2$ is obviously implied by P_I and this completes the proof of point 2, and thus the whole correctness proof.

The previous proof of correctness may seem to be tedious and cumbersome, and this may discourage the reader from applying formal correctness techniques in practice. However, notice that the example was nontrivial, and we took care of a lot of details mainly for didactic purposes. It is likely that after gaining experience with the method, the user can easily manage correctness proofs by collapsing several trivial steps into a few ones. In addition, one may be aided by computer-based tools that can take care of many trivial details.

Remark*

In the development of the previous correctness proof we applied axiom $\overline{\text{A1}}$ for backward substitution through statements of the type $a[x] := t$ even in the case where the involved assertions contained expressions as array indexes. We must warn the reader that such a procedure is not always safe, as the following example shows.

Let P be $a[a[2]] = 1$ where an indexed variable is the index of yet another indexed variable. In this case, applying $\overline{\text{A1}}$ to the statements $x := a[2]$; $a[x] := 1$ and to P would produce

$$\{(\textbf{if } a[2] = a[2] \textbf{ then } 1 \textbf{ else } a[a[2]]) = 1\} x := a[2]; a[x] := 1\{a[a[2]] = 1\}$$

that is,

$$\{T\} a[a[2]] := 1\{a[a[2]] = 1\}$$

which is contradicted if, before execution of the statement, $a[1] = a[2] = 2$.

Instead of modifying $\overline{\text{A1}}$, we circumvent the problem by means of a little trick. In fact, observe that $a[a[2]] = 1$ can be rewritten as $\exists \bar{y}(a[\bar{y}] = 1 \land \bar{y} = a[2])$. Now, by applying $\overline{\text{A1}}$ we obtain

$$\{\exists \bar{y}((\textbf{if } \bar{y} = a[2] \textbf{ then } 1 \textbf{ else } a[\bar{y}]) = 1 \land \bar{y} = (\textbf{if } 2 = a[2] \textbf{ then } 1 \textbf{ else } a[2])))\}$$
$$x := a[2]; a[x] := 1$$
$$\{\exists \bar{y}(a[\bar{y}] = 1 \land \bar{y} = a[2])\}$$

This properly shows that $a[2] = a[1] = 2$ as a precondition gives a contradiction (it imposes $\bar{y} = 2 \land \bar{y} = 1$).

Observe that if an array index in a program assertion P is an expression e not involving other indexed variables, the foregoing caution is useless. In fact, let P denote a predicate involving some free occurrence of $a[e]$. If we apply the procedure we have just discussed, we obtain

$$\{\exists \bar{y}(\bar{y} = e \land P_{a[e]}^{\text{if } \bar{y}=x \text{ then } t \text{ else } a[\bar{y}]})\} a[x] := t \{\exists \bar{y}(\bar{y} = e \land P)\}$$

where the precondition is clearly still equivalent to

$$P_{[a[e]]}^{\text{if } e=x \text{ then } t \text{ else } a[e]}$$

Thus—a posteriori—we confirm the procedure used in Example 5.4.   □

Exercises

5.8   Prove steps 1.2, 2, and 3 of the proof of point 1 of Example 5.4.

5.9   Write a program to state whether a positive integer x belongs to a given multiset, represented by an array $a[i]$, with $i = 1, \ldots, n$. If it does, the variable *ind* should contain the value of an index i such that $a[i] = x$. Prove the correctness of your program.

5.10   Prove the correctness of the following sorting program (Bubble Sort).

```
BUBSORT:   begin
               i := n;
               while i > 1
                   do j := 1;
                       while j < i
                           do k := j + 1;
                               if a[j] > a[k]
                               then x := a[k]; a[k] := a[j]; a[j] := x
                               fi;
                               j := j + 1
                           od;
                       i := i - 1
                   od;
           end
```

5.11   Write a program to check whether two arrays $a[i]$, with $i = 1, \ldots, n$, and $b[j]$, with $j = 1, \ldots, m$, contain the same elements (i.e., each element in a is also in b and conversely). Prove the correctness of your program.

5.12*   Modify the foregoing program of Exercise 5.11 by requiring in addition that all elements occur the same number of times both in a and in b (in this case a and b must have the same number of elements).

5.13*   Prove that the program of Example 5.4 is correct also with respect to an output predicate stating that a is a true permutation of b (remember we used a weaker predicate for the sake of simplicity).

5.3   The Termination Issue

The correctness proofs derived so far are called *partial correctness proofs* since the notation

$$\{Pre\}S\{Post\}$$

means that S guarantees that *Post* holds after its execution provided that *Pre* holds before *and S terminates*. But the proof of $\{Pre\}S\{Post\}$ does not imply that s will eventually terminate. As a consequence, a program fragment that never halts is partially correct with respect to any pair $\langle Pre, Post \rangle$ of assertions.[7] This is consistent with the fact that $\Omega \subseteq f$, where Ω is the undefined function and f is the least fixed point of any (recursive) program. In other terms, the mathematical tools developed so far to define formal semantics adopt the convention that any computation can reach any result as far as it is not yet terminated.

We say that S is *totally correct* with respect to the pair of assertions $\langle Pre, Post \rangle$ if *Pre* guarantees that S will eventually halt and $\{Pre\}S\{Post\}$ holds. The reason why the theory developed in the previous section enables us to prove only partial correctness instead of total correctness is due to the semantic definition of the **while** construct. In fact, it is defined in such a way that *IR4* is valid whenever the loop terminates, but it does not imply termination.

For example consider the following program fragment

P: $x := n$;
    $y := m$;
    $c := 0$;
    while $x \neq 0$
        do $x := x - y$;
           $c := c + 1$
        od

Clearly, P computes $c = n/m$ if and only if m divides n, but it never halts if this is not the case.

If we choose the predicate

$$J : n - y \cdot c = x \wedge y = m$$

we immediately verify that J is a loop invariant for P. Thus

$$\{n - y \cdot c = x \wedge y = m\} \textbf{ while } x \neq 0 \textbf{ do } x := x - y; \, c := c + 1 \textbf{ od}$$
$$\{n - y \cdot c = x \wedge y = m \wedge x = 0\} \supset \{n = m \cdot c\}$$

Furthermore,

$$\{T\}x := n; \, y := m; \, c := 0\{J\}$$

---

[7]Recall that $A \supset B$ is always true if A is false.

and, therefore,

$$\{T\}P\{n = m \cdot c\}$$

Thus, under the precondition T (i.e., *always*) $n = m \cdot c$ when P terminates.

This definitely shows that, in order to rely on our correctness proofs, we need to enrich partial correctness proofs with *termination proofs*. Let us stick for awhile to the above program P: consider a new assertion

$$J' : \exists \bar{k} \, (x = y \cdot \bar{k} \wedge x \geq 0 \wedge y > 0 \wedge \bar{k} \geq 0)$$

J' defines a subset of integers as possible values of x, namely the multiples of y.

We can easily prove J' invariant for P's loop. To do so, first we backwards substitute J' through the loop body:

$$\{\exists \bar{k}(x - y = y \cdot \bar{k} \wedge x \geq y \wedge y > 0 \wedge \bar{k} \geq 0)\}x := x - y; \; c := c + 1$$
$$\{\exists \bar{k}(x = y \cdot \bar{k} \wedge x \geq 0 \wedge y > 0 \wedge \bar{k} \geq 0)\}$$

Then we prove the following sequence of (more or less immediate) implications

$$J' \wedge x \neq 0 \equiv$$
$$\exists \bar{k}(x = y \cdot \bar{k} \wedge x \geq 0 \wedge y > 0 \wedge \bar{k} \geq 0) \wedge x \neq 0 \supset$$
$$\exists \bar{k}(x = y \cdot \bar{k} \wedge x > 0 \wedge y > 0 \wedge \bar{k} > 0) \supset$$
$$\exists \bar{k}(x - y = y \cdot (\bar{k} - 1) \wedge x > 0 \wedge y > 0 \wedge \bar{k} > 0) \supset$$
$$\exists \bar{h}(x - y = y \cdot \bar{h} \wedge x > 0 \wedge y > 0 \wedge \bar{h} \geq 0) \supset$$
$$\exists \bar{h}(x - y = y \cdot \bar{h} \wedge x - y \geq 0 \wedge y > 0) \wedge \bar{h} \geq 0) \supset$$
$$\exists \bar{h}(x - y = y \cdot \bar{h} \wedge x \geq y \wedge y > 0 \wedge \bar{h} \geq 0)$$

which is exactly the precondition of the loop body that guarantees J' invariant. In conclusion, if y divides x before the loop, so happens at loop exit; thus the following theorem for P holds.

$$\{\exists \bar{k}(n = m \cdot \bar{k} \wedge \bar{k} \geq 0 \wedge m > 0)\}P\{n = m \cdot c\}$$

and this result has been proven by a partial correctness proof.

Observe, however, that now we also know that if the predicate $\exists \bar{k}(n = m \cdot \bar{k} \wedge \bar{k} \geq 0 \wedge m > 0)$ holds before P's execution, then x always ranges over the positive (or null) multiples of m. On the other hand, it also happens that, at every iteration, x is decreased by the positive integer $y = m$. Thus we can conclude that x must eventually reach the null value, thus determining the exit from the loop.

The previous example can be generalized to the following proof method.

Termination proof method for while programs

Let $L = $ **while** C **do** L_B **od** be any loop within a program P, where C is the loop condition and L_B is the loop body. Let $\bar{x}$ denote the collection of P's variables and let X denote P's state space. For example if P operates on variables x, y (of type integer) and u (of type Boolean), then $\bar{x} = \langle x, y, u \rangle$, and $X = \mathbb{Z} \times \mathbb{Z} \times \{$*true*, *false*$\}$. Let $\bar{x}'$, $\bar{x}''$ denote the value of $\bar{x}$ before and after execution of the body, respectively.

If there exist:

1. A well-founded set $\langle \mathcal{W}, \succ \rangle$ (see Section 0.1.1 for a definition of a well-founded set).
2. A (possibly partial) function $f: X \to \mathcal{W}$.
3. A loop invariant J, (i.e., a predicate such that $\{J \wedge C\}L_B\{J\}$) for which $J \supset f(\bar{x}) \in \mathcal{W}$.

Furthermore, if

4. $J_{\bar{x}}^{\bar{x}'} \wedge C_{\bar{x}}^{\bar{x}'} \supset (f(\bar{x}') \succ f(\bar{x}''))$.

Then we conclude that if J holds before L's execution, L *does terminate* and $J \wedge \neg C$ holds after L's execution. Thus L is *totally correct* with respect to precondition J and postcondition $J \wedge \neg C$.   □

With reference to the previous example, we can assume the conjunction $J \wedge J'$ as the loop invariant for the total correctness proof. By letting $\langle \mathcal{W}, \succ \rangle = \langle \mathbb{N}, > \rangle$, $f(x, y) = x$, we immediately verify that conditions 1 through 4 hold. Thus P terminates and is correct with respect to the precondition $\exists \bar{k}(n = \bar{k} \cdot m \wedge \bar{k} \geq 0 \wedge m > 0)$. Notice that, if J' does not hold at entry of L, it is not guaranteed that $f(x, y) \in \mathbb{N}$ as x may become negative.

The foregoing proof method for termination is intuitively sound (i.e., if a loop verifies conditions 1 through 4 for some $\langle \mathcal{W}, \succ \rangle$, f and J, it actually terminates). A formal treatment of this topic, however, is beyond the scope of this introductory text. A few more remarks are given later in Section 5.4.

5.3.1* Further Insights into Termination Proofs

Let us go a little further into the termination issue through the following examples.

Example 5.5

Let us go back to the *binary__search* algorithm presented in Example 3.2. Below we give a slight modification of the algorithm, coded in SMALG.

```
BINSEARCH:   begin
                i := 1, j := n; found := 0;
                while i ≤ j do h := i + j; k := h div 2;
                            if y = a[k]
                            then found := 1; i := j + 1
                            else if y < a[k]
                                       then j := k − 1
                                       else i := k + 1
                                       fi
                            fi
                        od
             end
```

Again, notice that we have been forced to code the logical variable *found* as an integer, because of SMALG's limitations. Furthermore, we removed the test on *found* from the loop condition. The same effect was achieved by the assignment '$i := j + 1$' in the case where $y = a[k]$. We apologize for our tricky programming style, but our choice has been motivated both by SMALG's syntactic limitations and by the goal of making the termination proof easier. These limitations are removed in Exercise 5.14.

We leave to the reader as an exercise to prove partial correctness of *BINSEARCH* with respect to precondition $\{n \geq 1\}$ and postcondition

$$\left\{\exists \bar{k}\left((1 \leq \bar{k} \leq n \wedge y = a[\bar{k}]) \supset found = 1\right) \wedge\right.$$
$$\left.\not\exists \bar{k}\left((1 \leq \bar{k} \leq n \wedge y = a[\bar{k}]) \supset found = 0\right)\right\}$$

Let us prove the termination of *BINSEARCH* by applying the method given in Section 5.3. There is only one loop to consider. An obvious choice of the pair $\langle \mathcal{W}, \succ \rangle$ is $\langle \mathbb{N}, > \rangle$.

As a first try, let us define function f as $f(\bar{x}) = j - i$, where $\bar{x}$ denotes the collection of *all* program variables of *BINSEARCH*. The reasons of our choice is that, at each step, the program searches subarray $a[i \ldots j]$ whose size is montonically decreasing. However, we immediately realize that, if at loop exit *found* = 1, then $f(\bar{x}) = -1 \notin \mathbb{N}$.

This failure suggests to change f's definition into $f(\bar{x}) = j - i + 1$. The predicate $J : j \geq i - 1$ implies $f(\bar{x}) \in \mathbb{N}$. Since J is easily proved invariant for the loop, we are left with point 4 of the termination proof method; that is, we must prove that $j' \geq i' - 1 \wedge i' \leq j' \supset (j' - i' + 1) > (j'' - i'' + 1)$ (Notice that we can drop predicate $j' \geq i' - 1$ from the previous formula since it is implied by $j' \geq i'$.)

Let h', h'', k', and k'' denote the values of h and k before and after execution of loop body, respectively. Let us consider the three possible cases.

1. $y = a[k'']$: in this case $i'' = j' + 1$, $j'' = j'$.
2. $y < a[k'']$: in this case $i'' = j'$, $j'' = k'' - 1$.
3. $y > a[k'']$: in this case $i'' = k'' + 1$, $j'' = j'$.

Since $k'' = (i' + j')$ **div** 2 it is easy to verify that in all three cases $(j' - i' + 1) > (j'' - i'' + 1)$ is implied by $i' \leq j'$. In fact, in case 2 we have $j'' - i'' + 1 = (i' + j')$ **div** $2 - 1 - i' + 1 \leq (2j')$ **div** $2 - i' = j' - i' < j' - i' + 1$. The remaining cases are left to the reader as an exercise.

Exercise

5.14 Build a SMALG program closer to the original Pascal program of Example 3.2. This could be obtained by introducing the "pseudo-Boolean" variables *iLeqJ*, *notFound*, and *iLeqJandNotFound*, which have value 1 when $i \leq j$, *found* = 0, $i \leq j \wedge$ *found* = 0, respectively; 0 otherwise. Prove the termination of your program.

Hint: In this case the previous choices for $\langle \mathscr{W}, \succ \rangle$ and f do not work because, when $y = a[k]$, i and j are not affected and the value of f does not decrease.

Therefore, we suggest you to choose $\mathscr{W} = \mathbb{N} \times \{0, 1\}$ and to define f as $f(\bar{x}) = \langle j - i + 1, notFound \rangle$. The ordering on $\mathscr{W}$ must be arranged in such a way that $f(\bar{x})$ is decreased at each loop iteration.

Example 5.6

Consider the problem of stating whether the ratio between two positive integers m and n has a finite or a periodic decimal representation. For instance, 2/5 is .4 —i.e., it has a finite decimal representation—whereas 2/3 is .666... —i.e., it is a periodic number.

A simple algorithm solving this problem is sketched below. First, the remainder of integer division m **div** n is stored in variable *rem*. Then, if *rem* is other than 0, we compute the value of $(rem * 10^r)$ **div** n, where r is the minimum integer such that $rem \cdot 10^r \geq n$. The procedure is repeated until either $rem = 0$ or *rem* equals one of the previously assumed values. In order to perform this test the sequence of values assumed by *rem* is stored into the array *remSet*.

A SMALG program coding of the foregoing algorithm is given as follows.

```
PERTEST:   begin
             rem := m mod n; k := 1; remSet[k] := rem; notRepeated := 1;
             if rem = 0 then notRemZero := 0 else notRemZero := 1 fi;
             doubleNot := notRemZero * notRepeated;
             while doubleNot = 1
                       do while rem < n do
                                          rem := rem * 10
                                          od;
                          rem := rem mod n;
                          k := k + 1;
                          remSet[k] := rem;
                          i := 1;
                          while i < k
                               do if remSet[i] = remSet[k]
                                  then notRepeated := 0
                                  fi;
                               od;
                          if rem = 0 then notRemZero := 0 fi;
                          doubleNot := notRemZero * notRepeated
                       od
```

We leave to the reader the following proofs.

Exercises

5.15 Prove the partial correctness of *PERTEST*.

5.16 Prove the termination of the two inner loops of *PERTEST*.

Now we face the problem of proving termination of the main loop. Intuitively, termination is guaranteed by the fact that the set of possible remainders of the division by n has exactly cardinality n. Because the set $\{remSet[i] | 1 \le i \le k\}$ is a subset of such set and its cardinality is incremented at each loop iteration, the loop must eventually terminate.

More formally, let us assume $\mathcal{W} = \mathcal{P}(\{0, 1, \ldots, n-1\})$ and $\subset$ as $\succ$; that is, $x \succ y$ means $x \subset y$. Clearly, $\succ$ is a well-order for $\mathcal{W}$ since $\mathcal{W}$ is finite. Then we define f as $f(\bar{x}) = \{remSet[i] | 1 \le i \le k-1\}$ (why did we use $k-1$ instead of k?). $f(\bar{x}) \in \mathcal{W}$ by definition. In order to prove that $f(\bar{x}') \succ f(\bar{x}'')$ is implied by $doubleNot' = 1$ and by a suitable loop invariant, notice that $f(\bar{x}') = \{remSet'[i] | 1 \le i \le k'-1\}$, $f(\bar{x}'') = \{RemSet''[i] | 1 \le i \le k''-1\}$, with $k'' = k'+1$.

Furthermore, $doubleNot' = 1$ implies $notRepeated' = 1$ and, in turn, this implies the predicate $\forall \bar{p}, \bar{r}(1 \le \bar{p}, \bar{r} \le k' \wedge \bar{p} \ne \bar{r})^8 \supset remSet'[\bar{p}] \ne remSet'[\bar{r}]$. (Prove this claim as an exercise.) This means that as far as the loop is repeated all elements of $remSet$ are different. Thus $f(\bar{x}'') = \{remSet''[i] | 1 \le i \le k''-1\} = \{remSet'[i] | 1 \le i \le k'\}$ properly contains $f(\bar{x}')$.

Notice that Example 5.6 provides a proof that a rational number has either a finite or a periodic decimal representation. Thus, we have proven an important result of number theory as a corollary of a program termination proof!

Exercises

5.17 Prove the termination of the program computing the greatest common divisor of two positive integer numbers given in Example 5.2.
Hint: Assume $f(x, y) = |x - y|$.

5.19 Prove the termination of the sorting program of Example 5.4. Observe that the termination of the external loop is a trivial fact, once termination of the inner loop has been proved, which, in turn, is rather obvious.

5.19 Write a program that evaluates the largest Fibonacci number (see Exercise 4.29.2) not exceeding a given constant n. Prove total correctness of your program.

---

[8] This is a natural short notation for the wf $\forall \bar{p} \forall \bar{r}(1 \le \bar{p} \wedge 1 \le \bar{r} \wedge \bar{p} \le k' \wedge \bar{r} \le k' \wedge \bar{p} \ne \bar{r}) \ldots$.

5.20   Write a SMALG program that receives as input a suitable encoding of a finite-state automaton A and a positive integer n and produces as output all the strings x such that $x \in L(A)$ and $|x| \le n$. Prove its termination.

5.4*   The Soundness and Completeness Issues

In Section 5.2 we have derived proof rules for simple programming language constructs on the basis of their intuitive semantics. Obviously, proof rules must be *sound*, that is, their application must produce assertions that must be true under a chosen interpretation. For instance, we showed that the application of axiom A1 to assertions with quantifiers is not sound if we are not careful. The present section briefly addresses the problem of guaranteeing the soundness of the given proof system and its completeness (i.e., the possibility of actually proving truths about programs within the formalism).

Since we have defined Hoare's system syntactically as an enrichment of first-order axiomatization of arithmetics, now we must formally define the soundness of the system by means of a suitable extension of the notions of logical validity and consistency introduced in Section 0.2.3. Notice that we do not care about consistency of Peano's arithmetic, since this result is already well known. Actually, the deductions we made on program correctness did rely on consistency of arithmetic but were, of course, independent of the particular first-order theory chosen to axiomatize arithmetic. Thus, we introduce a notion of soundness that is, in some sense, independent of the axiomization used to make deductions on program assertions. For the sake of simplicity we restrict our attention to the case of SMALG without indexed variables.

Let H denote the formal theory, or system, containing only axiom A1 and proof rules *IR1* through *IR4*. Let *WA* denote the set of arithmetic wfs, which is contained in the set of H's wfs. *Asserted programs* (i.e., wfs of H not in *WA* of the type $\{ Pre \} S \{ Post \}$, where *Pre*, *Post* $\in WA$ and S is a program fragment) are denoted by the letters φ, ψ. An interpretation $\mathscr{I}$ of *WA* and its domain D are defined according to the rules given in Section 0.2.3. In particular $\mathscr{I}_0$ will denote the standard interpretation of Peano's arithmetic with $D = \mathbb{N}$. (For simplicity, we restrict our attention to $\mathbb{N}$. In order to deal with $\mathbb{Z}$, see footnote 2.) By following the usual notation, a *universal state s* is defined as a function from the set of variables of H into D or, equivalently, as a sequence of elements in D as in Definition 0.5 of Section 0.2.3. For any state s and assertion $A \in WA$ we write $\models A(s)$ to denote that s satisfies A under the interpretation $\mathscr{I}$. Notice that $\underset{\mathscr{I}}{\models} A(s)$ does not depend on the value of s for bound variables of A (see Section 0.2.3). As a consequence, for a given program P, define a *state s of P* as the restriction of a universal state to P's variables and use the same convention as in Section 5.2.1 to denote quantified variables in program assertions in such a way that a quantified variable will never be a program variable. Then the notion of an "assertion A is true in the state s under the interpretation $\mathscr{I}$" is defined by $\underset{\mathscr{I}}{\models} A(s)$. Now, for any program fragment S we know that we can define its semantics $\mathscr{S}em_S$ as a partial function from P's states to P's states. For instance, by using the formalism of denotational semantics of Section 4.6.3, $\mathscr{S}em_S(s) = f_{\langle \text{StatList} \rangle}(S, s)$.

We are now ready to introduce the main definitions on the soundness of H.

Definition 5.1

An asserted program $\varphi = \{ Pre \} S \{ Post \}$ is said to be *true* under interpretation $\mathscr{I}$ if and only if for any states s and s'

$\underset{\mathscr{I}}{\models} Pre(s)$ and $\mathscr{S}em_S(s) = s'$ imply $\underset{\mathscr{I}}{\models} Post(s')$ ☐

Definition 5.2

H is said to be *sound* if and only if for any finite $\Gamma \subseteq WA$, for any interpretation $\mathscr{I}$, and for any asserted program φ the fact that all assertions in Γ are true under $\mathscr{I}$ and $\Gamma \vdash \varphi$ implies that φ is true under $\mathscr{I}$. ☐

Notice that Definition 5.2 is based on the truth of assertions in Γ, no matter if and how they can be proved as theorems in a suitable axiomization of arithmetic.

The treatment developed so far should have provided enough evidence for the following statement.

Statement 5.1

H is sound. ☐

Indeed, a formal proof of Statement 5.1 can be obtained by induction on the structure of programs using a formal definition of SMALG's semantics, say denotational semantics. The kernel of the inductive proof consists of verifying that any instance of axiom A1 is a valid asserted program (i.e., it is true under all interpretations). This is an immediate consequence of the definition of $f_{\langle \text{AssStat} \rangle}$ given in Section 4.6.3.

Similarly, it is quite easy to prove that rules *IR1* through *IR4* preserve the truth of asserted programs for any $\mathscr{I}$; that is, if $\varphi_1, \varphi_2, \ldots, \varphi_n$ are true under $\mathscr{I}$ and $\dfrac{\varphi_1, \varphi_2, \ldots, \varphi_n}{\varphi}$ then φ is true under $\mathscr{I}$. We leave the details of such proof as an exercise for the reader.

The issue of completeness is more difficult to address than soundness. First of all, the whole proof system will obviously suffer due to arithmetic's intrinsic incompleteness, as stated in Section 0.2.4.3 (Gödel's Incompleteness Theorem). Thus, since the proof of an asserted program may require the proof of arithmetic truths, the same incompleteness is inherited by Hoare's system. On the other hand, as we did for soundness, we would like to state the completeness of the proof system with respect to the language semantics, without including the properties of arithmetic. This leads to the following definition, which can be seen as the completeness counterpart of Definition 5.2.

Definition 5.3
Let $Tr\mathscr{I}$ denote the set of assertions true under the interpretation $\mathscr{I}$. Then H is said to be *relatively complete* if and only if for any interpretation $\mathscr{I}$ and asserted program φ, if φ is true under $\mathscr{I}$, then $Tr\mathscr{I} \vdash \varphi$. $\square$

Intuitively, the previous definition states that H is complete if and only if all truths about programs can be proved in H on the basis of truths about the interpretation $\mathscr{I}$ of arithmetic, no matter whether such arithmetic truths can be proved within the whole proof system also containing the arithmetic axioms.

Unfortunately, it can be shown that H is not complete even in this restricted sense. We just mention this result without proving it. Several arguments showing H's incompleteness can be found in a more specialized literature to which we refer the interested reader in the bibliographic remarks. The same literature shows that some appropriate kind of completeness can be proved for H or other similar proof systems for asserted programs.

Finally, the same issues of soundness and completeness should be addressed also for termination proof methods. Again, we choose not to go into this topic but to refer the advanced readership to the appropriate literature. We simply inform the reader that, unlike partial correctness, termination turns out to be interpretation dependent, since there exist programs that can terminate or not depending on the chosen interpretation for arithmetic formulas. However, within particular interpretations, soundness and completeness of some termination proof methods can actually be shown.

5.5*   **The Synthesis of Correct Programs**

The examples presented in Section 5.2 could give the impression that formal analysis of programs is a hard and intricate job even for rather simple programs. We claim that the real difficulty is in analyzing from scratch already existing programs, whether we are using formal techniques or not.

It is now generally accepted in the software engineering literature that a program, even a well-documented program, shows just the last step of the design activity that led to its development and—very often—it does not show the principles that should explain its behavior. On the other hand, once the deep meaning of a program has been caught, its translation into formal assertions to be proved (or disproved) is a rather straightforward job. The lesson is that program analysis and synthesis should be developed as two parallel and strictly integrated activities. That is, starting from predicates we derive a program and, in turn, we check its correctness against the given predicate. In other terms, we develop a program jointly with its correctness proof in an interplay between program derivation and formal program verification.

Once again, the purpose of this text is not the development of good programming techniques—a software engineering problem. Rather, we are interested in providing robust theoretical foundations to programming. Therefore, we present only a few examples to show how the use of formal correctness proofs can—and should—be integrated with the programming activity. An elementary knowledge of structured programming techniques will certainly be helpful to understand the following examples.

Example 5.7

Consider the problem of merging two sorted arrays a and b of n nonnegative integers into a sorted array c containing all elements of a and b. Let us first state the requirements for a *MERGE* program in terms of an informal Hoare-like notation:

$$\{ ordered(a) \wedge ordered(b)\} MERGE \{ ordered(c)$$
$$\wedge \text{ all elements occurring in } a \text{ or } b \text{ occur in } c, \text{ and conversely}\},$$

where a, b, and c denote array variables. Strictly speaking, the above informal postcondition adequately captures the usual meaning of the term "merge" only if a and b have disjoint sets of values. In fact, a program transforming $a = \{3,5\}$ and $b = \{5,6\}$ into $c = \{3,3,5,6\}$ would satisfy the above postcondition even if the correct merge of a and b would be $\{3,5,5,6\}$. However, for the sake of simplicity, we will stay with the foregoing weaker requirement for a *MERGE* program, as we did in a similar case in Example 5.4. If we assume as a further precondition that a and b do not contain multiple occurrences of the same value and that no value occurs in both a and b, then our postcondition becomes perfectly adequate.

Let us now formalize the above pre- and postconditions as follows.

- For any array z, *ordered*(z) is an abbreviation for

$$\forall \bar{p}((1 \leq \bar{p} < r) \supset z[\bar{p}] \leq z[\bar{p} + 1])$$

where r is the size of the array.
- "Any element occurring in a or b occurs in c and conversely" is specified by the predicate: $c = union(a, b)$; that is

$$\forall \bar{x}(\exists \bar{i}((1 \leq \bar{i} \leq n) \wedge (a[\bar{i}] = \bar{x} \vee b[\bar{i}] = \bar{x})) \equiv$$
$$\exists \bar{j}((1 \leq j \leq 2n) \wedge c[\bar{j}] = \bar{x})).$$

A simple and natural way to design *MERGE* is the following: Let arrays a and b be partitioned into a lower part, *al* and *bl*, and an upper part, *au* and *bu*. Let *cl* store the result of merging of *al* and *bl*. During program execution, *al* and *bl* should range from empty subarrays to full a and b, respectively, in such a way that eventually *cl* will become the desired c. This will be obtained by means of some loop, say L. At each iteration, L will change *al*, *bl*, *au*, *bu*, and *cl* in such a way that *cl* remains ordered. If we choose the natural policy of changing the previous arrays by appending elements (i.e., the first element of *au* (*bu*) becomes the last element of *al* (*bl*) and also of *cl*), it is clear that *cl* remains ordered if all its elements are invariantly less than or equal to all elements of *au* and *bu*. This immediately suggests an invariant assertion for *L*, before *L* is actually defined as a sequence of SMALG statements.

Assuming *ii* and *jj* as two program variables that denote the lengths of the lower parts *al* and *bl*, the invariant for *L* can be written as

$$I: 0 \leq ii, jj \leq n \wedge cl = union(al, bl) \wedge ordered(cl) \wedge (cl \leq [au, bu])$$

where

- $0 \leq ii, jj \leq n$ is a short notation for $0 \leq ii \wedge ii \leq n \wedge 0 \leq jj \wedge jj \leq n$;
- $cl = union(al, bl)$ stands for

$$\forall \bar{x}\big(\exists \bar{i}\big((1 \leq \bar{i} \leq ii \wedge a[\bar{i}] = \bar{x}) \vee (1 \leq \bar{i} \leq jj \wedge b[\bar{i}] = \bar{x})\big) \equiv$$
$$(\exists \bar{j}(1 \leq \bar{j} \leq ii + jj \wedge c[\bar{j}] = \bar{x}))\big);$$

- $ordered(cl)$ stands for

$$\forall \bar{p}(1 \leq \bar{p} < ii + jj) \supset c[\bar{p}] \leq c[\bar{p} + 1];$$

and $cl \leq [au, bu]$ stands for

$$(ii < n \supset c[ii + jj] \leq a[ii + 1]) \wedge (jj < n \supset c[ii + jj] \leq b[jj + 1]).$$

Notice that *I*, the main invariant assertion, is not only a candidate support for a correctness proof to be associated to *MERGE*, but it is also a milestone in the design of *MERGE* itself as it suggests much of the structure to be given to the program.

At this point, we are ready for the following refinement of the original goal.

$\{ ordered(a) \wedge ordered(b)\}$
begin $ii := 0;\ jj := 0;$
      $\{ J:I \wedge ordered(a) \wedge ordered(b)\}$
      while $ii + jj < 2n$
          do
          L_B
          od
      $\{ J \wedge ii + jj \geq 2n\}$
end

Now backwards substitution of *I* through $ii := 0;\ jj := 0$ trivially evaluates to T so that initialization guarantees *J*. Also, the assertion $J \wedge ii + jj \geq 2n$, which holds at the loop exit, obviously guarantees that the program produces the desired result (since $J \wedge ii + jj \geq 2n$ implies $ii = n \wedge jj = n$).

Thus our next job is to the design a loop body L_B such that *J* is invariant (i.e., $\{ J \wedge ii + jj < 2n\}\ L_B\ \{J\}$ holds). Intuitively, this can be obtained if at each iteration of L_B a new element is added to *cl*—the portion of *c* constructed so far—which is the minimum between $a[ii + 1]$ and $b[jj + 1]$. In the former case, $a[ii + 1]$ is conceptually removed from au and appended to both al and cl; in the latter case this happens to $b[jj + 1]$. This is translated into the following implementation of L_B.

L_B: $ki := ii + 1$; $kj := jj + 1$; $z := ii + jj$; $z := z + 1$;
   if $a[ki] < b[kj]$
   then $ii := ii + 1$; $c[z] := a[ki]$
   else $jj := jj + 1$; $c[z] := b[kj]$
   fi

(Shortly, we will see that this implementation contains an error. Can you anticipate it?) Let us check whether J is invariant. First notice that $ordered(a) \wedge ordered(b)$ certainly holds at each point of L_B since a and b are not affected by the program. So we can use them whenever needed but we do not have to worry about proving their invariance. Therefore, let us concentrate on I. Let us first consider the portion of I: $0 \le ii$, $jj \le n$, which is backwards substituted through L_B. It is immediate to realize that I is invariant if

$$J \wedge ii + jj < 2n \supset ((a[ii + 1] < b[jj + 1] \supset 0 \le ii + 1, \; jj \le n) \wedge$$
$$(a[ii + 1] \ge b[jj + 1] \supset 0 \le ii, \; jj + 1 \le n))$$

This cannot be proved if $a[n + 1]$ and $b[n + 1]$ are not defined. This fact shows the little error of our program: $ii + 1$ and $jj + 1$ are computed with no guarantee that they do not exceed n.

Instead of modifying L_B, which would force us to distinguish among the three cases $ii = n$, $jj = n$, and $ii < n \wedge jj < n$, we *conventionally define* $a[n + 1] = b[n + 1] = \tilde{m}$, where $\tilde{m}$ is a value such that $a[i] < \tilde{m}$ and $b[i] < \tilde{m}$ for all i, with $1 \le i \le n$. Accordingly, the clause $cl \le [au, bu]$ in I simply becomes $c[ii + jj] \le a[ii + 1] \wedge c[ii + jj] \le b[jj + 1]$. J is redefined as J: $I \wedge ordered(a) \wedge ordered(b) \wedge$

$$(a[n + 1] = b[n + 1] = \tilde{m}) \wedge \forall \bar{p}((1 \le \bar{p} \le n) \supset a[\bar{p}] < \tilde{m} \wedge b[\bar{p}] < \tilde{m})$$

where I has been slightly modified as we discussed before. Again, notice that the part of J other than I is obviously invariant through L_B. Therefore, let us try to prove I invariant, that is,

$$\{J \wedge ii + jj < 2n\} \; L_B \; \{I\}$$

In order to simplify the proof, we separately handle the clauses

P1: $0 \le ii$, $jj \le n$
P2: $cl = union \; (al, bl)$
P3: $cl \le [au, bu]$
P4: $ordered(cl)$

Let P1′, P2′, P3′, and P4′ be the results of backwards substituting P1, P2, P3 and P4 through L_B, respectively. If we show that $J \wedge ii + jj < 2n \supset$ Pi', $i = 1, \ldots, 4$ the proof will be complete.

1. P1′ is

$$(a[ii + 1] < b[jj + 1] \supset (0 \le ii + 1 \le n \land 0 \le jj \le n)) \land$$
$$(a[ii + 1] \ge b[jj + 1] \supset (0 \le ii \le n \land 0 \le jj + 1 \le n))$$

This is implied by $J \land ii + jj < 2n$. In fact, $ii + jj < 2n$ guarantees that ii and jj cannot be both equal to n. Thus a $[ii + 1] \ge b[jj + 1]$ implies that $b[jj + 1]$ is not $\tilde{m}$, since, otherwise, it should be $b[jj + 1] = a[ii + 1]$ and therefore $ii + 1 = jj + 1 = n + 1$. Therefore, $jj + 1 < n + 1$. $a[ii + 1] < b[jj + 1]$ implies, a fortiori, $ii + 1 \le n + 1$.

2. P2′ is

$$a[ii + 1] < b[jj + 1] \supset$$
$$\left(\forall \bar{x}\left(\exists \bar{i}\left((1 \le \bar{i} \le ii + 1 \land a[\bar{i}] = \bar{x}) \lor \right.\right.\right.$$
$$\left.\left(1 \le \bar{i} \le jj \land b[\bar{i}] = \bar{x}\right)\right) \equiv \exists \bar{j}(1 \le \bar{j} \le ii + jj + 1 \land$$
$$\textbf{if } \bar{j} = ii + jj + 1 \textbf{ then } a[ii + 1] = \bar{x} \textbf{ else } c[\bar{j}] = \bar{x})))$$
$$\land$$
$$a[ii + 1] \ge b[jj + 1] \supset$$
$$\left(\forall \bar{x}\left(\exists \bar{i}\left((1 \le \bar{i} \le ii \land a[\bar{i}] = \bar{x} \lor \right.\right.\right.$$
$$\left.\left(1 \le \bar{i} \le jj + 1 \land b[\bar{i}] = \bar{x}\right)\right) \equiv \exists \bar{j}(1 \le \bar{j} \le ii + jj + 1 \land$$
$$\textbf{if } \bar{j} = ii + jj + 1 \textbf{ then } b[jj + 1] = \bar{x} \textbf{ else } c[\bar{j}] = \bar{x})))$$

$J \land ii + jj < 2n$ implies P2′. In fact, consider the case $a[ii + 1] < b[jj + 1]$. Then, from $J \land ii + jj < 2n$ we deduce that, for all $\bar{x}$, if there exists an i such that $1 \le \bar{i} \le ii \land a[\bar{i}] = \bar{x}$ or $1 \le \bar{i} \le jj \land b[\bar{i}] = \bar{x}$, then $\exists \bar{j}(1 \le \bar{j} \le ii + jj \land c[\bar{j}] = \bar{x})$. Instead, if $\bar{i} = ii + 1 \land a[\bar{i}] = \bar{x}$, then the predicate

$$\exists \bar{j}(1 \le \bar{j} \le ii + jj + 1 \land$$
$$\textbf{if } \bar{j} = ii + jj + 1 \textbf{ then } a[ii + 1] = \bar{x} \textbf{ else } c[\bar{j}] = \bar{x})$$

is satisfied by $\bar{j} = ii + jj + 1$.
Conversely, suppose

$$\exists \bar{j}((1 \le \bar{j} \le ii + jj + 1) \land$$
$$\textbf{if } \bar{j} = ii + jj + 1 \textbf{ then } a[ii + 1] = \bar{x} \textbf{ else } c[\bar{j}] = \bar{x}).$$

If $1 \le \bar{j} \le ii + jj$, then $c[\bar{j}] = \bar{x}$ holds and this implies $\exists \bar{i}(1 \le \bar{i} \le ii \land a[\bar{i}] = \bar{x} \lor (1 \le \bar{i} \le jj \land b[\bar{i}] = \bar{x})$. If $\bar{j} = ii + jj + 1$, then $a[ii + 1] = \bar{x}$ holds and thus $\exists \bar{i}(1 \le \bar{i} \le ii + 1 \land a[\bar{i}] = \bar{x})$ is satisfied by $\bar{i} = ii + 1$.
The case $a[ii + 1] \ge b[jj + 1]$ is completely similar.

3. After some simplification, which should be checked by the reader, P3′ becomes

$$(a[ii + 1] < b[jj + 1] \supset (a[ii + 1] \le a[ii + 2] \land a[ii + 1] \le b[jj + 1])) \land$$
$$(a[ii + 1] \ge b[jj + 1] \supset (b[jj + 1] \le a[ii + 1] \land b[jj + 1] \le b[jj + 2]))$$

In the case $a[ii + 1] < b[jj + 1]$, $a[ii + 1] \le a[ii + 2]$ is implied by $ordered(a)$ and by $ii < n$ as we proved in the above point 1; $a[ii + 1] \le$

$b[jj + 1]$ is implied by $a[ii + 1] < b[jj + 1]$. The case $a[ii + 1] \geq b[jj + 1]$ is similar.

4. After some simplification, which should be checked by the reader, P4'

$$a[ii + 1] < b[jj + 1] \supset (\forall \bar{p} (1 \leq \bar{p} < ii + jj + 1) \supset$$
$$(\textbf{if } \bar{p} = ii + jj \textbf{ then } c[\bar{p}] \leq a[ii + 1]$$
$$\textbf{else } c[\bar{p}] \leq c[\bar{p} + 1])$$
$$\wedge$$
$$a[ii + 1] \geq b[jj + 1] \supset (\forall \bar{p} (1 \leq \bar{p} < ii + jj + 1) \supset$$
$$(\textbf{if } \bar{p} = ii + jj \textbf{ then } c[\bar{p}] \leq b[jj + 1]$$
$$\textbf{else } c[\bar{p}] \leq c[\bar{p} + 1])$$

Let us consider the case $a[ii + 1] < b[jj + 1]$.

For $1 \leq \bar{p} < ii + jj$ the first member of the conjunction is implied by *ordered*(cl). For $\bar{p} = ii + jj$, $c[\bar{p}] \leq a[ii + 1]$ follows from P3.

The case where $a[ii + 1] \geq b[jj + 1]$ is similar.

The proof is now complete.

Example 5.8 (Merge-Sort)

Once again, let us consider the problem of sorting an array a of n elements. We will develop a new sorting algorithm, coded in SMALG, based on the previous example of *MERGE*. The algorithm is called *MERGE-SORT*. It will be developed jointly with its correctness proof, in order to show how structured programming techniques can be enhanced by formal methods. For the sake of simplicity, we will assume $n = 2^k$ for some integer k.

Suppose we know that the array a is partitioned into j ordered subarrays $a_1, \ldots, a_j$ of size m; that is,

$$a_1 = a[1..m], \ a_2 = a[m + 1..2m], \ldots, a_j = a[m \cdot (j - 1) + 1..n]$$

For simplicity, we also assume that $m = 2^h$ for some $0 \leq h \leq k$. Observe that this is trivially true for any array of size $n = 2^k$ with $j = n$ and $m = 1$, because any one-element array is automatically sorted. Also, observe that if we perform the *MERGE* of a_i and a_{i+1} for $i = 1, 3, \ldots j - 1$ we obtain a rearrangement of a, which is now partitioned into $j/2$ ordered subarrays.

This can be immediately translated into the following kernel of a sorting algorithm, based on the properties of *MERGE*.

MERGE-SORT: Initialize j to n; that is, partition a into
n one-element sorted subarrays;
    while $j > 1$
        do for all odd values of i from 1 to $j - 1$
            do *MERGE* a_i with a_{i+1} **od**;
            $j := j$ **div** 2
        od

Before detailing the above algorithm, we integrate it with appropriate assertions. Let us define $p\_ordered\,(a, i, j)$:

$$\forall \bar{p}((n/j \cdot (i - 1) + 1 \leq \bar{p} < n/j \cdot i) \supset a[\bar{p}] \leq a[\bar{p} + 1]) \wedge$$

$$\forall \bar{p}((n/j \cdot (i - 1) + 1 \leq \bar{p} \leq n/j \cdot i) \supset$$

$$\exists \bar{r}((n/j \cdot (i - 1) + 1 \leq \bar{r} \leq n/j \cdot i) \wedge a[\bar{p}] = b[\bar{r}])) \wedge$$

$$\forall \bar{r}((n/j \cdot (i - 1) + 1 \leq \bar{r} \leq n/j \cdot i) \supset$$

$$\exists \bar{p}((n/j \cdot (i - 1) + 1 \leq \bar{p} \leq n/j \cdot i) \wedge a[\bar{p}] = b[\bar{r}]))$$

which is a formal way to state that the portion of a included between the $(n/j \cdot (i - 1) + 1)$-th and the $(n/j \cdot i)$-th element is ordered and consists of all elements included within the same portion of b, where b denotes the initial arrangement of a. This is the version of *MERGE-SORT* annotated with assertions.

MERGE-SORT: **begin** $\{\exists \bar{k}(n = 2^k)\}$
$\qquad\qquad\qquad j := n;$
$\qquad\qquad\qquad \{I_{\text{EXT}}: \forall i(1 \leq \bar{i} \leq j) \supset p\_ordered\,(a, \bar{i}, j) \wedge \exists \bar{h}(j = 2^{\bar{h}})\}$
$\qquad\qquad\qquad \textbf{while } j > 1$
$\qquad\qquad\qquad\qquad \{I_{\text{EXT}}\}$
$\qquad\qquad\qquad \textbf{do}$
$\qquad\qquad\qquad L_{\text{EXT}}$
$\qquad\qquad\qquad \textbf{od}$
$\qquad\qquad\qquad \{I_{\text{EXT}} \wedge j \leq 1\}$
$\qquad\quad$ **end**

Clearly, backwards substitution of I_{EXT} through $j := n$ yields the required precondition. Furthermore, $I_{\text{EXT}} \wedge j \leq 1$ implies $i = j = 1$ and $ordered(a)$ (predicate $ordered$ has been introduced in Example 5.7). Thus the problem is to design L_{EXT} in such a way that it terminates and keeps I_{EXT} invariant. Let us try the following derivation.

L_{EXT}: $i := 1;$
$\qquad \textbf{while } i \leq j - 1$
$\qquad L_{\text{IN}}$: **do** "merge $a[n/j \cdot (i - 1) + 1..n/j \cdot i]$
$\qquad\qquad\qquad$ with $a[n/j \cdot i + 1..n/j \cdot (i + 1)]$";
$\qquad\qquad\qquad i := i + 2$
$\qquad\qquad \textbf{od};$
$\qquad j := j \textbf{ div } 2$

L_{EXT} contains an internal loop whose body is L_{IN}. As we did before, let us try to define an appropriate invariant before going into the implementation of L_{IN}. Intuitively, the purpose of L_{IN} is to provide a new partitioning of a. This is obtained by merging two consecutive subarrays into a new larger subarray. A candidate invariant I_{IN} is therefore the following (with the obvious meaning of $odd(i)$).

$$I_{IN}: \forall \bar{z} \left(1 \le \bar{z} \le \frac{i-1}{2} \supset p\_ordered(a, \bar{z}, j/2) \; \wedge \right.$$

$$\left. i \le \bar{z} \le j \supset p\_ordered(a, \bar{z}, j) \right) \wedge i \le j + 1 \wedge odd(i) \wedge \exists \bar{h}(j = 2^{\bar{h}})$$

The reader should prove that if I_{IN} is actually an invariant assertion for the internal loop, then the entire program is correct. Our problem is then to design a suitable L_{IN} such that I_{IN} is actually invariant. Let us define the following L_{IN}.

$$x := a[n/j \cdot (i-1) + 1..n/j \cdot i]$$
$$y := a[n/j \cdot i + 1..n/j \cdot (i+1)]$$

merge x and y into z (by using program *MERGE* of Example 5.7);

$$a[n/j \cdot (i-1) + 1..n/j \cdot (i+1)] := z$$
$$i := i + 2$$

Arrays x, y, and z are used to store temporary array values, and, for simplicity, we have used only one SMALG statement to denote an array assignment. The reader can easily expand such assignment into a loop of simple assignments.

It is easy to verify the following proof steps.

1. $\{ p\_ordered(a, i, j) \} x := a[n/j \cdot (i-1) + 1..n/j \cdot i]$
   $\{ ordered(x) \wedge x = perm(b, i, j) \}$
   Where $x = perm(b, i, j)$ stands for

   $$\forall \bar{p}(n/j \cdot (i-1) + 1 \le \bar{p} \le n/j \cdot i) \supset \exists \bar{r}((1 \le \bar{r} \le n/j) \wedge (b[\bar{p}] = x[\bar{r}])) \wedge$$
   $$\forall \bar{r}(1 \le \bar{r} \le n/j) \supset \exists \bar{p}((n/j \cdot (i-1) + 1 \le \bar{p} \le n/j \cdot i) \wedge (b[\bar{p}] = x[\bar{r}])).$$

2. $\{ p\_ordered(a, i+1, j) \} y := a[n/j \cdot i + 1..n/j \cdot (i+1)]$
   $\{ ordered(y) \wedge y = perm(b, i+1, j) \}$

3. $\{ ordered(x) \wedge ordered(y) \wedge x = perm(b, i, j) \wedge y = perm(b, i+1, j) \}$
       merge x and y into z; $a[n/j \cdot (i-1) + 1..n/j \cdot (i+1)] := z$
   $$\{ p\_ordered\left(a, \frac{i+1}{2}, j/2 \right) \}$$

4. $\left\{ \forall \bar{z} \left(1 \le \bar{z} \le \frac{i+1}{2} \supset p\_ordered(a, \bar{z}, j/2) \right. \right.$

   $$\left. \left. \wedge \, i + 2 \le \bar{z} \le j \supset p\_ordered(a, \bar{z}, j) \right) \wedge i \le j - 1 \wedge odd(i) \right\}$$

   $i := i + 2$

   $$\left\{ \forall \bar{z} \left(1 \le \bar{z} \le \frac{i-1}{2} \supset p\_ordered(a, \bar{z}, j/2) \right. \right.$$

   $$\left. \left. \wedge \, i \le \bar{z} \le j \supset p\_ordered(a, \bar{z}, j) \right) \wedge i \le j + 1 \wedge odd(i) \right\}$$

Finally, by observing that

i. $\forall \bar{z} \left(1 \le \bar{z} \le \dfrac{i+1}{2} \supset p\_\!ordered(a, \bar{z}, j/2) \right) \equiv$

$\forall \bar{z} \left(1 \le \bar{z} \le \dfrac{i-1}{2} \supset p\_\!ordered(a, \bar{z}, j/2) \wedge p\_\!ordered\left(a, \dfrac{i+1}{2}, j/2 \right) \right)$

ii. $\forall \bar{z} \left(1 \le \bar{z} \le \dfrac{i-1}{2} \supset p\_\!ordered(a, \bar{z}, j/2) \wedge \right.$

$\left. i \le \bar{z} \le j \supset p\_\!ordered(a, \bar{z}, j) \right) \supset$

$\forall \bar{z} (1 \le \bar{z} \le j \supset p\_\!ordered(a, \bar{z}, j))$

it is easy to prove

$\{ I_{IN} \wedge i \le j - 1 \} L_{IN} \{ I_{IN} \}$

and this completes the proof.

Exercises

5.21 Develop a program computing the greatest common divisor of two positive integers hand in hand with its correctness proof.

5.22 Develop a bubble-sort program (see Exercise 5.10) hand in hand with its correctness proof.

5.6 Towards a Proof-System for a Real-Life Programming Language

Throughout this text we focused the reader's attention on conceptually relevant aspects of theoretical computer science as tools to be applied in the practice of computer programming. Although we devoted much effort to motivational issues, the technical details involved in the application of these tools to real, practical cases have been systematically set aside and delayed to further specialized studies. This is the reason why Hoare's formal method for proving program correctness has been presented for a toy language, which is just a kernel of today's ALGOL-like languages. Here, we give the reader just a glimpse of the problems arising when we address formal program verification for real-life programs written in a real-life programming language.

When programs grow to solve complex problems, they generally increase in size, number of used variables, number of subprograms, nesting levels, etc. In one word: complexity. Accordingly, the complexity of program analysis—be it formal or not—increases in a way that may be more than proportional to, say, the size of the program. The only way to master complexity is through a rigorous application of modularization principles and of structured programming methodologies.

As far as the programming language is concerned, let us consider the problems arising when we try to extend our toy language to cover all of—say—Pascal. As for any real programming language, Pascal exhibits a number of features that have been ignored in our toy language. For all of them, one must give an adequate set of proof rules defining their semantics. Here we review some of them.

1. Although the **if-then-else** and **while** constructs are sufficient to reach the computational power of Turing machines, real-life languages provide a richer set of control structures, such as the **case** statement and the **repeat...until** statement.

   The **case** statement has the following structure.

   case e **of**
   $$L_1 : S_1;$$
   $$L_2 : S_2;$$
   $$\cdot$$
   $$\cdot$$
   $$\cdot$$
   $$L_n : S_n$$
   end

   where, for $i = 1, \ldots, n$, S_i is a statement and L_i is a value of expression e. The semantics of **case** statement is easily described by the following simple proof rule

   $$\frac{\{P \wedge (e = L_i)\} S_i \{Q\}, \forall i = 1, \ldots, n}{\{P \wedge e \in \{L_1, \ldots, L_n\} \wedge (i \neq j \supset L_i \neq L_j)\} \text{ case } e \text{ of } L_1 : S_1; \ldots; L_n : S_n \text{ end } \{Q\}}$$

   The **repeat** statement has the following structure.

   repeat SL
   until B

   where SL is a statement list and B is a Boolean expression. The semantics is easily described by the rule

   $$\frac{\{P\} S \{Q\}, Q \wedge \neg B \supset P}{\{P\} \text{ repeat } S \text{ until } B \{Q \wedge B\}}$$

   where P is the loop invariant.

2. Pascal requires any variable occurring within a statement to be declared with a statically associated type. This allows the compiler to verify that the variable is properly used (e.g., a record is not added to an integer). This is one aspect that falls under the term static semantics discussed in Section 4.5. Static semantics rules are easily described via Hoare's style axioms. For example, suppose that

a hypothetical language

a. Allows only integer type variables.

b. Does not contain procedures.

c. Imposes the user to declare any used variable.

The following rule could be attached to an identifier declaration according to the SMALG definition (see Section 4.5)

$$\{ id \notin ID_M \} \, id \, \{ id \in ID_M \}$$

Accordingly, the rule for the assignment statement can be modified as follows

$$\{ P_x^{f(x_1, \ldots, x_n)} \wedge Q \} \, x := f(x_1, x_2 \ldots x_n) \, \{ P \wedge Q \}$$

where $Q = \{ x, x_1, \ldots x_n \} \subseteq \{ ID_M \}$.

Since static semantics can be checked by the compiler, we can ignore these rules and use axioms in our proof for run-time correctness. For exactly the same reason, the clause $i \neq j \supset L_i \neq L_j$ can be deleted from the axiom for the **case** statement.

3. Procedures (and functions) are an essential abstraction tool. In the simplest case of a parameterless procedure containing no calls to further procedures, the proof rule to be associated to a procedure call is easy to derive. Let **procedure** *proc*; **begin** S **end** be a procedure declaration with no formal parameters, where S—a statement list—denotes *proc*'s body. If we wish to prove $\{P\} \, proc \, \{Q\}$ for any call to *proc*, we just need to prove $\{P\} \, S \, \{Q\}$. Thus, we have the rule

$$\frac{\{P\} S \{Q\}}{\{P\} \, proc \, \{Q\}}$$

Things become more and more complex as we start dealing with parameter passing, scope rules, recursion, procedures as parameters, etc. Again, the reader is referred to the bibliography for a treatment of this topic.

Let us just add one remark. Most programming languages (including Pascal) allow function calls to occur within an expression. Unlike mathematical functions, Pascal functions may produce *side effects*; that is, besides returning a result they can modify the value of some nonlocal variable or parameter passed by reference. Consequently, the axiom A1 is invalidated. In fact, suppose the body of function *func*(x, y) contains a statement $z := expression$, where z is a nonlocal variable of *func*. The effect of $w := func(a, b)$ cannot be described by

$$\{ P_w^{func(a, b)} \} \, w := func(a, b) \, \{ P \}$$

because it would consider z unaffected by the function call.

We have given only a sample of the problems we should face when we wish to cover all of the details of a real-life programming language. Others are presented in the following exercises. The conclusion is that there is a long way from the formal definition of a toy language to the formal definition of a real programming language; some of the steps are simple exercises, others are just a tedious job, still others require additional conceptual insight. In practice, a difficulty in formally defining a language feature reflects a difficulty in deeply understanding and/or implementing it. This is the case of a powerful and useful language feature such as passing procedures as parameters, and also of often blamed and undesirable features such as **goto** and side effects in function calls.

Exercises

5.23   Give proof rules for
a. The Pascal **for** statement.
b. The FORTRAN DO statement.

5.24*   Try to develop a proof rule for the **goto** statement. If you do not succeed, you should refer to the suggested bibliography.

5.25   Give a formal description of static semantics of procedure calls in Pascal.

5.26   Introduce formal rules describing I/O statements in Pascal. *Hint*: I/O statements are nothing else than assignment statements between external and internal data structures.

5.27   Give a correctness proof of the Pascal program of Figure 2.1*a*, which codes the same algorithm as the SMALG program of Example 5.4.

5.7 * Proving Further Program Properties: The Case of Complexity

The examples presented so far were all devoted to the proof of assertions through which we intended to capture the meaning of a program: This is why we have called them *correctness proofs*. However, it should be clear that the method is well suited to proving any program property, provided that such property can be expressed by means of first-order formulas involving program variables. In this section, we present an example showing that time complexity bounds—and even termination—can be obtained by means of Hoare's proof rules as a *refinement of correctness proofs*. In general, it turns out that any property concerning the program behavior of a program can be formally analyzed by first introducing, if necessary, suitable new state variables that capture the desired property (such as time or space consumed), then trying to prove predicates on these state variables. Once again, the crucial point of the analysis is the invention of invariant assertions.

Figure 5.1 shows the *sort-by-straight-insertion* algorithm discussed in Example 5.4, augmented with the predicates needed for the proof of the desired postcondition P_{O1}.

Now, let us try to evaluate the time spent by the program to compute its solution. This can be done by introducing into the program a new *time counter*

$\{P_I : 1 \leq n\}$

$PSORT:$ **begin**

$\qquad i := 2$

$\qquad \{I_{\text{EXT}} : 1 \leq i \leq n + 1 \wedge \forall \bar{p}((1 \leq \bar{p} < i - 1) \supset a[\bar{p}] \leq a[\bar{p} + 1])\}$

$\qquad$ **while** $i \leq n$

$\qquad$ **do**

$\qquad\qquad x := a[i];\ a[0] := x;\ j := i - 1;$

$\qquad \{I_{\text{IN}} : \ \forall \bar{p}(((1 \leq \bar{p} < j) \supset a[\bar{p}] \leq a[\bar{p} + 1]) \wedge$

$\qquad\qquad\qquad ((j + 1 \leq \bar{p} < i) \supset a[\bar{p}] \leq a[\bar{p} + 1])) \wedge$

$\qquad\qquad x \leq a[j + 1] \wedge 0 \leq j < i \wedge x = a[0] \wedge (j < i - 1 \supset a[j] \leq a[j + 1])\ \}$

$\qquad\qquad$ **while** $x < a[j]$

$\qquad\qquad$ **do**

$\qquad\qquad\qquad k := j + 1;\ a[k] := a[j];\ j := j - 1$

$\qquad\qquad$ **od;**

$\qquad \{I_{\text{IN}} \wedge x \geq a[j]\}$

$\qquad\qquad k := j + 1;\ a[k] := x;\ i := i + 1$

$\qquad$ **od**

$\qquad \{I_{\text{EXT}} \wedge i > n\}$

$\qquad$ **end**

$\{P_{O1} : \forall \bar{p}((1 \leq \bar{p} < n - 1) \supset a[\bar{p}] \leq a[\bar{p} + 1])\}$

FIGURE 5.1 An asserted SMALG program coding algorithm *sort-by-straight-insertion*

variable t and by updating it as a consequence of execution of the original statements of program *PSORT*. Thus we obtain a new program *PSORT*, given in Figure 5.2.

First notice that the new variables t and tt and constants $k0$, $k1$, and $k2$ do not affect the program's behavior. In fact, intuitively, they do not affect the value of any original variables; more formally, the correctness proof for *PSORT* still

$PSORT_t:$ **begin**

$\qquad\qquad t := k0;$

$\qquad\qquad i := 2;$

$\qquad\qquad$ **while** $i \leq n$

$\qquad\qquad$ **do** $x := a[i];\ a[0] := x;\ j := i - 1;$

$\qquad\qquad\qquad tt := 0;$

$\qquad\qquad\qquad$ **while** $x < a[j]$

$\qquad\qquad\qquad$ **do** $k := j + 1,\ a[k] := a[j];\ j := j - 1;$

$\qquad\qquad\qquad\qquad tt := tt + k1;$

$\qquad\qquad\qquad$ **od**

$\qquad\qquad\qquad k := j + 1;\ a[k] := x;\ i := i + 1;$

$\qquad\qquad\qquad t := t + tt + k2$

$\qquad\qquad$ **od**

$\qquad$ **end**

FIGURE 5.2 A modified version of *PSORT*

holds for $PSORT_t$. Second, observe that constants $k0$, $k1$, and $k2$ represent the time necessary to compute $i := 2$; $i \leq n$, $x < a[j]$; $k := j + 1$; $a[k] := a[j]$; $j := j - 1$, and $i \leq n$; $x := a[i]$; $a[0] := x$; $j := i - 1$; $k := k + 1$; $x < a[j]$; $a[k] := x$; $i := i + 1$, respectively. In principle, $k0$, $k1$, and $k2$ may also depend on the value of program variables. However, we may assume here that the main factor which dominates P's time complexity is the number of accesses to array a, to which we attach a conventional cost 1. Thus $k0 = 0$, $k1 = 3$, and $k2 = 4$. Under these assumptions, the value of variable t at the end of $PSORT_t$ clearly represents the time spent to run $PSORT$, and time complexity analysis is reduced to proving assertions on variable t.

What is interesting here is that a complexity proof involving variable t can be obtained incrementally as an enrichment of the original correctness proof. Such an enrichment is obtained by

a. Adding a new invariant CI_{IN} to I_{IN}. A simple intuitive analysis suggests CI_{IN}: $tt = 3(i - 1) - 3j$. It is immediate to verify that

$$\{ I_{IN} \wedge CI_{IN} \wedge x < a[j] \}$$
$$k := j + 1; \ a[k] := a[j]; \ j := j - 1; \ tt := tt + k1$$
$$\{ I_{IN} \wedge CI_{IN} \}$$

b. Observing that $0 \leq j < i$ in I_{IN} implies $0 \leq j \leq i - 1$ and therefore also

$$\overline{CI}_{IN}: 0 \leq tt \leq 3(i - 1)$$

is an invariant for the internal loop.
This suggests an additional invariant for the external loop

$$CI_{EXT}: 4(i - 2) \leq t \leq 4(i - 2) + \sum_{r=2}^{i-1} 3(r - 1)$$

Again, it is easy to verify that $I_{EXT} \wedge CI_{EXT}$ is actually invariant for the external loop.

c. Verifying that CI_{EXT} reduces to T by backwards substitution through $t := k0$; $i := 2$ and that

$$I_{EXT} \wedge CI_{EXT} \wedge i > n$$

implies

$$4(n - 1) \leq t \leq 4n - 4 + 3 \cdot \left(\frac{n \cdot (n - 1)}{2} \right)$$

In conclusion, we have formally derived $PSORT$'s lower and upper time complexity bounds starting from its correctness proof.

The reader must be aware that our proof is still a partial correctness proof: Thus, the computation time for PSORT is limited by the obtained upperbound *only if* P terminates. This may sound somewhat confusing, but little concentration should convince the reader of its truth. As a further exercise, the reader can easily prove a complexity formula $t \le 99/2$ for the program below, where t is again a newly added variable to describe time behavior.

P': $a := 1$; $t := 0$;
    while $a \ne 100$
    do $a := a + 2$; $t := t + 1$
    od

Clearly P' never halts even if $t \le 99/2$ can be easily proved.

5.7.1* Termination as Corollary of Complexity

Consider a loop of the form

$t := 0$;
L: **while** *cond* **do**
    L_B: $\ldots$;
        $t := t + k_L$
    od

where t has been added to the original program variables as we did before.

Suppose that through conventional partial correctness techniques we have been able to prove $t \le f(\bar{y})$ at loop exit, where $\bar{y}$ denotes a vector of program variables *not modified* within L_B, and f is a *total positive function*. Observe that the set

$$\mathscr{W} = \{ z \mid 0 \le z \le f(\bar{y}) \}$$

is well ordered by $<$ for any value of $\bar{y}$.

Therefore, if for any loop invariant I we can prove

$$\{ I \wedge cond \wedge t \in \mathscr{W} \} L_B \{ I \wedge t \in \mathscr{W} \}$$

and if t is increased within L_B, then we can conclude termination of L_B.

For instance, above we have verified that $tt \le 3(i - 1)$ is an invariant for the innermost loop of *PSORT*. Thus, tt always ranges in the well-founded set $\{ z \mid 0 \le z \le 3 \cdot (i - 1) \}$ for each $i \ge 2$. Since tt is incremented within the loop, the loop itself must terminate eventually.

Although the opposite might sound more natural, the termination proof has been obtained as a corollary of complexity proof, which in turn has been developed as a corollary of partial correctness proof.

Exercises

5.28 State complexity formulas for the programs of Examples 5.2, 5.5, 5.6, 5.7, and 5.8. Prove also their termination by means of the above method.

5.29 Prove complexity formulas and termination for the programs of Exercises 5.6, 5.7, 5.10, and 5.11.

5.8 Proving Program Properties through Denotational Semantics

So far, we examined the most widely known method for proving program properties, namely Hoare's method. Several other methods have been proposed in the literature. A large number of them is based on the use of logical formulas and on their transformation through programming language constructs. Such methods are generally referred to as *axiomatic methods*. A few references thereon are given in the Bibliographic Remarks.

A rather different way of reasoning on programs exploits a functional programming style and is mainly based on recursion and induction. In this section, we just try to give the flavor of such inductive methods by choosing the simplest method, namely *computational induction*, and by applying it to simple examples. Not surprisingly, we base our presentation on McCarthy's formalism, which is the natural framework for inductive reasonings, even if the philosophy of the method can certainly be extended to more conventional programming languages.

The main idea of the method consists in trying to prove properties of a recursive program P by induction on the level of recursion. Let τ denote the continuous operator associated with P in the natural way, as we saw in Section 4.6. For simplicity, we restrict our attention to the case where $\tau: [D^{\wedge} \to R^{\wedge}] \to [D^{\wedge} \to R^{\wedge}]$: This will allow for a general enough treatment. As usual, let f_τ denote the LFP of τ.

Suppose we wish to prove that a property φ holds for f_τ. If we succeed in proving that φ holds for Ω (i.e., $\tau^0[\Omega]$), and that if φ holds for $\tau^i[\Omega]$, then it holds for $\tau^{i+1}[\Omega]$ too, then we can deduce that φ holds for any $\tau^i[\Omega]$. At this point, one might try to "go to the limit," and say that φ holds for $f_\tau \equiv$ LUB $\{\tau^i[\Omega]\}$ as well. However, we warn the reader that such a limit operation is not always admissible as it is shown by the following example.

Example 5.9

Consider the following recursive program over the natural numbers.

$TIM(x, y) \Leftarrow$ **if** $y = 0$ **then** x **else** $x + TIM(x, y - 1)$

Clearly the LFP of the associated continuous operator is f_τ given by

$f_\tau(x, y) = x \cdot y.$

Consider now the property

$\varphi(TIM): TIM(x + z, y) \equiv TIM(x, y) + TIM(z, y)$

which states distributivity of the sum with respect to multiplication. Clearly φ holds for Ω as $\Omega(x + z, y) \equiv \perp \equiv \Omega(x, y) + \Omega(z, y) \equiv \perp + \perp$. Furthermore, suppose

$\tau^i[\Omega](x + z, y) \equiv \tau^i[\Omega](x, y) + \tau^i[\Omega](z, y)$

Then

$$\tau\left[\tau^i[\Omega]\right](x+z,\,y) \equiv \text{if } y=0 \text{ then } x+z \text{ else } x+z+\tau^i[\Omega](x+z,\,y-1)$$
$$\equiv \text{if } y=0 \text{ then } x+z \text{ else } x+z$$
$$+\tau^i[\Omega](x,\,y-1)+\tau^i[\Omega](z,\,y-1)$$
$$\equiv \text{if } y=0 \text{ then } x \text{ else } x+\tau^i[\Omega](x,\,y-1)$$
$$+ \text{if } y=0 \text{ then } z \text{ else } z+\tau^i[\Omega](z,\,y-1)$$
$$\equiv \tau^{i+1}[\Omega](x,\,y)+\tau^{i+1}[\Omega](z,\,y)$$

Thus, φ holds for $\tau^i[\Omega]$, for every i. Moreover

$$f_\tau(x+z,\,y) \equiv (x+z)\cdot y \equiv x\cdot y+z\cdot y \equiv f_\tau(x,\,y)+f_\tau(z,\,y)$$

Thus, in this case, φ holds for any $\tau^i[\Omega]$ as well as for f_τ. On the other hand, consider the property

$$\psi(TIM): \exists y \in \mathbb{N}(TIM(x,\,y) \equiv \perp)$$

Clearly, ψ holds for any $\tau^i[\Omega]$. In fact, $\tau^i[\Omega](x,\,y) \equiv \perp$ for $y > i$. However, ψ does not hold for f_τ as $x \cdot y \neq \perp$ for every $y \in \mathbb{N}$.

In general, we can state the following.

Definition 5.4
A k-ary relation over $[D^\wedge \to R^\wedge]$ is said to be *admissible* if and only if for any k continuous operators $\tau_j \colon [D^\wedge \to R^\wedge] \to [D^\wedge \to R^\wedge]$, where $j = 1, \ldots, k$, $\varphi(\tau_1^i[\Omega], \ldots, \tau_k^i[\Omega])$ for all i implies $\varphi(\text{LUB}\{\tau_1^i[\Omega]\}, \ldots, \text{LUB}\{\tau_k^i[\Omega]\})$. □

It is not surprising that admissibility (i.e., preservation of a property through a limit operation), is guaranteed by some sort of continuity of φ, as the following statement states formally.

Theorem 5.2
If φ is of the form

$$\bigwedge_{i=1}^{n} \alpha_i[F_1, \ldots, F_k] \subseteq \beta_i[F_1, \ldots, F_k]$$

where α_i and β_i are continuous operators on $[D^\wedge \to R^\wedge]^k$, then φ is admissible.

Proof
Assume φ is $\alpha[F] \subseteq \beta[F]$ (the extension to the general case is immediate, but requires a heavier notation). By hypothesis, let $\alpha[\tau^i[\Omega]] \subseteq \beta[\tau^i[\Omega]]$ for any i. We have to show that $\alpha[\text{LUB}\{\tau^i[\Omega]\}] \subseteq \beta[\text{LUB}\{\tau^i[\Omega]\}]$.

Since β is monotonic, $\tau^i[\Omega] \subseteq \text{LUB} \{\tau^i[\Omega]\}$ for any i implies that $\beta[\tau^i[\Omega]] \subseteq \beta[\text{LUB} \{\tau^i[\Omega]\}]$ for all i. Thus, $\alpha[\tau^i[\Omega]] \subseteq \beta[\text{LUB} \{\tau^i[\Omega]\}]$ for all i, so that $\beta[\text{LUB} \{\tau^i[\Omega]\}]$ is an UB of $\{\alpha[\tau^i[\Omega]]\}$, which is a chain. This implies $\text{LUB} \{\alpha[\tau^i[\Omega]]\} \subseteq \beta[\text{LUB} \{\tau^i[\Omega]\}]$. But, since α is continuous, $\alpha[\text{LUB} \{\tau^i[\Omega]\}] \equiv \text{LUB} \{\alpha[\tau^i[\Omega]]\}$ and this completes the proof. ∎

Note that for any F, $\alpha[F] \equiv \beta[F]$ is equivalent to $\alpha[F] \subseteq \beta[F] \wedge \beta[F] \subseteq \alpha[F]$ so that an immediate application of the above theorem is for proving equivalence of recursive programs. In fact, let P and Q be two recursive programs and let τ and ρ be the corresponding continuous operators. If we succeed in proving that $\tau[\Omega] \equiv \rho[\Omega]$ and that for any i, $\tau^i[\Omega] \equiv \rho^i[\Omega]$, implies $\tau^{i+1}[\Omega] \equiv \rho^{i+1}[\Omega]$, or that for any $f, g \in [\hat{D} \to \hat{R}]$, $f \equiv g$ implies $\tau[f] \equiv \tau[g]$, then we can deduce that the property φ (F, G): $F \equiv G$ holds for $F \equiv f_\tau$ and $G \equiv f_\rho$ (i.e., the two recursive programs P and Q are equivalent).

Let us give now a few examples showing how the foregoing method (called *computational induction method*) can be used to prove admissible properties of recursive programs.

Example 5.10

Consider the following two recursive programs over the natural numbers

P: $F(x, y, z) \Leftarrow \textbf{if } x = 0 \textbf{ then } y \textbf{ else } F(x - 1, y + z, z)$
Q: $G(x, y) \Leftarrow \textbf{if } x = 0 \textbf{ then } y \textbf{ else } G(x - 1, y + 2x - 1)$

Denote by τ and ρ the two continuous operators defined by P and Q, respectively. We wish to show that the following property holds on f_τ and f_ρ, namely, $f_\tau(x, 0, x) \equiv f_\rho(x, 0)$. Incidentally, notice that $f_\tau(x, 0, x) \equiv f_\rho(x, 0) \equiv x^2$. The computational induction method requires to how that $\varphi(F, G)$: $F(x, 0, x) \equiv G(x, 0)$ holds

1. For $F = \Omega$, $G = \Omega$, it is a trivial truth since $\Omega(x, 0, x) \equiv \Omega(x, 0) \equiv \bot$
2. $f(x, 0, x) \equiv g(x, 0)$ implies $\tau[f](x, 0, x) \equiv \rho[g](x, 0)$.
   Actually,

   $\tau[f](x, 0, x) \equiv \textbf{if } x = 0 \textbf{ then } 0 \textbf{ else } f(x - 1, x, x)$
   $\rho[g](x, 0) \equiv \textbf{if } x = 0 \textbf{ then } 0 \textbf{ else } g(x - 1, 2x - 1)$

Here we run into difficulties since there is no apparent way of proving $f(x - 1, x, x) \equiv g(x - 1, 2x - 1)$ from the induction hypothesis. Thus, we use a little trick and generalize the property to be proved; namely we try to prove

$$\psi(f_\tau, f_\rho): f_\tau(y, x(x - y), x) \equiv f_\rho(y, x^2 - y^2)$$

Now, by letting $y = x$, φ will follow. Here are the two steps of the proof.

a. $\psi(\Omega, \Omega)$ is trivially true.
b. Assume that $f(y, x(x - y), x) \equiv g(y, x^2 - y^2)$.

$\tau[f](y, x(x - y), x)$
$\equiv$ **if** $y = 0$ **then** $x(x - y)$ **else** $f(y - 1, x(x - y) + x, x)$
$\equiv$ **if** $y = 0$ **then** x^2 **else** $f(y - 1, x(x - (y - 1)), x)$
$\equiv$ **if** $y = 0$ **then** x^2 **else** $g(y - 1, x^2 - (y - 1)^2)$
$\equiv$ **if** $y = 0$ **then** $x^2 - y^2$ **else** $g(y - 1, (x^2 - y^2) + 2y - 1)$
$\equiv \rho[g](y, x^2 - y^2)$

The foregoing example shows that some ingenuity is necessary in order to obtain the desired proof of properties by means of the computational induction method. This is essentially due to the need that the induction on the property in some sense parallels recursion in the LFP computation. Let us further investigate this issue in the following example.

Example 5.11

Consider the problem of building the reverse of an array of n elements, that is, an array whose first element is the nth element of the input array, the second element is the $(n - 1)$th element, and so on.

In order to state the problem in a formal way, let us refer to the notation introduced in Example 4.14. With reference to that notation, we define

- The set A of all arrays represented as functions $a : (\mathbb{N} - \{1\}) \to (\mathbb{N} \cup \{\perp\})$, such that for any $a \in A$, there exists an element of $\mathbb{N}$, denoted as $CARD(a)$, such that $1 \le i \le CARD(a)$ implies $a[i] \in \mathbb{N}$, whereas $a[i] = \perp$ for $i > CARD(a)$. $\varnothing$ denotes the unique element of A such that $CARD(\varnothing) = 0$
- The function $REVERSE: A \to A$ given by

if $CARD(a) = 0$ **then** $REVERSE(a) = \varnothing$
  else $REVERSE(a)[CARD(a) - i + 1] = a[i]$,
    for $1 \le i \le CARD(a)$
      $REVERSE(a)[i] = \perp$, for $CARD(a) < i$

Let us define now a recursive program P to compute the function $REVERSE$. We define P with the help of some simple auxiliary functions, namely:

- $TAIL: (A - \{\varnothing\}) \to A$, defined by
  if $CARD(a) = 1$ **then** $TAIL(a) = \varnothing$ **else** $TAIL(a)[i] = a[i + 1]$ for all i
- $FIRST: (A - \{\varnothing\}) \to \mathbb{N}$, defined by $FIRST(a) = a[1]$
- $\cdot : A \times \mathbb{N} \to A$ (with infix notation), defined by
  $(a \cdot x)[i] = $ **if** $i = CARD(a) + 1$ **then** x **else** $a[i]$

P is defined by

$P:\ REV(a) \Leftarrow \text{if } CARD(a) = 0 \text{ then } \varnothing \text{ else } REV(TAIL(a)) \cdot FIRST(a)$

Let us now prove that P actually computes $REVERSE$, that is, $REVERSE \equiv f_\tau$, f_τ being the LFP of the operator $\tau: [A\hat{} \to A\hat{}] \to [A\hat{} \to A\hat{}]$ defined by P. Intuitively, it should be clear that some proof based on induction on $CARD(a)$ should be possible since the statement clearly holds for $CARD(a) = 0$ and, if P succeeds in computing $REVERSE(a)$ when $CARD(a) = h$, then for $CARD(a) = h + 1$, $REVERSE(a)[h + 1 - i + 1] = a[i]$, $i = h + 1, h, \ldots, 2$, that is, the sequence $\{REVERSE(a)[h + 2 - i] | i = h + 1, \ldots, 2\}$ is just

$REVERSE\ (TAIL(a))$ and $REVERSE(a)[h + 1] = a[1] = FIRST(a)$.

However, some formal obstacles forbid an immediate application of the computational induction method to the property $\varphi(REV): REV(a) \equiv REVERSE(a)$. In fact, $REVERSE$ is a constant element of $[A\hat{} \to A\hat{}]$ and for any i, $\tau^i[\Omega](a) \equiv \perp$ if $CARD(a) > i$.

A first way out of this problem consists of proving that the predicate $\psi(REV): REV \subseteq REVERSE$ holds for f_τ.
$\psi(f_\tau)$ can be proved by means of computational induction. In fact,

1. $\Omega \subseteq REVERSE$ is obvious.
2. Let now f be any function in $[A\hat{} \to A\hat{}]$. Assume that $\psi(f)$ holds, that is $f \subseteq REVERSE$. This means that for any a, if $f(a)$ is defined (notice that $\varnothing$ is not $\perp$), then

$\text{if } CARD(a) = 0 \text{ then } f(a) = \varnothing$
$\qquad \text{else } f(a)[CARD(a) - i + 1] = a[i], \text{ for } 1 \le i \le CARD(a),$
$\qquad\qquad f(a)[i] = \perp \text{ for } CARD(a) < i$

Let us show that ψ holds for $\tau[f]$, that is, for any a,

$\text{if } CARD(a) = 0 \text{ then } \varnothing \text{ else } f(TAIL(a)) \cdot FIRST(a) \subseteq REVERSE(a)$

This is trivially true if $CARD(a) = 0$. Otherwise, if $f(a) \ne \perp$, so is $f(TAIL(a))$. (If $f(a)$ is $\perp$ and $CARD(a) > 0$, then, again $\psi(\tau[f]a)$ holds in a trivial way). Thus, $f(TAIL(a)) \equiv REVERSE(TAIL(a))$ and

$f(TAIL(a)) \cdot FIRST(a) \equiv REVERSE(TAIL(a)) \cdot FIRST(a)$.

Let b be the array $REVERSE(TAIL(a)) \cdot FIRST(a)$, and let $h + 1 = CARD(a)$, $h \ge 0$. For $i = 1, \ldots, h$ we have
$b(i) = REVERSE(TAIL(a))[i] = TAIL(a)\,[CARD(TAIL(a)) - i + 1] = a[h + 1 - i + 1] = REVERSE(a)[i]$.
For $i = h + 1$, we have $b[i] = a[1]$.
thus $\tau[f](a) \equiv REVERSE(a)$ if $f(a) \ne \perp$ and $CARD(a) > 0$.

We can conclude $\tau^i[\Omega] \subseteq REVERSE$ for all i and $f_\tau \subseteq REVERSE$.

At this point we can convince ourselves of the apparent fact that for any $a \in A$, there exists an i such that $\tau^i[\Omega](a) \neq \bot$ and therefore $f_\tau \equiv REVERSE$. However, proving a LFP to be total or $\supseteq g$, where g is a total function, by means of computational induction leads to some difficulties since, in general, $\tau^i[\Omega]$ is not total for any i even if LUB $\{\tau^i[\Omega]\}$ is total.

An alternative solution consists of transforming the definition of $REVERSE$ given above as a constant element of $[A^\wedge \to A^\wedge]$ into a recursive definition through a suitable operator. For instance, we could introduce a unit element u with respect to an operation $\square$ in $A^\wedge$. That is, $u \square a \equiv a \square u \equiv a$, for any $a \in A$ and $\bot \square a \equiv \bot$ for any a.

Then we could define $\overline{REVERSE}$ as $\overline{REVERSE}(a) \equiv f_\rho(a) \,\square\, REVERSE(a)$ where f_ρ is the LFP of the operator ρ on $[A^\wedge \to A^\wedge]$

$\rho : F(a) = \textbf{if } CARD(a) = 0 \textbf{ then } u \textbf{ else } F(TAIL(a))$

It is clear (but this cannot be proved by means of usual computational induction!) that $\overline{REVERSE} = REVERSE$.

On the other hand, if we assume $\overline{REVERSE}$ as a new *definition* of the reverse function, it is now possible to use computational induction to completely prove that $f_\tau \equiv \overline{REVERSE}$. This verification is left to the reader as an exercise.

Exercises

5.30   Let $a, b \in A$

Define the infix operator $\circ : A \times A \to A$ as

$c = a \circ b$ if and only if $c[i] = a[i]$ for $1 \leq i \leq CARD(a)$
$\qquad\qquad\qquad\qquad\qquad\qquad\qquad c[CARD(a) + i] = b[i]$ for $i > CARD(a)$

  1.1   Build a recursive program computing $a \circ b$ for any $a, b \in A$.
    Hint: Use the previous functions $TAIL$ and $FIRST$.
  1.2   Prove its correctness with respect to the foregoing definition.
  1.3   Prove that $(a \circ b) \circ c = a \circ (b \circ c)$ (associativity of $\circ$) by means of computational induction applied to your recursive program (not directly on the definition).

5.31   Extend Example 5.11 to prove that

$REVERSE\ (a \circ b) \equiv REVERSE(b) \circ REVERSE(a).$

5.32   Extend Example 5.11 to prove that $REVERSE\ (REVERSE(a)) \equiv a$.

5.33   Define the following operations on arrays.

  - $FRONT : (A - \{\varnothing\}) \to A$, is given by
    $FRONT(a)[i] = a[i]$ for $1 \leq i \leq CARD(a) - 1$,
    $FRONT(a)[i] = \bot$ for $i \geq CARD(a)$
  - $LAST : (A - \{\varnothing\}) \to \mathbb{N}$, is given by
    $LAST(a) = a[CARD(a)]$

Prove the equivalence of the following recursive programs computing

$$\sum_{i=1}^{CARD(a)} a[i]$$

$P_1: SUM(a) \Leftarrow \textbf{if } CARD(a) = 0 \textbf{ then } 0 \textbf{ else } FIRST(a) + SUM(TAIL(a))$

$P_2: SUM(a) \Leftarrow \textbf{if } CARD(a) = 0 \textbf{ then } 0 \textbf{ else } SUM(FRONT(a)) + LAST(a).$

5.9 Concluding Remarks

In this chapter, we have introduced some formal methods to tackle the problem of program correctness or, more generally, formal analysis of program properties. Although we claimed that the practical methods, techniques, and tools concerning the application of formalisms to the real programming activity are beyond the scope of this text, it is worth adding a few conclusive remarks to what we have already discussed.

We emphasized that as soon as programs reach a nontrivial complexity (as in Examples 5.4 through 5.8), their formal analysis becomes considerably complex too. Many of our readers will probably raise objections of this kind "If even for the relatively simple *MERGE* and *MERGE-SORT* programs correctness proofs are often longer than the programs themselves, what about large programs of thousands of statements?"

As we already mentioned, this is a serious objection. However, besides repeating our leitmotiv that the use of formal tools should be integrated with software engineering methodologies, we wish to focus the reader's attention on the following remarks.

1. Quite often, the apparent simplicity of an informal description versus a formal one hides some trap. For example, the reader should try to give a *precise informal* definition of the merge of two arrays, being sure to tackle all possible cases, and compare it with the formal one. In the authors' experience, a formal description and analysis following an informal analysis is valuable indeed since it often discovers some subtle mistakes.
2. Quite often, predicates are overly complicated formulas, because they have been completely detailed for didactic purposes. However, abstraction mechanisms can be applied to first-order formulas in much the same way as we do for Pascal programs. Thus, once the essential properties of a program fragment and related formulas have been stated, they can be used as if they were mathematical lemmas. We gave an example of this in Example 5.8.
3. Once sufficient experience is reached in the use of formal methods, many details become obvious and can be substituted by faster informal reasoning. Formal steps are left to the analysis of critical points. For instance, during the analysis of a sorting program we realize immediately that a fragment, say a

loop, maintains the property that an array *a* is a permutation of an array *b*. Consequently, a part of the proof can be skipped. This happens quite frequently also in mathematical proofs, which contain statements such as "It is clear that...." If such sentences were systematically replaced by their formal specification, formal proofs would become several order of magnitudes longer and more difficult to read. The goal is to develop an intuitive feeling of where one should be completely formal and where being formal does not provide any new insights but only adds to the details to be handled.

4. Formal program verification can be supported by computer-based tools. In this case, all trivial details are handled automatically and the user is only requested to direct the system in making conceptually critical deductions.

5. Finally, we should recall that formal analysis techniques have been successfully applied in practical cases (see the Bibliographic Remarks). Furthermore, there is some experimental evidence that an exposure to formal tools improves the programmer's capabilities even in informal analysis.

Chapter Summary

This chapter has been devoted to the general issue of proving formal properties of computer programs. Most of our discussion was based on Hoare's axiomatic method. We defined and illustrated the two key concepts of partial correctness and termination, and we emphasized that, in both cases, mathematical proofs are heavily based on human ingenuity, which must identify the deep essence of loops in terms of invariant assertions.

Programs can be developed hand in hand with their correctness proof. Informal reasonings on program derivation are formalized via assertions and then assertions are refined into programming language statements. This approach has been illustrated through examples to show how it can be used to derive programs that are guaranteed to be correct in the first place.

We stressed that Hoare's method can be applied to proving program properties other than correctness (e.g., computational complexity). Also, we discussed the relationship between program complexity proofs and termination proofs.

Finally, we presented the method of computational induction to prove properties of recursive programs written using McCarthy's formalism.

Further Exercises

5.34 Build a SMALG program that states whether a given sequence of positive integers is contained in another sequence. Prove the total correctness of your program and analyze its time complexity.

5.35 The following program is intended to check whether two given sequences, *sa* and *sb*, of $n > 0$ positive integers, possibly with repetitions, are a permutation of one another. State in which cases the program does not terminate, remove the error, and prove total correctness of your new program.

PERMCHECK: **begin**

$i := 1,\ j := 0,\ k := 0;$

while $i \leq n$ **do** $jj := j + 1;$

$\quad$ **if** $sb[jj] = 0$

$\quad$ **then** $h := j + 1;\ j := h$ **mod** n

$\quad$ **else if** $sb[jj] = sa[i]$

$\qquad$ **then** $sb[jj] := 0;\ k := k + 1;$

$\qquad h := j + 1;\ j := h$ **mod** $n;\ i := i + 1$

$\qquad$ **else** $h := j + 1;\ j := h$ **mod** n

$\qquad$ **fi**

$\quad$ **fi**

od;

if $k = n$ **then** *perm* $:= 1$ **else** *perm* $:= 0$ **fi**

end

5.36 Perform a complexity analysis for the program of Exercise 5.35 (in the subdomain where it terminates) and for your own version.

Sketchy Solutions to Selected Exercises

5.5 Proof of point a of Example 5.2.
First notice that for any $\bar{k}$,

$$x > y \wedge \exists \bar{x}_1, \bar{y}_1 \left(x = \bar{x}_1 \cdot \bar{k} \wedge y = \bar{y}_1 \cdot \bar{k} \right) \supset$$
$$x - y > 0 \wedge \exists \bar{x}_1, \bar{y}_1 \left(x - y = (\bar{x}_1 - \bar{y}_1) \cdot \bar{k} \right)$$

Thus, $\exists \bar{\bar{x}}_1, \bar{\bar{y}}_1 (x - y = \bar{x}_1 \cdot \bar{k} \wedge y = \bar{\bar{y}}_1 \cdot \bar{k}$

On the other hand, suppose by contradiction that $\bar{k}$ is not the greatest common divisor. Then

$$\exists \bar{h}, \bar{x}_2, \bar{y}_2 \left(\bar{h} > \bar{k} \wedge x - y = \bar{\bar{x}}_2 \cdot \bar{h} \wedge y = \bar{\bar{y}}_2 \cdot \bar{h} \right)$$

This would imply

$$x = \bar{\bar{x}}_2 \cdot \bar{h} + \bar{\bar{y}}_2 \cdot \bar{h} = \left(\bar{\bar{x}}_2 + \bar{\bar{y}}_2 \right) \cdot \bar{h} \wedge y = \bar{\bar{y}}_2 \cdot \bar{h}$$

and thus

$$\exists \bar{h}, \bar{x}_2, \bar{y}_2 \left(\bar{h} > \bar{k} \wedge x = \bar{x}_2 \cdot \bar{h} \wedge y = \bar{y}_2 \cdot \bar{h} \right)$$

thus contradicting I.

5.8 *Step 1.2*: Proof that $I_{\mathrm{IN}} \wedge x < a[j] \supset I_{\mathrm{IN}}^*$.

1. $x < a[j]$ implies $x \leq a[j]$.
2. $x = a[0]$ implies $x = a[0]$.
3. $j < i$ implies $j - 1 < i$.

4. $j = 0$ implies a contradiction between $x < a[j]$ and $x = a[0]$ so that $x < a[j]$ implies $j \neq 0$ and $0 \leq j \wedge j \neq 0$ implies $0 \leq j - 1$.

5. $\forall \bar{p}(1 \leq \bar{p} < j) \supset a[\bar{p}] \leq a[\bar{p} + 1]$
   obviously implies
   $\forall \bar{p}(1 \leq \bar{p} < j - 1) \supset a[\bar{p}] \leq a[\bar{p} + 1] \wedge a[j - 1] \leq a[j]$.

6. $\forall \bar{p}(j + 1 \leq \bar{p} < i) \supset a[\bar{p}] \leq a[\bar{p} + 1]$
   implies that
   $\forall \bar{p}(j \leq \bar{p} < i) \wedge \bar{p} \neq j \wedge \bar{p} \neq j + 1 \supset a[\bar{p}] \leq a[\bar{p} + 1]$.

7. If $\bar{p} = j + 1$, then $j < i - 1$ and therefore $a[j] \leq a[j + 1]$, but also $a[j + 1] \leq a[j + 2]$ and so $a[j] \leq a[j + 2]$.

8. Finally if $p = j$, then $a[\bar{p}] = a[j] \supset a[\bar{p}] \leq a[j]$.

Step 2: Proof that $I_{\text{IN}} \wedge x \geq a[j] \supset I_{\text{EX}}^{*}$.

1. $\bar{p} \neq j \wedge \bar{p} \neq j + 1$ in a trivial way.
2. $\bar{p} = j + 1$ by $x \leq a[j + 1] = a[\bar{p}] \leq a[\bar{p} + 1]$.
3. $\bar{p} = j$ by $a[\bar{p}] = a[j]$ and $x \geq a[j]$.

Notice that $0 \leq i \leq n$ is obviously invariant in the inner loop. It has not been explicitly mentioned in I_{IN} in order to make the notation not too heavy.

Step 3: Proof that $I_{\text{EX}} \wedge i \leq n \supset \bar{I}_{\text{IN}}$.

$\bar{I}_{\text{IN}}$ is the predicate $\forall \bar{p} (1 \leq \bar{p} < i - 1) \supset a[\bar{p}] \leq a[\bar{p} + 1] \wedge 0 \leq i - 1$. In fact, backwards substitution of $j + 1 \leq \bar{p} < i$ through $j := i - 1$ gives F so that $(1 \leq \bar{p} < i) \supset a[\bar{p}] \leq a[\bar{p} + 1]$ is always T. The same happens for $j < i - 1$.

5.35 *PERMCHECK* exits the loop only if *sb* is a permutation of *sa*. A correct version of the program is the following.

```
begin
i := 1; k := 0;
while i ≤ n do j := i + 1;
                while j ≠ i do
                            if sb[j] = 0
                            then h := j mod n; j := h + 1
                            else if sb[j] = sa[i]
                                      then sb[j] := 0; k := k + 1; j := i
                                      else h := j mod n; j := h + 1
                                      fi

                       fi
                od;
                   i := i + 1
              od;
if k = n then perm := 1 else perm := 0 fi
end
```

5.36 Both *PERMCHECK* and its correction are $\Theta(n^2)$, whenever they terminate, under the uniform cost criterion.

Bibliographic Remarks

A large amount of scientific literature is devoted to the topic of formal analysis of program properties. The original ideas are due to the pioneering works by McCarthy (1963a, b) and Floyd (1967a). Their ideas have been the starting point of much research. Most significant are the works by Hoare (1969), Manna (1969), Burstall (1969). In particular, Hoare (1969) first proposed a proof method for ALGOL-like languages, which was presented in this text. Manna (1974) presents both Floyd's and Hoare's methods. It also includes the presentation of proof methods based on computational induction which was originally proposed by Burstall (1969, 1974). Example 5.10 is borrowed from there.

Several modifications of the methods presented here have been proposed. Among them let us refer to the intermittent assertion method by Manna and Waldinger (1978) and the weakest precondition method by Dijkstra (1976).

The extension of the original proof rules to real-life programming constructs required a lot of work and exhibited many unexpected difficulties. A survey of Hoare-style proof rules is given in Apt (1981), while de Bakker (1980) is a careful comprehensive view of the field.

We warn the reader that several errors and inaccuracies are often present in the literature in the description of intricate cases. For instance, axiom A1 is frequently specified by saying that P_x^t is "the result of substituting all free occurrences of x in P by t", which has been shown to be an error. The paper by O'Donnell (1982) points out some weaknesses in the published rules for the **goto** statements.

In this chapter, we have not discussed correctness of concurrent programs —an important and active research area. Seminal approaches have been proposed by Hoare (1972, 1974), Owicki and Gries (1976), and Apt, Francez, and De Roever (1980). However, a sound formal basis for these methods has not been achieved yet.

The idea of combining the use of formal tools with techniques for reliable program synthesis is mainly due to Dijkstra (1976). Further examplification of such an idea is provided by the texts by Alagic and Arbib (1978) and Gries (1981).

Within the academic world, some languages have been defined with the express goal of supporting program correctness proofs: Gypsy (see Good, Cohen, and Hunter (1978) and Alphard (see Wulf, London, and Shaw (1976)) are two notable examples.

In most of this chapter, we used first-order logic as a *specification language*, that is, a language to express the requirements a program must satisfy in order to be considered correct. Other specification languages exist that are based on different formalisms such as (heterogeneous) algebras. This latter formalism has been first proposed by Birkhoff and Lipson (1970) and subsequently applied by several researchers to computer science concepts (see ADJ (1975), Guttag (1977), and Burstall and Goguen (1977)).

Alternatively, some researchers tend to see specification languages as true, *very high-level* programming languages. PROLOG (see Clocksin and Mellish

(1984)) is an example of a programming language based on the formalism of first-order logic (see also Kowalski (1979)). The so called Fifth Generation Project (see McCorduck (1983)) is strongly based on this idea.

Computer-based environments supporting formal program verification have been developed and extensively experimented for research purposes. Among the published examples of real-life, complex programs that have been formally verified we mention the security kernel of an operating system by Walker, Kemmerer, and Popek (1980).

CHAPTER SIX

Nondeterminism and Parallel Computation

6.1 Introduction

Throughout this text we have presented some basic mathematical tools that can be used in modeling and solving some computer science problems. We also claimed that the computer scientist, more than the engineer of other technological fields, must be ready and able to use, adapt, modify, and maybe even invent theoretical models according to the particular application under study. Consequently, an important skill of the computer scientist is not only the ability to apply models but also a critical attitude in the application of the models. We have seen a typical example of this when we have studied computational complexity in Chapter 3.

This chapter is devoted to examplifying some nontrivial problems in the choice and use of appropriate models for the description and solution of typical computer science applications. The chosen framework for such an examplification is the use of nondeterministic models that have already been introduced and shortly discussed in previous chapters. It goes without saying that this choice is largely based on the authors' personal taste and experience, although there is a general agreement on the relevance and usefulness of nondeterministic models.

The style of the presentation will differ from the previous chapters. In fact, our goal here is just to introduce and discuss problems without trying to provide a systematic framework, a job that still requires much research activity.

The next section starts with a few examples of how known algorithms can be restated in a nondeterministic fashion (Section 6.2.1). We also discuss their nondeterministic computational complexity. Furthermore, we analyze how nondeterministic algorithms can be executed by deterministic processors and, in particular, by a parallel (or concurrent) system, that is, a system where computations are performed by several processors working in parallel. The idea of speeding up computations by means of parallel processors is examplified in Section 6.2.2. Finally, Section 6.2.3 presents a language construct for nondeterministic programming and introduces the problem of proving correctness of nondeterministic programs.

Section 6.3 develops the theme introduced in Section 6.2.2 further. It motivates the need for concurrent systems through practical examples and introduces the problems of describing and analyzing them formally.

6.2 The Use of Nondeterminism and Parallelism in Classical Programming

In Section 2.4, we claimed that in general an algorithm is assumed to be *deterministic*, that is, for given state and input of the abstract processor the next state is uniquely determined. However, there are cases where we can take an advantage by eliminating this constraint. It is clear that the term "advantage" should not be intended as an increase of computational power—in Section 1.7 we have seen this is not the case—but as an increase of expressive power, or descriptive conciseness, or even simplicity of analysis. In this section, we give two different examples that show that nondeterministic models can have quite different applications and use.

6.2.1 Nondeterministic Algorithms for Search Problems

In Section 3.9.2, we have examined the problem of finding a path, if any, connecting vertices v_0 and v_1 of a given directed graph. Several, more or less abstract, versions of algorithms solving such a problem have been proposed and analyzed from the point of view of complexity. Let us just recall from Section 3.9.2 that the core of the search consists of incrementally building the set $\overline{V}_0$ of all reachable vertices from v_0. Since it is not known a priori whether or not a vertex v_i is in a path from v_0 to v_1, all elements of $\overline{V}_0$ must be considered as candidate members of such path until v_1 is reached or is proved not to be reachable from v_0.

Suppose now we are provided with a nondeterministic abstract processor to run our algorithms, such as a nondeterministic TM, or a nondeterministic RAM, or a nondeterministic version of SMALG that could be defined based on some nondeterministic modification of SMALM. For example, we could introduce a construct **or**, where *s1* **or** *s2* states that SMALM can nondeterministically choose to execute either statement *s1* or statement *s2*. Whichever formalism we chose, a one-to-many transition relation is defined on the abstract processor's state space.

If we relax the requirement that an algorithm be deterministic, some interesting alternatives to the above-mentioned search algorithms can be found. For example, consider the following one.

A nondeterministic algorithm for finding a path in directed graphs

Step 1: Let v_0 be the initial vertex and let v_1 be the target vertex to be reached from v_0. Let v denote a current vertex. Initially, v is v_0.

Step 2: If $v = v_1$ then halt with success otherwise let v' be any vertex adjacent to v. Then assign v' to v (i.e., v' becomes the new value of v).

Step 3: Repeat step 2 until a success is obtained. □

It is clear that the core of the algorithm is in the nondeterministic choice of *any* node adjacent to v. We write $v \vdash v'$ if there is a move of the processor executing the above algorithm which, having v as the current vertex, assigns v' to v. This occurs if and only if v and v' are adjacent. Thus, the algorithm is clearly correct because there exists at least one possible sequence of moves such that $v_0 \overset{*}{\vdash} v_1$; that is, $v_1 = v$, if and only if v_1 is reachable from v_0. In general, of course, there will be also infinitely many other sequences $v_0 \overset{*}{\vdash} v$ that fail the test $v_1 = v$ (this is exactly as in the definition of acceptance of a string by a nondeterministic Turing machine).

What are the advantages of the above nondeterministic algorithm with respect to deterministic versions of Chapter 3? Apparently, it is more compact and short, more natural and simple. This is very often the case for nondeterministic algorithms, as the following example shows. Consider the following practical case of a nondeterministic choice where the processor is a human (e.g., you). Imagine you are looking for a street in a town with no other support than the signals containing the street name placed along the streets themselves. No map, no person to ask for direction, and no way to remember previous experience available. In this case, your only possibility is just to walk around, hoping to find the desired street sooner or later. Therefore, the essence of the search algorithm is just to try. The rest is *heuristics* (or *tactics*) to increase the speed of reaching the goal. Going further into the example, your search of the street could become more fruitful if you were provided with pencil and paper by means of which you could build a map of the town during your walk. The map is the equivalent of the set of reachable vertices from v_0. Thanks to the map your search could become less blind, and you would be guaranteed to find the street, sooner or later.

In summary, we may say that the nondeterministic algorithms are *more abstract* than the corresponding deterministic versions, which could just be seen as refinements or even implementations of the original specification. Thus, nondeterministic programming can be used as a more abstract tool to describe problem solution. Whenever it may be useful, the programmer may forget about specifying a unique sequence of moves for the processor that lead to a problem solution. One just defines a general, nondeterministic strategy to look for the solution, leaving to a later stage its translation into a deterministic algorithm that can be run effectively on an actual computer.

Unfortunately, things are more intricate when we look at the problem from the point of view of computational complexity, say time complexity. From Chapter 3 we know that it is quite difficult to obtain statements of general validity. In particular, in Section 3.6, we learned that it is not known yet whether a nondeterministic algorithm of time complexity $\Theta(T)$ can always be translated into a deterministic version of complexity $\Theta(P \circ T)$, P being a polynomial function. If this were the case, we would obtain $\mathscr{P} = \mathscr{NP}$ and a lot of problems would become tractable, thanks to the existence of efficient nondeterministic algorithms for their solution. Unfortunately, the conjecture is $\mathscr{P} \subset \mathscr{NP}$. Thus, results on time complexity of nondetetministic solution do not give any insight into the complexity we can reach with its deterministic counterparts.

To illustrate this point, as a simple exercise let us modify the above algorithm in order to find Hamiltonian circuits. Recall that a path $v_0 \vdash v_{i_1} \vdash v_{i_2} \vdash \cdots \vdash v_1$ in a graph is called a *Hamiltonian circuit* if and only if $v_1 = v_0$ and every vertex of the graph occurs therein just once, except for v_0, which occurs twice. We assume the convention that if the set of vertices V consists of just v_0, a Hamiltonian circuit exists only if an edge $v_0 \vdash v_0$ exists.

A nondeterministic algorithm for finding Hamiltonian circuits in directed graphs

Step 1: Let v_0 and v be defined as in the previous nondeterministic algorithm. Set v to v_0. Also, define the variables CP (current path) and CPS (current path set, which denotes the set of vertices belonging to the sequence CP).

$CP \in V*$ is initialized to $\langle v_0 \rangle$.

Step 2: Let v' be any vertex adjacent to v.

    if v' is in CP
    then if $v' = v_0$ and $CPS = V$
        then halt with success
        else halt with failure
            {a non-Hamiltonian circuit has been discovered}
        fi
    else append v' to CP;
        set v to v'
    fi

Step 3: Repeat step 2 until a success or a failure is obtained.   □

It is fairly simple to realize that if a Hamiltonian circuit exists, then a sequence of moves exists in the nondeterministic execution of the algorithm that finds such a circuit by repeating step 2 a number of times that equals the length $n = |V|$ of the circuit. Furthermore, the test $CPS = V$ can clearly be executed in time $\Theta(n)$ while all other operations of step 2 require a bounded amount of time. Therefore, time complexity of the above algorithm is $\Theta(n^2)$. On the other hand, we mentioned in Chapter 3 that the Hamiltonian circuit problem is a classical $\mathcal{NP}$—complete problem. Thus, at the present state of the art we cannot deterministically solve it in polynomial time.

It is interesting to analyze how nondeterministic algorithms can be executed by means of a deterministic abstract processor. Such a processor can proceed in the following way: As far as the algorithm is deterministically specified, execution proceeds conventionally. Whenever a nondeterministic alternative with, say, k branches occurs, it creates k copies of itself and of its state. Each copy takes one among the k different choices and from this point on it behaves just as if it were the processor that generated it. During execution the number of copies (i.e., processors) can obviously grow in an unbounded way. Clearly, the algorithm is correct with respect to the problem if at least one copy eventually finds the problem's solution.

This is still an ideal picture and can hardly be viewed as a practical implementation of a nondeterministic algorithm. However, the tremendous evolution of hardware technology is leading to a dramatic decrease of hardware costs, in particular CPUs and main memories. In the future, we can even imagine that such a components will be available almost for free and therefore the foregoing ideal mechanism of processor duplication could become a viable solution. In some sense, we would obtain a hardware implementation of the software simulation described by Theorem 1.25.

For awhile, let us suppose, we have an arbitrary amount of physical processors for free. Notice that it would be a mistake to conclude that in such an ideal case our nondeterministic algorithm for finding Hamiltonian circuits can run in time $\Theta(n^2)$. In fact, at each nondeterministic move we should take into account the time necessary to copy the state from the father processor to its sons (the generated copies). In the case of our example, a natural way of realizing state duplication would require a time proportional to the size of CPS that is not greater than $|V| = n$. In fact, we may assume that the copy operation does not depend on the number k of sons, since such k copies may be done in parallel. Therefore, we would obtain an overall $\Theta(n^3)$ complexity by implementing the nondeterministic algorithm by means of an unbounded number of deterministic processors. Even if this does not reach the theoretical nondeterministic complexity, it is obviously a much better performance than that of existing deterministic algorithms that do not have polynomial time complexity.

Once again, this is still an ideal case since we cannot assume we have a sufficient amount of processors to implement the above procedure for *any* value of n. However, the foregoing reasoning can help us estimate what gain may be expected from an increase of the number of computational devices.

The idea of improving computational efficiency by means of an increased number of processors can be further exploited and generalized in several ways. We give just the flavor of what can be obtained through a simple example in the next section.

6.2.2   Parallel Computation: An Example

Consider the problem of computing the determinant Δ of a $n \times n$ matrix A. We give as follows a recursive description of the most "natural" algorithm computing the mathematical definition of determinant (i.e., the one that is closest to its specification). It is clear that such an algorithm is not the "best" from the efficiency point of view, but the focus here is on improving the efficiency of a given algorithm by means of an increased number of processors, not on finding the most efficient sequential algorithm to solve a given problem.

For a given $n \times n$ matrix $A = \{a_{ij} | 1 \le i, j \le n, n > 1\}$, define A_{ij} as the $(n-1) \times (n-1)$ matrix resulting from erasing the ith row and jth column from A. $\Delta(A)$ can be defined recursively in the following way.

$$\Delta(A) \Leftarrow \textbf{if } n = 1 \textbf{ then } a_{11}$$
$$\textbf{else } (-1) \cdot \sum_{j=1}^{n} (-1)^j a_{1j} \cdot \Delta(A_{1j})$$

This can be rewritten as follows in a more imperative style but still maintaining the basic recursive definition.

Recursive algorithm computing the determinant of an n × n matrix

Step 1:   If $n = 1$, then $\Delta(A)$ is exactly the only element of A. Otherwise,

Step 2:   Compute $\Delta(A_{1j})$ for each j, with $1 \le j \le n$.

Step 3:   For each j multiply a_{1j} by $\Delta(A_{1j})$, and by $(-1)^j$. Let t_j denote the result of this operation.

Step 4:   Execute $(- \sum_{j=1}^{n} t_j)$ and assign the result to $\Delta(A)$. $\square$

Let us compute the time complexity T of the above algorithm as a function of n. For the sake of simplicity, we assume the uniform cost criterion as we are interested in complexity with respect to the size of the matrix. Such a measure is clearly not affected by the choice of the cost criterion. The logarithmic cost criterion would instead be necessary if we were interested in complexity with respect to the values of elements a_{ij}.

On the basis of the recursive definition of Δ, we can easily obtain a recursive definition of T. In fact, if $n = 1$, then the computation of Δ takes a constant amount of time; as usual we can assume the conventional value 1 for such a constant. If $n > 1$, we must first compute $\Delta(A_{1j})$, for all $j = 1, \ldots, n$, which will take a time $n \cdot T(n-1)$. After this, we must perform n multiplications and n additions.
We thus obtain

$$T(n) = \textbf{if } n = 1 \textbf{ then } 1 \textbf{ else } n \cdot T(n-1) + 2n$$
$$= \textbf{if } n = 1 \textbf{ then } 1 \textbf{ else } n \cdot (T(n-1) + 2).$$

Since T is clearly not a constant function of n, we can assume the expression

$T(n - 1)$ as equivalent to $T(n - 1) + 2$ for $n \to \infty$. Thus, we obtain that T is $\Theta(n!)$.

Suppose now that an unbounded number of processors is available. We can, therefore, give the following modified parallel version of the above algorithm.

Parallel computation of $\Delta(A)$

Step 1: If $n = 1$, then $\Delta(A)$ is exactly the only element of A. Otherwise,

Step 2: Get n more processors (called *children processors*) and make the jth of them compute $\Delta(A_{1j})$, where $1 \le j \le n$, by means of the present algorithm.

Step 3: When each of processor outputs its result, say r_j, perform

$$t_j := (-1)^j \cdot a_{1j} \cdot r_j$$

Step 4: Execute $(- \sum_{j=1}^{n} t_j)$ and assign the result to $\Delta(A)$. ☐

This is certainly not the only possible parallel implementation of the previous sequential algorithm; it is just one simple solution that is used here to derive some general considerations.

Let us take a look at complexity of this parallel program. If $n = 1$, then obviously $T(n) = 1$, as before. If $n > 1$, the "father" processor waits a time $T(n - 1)$ in order to have all $\Delta(A_{1j})$ computed by its children working in parallel (in fact, $T(n - 1)$ is the maximum amount of time a processor can spend to compute the determinant of an $(n - 1) \times (n - 1)$ matrix). After the father receives the results from its children, it takes a time proportional to n, say n, to compute the desired result. Thus, we have

$T(n) = $ **if** $n = 1$ **then** 1 **else** $n + T(n - 1)$

which immediately shows that T is $\Theta(n^2)$.

Again, we have obtained a dramatic improvement in time efficiency thanks to the use of an unbounded number of processors. And again, this improvement of time efficiency is paid in terms of the number of processors. In fact, in order to compute $\Delta(A)$, A being of order n, we need the initial processor plus its n children. Each child, in turn, needs $n - 1$ children and so on. Thus the total number of used processors is

$N(n) = 1 + n + n \cdot (n - 1) + n \cdot (n - 1) \cdot (n - 2) + \cdots + n!$

and N is $\Theta(n!)$.

If we roughly define a *global complexity* C by $C(n) = T(n) \cdot N(n)$, we must recognize that C does not improve here, nor in the search problem, by increasing the number of processors. On the contrary it increased slightly in both cases.[1]

---

[1] Note that in the examples we refer to two different implementations of the same "abstract algorithm," namely a sequential versus a parallel implementation. It is certainly possible to find smarter parallel algorithms with better global complexity.

However, this definition of the global complexity C is not entirely satisfactory. In fact, the "real costs" accounted by T and N are not equivalent; the present trend in hardware costs is such that we might be willing to pay a higher N in order to save T.

Before closing this section, let us return to the question of unbounded parallelism. The hypothesis to have an unbounded number of available processors is clearly unrealistic but allows us to obtain a good estimate of how much can time efficiency be improved by exploiting parallelism. Instead, suppose we are given a large but fixed number of processors, say K. What gain in speed could we expect to achieve by using K processors to run an algorithm, whose time complexity is T_1 when executed by a single processor? It can be shown that, in general,

$$T_K(n) \ge \frac{T_1(n)}{K}$$

and that there are cases where $T_K(n) > T_1(n)/K$ where $T_k(n)$, with $k = 1, 2, \ldots$ denotes the time necessary to run an algorithm by means of k processors.

We refer the reader to the specialized literature for a formal proof of this statement. As an intuitive justification, consider that the total amount of work cannot be divided by more than K in such a way that, if it is equally distributed among K processors, each of them will take at least time $T_1(n)/K$, otherwise some of them will take more. In order to justify that in many cases it is even $T_K(n) > T_1(n)/K$, consider that it may be necessary to spend some time to synchronize processors, as well as to collect and integrate the results of separate jobs performed by the several processors, as it was the case of the above parallel computation of $\Delta(A)$. From a theoretical point o view, this result compares negatively with the linear speed-up theorem that instead claims that any purely sequential computation can be arbitrarily speeded up (in a linear way) by a suitable increase of processor's complexity.

Exercise

6.1 Give a parallel version of the *merge–sort* algorithm discussed in Example 5.8. Compute the gain in time efficiency and the number of needed processors in terms of the array's length n.

6.2.3 Nondeterministic Programming Languages and Correctness Proofs: A Brief Introduction

Throughout this text, the main programming constructs used to control the execution flow of a program have been the **if-then-else** selection and the **while-do** repetitive construct. Such constructs are universally accepted as appropriate basic mechanisms for structured programming. In this section we briefly discuss the statements that may be used to describe nondeterministic algorithms in a clear and useful way.

We introduce the discussion by means of an example. Suppose that an algorithm specification at a certain point says

In state 1   do S_1
In state 2   do S_2
In state 3   do S_3

If states 1, 2, and 3 can be determined at the algorithm specification time, then the Pascal **case** construct will be appropriate to code such specification. However if this is not so, the above construct will be of no help. For instance, a specification of the type

In case $x > y$ do S_1
In case $x = y$ do S_2
In case $x < y$ do S_3

should be coded in SMALG as

if $x > y$
then S_1
else if $x = y$
    then S_2
    else S_3
    fi
fi

where the nested syntactic structure of the program does not reflect the real specification (consider the situation where there are 10 branches instead of 3).

For this and other reasons, Dijkstra proposed a more symmetric conditional construct of the type

if $G_1 \rightarrow S_1$
   $\Box G_2 \rightarrow S_2$
     $\cdots$
   $\Box G_n \rightarrow S_n$
fi

where G_i are conditions, that is, functions from the program's state into $\{T, F\}$ called *guards*, S_i are (structured) statements, and the construct $\Box G_i \rightarrow S_i$ is called a *guarded command*.

A first intuitive and rough definition of the semantics of the above conditional construct is intuitively—operationally—defined as follows: "Perform a command S_i whose guard G_i is true; at least one guard must be true." For example, the statements

if C **then** S_1 **else** S_2 **fi**

and

if C **then** S **fi**

can be translated into

if $C \rightarrow S_1$
    $\square \neg C \rightarrow S_2$
fi

and

if $C \rightarrow S$
    $\square \neg C \rightarrow null^2$
fi

respectively.

Thus, the above example may be coded as

if $x > y \rightarrow S_1$
    $\square x = y \rightarrow S_2$
    $\square x < y \rightarrow S_3$
fi

Observe that the definition of guarded commands does not forbid more than one guard to be true. (In some sense, this is necessary because it would be quite difficult to enforce such requirement in the language.) This is where nondeterminism shows up in the language: *Any* command with a true guard may be chosen for execution.

Nondeterministic languages can have beneficial effects on program readability and elegance. They support abstract algorithm specifications, whereas deterministic languages very often overspecify algorithms. As a very simple example, consider the following fragments that describe the computation of the maximum of two integers. Fragment $F2$ clearly gets closer to our intuitive idea of what a desirable specification is than fragment $F1$.

$F1$: **if** $x \leq y$
    then $min := x$
    else $min := y$
    fi

$F2$: **if** $x \leq y \rightarrow min := x$
      $\square y \leq x \rightarrow min := y$
    fi

---

[2] *null* is defined as the empty statement list.

Anyway, our purpose here is not to discuss the appropriateness of a programming construct against another one but to carefully analyze the consequent semantic issues. If $G_i \rightarrow S_i$, where $1 \leq i \leq n$, are the guarded commands of a guarded **if** statement, the semantics require that we nondeterministically select an integer i, if any, such that G_i is true and execute the corresponding S_i. If no guard evaluates to true, the program is in error. No assumption is made on the evaluation order of guards $\{G_i\}$, nor it is required that all $G_i's$ are evaluated. For instance, a correct implementation of the foregoing semantics could choose the (lexically) first true G_i without further considering the remaining guards. Observe that in order to have a reasonable semantics it is strictly necessary that the evaluation of guards is free from side effects.

Let us turn now to a formal definition of semantics of guarded commands. For simplicity, we briefly discuss here the case of axiomatic semantics. Whenever the program reaches a nondeterministic guarded **if** statement, the associated semantic rule must ensure that program correctness does *not* depend on knowledge of the branch that is chosen nondeterministically. For example, the above fragment $F2$ must be proven correct with respect to precondition *true* and postcondition $m = min\{x, y\}$ no matter which guarded statement is selected for execution in the case $x = y$.

The following axiomatic proof rule describes the semantics of a guarded **if** statement and replaces rule $IR3$ for the traditional conditional statement.

Guarded Command Proof Rule

$$\frac{\bigwedge_{i=1}^{n} [\{(P \wedge G_i)\} S_i \{Q\}]}{\left\{ P \wedge \left(\bigvee_{i=1}^{n} G_i \right) \right\} \textbf{if } G_1 \rightarrow S_1 \square \ldots \square G_n \rightarrow S_n \textbf{ fi } \{Q\}}$$

The foregoing proof rule clearly allows us to carry over correctness proofs in a deterministic way even if the abstract processor executing the command is nondeterministic. For instance, the formal proof of

$$\{T\} \textbf{ if } x \leq y \rightarrow m := x \square y \leq x \rightarrow m := y \textbf{ fi } \{m = min\{x, y\}\}$$

is immediate.

One more comment is in order. In Section 6.2.1, we discussed a nondeterministic search algorithm and we saw that any correct deterministic implementation must be able to find a solution if the nondeterministic algorithm does. In the case of the search algorithm, this required a correct implementation to check *all* possible outcomes of a nondeterministic choice. This was a direct consequence of our definition of a correct nondeterministic algorithm as an algorithm for which there exists an execution path leading to a solution. Here things are very different: Any possible choice that may be selected nondeterministically must lead to an acceptable state. Thus, any implementation that chooses one among the guarded statements according to some policy (e.g., the first in lexical order) is acceptable.

Exercises

6.2 Following Dijkstra, we can introduce a *guarded loop* whose format is

> **do** $G_1 \rightarrow S_1$
> $\quad \Box G_2 \rightarrow S_2$
> $\quad \Box$:
> $\qquad \vdots$
> $\quad \Box G_n \rightarrow S_n$
> **od**

The intuitive semantics of the guarded loop is the following: "As far as at least one guard G_i evaluates to true, nondeterministically execute any S_i whose guard is true. Repeat the foregoing process until all guards are false." Formalize these semantics by means of a suitable proof rule.

6.3 Modify the semantics of the guarded **if** statement by allowing that no guard evaluates to true. In such a case, execution flow simply skips the **if** statement instead of producing an error. Provide a new Guarded Command Proof Rule that is adequate to the previous semantics.

6.4 Write a program to evaluate the greatest common divisor of two positive integers using Dijkstra's guarded commands. Prove the correctness of your program.

6.5 Write a program to find a possible path between any two nodes in a graph by using Dijkstra's guarded commands. Prove its correctness.

6.3 Concurrent Computations and the Use of Nondeterministic Models

In Chapters 1 through 5 of this text, we viewed the typical computer science problem as the sequential computation of a function from given input values into well-defined output values. We always viewed such sequential computation as a sequence of elementary steps performed by some abstract processor, which has been described formally by different mathematical models such as TMs, RAMs, or SMALMs. Such a view of automatic problem solving is quite satisfactory in many typical and traditional computer science applications. For instance the problems of computing payrolls, computing the determinant of a square matrix, finding the best way of distributing goods in a network of stores, etc. are perfectly described, analyzed, and solved within the foregoing sequential framework. As we have shown in Section 6.2.2, the only reason to adopt parallel processing in this class of problems is to reduce execution time. However, there are other classes of problems that do not fit naturally in the above framework. That is, they are *intrinsically* nonsequential. These are a few examples.

Example 6.1   Multiprogramming Environments

Consider a standard computer system used in universities to teach programming. Very often, such a system consists of a single computer (a mainframe) equipped with mass storage and many terminals. When a student is sitting at a terminal designing—say—a Pascal program, he or she does not realize that the same computer is shared, at the same time, by several other students. From the student's viewpoint interaction occurs with an abstract Pascal processor that is able to compute results according with the semantics of the submitted program. Furthermore, the student may have private files stored into mass storage so that the function computed by the program may depend not only on the input stream but also on previously stored values. In general, if n terminals are active at a given time, n different students will have n identical but distinct abstract Pascal machines to interact with. Each of these machines will perform the sequential computations required by the student's program.

We do know, however, that all students actually work on the same physical machine. It is the operating system's job to provide each user with a set of *virtual resources* (CPU, main memory, mass storage, etc.). Thus, thanks to the operating system and the Pascal compiler, each student can work as if he or she had a private Pascal processor and private files without bothering with the fact that possibly many other students access the same processor and the same memory devices at the same time. Students can refer to the semantics of Pascal to analyze programs, without knowledge of the underlying physical computer structure.

Let us take now the viewpoint of the operating system's designer. It is clear that the designer cannot view the machine as an abstract Pascal processor. At the other extreme, one might choose to model the multiprogrammed computer by means of a RAM-like machine having as many inputs and outputs as there are terminals connected to the computer. Although it is true that the physical multiprogrammed machine is indeed a deterministic machine provided with several inputs and outputs, such a view is definitely too low level to be useful in practice. Since the incoming inputs from the terminals are completely unrelated from one another, a model that explicitly considers all possible input combinations—for example, terminal 1 is inputting A, terminal 2 is inputting 2, terminal 3 is off, etc.—would simply be unmanageable. Instead, what is needed is a model that helps seeing the executions of users' programs as *independent* and *concurrent processes*.

Each process is a purely sequential activity; it works on its own memory and performs its own computation. However, we should not forget that some interactions do occur among different processes as they compete for access to common resources. One such common resource is the CPU. In the case of a uniprocessor machine, only one process can be executed at any given time and the operating system must schedule assignment of the CPU to processes according to some policy in order to let processes proceed in their computations.

Example 6.2   Shared Database Environments

Some of the most relevant applications of modern computer systems are in the field of databases. A typical architecture of a database (DB) is shown in Figure 6.1. A single computer is provided with a large amount of mass storage. Such a storage supplies a *logical view* of the data stored therein, which reflects the meaning of the data, and does not depend on the physical organization of memory devices (e.g., tracks and sectors of a disk). For instance, the DB of a bank may contain data on checking accounts. Each record of the file contains a description of a particular checking account (see Figure 6.2).

In general, many users may access the same DB through different terminals (i.e., the DB is *shared*). In the case of a bank, checking accounts can be accessed by several tellers at the same time. The operations performed on the DB by the

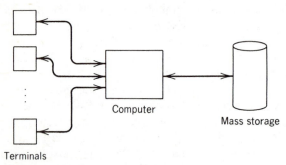

Terminals

FIGURE 6.1   Physical view of a DB.

Checking account number	Customer name	Balance	Other information
10657	SMITH	$1000	. . . . .

Transaction: deposit $500 into checking account no. 10657

10657	SMITH	$1500	. . . .

FIGURE 6.2   Logical view of the execution of a transaction on a DB.

users are usually called *transactions*. Again, transactions are defined in a logical way rather than in terms of physical changes of the information stored on the disk's tracks and sectors (see Figure 6.2). The most relevant difference between a DB environment and the previous case of a multiprogramming environment is that here many users compete not only for accessing the same physical resources but also for accessing logical items of the DB. For instance, several tellers might wish to perform some transactions on the same checking account independently and concurrently. This clearly adds further difficulties to the problem of defining a model suitable to describe, analyze, and design DBs.

A fundamental problem to solve here is that of supporting *atomicity* of transactions, which guarantees *consistency* of the system. These concepts are illustrated by the following example: Suppose that several customers (e.g., X and Y), have the right to perform transactions on the same checking account, say N. Suppose that N's balance is $1000 and X and Y contemporarily request to withdraw $800 at different banking sites.

Both X and Y request to perform the same transaction that might be implemented as

Step 1: Check if balance is greater than the requested amount.
Step 2: If so, accept the request and decrease the balance accordingly.

If we operate in a multiprogramming environment, the operating system might decide to interleave the execution of the two transactions in the following way.

- X executes step 1 and obtains a positive answer.
- Y executes step 1 and obtains a positive answer too (this happens because X has not changed the balance yet).
- X updates N's balance to $200.
- Y updates N's balance to $ - 600$, which is an *illegal state*.

In order to avoid such problems the system must guarantee atomicity of transactions (i.e., all steps of the transactions must be executed *as if* they were executed in a purely sequential, noninterruptible manner by the physical processor). Notice that atomicity is only a logical requirement because, in many practical cases, it would be impossible to dedicate the processor to execution of a single transaction (which may be long and complex) until the transaction itself has been completed.

In conclusion, in order to model shared database environments, one needs a model that is suitable to describing several activities that *concurrently and unpredictably* may access shared objects. The execution flow of such activities must guarantee the required consistency constraints.

Example 6.3   Real-Time Process Control Systems

Real-time systems are typical of process control applications, such as nuclear (chemical, electrical, ...) plants control, aircraft navigation control, weapon systems, etc. In these applications, incoming signals from the environment reach the system in a concurrent and unpredictable way and very often the system is expected to react to such signals within tight time constraints (real time). High reliability is another requirement of many such systems, since often they operate in extremely critical environments.

Modeling real-time and concurrent system is not an easy task. The same models that can be used to describe concurrent systems are not adequate here. In particular, the problems involved in specifying time constraints, and proving an implementation correct with respect to its specification, are still in the research stage.

Example 6.4 Semantics of Concurrent Programming Languages: Examples from Ada

Several modern programming languages support execution of concurrently executable program units. The underlying physical machine that executes the concurrent languages provides true concurrency if it is a multiprocessor. Otherwise, it may simulate concurrency by interleaving execution among the various units, as we saw in Example 6.1.

Ada is probably the best known example of a concurrent programming language. Ada concurrent units (called *tasks*) can interact—exchange information—by means of a language feature called *rendezvous*. In what follows, we briefly outline this feature in a simplified, incomplete, and informal fashion.

A task may possess *entries*, which may be called by other tasks. Syntactically, an entry call is exactly like a procedure call. A task possessing an entry may execute an *accept* statement, which accepts execution of a given entry call. A task *T1* issuing an entry call and a task *T2* accepting such entry call establish a rendezvous. During rendezvous, possible input parameters are passed from *T1* to *T2*, the entry's body is executed (as if it were a procedure's body), possible output parameters are passed back from *T2* to *T1*, and then *T1* and *T2* proceed concurrently. In general, tasks *T1* and *T2* are not ready to rendezvous at the same time. If *T1* issues the entry call before *T2* accepts it, then *T1* waits (its execution is suspended) until *T2* reaches the accept statement for that entry. When this happens, the rendezvous occurs. Similarly, if *T2* reaches an accept statement before a corresponding entry call is issued by *T1*, then *T2* waits until the rendezvous occurs.

Figure 6.3 sketches the case of two tasks MASTER and SERVER. MASTER issues an entry call to ORDER, which transfers parameter P to SERVER. Task SERVER executes a never-ending loop which repeatedly accepts and processes orders from MASTER.

Several tasks may issue calls to the same entry of some other task. In such case, entry calls are put in a queue associated to the entry; the queue is handled in a fifo fashion.

The example of Figure 6.3 illustrates the simplest example of a rendezvous. The accepting task SERVER performs an **accept** statement unconditionally; that

```
task MASTER            task SERVER
  .                      .
  .                      .
ORDER(P);              loop
  .                         accept ORDER(P) do
  .                             PROCESS(P);
                            end ORDER;
                        end loop
```

FIGURE 6.3   An Ada fragment.

is, SERVER enters a waiting state as soon as it reaches the **accept**, until MASTER issues the call to ORDER.

Suppose now that SERVER can perform two services, corresponding to ORDER__1 and ORDER__2, and chooses either one or the other according to the requests issued by its masters. A possible new description of SERVER is sketched in Figure 6.4.

The program of Figure 6.4 introduces a new kind of statement (**select**) that specifies a nondeterministic choice between several alternatives. More precisely, it specifies acceptance of a rendezvous on any entry for which a call is pending; if no entry call is pending, then execution is suspended until an entry call is issued.

In many practical cases, one wishes to specify a timeout for an entry call. For example, the MASTER task of Figure 6.3 may be rewritten as in Figure 6.5.

The fragment of Figure 6.5 illustrates the case of a *timed entry call*. If a rendezvous cannot be started within the specified time limit (1.5 seconds), then the branch prefixed by **delay** 1.5 must be chosen and DO__SOMETHING__ELSE is executed.

```
task SERVER
  .
  .
loop
   select
        accept ORDER_1 (P1) do
  .
  .
        end ORDER_1;
   or
        accept ORDER_2 (P2) do
  .
  .
        end ORDER_2;
   end select
end loop;
```

FIGURE 6.4   The Ada task SERVER.

task MASTER
:
:
select
    ORDER(P);
or
    delay 1.5;
    DO_SOMETHING_ELSE;
end select;   **FIGURE 6.5**   The Ada task MASTER.

This is just a sample of the Ada features supporting specification of concurrent programs. Our scope here, however, is not to cover all of the details of concurrency but rather to address the issue of formally defining the sample constructs we have seen so far.

It is easy to realize that the theory developed in Chapters 4 and 5 cannot be applied here in a straightforward fashion. In fact, even if we assume that the underlying processor executes instructions one at a time, we cannot predict which instruction will be executed after an instruction completes its execution.

On the other hand, formal models to specify concurrency are definitely needed. We need them in many cases, such as in reasoning about concurrent programs, understanding precisely the issues involved in their compilation, proving compiler correctness, and so on.

Example 6.5   Physically Distributed Computing Systems

In many computer applications, the data to be elaborated are naturally distributed over physically different places. A typical example is the case of a bank that has several agencies where some data (e.g., on customers' checking accounts) are intrinsically needed and routinely accessed only in one single peripheral location. The traditional solution has been to centralize data into a unique computer system (a DB) connected to peripheral locations via remote terminals. More recently, advances in hardware and software technology have made possible the implementation of *distributed systems* consisting of several physical processors—often situated at different places—cooperating in the realization of a single integrated application.

A typical example is a *distributed database* (DDB). Unlike centralized DBs, here several independent systems have their own data, their own processors, and their own users; but systems are also connected to one another by means of a *network*. In this way, individual systems can communicate and cooperate to perform some common activity, such as performing an electronic fund transfer from one checking account into another located at a different site (see Figure 6.6).

Modeling distributed systems raises new problems, even with respect to other previously considered unconventional computing systems. In fact, on one

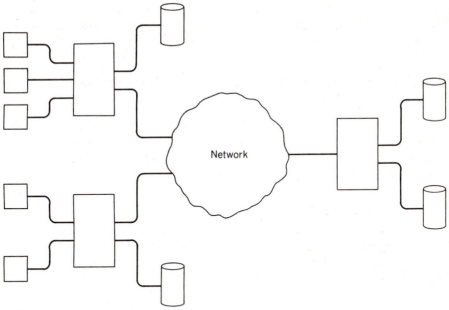

FIGURE 6.6 A distributed system.

hand, each node of the system can be seen as a single processor that interacts with its own interfaces, one of them being the network. On the other hand, it is clear that in many cases we are explicitly interested in modeling the set of all cooperating processors as a whole. The partial effect of an electronic fund transfer on a single node of the banking system is obviously far from providing an adequate information.

A typical difficulty arising in the modeling of a distributed system is the following. Suppose you describe the system by means of an evolutionary model (e.g., a finite-state machine). A natural approach defines the system's state space X as the Cartesian product of each processor state spaces: $X = X_1 \times \ldots \times X_n$. However, it is hard to talk about the system's state at a given time t, t being either continuous or discrete. For example, suppose that each processor has a machine cycle of 100 nsec. Because the light's speed is 300.10^6 m/sec, it is physically impossible to know—at exactly the same time—the state of two processors that are distant even a few hundred meters each other. Again, we are faced with a nondeterministic knowledge of the system as each processor knows at any instant about the rest of the system only the information it gets from the network.

We already claimed that no unified framework is presently available to model and analyze nonsequential computing systems of the type previously introduced.

In order to give the reader just the flavor of what kind of problems one is likely to face when designing or analyzing such systems, the next section discusses the use of a particular model, namely Petri nets, in some of the foregoing cases.

6.3.1   Petri Nets and the Description of Operating Systems

An oversimplified example of how a Petri net can model the behavior of a multiprogramming system has been given in Section 1.7.3. Still remaining in the realm of toy examples, let us refer here to a slightly more complex system. Suppose that tasks to be run are generated via two different terminals T_1 and T_2. After being generated, a task can run only if

i. The CPU is available.
ii. One memory bank is available. (We suppose that the system is provided with two different memory banks B_1 and B_2. For the moment, we suppose also that B_1 is exclusively used by tasks generated via T_1 and B_2 by tasks generated via T_2.)

After execution tasks need the printer in order to output hard-copy results (we suppose there is only one printer).

A Petri net model of such system is given in Figure 6.7, where places denote resources (the presence of a token in a place denotes availability of the resource) and transitions denote operations of the operating system. In particular, a token is initially present in *CPU* (the CPU is available), *PRINTER* (the printer is available), B_1 and B_2 (both memory banks are available), S_1 and S_2 (a task can be created both via terminal T_1 and terminal T_2). Creation of a task via terminal T_i ($i = 1, 2$) is modeled by the firing of transition t_i. A task can be run (that is, transition s_i can fire) only if the required resources are available. After running, a task prints results (that is, transition p_i fires).

Let us briefly comment on the adequacy of the Petri net model.

1. The intrinsic nondeterminism of the model allows us to capture concurrency of some events. For example, it is clear that once a task execution has been started, the request to generate a new task at the same terminal can be accepted immediately. This corresponds to the fact that after the firing of, say, s_1, the model does not impose any ordering on the firing of t_1 and p_1.
2. The Petri net description of the system hides the scheduling decision of which task is actually chosen for execution each time both transitions s_1 and s_2 can be fired. This can be considered as an abstract view of the system where such a choice is considered as an implementation detail. However, the model of Figure 6.7 allows the repetition of the firing sequence of transitions t_1, s_1, and p_1 an unbounded number of times with no occurrence of s_2 and p_2. In such case, the task associated with terminal T_2 would *starve*.

   The simplest scheduling decision solving the above problem consists of alternating the choice of s_1 and s_2 (see Figure 6.8). Unfortunately, this

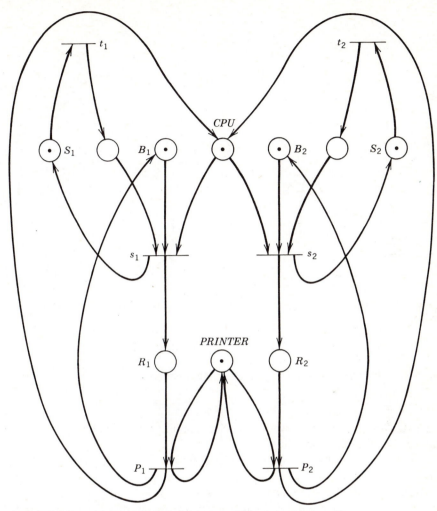

FIGURE 6.7 A Petri net describing a multiprogramming system.

solution shown in Figure 6.8 has its own drawbacks. Immediately after s_1 fires, a token is in E_2 and prevents s_1 from firing until after s_2 fires. However, if t_2 does not fire (for e.g., terminal T_2 is off), s_2 will never fire, and this prevents s_1 from firing too, while it is clear that in such case s_1 should be enabled. A capability is needed to establish the following policy: After s_1 is fired, "if s_2 is enabled then s_2 fires, else s_1 fires, if enabled."

This policy cannot be modeled by a Petri net in the general case. In fact, it can be shown that, if the firing of a transition could depend on another transition being enabled or not, then the Petri net model would reach the same computational power as TMs. On the other hand, it has also been proved that

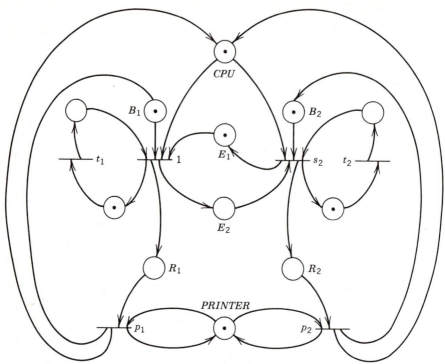

FIGURE 6.8   A Petri net describing an alternating scheduler.

Petri nets are strictly less powerful than TMs and this prevents the model from having the foregoing capability.

Another feature that cannot be modeled by Petri nets is a priority policy. Suppose you wish to state that if two (or more) transitions t_1 and t_2 are both enabled then only t_1 can fire. Such a statement is clearly similar to the previous one, and, therefore, it should not be surprising that Petri nets cannot model it. The interested reader is referred to the specialized literature for a rigorous treatment of this topic.

We must conclude that some features of concurrent systems—typically, those related with scheduling decisions—cannot be modeled adequately by an intrinsically nondeterministic model such as Petri nets.

3. Consider the following modifications of the above system.

- The physical processor is a multiprocessor providing two different CPUs that can be used to run tasks generated by T_1 and T_2, interchangeably.
- The available memory is still partitioned in two different banks, but it may happen that any task, during execution, needs one more memory bank in order to proceed.

The new system is modeled in Figure 6.9, which describes the initial marking

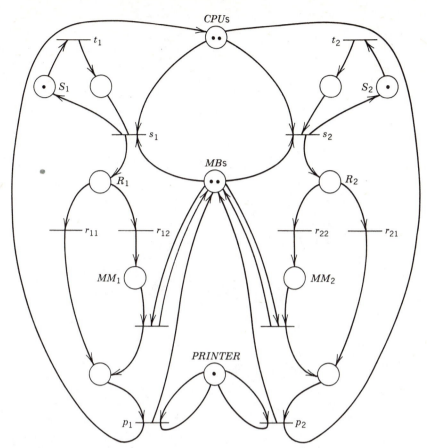

FIGURE 6.9 A Petri net describing a system with two CPUs and two memory banks.

of the Petri net. In particular, CPUs and memory banks are represented by means of one place with two initial tokens, places MM_1, MM_2 denote a situation where more memory is needed in order to proceed in execution. The exit branches of R_1, R_2 denote the possible alternatives during task execution: In one case, execution can proceed with no need for more memory, in the other case, more memory is needed. Since the usage of the memory banks cannot be predicted, our model presents a nondeterministic choice between r_{11} and r_{12} (r_{22} and r_{21}, respectively).

Let us examine the behavior of the system on the basis of its description of Figure 6.9. It is immediate to realize that if the firing sequence of transitions t_1, s_1, t_2, s_2, r_{12}, r_{22} occurs, no more transition is enabled; thus the system cannot evolve any more. This situation is called a *deadlock*. In our case, the deadlock is due to the fact that task T_1, after having obtained one CPU and one memory bank, needs one more memory bank to proceed. But task T_2 is

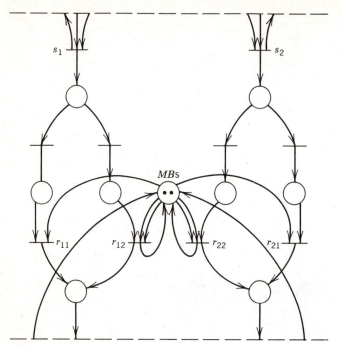

FIGURE 6.10   A deadlock-free modification of the PN of
Figure 6.9. The rest of the net is as in Figure 6.9.

exactly in the same situation so that no more memory is available for either
task.

   Let us focus our attention on branches r_{11}, r_{12}, r_{21}, and r_{22}. If they were
changed as shown by the Petri net fragment of Figure 6.10, deadlock would be
eliminated. However, this solution is correct only if the program can anticipate
whether or not it will need two memory banks. In such a case, if two banks are
needed by the program, they are not acquired piecewise (as in the case of
Figure 6.9) but rather as a unique larger resource.

4. A partial deadlock may occur. For example, suppose that in our system task
   T_2 enters a nonterminating loop as it is shown by the new modification of
   Figure 6.9, namely Figure 6.11. In such a case the firing sequence
   $t_1, s_1, t_2, s_2, r_{12}, r_{21}, l$ would lead the system in a state where task T_2 could
   continue to perform ll forever, leaving task T_1 locked. In this case, the system
   is not in deadlock since at least one transition is enabled, but task T_1 is in
   starvation since m_1 will never be enabled. It must be pointed out that this
   kind of starvation differs from that described in point 2. In fact, here it is
   simply impossible to let T_1 proceed while in the other case T_2 was actually
   enabled to proceed but it was possible that a nondeterministic choice, hidden
   to the user, never scheduled it for running.

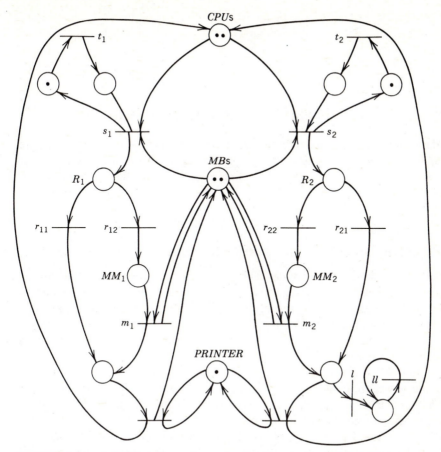

FIGURE 6.11 A PN that can enter a deadlock and a partial deadlock.

To summarize, these points have shown some appropriate features of Petri nets —and in general of nondeterministic evolutionary models—in the description of a type of concurrent systems. However, we also pointed out some weaknesses of the model.

Exercises

6.6 Suppose that the system in Figure 6.7, after execution, leaves results to be output into a (unique) buffer, and thus makes memory banks reusable without waiting for printing. Modify the model of Figure 6.7 accordingly. Which events may occur concurrently in this case?

6.7 Show that in case 3 if only one CPU (respectively, memory bank) where available, deadlock would be (respectively, would not be) avoided.

6.8 Consider a system of the type of Figure 6.9 with n terminals T_i, two CPUs, and m MBs. What is the minimum value of m to guarantee the absence of deadlock?

6.3.2 Describing Shared DBs by Means of Petri Nets

The description of a shared DB by means of Petri nets is conceptually quite similar to the previous case of a multiprogramming environment. In fact, in both cases the accent is on the way a discipline is imposed to the access of shared objects: Here, a shared object may be a record describing a checking account instead of a memory bank or a CPU.

6.3.3 Real-Time Systems and Petri Nets

Figure 6.12 is a simple Petri net describing a process control system. A computer system (CS) serves two incoming service request streams (r_1 and r_2). A request is represented by a token flowing through r_1 and r_2. Only one request at a time may be chosen (transitions c_1 and c_2 represent a choice). Once a request is selected, the corresponding service (P_1 or P_2) must be processed and an answer is eventually delivered (a_1 or a_2).

The problem with such a model is that time is not taken into account at all. Therefore, we cannot answer crucial questions of the type: "If incoming signals have a frequency of at most, say, 4 per second, is the system able to send an answer within an acceptable time limit?"

In order to support the analysis of real-time systems, a suitable modification of a Petri net (called a *timed Petri net*) has been defined. Informally, a timed

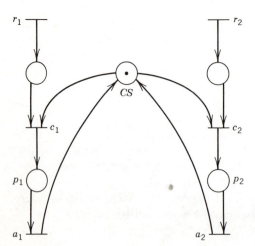

FIGURE 6.12 A PN describing a process control system.

Petri net is a net whose transitions are labeled by a pair $\langle t_{min}, t_{max} \rangle$, where $0 \leq t_{min} \leq t_{max} \leq \infty$. Once enabled, a transition does fire within a time t, $t_{min} \leq t \leq t_{max}$.

Let us try to apply this augmented model to the description and analysis of our real-time system. The fact that there are, at most, four incoming signals in one second for each input stream is described by labeling r_1 and r_2 with $t_{min} = 0.25$ sec, (we ignore t_{max}). Furthermore, we assume that, for any choice c_i, $t_{min} = 0$, $t_{max} = t_c$ and responses are evaluated within $t_{min} = t_{p1}$ and $t_{max} = t_{p2}$. If we know a priori that no "contemporary" requests from r_1 and r_2 will ever occur (i.e., c_1 and c_2 will never be both enabled), it is immediate to state that the system will timely react to any request if $t_{p2} + t_c \leq 0.25$ sec.

In the general case, however, things become more critical. In fact, if c_1 and c_2 are both enabled at some time $\bar{t}$, only one of them, nondeterministically, fires within a time less than or equal to t_c. After that, the other one is disabled and this may prevent it from firing within the assumed time t_c. Thus, it may happen that a transition, once enabled, does not fire within its t_{max}. It might even never fire. So we are faced with the same problems we saw in the case of multiprogramming system. Here, however, real-time constraints make them even more severe.

Some time analysis can actually be performed on the basis of timed Petri nets, even though not in a completely satisfactory way.

1. Suppose that

   $t_{p2} \leq 0.05$ sec, $t_c \leq 0.05$ sec

   In this case a straightforward analysis of the model shows that

   1.1 The system will respond to any incoming request correctly,
   1.2 In the worst case, the time elapsed from the firing of r_1 and the consequent firing of a_1 will be 0.2 sec.

   In fact, the worst case is clearly when r_1 and r_2 fire at the same time. Thus the sequential firing of, say c_1, a_1, c_2, a_2 will take at most 0.2 sec, leaving the system ready to react to next requests. Thus, the time reaction of the system is appropriate if reacting within 0.2 sec to any incoming request is sufficient.

2. Suppose that

   t_{min} is 1 sec for r_1 and 0.5 sec for r_2

   Furthermore, let $t_{min} = 0$ for both c_1 and c_2, as before, and $t_c = 0.2$ sec, $t_{p2} = \frac{2}{15}$ sec, so that $t_{p2} + t_c = \frac{1}{3}$ sec. Intuitively, the system should be able to react to any sequence of requests with time response ≤ 1 sec. In fact, at most three events per second can be generated by r_1 and r_2, which is exactly the minimum performance guaranteed by the system.

   Observe, however, that the following sequence of transition firings could occur at times t_0, t_1, t_2 and t_3.

   t_0: r_1 and r_2 contemporarily fire.
   $t_1 = t_0 + \frac{1}{5}$: c_1 fires as a consequence of the nondeterministic choice between c_1 and c_2.

$t_2 = t_0 + \frac{1}{3}$: a_1 fires. At this time, c_2 is enabled while c_1 is not.

$t_3 = t_0 + \frac{1}{2}$: r_2 fires again before c_2 fires. This may happen because $\frac{1}{2} < \frac{1}{3} + \frac{1}{5}$. Thus, at time t_3, we have two tokens in the output place of r_2, which means that two incoming signals occurred before reaction to the first one. If a requirement of the system is that it must be able to react to any event generated by r_i before a new event is generated by the same transition, then such requirement is not fulfilled. Notice that this kind of requirement is typical in systems based on the interrupt mechanism: An interrupt must be served before a new one is generated by the same device, otherwise the former is lost. According to the model of Figure 6.12, there is no way to prove that in no case more than $\frac{1}{2}$ sec may elapse between the firing of r_2 and c_2 what is particularly unpleasant.

Observe, however, that such inability is not intrinsic in the "system" but is due to the lack of information provided by the model. In fact, suppose that the choice between firing c_1 and c_2 is implemented by the following policy: If at any time $\bar{t}$ both c_1 and c_2 are enabled, then c_2 will fire. However, both transitions must respect t_c (i.e., none of them can remain enabled for more than 0.2 sec without firing). This implies that if c_1 has been enabled for 0.1 sec when c_2 is enabled, then c_2 will fire within 0.1 sec after being enabled. Of course, this is due to the requirement that scheduling decisions do not alter time constraints on the firing of transitions.

Assuming the foregoing policy, we are able to prove that in no way there will be more than one token in the output places of r_1 and r_2, provided that initially they are empty and CS contains one token. In fact, let t_{r_i} denote any time when transition r_i fires and t'_{r_i} the next time when r_i fires. Then $t'_{r_1} - t_{r_1} \geq 1$ sec, $t'_{r_2} - t_{r_2} \geq 0.5$ sec.
The following cases are possible.

2.1 $t_{r_1} + 0.2 < t_{r_2} < t'_{r_1}$

In this case, at time t_{r_2}, c_1 has already fired and it is not yet reenabled. Thus, after at most $\frac{2}{15}$ sec (the time needed to fire a_1) c_2 is enabled and will fire after at most 0.2 sec. Consequently, at time $t_{r_2} + \frac{2}{15} + \frac{1}{5} + \frac{2}{15} = t_{r_2} + \frac{7}{15}$, a_2 will fire and a new token will be in CS. Since $\frac{7}{15} < \frac{1}{2}$, $t_{r_2} + \frac{7}{15} < t'_{r_2}$; thus a new token will not yet be in the output place of r_2.

2.2 $t_{r_1} \leq t_{r_2} \leq t_{r_1} + \frac{1}{5}$

In this case, if c_1 fired before time t_{r_2}, then we can apply the same reasoning as in the case 2.1. Instead, suppose that at time t_{r_2} both c_1 and c_2 are enabled. Then c_2 will fire at time $t_{c_2} \leq t_{r_1} + \frac{1}{5}$. Thus a_2 will fire at $t_{a_2} \leq t_{r_1} + \frac{1}{3}$. At time t_{a_2}, c_1 will again be enabled while c_2 will not because $t_{r_1} + \frac{1}{3} < t_{r_2} + \frac{1}{2} \leq t'_{r_2}$. Now, if c_1 fires at time $t_{c_1} \leq t_{r_1} + \frac{1}{3} + \frac{1}{5}$ and $t_{c_1} < t'_{r_2}$, then we are back in the same state as in case 2.1 and the behavior proceeds as in that case. Otherwise, suppose that at time $t'_{r_2} = t_{r_2} + \frac{1}{2}$, c_1 did not fire yet. (The reader can easily verify that this can actually happen.) In this case, c_2 will fire again at time $t'_{c_2} \leq t_{a_2} + \frac{1}{5} \leq t_{r_1} + \frac{1}{3} + \frac{1}{5} = t_{r_1} + \frac{8}{15}$, and this prevents c_1 from firing. Again, a_2 will fire at $t'_{a_2} \leq t_{r_1} + \frac{8}{15} + \frac{2}{15} = t_{r_1} + \frac{10}{15}$. Thus, at t'_{a_2}, c_1 is enabled for the third time. This time, however, it will eventually fire at $t_{c_1} \leq t'_{a_2} + \frac{1}{5}$ because $t_{r_1} + \frac{10}{15} + \frac{1}{5} < t'_{r_2} + \frac{1}{2} = t_{r_2} + 1$. Thus, both c_1 and c_2 will eventually fire as requested, no matter what sequence of firings occurs for r_1 and r_2, since from now on the system will repeat the same behavior as in cases 2.1 and 2.2.

We will not try to derive general conclusions from the previous example. However, our discussion should have shown that Petri nets—and nondeterministic models in general—are an attractive formalism to describe concurrent systems. However, in some cases, nondeterminism provides "too much" abstraction and hides system features that are critical to reason about the model's behavior. Abstraction becomes even more critical in the case of real-time systems where system performance heavily depends on hidden scheduling policies.

6.3.4 Describing Semantics of Concurrent Programming Languages: Examples from Ada

Petri nets can be useful to model the semantics of a concurrent program. In this section, we illustrate an application to the constructs of the Ada programming language presented in Example 6.4.

The rendezvous of the two processes MASTER and SERVER of Figure 6.3 can be modeled as in Figure 6.13. We assume that a token appears in place MASTER__CALL when the MASTER task issues the entry call ORDER(P). Also, a token appears in place SERVER__ACCEPT when the SERVER task performs an "**accept** ORDER(P)". The RENDEZVOUS transition fires only if the MASTER has issued an entry call and the SERVER has performed an **accept**. After RENDEZVOUS, the MASTER resumes execution and the SERVER continues from the "**end** ORDER" on.

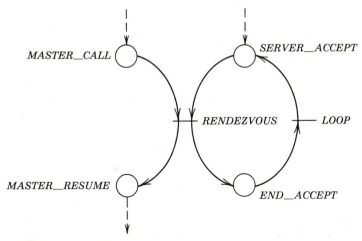

FIGURE 6.13 A PN modeling the fragment of Figure 6.3.

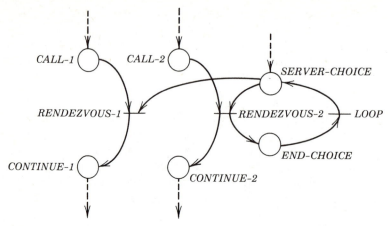

FIGURE 6.14   A PN describing a nondeterministic rendezvous.

Transition RENDEZVOUS models the execution of the **accept** body in a very concise way: In fact, here we are interested in modeling the synchronization of the two tasks, not the meaning of their sequential steps of computation.

Nondeterministic **accept** statements can be modeled in a natural way by means of Petri nets. For example, the behavior of task SERVER of Figure 6.4 can be described as in Figure 6.14. We assume that a token appears in CALL__1 (and/or CALL__2) if an entry call is issued to ORDER__1 (and/or ORDER__2). Also, a token appears in SERVER__CHOICE when the SERVER reaches the **select** statement. It is clear from Figure 6.14 that either RENDEZVOUS__1 or RENDEZVOUS__2 will be chosen nondeterministically if both calls have been issued.

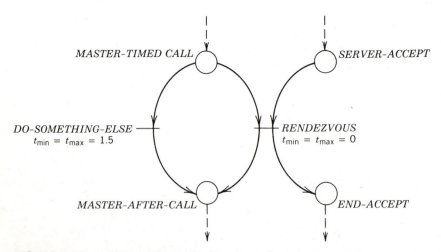

FIGURE 6.15   A PN modeling a timed entry call.

The case of timed entry calls is also easy to model if we use the formalism of timed Petri nets. For example, the case of Figure 6.5 can be modeled as in Figure 6.15. Transition DO__SOMETHING__ELSE fires if and only if 1.5 sec elapsed since a token appeared in the place MASTER__TIMED__CALL. Since transition RENDEZVOUS can and must fire as soon as it is enabled, the semantics of the timed entry call results in a time-out for the task MASTER.

Things become more involved if several tasks can issue calls to the same entry. In such a case, entry calls must be processed according to a first-in-first-out policy and, unfortunately, this cannot be modeled by a single place that accumulates tokens as entry calls are issued. In fact, there is no way to specify that entries must be processed according to their arrival time.

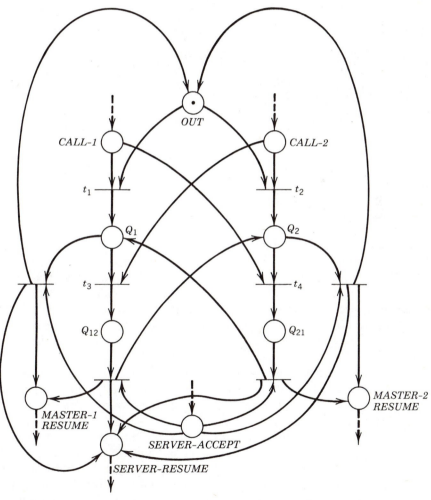

FIGURE 6.16 A PN describing the FIFO policy for serving two entry calls.

Figure 6.16 illustrates the case where two master tasks MASTER__1 and MASTER__2 call the some entry E of task SERVER. The presence of a token in place SERVER models the fact that the SERVER task is ready to accept a call to E. A token appears in place CALL__i, where $i = 1, 2$, when task MASTER__i issues E's call. A token appears in place *OUT* when no task MASTER__i is interacting with task SERVER. Initially, a token is present in *OUT*. A token appears in place Q_i, where $i = 1, 2$, when only an entry call issued by task MASTER__i is pending. A token appears in place Q_{ij} when two calls issued by tasks MASTER__i and MASTER__j are pending, in exactly this order. The reader is invited to examine the Petri net of Figure 6.16 carefully in order to understand that, if transitions $t_1, \ldots, t_4$ have $t_{min} = t_{max} = 0$ (i.e., they fire as soon as they are enabled), then the net properly models the first-in-first-out queue of, at most, two entry calls.

Exercises

6.9   How can you model the rendezvous in the general case where n calls can be queued in an entry? What is the reason of the difficulties you face? What happens if an unbounded number of entry calls can occur?

6.10   Let us change the semantics of Ada's rendezvous by allowing a nondeterministic choice of pending entry calls. Give a formal description using Petri nets.

6.3.5   Describing Distributed Systems by Means of Petri Nets

In a distributed system, computations are performed in a *physically concurrent* way by several autonomous processing *nodes*. However, because nodes cooperate to perform a unique complex computation, it is clear that some *synchronization* among them is necessary. For instance, in a distributed data base it may be necessary to collect data from several nodes in order to realize, say, a fund transfer between different checking accounts. Once again, we derive some considerations on the problem of modeling distributed systems by applying the Petri net formalism.

Several nodes are pairwise connected through bidirectional channels. Each node is provided with two or more *double ports*. Each double port is a pair of *buffers*, an input buffer and an output buffer connected with a *channel*. Figure 6.17 completes our informal description.

A single node is modeled by a Petri net of the type in Figure 6.18, where IB_i represents an input buffer, OB_i represents an output buffer, for $i = 1, 2$, *im* (*om*) represents the arrival of an input (output) message, and E represents the elaboration unit. The behavior of such network should be fairly obvious thanks to the similarity with previous examples. We only notice here that as a conse-

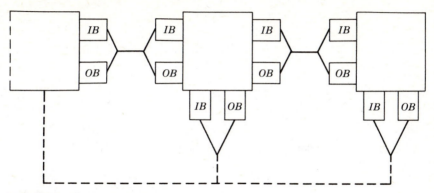

FIGURE 6.17 A distributed system.

quence of receiving an input message through port i, an output message can be nondeterministically produced in any output port j (i included).

Observe now that a bidirectional channel of the type shown in Figure 6.17 can be represented by a Petri net of the type of Figure 6.19, where im_s and om_s, for $s = i, j$, are the same as in Figure 6.18. Figure 6.20 integrates Figures 6.18 and 6.19 into a description of the fragment of distributed system comprising two nodes and their interconnection.

We assume that initially some nodes have one token in CPU—that is, they are waiting for messages—whereas others have one token in E, that is, they are already active.

Let us first consider the viewpoint of the single node. The only way an observer located in a node can obtain information on the whole system state is by

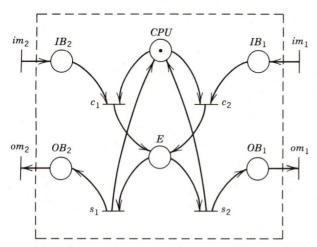

FIGURE 6.18 A PN modeling a node of a distributed system.

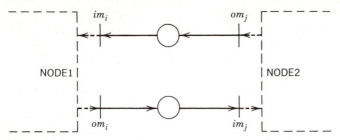

FIGURE 6.19 A PN modeling a channel of a distributed system.

means of the messages exchanged through the ports. The model of Figure 6.18 correctly captures the uncertainty concerning the incoming of messages from the outside world: This corresponds to the possibility of a totally nondeterministic firing for im_1 and im_2. Observe, however, that such uncertainty slightly differs from the nondeterministic choice between the firing of c_1 and c_2, in Figure 6.12, which was an abstraction from internal scheduling policies.

In both cases, nondeterminism corresponds to a *lack of observability*. However in the former case—let us call it *external nondeterminism*—the lack of observability is intrinsically due to the fact that an observer can only know about the global system through what it receives from the ports. In the latter case—let us call it *internal nondeterminism*—it is due to an explicit decision to hide some implementation detail.

Notice that we can analyze the system as a whole following the model of Figure 6.20. We might try to capture the notion of a global system state through the marking of the Petri net. However, we must recall that there is no way to give a precise meaning to the sentence "the global system state at time t is $x(t)$."

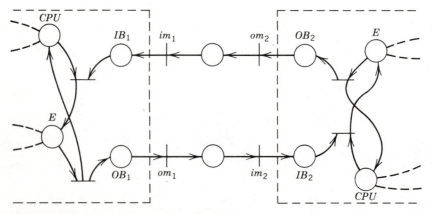

FIGURE 6.20 A combination of the PNs of Figures 6.18 and 6.19.

Thus, there is no possibility to say, for example, that the marking of a node n_1 is $m_1(t)$ and—at exactly the same time—the marking of node n_2 is $m_2(t)$. A better view of a Petri net as a model for a distributed system is as a *partial ordering*. For example, consider how NODE1 in Figure 6.19 can interpret the firing of im_1 at time t (NODE1's time!). If im_1 fires at time t in NODE1 there is no way for NODE1 to know what the marking of NODE2 is at time t. The only certainty we can have in NODE1 is that om_2 must have fired at some time $t' < t$.

Thus, the place between om_2 and im_1 imposes a precedence relation between the firing of om_2 and the firing of im_1. This view of Petri nets emphasizes a very important aspect of the description of concurrent activities, namely their synchronization on events: An activity A_1 cannot reach a given state if previously some defined event did not occur.

Exercise

6.11 Outline the problems that may arise if you try to perform a real-time analysis of a distributed systems. Base your remarks on a Petri net model for the distributed system.

Chapter Summary

In this chapter we have briefly addressed the problems arising in modeling and analyzing nonstandard computing environments. Without trying to treat them in a general and systematic way, we discovered that the use of nondeterministic models can be quite fruitful.

Petri nets have been chosen as a reference nondeterministic model, but many of the comments we gave are general enough to remain valid for other nondeterministic evolutionary models. If we decide to abandon evolutionary models, things become even more intricate. In fact, it has been observed that denotational techniques are difficult to apply to concurrent or nondeterministic computations. We refer the reader to a more advanced literature addressing such problem and for an overview of the most promising research directions.

Further Exercises

6.12 Write a nondeterministic algorithm that recognizes a regular language, based on a nondeterministic finite-state recognizer. Does time complexity change with respect to a deterministic algorithm solving the same problem?

6.13 A binary tree is sorted if, for each node n, the value associated to n is greater than the value associated to its left child and less than the value associated to its right child. Write a parallel algorithm to evaluate whether a binary tree is sorted. Evaluate time complexity of your algorithm.

6.14 A binary tree of $k = 2^n - 1$ nodes, for $n \geq 1$, is balanced if the distance of each leaf node from the root (i.e., the length of a path from the root to the node) is $n - 1$. Evaluate time complexity of the parallel algorithm of Exercise 6.13 when applied to a domain of balanced binary trees and compare it to its worst-case complexity in the general case.

6.15 A traffic light controls the intersection of two crossing roads. Use a Petri net to describe the change of state of the traffic light and the traffic flow of cars on the two roads.

6.16 (Inspired by an exercise of Gehani (1983).) Slightly modify the requirements of Exercise 6.15 in the following way. One of the two roads is a lightly used side road, and normally the traffic light is green for the main road and red for the side road. The light changes to red for the main road and green for the side road only if there is a request to cross the main road. In such a case, the traffic flow on the main road can be stopped by the traffic light only if the main road has had the green light for at least 3 minutes; then the light becomes green for 30 seconds. You may assume that there is always, at most, one request to cross the main road.

6.17 Slightly modify the requirements of Exercise 6.16 in the following way. There can be any number of vehicles that wish to cross the main road. The first vehicle arriving at the crossing point issues the request to set the traffic light to green. When the light is green all vehicles can cross the main road (you may assume that crossing the road takes a null time). You may assume that, once enabled, vehicles can cross the main road in any order.

6.18 Slightly modify the requirements of Exercise 6.17 in the following way: Once enabled by the traffic light, vehicles can cross the main road in the same order they arrived at the crossing point. (See also Exercise 6.9.)

6.19 The problem of the dining philosophers (due to E. W. Dijkstra). Five philosophers spend their lives alternating between eating and thinking. They eat at a circular table, which is set with five dishes and five forks. For some unknown reason, each philosopher needs two forks to eat, and forks may be picked up one at a time. After eating, a philosopher puts the forks down and starts thinking. Forks are reused by hungry philosophers without any particular care. Model this problem using Petri nets. Describe why and how a deadlock may occur.

6.20 Show how Petri nets can model the problem of transaction atomicity in a shared DB.

Sketchy Solutions to Selected Exercises

6.19 A PN describing the problem of the dining philosophers is given in Figure 6.21. Details such as dishes and the thinking of a philosopher are not explicitly modeled because they are irrelevant.

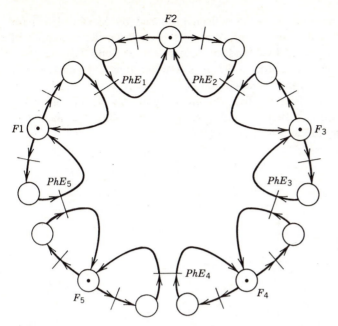

FIGURE 6.21 A PN modeling the dining philosophers. *PhE_i* denotes that the *i*th philosopher is eating. Places F_i denote forks.

Bibliographic Remarks

The use of nondeterministic models for describing and analyzing computing systems has been restricted for a long time almost exclusively to the fields of artificial intelligence and theoretical computer science. For instance, it is worth mentioning nondeterministic control structures due to Floyd (1967b) and some typical artificial intelligence programming languages suitable for symbolic information processing, and automatic theorem proving that are based on nondeterministic abstract machines: PLANNER, due to Hewitt (1969) and PROLOG, due to Colmeraurer (1970, 1985), are classical examples thereof.

Some significant studies devoted to discovering how much gain in computational efficiency can be achieved by making computations parallel are Kraska (1972), Kuck, Muraoka, and Chen (1972), and Leighton (1984).

Dijkstra (1976) first proposed the use of guarded commands as a basic control structure. Subsequently, Hoare (1978, 1980) suggested to extend the use of guarded commands to program concurrent computations. Dijkstra (1968), Hoare (1972, 1974, 1978), Brinch Hansen (1975), and a few others first tried to apply rigorous and possibly formal methodologies to the design of concurrent systems.

For a general bibliography on Petri nets and their applications the reader is referred to the bibliographic remarks of Chapter 1. Timed Petri nets are not widely used in the literature. They have been proposed by Merlin (1975) for analyzing real-time systems. The use of Petri nets to describe the semantics of Ada's tasks has been proposed by Mandrioli, Zicari, Ghezzi, and Tisato (1985). Queueing theory (see e.g., Kleinrock (1975)) is another formal framework for handling real-time problems from a stochastic point of view.

A significant sample of recent advanced literature on models for concurrent and distributed computing systems is Milne and Milner (1979), Astesiano and Reggio (1985), and Degano and Montanari (1983).

Bibliography

ADJ (1975)
Goguen, J. A.; Thatcher, J. W.; Wagner, E. G.; Wright, J. E.
Abstract Data Types as Initial Algebras and the Correctness of Data Representation.
Proc. of the Conference on Computer Graphics, Pattern Recognition and Data Structures.

ADJ (1977)
Goguen, J. A.; Thatcher, J. W.; Wagner, E. G.; Wright, J. B.
Initial Algebra Semantics and Continuous Algebras.
Journal of the ACM, Vol. 24, No. 1, pp. 68–95.

Alagic, S.; Arbib, M. (1978)
The Design and Analysis of Well Structured and Correct Programs.
Springer-Verlag, New York.

Aho, A. V.; Hopcroft, J. E.; Ullmann, J. D. (1974)
The Design and Analysis of Computer Algorithms.
Addison Wesley, Reading, MA.

459

Apt, K.; Francez, N.; DeRoever, W. (1980)
A Proof System for Communicating Sequential Processes.
ACM Trans. on Progr. Lang. and Syst., Vol. 2, pp. 359–385.

Apt, K. (1981)
Ten Years of Hoare's Logic: A Survey—Part I.
ACM Trans. on Progr. Lang. and Syst., Vol. 3, No. 4, pp. 431–483.

Astesiano, E.; Reggio, G. (1985)
The SMoLCS Approach to the Specification of Concurrent Systems.
CNET–Distributed Systems on Local Networks.
ETS-Pisa, Vol. 2, pp. 237–254.

Bar-Hillel, Y.; Perles, M.; Shamir, E. (1961)
On Formal Properties of Simple Phrase Structure Grammars.
Z. Phonetik. Sprachwiss. Kommunikationsforsch, Vol. 14, pp. 143–172.

Birkhoff, G.; Lipson, J. (1970)
Heterogeneous Algebras.
J. Combinatorial Theory, Vol. 8, pp. 115–133.

Bjorner, D.; Jones, C. (1982)
Formal Specification and Software Development.
Prentice-Hall, Englewood Cliffs, NJ.

Böhm, C.; Jacopini, G. (1966)
Flow—Diagrams, Turing Machines, and Languages with Only Two Formation Rules.
Communications of the ACM, Vol. 9, No. 5, pp. 366–371.

Brady, J. (1977)
The Theory of Computer Science: *A Programming Approach.*
Chapman and Hall, London.

Brassard, G. (1985)
Crusade for a Better Notation.
ACM-SIGACT News, Vol. 17, No. 1, pp. 60–64.

Brinch-Hansen, P. (1975)
The Programming Language Concurrent-Pascal.
IEEE Trans. on Software Engineering, Vol. SE-1, pp. 199–207.

Burstall, R. M. (1969)
Proving Properties of Programs by Structural Induction.
Computer Journal, Vol. 12, No. 1, pp. 41–48.

Burstall, R. M.; Landin, P. J. (1969)
Programs and Their Proofs: an Algebraic Approach.
Machine Intelligence, Meltzer, B. and Michie, D., eds., Vol. 4, pp. 17–43.
Edinburgh University Press.

Burstall, R. M. (1970)
Formal Description of Program Structure and Semantics of First-Order Logic.
Machine Intelligence, Meltzer, B. and Michie, D., eds., pp. 79–98.
Edinburgh University Press.

Burstall, R. M. (1974)
Program Proving as Hand Simulation with a Little Induction.
Proc. IFIP Congress, Amsterdam, pp. 308–312.

Burstall, R. M.; Goguen, J. A. (1977)
Putting Theories Together to Make Specification.
Proc. 5th Int. Joint Conf. on Art. Int., pp. 1045–1058.

Chomsky, N. (1956)
Three Models for the Description of Language.
IRE Trans. on Information Theory, Vol. 2, No. 3, pp. 113–124.

Chomsky, N. (1959)
On Certain Formal Properties of Grammars.
Information and Control, Vol. 2, No. 2, pp. 133–167.

Chomsky, N. (1963)
Formal Properties of Grammars.
Handbook of Math. Psych., Vol. 2, pp. 323–418.
John Wiley and Sons, New York.

Church, A. (1936)
An Unsolvable Problem of Elementary Number Theory.
American J. of Mathematics, Vol. 58, pp. 345–363.

Church, A. (1941)
The Calculi of Lambda—Conversion.
Princeton University Press.

Church, A. (1956)
Introduction to Mathematical Logic.
Princeton University Press.

Citrini, C.; Crespi-Reghizzi, S.; Mandrioli, D. (1986)
On Deterministic Multipass Analysis.
SIAM J. on Computing, Vol. 15, No. 3, pp. 668–693.

Clocksin, W. F.; Mellish, C. S. (1984)
Programming in Prolog, Second Edition.
Springer-Verlag, Berlin.

Colmeramer, A. (1970)
Les Systèmes-q ou un Formalisme pour Analyser et Synthétiser des Phrases sur Ordinateur.
Internal Report 43.
Departement d'Informatique, Université de Montreal.

Colmeramer, A. (1985)
Prolog in 10 Figures.
Communications of the ACM, Vol. 28, No. 12, pp. 1296–1310.

Cook, S. A. (1971)
The Complexity of Theorem Proving Procedures.
Proc. Third Annual ACM Symp. on the Theory of Computing, pp. 151–158.

Cook, S. A. (1973)
A Hierarchy for Nondeterministic Time Complexity.
Journal of Comp. and Syst. Sc., Vol. 7, No. 4, pp. 343–353.

Cook, S. A.; Reckhow, R. A. (1973)
Time Bounded Random Access Machines.
Journal of Comp. and Syst. Sc., Vol. 7, No. 4, pp. 354–375.

Davis, M.; Hersh, R. (1973)
Hilbert's 10th Problem.
Scientific American, Vol. 229, No. 5, pp. 84–91.

De Bakker, J. W. (1980)
Mathematical Theory of Program Correctness.
Prentice-Hall, Englewood Cliffs, NJ.

Degano, P.; Montanari, U. (1983)
A Model for Distributed Systems Based on Graph rewriting.
Internal Report, Collana CNET, N. 111.

Dekker, J. (1955)
Productive Sets.
Trans. Amer. Math. Soc., Vol. 78, pp. 129–149.

Dekker, J.; Myhill, J. (1958)
Some Theorems on Classes of Recursively Enumberable Sets.
Trans. Amer. Math. Soc., Vol. 89, pp. 25–59.

Dijkstra, E. W. (1968)
Co-operating Sequential Processes.
Programming Languages, Genuys, F., ed., pp. 43–112.
Academic Press, New York.

Dijkstra, E. (1976)
A Discipline of Programming.
Prentice-Hall, Englewood Cliffs, NJ.

Floyd, R. W. (1967a)
Assigning Meaning to Programs.
Proc. Symp. in Applied Mathematics, J. Schwartz, ed.
Mathematical Aspects of Computer Science, Vol. 19, pp. 19–32.
Amer. Math. Soc., New York.

Floyd, R. W. (1967b)
Nondeterministic Algorithms.
Journal of the ACM, Vol. 14, No. 4, pp. 636–644.

Garey, M. R.; Johnson, D. S. (1978)
Computers and Intractability: a Guide to the Theory of NP-Completeness.
W. H. Freeman, San Francisco.

Gehani, N. (1983)
ADA, An Advanced Introduction.
Prentice-Hall, Englewood Cliffs, NJ.

Ghezzi, C.; Jazayeri, M. (1987)
Programming Language Concepts, Second Edition.
John Wiley and Sons, New York.

Ginsburg, S. (1966)
The Mathematical Theory of Context-Free Languages.
McGraw-Hill, New York.

Ginsburg, S.; Greibach, S. A. (1966)
Deterministic Context-Free Languages.
Information and Control, Vol. 9, No. 6, pp. 563–582.

Gödel, K. (1930)
Die Vollstänigkeit der Axiome des Logischen Funktionen-kalküls.
Monatshefte für Mathematik und Physik, Vol. 37, pp. 349–360.

Gödel, K. (1931)
Über Formal Unentascheidbare Sätze der Principia Mathematica und Verwandter Systems, I.
Monatshefte für Mathematik und Physik, Vol. 38, pp. 173–198.

Gödel, K. (1934)
On Undecidable Propositions of Formal Mathematical Systems.
Princeton University Press.

Good, P. I.; Cohen, R. M.; Hunter, L. W. (1978)
A Report on the Development of Gypsy.
Proc. ACM National Conference 1, pp. 116–122.

Gordon, M. J. (1979)
The Denotational Description of Programming Languages: *An Introduction*.
Springer-Verlag, New York.

Gries, D. (1981)
The Science of Programming.
Springer-Verlag, New York.

Gross, M.; Lentin, A. (1967)
Notions sur les Grammaires Formelles.
Gauthier-Villars, Paris.

Guttag, J. (1977)
Abstract Data Types and the Development of Data Structures.
Communications of the ACM. Vol. 20, No. 6, pp. 396–404.

Harrison, M. (1978)
Introduction to Formal Language Theory.
Addison Wesley, Reading, MA.

Hartmanis, J.; Stearns, R. E. (1965)
On the Computational Complexity of Algorithms.
Trans. Amer. Math. Soc., Vol. 117, pp. 285–306.

Hasenjäger, G.; Scholz, H. (1961)
Grundzüge der mathematischen Logik.
Berlin–Göttingen–Heidelberg.

Hennie, F. (1965)
One-Tape Off-Line Turing Machine Computations.
Information and Control, Vol. 8, No. 6, pp. 553–578.

Hewitt, C. (1969)
PLANNER: A Language for Manipulating Models and Proving Theorems in a Robot.
Proc. of the First Int. J. Conf. on Art. Int., pp. 295–303.

Hoare, C. A. (1969)
An Axiomatic Basis of Computer Programming.
Communications of the ACM, Vol. 12, No. 10, pp. 576–580.

Hoare, C. A. (1972)
Towards a Theory of Parallel Programming.
Operating Systems Techniques, pp. 61–71.
Academic Press, New York.

Hoare, C. A. (1974)
Monitors: An Operating System Structuring Concept.
Communications of the ACM, Vol. 17, No. 10, pp. 549–557.

Hoare, C. A. (1978)
Communicating Sequential Processes.
Communications of the ACM, Vol. 21, No. 8, pp. 666–677.

Hoare, C. A. (1980)
A Model for Communicating Sequential Processes.
On the Construction of Programs, McKeag and McNaughton, R. eds., pp. 229–243.
Cambridge University Press.

Holt, A.; Commoner, F. (1970)
Events and Conditions.
Record of the Project MAC Conference on Concurrent Systems and Parallel Computation, pp. 1–52.

Hopcroft, J. E.; Ullman, J. D. (1969)
Formal Languages and Their Relation to Automata.
Addison Wesley, Reading, MA.

Hopcroft, J. E.; Ullman, J. D. (1979)
Introduction to Automata Theory, Languages, and Computation.
Addison Wesley, Reading, MA.

Hopcroft, J. E. (1981)
Recent Directions in Algorithmic Research.
Proc. 5th Conf. on Theor. Comp. Sc., Deussen, ed., p. 123.
Springer Verlag, New York.

Karp, R. M. (1972)
Reducibility among Combinatorial Problems.
Complexity of Computer Computations, pp. 85–104.
Plenum Press, New York.

Karp, R. (1986a)
Combinatorics, Complexity and Randomness.
Communications of the ACM, Vol. 29, No. 2, pp. 98–109.

Karp, R. (1986b)
Piecing Together Complexity.
Communications of the ACM, Vol. 29, No. 2, pp. 110–111.

Kleene, S. C. (1952)
Introduction to Metamathematics.
Van Nostrand Reinhold, New York.

Kleene, S. C. (1967)
Mathematical Logic.
John Wiley and Sons, New York.

Kleene, S. C.; Post, E. (1954)
The Upper Semi-Lattice of Degrees of Recursive Unsolvability.
Ann. of Mathematics. Vol. 59, pp. 379–407.

Kleinrock, L. (1975)
Queueing Systems, Vol. 1: Theory.
John Wiley and Sons, New York.

Knuth, D. E. (1969–1973)
The Art of Computer Programming, Vols. 1, 2, 3.
Addison-Wesley, Reading, MA.

Knuth, D. E. (1976)
Big Omicron and Big Omega and Big Theta.
ACM-SIGACT News, Vol. 8, No. 2, pp. 18–24.

Kolence, K. (1985)
An Introduction to Software Physics.
McGraw-Hill, New York.

Kowalski, R. (1979)
Logic for Problem Solving.
Artificial Intelligence Series, Nilsson, N., ed.
North Holland, Amsterdam.

Kraska, P. W. (1972)
Parallelism Exploitation and Scheduling.
Ph.D. thesis, Univ. of Illinois at Urbana-Champaign, Dept. Computer Sci. Rep. 518.

Kuck, D. J.; Muraoka, Y.; Chen, S. (1972)
On the Number of Operations Simultaneously Executable in FORTRAN-like Programs and Their Resulting Speed-up.
IEEE Trans. Computers. Vol. C-21, pp. 1293–1310.

Leighton, T. (1984)
Tight Bounds on the Complexity of Parallel Sorting.
Proc. 6th ACM Symp. on Theory of Computing, pp. 71–80.

Lewis, H.; Papadimitriou, K. (1981)
Elements of the Theory of Computation.
Prentice-Hall, Englewood Cliffs, NJ.

Lipton, R.. (1976)
The Reachability Problem Requires Exponential Space.
Research Report 62, Department of Computer Science, Yale University, New Haven, CT.

Lucas, P.; Walk, K. (1969)
On the Formal Description of PL/1.
Annual Review of Automatic Programming, Vol. 6, No. 3, pp. 105–182.

Luecker, G. S. (1981)
Algorithms with Random Input.
Proc. 13th Symp. Interface, Eddy, W. F., ed.
Springer Verlag, p. 68.

MacLane, S.; Birkhoff, G. (1970)
Algebra.
The MacMillan Company, New York.

Mandrioli, D.; Zicari, R.; Ghezzi, C.; Tisato, F. (1985)
Modeling the ADA Task System by Petri Nets.
Computer Languages, Vol. 10, No. 1, pp. 43–61.

Manna, Z. (1969)
The Correctness of Programs.
Journal of Comp. and Syst. Sc., Vol. 3, No. 3, pp. 119–127.

Manna, Z. (1974)
Mathematical Theory of Computation.
McGraw Hill, New York.

Manna, Z.; Waldinger, R. (1978)
Is "Sometime" Sometimes Better than "Always"?
Communications of the ACM, Vol. 21, No. 2, pp. 159–172.

Manna, Z.; Waldinger, R. (1985)
The Logical Basis for Computer Programming.
Addison-Wesley, Reading, MA.

Markov, A. (1954)
The Theory of Algorithms.
Tr. Mat. Inst. Steklow, Vol .XLII.

McCarthy, J. (1960)
Recursive Functions of Symbolic Expressions and Their Computations by Machine.
Communications of the ACM, Vol. 3, No. 4, pp. 184–195.

McCarthy, J. (1963a)
A Basis for a Mathematical Theory of Computation.
Computer Programming and Formal Systems, Brafford, P., and Hirschberg, D., eds., pp. 30–70.
North-Holland Publishing Company, Amsterdam.

McCarthy, J. (1963b)
Towards a Mathematical Science of Computation.
Information Processing: *Proc. of IFIP Conf*. 1962, pp. 21–28.
North-Holland Publishing Company, Amsterdam.

McCarthy, J.; Abrahams, P.; Edwards, D.; Hart, T.; Levin, M. (1965)
LISP 1.5 *Programmer's Manual*.
The MIT Press, Cambridge, MA.

McCorduck, P. (1983)
An Introduction to the Fifth Generation.
Communications of the ACM, Vol. 26, No. 9, pp. 629–630.

McNaughton, R.; Yamada, H. (1960)
Regular Expressions and State Graphs for Automata.
IEEE Trans. on Electronic Computers, Vol. 9, No. 1, pp. 39–47.

Mendelson, E. (1964)
Introduction to Mathematical Logic.
Van Nostrand Reinhold, New York.

Merlin, P. (1975)
A Methodology for the Design and Implementation of Communication Protocols.
IEEE Trans on Communications, Vol. COM 24, pp. 614–621.

Milne, G.; Milner, R. (1979)
Concurrent Processes and Their Syntax.
Journal of the ACM. Vol. 26, No. 2, pp. 302–321.

Minsky, M. (1967)
Computation. Finite and Infinite Machines.
Prentice-Hall, Englewood Cliffs, NJ.

Myhill, J. (1957)
Finite Automata and the Representation of Events.
WADD TR-57-624, pp. 112–137.
Wright Patterson AFB, Ohio.

Nerode, A. (1958)
Linear Automaton Transformations.
Proc. AMS, Vol. 9, pp. 541–544.

O'Donnell, M. J. (1982)
A Critique of the Foundations of Hoare-Style Programming Logic.
Communications of the ACM, Vol. 25, No. 12, pp. 927–934.

Owicki, S.; Gries, D. (1976)
Verifying Properties of Parallel Programs: An Axiomatic Approach.
Communication of the ACM, Vol. 19, No. 5, pp. 279–284.

Peano, G. (1891)
Sul concetto di numero.
Rivista di Matematica, Vol. 1, pp. 87–102 and pp. 256–267.

Peterson, J. L. (1977)
Petri Nets.
Computing Surveys, ACM, Vol. 9, No. 3, pp. 223–252.

Peterson, J. (1981)
Petri Net Theory and the Modeling of Systems.
Prentice-Hall, Englewood Cliffs, NJ.

Petri, C. (1962)
Kommunication mit Automaten.
PhD. Dissertation, University of Bonn.

Pnueli, A. (1979)
The Temporal Semantics of Concurrent Programs.
In *Semantics of Concurrent Computation*, Kahn, G., ed., pp. 1–20.
Springer-Verlag, New York.

Post, E. (1936)
Finite Combinatory Processes—Formulation 1.
Journal of Symbolic Logic, Vol. 1, pp. 103–105.

Post, E. (1947)
Recursive Unsolvability of a Problem of Thue.
Journal of Symbolic Logic, Vol. 12, pp. 1–11.

Rabin, M. O. (1976)
Probabilistic Algorithms.
Algorithms and Complexity: New Directions and Recent Results. Traub, J., Ed.,
pp. 21–40.
Academic Press, New York.

Rabin, M. O. (1977)
Complexity of Computations
Communications of the ACM, Vol. 20, No. 9, pp. 625–633.

Rice, H. (1953)
Classes of Recursively Enumerable Sets and Their Decision Problems.
Trans. of the Amer. Math. Soc., Vol. 74, pp. 358–366.

Rogers, H. (1967)
Theory of Recursive Functions and Effective Computability.
McGraw Hill, New York.

Rosser, J. (1936)
Extensions of Some Theorems of Gödel and Church.
J. of Symbolic Logic, Vol. 1, pp. 87–91.

Savage, J. E. (1976)
The Complexity of Computing.
John Wiley and Sons, New York.

Scott, D. (1970)
Outline of a Mathematical Theory of Computation.
Fourth Annual Princeton Conf. on Inf. Sci. and Syst., pp. 169–176.

Scott, D.; Strachey, C. (1971)
Towards a Mathematical Semantics of Computer Languages.
Tech. Mono. PRC-6, Oxford University Press.

Shannon, C. (1938)
A Symbolic Analysis of Relay and Switching Circuits.
Trans. Amer. Inst. Elect. Eng., Vol. 57, pp. 713–723.

Shannon, C. (1956)
A Universal Turing Machine with Two Internal States.
Automata Studies, Shannon, C. and McCarthy, J., eds.
Princeton University Press.

Schützenberger, M. (1963)
On Context-Free Languages and Pushdown Automata.
Information and Control, Vol. 6, No. 3, pp. 246–264.

Stoy, J. E. (1977)
Denotational semantics: *The Scott–Strachey Approach to Programming Language Theory*.
MIT Press, Cambridge, MA.

Strachey, C. (1964)
Towards a Formal Semantics.
Formal Description Languages for Computer Programming, Steel, T., ed.,
pp. 198–200.
North Holland, Amsterdam.

Tarski, A. (1955)
A Lattice-Theoretical Fixpoint Theorem and Its Applications.
Pacific J. Math, Vol. 5, pp. 285–309.

Turing, A. (1936–1937)
On Computable Numbers, with an Application to the Entscheidungsproblem.
Proc. London Math. Soc., Vol. 42, pp. 230–265 and Vol. 43, pp. 544–546.

Vitanyi, P.; Meertens, L. (1985)
Big-Omega versus the Wild Functions.
ACM-SIGACT News, Vol. 16, No. 4, pp. 56–59.

Walker, B. J.; Kemmerer, R. A.; Popek, G. J. (1980)
Specification and Verification of the UCLA UNIX Security Kernel.
Communications of the ACM, Vol. 23, No. 2, pp. 118–131.

Wirth, N. (1981)
Pascal-S: A Subset and its Implementation.
Pascal—The Language and Its Implementation, Barron, D., ed., pp. 199–260.
John Wiley and Sons, New York.

Wulf, W.; London, R. L.; Shaw, M. (1976)
An Introduction to the Construction and Verification of Alphard Programs.
IEEE Trans. on Software Engineering, Vol. SE-2, pp. 253–265.

Index